THESE WERE MY PEOPLE
WASHABUCK —
AN ANECDOTAL HISTORY

VINCENT W. MACLEAN

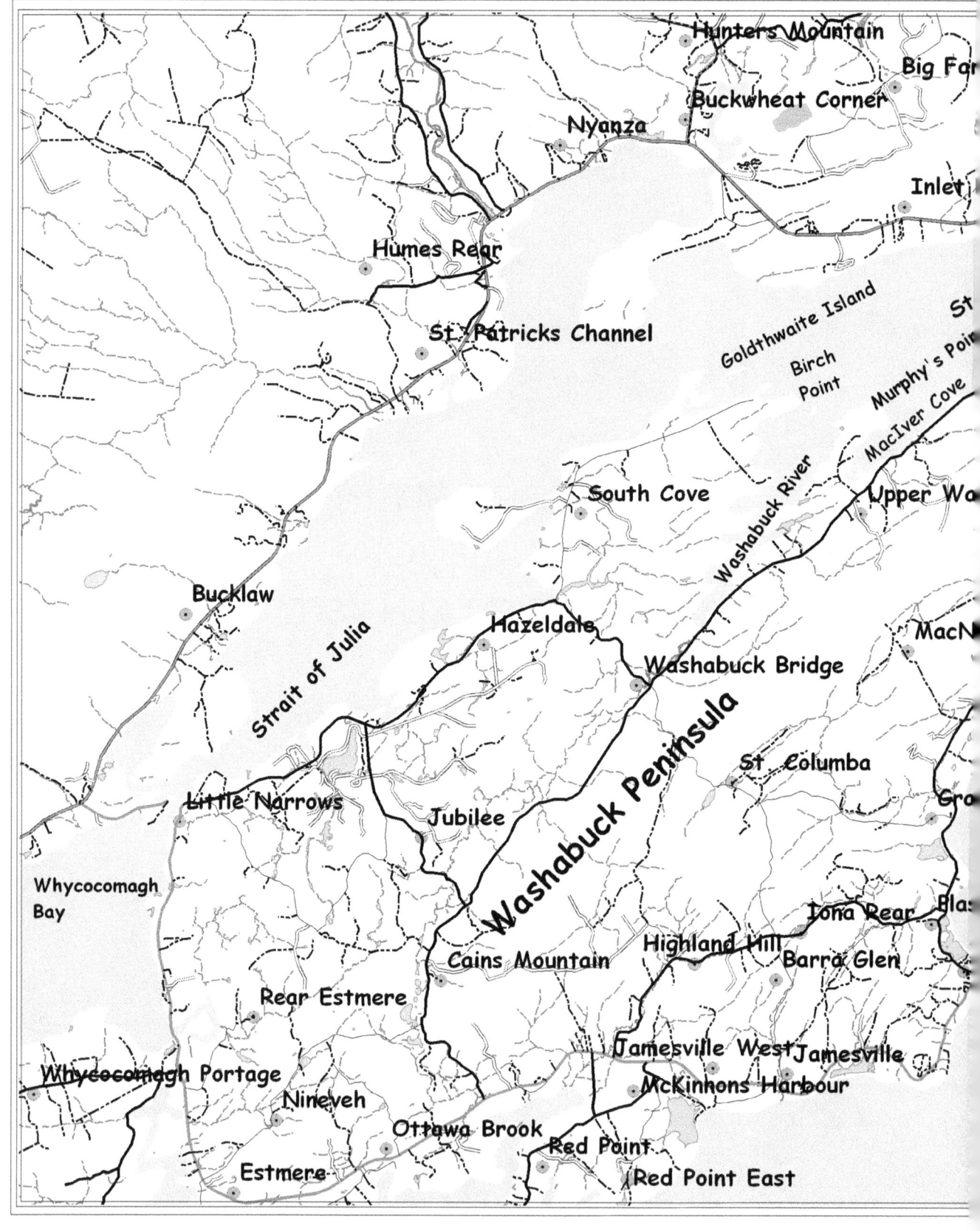

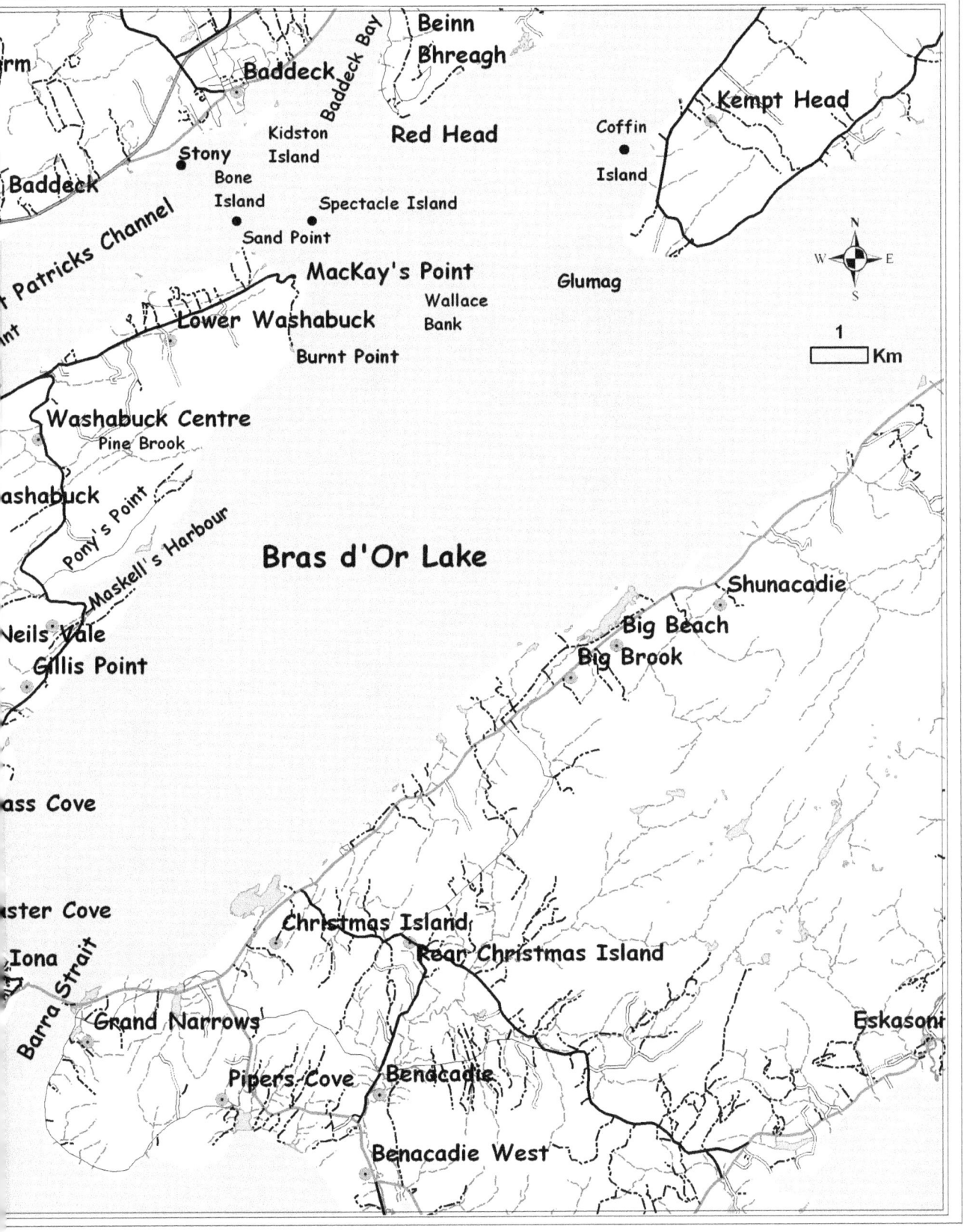

To the memory of the exceptional women in my life
Whose love, kindness and compassion,
Each in her own amiable way
Made this work possible

My grandmothers
Sarah Liza MacDonald
and
Theresa MacLean

My mother
Rose

My mother-in-law
Mary Ann MacKenzie

and also to

My sister
Judi

My wife
Charlotte

My daughters
Susan and Jill

My daughter-in-law
Stephanie

and

My granddaughters
Skyler, Ellie and Mallory

THESE WERE MY PEOPLE WASHABUCK — AN ANECDOTAL HISTORY

VINCENT W. MACLEAN

CAPE BRETON UNIVERSITY PRESS
SYDNEY, NOVA SCOTIA

CAPE BRETONIANA RESEARCH SERIES
Made possible, in part, through
THE ROBERT J. MORGAN GRANT-IN-AID PROGRAM
BEATON INSTITUTE, CAPE BRETON UNIVERSITY

Copyright 2014 Vincent W. MacLean

All rights reserved. No part of this work may be reproduced or used in any form or by any means, electronic or mechanical, including photocopying, recording or any information storage or retrieval system, without the prior written permission of the publisher. Cape Breton University Press recognizes fair dealing uses under the *Copyright Act* (Canada). Responsibility for the research and permissions obtained for this publication rests with the authors.

Cape Breton University Press recognizes the support of the Province of Nova Scotia, through Film and Creative Industries Nova Scotia and the support received for its publishing program from the Canada Council for the Arts Block Grants Program. This book was made possible, in part, through the Robert J. Morgan Grant-in-Aid Program and the Beaton Institute at Cape Breton University. We are pleased to work in partnership with these bodies to develop and promote our cultural resources.

Cover images – For descriptions and sources, see page vi.
Cover design – Cathy MacLean Design, Chéticamp, NS
Layout – Mike Hunter, Port Hawkesbury and Sydney, NS
First printed in Canada.
Second printing, 2014.

Library and Archives Canada Cataloguing in Publication

MacLean, Vincent W., 1944-, author
       These were my people : Washabuck : an anecdotal history / Vincent W. MacLean.

Includes bibliographical references and index.
Issued in print and electronic formats.
ISBN 978-1-927492-90-1 (pbk.).--ISBN 978-1-927492-91-8 (pdf).--ISBN 978-1-927492-92-5 (epub).--ISBN 978-1-927492-93-2 (mobi)

1. Washabuck (N.S.)--History--Anecdotes. I. Title.

FC2349.W36M32 2014   971.6'93   C2014-904130-6
  C2014-904131-4

Cape Breton University Press
PO Box 5300, 1250 Grand Lake Road
Sydney, NS B1P 6L2 CA
www.cbupress.ca

Table of Contents

Notes from the Editors –	vi
Acknowledgements	vii
Foreword, by A. J. B. Johnston	ix
Introduction	xi
Chapter 1 – Washabuck –	1
Chapter 2 – Early Residents, Visitors and Neighbours –	4
Chapter 3 – The Gaels –	14
Chapter 4 – Surveyors, Land Grants and Early Land Owners –	28
Chapter 5 – Stores, Merchants and Shopping –	40
Chapter 6 – Education –	55
Chapter 7 – Religion –	83
Chapter 8 – Post Offices and Courier Services –	129
Chapter 9 – Vessel Construction –	140
Chapter 10 – Transportation –	148
Chapter 11 – Communications –	193
Chapter 12 – Alphas and Omegas –	213
Chapter 13 – Fires & Firefighter Services –	220
Chapter 14 – Forestry, Farming and Fishing –	224
Chapter 15 – Murder –	255
Chapter 16 – Melodic Memories –	263
Chapter 17 – Islands –	277
Chapter 18 – Community Organizations –	291
Chapter 19 – Military Salute –	308
Chapter 20 – Politics –	319
Appendix –	337
Notes –	350
Bibliography –	378
Index –	383

Notes from the Editors

Responsibility for the research and permissions obtained for this publication rests with the author. Every effort has been made to correctly identify the source of images and to seek permissions. In a book with a great many images, there may be errors or oversights. CBU Press and their authors recognize our mutual obligation with respect to rights and permissions and apologize for any shortcomings that may later be discovered.

Here and there, image quality may be lacking, but such is the nature of historical research. Clippings, copies, old photos and less-than-desirable lighting are all factors in collecting; we have done our utmost to put the images in the best light possible.

Where other sources have been used, we have tried to remain true to their originator. From time-to-time such passages may reflect terms and attitudes acceptable at the time, but may not reflect the attitude or ideals of the editors; they have been left intact for their historical value.

Cover images

Front cover, top: Washabuck, Cape Breton Island, as taken from on top of Beinn Bhreagh in 1938, where Spectacle Island and Bone Island front its shoreline on a calm St. Patrick's Channel. In the distance on the far left is the Barra Strait, dividing the communities of Grand Narrows and Iona, while on the right, MacIver's Cove can be seen in the distance. Photo courtesy of the estate of Margaret Fay Shaw, Canna Collections, National Trust for Scotland, U.K.

Front cover, bottom: A group of well-wishers and merry-makers attend the 1939 wedding of Andrew and Helen (MacKenzie) MacLean at the bride's homestead in Washabuck Bridge. Back Row L-R: Murdock (Peigag) MacKinnon, MacKinnon Settlement; Dan MacDougall; Charlie Beaton, Port Hastings; Annie "Sister" MacKenzie; Isabelle MacLean, Derby Point; Mary Ann MacKenzie (nearly obscured), Veronica MacKinnon, Barra Glen; Caluman MacNeil (partially hidden), Celia Murphy, Elizabeth "Lizzie" MacNeil, Cassie MacDougall, Dan MacKinnon, Macie MacKenzie, Simon MacKenzie (bent over), Jimmy "Caluman" MacNeil; Front Row L-R: Danny Murphy, Hector MacKinnon, Theresa MacDougall, Roddie MacKinnon: The car is a 1929 Plymouth owned by Murdock Peigag, one of the first cars owned in the Barra Glen area. Photo courtesy of Hector MacKenzie.

Map pages ii, iii provided by Joel Taylor, Port Hawkesbury, with information provided by the author.

Map pages 415, 416: Detail of Washabuck Peninsula from an A. F. Church and Co. topographical map of Victoria County, Bedford, N.S. 1884-1887. Courtesy of Department of Natural Resources, Baddeck, CB.

Back cover: Washabuck Waterfalls, CB. Photo by and courtesy of Wally Ellison, West Bay Road, CB.

Acknowledgments

Every writer is indebted to many people. In addition to those mentioned elsewhere, the people listed below are those who have assisted me, along this long, enjoyable, obsessive, trek. Some have long since passed into eternity; nevertheless, their perception of an event, situation or happening, helped flavour the contents within. To all I am so grateful. In no particular order they include:

Don Morrison, Baddeck, Ann Marie MacNeil, Grass Cove; Mickey Ben Neilach MacNeil, Iona; S. R. and Annie MacNeil, Barra Glen; Maxie MacNeil, Highland Hill; Evelyn MacNeil, Gillis Point; Public Archives of Nova Scotia staff, Halifax; Wendy Arseneau, DNR, Baddeck; Joan MacInnes, Archivist, Municipality of Victoria, Baddeck; Rodney Chaisson, Pauline MacLean, Katherine MacLeod, and Jim Watson, Nova Scotia Highland Village Museum, Iona, with a special salute to Jim Watson for his assistance with Gàidhlig editing; Jim St. Clair, Mull River; Peter F. and Bea MacLean, Iona; Honey and F. X. MacNeil, Iona; Joan Gillis, Jamesville; Hector MacKenzie, Hugh Campbell, Roddie J. MacDonald, Washabuck; Mary (Alfred) MacDonald, Baddeck; Mickey (Red Rory) MacLean, Washabuck and Baddeck; Mary Dan D. MacNeil and Danny MacNeil, Grass Cove; James MacDonald, Twining Street, Baddeck; Murdock (Rabbit) MacRae, Baddeck; W. James MacDonald, Baddeck; Joe (Red Rory) and Josie MacLean, Washabuck, Professor A. A. "Tony" MacKenzie, Egerton; Rose MacDonald and Mary C. MacDonald, Washabuck; Anna Long, Bonnie Thornhill and Tom Wilson, Baddeck; Jessie MacKinnon, Little Narrows.

Peter (Jack) MacLean, Benacadie; Mickey (John H) MacNeil, Jamesville; Wanda and Ricky MacDougall, Washabuck; Susan MacLean and Kelly McNenly, Sydney Forks; Ben and Carmie MacLean, Washabuck; Lauchie MacLean, Bedford; Terry A. MacGillivray, Halifax and Antigonish; Gordon "Lighthouse" MacLean, Sugar Camp; Kathy MacKenzie and Jennifer Clifton with Special Collections staff, Angus L. Macdonald Library, Antigonish; Jane Arnold, Anne MacNeil and Catherine Arseneau, Beaton Institute, CBU, Sydney; Madeline Harvey, Parks Canada, Baddeck; Waneta MacNeil, NSCC, Port Hawkesbury; Calum and Rhoda MacNeil, Mairi Ceit MacKinnon and Angus Brendan MacNeil MP, Isle of Barra, Scotland; Archie MacLean, Irene MacLean, Donnie MacKinnon, Washabuck; Walter and Eileen Matheson, Little Narrows; Norm Macdonald, Cape Breton Genealogy and Historical Society, Sydney.

Joel Taylor, Port Hawkesbury GIS specialist, for his mapping skills; Robin Stuart, Englishtown; Anita and Larry (Murdock) MacNeil, Iona and Little Narrows; Roderick MacNeil, Gillis Point; Michael A. and Rose MacLean, MacKay Point; Murdell MacNeil, Iona; Michael Dan MacNeil, Jamesville; Quentin MacDonald, Washabuck; Vincent J. MacLean, East Bay; Murray Chisholm, Whycocomagh; Ewen MacLean, Baddeck Bridge; Billy and Reid MacKay, Big Baddeck; Sadie Marie MacNeil, Ottawa Brook; Roslyn MacRae, Baddeck; Halifax researcher Virginia Clark; Michael and Shirley MacNeil, Sydney; Martin MacLean, Millville; Chrissy and Gerard MacNeil, Washabuck; Mary and Clarence Roberts, Baddeck; Kyle and Anita MacNeil, Mira; Pat Chafe, Glace Bay, for her melody transcriptions; Jocelyn Bethune, Baddeck for her copy editing; Historian A. J. B. Johnston, Truro, for his considerate remarks delivered in the Foreword, and Editor-in-Chief Mike Hunter, Cape Breton University Press, Sydney, for his understanding, foresight and assistance.

A specific thank you to the authors, publishers and photographers listed in the bibliography, notes and elsewhere, who generously granted permission for reproduction and extracts from their works. Special thanks to son Calum, who critiqued an early draft, as well as to Marie MacLean, Lower Washabuck, and Rod C. MacNeil, Barra Glen, for their timeless knowledge, suggestions and continuous encouragement. A very special thank you and salute to Marjorie Andrews, New Hampshire, daughter of Marjorie MacLean, widow of Alex D. MacLean, for the legal conveyance of copyrights to me pertaining to Alex D. MacLean's manuscripts. *Moran taing*!

And first, last and foremost, I am especially grateful to my wife Charlotte, for her insight, suggestions, love and tolerance as she permitted me to entomb myself for long periods of time in the catacomb of our home. *Tapadh leibh.*

V.W.ML.

Foreword

I was not far into Vince MacLean's manuscript for this book before I began to feel I'd made a serious error: During the near quarter-century I lived on Cape Breton Island I'd not once been to Washabuck, Birch Point or St. Columba. Such is life of course; sometimes we miss out on opportunities and regret it later on. I'm certain now that if only I'd read this book, or spoken with Vince MacLean before I moved off-Island back in 2000, I'd have made sure I spent some time in and around Washabuck to take in the place he writes so eloquently about, if only to see how exactly its seascape meets the sky.

Then again, the people, places and events Vince MacLean brings to life in these pages are not exactly there to be visited anymore. The Washabuck of this book is the Washabuck that was, and as it now still lives on in Vince MacLean's mind, thanks to a lifetime of listening to oral traditions and of conducting his own in-depth research of every written source he could find. In the end, what he's produced is much more than a study of a community with geographical coordinates on a map. It's a compelling examination of both a place and its time, and that time spans a few centuries. At its deepest level, or so it seems to me, *These Were My People* is a celebration of *his* people and of life itself, as seen through the distinctive prism of a distinctive corner of the Isle.

Though the author chose not to call the book an encyclopedia, he might have done. A Washabuckopedia, if I am permitted to invent a term. And like an encyclopedia, thanks to the detailed breakdown offered in the table of contents, readers could, if so inclined, pick and choose the subjects they wish to absorb and enjoy. Or, best of all, just sit back and take in the entire book just as the author hoped and planned.

As I turned the pages I was caught up in the author's immense talent for sharing what he's gathered. Within these pages are countless fascinating tales about all aspects of life in Washabuck. It's clear that Vince took delight in soaking up the stories he heard and the documents he read. There's humour as well as serious stuff here, and he presents it all with a definite voice and tone. It's almost as if you can hear a background sound of the kettle coming to a boil for a pot of tea. I've not met Vince in person, but I imagine there's a slight Cape Breton lilt to his voice, which reflects the even stronger lilt of his Scottish forebears.

One final thought: it strikes me that this book could be a model for historians and storytellers in other communities on Cape Breton Island, or elsewhere. Easier said than done, of course, for a book like *These Were My People* is not the product of a few weeks or months. It takes years, and requires someone special like Vince MacLean to be collecting the stories and making sense of them as well as spending long hours in the archives. The end result, this book, is a treasure house.

A. J. B. Johnston, 2014

Introduction

"There comes a voice that awakes my soul. It is the voice of years that are gone; they roll before me with their deeds." – Ossian

I was perhaps all of ten years old – home from school, recuperating from one of those by now, usually innocent but inescapable childhood illnesses, when my mother asked me if I felt up to reading *The Highland Heart in Nova Scotia*. It was about life in Washabuck in pioneer times she explained. I was feeling better and agreed. Unaware that what would follow would spark a lifelong interest and forever be a part of my life.

"Is the mail from Washabuckt in yet?"[1]

This simple question, posed with outrageous bravado, triggered a wisp of smirk to flit across my now, pock-marked face. The baffling, melodramatic utterance, accompanied with counter thumping, directed at the mail clerk in the grandiose foyer of the old Waldorf-Astoria by a former Washabucker in the early 1900s, endeavouring to impress his friend newly arrived from Cape Breton with his own feigned familiarity to Fifth Avenue and New York City, puzzled me perhaps, almost as much, as it surely had the startled employee![2]

I was immediately hooked, altogether totally delighted that such a book existed. Not only did it tell the story of my people in an entertaining, delightful and informative fashion, it was penned by Washabuck native, long-time managing editor of the *New York Times*, Neil F. MacNeil. I devoured it despite my illness and tender years. Now, sixty years later, I still savour the rereading of this Cape Breton classic.

Looking back, I ask myself, what were the major factors that influenced my lifelong interest in the relics and history of my bucolic community and hearty people?

I have to give unqualified credit to my parents for instilling in me the desire to read. I remember each of them after a day full of manual labour, taking turns reading children's storybooks to me in the nightfall's dimness, aided by the yellow dancing shadows stuttering from the kitchen's pungent kerosene lamp. One, a story about a girl named Nan whom I seemed to have bonded with, even at such an early age, as she romped through green hay fields overcome with an intense medley of flowers, cavorting with her constant companion, a brown and white spaniel named Zipper. The other, a book entitled, *The Mystery of Lakeside Camp*, recounted the saga of a youthful sleuth displaying his doggedness in resolving a cold case involving a stolen precious necklace. To my continuing delight and as a result of my unending requests, both of these stories were read and reread to me a multitude of times. That simple yet effective initiative by my parents instilled in me a powerful desire to read. I impatiently bided my time until I could learn for myself. As things turned out – books, reading and second-hand stories proved to be great escapes and were to have a profound impact upon my life.

Around 1945, Joe MacNeil (1877-1948), a grand uncle of mine, arrived back home from a lifetime spent as a sourdough, panning alluvial streambeds for that elusive golden motherlode, first in the wilds of the Klondike along the Yukon River and later in Alaska. He built a trapper's cabin in nearby Iona and it was there that he died in 1948. But when I was four years old, he would offer me peppermints to dance a few barefoot steps as my father played *Lord MacDonald* on the fiddle. He'd laugh as I rushed to the water bucket, for a dipper of "cold" (as I called it), to douse the fervent consequent of chewing those fiery peppermints.

I remember Uncle Joe as a rangy man of average height with broad shoulders, his balding head usually adorned with a flat brimmed hat, and a twinkle in his eye. Joe returned to Cape Breton with little more than the clothes on his back, a bruised valise sheltering some battered belongings and paraphernalia of the gold rush era, remnants of miner's apparel: gold pan and scales, a few gold nuggets along with some gold dust snugly secured in a dilapidated leather poke, a grizzly bear's tooth, a smattering of photographs of his late family and the snowy north country. Each wonderful and awe-inspiring saga, stories of a lifetime, filled with adventure and heartbreak.

Snippets of tales involved the navigating of raging rivers, the scaling of snowy mountain passes and of marauding wolf packs. Wolverines were an animal we were totally unfamiliar with, but apparently they viciously plundered Uncle Joe's food caches. We heard of the exhilaration of hunting mountain sheep and of being eyeball to eyeball with grizzlies with bad breath. These stories still race through the archives of my earliest recollections. A good story is enjoyed by most, especially children, and many from those older generations had perfected the nuances that enhance storytelling, *sgeulaichean* the Gaels called them, and Uncle Joe certainly had honed his repertoire to a Gillette's edge.

It was my grandmothers though, both of them descendants of Washabuck MacNeil pioneer families, that proved to have, indirectly and unwittingly, the leading influence on my lifelong interest in local history, lore and genealogy. My mother Rose (1912-1999) was born in Upper Washabuck, the third eldest in a family of fourteen. She grew into adulthood familiar with all the families there and how they were entwined and related; whether through wedlock, kinship or friendship, and to what degree. She and her siblings were the benefactors of listening unceasingly, to their mother Sarah Liza MacDonald (1886-1961) and their aunt Annie (Ranald) MacDonald (1852-1925) along with neighbouring women, discuss relationships as they went about their endless daily and seasonal chores of mothering and housekeeping. This was the fare then of everyday conversations spent over a cup of hot tea, a feed of baked eels speared through the winter's ice, the washing of heavy bedclothes during the springtime months in the nearby "washing brook," or while simply seeing to the incessant, home and farm chores that required constant tending.

In 1943 my parents married. My father Michael was the eighth in a family of twelve and my mother moved into his family's ancestral home at MacKay Point, on the eastern end of Washabuck. Michael's mother Theresa (1875-1951) was to live another six years with us after my birth. During that time my mother gleaned much of my paternal grandmother's genealogical knowledge that she readily shared with my mother, about her own people at Washabuck Centre and the folks of Lower Washabuck, including those individuals who had "moved away" and how they too were related, intertwined and connected.

I remember both my grandmothers well. I recall the frequent topic of relationships and their invariable use of the patronymic – *sloinneadh* as its expressed in Gàidhlig, the manner of describing one's pedigree. As it was gutturally rhymed off, it identified and described the genealogical lineage of each family or a particular family member, ensuring subtle distinction from other individuals or families with similar surnames, that was such a widespread characteristic of Gàidhlig-speaking people. In addition to one's Clan name the majority of people were intimately identified by their father and grandfather's Christian names or on occasion their mother or grandmother's name, and very often by their occupation or some descriptive peculiarity.

Until her marriage, my maternal grandmother was known as Sarah *Liosaidh ni'n Ruairidh, 'ic Iain 'ic Ruairidh 'ic Dhòmhnuill 'ic Ruairidh (MacNill)* and thereafter she was usually referred to as Sarah Liza *bean Aonghais Raghnaill `ic Raghnaill Mhóir (MacDhòmhnuill)*, she now being identified as Sarah Liza, wife of Angus Ranald son of Ranald *Mór* (MacDonald), pioneer.

My paternal grandmother was referred to as Theresa *Mhìcheil Eòin*, she was *Theresa ni'n Mhìcheil 'ic Eòin* (MacNill), Theresa daughter of Michael son of *Eòin* (MacNeil), pioneer. Upon her marriage she was referred to as Theresa *bean Bhincent 'ic Pheadair 'ic Caluim 'ic Lachainn (MacGhill-Leathain)*, Theresa wife of Vincent, Peter, Calum, Lachlan (MacLean), and so it went.

This genealogical characteristic, the oral tradition of the family patronymic, the identification of a person by referring to the immediate predecessors of an individual, rather than referring to someone in the ancient past, was a distinction that went back generations certainly well beyond 1817, when many of the Gaels first arrived in Washabuck.

Gàidhlig was not spoken in our home in my time. My grandmothers were both fluent Gàidhlig speakers and singers though, and while my mother could understand it, she spoke but a few words. As did my father. The family *cù* was similarly handicapped. Unfortunately, we did not learn Gàidhlig as children and later on my own feeble attempts wrestling with the language proved futile. Perhaps that whole sorry situation could best be summarized by citing the eloquent Gàidhlig speaking Presbyterian Minister of Little Narrows, Rev. A. D. MacKinnon (1898-1985) when completing a presentation in Gàidhlig, he would add in English (tongue only partially in cheek) that, "If you have failed to understand what has just been said, your education has been sadly neglected!" *Gu dearbh!*

Due to the influence of both my grandmothers, my mother was well versed and comfortable with the genealogy of many of Washabuck's people. As a result of listening to her speak so enthusiastically and convincingly about the genealogy of so many families, I soon realized this was something I too enjoyed. Over passing decades I succeeded in achieving, by mere association and assimilation, a degree of knowledge about these relationships that my mother always chatted about. The strong sense of family fraternity somehow penetrated my own genetic makeup.

Again, with hindsight that now spans decades, these conversations proved invaluable to me as I prepared this work. Today, the one thing I can honestly (and selfishly) say that I miss most by my mother's passing is the absence of those informative, easy conversations about kith and kin that somehow seemed (just as the cream rises naturally to the top of the cream can) to always flow to the forefront, whether during a keen game of cribbage or while simply enjoying a cup of tea.

Then, my future mother-in-law Mary Ann MacKenzie (1901-1983) entered into this ever broadening genealogical mosaic. Mary Ann was from Washabuck Bridge on the western end of Washabuck. Her daughter Charlotte was the baby in the family of twelve. In due course we committed holy deadlock, so now there was an additional family, an exploding clan of in-laws, with whom I was to become very well acquainted.

Mary Ann was born a Devoe. Her father was Simon, the son of Peter Devoe of Little Bras d'Or who had married Christy Murphy of MacKinnon's Harbour. Simon Devoe married Ellen MacKenzie of Washabuck and their daughter Mary Ann, my mother-in-law, married John Stephen MacKenzie a grandson of a union of two other MacKenzie families, one from Washabuck and the other from North Lake Ainslie. John Stephen's father, Charles "Framer," had married Ann (Stephen "Rogers") MacNeil from nearby Highland Hill.

Just to keep this genealogical cauldron boiling and the milieu challenging, two of Charlotte's six sisters married distant MacLean cousins from Washabuck, one of them bearing a family of eight, and the other sixteen children. As well, the MacKinnon family, early pioneers of Washabuck and later of nearby Cains Mountain, was closely related to my mother's MacDonalds and the above mentioned MacKenzie families, and they delivered a family of twenty-one, eighteen of them surviving infancy to be put on the road for adulthood. Fruitfulness, propagation and birthdays prevailed.

So, I had two reasons (as if I needed a second one) for visiting "The Bridge" as the MacKenzie home was called, because of its location adjacent to the tarnished iron highway bridge spanning Washabuck River. Mary Ann MacKenzie was blessed with a sense of humour, a fabulous memory, a singing voice that soothingly enhanced any Gàidhlig lullaby, and she raised one of the most musically talented families that have ever come from Cape Breton Island. Among her precociously talented horde of harmonic grandchildren, are The Barra MacNeils and members of Slàinte Mhath, two musical bands that have shared superbly in revealing the infectious Celtic music of Cape Breton Island to the planet.

Mary Ann kindly and patiently shared with me various stories of the pioneer people of Washabuck and tales of "days gone by."

Unfortunately, I knew neither of my grandfathers. Both died before I was born. My Grandfather and namesake Vincent MacLean died in 1943 a year prior to my birth, and Grandfather Angus Ranald MacDonald had passed away in 1934. Charlotte's father John Stephen MacKenzie (1895-1945) died when she was but three months old. This probably accounts for the preponderance of matriarchal influence on this work. Certainly though, my own father Michael A. (1911-2007), an admirable dance fiddler was adept at spinning a yarn and some of his reminisces have woven their way into this work.

An enjoyable and significant male influence upon my education occurred during my years at St. Francis Xavier University. During a four year period I was among a plethora of students who were privileged to benefit from the gifted influence of Major Calum I. N. MacLeod, Professor of

Celtic Studies. I shared an amicable and buoyant friendship with him and his supportive and entertaining wife, Iona. We quickly developed a rapport which was to extend well beyond university days until his untimely death in 1977. MacLeod arrived in Nova Scotia in the late 1940s to teach Gàidhlig at Colaisde na Gàidhlig (The Gaelic College, St. Anns). He soon became Gàidhlig advisor to the provincial Department of Education and eventually a professor at the Antigonish University.

As a youth in Scotland he had demonstrated his athletic prowess by excelling at the Scottish game of shinty. Later as a rotund university professor clad in his MacLeod tartan kilt with green tunic and tam, he brought a commanding presence to any event, exhibiting a dour demeanour which belied a keen mind and an impish sense of ribald humour. A former Major with the British intelligence service during the Second World War, Major MacLeod was a Celtic scholar, a piper, a Gàidhlig author, a gifted, distinguished – and a crowned – Gàidhlig Bard.

The Major as he was affectionately addressed, shared with his youthful disciples his deep love for Celtic heritage, its turbulent history and its venerable literature, including a fervent appetite for us to acquire the Gàidhlig language. He explained the particular roles the Celts had played throughout the mists of ancient history and detailed for us why so many of their descendants were now living in Nova Scotia. Until that time, I had no real understanding of why our ancestors had left their homeland.

The failed Jacobite Rebellion of 1745 under "Bonnie Prince Charlie" and the ruthless consequences of that undertaking, including the dismantling of the social, economic and hereditary structures, were laid bare. The prohibition of the wearing of Highland dress, the elimination of the of bearing of arms, and the new emphasis placed upon the use of the English language especially for "disloyal" chiefs, together with the continuing religious repercussions stemming from the intensified Scottish penal laws, brought veracity and a new reality to our Celtic education. These reasons coupled with the Highland Clearances – the enforced removal of Highland families from their crofts to be replaced with sheep to supply the increased demand for wool in England – and then the failure of the kelp industry in the Hebrides to sustain the population in the early decades of the 1800s, all added to the confused medley that explained in a directly discernable fashion, why our people had emigrated from their ancient *taighean dùbha* to eke out a new existence in a fresh homeland.

In the mid-seventies, after a sojourn of about a dozen years, my wife and I returned from exile with our young family to take up permanent residence in Washabuck. We became re-acquainted with Steven Rory (S. R.) MacNeil, who, was by that time the retired curator of the Nova Scotia Highland Village Museum at Iona. He had been compiling a book about the genealogy of the pioneer people and their descendants that lived in

Iona and surrounding communities. The published work was entitled, *All Call Iona Home*. During the first of what proved to be many enjoyable and informative visits to their home over the next number of years, S. R. asked me if I would assist him with the genealogy of the Washabuck people.

I gladly agreed. I helped him with some minor bits and pieces of genealogy that had been kindly shared with me by senior Washabuck residents, fourth and fifth generation descendants of the pioneers, including Marjorie and Kaye MacLean, Murdock MacInnis, Malkie MacDonald, Archie MacIver, Neillie Devoe, Joe (Red Rory) MacLean, Archie MacLean, Mick-John MacLean, Jimmy MacKinnon, and of course my mother and mother-in-law. These individuals and others, each in their own personable, enthusiastic, and enjoyable manner, gladly responded to my oft-times grasping and confused questions. I'd arrive back home late at night, but not before sometimes savouring a *dileag*, and always the tea, with sheets of paper filled with bits and pieces of information – *gibeagan*, as it could may be expressed in Gàidhlig.

It was my aunt and Godmother Kaye MacLean that shared with me a spare copy of a tattered sixteen page typeset booklet entitled, *Early Days in Lower Washabuckt* (ca. 1939) penned by A. D. MacLean. It tweaked my interest. The book provided basic information about some of the first pioneers in Lower Washabuck, including data on early schools, post offices and a store.

So, who was A. D. MacLean? A. D., Alex D., or "Little Alec"(1889-1974) as he was variously called, was a grandson of the first MacLean born in Washabuck.

For many years Alex D. served as local newspaper correspondent for a number of newspapers including: *The Casket*, *The Post Record* and *The Victoria-Inverness Bulletin*. He took an in-depth interest in political happenings of the day, the history of his community, the broader community, and his ancestors.

Alex D. deserves special mention in this discourse, as much of the primary written sources for this work can be credited to him. He penned an unpublished manuscript, comprising some seventy typewritten foolscap pages describing local events, with tales and genealogy of the community of Washabuck. It is entitled *The Pioneers of Washabuckt*, his preferred way of spelling the community name.

In later years, Alex D. undertook the daunting task of compiling a manuscript called *History of Victoria County*. Much of this work is a duplication of Patterson's *History of Victoria County* first published in1885. Alex D. though, added some very colourful, detailed, informed and pertinent information to Patterson's edition.

Alex D., whom any reader can easily glean from his writings, was as staunch a Conservative in politics as he was rabid a Catholic in religious persuasion. He authored an entertaining, authentic rendering of a now almost forgotten municipal election that occurred in the Washabuck district in 1937. He did not write it under his own by-line as he had his other works but it was common knowledge that it was indeed authentic Alex D. at his best. He capitalized on what was considered (certainly at that time) a serious political happening and did it justice with his enlivened hand, gratefully capturing for posterity in a mirthful manner, an exemplary rendition of an old-time, if unusual, Cape Breton election. "The Three Rorys' Election" is printed in its entirety in the last chapter.

So I salute Alex D. MacLean. Much of the early oral history of the community of Washabuck would have been forever lost had it not been for his interest in its people, and his efforts in preserving in writing, facts and incidents of the community. Whatever errors may exist in MacLean's efforts, they were certainly honest ones, as he did his utmost best, working with the information that was available and shared with him. His work provided me with a solid foundation to shingle together this volume. A number of his colourful stories have been incorporated throughout this work.

Another storyteller, and genealogist without peer, whose works have played a significant role in this endeavour was Francis Hector MacNeil (1867-1954) of Iona and New Waterford He was a son of Hector (Rory, Donald) MacNeil, his great-grandfather Donald being one of the original four pioneer MacNeils to settle in Iona. Francis Hector married Mary MacNeil, (1865-1935) daughter of Murdock (*Dhòmhnaill Eòin*) MacNeil of nearby MacNeil's Vale in 1889. They had a family of twelve, seven boys and five daughters.

Francis Hector compiled two unpublished sketches of genealogy that outline the pioneers of these areas and their descendants. "The MacNeils of Iona" and "The MacDonalds of Saint Columba and Washabuck" are typewritten essays of fifteen and eleven pages respectively. Both documents are undated and do not bear Francis Hector's byline, although again, there is no doubt about their authenticity and the authorship. Both were assembled ca. 1939-1940.[3] Interest in his genealogy continues to be perpetuated today by one of his own great-grandsons, Vince MacNeil of Halifax.

It is noteworthy that Francis Hector's own father, Hector R., who died in New Waterford in 1925 at the age of 91 years, was married four times and was predeceased by all his wives. He is buried in Iona. Hector R. was another acknowledged, excellent source of local oral history for Alex D. MacLean.

Another Hector, Hector MacKenzie of Washabuck Bridge, recalls the genealogical abilities of Francis Hector MacNeil. Hector, with his mother Mary Ann and Mickey MacDougall, a neighbour and chauffeur for the occasion, attended the wake of Murdock A. MacNeil. Murdock A. of Gillis Point, a bachelor, had died in early November 1950 and as was the usual practice, the wake was held in the deceased's home. Murdock A. was a veteran of both world wars – wounded three times, and had spent the balance of his life employed as a carpenter. Hector finishes his story:

> It was one of those clear, cool, crisp evenings in November. The early winter snows had yet to arrive. In fact, as I remember it, there was almost no snow at all that winter. Anyway, there was a crowd sitting around the wake house, at various times praying, discussing the weather of the day and the events of the season. Everyone was dressed in their better clothes, some in suits. Various mourners were to remain for the all-night-vigil, the typical practice at that time, sitting up as a show of respect to the deceased. The aroma of food, tea, and pipe tobacco permeated the house. Francis Hector was there holding court. In response to my whispered query, mother told me who he was. This was the first and only time I recall ever seeing Francis Hector, although I had heard much about him. He held the rapt attention of most, with his obvious command of genealogical relationships and stories of days of old. The Gaelic was flowing along with the English, both languages being used interchangeably. Murdock A.'s life-long neighbours were there; John Neillie, John Alec, John Allen, John P., Jimmy John D. – all MacNeils, and John Archie – a MacDonald from St. Columba. [Another John could be found outside!]
>
> These individuals amongst others were there, themselves all ardent genealogists; and they were obviously mesmerised by Francis Hector, who was spinning it off as if he was reading from a teleprompter. There was nothing these old timers enjoyed more; and the further back one could go with names, right back to Scotland even, well then the better they liked it. Names you could really not understand in English were readily understood in Gaelic. The Gaelic definitely put the stamp on a name or a family, and Francis Hector was obviously a master at it, and certainly that night as I remember it, he commanded everyone's attention and respect.[4]

Francis Hector's genealogy on the "MacDonalds" proved invaluable in outlining early pioneer families in Washabuck and St. Columba, and one of Washabuck's little-known tragic stories related by him that November evening, is included within these pages.

Two other primary sources pertaining mostly to early times in both Washabuck and St. Columba, include "The Story of Pioneers and Progress in Our Community" by Anna Murphy, a handwritten eighth grade history project of eleven pages from 1930 and a similar beautifully handwritten nine-page document dated 1935 entitled "Settlement and Development of our District," by Frances MacDougall, both students in the community during that time. Each of these documents adds important social fibre to the story of early days of Washabuck with collaborative information gleaned from community elders. These novice authors have certainly earned my respect and gratitude for their superb efforts, which in turn have proven so valuable for this narrative.

I would be remiss if I did not mention the worthy role played by the work entitled, *History of Christmas Island Parish* by Archibald J. MacKenzie, published in 1926. Perpetuating the memories of the pioneers from there and surrounding communities, so many of them expatriates from the shores of the Isle of Barra, MacKenzie's opus (and the revised, more recent 1984 edition, by MacKenzie's son Archie Alec and granddaughter Marion Rothe) has been helpful in resolving a number of genealogical hurdles pertaining to, in particular the MacNeil and MacKenzie families, pioneers of Christmas Island with relatives that subsequently settled in Washabuck.

Another transgression that must be confessed occurred when it came time for me to do some actual writing for the endeavour. I found amongst the staggers and jags and endless "odd jobs," every conceivable reason to procrastinate. I haven't interviewed this old timer yet. I can't type. I need to buy a computer. I should visit Scotland. I don't know where to start. Well, that last statement was at least partially true. I did not really know where to start. I used that excuse for the longest time, until by chance, I mulled over a couple of amusing stories my father had shared with us. The lessons from each I eventually linked and realized somewhat embarrassingly that they applied perfectively to my own procrastination. I finally took them to heart and used their influence to combat my own self-imposed inertia. Surprisingly, to a degree it worked.

Dad and his siblings used to exchange visits with the Pauls as the family were known. They were a MacLean family, related to us, most of whom were either deceased or had vacated Washabuck by 1950. Murdock Paul (1861-1947) a beloved bachelor lived with his spinster sisters Kate and Ellie-Ann and their faithful dog Dixon, while another bachelor-brother, Malcolm, lived on the neighbouring farm. Both were tall men. Malcolm could play the fiddle but was better noted for being a deft, if coy, step-dancer. He was also looked upon admiringly, as being the most skilled hand-scyther in the entire community. Murdock was a tall reedy man with an oversized drooping moustache and head full of thick white hair usually adorned with a broad-brimmed fedora. He was described as a fine and likeable gentleman, who was naturally funny, with an explosive laugh that seemed to spring from his bootstraps. He enjoyed telling a story and could deliver one with flair.

Gàidhlig of course had been the family's mother tongue but over the period of his lifetime Murdock had learned to converse in a limited way in English but understandably, the grammar was not always quite up to scratch, particularly when he became animated. Profanity was Murdock's other speciality. Let's just say that he was proficient in *three* languages.

Dad recalled that when Murdock Paul told a story he seemed to always start in the middle of it and then somehow, he'd work the tale from both directions. This was not an intentional ploy on his part, but rather one that probably developed from his thinking in Gàidhlig, while attempting to express himself in English. Murdock's stories, amusing enough in themselves, took on even more comical dimensions in his relating them, because of his own singular style.

Dad's second story referred to how his own father successfully dealt with a problem. His father had a relatively large farming operation. Consequently, he would have fields of hay and oats to slash at harvest time. One of the neighbouring Brown brothers, Johnny (1884-1959), arrived at the house in October looking for work. My grandfather liked Johnny very much and asked him if he could handle a hand scythe. Johnny replied that he could and so grandfather gladly and gratefully put him to work. There were acres and acres of oats to harvest. Grandfather showed Johnny where to start and told him to, "Go to it!"

When grandfather returned a few hours later he was totally dismayed at the scene that played out before his eyes. He had never witnessed such devastation from the use of a hand scythe. Normally, the mower begins at the edge of a field and then proceeds forward along the field, swinging the handle with its razor-sharp scythe from right to left in front of him, effectively severing the crop at the base of the stalk. A swath is cut for a predetermined distance and then returns to the point of beginning and repeats the whole procedure in a neat and orderly fashion.

As with so many skills, hand-scything is an acquired one, and at that time especially, most men were skilled and some were extremely proficient at it. But all took pride in doing a good job, for they knew the quality of their work would eventually become part of the everyday gossip throughout the community.

What was Grandfather to do? He pondered for a few moments musing over his options; then suddenly asking Johnny to follow him, he strode into the centre of the large oat field and again told him, "Go to it!" The problem was immediately resolved, as the errant but willing worker now proceeded to successfully slash the oats in an ever-broadening circular fashion.

I realized I must now apply a similar solution to my own problem. Proceed like Murdock Paul and Johnny Brown from somewhere in the middle of this work and hope that the various components would eventually find some sense of order and perspective. It took a long time but the challenge finally staggered toward a measure of triumph.

Many years ago, in youthful wanderlust, I wound my way to British Columbia. I worked on several construction projects in its wilderness, attempting to pay off overdue tuition bills from university days. While there, I chanced upon a labour of love written by two long-time residents of Hudson Hope. The superb volume was entitled *This Was Our Valley*. I mention this because upon much reflection, the *Valley* in the book's title hinted to me what perhaps, could make a suitable title for this work. It is about the people – *my people* – the people that settled here and were born here, laughed and wept here, prayed to their God, danced in the aisles, and in due course died here and elsewhere.

Why *my people*? I reflected upon the number of relatives I had; innumerable uncles and aunts, alongside ancient grand-uncles and antiquated grand-aunts, some maidenly and others less so; shirt-tail cousins of every degree, many of them within kissing distance. And Charlotte's people, in-laws to no end with their seemingly far-flung, unending, vibrant families. I couldn't swing the proverbial dead cat by its limp tail at a local shindig, funeral reception or community fracas without striking scores of relatives and immediately insulting twice that number.

It was impossible then for me to write about my community and the residents from my community without referring to people related to me from some quarter of wind, or to some nth degree, whether by blood or marriage or friendship, the lovable knave, hero, leader, midwife, warrior, rascal or follower, oft times like pipe tobacco, they emitting an aroma encompassing a host of these blended characteristics, a goodly share of them striking startlingly close to home. Whatever, if one searched keenly enough, there always seemed to be a connection. For these reasons then, the title eventually evolved and displayed itself: *These Were My People*.

Today, people ask, "Well, how long have you been working on this history?" When I reply, "Oh, about fifty years," I inevitably receive back in response a quizzed look framed below a cocked eyebrow. (I didn't want to rush it.) But the truth is, I have been researching it after a fashion since my boyhood years; asking questions, scribbling quick notes to myself, recording conversations with willing participants, haunting cemeteries in company with the ghosts, gathering related documents, collecting manuscripts and faded newspaper clippings, finding blurred photographs along with musty books.

It was my goal to mingle a warm anecdotal approach with salient facts for future generations in particular, as a result of saving historical and archival documents and local lore, bundling that information, ensuring a reasonable degree of authenticity and enthusiasm, while showcasing and displaying the accounts through Washabuck's eclectic cast of compelling characters – these were my people.

1 – Washabuck

Islands embrace this ball of spinning mud we call planet Earth. Some are enormous continents onto themselves; others are nondescript bikinis of sand. Still others, like Cape Breton Island with its combination of rugged, picturesque landscapes and intoxicating vistas, enthral the world and imprint upon the eye of the beholder, whether they be permanent resident, a seasonal tenant or the discriminating tourist.

A quick glance of a map of Cape Breton Island from the perspective of a spiralling bald eagle reveals the uniqueness of this island. Its exterior coastline surrounded by the salty waters of the western North Atlantic, while its geographic interior is dominated by a resplendent, luminous, brackish sea, called the Bras d'Or Lake. The Lake displays itself like a giant octopus with some of its narrow tentacles groping seaward toward the Atlantic in the form of two natural passages and a man-made canal.

"The Lakes," as they are referred to locally, are composed of two bodies of water comprising some 1165 square kilometers; The "Big Lake" to the south is approximately thirty-five kilometres in diameter and the smaller "Northern Basin" which forms a dogleg to the west known as St. Patrick's Channel and delineates the Washabuck peninsula. These natural reservoirs are linked at the Island's centre by the Barra Strait *(Caolas nam Barrach)*, a deep, narrow, body of churlish water, named for the Isle of Barra in Scotland, the original home of so many of the transplanted Gaels that settled here on its shores more than two centuries ago and whose descendants today continue to live along its scenic watershed. St. Patrick's Channel gradually tapers into the Strait of Julia *(Caolas nam Sìlis)* at Little Narrows before tethering itself at its most western point to Whycocomagh Bay.

Nestled along the north side of this prominent peninsula, defined by St. Patrick's Channel, lay the rural hamlet of Washabuck. This peninsula is an integral portion of the Central Cape Breton landmass. The Washabuck

Peninsula is easily identifiable as it is essentially surrounded by the Lakes with the sole exception of an isthmus to the westward called Portage. The Mi'kmaq called this neck of land *Sgitegengtg,* which means "pull canoes." Across this narrow, time-worn, land-corridor, the Mi'kmaq of old would carry their canoes, avoiding a tedious round-about journey of sixty-five kilometres. The Washabuck Peninsula forms the southernmost portion of the Municipality of Victoria, (that in 1851 became a separate county, apart from Cape Breton County), and owing to the three kilometre-wide St. Patrick's Channel, is physically separated from the remainder of the municipality and the county seat in the neighbouring village of Baddeck.

The community of Washabuck is fifteen kilometres in length and lies in an east-westerly direction along the northern shore of the peninsula; the more eastern portion faces Alexander Graham Bell's Beinn Bhreagh, the village of Baddeck, Spectacle Island and Baddeck Bay, where the snarling north winds of March, *an giobagan,* come from. The more westerly part of the community lay along both banks of the meandering Washabuck River that leisurely empties eastwardly, into St. Patrick's Channel.

Washabuck shares the peninsula with the neighbouring, now sadly, mostly uninhabited communities of Murphy Point, St. Columba, Cain's Mountain, Birch Point, MacNeils Vale and Ponys Point. In a generally counter-clockwise direction around the peninsula, other thriving, entangled settlements include, South Cove (The Grant), Hazeldale, Jubilee, Little Narrows, Estmere, Ottawa Brook, MacKinnon Harbour, Red Point, Jamesville, Highland Hill, Barra Glen, Iona Rear (*Cùl Beag*), Iona and Grass Cove, which leads you back through Gillis Point and Gillis Point East to Washabuck.

Washabuck itself is composed of a series of subdivisions. From MacKay Point on its most eastern promontory, through in a westerly direction to Lower Washabuck, Washabuck Centre, Rear Washabuck Centre, Upper Washabuck, Murphy Point, Washabuck Bridge, St. Columba and Birch Point. In pioneer days Washabuck Centre and Rear Washabuck Centre were considered part of Lower Washabuck. With seemingly as many boroughs as the city of Boston, the Washabuck community, even as late as 1901, was rife with a federal census count of 435 residents. St. Columba was known as Grand Narrows Rear until it received its own Post Office in 1903. For the purposes of this work, the peoples from Barra, South Uist, and Lewis, who settled in Birch Point and St. Columba, are included. These two settlements lay immediately adjacent to Washabuck and both were settled about the same time and their people were certainly considered Washabuck residents in pioneer days.

The name Washabuck is said to be of Mi'kmaw origin. The most likely meaning is *"an angle of land* (Washabuck peninsula) *formed between a river* (Washabuck River) *and a lake"* (Bras d' Or Lake). There is also a Native word "Wosobachuk" which means *"placid water"* which could very well be the term from which the name is derived.[1] There have been numerous spellings – most of them jawbreakers – each one being more challenging and daunting than the next. A common spelling in pioneer times found on early documents was Watchabaktchkt, Astchbuckt or Washabuckt. Today however, most residents, along with governments, their departments and agencies, seem content and comfortable with its spelling in its as yet simplest arrangement – *Washabuck*.

1-1 Cartoon depicting Washabuck, Montreal *Star Weekly*, 1970.

2 – Early Residents, Visitors and Neighbours

The Mi'kmaq

Undeniably, the Mi'kmaw people were the first here. For how long, no one knows for sure, but certainly for thousands of years, perhaps for as many as 11,000.[1] Their language endowed prominent geographic points of interest with appropriate names. Patterson, in his *History of Victoria County* first published in 1885, states: "It must be remembered that every prominent object, whether hill or river, streamlet or lake, headland or island, had its appropriate designation which is still in use among them."[2]

Their words for the places of the Washabuck peninsula include: *Oatjepagtjeg gisna Oatapagtjig* which in Mi'kmaw means "shining waters," one of their descriptions of Washabuck. *Toitgetjg gisna Teoitgitjg* is Little Narrows which literally means "little narrows"; *Gamiteoigt* is the name for Iona which appropriately enough means "across the narrows," *Ilpanogotimg gisna Ilpaligotimg* for MacKay Point which means "packing away" or "fixing up your pack to get off!"[3]

Authors George Patterson and Stephen Davis, write that the Mi'kmaq had a descriptive language with a rich oral tradition, one that was not a written language prior to the arrival of the Europeans.[4] It was described by Uniacke as "remarkably soft and melodious."[5] Mi'kmaw historian, Daniel N. Paul observes:

> The Micmac were known by the early French settlers as the Souriquois, "the salt water men," to distinguish them from the Iroquois, who inhabited the fresh water country.[6]

Robert Morgan writing in *Early Cape Breton* states that:

> The only other inhabitants of Cape Breton were the Mi'kmaq Indians who hunted and gathered berries; around 450 of them lived on Cape

Breton around 1800; of this number, 130 were able hunters who used the bow and arrow, but could hurl their tomahawks with precision eight to ten yards.[7]

Certainly, the Mi'kmaq were in sufficient numbers to be reckoned with as demonstrated, ca. 1800, when a flotilla of forty or fifty armed canoes, laden with men, women and children, approached the first four Barramen to arrive on the shores of the strait, at what is today Iona. The Barramen had begun the formidable chore of clearing land and burning brush in preparation of building a shelter and planting potatoes.

The Gaels were challenged by the Mi'kmaw Chief as to why they were burning brush on their lands. An altercation was avoided when, at last minute, the Gaels knelt, made the sign of the cross and displayed a crucifix. The Mi'kmaq reconsidered their hostile intentions and bloodshed was averted. The Mi'kmaq were also Catholic having been Christianized centuries earlier by French Missionaries. Realizing that the Barramen were Catholic as well, their anger and fear abated. Arms were set aside and a meal of eels and salt was jointly prepared and shared, and peace, harmony and cooperation prevailed.[8]

2-1 *The Barraman's Feast*. A conjectural painting by Terry MacDonald, New Waterford/Inverness CB (2002), depicting the evolving lifestyles of the pioneer Gael in their new homeland, coupled with an early meeting between the native Mi'kmaq and first Gaels at what is now Iona, ca. 1800. Photo courtesy of the Nova Scotia Highland Village Society, Iona, Cape Breton. See appendix 1 for a more complete description.

EARLY RESIDENTS, VISITORS AND NEIGHBOURS

Not a few Gàidhlig families staved off starvation through a hungry pioneer winter and leaned gratefully upon the traditional skills and wilderness lore of compassionate Mi'kmaq. Morgan writes in *Early Cape Breton*:

> ...the Indians feed the people the first winter with moose meat and dogfish and that sort of thing, eels. I don't know if they could have survived without the assistance of the Indians the first winter. That was how difficult the situation was.[9]

Expressions of appreciation for the life-saving help provided by the Mi'kmaq toward European pioneers who were floundering through dire circumstances, has received scant acknowledgement from English historians.

An appreciation of the Mi'kmaw Nation's perspective on Atlantic Canada history and their own historic "bloody relationship" with the English Crown, can perhaps better provide the inquiring reader with a more balanced understanding as to why the Mi'kmaq would have felt so naturally threatened and angry with the Highlanders at Iona, who they perceived as encroaching "Englishmen."[10] The fact of the matter was that the Mi'kmaq simply did not trust the English. As Davis informs in *Mi'kmaq: Peoples of the Maritimes*, the Mi'kmaq

> ...chose to cooperate with the French. Trading relationships grew with the French and French missionaries were accepted. A growing dependence on French goods and conversions to Catholicism led to natural alliances with the French.[11]

A later witness and neighbour of the Washabuck area was Robert Elmsley, who arrived in Baddeck via Sydney in March 1840. He was born in Brechin, Scotland, seventeen years earlier, eventually married, had a family of five children and died in Baddeck in June 1903. He operated a store for a number of years and served as the local Postmaster in Baddeck. He also kept a diary from 1855 until 1889.

Elmsley encountered Mi'kmaw encampments on the western end of what is now Kidston Island, which is located less than three kilometres across St. Patrick's Channel from Washabuck. They had a large encampment on Graveyard Point, opposite the western end of Kidston Island. It was on this Point that the Mi'kmaq buried some of their dead.

Elmsley is totally captivated by the natives and relates in his diary:

> On looking around I observed Indian encampments, in various situations, and at once became enamoured with the scene. [They] would offer for sale bunches of lovely smoked and dried trout ... also eels, lovely quill boxes [and] baskets. Oh, what a sight! It excelled Robinson Crusoe and all his adventures.[12]

Historian James B. Lamb writes:

European fisherman found that the Micmac Indians of Cape Breton were already sailors of a sort, equipping their larger canoes, from 18 to 24 feet, with a single square sail of bark or hide in order to take advantage of the winds in sheltered water.[13]

It was a scene Elmsley witnessed firsthand:

> At this time, dozens of Indian canoes, under sail, were to be seen, sailing to and fro, from Boularderie Head enroute to and from Little Bras d'Or, and the scene was enchanting in the extreme.[14]

On the north side of St. Patrick's Channel is a large cove that at one time was called Indian Bay into which flow, Baddeck and Middle Rivers. Today, as scant as detailed evidence is, archaeologists can determine from middens, (the remains of shells and bones) and from pieces and shards of small tools and pottery left behind by generations of First Nations people, what foods had played a key role in their diet, and to a great extent how they lived. Patterson records that

> Various large quantities of relics, including stone axes and pestles were found many years ago on a farm occupied by Daniel MacDonald on Long Point on the north side of St. Patrick's Channel. From the quantity of these remains we are warranted in believing that here also they were accustomed to gather in large numbers.[15]

Uniacke writes about their wi'kuom (wigwam) encampments:

> In the summer and autumn the Indians are scattered throughout the country or upon the shores of the lakes and harbours, where they live chiefly by fishing and hunting: but towards the winter they draw near to the towns and villages, and pitch their camps in their neighbourhood. A number of wigwams thus assembled on the margin of a lake or river, or in the retired parts of the road amongst the woods, form quite a picturesque sight.[16]

Archaeologist J. S. Erskine of Wolfville, Nova Scotia, uncovered evidence of ancient Mi'kmaq campsites in the nearby community of Little Narrows, during his explorations on its northern point peninsula in that community, between 1961 and 1966. He records, "The site was on a sand spit beside a tidal lake. Indians have camped there in this century [20th] to spear and smoke eels."[17] Pieces of pottery, arrowheads, and a broken long spear point were uncovered. Erskine relates later that he realized that he had dug through 3,000 years of aboriginal Indian history in just a depth of six inches of soil.

Almost directly opposite Indian Bay, Washabuck River empties itself into the south side of St. Patrick's Channel. Alex D. MacLean wrote that he had in his own possession a tomahawk that was salvaged from Washabuck River.[18] It takes really no stretch of one's imagination to realize how easily accessible and what compatible encampment sites, the Washabuck shoreline provided to the Mi'kmaq.

The Mi'kmaq were known to help Scottish pioneers in dire need; kindness that was often reciprocated. What follows is a narrative from Alex D MacLean:

> Archibald MacKenzie (*Gilleasbuig mac Eachainn*) settled on Birch Point in 1821. He was the grandfather of "Red" Archie MacKenzie who lived at Birch Point and passed away on March 5th, 1928, at the age of 81 years. Red Archie and his wife Sarah were noted for their hospitality, and none knew this better than the Indians who lived on the Reservation on the north side of St. Patrick's Channel. When the Mi'kmaq were short of provisions or in any sort of difficulty, they managed to get in touch with Red Archie and his wife. In winter this would be quite simple, they simply walked across the ice; in summer they sailed across, easier still if the wind was right. One of the natives was known as 'Little Joe' and do not think that I am exaggerating when I say he was known throughout the length and breadth of Cape Breton Island. He lived to be a great age. He was born in 1819, the same year as Queen Victoria, as he was quite proud to say.
>
> Red Archie and Little Joe (his correct name was Joseph Paul) were always great friends and often Little Joe would find his way across St. Patrick's Channel to Birch Point if he needed anything. My story deals with a particular time when Little Joe's wife was sick. She had been sick for a long time, and whenever the old Indian came to visit them, Mrs. MacKenzie would always make sympathetic inquiries about her and Little Joe would have a full basket returning home.
>
> One day in the winter, Little Joe crossed the ice; there was an excellent walking crust everywhere. When he arrived at Archie MacKenzie's, Little Joe wore a woebegone expression, and he informed the MacKenzie's that his wife had died early that morning. They were all sympathy, and Mrs. MacKenzie lost no time making up a basket of goods which she knew would be very acceptable at the wake. Little Joe was very grateful and about to start off, but just as he was leaving he turned to Mrs. MacKenzie and asked: "S'pose you have no candles?" The old lady had plenty of candles and she upbraided herself for not thinking of them herself. Of course they would need candles at the wake. She gave him a parcel of home-made tallow candles and off he went.
>
> Later in the morning one of their sons was outside and he was surprised to see bits of string rolling about on the crust. He was puzzled and examined them closer. He soon realized what the pieces of string meant. They were the wicks of the candles that had been given to Little Joe. He had eaten the tallow and tossed the wicks. It is a well-known fact that Indians regard tallow as a delicacy. Later it was learned that Little Joe's good wife was still very much alive.

Coincidently, Little Joe died on March 5, 1928, the same day and year as Red Archie. He was 109 years old. The Micmac sleeps his last sleep in the cemetery on the Nyanza Reservation [Wagmatcook], while Red Archie and his good wife Sarah rest side by side in Holy Rosary Cemetery, Washabuck.[19]

For potable water, for seasonal hunting, for gathering and for normal livelihood activities, a better setting than Washabuck River would be hard to find. Placid waters indeed, with deep inlets easily accessible by canoe, a peaceful river that teemed with an abundance of trout, smelt, eels and fattened oysters, and where sea-run species like salmon, shad, herring, mackerel, and cod (including tommy cod which spawns under the ice) schooled on a seasonal basis. In addition, lobsters were bountiful at that time in the Bras d'Or Lake and the Mi'kmaq had perfected a way of spearing them in shallow waters.[20]

The Washabuck River banks encircled by the primeval forest, furnished the gatherer with nuts and berries, wild roots and herbal medicinal plants. It certainly would be frequented by game and furbearers, while the nearby ponds and marshes hosted nesting, breeding and feeding places for a diverse array of migrating waterfowl, their eggs and broods.

Washabuck River is speckled with a myriad of natural coves and inlets. Not surprisingly, one of these superb anchorages is known as Indian Cove. As Stephen Davis writes in, *Mi'kmaq: Peoples of The Maritimes:*

> The natural resources of the Maritimes and the Native people's adaptation to them provided a lifestyle in harmony with the environment.[21]

Certainly Washabuck's shores displayed that same sylvan wilderness, one that the Mi'kmaq utilized, enjoyed, conformed with and left unsullied.

The French

The French were among the first Europeans to sail the Bras d'Or Lakes and visit the Washabuck area. We can be reasonably certain that fishermen from Portugal, Spain, Brittany, Ireland, and England, as well as the Scandinavian countries visited here long before Columbus dropped anchor in the Caribbean.

2-2 Aerial view of Washabuck River looking westward towards Washabuck Bridge. Photo courtesy of David Gillis, Scotsville, Cape Breton.

Lamb notes that, "There is a record in French archives of a catch of [codfish] being landed from America in 1497, just after Columbus's return, and its phrasing leaves no doubt but that the trade was already a long-established one."[22] In addition, according to an in-depth article about Cape Breton

Island in the July 1920 edition of *The National Geographic Magazine*, writer Catherine D. Mackenzie quotes an unnamed source saying "The French government valued Cape Breton as a 'nursery for her seamen'."[23]

In August 1629 an armed French ship under the command of Captain Charles Daniel of Dieppe had anchored in the snug anchorage of Sainte-Anne's Harbour [Victoria County], and he was so visually impressed with the harbour's assets that he, "determined to fortify it and make it strong enough to deter any further attempts by the British to menace the supply line and fisheries of New France."[24] Fort Sainte-Anne gradually evolved, garrisoned by forty soldiers and two Jesuits, who in subsequent years were complemented with a series of seven additional priests, who then began the long arduous challenge of Christianizing the Mi'kmaw communities along the Bras d' Or Lake and elsewhere. Trade was also begun between the French and the Mi'kmaq, and bales of fur were shipped back to France from Sainte-Anne's Bay.[25]

Then in 1634 another venture known as the Company of Cape Breton (Compagnie du Cap-Breton) was formed in France with a mandate to exploit the Island's resources particularly its furs and fishery, writes A. J. B. Johnston in his work entitled, *Storied Shores*. About 1636, the company's new outpost was established in what is now St. Peter's. It was situated directly on the portage trail between the Atlantic shore and Bras d'Or Lake, providing easier access to the ocean and the nearby Strait of Canso. This site proved to be a more advantageous location over Sainte-Anne for trading purposes with the Mi'kmaq.[26]

In addition to the economic and religious interest between the two peoples there was, not surprisingly, development of relationships between some French mariners and Mi'kmaw women.[27] Peter C. Newman writes about the loneliness of the Hudson Bay Company's frontiersmen describing similar relationships: "Native women were often coopted into causal sexual relationship though many liaisons resulted in 'country marriages' that lasted a lifetime."[28]

In February 1719, Louis-Simon de St. Aubin, Chevailer de la Boularderie (ca. 1674-1738) a French naval officer, relocated to Isle Royal (Cape Breton) with his wife, daughter and son Antoine. He had been granted a huge allotment of lands that included all of Boularderie Island after spending years in Port Royal (Acadia), successfully defending the settlement from raiding New England soldiers.

The Boularderie settlement flourished over the next several decades with the arrival of a hundred French settlers and fishermen in 1727. High quality wheat and other crops were farmed on 100,000 cleared acres (40,000 ha) of good farmland claimed from the densely forested island. A sawmill, together with a grist mill, dairy and a shipyard, all thrived. Coal was mined there, but the earliest activities focused on the fishing industry.

Following the death of Louis-Simon in 1738, the Boularderie Island settlement continued to thrive under son Antoine's leadership. Extensive orchards and vegetable gardens were planted, grew and flourished. These activities continued until 1758 when the English ravaged much of the settlement.[29] Boularderie Island, with Kempt Head area at its southwestern point, is but five kilometres from MacKay Point located on the easternmost part of Washabuck. It is reasonable to surmise that these French traders and fishermen, reconnoitred and investigated the entire Bras d'Or Lake shoreline, and must have been familiar with the coves and inlets skirting the Washabuck Peninsula.

Elizabeth MacLean (1868 -1961) who was born and raised on MacKay Point, Washabuck, often recalled that as a young child she heard the older generation speaking about remnants of fish-flakes found on Spectacle Island. It was assumed they were built and used by French fishermen for drying codfish. The drying process was at that time the only way of preserving fish for the long sail back across the Atlantic.[30]

In 1752, some 123 years after the settlement of Sainte-Anne's, and thirty three years after Louis-Simon settled Boularderie Island, the French made a feeble attempt to settle in the Grand Narrows area. Cape Breton historian Robert Morgan writes:

> The French called the Strait of Barra "Le detroit à la Jeunesse," and the area at Grand Narrows, "Pointe à la Jeunesse. This presumably referred to a French farmer who lived there. The land was good in the area, and since its location was so central, the government of Isle Royal (as Cape Breton was called during the French occupation between the years 1713-1758), tried to establish a settlement there in 1752. The settlement was only half-hearted and the people almost starved to death, after only one winter.[31]

Morgan writes that, had the French put more emphasis on developing agriculture at the interior of the Island, which they certainly would have done had they remained, Pointe à la Jeunesse, would have played a key role in the development of interior communications on the Island. As it was, the French were evicted in 1758, [and] the area was abandoned.[32]

In 1958, a 19th-century bayonet believed to be of French origin, was discovered on Cole Point on Washabuck River. A few years later, in 1964, an 18th-century French sword, was salvaged from the river. Both these artifacts were displayed during the 1970s as part of the Katherine McLennan Exhibits at Fortress of Louisbourg National Historic Site.[33] (See letter appendix 2) Other than a few sketchy late-night tales involving unlikely buried treasure, to my knowledge, these examples are the only extant signs of early French presence in the Washabuck area.

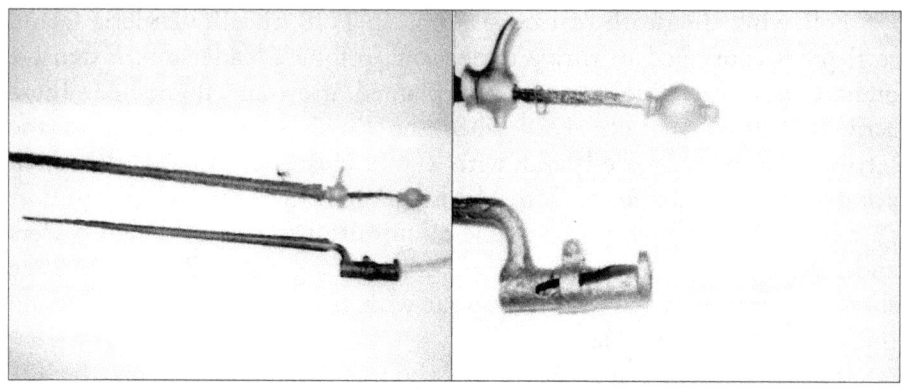

2-3 and 2-4 Artifacts believed to be of French origin. A 19th-century bayonet and an 18th century sword recovered from Washabuck River and displayed as part of the Katherine McLennan Exhibits at Fortress Louisbourg in the 1970s. Photos courtesy of Wanda MacDougall, Washabuck.

The Loyalists:

Between 1784 and 1800 Empire Loyalists played a significant role in the settlement of Cape Breton Island, including the County of Victoria. The Loyalists were led by Abraham Cuyler, a former Mayor of Albany, New York. One of his most prominent followers was Captain Jonathan Jones, of the King's Rangers of New York. Cuyler requested that Jones scout out possible suitable locations on Cape Breton Island for permanent settlement.

Some 140 Loyalists arrived in Cape Breton in late October 1784, and they over-wintered with some difficulty in Louisbourg and St. Peter's. In the following spring [Captain] Jonathan Jones surveyed the virtually uninhabited shoreline of the Bras d'Or Lakes and sailed up Baddeck River. He was impressed with what he saw, reported his findings and, in due course, the extended area was eventually settled with some twenty to thirty Loyalist families, all of whom were looking for land and any other available compensation, to atone for severe losses suffered as a result of their displacement by the American War of Independence.[34] Jones was made a Magistrate for the district of Louisbourg which at that time included Sydney and Baddeck and was awarded a grant of more than 2,000 acres at the mouth of Baddeck River. It was there that he, his wife and his family eventually settled and became known as the Jones Farm and later simply as "Big Farm."[35] In addition to two daughters, Esther and Sarah, Captain Jonathan Jones's sons were Jonathan Jr. and William; a son Thomas drowned while the family was living in Louisbourg.

In 1811, Jonathan Jones Jr. petitioned for a tract of land in Washabuck. This petition reads:

To His Honor Major General Napean President of His Majesty's Council and Commanding in Cape Breton;

The Memorial of Jonathan Jones (Junior): Humbly stateth: That Memorialist came to this Island with his father, an American Loyalist in the year 1784 and that he has resided here ever since, that he never received any land from Government except 350 acres being part of a lot of land formerly granted to Captain Bentinck, and supposed to be escheated but the escheated not having been compensated is claimed by the original grantee, so that Memorialist cannot improve the said 350 acres for fear of losing all his expense and trouble. Memorialist has therefore no land that he can call his own except 500 acres which he inherited from his father about 70 acres of which are cleared and improved. Memorialist further states that he wishes to erect a saw mill which he thinks may be of service to the public as well as himself, that he has discovered a brook on the south side of St. Patrick's Channel which he thinks may answer his purpose and humbly hopes that in consideration of the above mentioned circumstance and the loyally services and losses of his family that your Honor will be pleased to grant him 600 acres on the south side of the reservation which is on the south side of St. Patrick's Channel to enable him to carry out his plan into execution and he will as in duty bound ever pray.[36] (signed) Jon. Jones

A warrant of Survey was issued for the above lot of land by Major General Napean to Surveyor General Tom Crawley on November 4, 1811.[37] The request was granted, and Jonathan Jones Jr., proceeded to erect and operate the first water-powered sawmill in Victoria County, which was located below the highest (in a series of four falls) on the cascading Washabuck watercourse that eventually eases itself into placid Washabuck River.

2-5 Survey sketch of Jonathan Jones property, Washabuck Bridge-Cain's Mountain, 1811. Courtesy of the Registry of Deeds, Baddeck.

3 – The Gaels

>Once furled a standard to the breeze
>Where stood stout sons of Hebrides
>But unfulfilled were Fate's decrees
>On sad Culloden Moor.
>Yet n'er undaunted pluck went forth
>To found new homes, Dame Fortune court,
>Within this Garden of the North
>By bonny blue Bras d'Or.

Ronald Stephen MacDonald, 1934

1817 Lower Washabuck

The first influx of Gaels to settle in Washabuck arrived during the summer of 1817. Four families settled in Lower Washabuck, at the eastern end of the community. At that time, Lower Washabuck included Washabuck Centre and Rear Washabuck Centre. According to Alex D. MacLean,[1] three pioneers accompanied by their families arrived from the Isle of Barra. They were Lachlan MacLean, Donald MacKinnon and *Eòin* MacNeil. They were joined later that same year by George MacKay and his family who originally came from Caithness in northern Scotland. Recent information indicates that the MacKinnon family may have arrived later, perhaps as late as 1822.[2]

In August 1817, two ships arrived in Sydney from Scotland, the *Hope* with 161 passengers and the *William Tell* with 221 passengers. A third ship was expected in Sydney that season with 250 passengers from Barra.[3] She was probably the *Ann*.[4] According to a paper prepared by a youthful Washabuck scholar, Anna Murphy, the ship *Harmony* arrived in North Sydney in August 1817 as well. Each ship carried immigrants from Barra, many of whom settled in the Grand Narrow's area. Subsequently, three Barra families arrived in Upper Washabuck.[5] Simon Fraser was the ship's agent for both these vessels, Alex D. MacLean notes that Simon Fraser was the *Ann*'s captain.[6] The pioneers named below are believed to have arrived on the *Ann*[7] but passenger lists are not extant for either the *Ann* or the *Harmony*.[8]

Historian D. C. Harvey writes about the immigrants that arrived on the *Hope* and *William Tell*. Perhaps those who arrived on the *Ann* and the *Harmony* were afforded similar treatment.

> In 1817 the customs return show that two ships the Hope and the William Tell, arrived at Sydney with 382 emigrants from the island of Barra. Unlike the immigrants of 1802, these did not arrive unheralded. They had been assisted and probably encouraged to emigrate by one Simon Fraser, who asked the Colonial Secretary to recommend them to the care of Lieutenant Governor Ainslie.... He [Simon Fraser] had also advised the emigrants to provide a sufficient quantity of beef and meal for their passage across the Atlantic, and had sent them salt from Greenock, so that they could slaughter their own cattle for provisions. They, therefore, came to Cape Breton in comparative comfort, and with the reputation of "the best fisherman in Scotland." This is the first instance I have found of an emigrant agent directing Scots to Cape Breton.... In this instance he seems to have dealt fairly with the Barra people, except that he was accused of having assured them that the colony would supply them with provisions for the first twelve months, in addition to free land. Otherwise, he seems to have tried to get a good class of emigrants and to have them placed where they could follow the same vocation as in Scotland. These immigrants were settled near the Narrows at the expense of the poverty-stricken government, at a cost of £43, 14.6; Thirty-one pounds sterling for hire of schooners, and the balance for pork, flour and mutton. Thereafter, they had to eke out their own subsistence from the waters of the Bras d'Or, until they could harvest their first crop.[9]

3-1 Anna Murphy (1918-1989). Photo courtesy of Ann Marie MacKinnon, Sydney.

Lachlan MacLean

Pioneer Lachlan, a widower, was accompanied by his adult family of five sons and three daughters. Another son, Michael, remained in Barra. Michael was enlisted in the Royal Navy at the time that his father and siblings shipped for Cape Breton. Lachlan took up lands currently owned by the family of the late Joe (Red Rory) and Josie MacLean. Lachlan later donated a small portion of his property along its eastern line to the community, to be used as a cemetery.

It's worth noting here, that Lachlan's brother, Hector, remained in Barra. But one of Hector's sons, Charles (*Gobha*) settled some years later on the north side of Washabuck River. Another of Hector's descendants, Angus Brendan MacNeil of Barra (Scotland) is a Member of Parliament for the Outer Hebrides, representing the Scottish National Party in Westminster's Parliament since 2005. He and his family have exchanged visits with their Washabuck cousins a number of times, wondrously bridging the years and the generations across the broad North Atlantic, enhancing a current familial connection.

Lachlan's sons **Peter** and **Roderick** lived with their father on his property. Peter, who was unmarried, drowned in 1827. Roderick eventually married, and inherited his father's property and later his son Peter S. bought the adjoining western property that had been originally owned by John Ross. Lachlan's two sons, **Alexander** and **Calum** both married, with each owning two hundred acre lots in Lower Washabuck. Lachlan's second daughter **Jan** married Baptists Almon of George's River, Cape Breton County and a great many descendants of this marriage can be found in George's River and the Little Bras d'Or areas.

Lachlan's eldest son **Neil,** arrived with his wife and two children, Michael and Ann; a third child, an infant daughter had died during the voyage to Cape Breton and was buried somewhere along the Cape North coastline. They settled on lands at Washabuck Centre, inhabited today by descendants, including Carmie and Ben MacLean. Neil's wife, Annie, was a daughter of Neil *Geal* MacNeil.

Eòin MacNeil

Pioneer *Eòin* was married to Lachlan MacLean's eldest daughter **Mary** "*Mhór.*" They settled at Washabuck Centre. *Eòin* and his family established themselves on property at Washabuck Centre where four successive generations of the MacNeil family lived. This property in later years became distinguished as "Grandfather's Farm" having being identified as the pioneer homestead in the Cape Breton classic *The Highland Heart in Nova Scotia,* penned by that pioneer's great-grandson Neil F. MacNeil.

Donald MacKinnon

Donald was accompanied by his wife and their two sons, Neil and John. The eldest son was then seven years of age. Other family members included a second Neil, and a second Philip, Murdock, and Catherine who married Ranald (*Mór*) MacDonald. Donald, whose wife Mary was a daughter of Neil *Geal* MacNeil, (and a sister to Neil's (Lachlan) wife, Annie) settled on the property currently inhabited (2013) by Leo and Edie MacDougall and Dan Joseph and Charlene MacNeil among others. Murdock (Donald) MacKinnon married Catherine MacNeil from Big Beach and raised a family of four boys, in Upper Washabuck: Rory, Dan, Philip and Neil. Rory and Dan in turn, raised large families in Washabuck and Cain's Mountain.

George MacKay

Pioneer George and his family settled at the most eastern end of Washabuck on the prominent point of land that continues to so proudly bear the MacKay name. MacKay died ca. 1858. A few years later, his widow Mary sold the property to Lachlan MacLean's grandson Peter Francis (*Chaluim*) whose descendants continue to live there.

In 1939, Neil P. S. MacLean outlined in an article in *The Casket* newspaper what he had heard about George MacKay:

> I was informed that this man's name was Wallace McCoy and not George; later the surname was changed to McKay. Wallace had a son named John, who was the last occupant of the Outer Island [Bone Island] and the point commonly called Red Point, (*an rubha dearg*). He moved to Baddeck and his son George was a deep-water sailor. He, also, settled at Baddeck in later years and had a family.[10]

At the top of the hayfield at MacKay Point, is a place referred to by the immediate past generation of MacLean residents as, "Wallace's Clearing," and a rocky fishing shoal east of MacKay Point that is today referred to as "Wallace's Bank."

William Ross

William was one of four pioneer Ross brothers to settle in what became known as the "Ross Settlement" in Northeast Margaree Valley. Author John F. Hart, in his *History of Northeast Margaree*, describes that Ross was born in Ireland ca. 1768. He arrived in Cape Breton in 1790, later sold his farm there to a Miles McDaniel, and moved to Washabuck, where he later died.[11] His wife was Esther Mowatt (sometimes cited as Moore) and they had a family of eleven children. William Ross, age fifty years, is described in the 1818 census as living at St. Peter's Channel [*sic*], and having lands that were later taken up by Angus (*Eòin*) MacNeil at Washabuck Centre. Further reference is made about Ross in a petition by a William Wall in 1821, as Ross having lands adjoining the western line of the requested property by Wall. There is no evidence of William Wall actually living on this property. The Wall lands were subsequently taken up by the Barra pioneer Donald MacInnis and his family.[12]

John, one of William's three sons married Lachlan MacLean's youngest daughter Mary *Òg*. John Ross occupied the property adjoining the western side of that owned by Lachlan MacLean. John Ross, upon finding himself in debt to Mr. Plant, a merchant at North Sydney later returned to Margaree with his wife and family. John Ross signed his property over to Mr. Plant in payment of his debt. Peter S. MacLean, Roderick's son (Lachlan's grandson), was hired on as a clerk with Mr. Plant and later bought back the same property. The property is owned today by descendants of Peter

S. MacLean.[13] After his return to Margaree John Ross was referred to as John "Washabuck" Ross. One of his daughters Catherine "Kate," married James Murdock MacKenzie from Cain's Mountain and had a family. Their son William, married a widow, *Beatag* MacNeil, and raised a family on the original Alexander (Lachlan) MacLean lands in Lower Washabuck.[14]

Neil *Geal* MacNeil

Neil *Geal* arrived in Washabuck from Piper's Cove shortly after the other pioneers. One of Neil *Geal's* daughters, Annie, was the wife of Neil *Lachlann* MacLean. A second daughter, Mary, was married to Donald MacKinnon. Neil *Geal* settled near his daughter at Washabuck Centre and built a log home on the land now enclosed by Holy Rosary Cemetery. A third daughter Janey (*Sìne an Uillt*) married John MacNeil of Gillis Point. They lived on her father's property with a son, Neil *Geal's* grandson, who was referred to as "Red" Neil, *Niall Ruadh*. Red Neil later donated part of his grandfather's homestead for the cemetery, prior to his own death in 1917.[15]

Those lands are currently owned by brothers Roddie and Cyril MacLean, descendants as well, of Neil and Annie.

Donald MacInnis

There is record of a Donald MacInnis owning lands at Washabuck Centre at in 1817. There is also a record of a Marcella, who was a MacInnis, perhaps she was Donald's daughter. She had two sisters, Jane and another possibly named Mary.

Donald MacPhee

Marcella married *Dòmhnull MacPhì*. They lived on the property at Washabuck Centre that today bears her name, Marcella's spring (*Fuaran Mharsailidh*). Her husband Donald met death by drowning and he is believed to be the first of the pioneers buried in *Cladh Nìll Ghil*, the eastern portion of the property that was later enlarged and consecrated as Holy Rosary Cemetery. It

3-2 Lower Washabuck residents Malcolm (Stephen) MacLean on left and "Red" Rory MacLean on right, beside dignitaries visiting pioneer cemetery *Cladh Lachlann* ca. 1950: Next to Malcolm is Victoria County's long-time medical practitioner Dr. C. L. MacMillan, Inverness County MLA Rod MacLean and Sir Charles MacLean (1916-1990) 27th Chief of Clan MacLean from the Isle of Mull, Scotland. Photo by Alex D. MacLean. Courtesy of Carmie MacLean, Washabuck.

is thought that they had a family of two children, a daughter Catherine, and a son Donald.[16]

A few years after her husband drowned, Marcella sold her property to Washabuck residents Philip MacKinnon and Peter S. MacLean. She then went to live with a sister, an M. MacDonald, and ended her days in Boston, Massachusetts. Her son Donald MacPhee, resided at Sydney Mines/Glace Bay.[17] A portion of the property today is owned by the descendants of Peter S. MacLean while the balance is owned by descendants of Vincent MacLean (1871-1943). The other sister Jane, married a Campbell and had a family of at least one son, Hector, (*Eachmann Ban*) who died in Baddeck in 1922.[18]

MacPhee Brothers

Another pioneer family consisting of two MacPhee brothers, owned the property adjoining the John Ross property. They later sold it to Rory MacNeil, son of Neil (*Geal*) and relocated to Prince Edward Island. It is thought that these MacPhees were not related to the Marcella MacPhee mentioned earlier. Rory's daughter Ann and her husband John (*Murdock Beag*) MacNeil, owned the property until they relocated to Baddeck. They in turn sold it to Rory Ranald "Klondike" MacDonald whose descendants inhabit it today.

MacPhee Family

Alex D. relates a story about a third MacPhee family that lived in Lower Washabuck ca.1840-1845.

> The site of their home was east of the pioneer MacKinnon family property. The family consisted of the mother who was widowed, two sons and a daughter. It seems the property was indebted to a general merchant in Baddeck by the name of Charles J. Campbell and the poor woman was worried about not having the wherewithal to pay off the claim. One of her other neighbours used to continually play on these fears, so much so, that in time she decided to leave Washabuck and go to Prince Edward Island where she had relatives. So one morning Donald MacKinnon seeing no smoke from the residence discovered the house deserted and bare, with nothing left inside except a discarded bonnet on the floor. The widow owned a fair-sized boat so she with her family together with their personal and household affects sailed under cover of darkness without alerting the neighbours. It was afterwards learned that the family arrived at their destination without mishap.

According to Alex D., there seemed to be no connection[19] between this widow and the husband of the MacPhee woman who gave her name to the spring known as *Fuaran Mharsalaidhi*.[20]

MacIntosh

Sometime during the days of early settlers, a family by the name of MacIntosh lived for a time in Lower Washabuck, on lands between Roderick J. and Sarah MacLean's and MacKay Point, on the north side of the present highway. Mrs. Peter D. MacKenzie (Flora MacLean), formerly of Lower Washabuck, related that as a child, she and her sisters would look for their cows in this area, and that it was referred to by the "old people" of those times as, *Àite Fàs Mhic an Tòisich* – the vacant MacIntosh land.[21]

John C. Boyd

John C. of Lower South River, Antigonish County, was a school teacher. He married Christina (*Calum 'ic Lachlain*) MacLean and settled on a hundred acres of MacLean property in Lower Washabuck. They had a family. John C. drowned in Baddeck Bay. Christina's second husband was Cheticamp native Joseph A. Arsenault. They lived in Baddeck and had a family. The property today is still referred to as "Boyd's."

1817: Upper Washabuck:

Upper Washabuck embraces the territory extending from Holy Rosary Mission Church at Washabuck Centre for about a kilometre north west beyond Washabuck Bridge. In pioneer times, it included the areas later known as Birch Point and St. Columba. From the records and stories of the pioneers, we know that this section was settled in 1817, perhaps not quite as early as the settlement in Lower Washabuck, but a few months later.[22] Patterson in his *History of Victoria County* writes that:

> In the same year, [1817] but a little later three from the west of Lewis, by name **George McIver, Allan Munro and Donald McAulay**, arrived and began to clear lands in the same locality a little farther up St. Patrick's Channel.[23]

Alex D. MacLean writes that George MacIver occupied lands later owned by Joseph MacIver and Daniel Murphy respectively. According to Archie MacIver (1898-1984), George MacIver did not remain in Washabuck for any length of time but relocated to Pugwash on the Gulf Shore.[24] But it seems that **Colin MacIver and his wife Margaret Hayden,** who had settled first at Big Farm on Baddeck River, relocated to Upper Washabuck in 1817 in search of higher farming ground, and took over that property.[25] Allan Munro lived on the property now known as Murphy Point while Donald MacAulay lived on the property referred to as "The MacAulay Place," currently owned and divided between two MacDonald families, brothers Stephen and Quentin, and their Aunt Rose and her family.

Daniel Carmichael

Daniel settled in Upper Washabuck ca. 1817. He arrived in Washabuck via Ingonish and Baddeck. Born in Oban, Scotland, in 1787, he sailed for Cape Breton in 1810. Visiting Northeast Margaree he married **Sarah Ross**, daughter of David Ross, one of the four Ross Pioneer brothers of that area. Seven of their thirteen children were born in Washabuck (one is buried there) before he moved to a farm he purchased at Margaree Valley. It is known that Carmichael was still residing on the Washabuck property in 1832. He settled on the property that today is owned by Roddie and Laura MacDonald. Roddie is a great-great-grandson of **Alasidair** *(Glas)* **MacDonald,** believed to be originally from North Uist, who settled with his family upon this same property, subsequent to Carmichael relocating with his family to Frizzleton, Inverness County.[26]

It was during this time also that **Murdoch MacNeil** (*Murachidh Beag*), his brother **John MacNeil** (*Ian Ruadh*), and brother-in-law **Murdock MacKenzie** (*Murchadh mac Eachainn*) arrived and took up residence in what is today Washabuck Bridge area. **They and their families** arrived in North Sydney on the ship *Harmony* in August 1817.[27]

Robert Sutherland, a surveyor, lived for a time with his family on lands subsequently owned by Ranald *Mór* MacDonald. Sutherland is believed to have sailed to New Zealand in 1851.

Allan MacLean (*Ailean Leathaineach*) a native of mainland Scotland arrived in 1817 and settled in the St. Columba area,[28] along the Camp Road that ran to Highland Hill. He married **Flora** the sister of the MacDonald brothers, Rory, James, and Donald, who arrived in Upper Washabuck in 1821, and Michael who relocated there ca. 1825. Allan and Flora had a family of three, Michael, Alex and Catherine.

1821

The second major influx of pioneers arrived in Washabuck in 1821. Archibald J. MacKenzie writes about their sailing and crossing to Cape Breton:

> It was in the month of August 1821, that the ship *Harmony*, with three hundred and fifty immigrants on board, sailed from Barra to Canada. Only a portion landed in Cape Breton, and some went as far west as Stratford, in Upper Canada, as Ontario was known at that time..... In those days of slow sailing vessels, the record made by the *Harmony* on that occasion was remarkable. She sailed on a Friday and touched at Tobermoire to receive the ministrations of a priest for the wife of Donald McKenzie (Hector). On Sunday, Ireland was still in sight,

but appeared no larger than a "half-bushel measure," and on the third Sunday, they sighted Newfoundland.[29]

This crossing contrasts most favourably to the trials and hardships of the earlier immigrants on the ship *Hector*, who according to the passengers themselves, claimed that they were eleven weeks on their passage.[30] MacKenzie continues:

> When the *Harmony* landed in Sydney, Archibald and John McKenzie, with some of the other immigrants, came by way of East Bay to Piper's Cove and Grand Narrows to engage boats to take their families and their belongings to Christmas Island and Shunacadie. They got a boat from a Donald McEachern of East Bay, and one from Donald McNeil (Piper). Taking the way of Little Bras d'Or Strait, they sailed with the boats to Sydney, where they had left their friends in camps near the shore. In due time the boats returned loaded with men, women, children and their effects. As the "sgoth" conveying the McKenzies to their future homes in the New World tried to make a landing east of Christmas Island, it struck a shoal opposite the house of Rory McNeil (Governor), who had left Barra with the Pictou immigrants in 1802. He went to the shore to lend a helping hand, but when he recognized his sister, Mary, the wife of Hector McKenzie (Archibald), he could not restrain his feelings. He waded out to the boat, took his sister in his arms, and carried her to his house. It was when he returned to the boat that he found his speech to greet his other friends, and invite them to his house.[31]

This passage hints at the depth and range of emotions experienced and endured by our ancestors upon leaving their hearth and native homeland; of sailing off in ships of dubious seaworthiness across the gaping expanse of the North Atlantic Ocean. The trauma of leaving family members, friends and neighbours, knowing quite well that the chances of ever seeing one another again or revisiting their native land were practically nil.

The passage hints too at taxing routes and transportation hurdles that further stymied the pioneers before they achieved a final destination, after their Sydney harbour landfall. Francis H. MacNeil writes that the ship *Harmony* made a number of trips across the Atlantic from Scotland with immigrants. On that particular voyage, that arrived in Sydney on August 14, 1821 three families settled in Beaver Cove, and another three families settled at Shenacadie Harbour,[32] while Alex D. adds, that a large number of the Barra immigrants from this voyage settled on Southside Boularderie Island.[33]

The following pioneers arrived and settled in Upper Washabuck in 1821:

Hector MacKenzie and his son John, the great-grandfather and grandfather of Peter D. MacKenzie (1869-1956), a noted storyteller.

James MacDougall (*Seumas Muillear*) and young son **Alexander**.

Charles MacLean (*Teàrlach Gobha*) and **Archibald MacKenzie** (*Gilleasbuig mac Eachainn*), the latter settling at Birch Point.

Calum William MacDougall settled on the north side of Washabuck River opposite the other MacDougall property on the south side, referred to as Jim Alec's. This MacDougall family was known as "The Captain's," but they were not thought to be closely related to the neighbouring pioneer, **James MacDougall** or his family.

The MacDonald family immigrated to Cape Breton in 1821 and settled in Upper Washabuck, in what later became known as St. Columba. They were the family of **Alexander** and **Margaret (Gillis)** MacDonald. Alexander was a son of Archibald, who was a son of Andrew MacDonald of South Uist. It seems that Alexander MacDonald had relocated from South Uist to Barra (Scotland) shortly after 1770 for religious reasons. It was in Barra (Scotland), where he married Margaret Gillis and they had a family of four sons, Michael (*Mór*), Rory, James, Donald and a daughter, Flora. Son Michael did not come to St. Columba until ca. 1825.

Margaret Gillis (wife of Alexander MacDonald) was a daughter of John Gillis and sister of Hugh Gillis. Hugh was a native of Lorn, Argyllshire, and had relocated to Barra. He was killed while in the army, but his widow Ann MacIntyre and their family immigrated to Cape Breton in 1813, settling on the south side of Gillis Point Harbour (Maskells). It is undoubtedly after this particular family, that this district is called Gillis Point. Three years later this family relocated to Jamesville.[34]

Malcolm MacNeil (*Calum Ruadh*) lived on the property just west of Holy Rosary Church, later owned by Murdock Paul MacLean. Malcolm's wife was a MacNeil from the Grand Narrows area. Their son Michael, a bachelor, remained on the property during his lifetime and their daughter Ann "Nancy," married William Munro (*Uilleam Ailein*). They had no family.[35] Carmie MacLean recalls as a youth in the late 1940s, walking with her Aunt Marjorie MacLean on the back part of this same property. Marjorie remembered two family homesteads located in that area at one time. One site had an orchard that she referred to as "Murdock's orchard" (not Murdock Paul's), and another, an unknown family site, that was older and less visible, located further to the west. The previous generation had sometimes referred to these homesteads as belonging to the *bodaich* (old men). Unfortunately, nothing further is known about who these people were.[36]

A little later these settlers were joined by **Alexander** (Allie Donn) **MacAulay** and **William Matheson**.[37] A second **Malcolm MacNeil** (*Calum mac Iain Ruaidh*) who was John MacNeil's son, lived at Washabuck Bridge where Hector MacKenzie currently lives. His brother **James** married **Mary** *Bàn* of PEI[38] and lived next door. A second brother **Allan**, the father of Rev. John J. MacNeil, relocated to Arichat as a young man. Allie *Donn* was the son of Murdock MacAulay and was born at Red Head, now known as *Beinn Bhreagh*. Allie *Donn* later moved to Grand River, CB, to live with a married daughter and died there. His property ended up in possession of Rory J. MacNeil (*Iain 'ic Ruairidh Mhóir 'ic Dhòmhnaill 'ic Ruairidh*) of Iona, ca. 1870, and his descendants remain the owners.

William Matheson married **Ann MacLeod** from Big Baddeck and had a family of at least four children; a son Angus, and daughters, Elizabeth (Betsy) unmarried; Catherine, wife of Henry MacIver, and another daughter who was married to Murdock MacFarlane, Baddeck. Angus moved to Hunter's Mountain in 1869, married Rebecca Doherty, and had a large family, one of whom was Hugh G., known as Hoodie.[39]

Ranald *Mór* **MacDonald** (*Raghnall Mór*) arrived some years later and married **Catherine (Donald) MacKinnon** of Lower Washabuck. He bought the Sutherland property in Upper Washabuck that today remains in the possession of his descendants. Ranald *Mór* arrived in Washabuck purportedly from South Uist, and subsequently, via southside Boularderie Island.

Neil MacLean (*Niall Dubh*) and his brother **Allan**, were the sons of Donald (*Aonghais "Og" MacLean*) and their sister became the second wife of John (*Ruadh*) MacNeil, Washabuck Bridge; **Angus MacDonald** (*Aonghas an Tuathach*), **Roderick MacIntyre** (*Ruaridh Ùr*) and his mother were other pioneers.

Daniel MacLean, who was born in Scotland on June 1, 1834, settled on the property between Hector and John MacKenzie and Daniel Carmichael. His first wife died young, and he married Ann Jessome. There is no further information on this MacLean, except that between the two wives he had a total of nine children, two of them named Mary and Susan.[40]

Henry MacInnis was the first MacInnis to live in Upper Washabuck. He was an old man arriving in Cape Breton and he squatted first on lands fronting on Washabuck River. He had at least four children, Anna Belle, Christina, Donald and Malcolm. Donald (Henry) MacInnis had come first to the Whycocomagh area before he relocated to the Washabuck area where he took two lots of land, one for his father Henry and the other for his brother Malcolm. Henry (Pioneer) MacInnis relocated to South Cove. Donald bought a 200-hundred acre (80 ha) lot in South Cove ca. 1822 and had it granted. For that reason, South Cove is still referred to by local residents as "The Grant" simply because Donald's property is understood to be the first land on Washabuck Peninsula to have received Grant status from the Crown. Donald (Henry) MacInnis married Peggy MacIver, a daughter of Neil MacIver who was from the Isle of Lewis, while Malcolm (Henry) MacInnis married Jane (Donald "Piper") MacAulay, of Upper Washabuck.

Kenny MacRitchie and his brothers Murdo and Angus were the sons of John and Kirsty (MacLeod) MacRitchie from Uig, Isle of Lewis. Kenny lived in the Washabuck Bridge area[41] as (it is thought) did Donald Morrison and his wife, who had a family of twelve. A couple of their girls married MacRitchie men. Of the others, there is little detail. It is worth noting that on A. F. Church's topographical map of Victoria County ca. 1887, the St. Columba Road from Washabuck Bridge to Grass Cove is referred to as the Maccrutchie Road. The same map indicates a D. Morrison residence located at the South Cove/Washabuck Road intersection. Families from the Isles of Lewis and Harris settled throughout the Hazeldale, South Cove, Cains Mountain, and Little Narrows communities, and those early defining boundary lines with Washabuck Bridge still remain blurry.

"California" **Angus MacLean** (*Aonghas Nill Eachainn*) of Ottawa Brook, settled in Upper Washabuck ca. 1870 on the property homesteaded by pioneer William Matheson. Angus's wife Mary was a sister to Rory J. MacNeil. **Peter Murphy** (1) arrived from Mabou and settled here at about the same time and the Murphy name christened the Point of land they lived on. Prior to that time, the land was referred to as Munro's Point. **Peter Murphy** (2), settled at Washabuck Bridge arriving from Prince Edward Island via Humes Rear, Victoria County, around the turn of the last century. **Alexander "Framer" MacKenzie** from north Lake Ainslie and **John Brown** (ca. 1883) from Cape North, arrived in Washabuck during later decades as well.

John MacInnis from Humes Rear, Victoria County, married Annie (Dan) MacDonald from Nyanza, and settled at Washabuck Bridge. Their home had been owned, probably built by and lived in, by Kenny MacRitchie, who later moved to Glace Bay. The MacInnis's raised a family of seven children including Murdock, a bachelor, who lived there until his passing in 1994.[42]

As a young man, John MacInnis worked as a carpenter on the construction of Canada's Parliament Buildings.[43] According to Archie MacIver, Donald MacInnis (2) from Humes Rear had married Annie MacIver (a sister to Peggy MacIver married to Donald MacInnis (1) and they were the parents of John MacInnis mentioned above, so, obviously, were Murdock and his sibling's, grandparents.[44]

Michael MacDonald (*Mìcheal Mór mac Alasdair*) was married to **Catherine MacIntyre** of Barra. They immigrated to Cape Breton in 1817 with a family of one or perhaps two. He settled in Mabou. *"Beinn Mhìcheil"* near that community is named after him. The MacDonald's lived in Mabou for eight years where three more of their family were born. As mentioned earlier, his brothers Rory, James, Donald, and a sister Flora, had settled in Washabuck in 1821, and evidently the urge to be near them was strong so the family relocated from Mabou and in due course took up residency in St. Columba ca. 1825, on lands later owned by Michael E. MacDonald, having lived for a short time in the Washabuck Bridge area.[45]

Other St. Columba settlers included **Rory Neil MacNeil** and his family, **Roderick MacIntyre** (*Ruaridh Ùr*) and his mother.[46] **Jonathan Nash** relocated from Benacadie and in ensuing years, **Malcolm Campbell** and his brother **Rory** (a bachelor) and sons of Hugh Campbell, relocated from Barra Glen while **Caluman MacNeil**, the son of Angus MacNeil arrived there via Iona Rear.[47] There were apparently at one time, as many as seven families living on what was often mistakenly referred to, as the Highland Hill road, extending from the top of St. Columba Mountain through to Highland Hill.[48] One of these families could have been Rory Neil MacNeil referred to previously. There were also a couple of MacLean families, **Jane (*Sìne*) MacDougall** and a man referred to as *Gruaigean* (about whom nothing else is known). The St. Columba end of this road was frequently referred to (ca. 1921), as the Camp Road, or simply, Jane's Road.[49] On Church's map, the other end of this road is referred to as the Intervale Road, probably because it ended along the Intervale at MacKinnon Harbour.[50]

Another resident in Upper Washabuck was William Oram. It is believed he was a bachelor. It is not known exactly when he arrived in Washabuck or where he lived. But Alex D. MacLean, wrote that William was related to the Orams of Little Bras d'Or. He is primarily remembered today for the fact that a small pond located in Upper Washabuck is known as "Bill Oram's Pond."[51] In 1816, a **William Oram**, age twenty-one, petitioned for a lot on the south side of St. Patrick's Channel in the Bay of Waserbaurkchuch [*sic*]. He was a native of Cape Breton, a resident at Quebec, married with two step-children.[52] Could this be the same man? It is not known.

It is obvious that I have merely touched upon the lives of these intrepid Gaels; that further in-depth research awaits. Research into land petitions, widened genealogy, personal anecdotes, family lore, together with the pin-pointing of exactly where each pioneer family settled, deserves further ferreting.

3-3 Bill Oram's Pond, Upper Washabuck, ca. 2000.

4 – Surveyors, Land Grants and Early Land Owners

Fearless Adventurers

Surveyors names are forever linked with history of Canada through the early exploration and eventual development of this country including Major A. B. "Hells Bells" Rogers and David Thompson. Perhaps not as well-known, but equally as determined, Cape Breton Island was endowed with its own notable slate of capable, fearless and dedicated surveyors.

Robert Morgan, writing in *Early Cape Breton*, dedicates an entire chapter to early Cape Breton surveyors. Much of the following is culled from his in-depth research, as it details for the reader a quick review of why surveys evolved and how land grants were made available to the emigrants to Cape Breton including the Washabuck pioneers.

Morgan cites three reasons Cape Breton became so well surveyed between 1750-1850. European seaman were constantly sailing the waters around the island and felt the more that was known about the depths of its harbours – as well as the island's exact position in relation to Europe – the better for everyone involved. Early Cape Breton was settled by Europeans from France and Britain and the island played a pendulous role in the never-ending exchange of the "spoils of war" that occurred between these imperial powers. Finally, the influx of Acadian, Loyalist and Scottish immigrants in the 19th century demanded that a system of orderly land demarcation was necessary.

Four surveyors in particular are cited by Morgan as having played major roles in the pioneer surveying of the island, its coastline, harbours, its interior and its land grants.

In 1745, Joseph-Bernard Chabert de Cogolin, a French naval officer and career navigator, found himself off the coast of Cape Breton with inaccurate charts. Later, Chabert was sent to Louisbourg where he built an observatory, then plotted through "star shots" the accurate position of the island. With his findings published in 1753: "It was the first attempt to locate what is today the province of Nova Scotia with scientific accuracy."[1]

After Great Britain assumed control of Cape Breton in 1763 Samuel Holland was appointed to determine the island's assets. Holland, a Dutchman by birth, was one of the 18th century's great surveyors. As surveyor-general of Quebec and the Northern District of America, he surveyed the island for 14 years. He organized three surveying parties for various parts of Cape Breton Island and compiled the findings into one *Description*. Morgan writes that Holland divided the island into counties and townships:

> The accuracy of his surveys and the orderliness of his observations are beyond dispute … while his estimate of great potential of the fishing, gypsum, coal and lumbering industries on the island have been borne out for two centuries.[2]

Joseph Frederick Wallet DesBarres served under the British and surveyed thousands of miles of coastline along the western Atlantic. He accurately plotted shorelines and made soundings by employing the newly-developed technique of triangulation for measuring distances between points of land. His work, published in *Atlantic Neptune* in four editions, was praised for its accuracy, together with his artistic views of various shorelines and surroundings. DesBarres was appointed Lieutenant-Governor of Cape Breton in 1784 when it became a separate colony. He drafted a detailed design for the city of Sydney, some of which was achieved and to this day testifies to his genius as a surveyor.

Other lesser known surveyors included Thomas Hurd and Alexander Haire, who laid out the first land grants for the Loyalists settlers in the Sydney area. Morgan writes that the greatest of these Nova Scotia surveyors however, was Thomas Crawley. Captain Crawley served under Admiral Nelson in the British Navy. He came to Cape Breton in 1788 and was appointed surveyor-general of Cape Breton, a position he held for nearly thirty years.

Thousands of Scottish immigrants coupled with hundreds of Acadian immigrants from St. Pierre and Miquelon were to inundate Cape Breton Island during these decades. With simple surveying equipment, Captain Crawley, assisted by Captain William Cox and joined by Mi'kmaw guides in a canoe, meticulously plotted out baselines and planned land grant patterns throughout the island.

Because the Acadians wished to pursue the fishery, their grants tended to be six or seven acres along the shoreline; while married Scots received 200 acres and single men received 100 acres. Captain Crawley laid out the boundaries for three of Cape Breton's four counties as well as the three

Mi'kmaw reservations located at Waycobah, Wagmatcook and Eskasoni. He was the only appointee retained by Nova Scotia when Cape Breton was annexed by the mainland in 1820. In 1832, he compiled a listing of 7,374 land grant searches on Cape Breton.[3]

Following Cape Breton's annexation, the new government realized that the colony had been terribly inefficient in attempting to deal with the influx of its new immigrants to the island. Historian D. C. Harvey outlines:

> Inadequate records had been kept of even the titles to land and, when the government of Nova Scotia assumed control of the Island, they found that fully as much land had been occupied without any form of title as was held by grant, license or lease of the crown, that the new grants had been made of lands in which the process of escheat had not been completed, and that everything was in hopeless confusion.[4]

Even the Nova Scotia government's own resources after 1820 were stretched to the limit, and transportation around the Island consisted for the most part of blazed trails. The best and most practical means of travel and communication, particularly for communities along the Bras d'Or Lake, was by water, a situation to remain well into the next century. Heavy immigration poured into Cape Breton Island between 1815 and 1838, resulting in ever greater problems: poverty, smallpox and starvation coupled with an extreme strain on relief funds added to a lack of surveyed lands which resulted in squatter challenges, particularly in the back lands, as the front lands were already occupied.

Harvey continues:

> There still remained the problems of discovering, selecting and marking of suitable lots, of transporting the settlers to these new lots, and of protecting them against the ingenuity of squatters. It was natural that these problems should be recognized first by the men who were immediately responsible for the settlement of immigrants.

In 1828, Deputy Surveyor Robert McNab had written:

> Among the many difficulties the numerous Emigrants that arrive annually in this province have to experience, that of finding a suitable situation to settle themselves is not the least.[5]

Harvey quotes from a letter written in 1830 by Surveyor-General Captain Crawley to the Provincial Secretary in which he informs that office that Cape Breton was:

> ...threatened with a dreadful innundation [sic] from Scotland amounting to 3000 souls, and suggested that lots might be laid out for them in advance, to which they might repair at once, instead of lying about our beaches to be consumed by want and sickness.[6]

This was eventually done, but officials still encountered the ingenuity of the squatter, as related in 1831 by Crawley in a subsequent letter, when he advises his superiors that:

> I understand that flocks of squatters are on the watch to pounce on the best lots as soon as marked by the Surveyor, trusting that government will not incur any expense to eject them.[7]

These problems became more evident during the 1830s, as most of the front lands were settled by then and the remaining Crown lands had to be purchased. The problem had existed before 1820, but land was still plentiful and essentially free in those early years. It was also more accessible because it fronted on the water courses. By 1839 it was estimated that as much as half the population of Cape Breton was settled with only a license of occupation or without title at all.[8]

According to an archival description by Nova Scotia Archives:

> In 1749 Charles Morris was appointed the first Surveyor General to administer the granting of land. The Surveyor General was responsible for surveying of the boundary lines of land grants, roads, and other lands and the preparation of maps and plans. Deputy surveyors were appointed for each district or county. In 1827 a Commissioner of Crown Lands was appointed to oversee the sale of crown land and in 1851 the commissioner absorbed the position of Surveyor General.
>
> The existence of a separate Commissioner of Crown Lands for Cape Breton reporting directly to the Provincial Secretary, and distinct from the Commissioner of Crown lands for Nova Scotia, survived the demise of Cape Breton as a separate colony in 1820 and continued until 1847, when the *Crown Land Department Act* abolished the position of surveyor general of Cape Breton. In 1877 the Attorney General became ex office Commissioner of Crown Lands. In 1926 the Department of Lands and Forests was created and the functions of the commissioner were transferred to the new department."[9]

In a similar vein, Effie Bain in her manuscript *History of Baddeck* mentions that for years no land grants were issued in Cape Breton, mainly because neither France nor England would allow control of the island's suspected natural resources out of their control. In 1783 there was a policy to give land grants on the mainland. In 1784 land grants were provided with reservations to disbanded solders and Loyalists in Cape Breton. Lt. Governor DesBarres promised three years provisions for settlers who came to Cape Breton. But with the exception of a few previously issued land grants promised to disbanded solders, those plans never materialized as DesBarres was replaced before his plans were realized. A number of grants were issued during the Macarmick administration. No records were kept of land grants during 1784-1820 the period when Cape Breton was a separate colony. Settlers occupied the land while they waited or hoped for grants to be awarded them.[10] Bain continues:

> In 1790 issuing of land grants were discontinued except for those whose warrants had already been issued. In 1811 the practice of granting land to bona fide settlers were discontinued. Instead they gave Crown leases, terminable at will. In 1817, the land grant issuing policy was reinstated because so many settlers left. In 1820, when Cape Breton was re-annexed, Sir James Kempt visited the island to lay off lots of 100 acres for single men and 200 acres for married men.

> Free land grants were no more. People were allowed to occupy lots under "tickets of location" until they were prepared to pay for land grants and these were only given if and when improvements were made on the land. The kinds of improvements and its use were determined by the type of land issued: good farming, forested, etc. One stipulation: 150 acres to the head of the family plus 50 acres per child up to 200 acres, over that the charges was 5 shillings an acre.[11]

In Lower Washabuck in 1817, the pioneer MacLean clan settled on 200-acre (40 ha) lots for a grand total of 1,200 acres (485 ha) among them. Brothers Roderick and Peter lived with their father Lachlan on a 200-acre site (40 ha). Peter who was single, drowned in 1827, and did not own any property. The other brothers Neil, Calum and Alexander and daughter Mary *Mhor*, who was the wife of *Eòin* MacNeil, each owned 200 acres (40 ha) apiece; as did Lachlan's youngest daughter Mary *Òg*, wife of John Ross. In all cases the settlers found themselves with more land than they ever dreamed owning when they left Barra. As already noted, the government did not commence issuing land grants until 1820, and the evidence displays that these pioneers had taken the necessary steps to secure their lands by 1825.

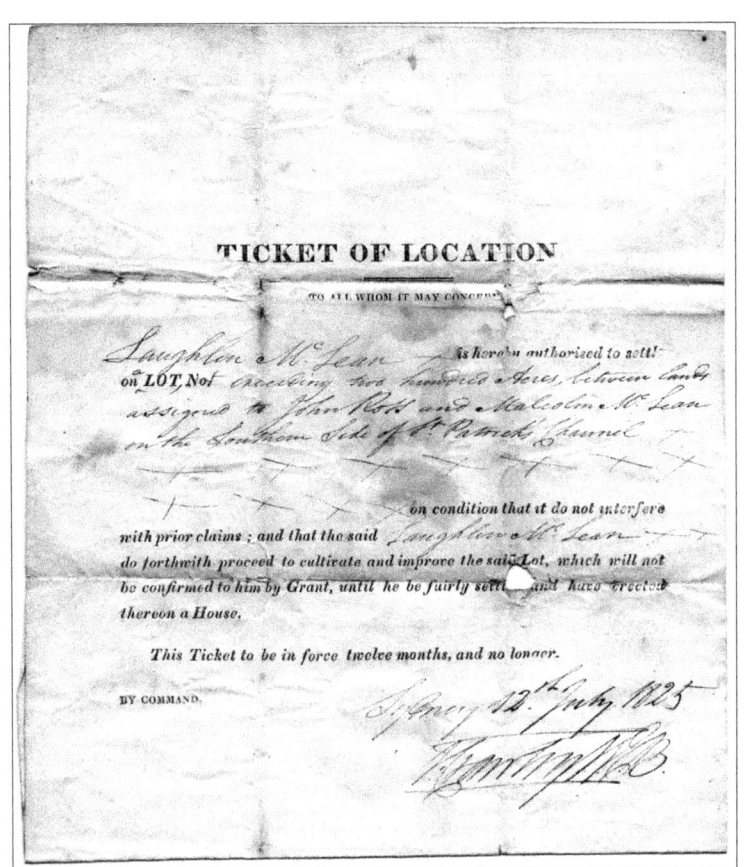

4-1 Lachlan MacLean's location ticket from Lower Washabuck, 1825. Courtesy of Lily MacIvor, great-great-granddaughter of Lachlan, Sydney, CB.

Upper Washabuck

Another compelling document encompassing 1,000 acres (404 ha) records the lands of five of the original pioneers of Upper Washabuck. This deed from the Crown is recorded in Book P page 102 on the 16th day of October 1832 and signed by Rupert D. George.[13]

It conveys to pioneers Daniel Carmichael, John McNeil, Murdock McNeil, James McDonald and Murdock McKenzie, certain pieces or parcels of land situate lying and being in the County of Cape Breton [Victoria did not become a separate county until 1851] in the following lots and proportion:

> To the said Daniel Carmichael a lot of land near the entrance of Watchabaktchkt Inlet south side of Saint Patricks Channel included within the boundaries that were established in the year one thousand eight hundred and twelve, beginning at a stake near the shore ... etc, etc.
>
> Then to the said John McNeil lot number two on the south side of Watchabaktchkt Inlet beginning at a blazed spruce tree on the margin of the Inlet, thence bounded by a line running by the magnet in the year 1826 south twelve degrees etc, etc.
>
> Then Murdock McNeil gets lot number three bounded by the magnet aforesaid [1826] etc, etc.
>
> Then James McDonald gets lot number four [...] running by the magnet aforesaid [1826] and
>
> Then to Murdock McKenzie a lot of land at the rear of the Jones' mile lot at the head of Watchabaktchkt Inlet ... running by the magnet in the year 1814 ... etc.etc.

4-2, 4-3 Survey sketches of pioneer grants of Upper Washabuck, 1832 and 1839. Courtesy of Registry of Deeds, Baddeck, CB.

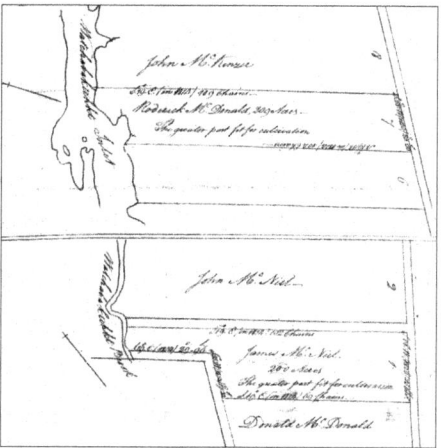

This document seems to indicate that these lots had been surveyed in the Washabuck area between 1812 and 1826, and that pioneer families were provided with Tickets of Locations until grants were awarded by the provincial government. Not surprisingly, all of these early surveyed lots included brooks or were adjacent to a ready source of fresh water.

Reference is made in the above deed to the Jones mile lot at the head of Washabuck Inlet. The request for the survey of these 600 acres of land (242 ha) for Loyalist Jonathan Jones Jr. was made of Surveyor General Captain Crawley by Major General Nepean, President of His Majesty's Council on November 4, 1811.[14]

So, we can be reasonably assured of surveying of lands happening around the Washabuck area as early as 1811.

Early Land Owners:

The 1818 census Rolls for Cape Breton Island includes the following Wasabackteh [sic] residents for the Division of Baddeck, dated June 20, 1818.

1) Daniel Carmichael, age 31, a married stone cutter from N. Breton
2) William Goold, age 24, married from Cape Breton
3) William Mathewson, age 33, married from N. Breton
4) David McQuillen, age 25, a single Joiner from the States
5) The name of William Ross is also included, age 50, a married carpenter from N. Breton listed as living at St. Peter's Channel.[15]

According to provincial Archivist Bruce Fergusson[16] the name of **John Cameron** precedes all others who "was undoubtedly one of the first settlers," in Washabuck before 1807. Robert Morgan includes the name of a Lieut. John Cameron among a list of Loyalists that settled in various parts of Cape Breton Island. Cameron is listed as arriving in Spanish River (Sydney) in 1783 from Liverpool, Nova Scotia, he being a Lieutenant with the King's Orange Rangers.[17] In 1807, the Cape Breton Land Grant papers outline a John Cameron petitioning Nepean for 300 acres of land at Whasbock (sic) on the south side of St. Patrick's Channel [sic].[18]

In March 1821, **William Wall** also petitioned Lieutenant-General Sir James Kempt, for a lot of land, not to exceed one hundred acres at Watchabaktcht, [sic] eastward of and abutting lands lately held by William Ross, on condition of immediate settlement. The petition continues:

> ...the petitioner is a native of England, twenty six years of age, unmarried and has resided eleven years in this Island, has never received any land from the crown nor holds any by purchase or otherwise, and prays that your Excellency will grant him a lot at Watchabaktcht to the eastward of and adjoining to lands lately held by William Ross which is neither improved nor claimed by any person but lies at the disposal

of the Crown and which petitioner has not agreed to let or otherwise transfer but intends to reside on and cultivate....

Based on the petition data, William Wall likely arrived on Cape Breton in 1810. In a petition of confirmation of lands in possession of Donald MacKinnon, reference is made, "To Donald MacKinnon for the lot no. 7, adjoining the eastern side of lands formerly occupied by W. Ross at the southern side of St. Patrick's Channel, being the lot formerly applied for by W. Wall, who resigned to petitioner."[19]

Local historian Neil P. S. MacLean wrote that a man by the name of **Carmichael** lived for a time at what is now Washabuck Centre, on property that was later taken up by Angus (*Eòin*) MacNeil. He relocated to St. Ann's or the Englishtown area of Victoria County.[20] No other information is known about him.

Rich in Acreage:

Pioneers now possessed an embarrassment of riches in acreage compared to the marginal crofts they had left behind in their homeland and they guarded their new possession vigilantly. In many cases the pioneers or their descendants never saw the back portions of their lands, as access was not easy and there was an abundance of timber and arable land surrounding their rustic residences. It wasn't until the mid-1980s and the advent of the local Route 223 Forestry Co-op Ltd. that easier access was possible through the construction of adequate woodlot roads and bridges in many of these properties in Washabuck.

Moolah for Memory

Roddie MacDonald recalls an often heard tale in his ancestral home about wood harvesting on the property abutting his great-grandfather Murdock (*Alasdair Glas*) MacDonald's lands in Upper Washabuck. This property was originally settled by Daniel Carmichael in 1817. According to family lore, the MacDonald family's patriarch *Alasdair Glas* had immigrated to Cape Breton from North Uist, Scotland.[21] It seems that William Dryden's lumber crew was working the adjacent property during the winter months and the property line was indistinguishable. The work crew didn't know where the property line was and even R. C., Murdock's son, couldn't ascertain where the line was. By this time, Murdock MacDonald was old and not well – he had lost the use of his legs and could no longer walk – but who as a young man knew exactly where the property lines were, agreed to be placed on a bob-sled and hauled by the family horse out to the old mountain trail. Sure enough, as fragile as his body had become Murdock still displayed an acuteness of mind and memory and indicated to Dryden, precisely the location of the old survey line. As it turned out, the logging crew were over the line and onto MacDonald's land by a fair margin. So in payment for the stray wood-cutting the princely sum of $ 5.00 exchanged hands. Murdock died in 1918.[22]

SURVEYORS, LAND GRANTS AND EARLY LAND OWNERS

A Priest who was a Land Surveyor

Alex D. MacLean unveils this tale about a priest who was a land surveyor and how he resolved a Washabuck property row.

Father John V. MacDonnell, familiarly known to the Barramen as *Maighstir Ian Dòmhnullach*, was parish priest in this section until he passed away in 1858. At that time, all of what is now the parish of Iona [St. Columba] was included in Christmas Island parish. It was during the pastorate of Rev. Father MacDonnell that Roderick MacDonald … who was my great-grandfather, went to his eternal reward. It seems that some time before his death he was involved in a dispute about a line-fence.

He claimed that his fences were erected as they should be, while the other party, Mrs. MacNeil, a widow, felt that she was deprived of about an acre of land. It seems that there was not much that the poor widow could do about it, as my great-grandfather was inclined to be rather dogmatic about anything that he took into his head. Some people would say he was plain bull-headed, and that this trait may be seen in some of his descendants unto this day. However, I prefer to say that he was inclined to be dogmatic, and let it go at that.

Anyway, there did not seem to be anything that the poor widow could do about it so the matter was allowed to drop. This was now the situation when Roderick MacDonald was on his death-bed. Now he was not so sure of things, and he was not so inclined to be so bull-headed … er, I should have said dogmatic. He was not at all sure that he was right. He exclaimed his doubts to Father MacDonnell who procured a surveyor's chain and went over the ground. The priest gave a decision that upheld the widow's contention, and she was awarded the disputed acre of ground. The fence was shifted."[23]

Early Washabuck Land Surveyors

The following surveyors and deputy surveyors for Victoria County carried out surveys throughout the Washabuck and St. Columba areas during and including the following time-frames:

> Captain Thomas Crawley 1804 and 1811 (also mentioned in the Donald MacKay Sand Point survey, 1836).
> D. B. McNab 1855, 1856 and 1862.
> Angus McKay 1872 and 1876.
> Peter H. Ross 1877 and 1880.
> Joseph S. McLean 1880, 1888 and 1911.[24]

Robert Sutherland

There is evidence that another early land surveyor owned, occupied, and surveyed, lands in the Washabuck area. There exist two deeds, the first dated August 1849 that reads in part:

> …between Robert Sutherland (L S) Senior of the township of Watchabaktchkt in the parish of St. Patrick in the County and Island

of Cape Breton and province of Nova Scotia of the one part and Charles Sutherland ... of the township aforesaid ... half of lot sixteen ... containing one hundred acres more or less ... for the sum of thirty five pounds of lawful money. The deed is signed by Murdock McAskill Esq., Magistrate, Justice of the Peace of the County of Cape Breton and witnessed by Allan McAulay and Murdock Matheson.[25]

The second deed is similar except it is dated April 30, 1850:

...between Robert Sutherland Senior and Charles Sutherland and Robert Sutherland Junior and Mary Sutherland ... for a lot of land in Washabuck for sixty five pounds ... which is then described ... encompassing two hundred acres being lot number seventeen ... again signed by Murdock McAskill J.P. and witnessed by Allan McAulay and another individual.[26]

Furthermore, the surveyor Robert Sutherland's (of whom little more is known) work is referenced on at least two later Returns of Survey. In the first, surveyor D. B. McNab in laying out a 200-acre lot (40 ha) for Colin McIvor [sic] in Upper Washabuck in June 1856, references McIvor's western line having been "trued" by Robert Sutherland. The second, in 1877, by Peter Ross, notes that the original western line between John MacNeil and Neil MacKinnon in Lower Washabuck was run by Sutherland.[27]

Alex D. MacLean gets the last word and provides more details ca. 1940:

Sutherland was a land surveyor. He lived on the property now divided between Mrs. Roderick MacKinnon, Mrs. Sarah E. MacDonald, and Roderick MacIsaac. It is thought that this family removed to the North Shore. Patterson in his, "History of Victoria County" states that a Sutherland who was a land surveyor, lived on the North Shore district in the early days. Patterson says distinctly that he was the first settler there. It is definitely known that he and his family went to New Zealand during the exodus that commenced in 1851. His lands in Upper Washabuck were sold to pioneer Ranald (*Raghnall Mór*) MacDonald.[28]

A. F. Church, Cartographer[29]

Ambrose Finson (A. F.) Church was a noted mapmaker whose county maps of Nova Scotia are renowned for the information they contain and for the unique way the information is displayed. They were prepared and published by Church between the years 1865 and 1888 under various contracts to the Nova Scotia Government.

A. F. Church was born in Maine, USA, in 1836 of Welsh ancestry. He became a civil engineer and worked for four years in Portland, Maine, with noted mapmaker Jacob Chace Jr. After Chace's death in 1865, Church offered to relocate to Nova Scotia and finish the proposed plans of the counties for the province. With that agreement with the government in hand, Church purchased from J. Chace Jr. and Co. and H. F. Walling of New

York, some surveys of a portion of Nova Scotia. He arrived in the province in 1865 to proceed with his work.

Church was described as bearded and a short man, who always wore a beaver hat. He was a respected resident of Dartmouth, and later Bedford, but he always retained his American citizenship. He was further described as quiet, learned man, and a bit of an eccentric. He had a number of unusual traits, including that he never emptied a teapot until it was too full of tea leaves to take water. Perhaps he was familiar with the old saying that tea leaves are like politicians, you can't tell if they are any good until they are in hot water.

His map of Victoria County was completed between 1883 and 1887, with a scale of one mile to the inch. His maps outline the locations of schools, wharves, and businesses, along with the residences and the roads that passed through the countryside. It is claimed that he got school children to help with his effort, by having the children fill in maps of where they lived. As a result, "his maps can be read with as much pleasure and interest as you might read a book."

Church and his wife had a family of five, a son and four daughters. Church ended his days living with his son in Rio de Janeiro where he died in February 1920.[30]

(For Church's map delineating the Washabuck district, see pages 415, 416.)

Geological Surveyor Hugh Fletcher

During the summer of 1876 extensive geological explorations and surveys were made within the Bras d'Or Lake watershed that included the lands of the Washabuck Peninsula along St. Patrick's Channel. These explorations were carried out under the direction of Hugh Fletcher assisted by his younger brother William and E. A. Bowes of Toronto, for the Geological Survey of Canada. Fletcher declares:

> The Washaback [sic] Hills lie between two basins of carboniferous rock. The Washaback Hills consist of gneiss, mica-schist, syenite, diorite, hornblende-rock, quartzite and felsite; all more or less foliated, and sometimes in exceedingly thin laminae...."[31]

> "Schistose rocks are well seen on the Washaback anticline in the cliffs of Little Bras d'Or Lake, between Burnt Point and Boulaceet Harbour...."

He then described in detail, a sequence of fifteen different types of rocks and mineral formations between the two mentioned areas, including "a rich pocket of copper and iron pyrites, sulphide of silver and gold was discovered and mined by a Mr. [Alexander] Cameron of Baddeck," at Boulaceet Harbour.[32]

The annual report details their mineral finds extending from Boulaceet Harbour around MacKay Point to Washabuck Bridge and beyond.

According to G. A. O'Reilly, writing in Nova Scotia Minerals Update, in an intriguing article entitled "From The Mineral Inventory Files, Three Graves in Margaree" states: "Fletcher was held in very high regard by the province's mining industry and his work often directly assisted mining operations."[33]

Much of the following biography is from O'Reilly's article.

Hugh Fletcher was born in England in 1848. He and his brother William immigrated to Canada with their father, a mining engineer, in 1860. He graduated from University of Toronto near the top of his class in 1872 with a degree in natural sciences. In 1875 Fletcher assumed responsibility for the geological mapping of Nova Scotia for the Geological Survey of Canada. Fletcher worked his entire career in Nova Scotia. Working with E. R. Faribault, they produced a series of 70 geological maps of the province, with Fletcher concentrating on the Cape Breton and northern Nova Scotia sectors.

It seems that Fletcher and his younger brother William, also a University of Toronto graduate, worked together on a mapping party in 1881. William drowned while attempting to ford the Margaree River in Inverness County to see his girlfriend, Christie MacLeod, who lived in Big Interval. Hugh Fletcher met Christie at his brother's funeral, and a year later they married. They had a family of two children. Christie died of tuberculosis in 1892 and is buried in the Margaree Centre Cemetery.[34] Her grave is between the two Fletcher brothers, William her first beau, and her husband Hugh, who died from pneumonia in Joggins, Nova Scotia, in September 1909.[35]

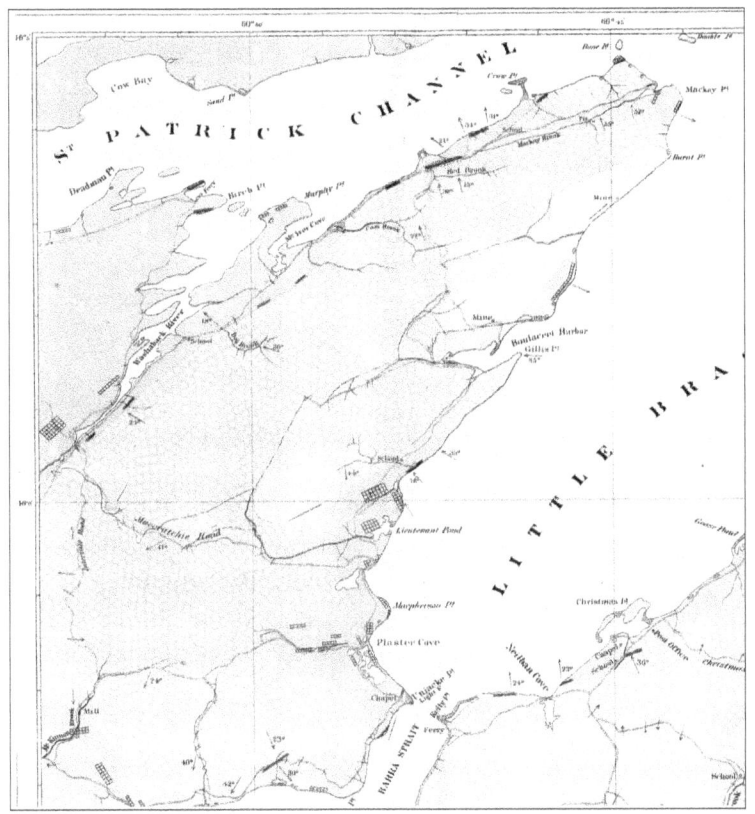

4-4 Detail of Hugh Fletcher's geological map outlining the Washabuck Peninsula. Courtesy of Lauchie MacLean, Bedford, NS.

SURVEYORS, LAND GRANTS AND EARLY LAND OWNERS

5 – Stores, Merchants, Shopping

During its two-century-long history, Washabuck has had eight stores. But for a long time, the community was solely dependent on shopping elsewhere, in villages that were only accessible by water.

Little Bras d'Or Gammell and Christie

In writing about early stores in Baddeck and area, diarist Robert Elmsley writes:

> ...There being no stores inside the Bras d'Or [Lakes] the settlers could procure no supplies unless at Arichat or Gammell's, hence the necessity of going there by water, which was done by clubbing.... The farmers in the country used to club together, procure a boat twice a year, and load their produce, and proceed to Mr. Gammell's, [at] Little Bras d'Or, who supplied them with every article required. This also applied to people of Whycocomagh as well as to those bordering on the lakes. It may be added that Gammell catered for North Sydney including miners.[1]

Alex D. MacLean commenting on Elmsley's observation explains: "The Mr. Gammell referred to was an influential merchant at Little Bras d'Or; he was afterwards associated with Mr. Christie, and the business was then known as Gammell & Christie."[2] Mr. Gammell's name was William and Mr. Christie's was John.

The village of Baddeck was not yet in existence. The only store on the Bras d'Or Lake was the one operated by James Duffus on Duffus Island, now known as Kidston Island. The year was 1827. The Washabuck pioneers had arrived ten years previously.

Alex D. MacLean relates the following story about a trek to Bras d'Or for staples turned tragic.

Perils of Shopping

The story is to the effect that one evening in 1827 about twilight Peter MacLean (*Peadar mac Lachlainn*) returned from visiting the store on Duffus Island, near Baddeck. He had hauled his boat up on the beach and was proceeding towards his home when he was accosted by a man, who addressed him in a friendly manner and called him by name. Peter did not recognize him. He was a stranger and Peter told him so. The stranger insisted that he should be able to recognize him, and finally informed him that he was his grandfather (or great-grandfather, at this time and distance it is no longer clear). Peter replied that this was impossible, as that person had died in Barra long before they had immigrated to this country.

After a short "conversation" the stranger informed Peter that he (Peter) was to meet death by drowning. He was told further that whoever would listen to and accept this story from him when he would first related it would be with him when he would be drowned. He was detained at the scene of this ghostly tryst all night, and that it was sometime about sunrise that he returned home. Later, he wished to tell his brother Malcolm of his experience, but Malcolm who was of a very peppery disposition, refused to listen to him. His brother Neil, who resided at Washabuck Centre, was always inclined to be skeptical, and was more so in this case.

His brother Alexander, who was of an independent turn of mind, and who perhaps recognized that that there were stranger things happening than they were aware of, agreed to listen to Peter and advise him if possible. Having heard the tale, he, like Malcolm and Neil, was of the opinion that it was the result of a delusion or some figment of the imagination and told him not to worry over such things.

It is now not clear how soon after this that Peter and Alexander prepared to go to Little Bras d'Or to where they were accustomed to journey when they wished to purchase supplies or to sell any of their farm or sea produce. There was no money in circulation in those days; all trade was on a barter basis. The store that they did business with was operated by a man named Gammell. Later this same business was conducted under the name of *Gammell and Christie*. On their way to Little Bras d'Or they called to see their uncle Roderick MacLean (brother of Lachlan), who had a farm on the Southside of Boularderie Island, about twelve miles below Kempt Head. After visiting with their uncle for a short time, they proceeded on their way to Little Bras d'Or.

There, they soon transacted their business, and started on the return trip. They were accompanied by a man named Cann, who they had met at Gammell's store, and who had asked for passage to Washabuck. His home was in Mabou, and this passage would make his journey much shorter.

The boat in which they made the trip was of a type commonly known as a Barra Boat or *Sgoth*, and was built by their father. The boat was rigged with two square sails. Away to the west of Long Island and about opposite to their uncle's home in Boularderie, they were caught in a black squall and their boat capsized. It is understood that they were beating against the wind when this happened, and we are also told that the sheets of the sails or at least of one of them was tied – a dangerous practice – instead of being held by one of the occupants.

They were all floundering in the water. Alexander helped to place the passenger Cann on the upturned boat, and told him to remain there until they could get assistance. Alexander and Peter then struck out for the shore. After proceeding a short way, the latter complained that he was becoming exhausted. Alexander then took him on his back and returned to the capsized boat and placed him astride her. There was no sign of Cann and it is certain that he slid off and perished.

Alexander again, then struck of for shore a distance of three or four miles. It was dark when this happened and daylight when Alexander managed to reach the shore a short distance below his uncle's house. The latter, like the great majority of the old people, was an early riser, and was up and about very early that morning. He was walking around outside his house when he saw a man walking along the shore bank. He did not recognize him but returned to the house and told his wife, who was still in bed, of seeing this man, adding that he was afraid that something had happened to his nephews who, he was aware, would be making their return journey. He went down to the beach where he found Alexander, who was stark naked, having to divest himself of all his clothing during the long and exhausting swim to land. The uncle returned to the house and secured some clothing for him, and after he had come to the house where he was given a warm meal, they both proceeded to the scene of the tragedy in the uncle's boat.

They recovered the overturned boat, but Peter like the passenger Cann, had disappeared. The sea was rough and the weather was cold, and it was surmised that the unfortunate men had become chilled and numbed and fallen into the sea. Their bodies were never recovered. Later, Alexander continued the journey home in the same boat. The tragedy occurred in 1827, ten years after the pioneers settled in Lower Washabuck.

But the question will remain to the end of time: "Who was it really, that met Peter on the beach that evening, and to him forecasted his death?"[3]

Stores of Grand Narrows

Archibald J. MacKenzie in his *History of Christmas Island Parish*, outlines the merchants that were in business at Grand Narrows in the early years of the settlement. Most of the residents of Grand Narrows were immigrants from the Isle of Barra, settling there ca. 1802. Since most transportation was by water, it is likely that Washabuck residents accessed Grand Narrows businesses on occasion. Following is a distilled version of MacKenzie's listing.

The first merchant at Grand Narrows was a Robert K. Masters, a native of Truro. He granted the beach opposite the land of Donald MacNeil, Red, for the purpose of using it in his fishing business. He was also a boat builder. The second merchant was Peter McIntyre who bought the acre lot on which the stores and residences of McNeil Brothers later stood. When the business failed, the principal creditor, James Campbell of Arichat, offered Allan McNeil, Blacksmith, the whole of the real estate of McIntyre, and, store and residence, for three pounds sterling. This was in 1838.

Later on, another merchant, the ninth one, was William Murray. He was a Lowland Scotsman and a Presbyterian. Murray came from Halifax and perhaps he is best known for being the father of the longest serving Premier in this Province. George H. Murray who was born in Grand Narrows in 1861 and in due course served as Premier of Nova Scotia for twenty-six years, representing the County of Victoria, in the House of Assembly. The Murrays moved to Sydney Mines in 1869.

Murray was followed by Rory MacNeil with his business in due course taken over by the firm of McDougall and McNeil. Then in 1888, the firm McNeil Brothers commenced business at Grand Narrows with John C. and Rory McNeil as principals.[4] (See appendix #3 for the complete listing)

Shopping in Baddeck

The first settlement in Baddeck began on the island opposite the village and was known to the Mi'kmaq as *Apategoitjity* or "the island facing the south cove."[5]

Patterson's *History of Victoria County* states that in 1819 James Duffus, a retired half-pay naval officer arrived from Halifax. Duffus had been advised by his brother-in-law Samuel Cunard to consider Sydney as a worthwhile business locale, but after inspection, decided to proceed up the lake and set up his trading post on Mutton Island, which he renamed Duffus Island.

The trading post flourished and people came from far and wide to do business with him. The question naturally arises, why did he set up business on that site? By this time the communities of Grand Narrows, Baddeck River and Washabuck had been well-established, and the island location was easily accessible by water, the only mode of transportation available to these pioneers.

Not long after, in 1820, Mr. Duffus was appointed a Magistrate and applied for a 400-acre grant (161 ha) on the "mainland" opposite his newly built home on the western end of the island. By 1824 he had established a successful branch business in Big Bras d'Or with his brother William. He died in 1833 however, after seeking medical aid in Halifax.[6] His son Alexander died in 1838, just five years after his father.

Then, his executors sent a militia Captain by the name of William Kidston from Halifax, to wind up his business affairs. Kidston didn't just end up Duffus" affairs but married his widow and with the passing of his stepson fell heir to all the Duffus property.

In the autumn of 1840, James Anderson arrived in Baddeck. He was originally from Halifax. He had come to Sydney in 1835, where he lived for five years before moving his goods to Baddeck. He began to do business in the old Duffus Stand, which he purchased from Mr. Kidston.

Later, as the population grew, it was felt a post on the mainland would be more convenient and have more advantages. Thus, the business was moved there to a location known by the Indian word *"Abadak"* meaning a place with an island near....[7]

Kidston transferred his goods and chattels to the mainland, where some years later Anderson followed him.[8] Two young men were clerks with Mr. Anderson; one, his nephew Robert Elmsley, and the other, a Charles J. Campbell, who later played a prominent political role in Victoria County.

Robert Elmsley

Robert Elmsley was born in Scotland in 1823. He came to Sydney, Cape Breton, in 1839, and arrived on Duffus Island near Baddeck over ice in March 1840. He was then 17 years old. Charles J. Campbell was already in charge of Mr. James Anderson's store on Duffus Island. One end of the store building was inhabited by William Kidston and his wife, and Elmsley describes the Island as "beautifully wooded from end to end … except for a small spot where a lovely garden had once existed…."[9] The store, situated as it was on the island, some hundred yards from the mainland, made it inconvenient for the customers to reach. When a customer did appear on the mainland shore, a signal was given and a canoe was sent over for them. In due course the patron was delivered back to the mainland free of charge with their purchases.

In May of 1841 Elmsley left Duffus Island and went to Mr. Taylor's place in Baddeck, where he ran the store for Mr. Anderson of Sydney. Robert Elmsley later became Baddeck's first Postmaster in May 1858. Merchandising must have been in the Elmsley family's genes, as two of Robert's other three brothers also ran businesses: James was a merchant operating in North Sydney in 1855, and George was a merchant in St. John's Newfoundland. A third brother was Dr. Joseph who was commissioned as Registrar of Deeds at Baddeck for two years, until he sailed off with his wife and family to New Zealand in 1859.[10]

It can be said that as the town of Baddeck became more established, the trade and business that used to go to little Bras d'Or and St. Peter's from Washabuck, was diverted to Baddeck.[11]

Washabuck's First Store / *Stòr a" Gràthaich*

Catriona (*Chaluim*) MacLean (1839-1933) of Lower Washabuck and Baddeck, used to tell of a store located on MacKay Point, and at that time she was the only one alive that could recall it. The store was only a small log structure and it was stocked with goods from a vessel that became caught in the early ice off MacKay Point and held there until spring breakup. The ship's owner was a man named McGrath from Newfoundland. When he realized his situation, he erected a rustic log shelter over a root cellar, transferred his goods into it and proceeded to set up shop. Before spring arrived he had apparently sold out his entire stock and later made a trip to replenish his supplies the following summer. He exchanged his "store goods" for produce. The pioneers referred to the store as *Stòr a' Gràthaich*.¹²

The store was located on what was then called *Rubh' a' Stòr*, but today is referred to as Sand Point, a sandy jib of land jutting into St. Patrick's Channel facing Bone Island. A photo taken in 2000 displays the indentation of the root cellar that was underneath the log structure. A "Return of Survey" dated October 1904 in favour of Arthur W. McCurdy for an Island [Bone Island] in the district of McKay's Point … references the [Sand] Point "…standing six chains and fifty links from *Rubh' A' Stòr* [sic] (Store Point) containing in all 1 3/4 acres."¹³

5-1 Remnants of the root cellar of *Stòr a' Gràthaich*, ca. 2000, at what today is called Sand Point, near MacKay Point.

Buying Washabuck's First Cow:

One of the handicaps for the early settlers was dealing with a lack of livestock. Alex D. MacLean tells about the first cow to come to Washabuck.

> At first the pioneers had no cows of their own and were forced to depend on goats for their milk supply. They were accustomed to go through the Big Lake, as they called it, to St. Peter's where they used to trade with Lawrence Kavanagh, a merchant in that village…. Learning that the Barramen had no cow, he offered them a young animal. They would certainly like to have the cow, but money was a rare article at the time … and the Barramen told him so. Kavanagh, who it was agreed by all, was a genial, warm-hearted gentleman, a trait to be found in most people of Irish extraction, told them to take the cow and that he would take payment in butter. I cannot say with any degree of definiteness which of the families was fortunate to get this cow, but I recollect very clearly about the late Mrs. Arsenault [nee Catherine (MacLean) Boyd] mentioning something about her father [*Calum mac Lachlainn*] bringing this cow to Washabuck. At any rate, the cow was bought by boat to Washabuck, and in the course of time paid for as per agreement.¹⁴

Catherine (*Catriona*) was the daughter of Calum, son of Lachlan MacLean. She married first school teacher John C. Boyd and in a second marriage Captain Joseph Arsenault.

STORES, MERCHANTS AND SHOPPING

William Dryden's Store

William Dryden was a lumber contractor from New Brunswick. He arrived in Upper Washabuck ca. 1909. His store was located at his mill at Cole Point, between the public road and the river. It was a two story building built by Dan MacKinnon and "Little" Jimmy (Stephen) MacDonald. Murray Steeves, a scaler for Dryden and also from New Brunswick, operated the store for him during the time period Dryden lumbered in Washabuck, perhaps for as long as ten years. Murray Steeves married Cassie MacRitchie, a sister of John Dan MacRitchie who was also a Washabuck Bridge merchant. Steeves and his wife resided upstairs in the building while the store operation was on ground level.

When Dryden finished lumbering in Upper Washabuck, he moved his operation to West Bay, Richmond County. But the store building was moved across the lake ice to Iona, where it became a garage for the St. Columba Pastor's car. This building also served to house a dynamo which provided early electricity for the parish buildings.[15]

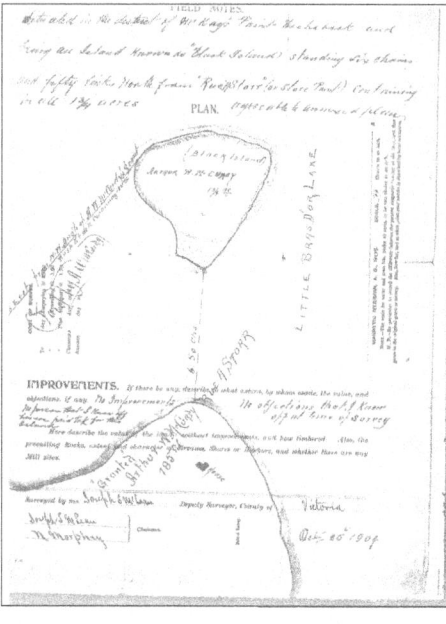

5-2 Survey plan describing Black Island [Bone Island] as being 6.5 chains from *Rue A Storr* [sic] (Store Point) dated October 25, 1904, surveyed by Victoria County deputy surveyor, Joseph S. MacLean. Courtesy Registry of Deeds, Baddeck, CB.

5-3 Catriona (*Calum Lachlann*) MacLean (1839-1933) on right, of Lower Washabuck, with her daughter Esther. Catriona first married John C. Boyd of Antigonish County. Following his death, she married Captain Joseph Arsenault.

John and Mary MacNeil's Store

John (*Iain mac Ruairidh*) MacNeil and his wife Mary (MacDougall) built and ran a successful general store operation at Washabuck Centre for many years. Their building was strategically located at the site of the government wharf. Mr. MacNeil had bought the property on each side of the right-of-way leading down to the wharf, and as a result he received all of the business moving through that particular nerve centre. At that time there was still a substantial piece of land east of the right-of-way which he kept fenced. Inside this area he kept livestock, including a particularly large black-spotted hog.[16] The MacNeil's lived upstairs in the building.

Both John (1846-1930) and Mary had prior marriages. "Little" Mary, who was a member of the MacDougall (Captain) family that inhabited the north side of Washabuck River, had first married Johnny Morrison from South Cove. Johnny had two brothers, Angus and Norman. Mary's mother, "Big" Kate was a sister to Malkie MacDonald's grandfather Murdock. The couple had lived in Maine and had a daughter Cassie. Mary's husband died there and the daughter remained in Maine after Mary returned to Washabuck. Later, the daughter was thought to have died from tuberculosis.

5-4 William Dryden's store was managed by Murray Steeves and his wife Cassie (MacRitchie) at Cole Point, Upper Washabuck. Once lumberman Dryden departed Washabuck, the store building was taken across the ice to Iona, where it served as a garage for St. Columba parish's clergymen. Courtesy Hector MacKenzie, Washabuck Bridge.

John MacNeil spent part of his youth at sea before he worked in the forestry industry in Maine He married there. He and his first wife relocated to western Canada, living in Telkwa, northern British Columbia, where they raised a family of three sons.[17] John's first wife died there. John returned home, while his three sons remained in the west.

Spiritual Libations

John MacNeil was well liked, both personally and as a businessman. In due course, he began to spend more of his time farming the beautiful piece of property that his wife Mary had inherited on north side Washabuck River, known as Pleasant Point. Mary spent most of her later years running the store. It was during this time that as a side-line venture, the duo began brewing and selling home-made beer. The beverage was branded under their commercial logo as Nixy Beer. It was a spruce beer and one that was appreciated by those who imbibed and savoured quality drinks. Salivating clients arrived on foot, on horseback, and in buggies and sleighs (some even paid fares), all craving the quenchable beverage. It was a common sight as they queued up at The MacNeil Agency on lazy Sunday afternoons and especially, during those rainy days.

5-5 A youthful "Little" Mary MacDougall whose second husband was John MacNeil.

Unfortunately, for John, Mary and their stalwart patrons, this entrepreneurial value-added venture, became the victim of its own success. After one particularly brisk business weekend, the amount of traffic on the Sunday road roiled the ire of a local temperance crank, causing a rather vigorous complaint to Pastor Father Duncan Rankin. The following Sunday morning Father Rankin in his most emphatic *Gàidhlig* railed and chastised the congregation in a long-hour's rant about the evils of liquor and the derivatives thereof. [No mention was made about church wine.] Finally, toward the end of the harangue, John MacNeil could bear it no longer. He stood at his pew and in a loud voice interrupted Father Rankin and exclaimed, *"'S mis' an duine! 'S mis' an duine!"* [I'm the man! I'm the man!] On that note he grabbed his hat and strode briskly out of the church.

So ended Nixy Beer and a budding Washabuck enterprise was squelched in its infancy. Perhaps though, it was simply a case of the dollar sign being trumped by the sign of the cross – an entrepreneurial spirit being nudged aside by The Holy Spirit. Whatever, a few weeks later all were back on good terms and remained so for the balance of their lives. Mary MacNeil passed away in April, ca. 1925. Her husband John died in 1930 and Father Rankin in 1954.

Effie Morrison's Store

Effie Morrison from Washabuck Bridge built and ran a successful general store there during the 1920s and 1930s. Not much is known about the operation; but it was a good sized building, built at a cost of $1,100.[18]

Image 5-6 John and Mary MacNeil in front of their Washabuck Centre store, ca. 1920.

Her store was just fifty feet (15 m) west of another general store run by her competitor, John Dan MacRitchie. The store site was at the corner at Washabuck Bridge intersection between the road and the river. Effie's store burned to the ground and she did not rebuild. She later ran a modest retail operation from her own home, located beyond Washabuck Bridge on a knoll to the left (Effie's Hill), as you proceed toward Little Narrows.

Effie – whose father was Murdock Morrison – married Murdock MacDonald, a brother to Norman Peter of South Cove. Her mother had died young and Effie was brought up by her aunt Mary Morrison. Effie's home, which doubled as her store, was a two story building that was vacated during the 1940s. Effie retired to Whycocomagh, and later to Sydney. The furniture remained inside the house until it was filched by vandals. As youngsters, Washabuck Bridge resident Charlotte MacKenzie and her older siblings, recall playing nearby and peering through the dusty window panes. Their mother always warned them to keep out of the house as there was a well in the cellar and accidents were always a concern.

John Dan MacRitchie's Store

John Dan MacRitchie ran a successful general store at Washabuck Bridge for years. John Dan's store was adjacent to and just east of, Effie store, by about fifty feet. Both stores functioned as prosperous enterprises because the settlement was well-populated at the time. MacRitchie's store was in operation prior to the First World War, but it too, like Effie's, burned during the 1920s. John Dan received about $3,000 from insurance for the building's loss. Shortly afterwards he rebuilt, but this time, in the neighbouring community of Little Narrows.[19] Today, that building functions as The MacKenzie Country Store and retails grocery staples and gasoline, under the proprietorship of owners Wayne and Louise MacKenzie, Hazeldale.

5-7 Effie Morrison, second from left, of Washabuck Bridge is joined by her affable neighbours from Upper Washabuck. On far left, *Ceiteig* (Mrs. Rory MacKinnon), next to Effie, Mary Ann (Mrs. Danny Murphy), Sarah Liza (Mrs. Angus Ranald MacDonald) and on right, Katherine (Mrs. Rory J. MacNeil) who was generally referred to as *muime* (Godmother) ca. 1940.

5-8 This photo is thought to be taken at the front of Effie Morrison's and John Dan MacRitchie's stores at Washabuck Bridge, ca. 1910. Courtesy of Beaton Institute, Cape Breton University, Sydney, NS.

Fleet-footed flannel-foots

John Dan, reminiscing about his mercantile challenges, mused that he found it necessary to be ever vigilant when dealing with customers. He dealt in feeds and basic farm equipment as well as dry goods and foodstuffs of all kinds. John Dan initially received much of his store supplies via the

STORES, MERCHANTS AND SHOPPING

5-9 John Dan MacRitchie and wife Margaret in front of their new store at Little Narrows, ca. 1930. (L-R) Norman MacAulay, Gordon MacLennan and John MacKinnon. To the right of Margaret are Katie Belle MacAulay and Louise "Honey" Mann. Courtesy of Norman MacAulay, Sydney, NS.

5-10 A faded invoice remnant from John Dan McRitchie's Washabuck Bridge store, itemizing a charge of $0.25 to neighbour Dan MacDougall for pipe tobacco, dated July 14, 1923. Courtesy of Lawrence MacDougall, Washabuck.

Washabuck Centre wharf. The wharf predated the River wharf by about seven to eight years.[20] He received and shipped most of his supplies and products by lake boat that delivered their cargos via the nearby government wharves. In the fall he would buy rabbits from the local boys, as he had a ready market in the Sydneys. In the following entry, John Dan recalls some tribulations as a merchant.

> One winter, I had bought what seemed to me to be an unusually large number of rabbits from the neighboring MacDougall brothers, but as usual, I just put them in general storage in the cool room at the back of the store for shipment later to Sydney. I realized upon checking on the situation, too late as it turned out, that these same rascals had found the door at the rear of my store unlocked, and that I had been buying back my own rabbits from them, a second and perhaps even for a third time. "You had to be on your toes to keep ahead of those scheming characters," exclaimed an exasperated John Dan.[21]

Dan Michael MacKenzie

Dan Michael ran a modest store operation out of his parents' home in Upper Washabuck. The store opened for business on May 17, 1927.[22] Dan Michael operated it for four or five years. He sold mostly staples like tobacco, molasses, kerosene, salt, sugar, flour and dry goods.[23]

Alec MacDonald's Store

Alec (Michael B.) MacDonald ran a store out of his home in St. Columba for a brief period. Alec's brother, John Archie, had bought a vacant building originally owned and operated by Joe (Allan) MacNeil in Iona. Joe (Allan) passed away in 1950. John Archie bought the building and had his brother Alec use it for a general store. When, the original Iona Co-op Store was destroyed by fire on December 5, 1954, the Co-op required a replacement immediately. John Archie sold his building and business to the co-operative. A number of items that were leftover items such as a measure of dry goods and canned products were sold for a short time from their St. Columba residence.

Washabuck Cooperative "Marjorie's"

In the 1930s, interest was awakened locally in the need and usefulness of the spirit of co-operation. So, in 1938, it was decided to organize a co-operative store at Iona, with a branch at Ottawa Brook. The first president was Father Donald Roberts, St. Columba parish curate, and the first Board of Directors comprised of: Roderick A. MacNeil (vice president) of Iona; George McCluskey, George Lewis and Hugh J. Murphy of Ottawa Brook; Neil J. MacNeil of Gillis Point and Dan M. MacKinnon of Upper Washabuck [Cain's Mountain] with Miss Cassie MacNeil of Iona, serving as secretary to the board.

    The Co-op was started from scratch. Property was purchased from John A. MacDonald in Iona and another piece was purchased from Donald Walker in Ottawa Brook. At a meeting held on June 20, 1938, Neil MacNeil, Baddeck, a man with many years merchandising experience, was appointed manager. Until his passing in 1961, Neil remained the co-operative's manager which by then had blossomed into a viable business. The first manager at the Ottawa Brook outlet was Hugh J. Murphy, followed by Charlie Lewis and Mary Walker.

    Shortly after, in 1942, a second co-operative branch opened in Washabuck.[24] It was run under the management of Marjorie MacLean (1897-1989) who remained its capable and sole manager until its closure ca. 1974. Residents referred to the Co-op simply as, "Marjorie's."

5-11, 5-12: Washabuck Co-op store buildings. If you peer closely, you'll glimpse a lonely gasoline pump, ca. 1958.

A vacant house, once the home of "Red" Neil MacNeil, was relocated and renovated for use as the Washabuck Co-op building. Carpenter, Jimmy MacKinnon later enlarged it with an addition. The Co-op's first ledger entry is dated the May 25, 1942, for Neil S. MacLean who sold 261/6 dozen eggs for 25 cents a dozen realizing a credit of $6.54. A few days later, Francis B. MacDonald sold two veal weighing 55 and 76 pounds respectively, at 10 cents per pound, for a credit of $13.95.[25] Eventually, business increased and volume improved with the sale of farm produce, salt fish and gasoline. No livestock or salt meat was ever sold. For three decades, the Co-op proved to be a convenient, viable and serviceable business for the community.

Raids

The Washabuck Co-op branch was burglarized on three occasions. The first time, RCMP officers rounded up and charged four North Sydney men with break, entry and theft, a day after the business was robbed. Marjorie's brother, Neil Stephen, had received a late night phone call from a passing neighbour who suggested that there might be a problem at the store. Neil phoned the RCMP who alerted the local ferry operators to be on the lookout for uncommon travellers. The surveillance paid off and the culprits were apprehended the following day at River Tillard, near St. Peter's. A quantity of clothing and dry goods had been taken. Marjorie recalled having marked a sales tag in a certain way and was able to identify the same at the ensuing trial, resulting in prison sentences.[26]

On another occasion a cigarette hole burned through a $2 bill enabled Marjorie to identify stolen Co-op cash at a hearing that saw a couple of young soldiers from Camp Gagetown charged with a $500 robbery. The store's safe had been cracked open with a piece of lead pipe and the firing of a .303 rifle. Marjorie's nephew, Joseph, recalled hearing that the bullet had ricocheted off the strong box and taken a piece out of the ear of one of the safe-crackers.²⁷ A guilty plea resulted in a two-year prison sentence for the duo.

The business was robbed a third time, and a variety of merchandise was stolen. Joseph and his brother Cyril, used to await the morning school bus at the store. "One morning when we arrived we found the front window broken and the store door open.... I remember there being a sense of, "broken into again," says Joe.²⁸ Those culprits were never apprehended. The three breaks occurred between the late 1950s into the mid-1960s.

5-13 Marjorie MacLean, long-time manager of the Washabuck Co-operative, during the last months of its operation, ca. 1974.

One of Marjorie's long-time admirers reminisced about her commitment, enthusiasm and dedication, toward the success of the Co-op store: "She was a terribly honest woman, but she saw to it that the Co-op was always on the winning side!"³⁰

Vanilla Jiggered

During all her years as store manager, Marjorie claimed she was never really afraid, but for one occasion. The episode occurred when a badly hung-over neighbour pleaded for her to give him some vanilla extract. She eventually gave him a bottle, but absolutely refused to give him a second one. He became violently angry at her, but eventually departed ... distressed, dispirited and downtrodden ... as Marjorie defiantly stood her ground.²⁹

Stories abound about the dedication and ingenuity of Marjorie MacLean in her role as manager of the Washabuck Co-op store. She was faithful manager who worked a six day week for 33 years, diligently serving her rural community. She was also a dedicated mother, community and church volunteer, superb baker, genealogist, seamstress, and sport enthusiast, deserving a volume unto herself. The following reminiscences will provide some hint of her directness, honesty, ingenuity and business acumen.

STORES, MERCHANTS AND SHOPPING

By the Pound

Local patron Jimmy, (Neil P. S.) MacLean (1902-1981), required a bag of livestock feed. He asked Marjorie for some. "Well, I've just sold the last of it!" she exclaimed. She suggested, however, that there may be remnants on the floor of the Washabuck Centre wharf shanty, which was sometimes used for bulk storage. The building, naturally, was a favorite haunt for wharf rats. "Go see what you can find," she suggested. So Jimmy, a veteran, hoping to salvage enough feed to tide him over until he got to a Baddeck supplier later in the week, grabbed a broom and swept up a combination of spilled feed and chaff, about 40 pounds, from off the shanty's floor. Jimmy proudly brought the bag to Marjorie to show how much he had managed to scrounge. She promptly weighed the bag and charged him the going price. But as Jimmy later related, "About half of it was rat shit!"

Unfazed

On another occasion, loyal Co-op member Danny Murphy (1874-1955), sent his young son Charlie to Marjorie's for a horse-collar pad. The long-standing price had been seventy-five cents, which was a lot of cash at the time for struggling farmers with large families. Danny gave his son a dollar and told him to bring back the quarter. Marjorie lamented that she did not think she had any collar pads left in stock - there apparently had been a run on them, but after rummaging about she uncovered a last one. A closer examination revealed that a rodent had being chomping on a corner of it. Marjorie was unfazed. She put on her seamstress hat and with her sewing kit made deft repair in quick time. She then charged Charlie eighty-five cents for the pad. When Charlie returned home with the refurbished piece of harness, his father inquired why he had to pay the extra ten cents for his pad. Charlie's droll response was simply, "It must have been the darning."

Resuscitated

This "Marjorie" story involved another loyal Co-op member Francis B. MacDonald. Frank (1907-1971) was dispatched on a mercy mission by his wife Margaret, for some onions for a dish that was in the throes of preparation. Again, the familiar refrain was heard: "Well, the last of them have just gone out the door!" said Marjorie. She suggested Frank check the store's dumpsite behind the building, as she had recently cleaned out the storage bin. Perhaps he might yet salvage one or two cast-offs, enough to piquant the evening's pending casserole. Given the urgency of his wife's request, Frank rummaged around outside until he succeeded in uncovering a few discarded onions that he hoped would appease his wife's immediate needs. But true to form, Marjorie weighed them and charged him the going rate.

6 – Education

Gàidhlig communities throughout eastern Nova Scotia placed a great emphasis on the importance of education for their youth. Education was looked upon as a means to expand and enhance the knowledge and employment stability of their youth and not as a substitute for action, wisdom or common sense. To that end, the widened Washabuck community witnessed the erection of at least a dozen school buildings over a 142-year period between 1830 and 1972.

Alex D. MacLean writes about pioneer education in 1939:

> In the early days most of the pioneers could not speak or read the English language. This led a great many unthinking persons to assume that they were illiterate. This was far from the truth. All the pioneers, at least those whom I have reference to, with very few exceptions, were well versed in Gaelic, and could read and write it with ease and fluency. This is borne out by the fact that their great-grandchildren, many of them, are able to read and write the Gaelic language, and they learned their first Gaelic lessons from books that were among the prized possessions of their grandfathers.[1]

Yet, by 1864, Nova Scotia schools were no longer permitted to teach Gàidhlig.

Kitchen Academy

John F. Hart in his detailed *History of Northeast Margaree*, Inverness County, writes. "At first, classes were held in the homes under the supervision of "schoolmasters' until school buildings could be erected."[2] Anna Murphy (1918-1989) of Upper Washabuck, as an eighth grade student in 1930, wrote a community history project entitled *The Story of Pioneers and Progress in Our Community*:

The first school master in Washabuck was an Irishman, a Mr. Doyle who went to the houses to teach children there for about two weeks. From there he would go to the next family where he remained for a similar period of time. His fee was two dollars for every child taught.[3]

Could this pedagogical initiative been the genesis of the term, "kitchen academy"?

Lower Washabuck

In 1939, Neil P.S. MacLean writes:[4]

The first schoolhouse in Lower Washabuck was built of logs of course and erected on the property owned by the McPhee brothers. My father, [Peter S. (1830-1916)] as well as all that generation went to this school as young children.

1830

At the Public Archives of Nova Scotia, there exists an 1830 Washabuck School Register. This invaluable document confirms school was in session in Washabuck that year and lists attendees and their ages. It delightfully also includes the names of the heads of the households, most of whom were the Gàidhlig pioneers of the community. See Appendix 4.

Excerpt from Register:

We this day have examined the School and do declare our satisfaction of the progress of the children and have nothing against the Teacher's conduct.

Washabuck, December 1830 Signed, George MacKay

Daniel Carmichael Trustees
Murdock MacNeil

This is to certify that the people have fulfilled their engagements and that no part of my salary has been collusively withheld by them and that my agreement was not made merely to obtain a part of the Provincial Bounty and also that the whole of my salary is paid in produce.

(Signed) Hugh MacAulay

     School District Number 6

Half yearly return of the school kept at Washabuck to the 1st day of Dec. 1830.
The school is supported by subscription.
The amount raised is £40 for the Teacher and £20 for the School house.
The name of the Teacher is Hugh MacAulay.
The Teacher's salary is at the rate of £60 per annum.
The allowance for Boarding, Lodging and Washing is at the rate of 8/per week.

The School has been kept from the first day of June last up to this date. The children who have attended the school are enumerated in the subjoined list.

The people have fulfilled their engagements with the Teacher and the Trustees.

No.	Children's Names	Age	Names of Parents
1	Hector MacKenzie	16	
2	Archie MacKenzie	10	Murdock MacKenzie
3	Neil MacNeil	16	
4	Hector MacNeil	11	John MacNeil
5	Margaret MacDonald	9	
6	Alex MacDonald	7	
7	John MacDonald	6	James MacDonald
8	Murdock MacKenzie	11	
9	Neil MacKenzie	14	John MacKenzie
10	Allan MacLean	14	
11	Angus MacLean	8	Donald MacLean
12	John Carmichael	10	
13	David Carmichael	6	
14	Duncan Carmichael	4	
15	Mary Carmichael	14	Daniel Carmichael
16	John MacIver	16	
17	Henry MacIver	18	
18	James MacIver	8	
19	Donald MacIver	5	Collin MacIver
20	William Munro	10	
21	Allan Munro	10	
22	Donald Munro	9	Allan Munro
23	Donald MacAulay	5	Donald MacAulay
24	Angus Matheson	9	William Matheson
25	Angus MacLeod	17	Angus MacLeod
26	Donald MacLean	12	
27	Peter MacLean	9	Neil MacLean
28	Alex MacNeil	13	John MacNeil
29	Neil MacKinnon	14	
30	Philip MacKinnon	8	Donald MacKinnon
31	Hector MacNeil	6	Murdock MacNeil
32	Michael MacLean	14	Widow MacLean
33	Alex MacDougall	16	James MacDougall
34	Peter MacLean	9	Alex MacLean
35	Rory MacNeil	15	Rory MacNeil [5]

Where was this school house of 1830 located? I am not sure, but it is probably the school referred to by Neil P. S. MacLean as the one his father Peter S. attended. That one was located on the McPhee brothers' property in Lower Washabuck, the property currently owned by Jimmy and Gerry MacNeil, Roddie and Clare MacDonald, descendants of Rory Ranald MacDonald.

I have no knowledge about Hugh MacAulay the school teacher. It is interesting to note however, that the surnames are all spelled "*Mac*" rather than "*Mc*," as that was the more common usage at that time. All of these heads of households were residents of Washabuck with the possible exception of Angus MacLeod. However, William Matheson's wife was a MacLeod and so it is possible that "young" Angus, the student, was perhaps William Matheson wife's brother.

Neil P. S. continues:

> How long this school was in operation I am unable to relate. It was afterwards that Lower and Upper Washabuck co-operated in building the schoolhouse near the site of the Holy Rosary Church. After the closing of this last schoolhouse, Lower Washabuck began to maintain its own schoolhouse and had school in a vacant house that Peter F. MacLean lived in before he moved [ca. 1861] to what is now called MacKays Point. School was kept in this house while they were preparing to build the present school house. This present school house was built according to the prescribed dimensions of the Education Office. At that time it was equipped with a large globe; maps of Palestine, Europe, England, Scotland and Ireland inclusive, a map of Canada showing the provinces including the North-West Territories, also one of Nova Scotia of a smaller size; home-made desks, a platform and teacher's desk and a clock. There were only three schoolhouses of these dimensions and equipment in the county of Victoria in those times, Lower Washabuck included. These three schoolhouses were drawing special grants which were denied smaller schools with little or no equipment.[6]

This school was in operation prior to 1867 and was located across the public road from the Peter S. MacLean residence. A new schoolhouse was opened nearby in 1949 and closed for good in 1972 when the students were sent to Rankin Memorial in Iona. Since Rankin closed in January 2007, students now attend *Sgoil Mhic Fhraing a" Chaolais* (Rankin School of the Narrows). The Lower Washabuck school building has been upgraded and is now used as the Community Centre.

Birthing Pains

Undoubtedly, the first co-operative educational venture in the community encountered some growing pains, including building a school house that

6-1 Lower Washabuck Students ca. 1915-1916. L-R: Front Row: Katie (Allan) MacLean, Mary Christine (Neil Peter) MacLean, Sadie (Allan) MacLean, Annie May MacNeil, MacNeil's Vale, Margaret Creighton (Agnes) MacDonald, Annie May (Neil Peter) MacLean, Mary Theresa (Neil Peter) MacLean: Second Row: Mary (Vincent) MacLean, Alexander (Vincent) MacLean, Michael Joseph (Allan) MacLean, James (Billy) MacKenzie, Michael Hector (Billy) MacKenzie, Frank (Agnes) MacDonald, R.R. (Agnes) MacDonald, Quentin (Agnes) MacDonald, Neil Stephen (Neil P.S.) MacLean Third Row: Leo (Vincent) MacLean, Murdock (Vincent) MacLean, Tommy (Billy) MacKenzie, Joseph (Agnes) MacDonald, George (Agnes) MacDonald, James (Neil P.S.) MacLean, Matt (Neil P.S) MacLean. Back Row: Lucy (Vincent) MacLean, Helen (Vincent) MacLean, Teacher, Katherine MacNeil, MacNeil's Vale, Mary Sarah MacNeil, Ranald (Agnes) MacDonald, Stephen (Agnes) MacDonald. Courtesy of Mary (Alfred) MacDonald, Baddeck, CB.

"was located near the [old] road and opposite to where Holy Rosary church stands today," advised Alex D. MacLean.[7] The property by this time would probably have been owned by the Paul MacLean family. This school opened ca. 1860. Alex D. explains further:

> The people of Lower and Upper Washabuckt got together as they were desirous of erecting a school. By a survey they determined that the site mentioned was the centre, and they built their school here. They all assisted in this undertaking. Some of them sent logs; some more furnished the required door and windows. However, as will sometimes happen in the best regulated communities, a disagreement arose between the people of the Upper and Lower sections. Michael MacNeil (*Eòin*) had contributed some logs as his portion, and early one morning he went to

the little school with his horse, and pulled his logs out of the building. My grandfather, Donald MacLean, (*Dòmhnull Nill "ic Lachlainn*) who was a carpenter, had contributed a window – the frame, sash and glass. Hearing that MacNeil had removed his logs, he went there to remove his window, but before he could carry out his plan, he was advised by a friend to leave things alone, as legal difficulties were likely to ensue. He heeded this good advice, and returned to his home. After a short period, this "tempest in a teapot" was stilled, and the little schoolhouse saw service again.[8]

The following list of teachers names, their home communities and years taught is not exhaustive.

Lower Washabuck School Teachers:
Hugh MacAulay – 1830
Norman MacNeil – Grand Narrows
John C. Boyd – Antigonish
Michael B. MacDonald – St. Columba, 1860

The following nine teachers taught school in Lower Washabuck from 1892. This listing was compiled by Marjorie MacLean of Washabuck Centre.[9]
Liza A. MacKenzie – taught 5 or 6 years
John Dan MacRitchie – Hazeldale, one term
Tina Miller
Annie Watson – Baddeck, 1910
John R. Matheson
Stanley MacDonald
Cassie (MacInnis) Cullens[10] – South Cove, 1912-1913
Annabelle MacAskill – Baddeck, 1913-14
Hanna MacDonald

Later teachers included:
Katherine MacNeil – MacNeil's Vale, *Ian Eachain's* daughter
Margaret Forbes – Antigonish, 1923-24
Katie A. (Frank) MacNeil – Gillis Point
Jessie Ann MacNeil (John Malcolm's sister) – Iona, 1922-23
Elizabeth A. "Red Lizzie" MacNeil – MacNeils Vale, 1914, 1917
Gertrude (Frank) MacNeil – Iona, (A good teacher)
Margaret MacNeil, (Frank B. MacDonald's wife) – MacNeils Vale
Hector MacLean, – "Lighthouse" Gillis Point
Bennie MacLean – Washabuck, 1939-40
Irene (John P.) MacNeil – Iona

Mary E. (MacLean) MacDonald – Washabuck, 1925, 1930 (2 sep. years)

Annie Helen MacLean – Washabuck, ca. 1931, 1933

Mary Ann (Arthur) (MacDonald) Campbell – Iona, half a year ca. 1932

Annie (Morrison) MacInnis – Iona, 1931

Katherine MacLean – Reserve Mines half a year, 1932

Helena (Brophy) MacDonald – Mulgrave, 1928-29

Susan Doucet – L'Ardoise

Sarah Margaret (Campbell) Bonvie – St. Columba

Catherine Morrison – Gillis Point

Mrs. Graves

Miss. Robinson – Glace Bay

Nubby (MacNeil) Murphy – Iona, 1944

Susan Langley – Antigonish Co.

Josephine (LaRusic) MacLean – Bay St. Lawrence, 1945

Vincent Kennedy – Inverness, 1949 last teacher in old school

The "old" school in Lower Washabuck closed in 1940 for a couple of years due to a lack of students. Washabuck Centre students, "Little" Marjorie MacLean and Roddie MacLean attended the Upper Washabuck School during those years. The school was later reopened with the return of Leonard MacKenzie and Raymond MacDonald who joined with Roddie and Marjorie to help make up the required minimum number of students.[11]

Theresa MacNeil – Gillis Point 1949-50, 50-51, 51-52 First teacher in new school

Dolly MacNeil – Big Beach 1952-53

Agnes (Rankin) MacDonald – Washabuck

Margaret MacDonald – Washabuck

Florence Morrison – Boisdale

Annette MacLean – Washabuck

Ann MacKenzie – Washabuck, School closed June 1972.

"Too Baaad"

St. Columba's Pastor Father Duncan Rankin was chatting with Iona resident Johnny MacGillivray at the Iona Co-operative store one day in the early forties. Father Rankin ruefully lamented the unfortunate situation that the Lower Washabuck schoolhouse was not able to open because of a lack of students, while at the same time the MacKinnon Harbour schoolhouse was crammed with students. The situation at the Harbour school was fostered by the fact that, Dan Angus and Margaret MacDonald of Red Point had twelve children, with more than half of them attending the Harbour school. Johnny MacGillivray's response to Father Rankin's observation was something to the effect: "Isn't it too baaad that Dan Angus is not living in Lower Washabuck?" Father Rankin's response was not logged.[12]

6-2 Last class of "old" Lower Washabuck School; springtime, 1949, standing before the new school building. Front Row: James MacLean, Patrice MacDougall, Betty MacKenzie, Bernie MacLean, Carmie MacLean, Mary MacDougall, Clare MacDonald, Nancy MacLean, Gerry MacDonald. Back Row: Roddie MacLean, Raymond MacDonald, Leonard MacKenzie and Teacher, Vincent Kennedy, Inverness, CB. Courtesy of Carmie MacLean, Washabuck.

6-3 Lower Washabuck's last schoolhouse (1949-1972).

6-4 Lower Washabuck students, December, 1964: L-R Back Row: Judi MacLean, Agnes MacDonald, Teacher, Shirley MacKenzie Second Row: Mary Belle MacKenzie, Alice MacLean (head turned), Joanne MacLean, Martina MacLean, Robert MacLean, Loretta MacLean; Third Row: Peggy MacDougall, Michelle MacDougall, Annie MacLean, Teresa MacLean, Darlene MacLean; Front Row: Beverly MacLean, Ernest MacDougall, Johnny MacKenzie, Louis MacLean, Lauchie (Michael Dan) MacLean, Jim MacLean. Courtesy of Roddie J. MacDonald, Washabuck.

Suitcase Teachers

"Suitcase teachers" boarded at community residences, spending a week or two with most households, occasionally accepting free board as partial compensation for a meagre salary. Food could be coarse, bedrooms (and beds) could be cold and uninviting and there was an expectation that the boarders would lend a hand with household and outdoor chores. Having to cover the distance to and from

Too Many Questions

In 1983, I visited with Annabelle MacAskill in her home in Baddeck. She was then 92 years of age. She recalled that she taught school in Lower Washabuck in 1913 and 1914 and the following year in Little Narrows. Later, she went into training to become a registered nurse. She recalled taking the local passenger ferry from Baddeck to Washabuck on Monday morning and then returning home on Friday evening. During the week she boarded at the nearby Rory Ranald and Agnes MacDonald's residence as did so many of the other school teachers of that time. I asked her how well behaved her Washabuck students were and she coyly replied; "Fine, except for the boys of the different MacLean families, who seemed to be forever scrapping amongst themselves."[13] Sometimes, one asks a question too many. Annabelle was simply a delight to chat with.

The MacLeans however, were not the only clan involved with shenanigans. The next to last school house in Lower Washabuck was located just across the public road from the homestead of Neil P. S. MacLean, who was the capable school secretary for the local trustees. Like most farms, his was blessed with a score of bovine, providing milk and an occasional beef roast. On more judicious occasions, an animal would be butchered for cash, a precious commodity itself. Neil P. S. also kept a bull. The animal, like all bulls, bore his responsibilities seriously, closely attending to the small herd that would be seen grazing in the nearby field, sometimes close to the school house.

The local MacDonald brothers (there were seven of them) were not particularly enraptured with a particular lady teacher it seems. As was her practice, the teacher, who happened to be boarding at a neighbouring home, would go home for her noon meal and return within the hour to complete the school day. On one occasion during lunchtime, the brothers noticed Neil P. S.'s herd was grazing particularly close to the school. The brothers, with diabolical refinement, lured the bull into the schoolhouse with fistfuls of an unknown elixir, and closed the door, imprisoning him. They high-tailed it for parts unknown and the rest of the student body cleared as well.

And so it was there, that as Ms. Teacher returned for the afternoon session, she discovered Mr. Bull. Not unlike the proverbial china shop, the classroom was in shambles. A local wag later commented the poor bull, though seemingly at ease within his new surroundings, had been reduced to chewing on a bearcat scribbler.[14]

A further prank involved another MacLean family (this is becoming embarrassing). Joe W. MacLean was next-to-youngest in a family of twelve, so when it came his turn to head off for his first day of school, he had a bevy of older siblings to educate him on proper etiquette. Obviously, first impressions were important. Every school had a pot-bellied stove in the centre of the room. When the new teacher arrived for her first day in class, she was greeted with a tousled calamity of black hair disguising a pair of matching dark eyes, peering intently at her from through the lid-opening of the top of the wood stove. The freshly minted student had been tutored to follow directions precisely, and he was conveniently just the right height and size to ensure success of the caper.[15] His novel début didn't seem to constrain him adversely though, for in later years Joe and wife Marguerite raised a prominent Sydney family, as he went on to experience a successful career serving as conductor, and later, yardmaster, with CN Rail out of the Island's depot, and he is regarded as one of Cape Breton Island's all-time renowned fiddle players.

the school house in red-sole gumshoes, teachers had it no easier than their students. Michael A. MacLean relates the following tale:

Occasionally a boarding house was unavailable. In one such case a certain female teacher was unable to secure appropriate lodging. No family would take her in. Most of the students disliked her because of last years" experience with her. This was really the crux of the problem. By cripers, as a last recourse she landed back at the previous year's boarding house much to the chagrin of the two brothers who were part of her last year charges, and had absolutely no desire in having her billeted at their home for yet another term, or even a part thereof, they having to share their nights and weekends with her, after having spent the school day with her.

The problem called for drastic action, so the brothers devised a scheme. Ghosts and ghost stories were a popular and frequent evening topic of conversation in many homes and this particular home was no exception. Although the teacher avowed her disbelief in such goings-on, the two brothers must have sensed some muted apprehension on her part.

The brothers' bedroom was on the second level with a window that opened over the shed-roof of a one story appendage. For a number of consecutive nights the brothers stealthily stole out upon the shed roof and made a bit of rattling noise against her window pane with a light chain attached to a piece of twine secured in turn to a length of alder.

The teacher complained on each occasion to the father, rousing him night after night expressing a woe of consternation, her brow furrowed, going on about hearing strange noises outside about her window. On each occasion she insisted that the father go outside and investigate for the source of the offending noise. Of course nothing was found, but after a week or so of this ritual, the father had arrived at the conclusion that the woman herself was losing it, and he was not too happy about his own nightly slumber being continually interrupted.

By the end of the following week the pedagogical fossil had cleared the premises with her valise, stating that she would return to neither her place of lodging nor her teaching position, much to the obvious delight of the two brothers, and the rest of the student body. The parents of the brothers were never made aware of what actually happened. The reality was though that the parents were probably as happy to see her pack her belongings and depart as were the brothers. Another teacher was eventually gotten and completed the school term.[16]

To be fair, families did their best to accommodate visiting teachers and appreciated their genuine efforts to further the education of their children. In the words of S. R. MacNeil, "As a general rule though, if a teacher was cross and could keep discipline, he or she could usually get hired."[17] Fortunately or otherwise, it seemed to be considered a teacher's best qualification.

Upper Washabuck

Frances MacDougall, a long-time, highly respected school teacher and former Washabuck resident, writes in a 1935 eighth-grade history project entitled "Settlement and Development of Our District":

> The first log school house [in Upper Washabuck] was built on James MacDonald's farm, the foundation of which can yet be seen. The next one was built farther east on Rory MacDonald's farm. The next one was built on Paul MacLean's farm, where the late M. B. McDonald of Saint Columba did his first teaching.[18]

This last schoolhouse was a co-operative venture, built near the church property at Washabuck Centre. Both James and his brothers Rory and Donald settled in Upper Washabuck in 1821. The fourth brother Michael settled in St. Columba in 1825.

Mary Ann (Devoe) MacKenzie could remember her mother Ellen (1868-1953) talking about an old schoolhouse across the road from Peter MacKenzie's in Upper Washabuck, but nothing more is known about the building except that its location is clearly noted on A. F. Church's topographical map of 1887.[19]

Mary Ann MacKenzie also remembers hearing her mother relate a story about a teacher named MacAulay who would walk to Washabuck from the South Cove area. He would cross over the properties on the north side of Washabuck River (lands later owned by Murdock MacInnis, the Brown family and Johnny Campbell) and take a rowboat across the river to reach the school on the south side. Tom Murphy, who lived on the north side, was known to put tar on his fence poles in an attempt to deter MacAulay, unsuccessfully as it turned out, from crossing his property.[20] Whoever said schoolteachers have it easy? Educators, even then, had challenges.

Two other schools were built in Upper Washabuck. One on the Rod MacIsaac property near the present public road; the last one, which was opened ca. 1916, was situated on a lot of Angus (Ranald) MacDonald property, adjacent to Mary C. MacDonald's place. This last school closed its doors for the final time upon the completion of the 1966 school term. The students were then sent to the Lower Washabuck School until that building closed in June 1972. Since then all Washabuck students have been bussed to Rankin Memorial and Rankin School of the Narrows in Iona.

Upper Washabuck School Teachers

Mr. Doyle tutored students in their homes for a fee of $2.00 per student, for a two week period. Michael B. MacDonald (Malkie MacDonald was a student of his) was thought to be the last teacher in the old school at Rod MacIsaac's.

6-5 Student body at school building located at Rod MacIsaac's, Upper Washabuck, ca. 1906-1907. L-R: Neillie Devoe, Joe MacIver, Peter M. MacNeil, Hector MacKinnon?, Dan Alec MacKinnon?, Jimmy Fraser, John D. MacLean, Angus MacKinnon, Dan Henry MacIver, Anna MacKinnon, Mary Ann Devoe, Liza Campbell, Teacher Kitty Margaret MacIver, Annie MacKinnon, Marjorie MacLean*, Tena Devoe, Christina MacIver, Mary MacIver, Dan Brown and Angus Brown.
*(Marjorie claimed she was not at school this day and says this student is Lizzie Ann MacNeil from MacNeil's Vale.) Courtesy of Hector MacKenzie, Washabuck.

Rev. Herdman, a Presbyterian Minister taught for one term, January to June for which he was paid $24.[21]

Norman MacNeil – Grand Narrows
John C. Boyd – Antigonish
Christine (Dolly) MacIver – Washabuck
Mr. MacAulay – Hazeldale
Liza (MacKenzie) Campbell – Birch Point, 1906-07
Christina MacKenzie – Middle River 1913-14
Mary Christine MacLean (Michael Charlie's daughter) – Baddeck
Mary Ann MacNeil – Barra Glen
Sarah Margaret MacNeil – Barra Glen, 1917-18
Jessie Ann MacNeil – Iona, 1918-19
Ida Wright – Hazeldale, 1919-1920
Mary Ann MacNeil – Barra Glen 1920-21, 1921-22
Sarah Margaret MacNeil – Barra Glen
Annie Davis – Inverness
Mary C. MacLean – Washabuck Centre, 1922-23
1923-24 no school

1924-25 no school
Florence MacDonald – Judique, 1917, 1925-26
Katie (M.D.) MacNeil – Iona, 1926-27
Kaye (Angus Ranald) MacDonald – Washabuck ca. 1926-27[22]
Florence MacDonald 1926-27 -West Bay Road or Stellarton
Kathy Anne MacDonald, 1927
Martha Rose Lahey – Main-a-Dieu, boarded at P.M. MacNeil's, 1929
Mary Jane MacNeil – Iona 1929-30
Marion Cameron – Glace Bay, 1927, 1930-1931

Upper Washabuck School Teachers, cont'd
Rose Cogswell – Evanston, 1931-1932
Annie Morrison (Mrs. John Francis MacInnis) – Iona, 1931
Frances Ann MacNeil – Washabuck, ca. 1931
Agnes Rankin – Creignish, 1932-33 and other years
Mary Catherine MacDonald – Iona, 1933-34
Martha MacDonnell – Antigonish
Anne Elizabeth MacCormack – 1940
Madeline (MacLean) Northen – Washabuck, 1940-1942 and half a term January-June 1946

Frances MacDougall – Washabuck, September-December 1945
Margaret MacDonald – Washabuck
Stanley MacDonald – South Cove
Neil Stephen (Neil P.S.) MacLean – Washabuck
Hector (Lighthouse) MacLean – Gillis Point
Teresa (Malcolm Dan) MacNeil – Iona
Martha E. (MacDougall) MacKinnon – Washabuck
Francis MacDougall – Washabuck, last year taught was 1964
Genevieve (Stephen Jim) MacNeil – Iona, 1965
Hugh (Arthur) Campbell – Iona, 1966
School closed, students conveyed to Lower Washabuck

6-6 Upper Washabuck students, ca. 1914. Front Row: L-R: Sally MacKinnon, Mary Ann MacDonald, Mary MacIver, Mary Ann Devoe, Katie Ann MacKinnon, Josephine MacNeil behind Frances Ann MacNeil, Leo MacKinnon, Johnny MacKinnon. Second Row: Mary Lizzie MacKenzie, Jamie MacIver, Jimmy MacKinnon, Jackie Whitehouse, Malcolm MacDonald. Back Row: Teacher Christina MacKenzie, Middle River, and Allan Stewart.

6-7 Upper Washabuck students, ca. 1935: Front Row: L-R: Margaret MacDonald, Alec MacDonald, Kathleen Murphy, Bertha MacIsaac, Marie MacKinnon, Gussie Murphy, Bernie MacKinnon, Johnny MacDonald Second Row: Angus MacDonald (Hidden),Tony McNaughton, Dan F. MacDonald, and Roddie MacKinnon? Third Row: Mary MacDougall, Teresa MacDonald, Frances MacDougall, unknown, (Head turned) Mary Agnes MacDonald, Margaret Murphy, Peter Murphy In Doorway: Joe MacDougall and Charlie Murphy. Courtesy of Frances MacDougall, Mabou, CB.

Birch Point

Mary Ann (Devoe) MacKenzie (1901-1983) attended school in the building located on the Rod MacIsaac property. She recalled that when she was little, she and her brother Neillie would row down the river and visit the ruins of an old school building at Deep Cove, on the north side of Washabuck River.[23]

Possibly, this is the school referred to as the MacKenzie's School in an 1898 register (See appendix 5).[24] Fifteen students were in attendance. Approximately fifty visitors had visited the school during the year as their names and addresses are recorded. Unfortunately, the page with the students'

6-8 Upper Washabuck students, 1964. Back Row: L-R: Mary Margaret MacDonald, Muriel MacKinnon, Stephen MacDonald, Melvin MacNeil Second Row: Gregory MacDonald, Patsy MacDonald, Sarah MacDonald, Ann MacDonald, Jim MacKinnon Front Row: Marlene MacDougall, Helen MacDonald, Carmella MacDougall. Courtesy of Quentin MacDonald, Washabuck.

and parents' names is missing. Liza MacKenzie of Birch Point, (later Liza Campbell of St. Columba) was the teacher at this school in 1905.

St. Columba

In 1876, school classes were held in John MacDonald's house. The teacher was John's wife Mary (MacNeil) formerly from Red Point. She taught two terms of six months each. This is one of the earliest educational programs in St. Columba.

St. Columba's first school house was located near the intersection of Fraser Road and St. Columba Road. It was situated in a hollow on the northerly side of the St. Columba Road. According to a 1935 school project prepared by Frances MacDougall,[25] the schoolhouse was built in 1881. Because two terms of school had been taught in John MacDonald's house, the Department of Education recognized St. Columba as an organized school section and consented to building a school.

Murdock (Michael D.) MacNeil of Iona reminisced to Jimmy (Caluman) MacNeil of St. Columba, that when his family started delivering the rural mail in 1926, this first school house was still partially standing. The second schoolhouse had already been built and in use at this time.[26] S. R. MacNeil adds that "we went to school there [St. Columba] when there was no school teacher in Barra Glen."[27] And St. Columba students went to school in Barra Glen when there was no school being held there.

John Malcolm MacNeil's sister, Jessie Ann of Iona, taught in St. Columba in 1916 and 1917. The Nash boys, Dan A. MacDonald and his siblings went to school there. As did Danny (John D.) MacNeil from Grass Cove,[28] Jimmy Caluman's adoptive mother Lizzie MacLean, John Peter MacDougall, of Washabuck Bridge, Dan MacDougall's youngest brother, who later moved to San Francisco.[29] For an entire year, Colin Campbell walked through the woods from his home in Jamesville to attend St. Columba School. Annie Catherine (Mrs. John Dan MacNeil) of Barra Glen attended school at St. Columba, as did Neil F. MacNeil and his brother Murdock of Washabuck Centre, who attended there for a year.[30] Hugh Campbell recalled the second school was built during 1924-25[31] while Jimmy Caluman recalled it opening in 1926.[32]

The St. Columba School Cup: (1933-34; 1934-35; 1935-36)

For many years, Fall Fairs were events that many people participated in with lively interest. The fairs were full of activities that represented a sampling of family life in rural communities, with families proudly displaying their wares. Farm animals, garden produce, crafts, pantry goodies, and samples of mending, darning, and knitting were some of the competitive categories School children participated in public speaking, spelling matches and displayed their work on posters and in scrapbooks. Sports included tug-of-war and races.

6-9 St. Columba School house (1926-1951). Courtesy of Joe (Jimmy Stephen) MacNeil, Grass Cove, CB.

The Fall Fair was a prelude to the 4-H program that developed at the end of the Second World War. This work was collected at a centre (i.e., Baddeck) at the end of the school term, judged and returned to the local Fair at the beginning of the next school year. Points were awarded. Additional points were accumulated and awarded at the Fair itself where students, in formation, displaying a banner to designate their school, performed required drills and routines. One outstanding banner made by Sarah Margaret Campbell of St. Columba for her school, was so well made, that the judges deemed she had bought it somewhere, and as a result refused to award her any points for her competence and extraordinary effort.[33]

If a school won the trophy for three successive years, it became the permanent property of that school, with full accolades and bragging rights to its students and teacher. Thus it was that under the competent leadership of teacher Martha MacDougall (Mrs. Dan Alec MacKinnon) of Upper Washabuck that St. Columba School won the cup in the successive years, 1933-34, 1934-35 and 1935-36. This trophy, today, is among artifacts displayed at the Nova Scotia Highland Village Museum in Iona. It would seem that their subsequent decline in many communities throughout the province could be directly attributed to the outbreak of the Second World War.[34]

The Grade 11 and 12 curriculum was offered in St. Columba School between 1938 and 1943. This accomplishment was achieved through the efforts of local resident and trustee secretary Liza Campbell, who was successful in recruiting a number of teachers with university degrees, which qualified them to teach the high school curriculum. A few students, including Liza's own children, Angus and Sarah Margaret, were successful in obtaining their Grade 11 certificates from St. Columba during this period. Other than MacKinnon Harbour School, St. Columba, was the only local

6-10 St. Columba students display their prized banner and trophy, awarded for winning the treasured Fall Fair Championship competition for three consecutive years. Because of the successive wins, the cup was named the St. Columba School Cup and could now be permanently displayed at the school. Courtesy of Joan Gillis, Jamesville, CB.

6-11 (Right) St. Columba students with teacher Martha MacDougall (Mrs. Dan Alec MacKinnon) in 1935. Back Row: Malcolm MacIvor, Dan Hughie MacDougall Middle Row: Kaye MacIvor, Mary MacIvor, Charles MacKenzie, Joan MacKenzie in front Simon MacKenzie. Courtesy of Joan Gillis, Jamesville, CB.

school that provided a high school curriculum for its students. During 1944-45 Hector MacKenzie and siblings attended Cain's Mountain School[35] as St. Columba School was closed due to insufficient enrollment.

St. Columba School Teachers

Jessie Ann MacNeil – Iona, 1916, 1917
Francis Ann MacNeil – Washabuck
"Girlie" (John P) MacNeil – Iona
Margaret (MacNeil) MacDonald – MacNeils Vale
Liza Campbell – St. Columba
Martha MacDougall – Washabuck, 1933-34, 1934-35, 1935-36
Kitty Griffiths – Bras d'Or
Joe I. MacLean – Gillis Point, 1938 and a quarter of 1939 (grades 11, 12)
Josephine Chisholm (Lanark), two years, taught Grades 11 and 12
Sarah Margaret Campbell [36] – St. Columba
Lucille MacNeil – Gillis Point, 1943-44
Reddy MacNeil – Gillis Point, 1944-45
Joan MacKenzie – Washabuck, ca.1946
Margaret (Frank M.) MacNeil – Barra Glen, 1948
Frances MacDougall – Washabuck, 1949-1951

The school closed for good in 1951. The MacKenzie sisters, Jean, Rose and Charlotte of Washabuck Bridge were the three last students in attendance that year with their teacher Frances MacDougall. The next fall, these students resumed classes and joined the ranks of the Upper Washabuck School roster with Francis MacDougall, again, as their teacher.[37] (See appendix # 6 for Collector's Roll for St. Columba School Section # 19.)[38]

High School

In 1919 the St. Columba parish in Iona was forty-six years old. The parish priest Father Rory MacKenzie, was concerned that there had been no seminarians from the area and blamed the lack of a high school in the area. Grades higher than grade eight had to be accessed in Antigonish or Sydney. As most youths were required for work around home and money was scant, few if any, went on for high school education.

6-12 St. Columba school teachers, sisters, Martha, center, and Frances, right, are visited at their Upper Washabuck homestead by cousin Michael R., his wife Rita, and their new daughter Patricia, 1942. Courtesy of Frances MacDougall, Mabou, CB.

So Father MacKenzie, together with neighbouring parish priests Father Angus R. MacDonald of St. Barra's at Christmas Island and Father Michael Gillis at St. Andrew's at Boisdale, decided that it was not an unrealistic dream for a high school to be founded to serve the three parish areas. Iona was selected to be the site of the new high school, mainly because it was central and students from Little Bras d'Or, Grand Narrows, Beaver Cove, Boisdale, and Christmas Island could access the school by railroad with the morning westbound train arriving at Iona about 8:30 a.m.; then return home on the evening train at 5:00 p.m. Students from Ottawa Brook and Washabuck were expected to reside in Iona while attending high school.

Through the combined efforts of the three priests and the assistance of local residents, the doors to the high school opened in September of 1920. An official *Act* of the House of Assembly was passed allowing for a high school to be founded in a rural community such as Iona. The Iona Federated High School (IFHS) was the first rural federated high school in Nova Scotia.

Dusty Roads and Windfalls:

Lawrence MacDougall began school at St. Columba in 1948. He remembers four other students attending that year, Agnes Nash along with Carl MacKenzie and two of Carl's sisters Jean and Rose. Margaret (Frank M.) MacNeil of Barra Glen was the teacher. "We walked those two miles [from Washabuck Bridge] every day. It was mostly an up-hill grind in the morning and of course the reverse in the evening."

To circumvent the tediousness of those long walks home, Lawrence and Carl would break off pieces of alder poles with branches attached, and drag them behind them on the dry dirt roads. "The best place for raising the most dust seemed to be over the flat at "Rory Neil's," recalled Lawrence chuckling with his infectious laugh. Another unique diversion involved the shaking of a jam-jar half full with luncheon milk, in a questionable effort to see how much butter would be churned in the bottle by the time they arrived home.

Lawrence relates that in those days there would be the occasional dual wheel truck driving through the St. Columba road. During the winter months, they left tire imprints embedded in the wet snow, which usually froze. These frozen tracks could result in excellent downhill sledding for the homeward part of the day's adventure.

An older cousin of Lawrence's, John A. MacDougall, made a small wooden sled for Lawrence earlier that year, a sled the seven year old faithfully towed to school each winter's morning. The bottoms of the wood runners were enhanced with metal, improvised from flour-barrel hoops. The sled although small was well crafted and resembled the luge models now used in Winter Olympics competitions. So given proper conditions, the downhill part of the homeward-bound trek could be completed in record time.

On one particular occasion, Lawrence had his sled cranked out at maximum velocity in one of the ice-encrusted dual-tire tracks, when he unexpectedly met John MacDougall's brother Joe, who was plodding along with his Apache horse and riding sleigh, up the steepest part of the mountain road, straddling the same frozen track. Lawrence's instant decision was to cast himself as flat as possible on his sled. In the blink of an eye, he skirted the horse's legs and hurled under the riding sleigh and between its runners. The decision proved to be a winning one as the body of the riding sleigh was high enough off the track to clear the speeding projectile. Joe MacDougall himself had no time to react, only to swear something, part of which Lawrence caught as he whipped by as "shit-a-devil," before the care and control of the sled itself went to the *deamhan*.

The sled and its occupant, now clear of the horse and sleigh, careened out of the frozen track and hurdled down an embankment amongst a thicket of small fir bushes. "I had a death grip on the sled but the bushes proved not to be the real problem as I suddenly encountered something I later learned was called a windfall," recalled Lawrence. But this time, reactive impulse was wrong and he hit the tree head on, with inevitable results, a bent nose and some loosened baby teeth, a couple of which were later lost prematurely. And so, the homeward-bound portion of that school day adventure came to a frenzied, bloody and bone-jarring conclusion. Lawrence also recalled that his school-bag was a small army kit-bag, salvaged by his Grandfather Dan MacDougall (1876-1963), from among his sons' over-seas military relics. Although the bag was relatively small, Lawrence recalls it seemed large for a seven year old.[39] Just another day in the life of a struggling St. Columba student.

Joseph A. McCarthy, a man who later served as principal at the Nova Scotia Normal College in Truro, was hired as the teaching principal at Iona. There was an enrolment of twenty-one students; one in grade eleven, three in grade ten and seventeen in grade nine. McCarthy taught all of the subjects in all of the grades. The first high school classes were held on the upper floor of the St. Columba Parish Hall (built ca. 1910). McCarthy writes:

> It was a very large open room with a low slanting ceiling, poorly lighted, poorly ventilated and in winter was heated by a large pot-bellied coal stove which smoked and inadequately heated the large school room.[40]

> My Grade XI pupil was very bright and needed a minimum of guidance from me. The three pupils in Grade X were also bright, but had no French or Latin and were inadequately prepared in the basics of other Grade IX work. Hence, much of the time they had to be grouped with those in Grade IX. Further, many of the Grade IX pupils, coming from small rural schools were ill prepared for the regular work of Grade IX. But one characteristic of all the pupils in the school was that they had a real desire to learn and were prepared to do everything possible to do so. It was a year of intensive work for all of us.[41]

In June 1921, the provincial examination results showed a successful year with nineteen out of twenty one pupils receiving provincial pass certificates. A remarkable achievement, indeed.

J. H. MacKenzie of Christmas Island, a nephew of Father Rory MacKenzie was a student. He later became a teaching principal of the IFHS. He recalled:

> In 1924 I obtained my Grade XI. That fall Alexander MacLean, Washabuct [sic], Sylvester Macdonald, Iona, and myself attended St. F.X. I believe we were the first students from Iona High to attend St. FX.[42]

For the 1922-23 school year, the downstairs of the parish hall was opened for classes. Using folding doors, they were able to create two classrooms. Grade 9 occupied one side of the room while grades 10 and 11 filled the other. Conditions had improved. Two teachers were hired and they alternated teaching subjects in both classrooms instead of strictly teaching in their own grades. One of the two served as principal while the other served as vice principal.

As a student, Margaret MacNeil from MacNeil's Vale (later Mrs. Francis B. MacDonald of Washabuck and a teacher herself), boarded at a home in Grand Narrows and walked the railway bridge spanning the Barra Strait, daily, to complete her high school education.[43] In 1926, Mary E. MacLean from MacKay Point boarded in Iona to complete her Grade 11. She completed her Grade 12 studies the following year by correspondence and then attended Teacher's Normal College that brought about, a lifelong career in the teaching profession.[44]

Iona School Conveyance

When transportation by automobiles began, students no longer had to board in Iona to attend high school. Such was the case in 1942 when students were taken daily from MacKinnon Harbour, Barra Glen, Ottawa Brook and Jamesville. Some years later, a similar conveyance was provided for Washabuck students. The principal at IFHS, William Cashman, who was married to Mary Rankin, also provided transportation services for the students on the Barra Glen route. Malcolm Dan MacNeil from Grass Cove relieved him of those duties, when the route was extended to include Washabuck students. Mr. Cashman remained Principal at IFHS for five years.

Malcolm Dan MacNeil had joined the RCMP during the war. He was assigned to watch the Grand Narrows Railway Bridge, as it was guarded at all times. At some point, (probably after D-Day), it was felt that it was no longer likely that a U-boat would torpedo the bridge, so guard service was discontinued. Malcolm Dan began his school transportation service in September of 1944 and continued it until June of 1952.

The service was tendered and when Malcolm Dan won the contract, he bought a used, seven passenger, 1936 Chevrolet from Sampson Motors in Sydney. It was somewhat difficult to buy a vehicle at that time as not many cars were being manufactured because of the war. According to Peter, Malcolm Dan's son, "this particular vehicle was a piece of junk and Dad and I spent more time underneath the car than in it." Peter added: "There were a few times when a distress call was put out to Father Rankin to borrow his brand new 1946 Monarch," which he never refused to loan.[45] Like Winston Churchill, the war years had not dampened Father Rankin's ability to somehow, secure a new vehicle.

At the beginning of the service Malcolm Dan would drive to Washabuck and return with those students before doing the Barra Glen-Ottawa Brook route. The trip was reversed for the evening run. A year or so later, a separate run began on the Barra Glen-Ottawa Brook route with Murdock (Michael D.) MacNeil becoming the designated driver of that vehicle. Peter recalls that after he had completed Grade 10, he took a year off school during 1947-48, driving the vehicle to assist his ailing father.

Gillis Point neighbour Roderick MacNeil mentions that Malcolm Dan's other son Norman, took his father's three-seater car to a winter square dance in Lower Washabuck with his date, Rita Murphy of Washabuck, who was boarding in Iona at the time. Roderick recalled that in those early days, "When there was no anti-freeze available the vehicles had to be drained during those cold nights." Norman was told to make sure to drain the radiator when he got to the dance, but of course he forgot. [There were undoubtedly more pressing matters on his mind].[46] But things turned out alright as it was yet early in the winter season, and the cooling system did not freeze up.

Over an eight-year period, Malcolm Dan had three vehicles. After he purchased the 1936 Chevrolet, he bought a former British army vehicle, a 1941 Ford station wagon with right hand drive. Peter remembers picking up walkers along the route who were startled when they attempted to get in on the right-hand side of the wagon, only to find the driver there. Lastly, Malcolm Dan drove a 1940 International panel that he ultimately used to relocate his family to Halifax during the summer of 1952, when he had obtained permanent work with Mount St. Vincent University.[47]

Michael B. MacDonald of Iona took over the transportation contract from Malcolm Dan, driving a four-door Chevrolet. His tenure as driver is fondly remembered by his youthful passengers, as he had a musical horn jury-rigged onto his vehicle.[49] Michael B. drove for a short time, perhaps two years, before he relinquished his duties due to illness. Neil James MacNeil of Gillis Point was the next driver and he used his own Ford van that had wooden benches for student seating. Neil James was noted for his aggressive driving. Perhaps his driving style was best described by former student Buddy MacDonald as he recalled with a laugh, "He drove like a mad whore!"[50]

The Long Horn

Charlotte MacKenzie of Washabuck Bridge recalls Neil James blowing the

---

Buckshot

Buddy and Andy MacDonald (1937-2005) recall one particular fall morning when the vehicle arrived at the bottom of the "Harbour Hill." The pair were Washabuck neighbours and Iona high school students at the time. Malcolm Dan was at the wheel and they were on their way to Iona. There was a good apple orchard located on a vacant farm at Harbour Hill which was easily visible from the road, and on this morning, there was a beautiful buck in the orchard. Malcolm Dan stopped the car, loaded his rifle, a 30-30 that he always carried with him during hunting season, and dropped the animal. With the help of the boys, he bled the deer and left it in the orchard until he completed delivery of his pupils to school. Then he returned to the site of the kill, dressed his trophy and couriered the carcass home to the family's larder.[48] Times have changed!

van's horn continuously from near the top of St. Columba Mountain, all along Mary *Bàn's* pioneer property, until he would arrive a few minutes later at the end of their long driveway. This was a prearranged signal between Neil James and her older brother Carl, to allow Carl time to hurl himself out of bed, don his socks, snatch his books (which apparently he never opened) and race down their long country lane to spring aboard the van, just as it skidded to a turbulent halt amidst a cloud of dust, even on the wet days. (Apparently, there was not a lot of time spent of toiletries or balanced breakfasts.)[51] Buddy MacDonald recalls the following students were also in the van: Agnes Nash, Andy MacDonald, Dougie Smith, Chrissy (Allan Alec) MacNeil, Joseph (Hector) MacDonald and Robert (Danny John D) MacNeil.[52]

Roderick MacNeil of Gillis Point and Joseph Neil MacNeil from Grass Cove were neighbours of Neil James. Both had their own vehicle and would occasionally pinch-hit for Neil James in an emergency. The road conditions were atrocious. During spring months, the transportation service could not run and Washabuck students, once again, had to board with Iona residents. Neil James subsequently took over driving a 30-passenger International school bus owned by the school board, and he continued driving that vehicle until early 1958, when he became local road foreman.

School Busing

Roderick MacNeil (1927-2009) assumed full time busing duties from Neil James MacNeil in early 1958. Ed Gowda, the director of busing for the regional school board suggested to Roderick that he should get his bus driver's license. Roderick agreed, providing Gowda would guarantee him the job for the full school year. Roderick provided successful service for that year and for the following thirty-one he was three decades dedicated to the school bus driving service, retiring in 1989. Roderick recalls in those early days, an inspector checking on the safety condition of school busses, which he claimed involved not much more surveillance than, "checking the tail lights and kicking the tires."

Icy-dicey

Roderick recounts the day he was involved in an accident with the bus at Dan Francis MacDonald driveway in Washabuck in the 1970's.

> It was a fine day but the dirt roads were slippery with ice and hard packed snow. When I got to Washabuck there were several big dump trucks hauling armour stone to MacKays Point. The Washabuck road was narrow and just a sheet of ice that day. When I got to Dan Francis's [MacDonald] gate there were four or five students disembarking there along with their older sister Marie, who was a teacher's aide at Rankin

Memorial at the time. One of the siblings was also slightly handicapped with leg problems. The pupils got out of the bus but were having a problem getting across the road in front of the bus because it was so slippery.

All of a sudden here comes a truck from the westward with its load of rock. I was obviously stopped, on my own side of the road with the red lights flashing, but the truck driver, well he could not do anything. I was thinking he was going to strike the whole bunch of them; the children were on the slippery road right ahead of him. If the driver tried to cut the truck to the high bank on the right, the truck would roll and he'd catch all the pupils with the load of boulders so instead he cut it sharply to the left in front of me but of course the truck didn't respond immediately because of the ice. It eventually answered to his evasive manoeuvre, but not quickly enough and it caught half of the front bumper of the bus and went over the embankment on the left side of the road.

There were not many students left on the bus at this time, a few of them got whiplash, nothing too serious, but it could have been a real mess. Because the truck went partially over the embankment at a right angle to the road, it did not roll or lose its load or go into the water. There were a lot of alders along the road as well which probably helped the situation. There was little damage to the truck but the bus received $1,500.00 worth.

The road job was a contract one so the more trips that were made the more the day was worth, so driver David Matheson [1951- 2011] from Little Narrows and his fellow drivers were doing their best to make the day worth their effort. Everyone was pretty shaken up and a bit rattled by what did occur, but even more so by the thought of the catastrophe that could have happened. Marie MacDonald delivered the remainder of the students to their homes with her own car that was parked at the road.[53]

Taxpayers

Roderick MacNeil's reminiscences continue:

> When I'd get up in the morning I would check which quarter the wind was blowing from, and you have a good idea then where you would probably run into trouble with snow drifts that day. I was stuck at Neil Stephen's [MacLean] gateway more than once and John D.'s [MacNeil] at Grass Cove with the east wind blowing hard and at Dan Joe Campbell's and Evelyn MacNeil's in Gillis Point. These snow banks were so high they would just be sloping downwards toward the narrow passageway that was the road.
>
> Brothers Angus and Dan F. MacDonald and Charlie Murphy of Washabuck were working in the woods out St. Columba and so we'd be

extra careful because we knew we'd be meeting each other somewhere along that road in the morning. It was so damn narrow. Malcolm Campbell used to stop me out there. He was alone then. "Bring me a pound of tea and a package of tobacco," he'd say and I'd pick that up for him at the Iona Co-op. I remember Dan MacDougall at Washabuck Bridge. He'd be sitting in his window with the pipe in his mouth. He'd be at the road the odd time. "Pick me up a loaf of bread and some milk *a dhuine*, he'd ask. I didn't mind doing that for those fellows.

When I came down St. Columba mountain road toward Washabuck Bridge, I'd always stop and wait there until the same time every morning [before I proceeded] to pick up the first pupils. I left home early. I might have to put the chains on, and if you didn't need them for the rest of the run, you'd have time enough to take them off. Those tires had a wide solid strip around the centre of them at that time, which made for poor traction and so they acted more like skis.

Dan MacDougall was staying at his daughter Cassie MacKenzie's in Lower Washabuck, in later years. I was over there butchering a pig for Cassie one day. I went in for the tea and Dan told me about an old alarm clock he had. Sometimes he'd forget to wind it before he went to bed and it would stop running around two o'clock in the morning. Then he added, "Well *a dhuine*, I'd just watch and reset it when the school bus went by and I was never out more than five minutes."

I must have been making twenty-five stops along the way picking up three, four and five students at each driveway. Today [2003] there may be two stops in Upper Washabuck and two in Lower Washabuck. I drove at least two generations of students and in some cases three. At the end I was chauffeuring the grandchildren of a few of them.

I'd pick up anyone walking on the road at that time. Malcolm (Stephen) MacLean would be sometimes arriving at MacKays Point in the afternoon, off the *Shenacadie* [mail boat], about the same time as I, so I'd pick him up. Neillie Devoe would be at Marjorie's [The Washabuck Co-op] with a bunch of groceries so I'd pick him up and drop him off at home. There would be church service in Washabuck at 8:30 a.m. on special occasions. I'd pick up a bunch of walkers and drop them off at the cross roads. It was a help to them. There was lots of room on the bus. The way I looked at it, they were all taxpayers. Of course insurance eventually stepped in and so that put an end to that.[54]

Roderick retired in 1989, and his son Anthony continues the family tradition.

Washabuck School Conveyance

With the closure of the Upper Washabuck schoolhouse in June 1966, students were then moved to Lower Washabuck School, until its closure in 1972. From then on all Washabuck students were bussed to Rankin Memorial in Iona. In the meantime, Washabuck resident Charlie Murphy (1919-1982) had successfully tendered for the student transportation contract, which continued until Washabuck's last schoolhouse closed for good. Charlie's first vehicle was an early 1960s Chevrolet sedan which he later replaced with a 1967 Pontiac.

Murphy's vehicle somehow always proved flexible enough to accommodate the full complement of sprightly students, since he made just the one morning and afternoon run. Although there were new pupils starting school each year, sufficient space was always available with departing older students graduating to Rankin. There was no use of seat belts and the rear doors of the vehicles did not always function as they should have, resulting in some students having to access the back seat through the front door, crawling over those bodies already sitting in the front seat. Thankfully, no accidents ever occurred, although icy road conditions were the norm during winter months.

If Charlie was indisposed or unable to drive, he had a crew of kind-hearted neighbours, including Dan F. MacDonald, Malkie MacDonald or Roddie MacDonald who gladly substituted as driver-for-the-day. Quentin MacDonald, then a student, laughingly recalls one particular morning Charlie stopped at the Washabuck Co-op at the request of a couple of young brothers. Their Dad had given them some currency to pick up something nutritional for their noontime lunch. To the delight of their peers, the brothers opted for a large bag of cookies, which they proceeded to share and destroy with delight, well-before the regular lunchtime....[55]

6-13 Roderick MacNeil, Gillis Point, CB (1927-2009).

Michael B – Teacher Extraordinaire

Michael B. MacDonald of St. Columba was the first teacher in the Washabuck Centre School, built circa 1860. Michael was born January 29, 1844. He was just sixteen years old when he began teaching and many students were older than he. Gàidhlig was the everyday language. One of the prescribed text books was entitled *A Guide to the English Tongue*.[56] By 1864, however, Nova Scotia schools were no longer allowed to teach Gàidhlig.

The name and reputation of Michael B. MacDonald is still revered today. The following description of the man, his ability, character and knowledge is delightfully described by Washabuck native Neil F. MacNeil, editor of the *New York Times* in his entertaining classic, *The Highland Heart in Nova Scotia*.

6-14 Students of both Upper and Lower Washabuck, 1968 at the Lower Washabuck School. Back Row L-R: Beverly MacLean, Roddie James MacLean, Louis MacLean, Jim MacLean Fourth Row L-R: Carmella MacDougall, Brenda MacDonald, Mary Lorraine MacDonald, Lucy MacDougall, Karen MacLean Third Row L-R: Wanda MacDougall, Cheryl MacDonald, Daniel MacLean, Dan E. MacDougall, Brian MacDougall, Quentin MacDonald: Second Row: Zina MacDonald, Maureen MacLean, Lauchie MacLean Front Row L-R: Eddie MacDougall and Blair MacDonald. Courtesy of Quentin, Rose and Ronald MacDonald, Washabuck.

The most respected teacher that Washabuckt had ever known was Michael B. MacDonald from St. Columba, a modest community in the mountain forests back of Washabuckt. He was known locally as Michael Fast, for every time he open his mouth, which was often, a torrent of words poured out, one crowding upon the other as if he had too much to say and no time to say it. Actually, he was a man of splendid character, wide knowledge and profound wisdom, and besides all this a great teacher, for he knew how to interest his pupils and to get them to learn. I had the good fortune to be with him for a year, and I learned more from him than I learned later in proud and noted preparatory schools and universities.

Michael Fast started his teaching career in a Washabuckt school while a mere boy and my father was one of his first pupils. Father had a deep affection for him ever afterwards; and he made certain that my brother and I had a chance to benefit from his wisdom. So we were sent to board with a neighbour in St. Columba and attended the little school by a brook in the trees. Michael Fast could have had other and better schools; but his brother had lived nearby and had died leaving a poor widow and a flock of boys, and he, a bachelor, took over the burden of supporting and educating them. This was no light task, for one of the boys was blind and one was a cripple and all were noisy and unruly and blessed with rapacious appetites. Michael Fast kept discipline in the home as he did in the school, but was always kind and patient. He had a big heart as well as an alert mind and rapid tongue. May his soul rest in peace! [57]

S. R. MacNeil was also a student of Michael B. MacDonald for two years, when he taught in the Barra Glen school house, a log building located halfway between Iona and Rear Iona.

This was the second Barra Glen school house, built in 1895, with the third one built ca. 1925. The first full ten-month school term was held in the second school in 1904-05 and Mary Margaret MacInnis is thought to have been the first teacher. In 1907 and 1908, Michael B. taught in Barra

Glen and brought his nephews Alec, John Archie and Murdock MacDonald with him to school. That made for a total of thirty-five students in school that year. In 1908 he took his nephews Peter and Michael John with him as well, accounting for at least five students attending from St. Columba. Michael B. taught in St. Columba for many years.

Michael B. MacDonald did not attend Teacher's College but finished his own education in Baddeck, Arichat and Sydney Mines. He was born in 1844 and died in the hospital at Whitney Pier, Sydney on May 29, 1921 at the age of 77 years. He taught school for just shy of 50 years, 16 years in Cape Breton County, and the balance in his native Victoria County. Michael B. is buried in St. Columba Parish cemetery adjoining the parish church.

Stephen Rory MacNeil states:

> He was a first-class teacher. He would teach to perfection any student that had an interest in learning. If you expressed an interest in wanting to learn, he would take an interest in you. He'd always ask, "Any trouble?" and would quickly help out the student that required help. If you were having trouble he'd send you to the board, wherein he would help you resolve the problem. We learned a lot just by watching his explanations to other students. We were in school each day longer than half past three.
>
> I remember one occasion when I was no longer in school but at home receiving some tutoring from my sisters. In other words, I was getting a little bit of the switch at home. Michael B. arrived at the house with some books for me. I got along fine with the help of my older sister, Antoine, but some of the questions eventually stumped her as well, so I then walked out to St. Columba to see Michael B.
>
> Well, when I arrived at his house, the widow Mary Ann MacDonald, John Archie's mother, told me Michael B. was in the woods with the boys cutting firewood. So, I followed their tracks to the woods, where I was greeted with handshakes all around and I related to him why I was there. But then I told him not to bother with my problem as they were busy cutting wood, and that I would drop by to see him at another time when he was not so busy. Michael B. would not hear of it. He told his nephews to continue doing what they were doing until noontime, when they would return home to eat. His firm comment to me was simply; "Do you think now, that anybody like you that came to me for help that I would stay here in the woods?" I came home with him and he sat with me until five o'clock.[58]

Neil P. S. MacLean saluted Michael B in the following:

> [He] showed in early youth promise of unusual mental attainments. He was especially gifted to lead, to mold and to develop the young mind and character. His interest was keen. He loved truth and honesty. He scored

sharply to the line and did not care where the chips fell. In eastern Nova Scotia many a man in the pulpit, many leading at the Bar of Justice and many in the medical profession owe their early start in life to the good teaching and wise council [sic] of the dear departed M. B. You came and labored for others without ostentation and with little worldly reward.[59]

S. R. MacNeil recalled hearing his father Michael (Stephen) and Michael B. reminiscing about a spelling match in which both had been involved. It was an annual duel between the "back-landers" of Barra Glen versus their worthy opponents, the "front-landers" from Iona. The Iona students had a reputation of being hard to beat. However, on this particular occasion the back-landers prevailed, as Michael B. and Michael (Stephen) proved to be the successful spellers. The Barra Glen community was naturally proud of this accomplishment, so much so, that as Michael (Stephen) was passing by his neighbour Malcolm Campbell's residence, Mr. Campbell congratulated him, and exclaimed, "It's too damn baaad I didn't have a drink for you! "[60]

As a final salute to Michael B. it's only fitting to acknowledge that it was he who wrote and delivered the address to Governor General Lord Stanley when His Excellency alighted at the Iona rail station on the gala occasion marking the opening of the Grand Narrows Railway Bridge on October 18, 1890.[61]

7 – Religion

Presbyterian

Perseverance, Dedication, Tenacity

During the early decades of the 1800s, the Protestant pioneers of Washabuck fared no better than did their Catholic neighbours in accessing clergymen. Like their Catholic peers, a working knowledge of the Gàidhlig language was essential for clergymen as the majority of Washabuck's Protestants were immigrants from the Isle of Lewis.[1] Mobility proved to be as formidable a challenge to the itinerant Presbyterian minister as to his Catholic counterpart where, "in the pathless wilds, forests and marshes of Cape Breton a distance of ten miles often implies a journey of forty."[2] Robert Burns DD, secretary to the directors of the Glasgow North American Colonial Society commented to the secretary of State for the British Colonies on the religious state of the Island of Cape Breton in 1834. He wrote:

> These interesting islanders have never enjoyed the privilege of a regular Gospel Ministry. They are divided from one another, here and there in small settlements, by large lakes, arms of the sea, mountains and forests.[3]

Perseverance, dedication and tenacity of purpose were the hallmarks of these pioneer Presbyterian ministers. Victoria County's renowned humanitarian and medical practitioner, Doctor C. L. MacMillan lauded their steadfastness:

> Travelling on horseback, winter and summer, along primitive paths in the forests, these ministers let nothing deter them from their monthly visits.[4]

In the Introduction to her history of the Presbyterian Church in Cape Breton 1798-1860, entitled *The Well-Watered Garden*, Laurie Stanley records:

> Prior to that date [1833] the rough-hewn Scottish communities of Cape Breton were almost completely devoid of religious leadership and the settlers themselves were largely indifferent to the traditional teachings of their faith.[5]

This hardscrabble description plays in sharp contrast to the revival realities of the following decades, Stanley writes, essentially for two reasons:

> …the subsequent arrival in Cape Breton of religiously-animated emigrants from Scotland, aroused by the religious revival in the Highlands, and the formation of the Edinburgh Ladies' Association, a missionary organization that single-handedly forged Cape Breton Presbyterians and altered the course of religious history in Nova Scotia.[6]

As a result, the tardy and languid start of Presbyterianism in Cape Breton was gradually replaced with a dedicated zeal that by 1880 had erased the religious indifference and replaced it with "spiritual rejuvenation"… and "vibrant ardour."[7]

House Churches

Rev. Archibald D. MacKinnon, the Little Narrows Presbyterian minister writes: "In the pioneer days of Cape Breton before churches were built worship services in various communities were held in the homes of people."[8]

Historian John F. Hart of Northeast Margaree observes, "In the absence of clergymen the early settlers met to hold services themselves, the elders taking turns in conducting worship."[9] Stanley also outlines:

> The almost complete absence of pastoral attention in Cape Breton gave a compensatory stimulus to family worship. In fact many settlers in Cape Breton developed a taste for this kind of worship in the familiarity and warmth of "house churches, with simple scripture reading, extempore prayer and unskilled singing."[10]

Rev. A. D. MacKinnon notes that like their Catholic counterparts, Presbyterian services took place in alternative settings.

> Dr. James MacGregor on the occasion of his second missionary journey to Cape Breton, in 1818, preached twice in barns in the West Bay community conducting services in both English and Gaelic.[11]

Early Churches

Obviously, the pioneers' first responsibility was to build themselves log homes. Then, simple log churches were erected. These served the spiritual purposes of the pioneers adequately until larger and more comfortable churches were built. The first Presbyterian Church in Cape Breton was constructed at St. Ann's by the Rev. Norman MacLeod congregation in 1821 or 1822.[12] MacKinnon comments further:

> It is generally admitted that the Presbyterian congregation of Mabou was one of the oldest in Cape Breton probably next to St. Ann's and that Malagawatch was in third place. It is reasonable to assume that the original churches in these congregations were the oldest Presbyterian churches in the Island.[13]

No Protestant church was ever erected in the community of Washabuck, simply we assume, because too few Presbyterian families lived here. Washabuck Presbyterian families attended services at Little Narrows, probably at Whycocomagh and on occasion at Baddeck. Like these Washabuck pioneers: "The early settlers at Little Narrows came to Cape Breton for the most part from the Island of Lewis.... In religion they were nearly if not all, Presbyterian."[14] The Protestant pioneers of Washabuck included following families: Carmichael, MacAulay, MacDonald, MacInnes, MacIver, MacKay, MacRitchie, Matheson, Morrison, Munro, Ross and Sutherland.

Pioneer Ministers

Rev. A. D. MacKinnon recalls other pioneer ministers:

> ...John MacLennan and Donald Allan Fraser travelled together throughout Cape Breton in 1827.[15] Rev. John Stewart arrived from Perthshire Scotland in 1834 and during his first year he visited most of the Presbyterian settlements on the Island preaching and ministering to the people in various communities for varying periods of time.[16] Rev. John MacLennan of St. John's Church Belfast Prince Edward Island made four visits to Cape Breton. The visits were made in the years 1824, 1827, 1829 and 1831 and he went from one community to another baptising children.[17]

From the Cape Breton Presbyterian baptismal records included in the records of Belfast church PEI, there were baptisms of two Washbug [sic] children that occurred in Wagamadkook [sic] on September 25, 1827. Similarly, baptisms of another six Washbug [sic] children occurred in Little Brodick [sic] now Baddeck on August 28, 1829, and five more the next day at Wagamdcook [sic]. Then on September 30, 1831, five additional Washbug children were baptised at Little Bradeck. The names of these Washabuck children with their birthdates and their parents" names are recorded in these Belfast records.[18] (See appendix 7).

This documentation indicates that Rev. MacLennan did not travel to Washabuck, at least not on those occasions, but rather the Washabuck pioneers toted their children to these neighbouring communities for baptism. This of course meant a trek across St. Patrick's Channel.

Rev. A. D. MacKinnon continues his discussion about pioneer religion:

> In the early days the Little Narrows congregation and the Whycocomagh congregation were associated. Rev. Peter MacLean one of the pioneer ministers from Scotland who arrived in Cape Breton in 1837 at the request of fellow Lewismen and settled at Whycocomagh. Mr. MacLean was born in Crowlista, in the island of Lewis and he took a special interest in the people of Little Narrows, who had come from Lewis a few years earlier, and he ministered to them while he was at Whycocomagh.[19]

Stanley asserts that understandably, "these spiritually intense and doctrinally enlightened settlers, some of them fresh from the Hebridean awakenings, were unwilling to settle without the oversight of a minister."[20]

Rev. MacLean was a dynamic force behind the Presbyterian awakening in Cape Breton and provided his congregations with a catalytic ministry.[21] Stanley maintains that the Cape Breton ministry of MacLean's is memorable because he awakened an eager desire for religious instruction and evangelicalism in half a dozen communities. Prayer meetings were organized; Scriptures were meticulously analyzed and memorized. Persons advanced in years learned to read for no other motive than to be able to read the "Holy Oracles."[22]

A burly and robust looking cleric, MacLean was a humble crofter's son. He cut an imposing figure as he "travelled to all his preaching engagements in morning coat, silk top hat, and white shirt and cuffs."[23] He was popular with his congregations who respected his stern sanctity which he tempered with his enthusiastic conciliation and healing message. Rev. MacLean returned to Scotland ca. 1842.[24]

Services

Presbyterianism as a Protestant denomination always laid more emphasis in its religious services on prayers and sermons, than on the administration of the sacraments.

> In Cape Breton the sacramental season re-enacted every year proved to be a potent means of enhancing religious feeling.[25]

Open air communion services were common in the early days. Rev. A.D. relates:

> The "long communion" was an annual event which lasted for five days, and which was attended by such large congregations, that where churches did exist, they were much too small to accommodate the people. It is said that in 1853, when Rev. Peter MacLean revisited Whycocomagh, he conducted a memorable communion service at which five thousand persons were present.[26]

Stanley adds that:

> ...another correspondent recalled witnessing a communion service at Whycocomagh when there were two hundred boats anchored in the bay and five hundred horses tied to the woods.[27]

Recompense

In pioneer times, Stanley states:

> Over worked and under paid was how most of the Scottish-born ministers saw their lot in Cape Breton. No cozy manse, no large purses, no verdant glebes were to be found there.[28]

American writer Charles Dudley Warner, writing in his 1874 travelogue *Baddeck and that Sort of Thing*, attended a Presbyterian service in Baddeck where he observed:

> [...the congregation] do not give their minister enough to keep his soul in his Gaelic body, and his poor support is eked out by the contributions of a missionary society.[29]

Nonetheless, these ministers soldiered on; it is intriguing to note that some of these missionaries provided solace to their faithful in further tangible and therapeutic manner as described by Victoria County's dedicated, and beloved itinerant medical practitioner of forty years, Dr. C. L. MacMillan (1903-1978).

> The clergy especially the Presbyterian ministers sent out from Scotland as missionaries had studied some principals of medicine during their college course. They regarded it as part of their ministerial duties to attend to the health of the people entrusted to their spiritual care. It was as important to ask about the Epsom salts, sulphur and molasses as it was to answer correctly, "What is effectual calling?" But these clergymen also probed deeply into the moral nature of their flock. And this attention to virtue I have no doubt, produced results that made for "the inculcation of those virtuous habits that redound to the health of the individual."[30]

7-1 Victoria County's long-time, beloved doctor and MLA, Dr. C. L. MacMillan.

Little Narrows Presbyterian Church

Very little information except the following brief reference seems extant, with regard to the first church that was located at Little Narrows. From an 1852 edition of *The Home and Foreign Missionary Record of the Free Church of Scotland*, the following entry:

> Whycocohah [*sic*], with two churches, about ten miles distant from each other, viz., Indian Rear and Little Narrows; upwards of 300 families, all adhering to the Free Church. Vacant."[31]

However, in these early days of pioneer settlement the congregations of Little Narrows and Whycocomagh shared much in one pastoral charge.[32] Walter Matheson (1931-2013), a dedicated church elder from Little Narrows, recalled hearing of a log church which sometimes doubled as a schoolhouse, located across the road from where the current church stands. Seating consisted of simple wooden planks and sometimes the minster doubled his responsibility by donning a schoolmaster's hat.[33]

Plans for dividing Cape Breton into ten parishes were drawn up by Reverend Alexander Farquharson, missionary to the island.[34] Rev. Farquharson's proposal (ca.1834) included a parish that encompassed the settlements of Washabuck and Whycocomagh with 160 families requiring two churches seven or eight miles apart.[35] The reality was that only about a dozen of those one hundred and sixty families lived in the area known as Washabuck.

The second church at Little Narrows was built in 1856 and was known for a period of time as Forrester Church, after Rev. Alexander Forrester, DD who delivered the first sermon preached in the building.[36,37]

The current Little Narrows Presbyterian Church was dedicated on July 16, 1950. Rev. John W. MacIvor, DD, of St. Louis Missouri, a native son of Little Narrows congregation, was the preacher for that occasion. During the ministry of Rev. A. D. MacKinnon, a manse and a hall were built at Little Narrows, two churches St. Andrew's in Whycocomagh as well as the present church in Little Narrows.[38]

7-2 Little Narrows Presbyterian Church, 1998. Photo by Roach, Donegal, Ireland.

7-3 Rev. A. D. MacKinnon, Little Narrows.

The second Little Narrows church was dismantled because it was believed that the structure was badly deteriorated. As it turned out, Dougald Matheson pulled the building down using a tractor. Some of the solid, structural framework was rescued and re-used in the present building. The current church was built on the same site as the second building, under the capable supervision of Norman Peter MacDonald of South Cove.[39]

The last Presbyterian resident to be buried in Little Narrows Cemetery was Murdock D. A. MacInnis, a descendent of Washabuck pioneers. MacInnis (1899-1994), a beloved, lithe, bon vivant bachelor, affectionately referred to by his Catholic neighbours as "The Thin Protestant," was laid to rest there in 1994. Prior to that, Joe (Dolly) MacIver (1899-1972) a former Washabuck resident who had relocated to Malden, Massachusetts, with his family in 1946, was buried at Little Narrows in 1972, alongside his wife Mary.[40]

7-4 Murdock D. A. MacInnis (1899-1994) Washabuck Bridge. Courtesy of Joan MacDonald, Washabuck.

Reverend James Colin MacIver

Another ordained minister with native ties to Little Narrows and South Cove is Reverend James C. MacIver. MacKinnon provides some biographical details:

> J. Colin MacIver was born at South Cove. His father was an elder in Little Narrows Church, as were his grandfather and great-grandfather. He was certified in 1961 by the Presbytery of Cape Breton to Presbyterian College. He taught school for some years and at the same time took courses extramurally from Acadia University. Along with his Arts degree, he received a degree in Education. He entered Presbyterian College in 1967 and graduated in 1970. He won a scholarship for highest standing in the first year, and the Calvin gold medal in the third year, as well as a number of prizes throughout his course. He was ordained by the Presbytery of Winnipeg, on July 26, 1970.[41]

> Reverend Colin served fourteen years as minister of Calvin Presbyterian in Winnipeg and Knox Presbyterian in Stonewall, before returning to his earlier profession of teaching. While he taught in Lower Sackville he attended the Anglican Church, and was drawn to their spirituality and as a result made a switch and was ordered a Deacon in the Anglican Church 1989 and a Priest in 1990. While continuing to teach he also served in the parishes of Stoney Mountain and St. Andrews, Manitoba. Colin retired from full time service in both professions in 2006, but currently does some substitute teaching.[42]

7-5 Rev. Colin MacIver with his Uncle Archie, Little Narrows, 1983. Courtesy of John and Linda MacIver, Little Narrows, CB.

Cladh nan Leòdhasach

The Presbyterians of Washabuck buried their faithful in *Cladh nan Leòdhasach* (The Lewis Cemetery) as it known in pioneer times. *Cladh nan Leòdhasach* is located on a section of property immediately west of Holy Rosary Mission Catholic Church bounded by the current highway, the waters of MacIver's Cove and Murdock Paul's brook. Most of Washabuck's Presbyterians found a final resting place here, although a few were buried in Baddeck, Middle River and Little Narrows. It is thought that the last interment to be made in this cemetery ca. 1925 is the infant daughter of Joe (Dolly) and Mary (MacInnis) MacIver.[43]

Neil F. MacNeil in *The Highland Heart in Nova Scotia* describes the Presbyterian cemetery:

> ...there were about twenty graves there in all, [ca. 1900] under beautiful trees, each with a modest headstone. The place had an atmosphere of repose and dignity....[44]

Marie MacDonald, a lifelong Washabuck resident lives near the pioneer cemetery. She recalls seeing at least 10 or 12 visible grave markers there, during her youth.[45] A number of these headstones were still standing during the 1960s but in 2000 only two marble headstones with fading inscriptions were visible. They read:

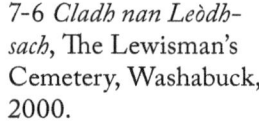

7-6 *Cladh nan Leòdhsach*, The Lewisman's Cemetery, Washabuck, 2000.

Robert Clarke
Died: Jan. 1847
A Native of Mirimachi
Age: 27
Wife: Ester McIver
Born at Washabuck
Died: 1907
Age: 82

William Munro
Born at Washabuck
May 14, 1819
Died Inlet Feb. 21, 1908
Also Brother
Daniel Munro
Died: 1848
Age 20

Although most of Washabuck's early Presbyterian's were buried in Washabuck, there are a few exceptions. George MacKay, whose name proudly adorns the most eastern point of Washabuck, was buried in the Knox "Auld Kirk" Cemetery in Baddeck ca. 1858. A young Carmichael boy was buried where he died after falling about forty feet from the high bank of MacDonald's Brook in Upper Washabuck and striking his head on a rock. His sole legacy is a large uninscribed field-stone that lies flat at his gravesite in mute witness.

Interestingly, the first burial in the older section of Middle River Cemetery is Angus MacKay who died at MacKay Point, Washabuck in 1820. The Protestant cemetery in Washabuck probably did not exist at that early date. The following newspaper item written by Charlotte D. MacRae of West Middle River was the 4th-place winner in a 1937 folklore contest and records the saga.

7-7 The fieldstone marking the young Carmichael's burial place, Upper Washabuck.

Pioneer Narrative:

> Angus MacKay lived in Loch Alsh in Scotland. He was comparatively well-off financially, being a proprietor of a hotel, or tavern, as they were called in those days.

> One evening as the family was retiring a knock was heard at the door. On opening it Mr. MacKay was surprised to see there a weary travel-worn man who requested food and a night's lodging. True to Highland hospitality he had to ask no more, but was taken in and he and his horse cared for.

> After the meal was over, the stranger proved to be quite talkative and entertained his host and hostess with many stories of adventure. It seemed he had just returned from Canada and many were the tales he told of the opportunities in that new land.

> Late at night all went to bed, although there was no sleep for Angus MacKay, for those stories kept running through his mind, and the idea became stronger and stronger that he and his family should seek their fortune in Canada. Having confided in his wife and finding that adventurous lady willing to accompany him, the next step was to interest

their neighbors in the enterprise. This did not require much persuasion for they were of the same spirit as themselves.

It was in 1820 that these hardy adventurers set out in a small sailing vessel bound for that New World and a new life. Many were the hardships endured. While crossing the Atlantic fever broke out among the passengers, due to unsanitary conditions prevailing on board the ship at that time. Alas for their bright plans for the future! Angus MacKay was one of the victims. For this reason he and his family were left at Washabuck, while the others went on. Being so carried away with the excitement of finding a suitable place for settlement, the plight of their friend and his family was forgotten. In a few days MacKay died, leaving his wife alone with her small family in a strange country. Wishing to have her husband buried among others of the Scottish Presbyterian faith, she wished to have his body taken to Middle River where a cemetery had been laid out.

In the true pioneer and Christian spirit her Catholic friends volunteered to help her convey the body of her husband to the cemetery at Middle River. Having crossed the Bras d'Or Lakes and entering Middle River, they were able to row up as far as Rock Pool (well known to tourist fishermen of today). From there they had to blaze their way along the bank of the river. Her friends went ahead with the coffin carried on their shoulders; the widow followed with her little children. Shortly after, they took up land on the east side of Middle River which is directly opposite the present school house at West Middle River. The MacRae and Campbell neighbors assisted Mrs. MacKay build her log cabin, cleared her land, and gave her food until her own family were able to carry on. When they became independent, one of their first acts was to place a headstone at their father's grave, where it may be seen still at the now overcrowded cemetery at Middle River, the first memorial for one to be buried there.

Today one may find people of Middle River, Baddeck, Sydney, and many towns of the Western Provinces who are the descendants of this Angus MacKay, among whom may be named:

Mrs. Malcolm Patterson, wife of Cape Breton's member of the local Assembly; Rev. Charles Crowdis, Halifax; Mrs. D. M. MacRae, Dawson City, Yukon; the family of Murdock MacKay near Calgary, Alberta; the widow and family of Major D. A. MacRae, Los Angeles; and the present teacher at West Middle River, Ruth L. MacKenzie.

Like so many of these early Scottish immigrants the MacKay's have done well in the country of their adoption.[46]

MacKay's headstone erected to his memory by his son Alexander stands in the lower section of the cemetery.[47]

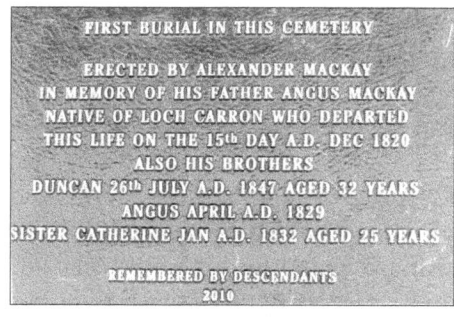

7-8, 7-9 Headstone for Angus MacKay found in Middle River, Victoria County. MacKay died at MacKay Point December 15, 1820. A recent plaque has been placed at the base of the headstone by his descendants.

Catholic

Too far

"Can you go a bit higher, Murdock? A little further? A bit further yet?" Murdock Paul was approaching the top portion of the spruce tree. Father Ronald MacLean was cajoling Murdock Paul MacLean, a distant cousin of his, to higher heights. Father Ronald was St. Columba Parish's first curate, appointed in 1924 and then parish Administrator in the following years. He had requested the local men attend for a day's clean-up of mundane tasks around Holy Rosary Mission Church grounds. The tasks included trimming the encroaching forest. It was blocking sunlight from entering the house of worship and threatening possible damage to the building itself should an untoward wind storm strike. The congregation needed uncluttered access around the structure so they could conveniently and safely hobble their horses and carriages. A group of the faithful showed up and the cleanup had gone well. All that was left was to sever the top from a tall spruce tree that was particularly close to the church vestry.

Father MacLean queried which man among them was willing to volunteer for the job. Peter MacKenzie, an un-swerving pillar of the local congregation, took command of the situation. He knew quite well that someone else would "volunteer" his own name if he didn't act quickly enough. So he volunteered the name of Murdock Paul, which was immediately greeted by a round of hearty applause. Murdock, now cornered, graciously agreed. A tall, reedy bachelor, he was a very agile man for his size. It was claimed once, that Murdock and several of his neighbours were sitting atop a five-pole panel of fence while taking a break from a task at hand. When the pole suddenly collapsed under their combined weight, Murdock, like a cat, was the only one of them that landed unscathed on his feet.[48]

Murdock's home was adjacent to the church property. It was renowned as a place of good humour, stories and cups of hot tea poured for its frequent visitors, provided by him and his two spinster sisters. Murdock was particularly noted for his propensity for swearing strikingly in both Gàidhlig and English, a practice that required little provoking. Everyone, including Father MacLean, was aware of this of course, so as Murdock approached the nose-bleed section of the lofty tree, Father MacLean mischievously prodded him to go a bit higher still.

A Mhuire, Mhuire! An diabhail! Grunnd ifrinn air, A Mhuire Mhàthair exploded Murdock into a petulant outburst of Gàidhlig imprecations angrily stirring this condensed and expurgated litany with a profane version of "Where do you want me to land, in Hell?" Father MacLean amidst much laughter of the knowing crowd said: "Oh, well that's far enough Murdock, far enough! Cut the top off there and come on down." The day's work and ruse had ended on a humorous note.[49]

7-10 (L-R) Father Charles MacKenzie, Vincentian Missionary of Philadelphia, PA; Peter D. MacKenzie and Father Ronald MacLean, St. Columba's curate and later administrator, ca. 1925. Photo taken at Peter MacKenzie's, Upper Washabuck. Courtesy of Archie MacLean, Washabuck.

Early Years

St. Columba parish had been established in 1873, with Father Alexander MacGillivray as its first pastor. Father Rory MacKenzie, St. Columba Parish priest (1901-1925) realized that the parishioners of Washabuck were labouring under a great disadvantage. They had to make a long journey to attend Mass at Iona. Road conditions were horrible and weather could be severe. By 1909, most of the construction of Holy Rosary Mission Church had been completed.

Before St. Columba was established, the Washabuck faithful had an even greater distance to travel to attend church services, to St. Barra parish at Christmas Island. John A. Macdougall of Glace Bay, a noted Gàidhlig scholar and a native of Christmas Island penned the following in the publication *Centenary of Christmas Island Parish* by Father Roderick MacKenzie. Macdougall recounts the diligence of those pioneers in attending Mass at Christmas Island:

> ...The "North Side" was established as a separate [parish in] August 1873 with the name Iona and the late Rev. Alexander MacGillivray became the first resident priest.... the hardships experienced by the good people of the "north" in coming to church were now removed. The attendance at Mass every Sunday at Christmas Island from across the water was marvelous in those days, considering the distances and the modes of travel.... At the break of dawn on Sunday morning many of them would leave their homes in the extreme western end of the parish and walk rough and stony paths to the ferry at Grand Narrows, ten or twelve miles, while a very few enjoyed the luxury of riding on horseback, and there were no carriages. They had to ferry in small boats across the strait which was usually rough owing to a very strong current, and again continue the tedious walk of three miles or more to Christmas Island.
>
> Others, left the shores of Washabuckt, the district along St. Patrick's Channel, walked along the rugged mountains until they came to the northern shores of the lake. Here they launched their boats, and engaged in a stiff row of four or five miles to Christmas Island. Often this was a perilous task, a strong breeze sweeping down the mountain side giving a short sharp choppy sea, exceedingly dangerous to boats, particularly when as they often were, overloaded with men and women. It was not unusual to see from fifteen to twenty boats landing directly below the Christmas Island Church. It must also be remembered that many of these people would be making that journey fasting, as they would want to receive Holy Communion that morning.[50]

First Church

The first Catholic Church built by Highlanders along the Bras d'Or Lake was constructed in Christmas Island in 1815. This 35 x 20-foot (10.7 x 6 m) log building was built close to the shoreline. The location is well identified today by a five foot high fieldstone cairn embossed with a bronze plaque erected in 1996 by Clan MacNeil.

First Priest

It is unknown whether any priest visited Washabuck before 1822. Mrs. Catherine (MacLean) (Boyd) Arsenault (1839-1933) of Baddeck and formerly of Lower Washabuck, was of

ON THIS SITE STOOD THE HIGHLAND SETTLERS FIRST
CATHOLIC CHURCH ON THE BRAS D'OR LAKES, 1814 CR.
The REVEREND WILLIAM DOLLARD WAS THE FIRST
RESIDENT PRIEST, 1820. FROM THIS MISSION SPREAD
The BEGINNING OF HIGHER LEARNING IN THE
DIOCESE OF ANTIGONISH, 1824.
ERECTED BY CLAN MACNEIL, 1996
ATLANTIC PROVINCES BRANCH

AIR AN LARACH SEO SHEAS A" CHEUD EAGLAIS
CHAITLICEACH A BH'AIG NA H-EILTHIRICH
GHAIDHEALACH AIR LOCH BHRAS D'OR, 1814 CR.
B'E AN T-URRAMACH UILLEAM DOLLARD A" CHEUD
SHAGART A SHUIDHICH AN SEO, 1820.
O'N TEACHDAIREACHD SEO, SGAOIL TOISEACH
ÀRD FHOGHLUIM AN "SGIR-EASBUIG ANTIGONISH, 1824
AIR A THOGAIL LE CLANN MHIC NEIL, 1996.
MEUR MHOR-ROINNEAN AN TAOBH SEAR

7-11 This rustic fieldstone embossed with bronze plaque at Cooper's Pond, Christmas Island, CB, identifies the site of the first Catholic Church erected by pioneer Gaels, along the Bras d'Or Lake shoreline.

the opinion that no priest came to Washabuck before 1822.[51] Bishop Plessis of Quebec had briefly visited the Gaels at Christmas Island and Grand Narrows in June of 1815. He was accompanied by three priests, but none of them could speak or understand Gàidhlig. Bishop Plessis was keenly aware then, that the Scottish settlers were spiritually handicapped by the lack of a priest.

> The Bishop determined to renew his efforts to find a priest to whose care he might soon confide these unintentionally neglected members of his vast flock; but nearly three years were to go by before he succeeded.[52]

Reverend William Dollard

In October 1817 Bishop Plessis finally succeeded in securing a young priest for the Gaels of the Bras d'Or Lakes and the Irish on the eastern communities of Cape Breton Island. Father William Dollard from County Kilkenny, Ireland, began his studies in Ireland and completed them in Quebec where he was ordained on October 12, 1817. He was immediately appointed assistant in Arichat with Father LeJamtel. The Bishop's intention was that Father Dollard spend time in the spring serving the Gaels living in the interior and eastern parts of Cape Breton.[53] He was also to serve the Mi'kmaq. And so it was, that by spending time among the Gaels that Father Dollard learned to converse better with them in their native language.

Father Dollard celebrated Mass in a newly built log barn at Washabuck Centre in 1822. The small barn was new and as yet unused and centrally located within the community on the property owned by Neil (*Geal*) MacNeil. Space was limited and so Father Dollard preached to the assembly outside.[54] Today, this piece of ground is a part of Holy Rosary Cemetery and the location of where the first Mass was celebrated is marked with a large crucifix which is clearly visible from the highway and St. Patrick's Channel.

Due to frail health, Father Dollard remained in Cape Breton until September of 1822. He returned to Quebec where he required a year to recuperate. Later, he did missionary work in New Brunswick and eventually became the first Bishop of Fredericton in 1843, later known as the Diocese of St. John. He died in Fredericton in 1851.[55]

Father Francois LeJamtel had become Pastor at Arichat in 1792 and several couples from Iona were married by him in Arichat in 1803. He accompanied them to Iona while on his way to Chéticamp, but the pioneers had yet to arrive in Washabuck.[56] Baddeck is less than three kilometers across St. Patrick's Channel and when a priest visited there, very often he was called upon to administer Sacraments in Washabuck as well. It is likely that priests like Fathers Remi Gaulin,[57] and Julian Courteau, (a French priest stationed in Chéticamp from 1826-1841 and would ride horseback to Margaree and Baddeck to visit Catholics who lived there) would also visit Washabuck. They had a working knowledge of Gaelic. Father Courteau would usually lodge in the home of Hector MacNeil (*Eachann Dubh*), formerly of Upper Washabuck and his wife, Virginia Marmout, a French woman from Arichat. Another priest that used to visit Baddeck from-time-to-time and who probably visited Washabuck was Father Eugene O'Rielly, who was stationed at North East Margaree. He died in 1859.[58]

The pioneers of Washabuck from Barra and South Uist were Catholic. They, with others of their faith that settled along the shores of the Bras d'Or Lakes in those early years, keenly felt the dearth of priests. Priests were scarce, their visits sporadic, unpredictable and unheralded. Couples wanting to get married often had to walk to Iona, find a ferryman to deliver them across the Barra Strait to Grand Narrows or Christmas Island where the priest resided. If the priest happened to be away, which was often the case, the couple would have to await his return. This in some instances meant waiting a week or more. Anna Murphy reveals: "It was quite com-

7-12 Charcoal sketch of Father William Dollard. He celebrated the first mass in Washabuck, 1822. Courtesy of Bishop J. E. Troy, Bishop of St. John, NB.

mon to see two able-bodied women take a young baby to Christmas Island to be baptized."[59]

Alex D. includes the example of Peter S. MacLean, who although born on June 29, 1830, was not baptized until four years later. In 1834 he, along with others about the same age, walked six miles to the home of Murdock (*Beag*) MacNeil at what is today called Washabuck Bridge. Years before, his parents, Roderick MacLean (*Ruaridh mac Lachlainn*) and his intended bride Ann MacIntyre, had walked to Sydney before they found an available priest to marry them, a distance of some sixty miles. There were no horses or carriages and for that matter no roads in those early days.[60]

Gradually between 1820 and 1873 the scarcity of priests became less critical. Although there is a lapse of twelve years between the visit of Father William Dollard to Washabuck in 1822 and the baptism of Peter S. MacLean and his peers in 1834, by 1843, Father Donald MacIsaac was appointed to serve the Ingonish area of Victoria County. In 1858, Father Donald MacKinnon became pastor of Grand Narrows shortly after his ordination. His territory comprised the present parishes of Christmas Island, Boisdale, Iona and Baddeck. He died at Christmas Island in May 1862, a victim of a fever contacted while administrating the last sacraments to one of his widely scattered flock. The sick parishioner was Catherine MacNeil, a young girl of nineteen who died at Washabuck Centre, the daughter of Roderick and Mary MacNeil and a sister to the renowned MacNeil Brothers Contractors in Boston. Father MacKinnon lived but two days after he contracted the fever.[61]

Washabuck Catholics were ministered to regularly after 1873 when Father Alexander MacGillivray was appointed the first resident parish priest of St. Columba which included Washabuck. Until that time, Iona had been known as *Seanntraigh* or *Saundrie*. This Cape Breton community reminded Bishop MacKinnon so much of St. Columba's Island, Iona, in Scotland, and he suggested its name be changed. This suggestion was readily accepted by parishioners and the name became Iona.

The scarcity of clergymen did not stymie the faith of the Catholic pioneers. They were only too aware of the challenges when they left Barra. Neil P. S. MacLean writing in *The Casket* addresses Alex D. MacLean's concern, lamenting the scarcity of priests in those early days.

> The pioneers were fully aware of the situation before leaving the old country and were prepared for the ordeal. They kept their religion in practice by gathering together on Sundays and holydays of obligation and would recite the rosary and many other prayers, teach the children their catechism, etc. and trust in God to do the rest. I have no doubt but their faith and their trust in God was far superior to ours, with all our advantages.[62]

St. Barra Parish: Pastors (1820-1873)

The following priests served St. Barra's parish from 1820 on and undoubtedly visited the whole Iona-Washabuck-MacKinnon Harbour area from time-to-time, as it was a part of that parish until 1873 when St. Columba parish was created.

> Fathers:
> William Dollard 1820-1822
> William Fraser 1822-1824
> William B. MacLeod 1824-1828
> Michael McKeagney 1828-1837
> John Grant 1837-1845
> Alexander MacSween 1845-1849
> Alexander MacGillivray 1849-1853
> James MacIntyre 1853-1853
> John V. MacDonnell 1853-1858
> Donald MacKinnon 1858-1862
> Donald MacIsaac 1862-1874

Father Donald MacIsaac was the last of the resident pastors at Christmas Island to have charge of both the north and south sides of the Barra Strait.[63] That is, until 2005 when Father Charles Donovan, OMI, and his successors began to serve both St. Barra and St. Columba parishes once again.

Washabuck Mass Houses

The priests that visited Washabuck in the early days made their headquarters at "Mass Houses." These houses included Murdock (*Beag*) MacNeil's and Angus (*Aonghas mac Ruaridh*) MacDonald's homes; later still, Murdock (*Murchadh Alasdair Glais*) MacDonald's of Upper Washabuck and the home of Roderick (*Ruaridh mac Lachlainn*) MacLean in Lower Washabuck.

When Father Alexander MacGillivray assumed his pastoral duties in the newly minted parish of St. Columba in 1873 he continued the practice of celebrating Mass in the Mass houses of Washabuck. The practice was continued by his successors Fathers Roderick Grant, Roderick MacNeil, John J. MacNeil and for a time by Father Roderick MacKenzie until the new Mission church was completed in 1909.

Alex D. MacLean relates a story as told to him by Upper Washabuck resident and storyteller extraordinaire, Peter D. MacKenzie (1869-1956). The story refers to a visit to Washabuck from missionary Father Angus Bernard MacEachern (later Bishop MacEachern) of Prince Edward Island.

> On this occasion Father MacEachern only spent an evening and part of the day with the little band of pioneers. The evening, we may be sure, would be spent hearing confessions, administering baptisms and

imparting religious instructions. Early the next morning he celebrated Mass in the home of Roderick (*Ruaridh mac Lachlainn*) MacLean. This house was only small, as all houses were in those days. When the Mass was ended, Father MacEachern asked the congregation to stand outside and that he would preach to them there.

At its conclusion, in taking farewell of them, he asked them if there were any questions that he could answer for them. He knew and they knew that a long time might elapse before they could see a priest again. There was a period of silence. Then one man spoke up, and said that he dreaded the thought of passing away without a priest to give him the last rites. At once they all spoke up, saying the same thing. Father MacEachern assured them that they would all have the privilege of receiving the last rites before they died, and my informant assured me that he was told that this was indeed the case.[64]

A Short Hour

An incident that occurred on the occasion of Father MacEachern's visit to Washabuck is related by Neil P. S. MacLean in an article to *The Casket* in October 1939.

When Father MacEachern arose in the morning he found that he had left his Mass book or missal at Murdoch [*Beag*] MacNeil's in Washabuck Bridge, six miles away, where he had said Mass the previous morning. He asked Roderick MacLean, in whose house he was to celebrate Mass, how he could procure the book so that he would not keep the congregation fasting too long. Roderick said, "I'll get it," and off he went for Washabuck Bridge on foot. The road at that time was only a path along the shore most of the way, and pioneers who occupied land along the route had this path crossed in innumerable places by brush fences. On and on Roderick went, not waiting to climb those barriers, but jumping over every obstacle. When he arrived at his destination, Mr. MacNeil asked him why he was on the route so early. Roderick gave him the message. It was then that Mr. MacNeil discovered the book. Roderick returned with the missal when the good priest was just after hearing the last confession. He looked at Roderick in amazement and said, "Why, what happened? Why did you not keep on and get the book?" Roderick handed him the book, and the priest looked at his watch. Roderick had taken exactly ten minutes less than an hour doing twelve miles under terrible odds. There was no heart or lung trouble in those times.[65]

When a priest arrived, it was sudden and unheralded. It was only rarely that a priest would be present to officiate at a funeral. When visiting the parishioners, he would give the last sacraments to those who were considered gravely ill and in danger of death.[66] Father Alexander MacGillivray who was Pastor at Iona and Baddeck (1873-1880), came from Baddeck to officiate at the funeral of a little boy. Francis Alexander MacLean, a son of Peter S. MacLean. He was only five years old and a favourite of Father MacGillivray's when he visited the community. There was no ferry running between Baddeck and Iona and the only way for Father MacGillivray to get to Baddeck every third Sunday was to travel to Washabuck and get the steamboat ferry from there. The lad was always in feeble health and the priest recognized that he would not live long. He requested that he be notified should the boy die. Word was sent to him when this happened and he came to Washabuck to officiate at the burial.[67]

Holy Rosary Mission Church

When Father Rory decided to build a church that would serve the Washabuck section of the parish, he received the hearty endorsement of the Washabuck Catholics. Although only a small building, the church stands on a commanding knoll just a short distance from where the first Mass was celebrated in 1822. In 1908 local men were quarrying and dressing the stone required for the foundation. The stone was procured near the shore not far from where the church stands. Early in 1909 those who had promised donations of timber and boards could be seen hauling their quota to the agreed upon site, which was then central for most Washabuck residents. The foundation was under the direction of a deft stone mason named Nicholson from the Grant (South Cove).

The construction of the church was supervised by experienced carpenters Archibald (*Ruadh*) MacKenzie of Birch Point and Donald (*Eòin a' Phlant*) MacNeil of Barra Glen. The local committee that oversaw the whole construction process was comprised of Washabuck residents, Neil P. S. MacLean, Peter MacKenzie and Rod MacKinnon.[68] The two carpenters supervised the many volunteers who helped to construct the church. In August 1909 the corner stone was laid by Father A. McD. Thompson, VG, who was delegated by the Diocesan Bishop, John Cameron.

On July 2, 1914, the church was dedicated with Msgr. Donald MacIntosh, VG, officiating, assisted by Father Dougald Gillis of Antigonish. Pastor Father Rory MacKenzie celebrated Mass. Later in the day the air was uplifted with the skirl of the bagpipes, played by piper Stephen B. MacNeil formerly of Gillis Point and then of Port Hawkesbury. A dinner was served. A great many people were in attendance from other sections of the parish, including Baddeck. The SS *Blue Hill* made a special trip from Baddeck for the occasion, disembarking her passengers at the Washabuck Centre wharf.

Some years after its completion it was found that the seating capacity was inadequate, so a gallery was added that provided more floor space. And so the little church provided accommodation for a couple of hundred people. A roomy vestry with penthouse above, complete with bed and wood stove, provided cozy sleeping quarters for priests that occasionally stayed overnight. This addition was completed shortly before Father Rory MacKenzie died in 1925.

The original pews and "Stations of the Cross" (now refurbished) that hang there today, were donated by the Rory (Ranald) MacDonald family[69] and the church bell was a donation from the Neil Peter MacLean family.[70] The current yellow birch pews were purchased by the Holy Rosary Ladies Society in 1964. In 1980 a new electric organ was donated to the church as a salute to Marjorie MacLean by her daughter and son-in-law Marjorie and Harold Andrews, an acknowledgment her lifetime of services rendered to the church.

St. Columba Parish: Pastors, Administrators, Curates: (1873-2011)
Alexander F. MacGillivray, First Pastor - August 23, 1873-October 29, 1880
Roderick Grant, Pastor - October 29, 1880-December 29, 1892
Roderick MacNeil, Pastor – December 29, 1892-December 3, 1894
John J. MacNeil, Pastor – December 4, 1894-October 13, 1901
Roderick MacKenzie, Pastor – October 13, 1901-December 4, 1925
Ronald MacLean, Curate – July 24, 1923-December 4, 1925
Ronald MacLean, Administrator – December 4, 1925-July 16, 1926
Duncan J. Rankin, Pastor – July 16, 1926-June 1, 1953
Samuel Campbell, Curate - July 25, 1927-August 7, 1929

7-13 Congregation of Holy Rosary Mission Church, on west side of the church ca. 1914. Photo by a MacKenzie from the States, formerly from Birch Point. Courtesy of Rose and Michael A. MacLean, Washabuck.

7-14 Statue of the Blessed Mother crowned by Washabuck teen Clare MacDonald at a memorable parish-wide celebration at Holy Rosary Mission Church. The special occasion saluted the Blessed Mother as "Our Lady of the Rosary," on the Feast of the Assumption, August 15, 1954.

Alexander J. Mac Donald, Curate – December 29, 1929-September 21, 1933
Michael J. MacKinnon, Curate – September 22, 1933-October 8, 1934
Daniel F. Roberts, Curate – October 10, 1934-June 8, 1939
Cyril H. Bauer, Curate – June 8, 1939-November 8, 1939
Bernard V. Chisholm, Curate - November 2, 1939-December 20, 1944
Francis N. MacIsaac, Curate – September 21, 1944-12 April 12, 1950
John Hugh MacDonald, Curate – April 12, 1950-July 5, 1950
Murdock J. MacKenzie, Curate – July 5, 1950-September 1, 1952
Andrew Hogan, Curate (Baddeck) – June 3, 1951-September 2, 1951 and June 20, 1952- September 10, 1952
Hugh D. MacDonald, Curate – September 1, 1952-July 7, 1954
Andrew Hogan, Curate (Baddeck) – June 17, 1953-September 1, 1953

From the time of Father Rankin's death to the present day St. Columba Parish has been served by the following priests:

Bernard Chisholm, Pastor	1953-1956
E. L. Sangster Macdonald, Curate	1954-1955
Dan E. MacDonald, Pastor	1956-1960
Pius M. Hawley, Administrator	1960-1961
John Archie Chisholm, Pastor	1961-1966
John A. MacLeod, Pastor	1966-1970
Gerald MacKenzie, Curate	1969-1975
Dennis Campbell, Pastor	1970-1976
Bernard MacDonald, Pastor	1976-1988
Everett MacDow, Pastor	1988-1992
Robert Donnelly, Administrator	1992-1992
Fred Morley, Pastor	1992-2005[71]
Charles Donovan, Pastor	2005- 2008
Ray Huntley, Pastor	2008 -2008
Agit Kerketta, Associate	2011-2012
Paul Abbass, Pastor	2008-2012

Tribute to the Lady of the Rosary

Alex D. MacLean writes of a memorable religious celebration observed by more than 500 St. Columba parishioners on August 15, 1954, at the Feast of the Assumption, a parish-wide pilgrimage to Holy Rosary Mission Church, Washabuck. Since Washabuck's Mission Church was one of very few in the Diocese of Antigonish dedicated to "Our Lady of the Rosary" special privilege was granted to the faithful to pay tribute to the heavenly Mother during the Marion Year.

> On the eastern side of the church an outside platform was erected which held a statue of the Virgin Mary with the child Jesus in her arms. A large procession of parishioners started walking from the Washabuck Cooperative store past Holy Rosary Cemetery the one-half mile to the church, under the direction of Pastor Bernard Chisholm and curate Father Sangster Macdonald. The rosary was recited as the procession wound its way to the church grounds, where the occasion was then highlighted by Our Lady's statue being crowned by a young Washabuck parishioner Clare MacDonald, as the Choir rendered appropriate music. The day's tribute was capped off with Benediction services being offered by Father Sangster Macdonald, and an inspiring sermon appropriate for the occasion that was preached by MacKinnon Harbour native, Father Lex Gillis, OMI.[72]

Cemeteries / *Cladh Lachlainn*

The remains of most of Washabuck's Catholic pioneers rest in the community's two cemeteries. The pioneer cemetery, known as Lachlan's Cemetery (*Cladh Lachlainn*), is located in Lower Washabuck. This burial ground was originally part of Lachlan MacLean's property. He donated the land to the community to be used for a cemetery. Members of the MacLean, MacKinnon, MacNeil and Murphy pioneer families, along with a number of Mi'kmaq, lay at rest in this burial ground. Oral tradition claims that perhaps as many as thirty five pioneers are interred there, including many young children.

When the cemetery was originally laid out, it was closer to the pathway that served as a road along the shoreline of St. Patrick's Channel. Today however, it is located away from the existing public road but nonetheless, easily accessible by a right of way constructed in 1977.[73] Alex D. observes in 1934:

> No one had been buried in the old cemetery for at least fifty years [1884] but when the moss and underbrush were removed, the graves were all plainly to be seen, and nearly all were marked with a large stone or boulder placed at the head and feet. Before the moss and underbrush that had been allowed to accumulate for more than half a century were removed, no trace of these markers could be seen. Our forefathers did

what they could to mark the last resting places of their departed, they marked them with boulders.[74]

Regrettably, around 1960, when further bush clearing was carried out on site with heavy equipment, these boulders and markers were pushed aside and as a result no headstones are now evident except a monument placed by residents in 1934. Alec D. MacLean describes further:

> In August 1934 a monument was unveiled by Washabuck residents to mark the last resting place of Lachlan MacLean, his family and his neighbours, Donald MacKinnon and John [*Eoin*] MacNeil and their families, all pioneers of Lower Washabuck. The monument, draped with the flag of St. Andrew was unveiled by eighty-four year old Mrs. Catherine Ann MacNeil [Mrs. George MacNeil] the oldest surviving great-grand daughter of Lachlan MacLean. Two well-known pipers, Pipe Major Alexander A. MacDonald of Inverness County and Piper Hugh MacKenzie of Christmas Island served as official pipers for the occasion, piping the procession of clergy to the cemetery, with the welcoming, poignant strains of "MacCrimmon's Lament," "The Land of the Leal" and "The flowers of the Forest." The occasion was honoured by the celebration of on open-air Mass by Bishop James Morrison together with many diocesan clergy and hundreds of descendants of the pioneers. This was the first time a Bishop of the Diocese visited Washabuck.
>
> The stones for the monument were obtained nearby, appropriately, from the remnants of the chimney of Alexander MacLean's former log home, he being one of Lachlan's sons. A metal box containing some documents was embedded in the concrete.

It was in July of 1934 that Alex D. MacLean in conversation with Pastor Father Duncan Rankin and a visiting mission priest Father George Bradley S. J. suggested to them that the cemetery might be given the name of a saint, so they agreed on the name, St. Peter's Cemetery.

Alex D. continues:

> Father Rankin asked me if I had any particular name in view and I said yes, Saint Peter, for two good reasons. First, because St. Peter was the Prince of the Apostles and secondly because every MacLean family in Washabuckt and elsewhere had the name "Peter" somewhere among their family names. And so it was! This name appeared on the gate to the cemetery while below it in Gàidhlig was the original name Cladh Lachlainn.[75]

7-15 Visiting cousins from the Isle of Barra are pictured with their Cape Breton relatives at *Cladh Lachlann*, the pioneer cemetery in 2006. L-R Francis and Peggy MacKinnon, Iona; Donnie MacKinnon, Washabuck; Rhoda and Calum MacNeil, Castle Bay, Barra; Mary Ceit MacKinnon, Castle Bay, Barra; D. F. MacDougall, Ottawa Brook; Vince MacLean, Washabuck and Hugh MacKinnon, Benacadie.

The inscription reads:
In This Cemetery Rests All That
Is Mortal
Of
Lachlan MacLean
The Progenitor of The MacLeans
of Washabuckt
Born In Barra, Scotland,
A.D. 1728
Died In Lower Washabuckt
A.D. 1842
Aged 114 Years

May His Soul Rest In Peace!

This following piece of poignant poetry was composed especially for the occasion of the unveiling of the Lachlan MacLean monument, by Ronald Stephen MacDonald. Mr. MacDonald was a resident of Montreal in 1934. His father was a native of Upper Washabuck and Alex D. MacLean attended school [residing] at his grandfather's home in Upper Washabuck for several years. MacDonald's parents at that time were residents of the United States. This poem is dedicated by its author as follows:

> A memorial poem written to honour Lachlan MacLean, his numerous distinguished progeny present at the memorial unveiling, Thursday, August 23, 1934. Also his neighbours, pioneers in the vicinity of Washabuckt, buried in the old cemetery he gave at Lower Washabuckt, Cape Breton, Nova Scotia.[76]

Cladh Nìll Ghil

A second pioneer cemetery evolved in the area of what is today known as Washabuck Centre (in pioneer days Washabuck Centre was considered part of Lower Washabuck.) This cemetery took its name from the fact that it was originally the site of the home occupied by Neil (*Geal*) MacNeil. Today, *Cladh Nìll Ghil* has been assimilated as the most easterly portion of Holy Rosary Cemetery.

The first interment at *Cladh Nìll Ghil* was Donald MacPhee. He was the husband of Marcella (MacInnis) MacPhee. They lived near what is known today as *Furan Mharsalaidh* (Marcella's Spring) at Washabuck Centre. Donald MacPhee drowned and was buried near where his body was recovered. Later on, further interments were made there and finally the site was recognized as a regular cemetery.

The Day of Lachlann MacLean

From Barra blest—far distant day
Came one to whom we homage pay,
Recalls anew the Pioneer way
Of Gallant Gaels of old!
What Scotland gave reaped greater gain
Emblazons high old Clan MacLean
Shines splendid lives in Faith's domain
Enriched with priceless gold

Clann Lachlann lives in lustrous lives,
Faith's flag aloft well reaps, revives,
And ancient glory rich survives,
To find its fruitage here
Clann Lachlann trills a troubled land-
Well kept, God's laws, each wise command,
Would warm from Folly's fatuous band,
By Sire's well spent career

Once furled a standard to the breeze,
Where stood stout sons of Hebrides,
But unfulfilled were Fate's decrees,
On sad Culloden moor
Yet n'er undaunted pluck went forth
To found new homes, Dame Fortune court,
Within this Garden of the North
By bonny blue Bras d'Or

Came first his God in Lachlan's heart,
"God's acre" gives! T'was princely part,
For here is limned our forebears chart
That brought to bloom the land.
Precursors true, Well carved their names,
O'er trackless wood, tenacious tames,
To fertile farms: Such work proclaim
High deed of heart and hand

Upraised, a stone by Lachlan's brood
To brave forebear: Their gift so good
Proclaims where pluck undaunted stood
To bare a Garden's breast.
'Tis hallowed ground! Here Destiny
Shall show its hundreds, glad to see
As years roll on that are to be
Their gift deeming fitting, best!

For here they sleep! Those iron men
That left their homes in isle and glen
They wait a worthy writer's pen
Heroic lives to show
A golden page for God they wrought,
Rich beauty rendered Him they brought,
Neath Highland homes vocations caught
God's choicer gems bestow!

Ronald Stephen MacDonald

In *Cladh Nill Ghil* there is a bronze plaque fastened to the interior of a four foot high concrete parapet enclosing the graves of the wife and daughter of Roderick (*Ruairidh Geal*) MacNeil.

> In memory of Mary MacNeil, wife of
> Roderick MacNeil of Lower Washabuck
> Born in Scotland
> Died August 15, 1844, Age forty years
> And her daughter Catherine
> Died August 10, 1862. Age nineteen years.

Mary, the mother, died perhaps in childbirth. Daughter Catherine died at 19 from a severe fever. Roderick is buried in St. Columba Cemetery in Iona. Roderick was the son of Neil (*Geal*) MacNeil, the pioneer of that property. The concrete enclosure was subsequently erected by Mary's sons, the MacNeil Brothers of Boston construction fame.

In 1873 Father Alexander MacGillivray was appointed Pastor of the newly created Parish of St. Columba. For unknown reasons, Father MacGillivray directed that thereafter all burials from the Washabuck area were to be made in Iona, at the St. Columba parish cemetery adjoining the parish church. This ruling obviously created additional hardship and stress on the bereaved Washabuck families. In many cases, one spouse was buried in Washabuck while the other was laid to rest in Iona. Today, many moss covered headstones in the old St. Columba Cemetery bear solemn testimony to Father MacGillivray's fiat.

It was not until 1901 when Father Roderick MacKenzie became pastor of St. Columba that Father MacGillivray's ruling was rescinded. Burials have since been made in Holy Rosary Cemetery. Notwithstanding, committals from the Washabuck area have over the intervening years been made in St. Columba Cemetery for personal and family reasons.

Holy Rosary Cemetery

The land that abuts the western side and now embraces *Cladh Nill Ghil* is called Holy Rosary Cemetery. This land was donated to the parish of St. Columba for cemetery purposes in 1917 by Neil (*Ruadh*) MacNeil a grandson of the original owner. It was blessed as consecrated ground on October 23, 1917, by Pastor Roderick MacKenzie assisted by Father John J. MacNeil, then Pastor of Dominion #4 Passchendaele. Father MacNeil was born at Washabuck Bridge and was the son of Allan J. and Sarah (MacLean) MacNeil. Their original home was located just a dozen or so metres east of where Hector MacKenzie's residence is today. The family relocated to St. Peter's shortly after Father MacNeil's birth in 1862.

During the summer of 1977, Holy Rosary Cemetery was doubled in size with the clearing and landscaping of a further piece of land between the existing cemetery and the public highway. In January 1988, deeds for both the old and new portions of the cemetery were transferred. These deeds were signed over to the parish by MacLean brothers, Rod and Cyril, the current owners of the surrounding properties. These surveys were carried out and finished during October 1986, under the direction of Washabuck resident and Nova Scotia Land Surveyor, Roddie J. MacDonald.[77]

Other Burial Sites

In addition to the Carmichael boy who was buried where he tragically died from falling off a cliff in Upper Washabuck, there are others known to exist through an oral tradition. Two young children buried in a field at Washabuck Bridge on the western side of the St. Columba Road. They were the children of Mary *Bàn*, from Prince Edward Island and her husband James MacNeil of Washabuck Bridge, a brother to Malcolm (*mac Iain Ruaidh*) MacNeil. William Oram is buried in an unmarked grave adjacent to the pond where he drowned and which still bears his name today.⁷⁸ More recently and in keeping with his wishes, the ashes of Ernest Matheson were scattered on the property of his brother and sister-in-law, Jimmy and Judi Matheson at MacKay Point.

Challenging Burials

Burials could be trying in "days gone by." Today we tend to take much for granted, with death and its accoutrements having become very sanitized.

7-16 Holy Rosary Cemetery, Washabuck. Courtesy of Rose MacDonald, Washabuck.

This first tale is related by Roddie J. MacDonald of Upper Washabuck, it was a family story told to him as a youth by his father Malkie (R. C.) MacDonald. In March 1918 the vigil of Malkie's own grandfather, Murdock (1828-1918) (*Alasidair Glas*), took place at Murdock's home where Roddie and his wife Laura reside today.

> When it came time for the burial in Holy Rosary Cemetery, for unknown reasons the only able-bodied men around were neighbour Peter MacKenzie, the deceased's son R. C. and twelve year old grandson, Malkie. The horse was hitched in the shafts of a single bob-sleigh, and the coffin secured to it. Malkie handled the reins propelling the make-shift hearse while both Peter MacKenzie and R. C. plodded ahead breaking the snow-bound road for the lonely *cortège*. Once the cemetery was reached, they found an impenetrable depth of frost in the ground and the coffin was "buried" deep in a drift of snow and there it remained, until the spring thaw permitted the remains to be fittingly buried.⁷⁹

A second tale involves similar challenges to bury Rory J. MacLean (1870-1934) of Lower Washabuck. Rory "Stephen" as he was commonly referred to, lived with his wife Sarah on the mountain in Lower Washabuck.

> The winter had been exceedingly cold. Rory took a severe pain in the abdomen the end of February. He was at home for several days before he went by horse and sleigh to Iona where he boarded an eastbound train for the Sydney City hospital. He proved too weak for surgery, however and after a two day hospital stay, he passed away.

> In the meantime the Island had been hit with a massive snowstorm. Rory's remains arrived in Iona by train but all roads were impassable.

Michael D. MacNeil of Iona, a relative of Rory's wife, decided to attempt an adventurous trek over the lake ice, taking the remains from Iona to MacKay's Point. They eventually succeeded by having one team break a track in the snow over the lake ice for the following team.

By the time they reached MacKays Point, the depth of snow was such that a track had to be broken by manpower on the road ahead of the teams for a mile or so distance back toward Rory's lane. This was done with the help of a crew of local men from Lower Washabuck. When the spectacle reached Rory's long, steep and snow-bound lane, the attendants decided it would be easier and more practical for all, men and teams alike, to unhitch the team from the pole and remove the top of the sleigh from its runners. The coffin was then lashed to just the runners. At that point the men took over the team's role and they duly delivered the remains via shaft and runners *on top* of the packed snow to the deceased's home.

Meanwhile, at Washabuck Centre, Neil Peter MacLean was in charge of digging the grave. Another swarm of residents, these from Upper Washabuck were slowly shovelling their own way eastward toward Holy Rosary Cemetery through the snow drifts. Despite the huge amounts of snow, Neil Peter nevertheless had a good idea where Rory's family plot was located and the digging began. During the excavation process, he encountered well over four feet (1.2 m) of frost under the recently accumulated snow. As one can imagine, Rory's grave was an exceptionally difficult one to dig – but unlike Murdock MacDonald's burial, the mass of manpower facilitated the Herculean undertaking.[80]

Pipers

The bagpipes have frequently played a prominent part at solemn church and burial services in the Washabuck district. Piper Roderick MacLean, son of progenitor Lachlan, is known to have piped at many funerals for both old and young in pioneer days. He played the lament at the funeral of his father Lachlan; at the funeral of his brother Neil, and at that of a sister. He also lived long enough to play strains of pathos at the funerals of three of his grandsons. One of the grandsons was the little boy Francis Alexander, mentioned earlier; the other two were the children of his son, Donald *(Dòmhnull mac Ruairidh)* who both died of diphtheria.[81]

This funerary custom has continued over the generations. More recently, Piper John MacLean of Halifax, a great-great-grandson of Piper Roderick MacLean, played at a special memorial service in July 1990 for all those buried in Holy Rosary cemetery. In September 2005, Piper Zackary MacLean great-great-great grandson of Piper Roderick MacLean sounded a poignant dirge for his deceased uncle, Francis MacLean of Sydney Mines, whose remains were being interred in Holy Rosary Cemetery

The pipes are not always associated with funerals. Piper Stephen B. MacNeil of Gillis Point and Port Hawkesbury shared his melodious repertoire with those assembled for the dedication of Holy Rosary Mission Church on July 2, 1914; while Pipe Major Alexander A. MacDonald of Inverness County and Piper Hugh F. MacKenzie of Christmas Island lent their harmonious strains of fervor in August 1934, for the celebration ceremonies that took place in *Cladh Lachlainn*.

The following Washabuck residents were identified as pipers: pioneer Donald MacAulay, who went by the sobriquet Donald "Piper," John Brown, Jimmy "Caluman" MacNeil of St. Columba, and "Piper" Rory MacDougall (1848-1936) of Upper Washabuck, who relocated to Ingonish. More recently, Wanda and Helen MacDonald along with Teresa MacLean and Mary "Lighthouse" MacLean were pipers with the Nova Scotia Highland Village Pipe Band between 1968-1984.

Holy Rosary Ladies Society

Shortly after Father Dan E. MacDonald was appointed as St. Columba's new pastor in 1956, he suggested the women of Washabuck create a society to service the requirements of Holy Rosary Mission Church and its cemeteries.

A brief initial meeting was held in Holy Rosary Church on Sunday June 3, 1956, to form the society. The elected officers were Irene MacLean (president), Frances MacDougall (secretary) and Marjorie MacLean (treasurer). A second meeting was held in Upper Washabuck School on Friday June 15, with twenty women present.

An Altar Society had existed in Washabuck years earlier, but most of its members had either died or relocated. It was decided that the new society's responsibilities should cover a wider field than that of an Altar Society. The new organization was to be known as the Holy Rosary Ladies Society to reflect that the Mission church had special devotion to Our Lady of the Rosary. Member's duties included cleaning the church, the caring and purchasing of altar linens and visiting the sick.

The first projects discussed included improving access to the church grounds, improving parking around the church and the purchasing of a Crucifix for the church altar. It was agreed to meet alternately in the school houses of Upper and Lower Washabuck on the third Friday of each month. The

7-17 Pioneer piper Roderick (*Lachlann*) MacLean, Washabuck. Courtesy of Annette (MacLean) Melanson, the piper's great-great granddaughter, Pomquet, NS.

annual dues were one dollar. High school girls were encouraged to attend but were not required to pay dues.

Suggested fund-raising activities included the usual – raffles, square dances, dinners, milling frolics, bingo, home cooking sales and concerts. It was however, the weekly winter forty-fives card games, held in both school houses and the homes of the Washabuck residents that provided the regular and major source of annual revenues.

Over time, other projects undertaken by the Society included renovation of the church sanctuary, improvements to the church basement and the installation of a central heating system to replace the old wood stove. Electrical wiring was installed prior to 1956. Much time and effort went into improving the Washabuck cemeteries, to improving the grounds, to the purchase and installation of grave markers where required, to the erection of a large cross and Corpus and general maintenance.

More recent activities carried out by the society included donations towards the parish debt, painting the interior and exterior of the church, purchasing carpet, repairing the church roof and chimney, erecting signs for the church and cemeteries, purchasing additional grave markers and surveying cemetery grounds.

In May 1981 the Society celebrated its 25th anniversary with a dinner and dance at the Washabuck Community Centre. The gala corresponded with the silver jubilee of Pastor Bernard MacDonald's ordination to the priesthood. Over the decades the Society had catered to a host of special events and occasions. The Society's women had addressed the needs of the Washabuck Mission and ably fulfilled the challenge that Father Dan E. had presented to them years earlier. Father Dan E. died suddenly on December 1, 1960. He is buried in St. Columba Cemetery, Iona.[82]

Reverend Sisters from the Washabuck Area:

Sisters Mary Ann and Annie MacLean

Sisters Mary Ann and Annie MacLean were the daughters of Peter S. and Jessie (MacDonald) MacLean of Lower Washabuck. They became Sisters of Sacred Heart, a cloistered Order. Mary Ann was born in 1860. She made her vows 1891 in Kenwood, Albany, New York and later served the Order in Rhode Island, Philadelphia, New York City and finally Grosse Pointe Farms Convent, Detroit, Michigan. She died in July, 1931. Her sibling, Sister Annie MacLean was born in 1863 and served the Order in Washington DC, New York and Providence, Rhode Island.[84] She died in 1955 and is buried in Torresdale, Pennsylvania.

Sister Mary Eulalia

Mary Ann MacLean was the daughter of Stephen and Mary (Gillis) MacLean of Lower Washabuck. Born in 1866, she became a Franciscan Sister and was employed with in the laundry room at St. Elizabeth's Hospital in Brighton, Massachusetts. As a result of an on-the-job accident Sister Eulalia lost an arm. On one of her return trips to Washabuck she brought

Holy Rosary Ladies Society: Charter members: (1956)

Rose MacLean	Eulalia MacLean	Cassie MacKenzie
Mary Ann MacLean	Josie MacLean	Irene MacLean
Margaret MacDonald	Rita MacDougall	Marjorie MacLean
Kaye MacLean	Mary Agnes MacDougall	Kathleen MacDonald
Mary Ann MacKenzie	Frances MacDougall	Ellen Ann MacLean
Mary Jane MacLean	Joan MacDonald	Martha MacKinnon
Sarah E. MacDonald	Bea MacNeil	Agnes MacDonald
Mary E. MacDougall	Katie MacKinnon	Mary Ann Murphy
Mary C. MacDonald	Jean MacKenzie	Norma MacNeil
Elizabeth MacDonald	Patrice MacDougall	Carmie MacLean
Betty MacKenzie	Josie MacDonald	Nancy MacLean
Clare MacDonald [83]		

7-18 Father Fred Morley, St. Columba Pastor (1992-2005) honours long-time members of the Holy Rosary Ladies Society, at the Society's final meeting November 22, 1998. Beside Father Morley is L-R: Rose MacLean, Irene MacLean, Joan Gillis, Annie MacKenzie, Josie MacLean, Clare MacDonald.

with her an orphan girl named Margaret Creighton, who would be raised by her sister Agnes and brother-in-law Rory Ranald MacDonald.

Sister Mary Osmund

Sister Mary Osmund became a Sister of Charity. She was born in St. Columba on August 21, 1876 to Allan and Sarah (MacNeil) MacDonald. She was christened Eliza A. She had first been with the Sisters of St. Martha for four years before joining the Sisters of Charity in Halifax in 1903. Sister Osmund spent fifteen years at Mount St. Vincent in Rockingham and then was assigned to St. John's Convent in New Aberdeen, Cape Breton. She died in St. Joseph's Hospital January 7, 1943 and is buried in St. Anne's Cemetery in Glace Bay, NS, No photo of her is known to exist.[85]

Sisters St. John and St. Joseph

Sisters Catherine and Christina were the daughters of Peter and Mary (MacNeil) MacNeil of Gillis Point East. Mary, their mother, was a daughter of Rory (Neil *Geal*) of Washabuck Centre. Her first marriage was to Michael (Murdock *Beag*) MacNeil of Upper Washabuck. They had a son Murdock. After her husband Michael died in 1872, she married Peter (*Niall mac Eachainn*) MacNeil of Gillis Point East. They raised a family of seven, four sons and three daughters. The family lived for a while on Inlet road but when her second husband died, the family moved to Dorchester, Mas-

Above, left to right
7-19 Sister Mary Ann MacLean. Courtesy of Madeline Northen, Little Narrows, CB.
7-20 Sister Annie MacLean. Courtesy of Madeline Northen, Little Narrows, CB.
7-21 Sister Eulalia (Mary Ann MacLean).
7-22 Sister St. John (Catherine MacNeil) (left) and her sister, Sister St. Peter (Christine MacNeil). Courtesy of Lucy (MacNeil) Hayes, Montreal, and her nephew, Neil MacNeil, Bethesda, Maryland, USA.

sachusetts. Mary died in 1916. Catherine and Christina became Sisters of the Congregation of Notre Dame, Catherine was known as Sister St. John and Christina as Sister St. Joseph. The two Sisters are buried in Montreal.[86]

Sister Mary Celestia

Mary A. MacNeil was born in Upper Washabuck a daughter of Rory J. and his second wife Katie (MacLean) MacNeil in 1900. She became a member of the Sisters of St. Martha, Antigonish, and died there in ca. 1961. She is buried in the adjoining cemetery at the St. Martha's Motherhouse.

Sister Mary Agnes Nash

Sister Agnes Nash was born a Livingston in Inverness County in 1935, but was adopted by Rachel and Mick-John Nash in St. Columba. She attended school in St. Columba and later at Rankin Memorial in Iona. In 1962, she joined the Sisters of the Congregation of Notre Dame. She taught school at several locations throughout Western Canada and ended her days at Holy Angels Convent in Sydney where she passed away on November 28, 2009.[87]

Sister Florence Elizabeth MacKenzie

Sister Florence was a daughter to Tommy and Cassie MacKenzie of Lower Washabuck. Born in December 15, 1943, Florence attended school at Lower Washabuck and later at Rankin Memorial in Iona before entering

Above, left to right
7-23 Sister Mary Celestia (Mary MacNeil).
7-24 Sister Agnes Nash. Courtesy of Rose MacDonald, Washabuck.
7-25 Sister Florence MacKenzie. Courtesy of Pat Timmerman, Washabuck.

the Sisters of the Congregation of Notre Dame in August 1962. After obtaining her teaching certificate from St. FX University she began a teaching career in New Victoria and River Ryan. Over the next ten years, she taught at Larry's River, Guysbourgh County. After a year of study in Toronto, Sister Florence returned to Guysbourgh County as school counselor at Port Felix, where she is currently employed.[88]

Clergymen with Washabuck Connections

Reverend John J. MacNeil

John J. MacNeil was born on Christmas day 1862 at Washabuck Bridge in a home that was located just a few yards east of Hector MacKenzie's home (2014). He was the son of Allan J. and Sarah (MacLean) MacNeil. His grandparents were John (*Iain Ruadh*) MacNeil and his second wife who was a MacLean woman from St. Columba, a sister to Neil (*Dubh*), and Alexander *(Lachlann)* and Mary (MacDougall) MacLean of Washabuck. The family relocated to St. Peter's while John James was still a child.

John received his early education at the public school in St. Peter's. For a number of years he was a deep-sea fisherman, sailing regularly to the Grand Banks. Later he became a book binder. In 1890 he entered St. Francis Xavier University and received his degree four years later. He joined the university staff while privately studying first year theology. He entered the Grand Seminary in Montreal and was ordained a priest on December 18, 1899. He was then thirty-seven years old.

Father MacNeil was the only person born in Washabuck to become a priest. He was also the first born to be ordained a priest from any of the communities that formed St. Columba parish.

Father MacNeil served many parishes with zeal and dedication during his lifetime. These included L'Ardoise, Bay St. Lawrence, Ingonish, Thorburn, Egerton and Lismore. He also served Port Hawkesbury and was responsible for Princeville, Creignish and Lower River Inhabitants. He became Pastor of St. Anthony's in Passchendaele in 1913 where he remained until he retired due to ill health in October 1937.

He was responsible for building St. Anthony's Church and the Convent bringing in the Sisters of Charity to augment the teaching staff of the parish school. He was a daily visitor at the local hospital and was ever a friend of the needy.[89] According to a brief referral in a genealogical article in the Clan McNeil publication *The Galley*, Father MacNeil was a widely known violinist, and taught music to his cousin Joe MacNeil of Arichat.[90]

The last four years of his life he served as Chaplain at St. Anthony's Home in Sydney. He died in 1941 and is buried in St. Anthony's Cemetery in Glace Bay.

Reverend Roderick (Rory) MacKenzie

Father MacKenzie was a son of (*Murchadh Bàn*) (John, Hector, Archibald) of Christmas Island and his wife Catherine MacSween of Beaver Cove. Roderick graduated from St. Francis Xavier University and the Grand Seminary in Quebec where he was ordained in 1890. He served as curate at Victoria Mines under his uncle Father Archibald MacKenzie and at Lourdes under Father W. B. MacLeod. He became pastor at Arisaig for six years and spent another two years in each of the parishes of Heatherton and Grand Mira. In 1901 he was assigned to St. Columba parish in Iona where he was pastor for twenty four years. In 1921 he was appointed Rural Dean for Victoria County.[91]

In 1924, following the death of Father Roderick (Rory) MacKenzie, Alex D MacLean recalled the priest's leadership, through the building of Holy Rosary Mission Church to his decision to once again grant permission for burials in Holy Rosary Cemetery.

7-26 Rev. John J. MacNeil, born at Washabuck Bridge, Christmas Day, 1862. Courtesy of St. FX University's Special Collection Archives, Antigonish, NS.

7-27 Rev. Roderick (Rory) MacKenzie. Courtesy Rod C. MacNeil, Barra Glen, CB.

> Father Rory MacKenzie pastor of St. Columba parish (1901-1924) went to his eternal reward in December 1924. His death occurred at Iona after a protracted illness, ending a faithful pastorate of more than a quarter of a century. His body rests as he wished in the parish cemetery not far removed from the church, and his grave is marked by an imposing monument, a mute testimony of the level of esteem of his flock. In the minds of many, the little church that stands today at Washabuck Centre overlooking the broad expanse of St. Patrick's Channel, is the most appropriate monument of the two, recalling as it does to them the memory of a gentle, self-sacrificing pastor, and one whose memory will ever be green in the minds and hearts of his people.[92]

We may say that Father MacKenzie provided for the living and the dead – he provided a place of worship for the former and a place of sepulture for the latter.[93]

Reverend Charles A. MacKenzie

Archibald MacKenzie (*Gilleasbuig mac Eachuinn*) arrived from Barra in 1821 and settled at Birch Point, Washabuck. His wife was Catherine MacKinnon a daughter of John MacKinnon, shoemaker, of Barra. They had a family of ten children. One of their daughters, Mary, married Alexander "Framer" MacKenzie from north Lake Ainslie, who settled in Washabuck. They in turn had a family of six children, one of whom was Hector. He married Margaret MacDonald a daughter of Donald MacDonald (*Calum Bàn*) of Grand Narrows and settled in the United States. One of their sons, Father Charles A. MacKenzie, CM, was the noted Vincentian Missionary of Philadelphia.

Father MacKenzie would drop in on his Washabuck cousins whenever he visited Cape Breton. In 1924, he preached a mission in Christmas Island.

"Father MacKenzie is a great missionary, and his sermons made a deep, lasting impression on the people of the parish," wrote Archibald J. MacKenzie the author of *History of Christmas Island Parish* in 1926. "They would never get tired listening to him, and the result was that the mission was a great success."[94] Most missionary priests in those times were noted for being powerful preachers and it seems Father Charlie could hold his own among the best of them.

Father Charlie preached a mission of several days at St. Columba parish in Iona as well around that time. In the late 1970s, John Rory MacNeil of Barra Glen related a tale about attending Father Charlie's sermons of fury and the powerful preaching abilities of the man as he exuberantly sermonized on, "Hell, fire, and the wrath of God," John Rory recalled:

> Each parishioner in attendance had little trouble imagining tongues of leaping hellfire, curling and caressing its way among the spindles of rail at the front of the church. You could smell smoke![95]

Charbroiled Faith

During October 1921 Father Charlie preached a three-day mission at Holy Rosary Church Washabuck.[96] Father Charlie had a head full of white hair, a sly set to his mouth and the ghost of a mischievous glimmer to his eye. St. Columba's Pastor, Father Rory MacKenzie, had delivered the Missionary to Holy Rosary Church before leaving him on his own for a couple of nights, safely ensconced in the cozy, if rustic penthouse above the vestry of the mission church. There, the first day and evening proved normal and uneventful, but it was during the following evening that untoward events unfolded.

The evening was quiet with the weather serene, the wood box was full and the studio's stove was performing to perfection. The pantry box had been well-provisioned by the local women. Services would begin again at eight the following morning and the small church would be jammed.

The church was situated adjacent to the farm of Murdock Paul MacLean. A hard working bachelor, Murdock was noted for his kindness, humour and exceptional capacity to swear wondrously at the slightest provocation. Murdock owned a few cattle, including a mature white-headed bull that was constantly causing his owner grief. Fences meant nothing to the bull. Like most farmers Murdock attempted to keep his farmland enclosed with the common post-and-pole fencing system that hopefully would maintain the small herd where he wanted them. But this particular bull had his own ideas. On more than one occasion he had stretched his master's short fuse past the outer limits of his vernacular. That evening proved no different as the cattle and bull were roaming close by in the hayfield abutting the church property.

The animal kingdom, like mankind, may occasionally perceive the other side of the fence to have greener grass. Murdock Paul's bull stretched his tongue for a lick of some just-out-of-reach elixir and caught his head between a couple of fence poles. Eventually, Murdock noticed the bull was missing, went searching and discovered him enjoying his pastoral freedom with several panels of fence partially pulled down around him. The ruinous scene was more than enough to set Murdock off on a blistering, blasphemous rant, venting tarnished imprecations upon the bull, promising to consign him immediately to the darkest and nethermost corner of eternity.

By coincidence, at the same moment, Father Charlie had stuck his own white head out of the church's loft window to catch a breath of fresh air. Father Charlie caught more than invigorating air, as Murdock Paul's profanity reached his ears, a tirade for the bull that included emphatic orders, "to immediately pull his goddamn white head back inside or he'd have the brook running red and rotten with his blood and guts before twilight faded." The startled Father Charlie had heard more than enough and quickly retreated, summarily slamming the window.

Whether or not Father Charlie ever learned what actually occurred doesn't really matter, but if he did, it certainly wasn't before he delivered the next morning's sermon of wrath, the likes of which Murdock Paul and his neighbours had never before endured. The tongues of the fires of Hell were particularly longer and the resultant heat hotter than any of the by-now, ghastly-faced congregation had ever before been subjected. With remorseless determination he castigated the assembly to the effect, that contrary to seemingly popular belief, The Father's celestial chambers consisted not only of heavenly rooms, but the bowels of Hell were for blasphemers and the profane alike.

Father Charlie's blistering words of excoriation that fateful morning have ever since remained the benchmark to which all subsequent Holy Rosary church sermons have been so drearily compared.[97]

Reverend Roderick A. MacEachen

Rory (John *Mór*) MacKinnon of Highland Hill married a sister of Michael (*Eòin*) MacNeil of Washabuck. Her name is not known. They had a family of two, a son John Bernard and a daughter Isabel. After the tragic death of her father, Isabel came to Washabuck Centre to live with her uncle and aunt, Michael *Eòin* and Mary MacNeil. Washabuck and her connections held a special place for Isabel. In due course, her children felt the same way. Correspondence was carried on regularly among these cousins throughout their lifetimes.[98]

Isabel first married Thomas MacNeil. They lived in Highland Hill. Thomas, along with three others, perished in a tragic boating accident on May 22, 1863 in the "Big" Lake. Isabel gave birth to a son Thomas Bàn, shortly after her husband's untimely death. She soon left Highland Hill and moved to Boston with her MacNeil cousins and finally to Ohio, USA. There she remarried Neil MacEachen, formerly of Mabou. They lived in Shawnee about eighty-five miles (137 km) from Columbus, Ohio.

Isabel and Neil had a family of six children, Mary Margaret, Sarah Ann, Roderick "Roddie," Isabella, John D. and Elizabeth. Of course, Roddie (1873-1965) was not a native of Washabuck but his grandmother had been and certainly his mother had spent her early years in Washabuck with her MacNeil cousins. Roddie was ordained a priest on August 11, 1901.

Fishy Time

Father MacEachen and his mother would visit their cousins in Washabuck. He enjoyed fishing with Vincent MacLean, his cousin Theresa's husband. He would relate with relish the story of how despondent he felt when he lost his gold-plated wrist-watch overboard while hand-lining for cod. And then, how jubilant he became, when after hauling aboard a particularly large fish, the cod coughed-up his so-recently lost timepiece onto the floor boards. The most hilarious part of the whole fish story though, was that his mother absolutely refused to believe her son's tale.[99]

Father MacEachen in addition to his priestly duties was a man of letters and a noted linguist. During November 1910, he preached a week's mission at Holy Redeemer Church, Whitney Pier, Cape Breton.[100]

Father MacEachen lived to be 91 years old. His obituary, carried in the July 2, 1965 edition of *The New York Times* mentions that he was a priest, professor, author, philanthropist, rancher and industrialist (no mention was made of his fishing exploits). Father MacEachen became a very wealthy man later in life, inheriting from his widowed sister Elizabeth, majority shareholder status in an Evansville, Indiana, steel mill company, the proceeds of which he later distributed to worthy causes in Florida.[101]

Centennial of Holy Rosary Mission Church

August 2009 saw the 100th anniversary commemorating the construction and the laying of the cornerstone for Holy Rosary Mission Church, Washabuck. Recognizing the approaching centennial, a committee of volunteers was struck a number of years previously. Committee members included: Carmie MacLean, Gerard MacNeil, Gus MacLean, Charlotte MacLean, Dan Joseph MacNeil and Ben MacLean.

During the years leading up to the celebration, substantial upgrades were made to the building and grounds. The committee oversaw fundraising from Washabuck residents and ex-residents who responded with enthusiasm and generosity to the request for financial help. As a result, the little Gothic

Revival church was given a complete makeover; structurally, it remains as sound as the day it was completed.

Committee members with the assistance of Clare MacDonald assembled and published a memorial booklet containing photos and stories of church happenings and the personalities involved in its first century of existence. The anniversary mass was celebrated on Friday August 7, 2009, by Pastor Paul Abbass and assisted by several priests who had formerly served the parish. A group picture was taken of the congregation outside the building, by photographer David Gillis, of Scotsville. Afterward, refreshments and a *ceilidh* were enjoyed by all at the community centre.

The following Sunday, a beautiful sunny afternoon, a service was held in Holy Rosary Cemetery, with mass celebrated by one-time St. Columba parish curate, Father Hugh D. MacDonald. Father Hughie is currently (2012) the oldest serving pastor in the diocese, serving in the parish of Creignish. He has just celebrated the Diamond Anniversary of his ordination. Regular week-end mass is no longer celebrated since 2000, with the exception of weddings, funerals and special events. Residents now attend church services at St. Columba in Iona.

Prejudices and Predicaments

Long Memories

When the pioneers left Scotland and came to this new land, there were some things they did not leave behind. They brought with them many of their prejudices. And often these biases continued rivalry and distrust among individuals, families and clans. Traces of these differences exist,

7-28 Rev. Roderick MacEachen.

7-29 Congregation of Holy Rosary Mission Church during its Centennial Anniversary, August 7, 2009. Photo by David Gillis, Scotsville, CB.

some of them until recently, although most of the reasons have been obscured by the mists of time. Then, their prejudices were simply a fact, indeed an intricate part of the Celtic culture; religious tenets and conflicts were deeply entrenched. Congregational distinctions were a source of friction between otherwise rational peoples – strife that scarred family relationships and communities and resulted in hurtful discrimination. Washabuck was no different. Religiously, about 70 per cent of the Washabuck pioneers followed Catholicism with the balance being adherents of Presbyterianism.

Catholic and Protestant communities remained almost as religiously divisive in Nova Scotia as they had been in Scotland. The Gaels settled in communities that reflected the commonalties of clan, family, kinship and religious affiliation. Most Scottish settlements on Cape Breton Island were originally clearly identified as being either Protestant or Catholic. Washabuck though, proved to be the rarer exception. In communities where Presbyterian and Catholic families lived in close proximity, religious discretion was usually observed. To quote Laurie Stanley author of *The Well Watered Garden*: "In such cases discrete settlement required discrete neighbourliness."[102]

It is well known from general comments of the past generation that the peoples of Washabuck got along very well with one another, even when it came to the practice of their respective faiths. Generally speaking, traditional generosity and the helping Highland hand seemed to have been maintained with religious differences over doctrine and dogma being treated with fitting respect. After all, their own humanity was what they shared in common and anything less would have been uncharitable.

For the most part that was the way it was in this area. Nonetheless, occasionally, an intrusion would develop that caused an eruption; a pot would boil over and spill its contents upon a smoldering situation. Those who crossed the line or "jumped the fence," were looked upon as betrayers to their respective faiths and worthy (to at least some) of derision. Following, are a couple of stories related here from the delicate hand of Alex D. MacLean that exemplify these prejudices and predicaments.

The Marriage of Paul MacLean

> The marriage of Paul MacLean (*Alasdair mac Lachlainn*) of Washabuck to Ann Carmichael of Whycocomagh was one of the romances of early days. Paul MacLean was a blacksmith and it was while he was learning his trade at Whycocomagh that he met his future wife. Everything was running smoothly with the young couple, with the exception of that very knotty problem: "How could they get married?" Paul was a Catholic, and Ann was a Presbyterian born and brought up a Presbyterian. [Was this then a double-barrelled affair, in the making?] Paul was not about to change his faith and Miss Carmichael knew only too well that her

parents would never consent that she would marry a Catholic or agree to her becoming a Catholic.

The courtship went on however and in due course there was a secret understanding reached between Paul and Ann that she would become a Catholic and later they would be married. When Paul ended his period of service as an apprentice blacksmith he returned to his home in Washabuck. Before he left Whycocomagh, it was arranged that on an agreed date, he would return with a boat and would be waiting for Ann at a designated place on the secluded beach.

The day arrived and Miss Carmichael told her parents that she intended visiting or spending the day with some friends or relatives that she wanted to see and who lived some distance away from her home. Permission was readily granted her to make this visit, but while she was getting ready, a younger sister suddenly decided that she would like to accompany her. Now, we can readily see that poor Ann was in a devil of a fix; she could not very well refuse to have her sister accompany her, this might arouse suspicion, and she could not get away without her, so there was nothing Ann could do but allow her sister to come with her.

Nevertheless, instead of proceeding to the home that she was supposed to visit, she went to the meeting place that herself and Paul had agreed upon previously and there found Paul waiting for her with his boat. She stepped into it, and a moment or two later was she was on her way to Washabuck. The sister who was left standing on the shore, stood dumbfounded for a moment, but soon recovered and ran off to inform her parents that Ann had run off with the papist. Paul MacLean and Ann Carmichael had pulled off a genuine elopement – possibly the first – in this part of the country.

When they arrived in Lower Washabuck, the intended bride went to the home of Paul's uncle, Malcolm MacLean, where she stayed for a time. Later, she found shelter in the homes of the other members of the MacLean family. During this time she was being instructed in the Catholic faith. In the meantime in Whycocomagh, the "heather was ablaze." A posse consisting of the father and his two brothers came to Washabuck and they vowed that they would have Ann with them when they returned. However, when they came across some of the MacLean's, men of about six feet in stature and who had a wide reputation as man-eaters, they decided that aggression had better give way to diplomacy. Accordingly, the posse retired to Whycocomagh.

Later, old Carmichael returned alone seeking to learn the whereabouts of Ann, but he was unable to even gain a glimpse of her. He could not locate her or find out where she was staying. One day while in Washabuck in his so-far fruitless quest, he came to a house in search of her; she was not to be seen, and the people of the house disclaimed all knowledge of her whereabouts. They liked the old fellow, who really was a mild-mannered gentleman, and they invited him to stay for dinner. The daughter was concealed in this house at this time, and many years later, she told her father that she was watching him that day as he was seated at the table eating.

In due course the intended bride and Paul were married by Father Donald MacIsaac. They thought their troubles were over, but they were overly optimistic. A few days after their marriage, when the young couple had commenced housekeeping for themselves they had visitors. Opening the door to a knock, they found Ann's father and his two brothers. They looked rather grim and in answer to the question as to what they wanted, they replied that they had come to take Ann home.

Paul MacLean was not a man of very rugged build but it is probable that the years that he spent at the blacksmith's anvil gave him some good brawn and able muscles. He told them that Ann was going to end her days with him and that before they could take her away, that they would have to fight him. He added that if they viewed the matters as they should, that he would welcome them into their home and he forthwith invited them to supper. They came in and were soon seated at the table. After the repast, Mr. Carmichael stood up. He wished the couple a long and happy married life, and said no one from Whycocomagh would ever bother them again. He kept his word.[103]

Oats and Oaths

Within fifteen or so years of their marriage, Paul and Ann relocated from Washabuck to Sydney Mines where he obtained employment as a blacksmith with the General Mining Association, which later became the Nova Scotia Steel and Coal Co. The couple had four children, three daughters and a son Alexander "Sandy." Sandy MacLean (1861-1940) related the following tale which occurred prior to the family's moving from Washabuck, to Alex D. MacLean.

When Sandy was about thirteen or fourteen years old his grandmother Carmichael died at Whycocomagh. It seems that her husband was left alone, so in time he came to Washabuck and asked his son-in-law Paul MacLean if he would be so kind as to let young Sandy go back to Whycocomagh with him. He added that he felt lonely and that the lad would be company for him and would be able to attend school there. Paul consented that he could go. Paul however laid the old man under a strict injunction that he was not under any circumstances to ask his grandson to attend Presbyterian services. The old man promised that this would be so.

Sandy recounted that after he arrived in Whycocomagh he felt all sense of loneliness depart. The surroundings were new and agreeable, and he got along fine with his new school friends. He was nevertheless unable to get accustomed to the family worship that the old man used to hold every morning and evening. Sandy in his own words said, "That his grandfather prayed and sang hymns to such an extent that he drooled at the mouth." The old gentleman was also very much averse to swearing or any form of profanity.

The Presbyterian services were held at Whycocomagh once a month in those days. As we have already seen, ministers among the Protestants were as scarce as priests among the Catholics in those times. The first Sunday the minister came to Whycocomagh following young Sandy's arrival at his grandfather's home, the minister was to hold service. His grandfather asked Sandy to accompany him to the church. He said that he did not ask to attend the services, but wished him to hold the horse while he was at the service himself. He explained that the horse was very restless and would not stand alone even though he would be hitched. Sandy obliged him, and fed the animal some oats while he stood by the horse or sat in the wagon throughout the service.

The next month the same thing happened. His grandfather asked him to come to the church to again hold the horse. When they got there, he noticed that the old man tied the horse with a stout rope. He then turned to the boy and said that the horse was all right now, that he could not break away. He said, "You may as well come in with me." Sandy replied, "No you promised my father that you would not ask me to go to your church." However, the old man insisted and so Sandy went in with him. Sandy related that he was kind of stubborn about it and would not sit alongside the old man, but rather sat down in a rear pew.

On the way home, Sandy began to consider how easy it was for the grandfather to put one over on him. He decided that he would have to leave and return to Washabuck. He thought about the situation for some time and eventually hit upon a scheme that would compel the old man to send him away. Next morning, he went outside to split some firewood. He purposely broke the axe-handle and coming into the house to effect repairs, he began to swear. The old man as he expected was horrified at the terrible swearing and reprimanded him severely. That night the prayers were longer than usual. The same thing happened the next morning. For the second time the axe-handle was broken. Sandy cursed and swore more that morning than he ever had before. That was the straw that broke the camel's back – or rather the old man's patience. He told Sandy to get his clothing ready, that he would have to go back to Washabuck. "I will not have anybody around me that will swear like that." And so it was that young Sandy gathered up his belongings and returned to Washabuck.[104]

The Burial of the *Tuathach*

Angus MacDonald was a native of North Uist. He was known locally in Washabuck as the *Tuathach* which simply means "Northerner" in *Gàidhlig*. Angus was Presbyterian as were most of the pioneers from North Uist. He however, married a Catholic woman and became a Catholic himself at the same time, abandoning his Protestant faith. His conversion to the Catholic religion seemed to be a matter of expediency though, for on his wife's passing, he ceased to practice his Catholic faith and did not return to his former Protestant religion. When Angus left the Presbyterian Church and became a Catholic his action was naturally very much resented by his Presbyterian neighbours, and this resentment continued on after his wife's passing and all through the time of neglect of the practice of his adopted faith. His religious affiliation had proven to be merely a nominal one. As a result the Protestants wanted neither part nor parcel of Angus. They would not traffic with a man who had turned Papist.

When death claimed the *Tuathach*, he was living among his Catholic neighbours. When they came to make arrangements for his funeral, they found themselves in a quandary. They suddenly realized that they could not give the deceased a Catholic burial, as he had neglected the practice of his adopted faith for years, and they at the same time knew that the Presbyterians would not wish to commit his body to the Protestant cemetery. The Protestants regarded Angus as a renegade, pure and simple. The about-to-unfold drama was barely tinged with charitable overtones.

It was finally arranged by the Catholics that they would take the *Tuathach's* remains early in the morning, just about dawn, and they would inter him in the Protestant cemetery without the knowledge or consent of the Presbyterians. Donald (*Dòmhnull Eòin*) MacKenzie was one of the conspirators who framed the plan. Accordingly, the little procession left the house very early in the morning. The coffin was carried on a sort of bier made out of two poles, and carried by four men, two on each side. This mode of conveyance was known as a *carrabag*. The redoubtable *Dòmhnull Eòin* was one of the pall-bearers. The procession was very near the Protestant cemetery when a figure detached itself from the shadows and halted the procession. This was John MacIver, one of the Presbyterians. He had reason to suspect that the Catholics would attempt a coup of some kind, and he and his neighbours were posted as sentinels. [The unfolding events certainly justified in his suspicions.]

The Catholic cemetery was only a short distance beyond the Protestant one, but MacIver was not at all sure that the *Tuathach* was to be buried in the Catholic cemetery. As mentioned, he stopped the procession and inquired of the bearers in *Gàidhlig* as to where they were going with the body? *Dòmhnull Eòin*, who acted as spokesman for the rest, replied in accents dripping with honey:

"A charaid tha sinn a' dol dhan chladh leis."
("Friend, we are going to the cemetery with him.")

Now it was obvious to all but a moron that they were enroute to the cemetery, and this calm reply nettled MacIver. Rather testily he replied:

"Tha mi 'ga fhaicinn sin, ach có fear!?
(Yes, I can see that, but to WHICH cemetery?)

Donald MacKenzie replied:

"A charaid, tha sinn a' dol gu cladh nan Leòdhasach leis."
(Friend, we are going to the Lewis Cemetery with him.)

This was what MacIver suspected and he began to protest rather vigorously, flailing his arms about and calling on the other Presbyterians to come forward to support him while shouting:

"Chan eil sinn-ne 'ga iarraidh idir! Chan eil sinn!"
(We don't want him at all! We don't want him at all!)

Donald MacKenzie merely shifted his burden to the other shoulder and calmly answered:

"Chan eil sin gu diobhar a charaid. Tha e 'dol ann co dhiubh."
(That makes no difference friend, he is going there anyway.)

That was that, and despite the vigorous protests and a fist fight between the opposing factions the remains of the *Tuathach* was laid to rest in *Cladh nan Leòdhasach*.[105]

Thistles

Finally, here is a bit of repartee with which to garnish these pious skirmishes. It seems that the thistle was in earlier days considered a symbol of the Catholic faith. Rev. John Hugh Gillis, PhD (1910-2006) of MacKinnon Harbour and St. Francis Xavier University, who was bestowed with the Church's rank of Monsignor a couple of years prior to his passing, shared this morsel in 1993.

> In my youth I often heard of the thistle as the symbol of our Catholic faith. We in our end of the parish mixed more frequently with Protestants (Little Narrows, Alba, Orangedale, Cain's Mountain). I often heard my father tell of a conversation in that part of the world between a Catholic and Protestant. The latter asked the Catholic: "Why do you use the thistle as the symbol of your Faith?" The Catholic replied: "That is the one flower you cannot wipe your arse with!"[106]

Come to think about it, with hindsight, perhaps an occasional daub of the virtuous thistle could have tempered some wayward happenings unveiled recently throughout the western world and ever closer to home.

7-30 An assembly of St. Columba parish men, attending a weekend spiritual retreat at Monastery, Antigonish County, NS, October 1959. Front Row: L-R Angus Gardiner, Hugh Campbell, John Dan MacNeil, Arthur Campbell, Retreat Master, Father Anastasias, John Alec (The Fiddler) MacNeil, John Murdock MacKinnon Second Row: Charlie Murphy, F.X. MacNeil, Arnold MacNeil, Collie MacNeil, Joe MacKenzie, Jerome MacKinnon, Bill McCormack, Andrew MacLean, Michael A. MacLean Back Row: Joseph Neil MacNeil, Hector MacKenzie, Alexander MacLean, Peter Murphy, Gordon MacLean, Jimmy (Hector) MacNeil, Columba MacNeil.

8 – Post Offices and Courier Services

In a 2005 *Cape Breton Post* article, history columnist Sandra Devlin succinctly outlined early postal service.

> A proud history of mail delivery dates back to the earliest of civilizations. Using a system of relay posts, the ancient Egyptians sent messages quickly over long distances. The Romans had fast horses and good roads which enabled them to ensure next-day delivery up to 280 kilometres away. When the French arrived in North America in the 16th century, messages were carried among the native people by messengers.
>
> The French adopted the native practice of using canoes to deliver dispatches between settlements. The modern postal system began in England with the introduction of the adhesive postage stamp by Rowland Hill in 1837. Hill also devised the uniform postage rate schedule based upon weight, rather than size, and made prepayment of postage both possible and practical.... Pre-confederation mail service was the successive responsibility of various private individuals, companies or government agencies...[1]

Early Post Offices

In his publication *The Nova Scotia Post: Its Offices, Masters and Marks: 1700-1867*, J. J. MacDonald writes:

> Ultimate control and authority resided in the General Post Office at London from the start of the system, with the opening of the Halifax office in 1754, until 1851, when the colony became responsible for all aspects of its own affairs. The chief officer prior to 1851 was designated the Deputy Postmaster General but after that date he assumed the title of Postmaster General of Nova Scotia.

Although Cape Breton Island was an independent colony from 1784 until 1820 it was never independent in postal matters as the Postmaster in Sydney reported to London through the Deputy Postmaster General in Halifax and was effectively under the latter's control.... That jurisdictional control of post office affairs and service by colony dated in Nova Scotia from 1754 until 1867.[2]

Frank Campbell describes the early postal system in this country in his work *Canadian Postal History*:

After Confederation of New Brunswick, Nova Scotia, and Canada East-West, in 1867, as Canada, the whole postal system was managed from Ottawa headquarters.[3]

Cape Breton had no separate postal system, being always managed with Halifax as a headquarters. [...] In 1801, A. C. Dodd was definitely appointed to be postmaster at Sydney. Some years after in [the Quebec] *Almanacks* the designation was "Cape Breton" rather than Sydney. In 1817 once a month trips to Halifax were the limit of service, and in 1821 a weekly trip to Halifax was started.[4]

Baddeck

The Baddeck post office officially opened on January 6, 1852. Historian Jim St.Clair outlines that it had previously been a "way office" since at least 1847[5] and probably as early as 1837.[6] A "way station" was simply a place where mail was gathered to be sent away and where incoming mail was left to be picked up, but the site itself provided no cancellation devices or other postal services, as would have a designated post office, under the jurisdiction of William Kidston, who had come to Baddeck from Halifax in 1835. Joseph Campbell was Baddeck's first [unofficial] postmaster. Robert Elmsley wrote that Thomas Battersly would arrive once a week from Sydney, on foot and "with a bag slung on his back … sometimes one letter or a paper" inside.[7]

Robert Elmsley subsequently served as the Baddeck postmaster from 1858 until November 1893. After the arrival of the railroad through Cape Breton Island [ca. 1890], Baddeck received mail by steamer from Iona and during the winter months by stage coach from the Orangedale railway station. The "old" Baddeck post office building opened its doors in February 4, 1887, and over its main doorway bears the bas-relief resemblance of the Honourable Charles J. Campbell who was Victoria County's Member of Parliament at that time.[8]

Iona

The most recent post office building on the Washabuck Peninsula was opened in Iona in June 1969, by Hon. Allan J. MacEachen MP. The building carries its identifying designation in three languages, Gaelic, English and French. Hon. Mr. MacEachen was assisted by Mr. Morrow of the office of Director Public Services, Halifax. Rev. Donald Sutherland and Rev. John A. MacLeod officiated at the blessing of the new building, according to Alex D. MacLean.[9] The day was a milestone in the history of Iona, the oldest Scottish settlement in Victoria County, added MacLean.[10]

The first post office in Iona was inaugurated in November 1851 as a "way station" and was known as Grand Narrows No. 1. Its first postmaster was Stephen McPherson who was followed by Stephen J. MacNeil (Red Stephen), and then in 1887 by Roderick A. MacNeil.[11] The name of the post office changed to Iona, in July 1891, with Roderick A. MacNeil as its postmaster.[12]

MacKay Point Post Office

Alex D. MacLean states the first postmaster in Lower Washabuck was Malcolm MacLean (*Calum mac Lachlainn*). Although Alex D.'s dates conflict somewhat with those of the official version, MacLean relates that Malcolm received his appointment in 1848 and the office was located in his house. A stalwart and uncompromising Conservative ... he retained the office until his death. He was succeeded by his son Michael, but in 1874, under the brief Liberal administration of Alexander MacKenzie, the post office was transferred to Angus MacNeil (*Aonghas mac Eòin*). By 1878, the Conservatives were in power once again and the post office reverted back to Michael MacLean and remained there until 1896, when a change in government caused the office to be closed permanently.[13] So for a period of forty-four years the Lower Washabuck post office was run out of the same home. The house was later occupied by Roderick D. MacLean and family.[14]

Neil P. S. MacLean puts his own interpretation on the changing post office locales, in his detailed *Casket* article of 1939. This post office was in the eastern end of Lower Washabuck and referred to as MacKay Point post office. It served only about three families. The remaining inhabitants for a further five miles [westward] were getting their mail at Baddeck from Robert Elmsley, the postmaster there. Since most of their shopping was done in Baddeck it was more convenient for these residents to pick up their mail at that location.

The post office at Upper Washabuck was kept by Angus MacDonald (*Aonghas mac Ruairidh 'ic Alasdair*). It opened on August 1, 1865, and was located about a mile-and-a-quarter (2 km) east of Washabuck Bridge. The Lower Washabuck post office was located about one mile from the eastern end. It was decided by the post office department to appoint Angus MacNeil as postmaster, as he was more centrally located in what is now Washabuck Centre and that location was more central between Upper Washabuck post office and MacKay Point. The people of this vicinity began to get their mail from then on at Angus MacNeil's post office.

```
                    McKAYS POINT
Open Jul. 1,1864   Closed Apr.30,1881   Reopened Jun. 1,1885 Closed
Oct.31,1897  Loc. 46/04N 60/44W  Serving Office: Ferry Landing.
Postmasters:
Jul. 1,1864-          1871      Michael McLean
     1871-Feb.11,1871           Malcolm McLean
Jun. 1,1871-Apr.30,1881         Malcolm McLean Jr.       office closed
Jun. 1,1885-Oct.31,1897         M. McLean                office reopened
```

This office may have been issued a second hammer for the reopening however, as 1885 was a "missing proof" year, no proof exists.

After a few years Hon. Charles J. MacDonald, post office inspector at Halifax arrived and closed McKay Point post office. When Angus MacNeil died, his son Alexander was appointed postmaster. Upon Alexander [Sandy] selling his property, the post office was then transferred to Rory Ranald "Klondike" MacDonald. After his death, his widow Agnes was appointed post mistress.[15]

8-1 MacKay Point Post Office Stamp. From Post Offices of Cape Breton, Volume 3, Victoria County, 1989. Courtesy of Carl Munden

Archival data states that the MacKay Point post office officially opened on July 1, 1864, and closed on April 30, 1881. It reopened on June 1, 1885, and finally closed for good on October 31, 1897.[16]

As Carl Munden so astutely discerns in the Foreword of his work on Cape Breton post offices:

> Two interesting points that kept reoccurring during the research were (i) the number of offices that were named after the pm rather than the location and (ii) the political ebb and flow of the Grits and Tories in regard to pm appointments. You can almost pick out the years in which the federal election caused a change of government."[17]

Lower Washabuck Post Office

8-2 Lower Washabuck Post Office Stamp. From Post Offices of Cape Breton, Volume 3, Victoria County, 1989. Courtesy of Carl Munden.

The Lower Washabuck post office officially opened on August 1881 at the residence of Angus [Eòin] MacNeil. Two of his sons were postmasters as well: Michael from 1894 until April 1895 and Alexander "Sandy" from 1904 until his resignation in May 1906. At that time, Rory Ranald MacDonald became the new postmaster at the post office which was operated from his home. He remained postmaster until his passing in 1909. His widow Agnes and son Francis B. became postmistress and acting postmaster respectively.

Francis B. resigned in 1947. The post office was then taken over by James A. MacLean, a Second World War veteran, and operated by his wife Irene until the onset of rural delivery in February 1959.[18]

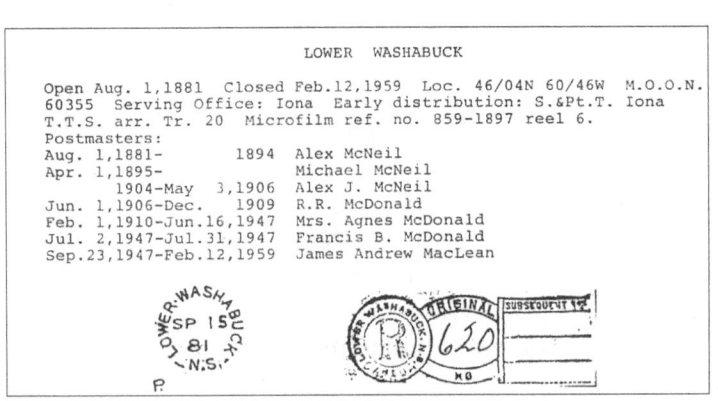

```
                    LOWER  WASHABUCK
Open Aug. 1,1881   Closed Feb.12,1959   Loc. 46/04N 60/46W  M.O.O.N.
60355  Serving Office: Iona  Early distribution: S.&Pt.T. Iona
T.T.S. arr. Tr. 20  Microfilm ref. no. 859-1897 reel 6.
Postmasters:
Aug. 1,1881-            1894     Alex McNeil
Apr. 1,1895-
      1904-May 3,1906            Michael McNeil
                                 Alex J. McNeil
Jun. 1,1906-Dec.        1909     R.R. McDonald
Feb. 1,1910-Jun.16,1947          Mrs. Agnes McDonald
Jul. 2,1947-Jul.31,1947          Francis B. McDonald
Sep.23,1947-Feb.12,1959          James Andrew MacLean
```

The Last Post

Lower Washabuck's last Post Mistress Irene MacLean recalls the mail being delivered by Murdock (Michael D.) MacNeil of Iona three times a week.

> He was a consistent and very dependable mail driver during those last years of local post offices. If he was running late due to late trains or bad road conditions he many times accepted my invitation to a meal. He especially enjoyed a salt cod dinner, a long-time Washabuck staple.

Irene, who arrived in Washabuck in 1946, remembers Murdock delivering the tri-weekly mail to Frank MacDonald's by horse and wagon or horse and sleigh, depending on the season.[19] When rural route delivery was introduced in 1959, Murdock delivered the mail daily six days a week. His wife, with daughter Anita, and later their sons, Jerry and Larry, faithfully continued the delivery service until ca. 2000 when the delivery was reduced to five days a week.

Irene did not consider the postal business a burden and adds:

> We had a small pigeon-holed wooden box in one corner of the living room and everything postal was kept in that location. There were no flyers in those days. The heaviest items were the seasonal Eaton and Simpson mail-order catalogues.[20]

Alex D. MacLean records that:

> The early postmasters were paid a stipend for their duties, initially $8.00 per annum which increased gradually to $10.00 and in later decades to $12.00. The postmaster was paid quarterly and not in cash but rather in the equivalent in postage stamps.[21] Cash was scarce!

Irene relates her experience.

> At the time of the introduction of Rural Route Delivery [1959] I was earning $13 a month as Postmistress which was paid in quarterly cheques of $39.00.[22]

Upper Washabuck Post Office

The Upper Washabuck post office officially opened on April 1, 1865, in the home of Roderick (*macAlasdair*) MacDonald. His sons Angus and Malcolm also served in the same capacity until they resigned and the post office was relocated on April 1, 1901, to the neighbouring residence of Kate MacNeil, wife of Rory J. MacNeil. Kate served as postmaster until May 1944 when her son Peter Malcolm took over the responsibilities. Peter and his wife Bea ran it until the arrival of rural route delivery on February 12, 1959.[23]

8-3(a, b) Upper Washabuck Post Office Stamp. From Post Offices of Cape Breton, Volume 3, Victoria County, 1989. Courtesy of Carl Munden.

8-4(a, b) Grand Narrows Rear and St. Columba Post Office Stamp. From Post Offices of Cape Breton, Volume 3, Victoria County, 1989. Courtesy of Carl Munden.

8-5 Washabuck Bridge Post Office Stamp. From Post Offices of Cape Breton, Volume 3.

8-6(a, b) Washabuck Centre Post Office Stamp. From Post Offices of Cape Breton, Volume 3, Victoria County, 1989. Courtesy of Carl Munden.

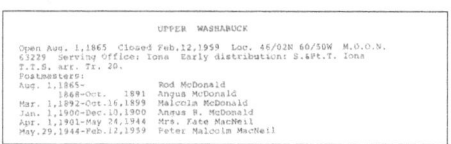

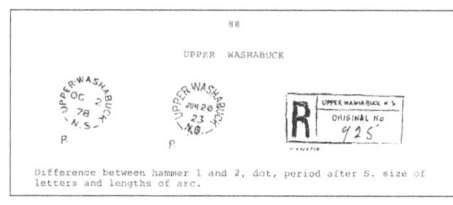

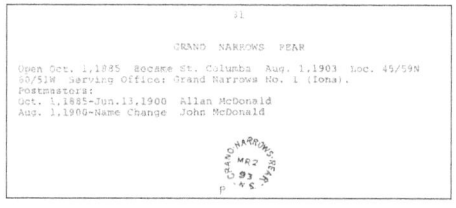

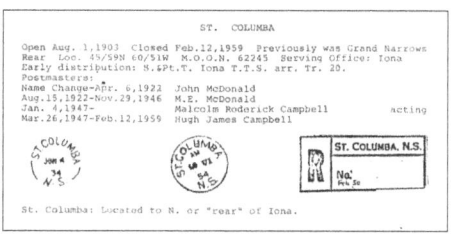

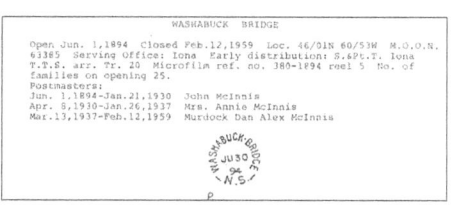

Grand Narrows Rear Post Office

Grand Narrows Rear (St. Columba) post office opened on October 1, 1885 at the residence of Allan MacDonald. Allan served as postmaster until June 13, 1900. On August 1, 1903 the name changed from Grand Narrows Rear to St. Columba Post Office and John MacDonald became the new postmaster.[24] He served until April 6, 1922 when the operation was transferred to the residence of Michael E. MacDonald who served as postmaster until November 1946. Malcolm Campbell filled in as acting postmaster until March 1947 when it was transferred to Hugh James Campbell, son of Malcolm and Liza. The service remained in the Campbell residence until the arrival of the rural route delivery in February 1959.[25]

Washabuck Bridge Post Office

Washabuck Bridge post office opened its doors on June 1, 1894 in the residence of John MacInnis. After John died, his widow Annie ran the service from April 1930 until January 1937, when she resigned the position in favour of her son Murdock. He became postmaster and continued the service until the arrival of rural delivery in February 1959.[26]

Washabuck Centre Post Office

Washabuck Centre post office began service on October 15, 1909, with Neil Peter MacLean serving as postmaster. Neil Peter served until May 1936, when the service was transferred to Roddie James MacLean's residence.

He provided the service until January 1941, when it reverted to Neil Peter MacLean's residence under the guidance of his son Neil Stephen, who served as postmaster until the arrival of rural delivery in February 1959.[27]

Mail Couriers

Neil P. S. MacLean writes in an article in *The Casket* in October 1939:

> There was but one courier from Little Narrows to MacKays Point. When Angus [*Eòin*] MacNeil got the post office [1881] they called there, thence by Peter S. MacLean's which was [the location of] the ferry to Baddeck. David Burton from Inlet Shore was the first courier to take the mails from Alba to Baddeck, calling at Angus MacNeil's post office semi-weekly. During the summer season and up to the closing of the ice on the [St. Patrick] Channel his teams were cared for by the ferry man [Peter S. MacLean]. When Mr. Burton gave up the job the mail contract was taken over by Roland Campbell, Eastmere [*sic*] or Alba as it is now called. Then Charles MacDonald was the courier, father of the ex-councilor Neil Hugh MacDonald, District 14. D[onald] Morrison etc. came next. Then the [Department] gave up sending the mails to Baddeck and the couriers returned home after depositing their mails at Lower Washabuck post office. The route of those times has changed. Now [1939] it leaves Iona, comes through St. Columba to Washabuck Bridge, thence to Upper and Lower Washabuck returning by way of Gillis Point and Grass Cove.[28]

8-7 Neil P. S. MacLean (1865-1947), Lower Washabuck. Courtesy of his granddaughter Lexie Reid, North Sydney, NS.

8-8 Alex D. MacLean (1889-1974) courtesy of Archie and Marie MacLean, Washabuck.

Alex D. MacLean continues:

> For many years the mails were conveyed from Iona and Alba through to Baddeck by way of "the little harbor" that fronts on the property of [Rory J. and Sarah MacLean]. The return trip was made by the same route. Some of the early mail carriers were the late John S. MacNeil, Iona, and later on his son, the late Francis X. MacNeil, also of Iona. For a time, Michael D. MacNeil (Red Michael), Iona, carried the mails. These former served in comparatively recent times. Before their day the mails were carried by John Gillis, Alba: Donald Morrison (Ban), Little Narrows. Another carrier was Murdock Morrison, an uncle of this Donald Morrison.[29]

Neil (P. S.) MacLean takes issue with Alex D, stating that, "The Saturday mail coming from Iona was discontinued long ago. This is the mail A. D. mentioned that was ferried from the little harbour."[30]

Some Washabuck residents used to pick up their mail at John MacNaughton's at St. Patrick's Channel as it had been a way station since 1855 and received full-fledge post office status in 1876. It remained open until 1968 when rural route replaced its services.[31]

The Michael D. [MacNeil] family of Iona had a role in delivering the rural mail. Michael D. was referred to locally as "Red Mike." He was also a highly regarded blacksmith. Documentation provided by the MacNeil

family outlines that Michael D. McNeil (blacksmith) began the services on April 1, 1926, between the Iona post office and Lower Washabuck post office three times a week. Courier service contracts in the "Conveyance of His Majesty's Mails" reveal there were some constraints:

> The route to be pursued in the conveyance of the Mails to be via the Post Offices at Grass Cove, St. Columba, Washabuck Bridge and Upper Washabuck to Lower Washabuck, returning via Washabuck Centre, Gillies [sic] Point East, McNeil's Vale and Gillies [sic] Point. Distance 31 1/8 miles (50 km). The mails to be conveyed by horse and vehicle.

The contract further stipulates that the courier is to:

> Leave Iona P.O. on Tuesday, Thursday and Saturday half an hour after the arrival of the mail train from Sydney and proceed over the described round route, serving the post offices named and performing the round trip within six hours and a quarter.

> Furthermore, the rate of traveling to be uniform so as the nature of the roads and the state of the weather will permit and the average speed of five miles per hour including stoppages.[32]

A further contract starting October 2, 1950, between His Majesty's Mails and Murdock McNeil, (Michael D.'s son), outlines the same information, the only difference that the mails were to be delivered on Monday, Wednesday and Fridays. The contract was in force until 1954 at a rate of 17.62 cents per mile (1.6 km).[33]

Perils of a Mail Driver

On occasion in those early years, Murdock's brother Francis (Michael D.) drove the mail. He delivered a newspaper to John MacNeil who along with his wife Mary *Beag* ran a general store at Washabuck Centre. On this particular day, Mary was away and John invited Francis into their living accommodations located above the store for a bite to eat. Francis gratefully accepted the invitation.

John MacNeil had just finished cooking a batch of eels. Typically, eels were parboiled for 10-15 minutes before being doused with salt and pepper and then oven-baked, slowly and subtly browned at a moderate temperature in the trusty old wood stove. They are considered a delicacy by many and were certainly a staple of the Washabuck community for generations. John had boiled his eels without baking them as he probably preferred them that way.

John placed the platter of boiled eels in front of Francis and went into the adjoining room to read the newspaper leaving Francis (who never did eat eels) alone to enjoy his meal.

Francis tried a few of the eels but he just could not stomach the plateful so he wrapped them in a piece of old newspaper that was on the table and jammed the remnants into the pocket of his heavy coat. He did not want to offend John's kindness by leaving the eels on the plate, so as Francis was taking leave, he expressed his thanks to John for his hospitality and of course the eels. "They were good, very good!" said Francis. John replied: "Well they must have been goddamn good, you even ate the bones!"[34]

The Mail Must Get Through

When Rural Route #1 delivery was introduced, it was for six days per week for a total distance of 33 miles (53) per return trip. Murdock was serving 49 customers for 305 days a year. A subsequent contract reduced the operating days to 253; the frequency of delivery was reduced to 5 days per week while he was serving 53 customers over an expanded route of 53.1 km, return trip.[35]

Road conditions could very often be horrible. Washabuck Bridge postmaster Murdock MacInnis related that one particular spring season in the 1960s, Murdock (Michael D.) faithfully delivered the mailbag on foot because of impassible road conditions. He recalled Murdock leaving his vehicle at Effie's Hill at Washabuck Bridge, toting the slung mailbag on his back, over the flat and up the steep rise to the MacInnis residence, a distance of a good 1,500 feet, for seventeen consecutive mail days.[36] Unwavering, mail driver Murdock made a point of ensuring that the mail always got through.

Murdock usually had company for the ride, including nephews Walter, Jackie and Hector MacNeil. On his retirement in 1971 his own family took over the contract. Wife Margaret sometimes drove accompanied by daughter Anita or sons Jerry and Larry. Larry recalls that he obtained his own driver's license in 1974 and from that point on, he delivered the mail.

> The route never varied except for weather or an emergency. I would very often have a passenger or if not, then Carl (Frank) [MacNeil] would jump in just to go for the drive as I fuelled up at Peter F.'s service station. Michael MacKenzie from Christmas Island would deliver the mail, which included the newspapers, to the Iona post office from the Sydney depot. Sorting would take us about an hour and I'd be on the road by eleven; drive through Gillis Point, up the New Glen road to Roderick's and Neil James's, then on to MacKays Point and from there to Murdock MacInnis's at Washabuck Bridge, before heading back over Washabuck Mountain as my father always called the St. Columba Road portion of the trek and return to Iona by 12:15 on a regular day.

Larry, like all the Michael D.'s, were car enthusiasts. He recalls the various vehicles the family used, which included 1972 and '74 Comets, a '72 Ambassador and a '78 Ford Station wagon. He also remembers driving a black '58 Ford, a blue '65 Ford and a '67 Ford that had at one time been a new car to Dr. Jim MacLean of Inverness.

8-9 A few members of the Michael D. MacNeil family, Iona L-R: Francis, Michael D., Murdock, Peter (a cousin) and Katie. Michael D. passed away in 1951. Courtesy of Murdock's daughter Anita MacNeil, Iona.

Murdock passed away in 1987 and the family ended the courier service a couple of months after his passing. Thus ended sixty one years of faithful, dedicated and dependable service by successive generations of the Michael D. family to a dispersed clientele throughout a desolate territory enduring less than stellar driving conditions, even on good days.[37]

Tribute

Murdock (Michael D.) and his wife Margaret MacNeil were fêted by the community-at-large at the Washabuck Community Centre on May 14, 1971, on his retirement as postal courier. The following excerpt of an address will give a sense of appreciation of the degree of gratefulness that the community felt toward Murdock and his family's years of service, dedication and commitment.

> The motto of the United States Postal Service which has been applied to postmen around the world, reads like this: "Neither snow nor rain nor heat nor gloom of night, stays these couriers from the swift completion of their appointed rounds."
>
> After forty odd years of delivering mail to Grass Cove, Gillis Point, Washabuck and St. Columba, I feel no hesitation in paraphrasing that famous motto in this manner: "Neither flood, nor mud, nor balky horse, nor broken culvert, nor flat tire, nor insufficient postage, has ever daunted our honoured guest in performing his duties in an efficient, dependable and praiseworthy manner."
>
> It is in this spirit of appreciation and gratitude that we have gathered here tonight, to recognize your service to the community over a long number of years. A period of service which began before many here tonight were born and which has seen a great many changes in the Postal System and in the community you have served.
>
> Although the Canadian Post Office has been modernized and the horsepower increased over a hundredfold, yet conditions of travel remain a vivid reminder, at times of earlier days.
>
> However, efficient dispatch of an important public service and unfailing devotion to duty are not the only or perhaps primary reason for our respect and commendation at this time. Instead, the many kindnesses you have shown, the many unpaid favours you have bestowed over

and above the call of duty – for these you will be especially remembered.

A drive to or from the train, a pick-up for a pedestrian, an errand run to save someone an inconvenience, a stubborn car started by a push or a tow or some expert advice – by all these and many too numerous to mention, all performed willingly and gladly and without complaint – you have placed us forever in your debt.

Our purpose here tonight and our small gift, is not an attempt to repay that debt. It is simply an expression, to you and your wife and family of our sincere appreciation and gratitude, and an opportunity for all those on your rural route to say. "Thank you, success in the future and God's Blessings."[38]

8-10 Murdock (Michael D.) and wife Margaret MacNeil are fêted at the Washabuck Community Centre by grateful residents for the family's unwavering loyalty as mail couriers. Murdock tests out his new retirement chair, while Archie, Michael A. and Martin MacLean, look on, May 14, 1971. Courtesy of Anita MacNeil, Iona.

9 – Shipbulding

The natural waterways of Cape Breton Island were the roadways of the Gaels, just as they had been for the ancient Mi'kmaq. Bras d'Or Lake which imprints itself so prominently upon the Island's geographic interior was the obvious, convenient and commodious thoroughfare for most of the transport. Indeed, the Bras d'Or provided not only a means of transportation, but also communication and livelihood for early residents. It was only natural that the pioneers, so many of them hardy fishermen and renowned as seamen, engaged in building and sailing small and large vessels for business ventures in their new domain around lakeshore.

In his diary, Robert Elmsley lists 49 vessels built in the Baddeck area between the years 1840 -1888.[1] At least three of those vessels and possibly a fourth were built along the shores of Washabuck.

Triumph

The first ship to be built in Lower Washabuck was the brig *Triumph*. This square-rigged ship with two masts was built at MacKay Point for James Anderson. He was a Sydney merchant who arrived in 1835 and soon relocated to Baddeck. In the earliest days of Baddeck, Anderson opened a store on Mutton Island, (later renamed Duke of Kent, then Duffus Island, then finally Kidston Island). Captain John Parker in his book *Cape Breton Ships and Men* recounts that Charles Kelly a shipwright from North Sydney built the brig for Anderson. The *Triumph*'s dimensions were 82.6 ft x 20 ft x 15.9 ft (25 m x 6 m x 4.8 m) and it was registered as being 205 tons. She was constructed in 1841.[2] Parker notes: "The following is by no means clear, yet a news item states that the work on the vessel was carried out in Washabuck but the [Shipping] register shows Baddeck as her birthplace." Parker avows, "I believe she was built at MacKays Point."[2] Robert Elmsley notes on page

155 of extracts of his diary "Brig launched at McKay's Point in September 1841."

The *Triumph* may have been built on Sand Point, located to the west of MacKay Point. Sand Point, as its name suggests is a sandy point of land that juts into St. Patrick's Channel adjacent to Bone Island. Since the water there is bold and deepens suddenly, this natural site would provide a logical and practical location to easily launch such a vessel.

Parker continues: "William Leslie was her master and an undated news item states that James Anderson was drowned off the coast of Portugal while a passenger in his own vessel but the fate of the brig was not given."[3] Elmsley notes that Anderson drowned at Oporto [Portugal].[4]

Alex D. MacLean writes that:

> While [the *Triumph*] was under construction this part of Washabuckt was visited by a disastrous fire, and a lot of valuable standing timber was destroyed. The new brig came very near going up in flames at the same time. Malcolm MacLean (*Calum mac Lachlainn*) unwittingly started the fire. The time of year was August, and everything was unusually dry. Malcolm while hewing a log paused from his labours to light his pipe and unnoticed, a spark fell either from his pipe or flint and soon the dry grass and chips which littered the ground were a roaring blaze. The fire could not be prevented from spreading and it did much damage before it burned itself out.[5]

Alexander

The schooner *Alexander* was the second vessel built in Lower Washabuck. It was built and owned by Alexander MacLean (*Lachlainn*) and his six sons. The family was skilled in several trades and was especially adept with the saw, axe and adze.

The Alexander was built in 1858 on the shore of the lands fronting the land of Alexander MacLean and which is today [2013] owned by the descendants of William and *Beatag* MacKenzie. The site is still today referred to as, "The Launch." The dimensions of the schooner were, 45.3 ft x 15.2 ft x 6.5 ft (13.8 m x 4.6 m x 2 m). She had a net tonnage of 24 tons [6]

The *Alexander* was launched in late 1858. Robert Elmsley jots in his diary on December 30, 1858 "*Alexander* came from Washabuck"[7] and on January 11, 1859, "Session Day. Very cold. *Alexander* came yesterday."[8] According to Alex D. MacLean the *Alexander* made her maiden voyage to Halifax. On this trip she was captained by Peter S. MacLean (*Peadar mac Ruairidh*) of Washabuck, a nephew of the owner Alexander MacLean.

On her second voyage the *Alexander* was lost at sea with all hands aboard. She was bound for Newfoundland with a cargo of livestock and produce. She was last seen sailing out Big Bras d'Or Channel on Christmas

Day 1859. No account of her was ever received and it was taken for granted that she foundered in a severe storm that raged off the Cape Breton coast at that time.[9]

Elmsley's entries in his diary for the week of December 23-31 1859 read:

> December 23: Dull, raw, snow squalls.
> December 25: Coldest day of the season, blows, drifts.
> December 26: Fine and clear
> December 27: Snow-storm, and continued until Thursday (29th). Very cold & wintery.
> December 31: Very cold and stormy [10]

Hector MacLean (*Eachann mac Nill Ghobha*) was Captain on the fatal voyage. Ronald MacSween was Supercargo. Both men were from Beaver Cove, Cape Breton Island. Lost as well were three of Alexander MacLean's sons, James, Nicholas and Michael. James was married and left a widow Catherine (MacNeil). They had no family.[11] She later married Hector R. MacNeil of Iona.[12]

A *Cumha,* a Gaelic song entitled *Lament for the Three Brothers* was composed in 1860 to commemorate the loss of the Alexander and her crew. It was composed by Peter MacLean a brother of James, Nicholas and Michael.[13]

Commemorative Songs

Lament for the Three Brothers:

9-1 Sheet music, "Lament for the Three Brothers" (Music transcriptions are included for the first verse and chorus. Each verse will dictate its own variation on the melody, reflecting the singer's personal style.)

CUMHA A' THRIUIR BHRAITHREAN

(Le Peadair Alasdair 'ic Lachlann, Washabuckt Iosal, C.B., 1860)

Och nan och, mo ageul dubhach,
Sinn 'nar naoinear fo mhulad;
na'm bu bhard mi cho fileant',
Gun deannain sa cumha;
Fhuair mi reausan an iomadach cas air,
Fhuair mi reasan, etc..

Fhuair mi reausan gun teagamh,
Ghuir an t-eug oiran, 's cha beag o,
Na fir threuna 'n am freagairt,
Sheasadh cruadal, "s nach taicheadh;
Cha tig 'nar n-eirig no sheasas an aite,
Cha tig 'nar n-eirig etc..

's e so gramhradh a' chruadail,
Thug air falbh thar a' chuain sibh;
Cha b'o moud a chuid Fuachd,
A dh'fhag mise cho truagh dheth;
ach g'un thuit leis thoirt bhuam mo
thruir bhraithrean.
Ach g'un thuit leis etc.

BBe sud soitheach no diachuinn,
'ga togail 's 'ga deanamh,
Ged a rinneadh 's am bhliadhn' I,
B'fhearr nach fhacas bior riamh dhi,
Mu'n do thuit a mach diubhail cho trath leath'
Mu'n do thuit a mach etc.

Dh' fhalbh criau oirr' cho tapaidh,
Ann am stiuradh 's pasgadh,
...' am an fheumach nach lapach;
Ged bhiodh i seideadh le frasan,
Mur a bhith cho re fhaisa 's a bha'm bas dhaibh.
Mur a bhith cho ro fhaisa etc.

Tha 'ur cairdean gu tursach,
's ur n-athair noo shunndach,
's tric no deoir air a shuilean,
'a beag an ioghnadh sin leamsa,
Dh'fhalbh an taic bha ri chul ri son uaith.
Dh'fhalbh an taic etc.

Tha ur mathair gu tursach,
's beag an t-ioghnadh i liathadh,
Dh'araich mic a bha ciatach,
's a bha foghainteach lionmhor,
's beag an diugh the dhe'n t-sianar an lathair,
's beag an diugh etc.

Och nan och mo sgeul duilich,
Sibh 'n ur sineadh 's an fheamainn,
Ann an siabun 's a ghainniamh,
Far nach dirich ur n-anail,
's mor an diubhail ur sgaradh bho'r cairdean.
's mor an diubhail etc.

Sud an turas bha cianail,
's mor an dolaidh a' thriall leis,
Thus i coignear do'n t-sionuidhe achd,
Oir 's coltach gur fior e.
's nach tig naidheachd gu siorruidh gu'r cairdean,
's nach tig naidheachd etc.

'S o gu'n robh 'n uair air a cumadh,
C'uim nach d'fhuair sibh o'n chunnart,
's gur cruaidh fhortanarh leinno,
Nach o'n uaigh rinn ur buinning,
Ach an cuan far hach fuirich sibh samhach,
Ach an cuan etc.

Sidh mi nis a co-dhunadh
Cha'n eil feum bhi gur n'iomndrainn,
OBn 's o toil righ na Dulaidh,
ur cuireadh gu ionnsuidh,
Bidh sinn leagte le umhlachd dha ordugh,
Bidh sinn leagte etc.

LAMENT FOR THE THREE BROTHERS.

(Peter MacLean, Washabuck, C.B., 1860)

Alas of all alas. My mournful story
We are nine of us in grief
If I was a poet of elegance
I would make a poem in praise of the dead
For that I have reason in many cases
For that I have reason in many cases

I got a reason undoubtly
Which put the death to us, and not trifling
The able men, in time of answering
Who would stand hardship and wouldn't run off
And cannot come in our time that will stand in their place
And cannot come in our time that will stand in their place

This is the winter of hardship
That took you from us across the ocean
It was not its cold
That left me so downcast
But to take away from me my three brothers
But to take away from me my three brothers.

That was a vessel of trouble
In building and designing
Although she was made in one year
It would be better if she was never seen
Before what happened so early with her
Before what happened so early with her

There went with her a crew so smart
In steering and warping sails
In time of need would not be slim
Altho it would be blowing with showers
If it was not so near death was to them
If it was not so near death was to them

Your relatives are in grief
And your father in low spirits
Often with tears in his eyes
Which is not strange to me
Gone is the support behind him
Gone is the support behind him

Your mother is lamenting
No wonder, she is so old
The mothered sons that was handsome
And was brave and valorous and many
Very few of the six are in sight today
Very few of the six are in sight today

Och na Och. My mournful story
You to be lying in entanglement
In drifting and in sandy bottom
Where your breath cannot rise
Great is the calamity you to be separated from your relatives
Great is the calamity you to be separated from your relatives.

That is the trip that was sorrowful
So great is the ruination that follows
That took five to eternity
As is likely to be true
That your story will never come to your relatives
That your story will never come to your relatives.

It was that the hour was counted
Was that you did not escape the danger
And so unfortunate for us
That it wasn't the grave that won you
But the ocean where you lie still
But the ocean where you lie still.

I will now come to a close
It's no use to be missing you
For it was the Will of the King of Glory
To invite you to Himself
We will now accept His Order with homage
We will now accept his Order with homage.

"The Schooner *Alexander*"

A second song was also composed to commemorate the loss of the *Alexander* and her crew. Its composer is unknown and the song would have been lost but that a close rapport existed among the people of Iona Rear, Barra Glen and Washabuck. The song was preserved orally by Mickey (*mac Bean Nilleig*) MacNeil (1917-1995) of Iona Rear who had learned it from his neighbour "Red" Neil MacNeil. Mickey agreed to record it in 1983. This song is entitled "The Schooner Alexander." Rod C. MacNeil of Barra Glen, a Gàidhlig authority and singer, made the comment at the time that: "Whoever composed the song was undoubtedly from the [Washabuck] area."[14][15]

9-2 S. R. (Stephen Rory) MacNeil, Barra Glen and Mickey (Bean Nilleig) MacNeil, Iona.

Ocean Lilly

Captain John Parker believed the *Ocean Lilly* was built at Big Bras d'Or in 1885.[16] When this issue was raised with him in 1972, Parker responded:

> [The] *Ocean Lilly* had her people and builders from Washabuck but her building place was noted in the Sydney Register as being at Bras d'Or. Years ago I met an old fellow at Bras d'Or who said he remembered this vessel being built at a site just above the present government wharf. It is said that quite a few others were built at the same place. I have since found that there have been about six building sites along both sides. Sometimes when you try to nail down a man he will tell you what you want to hear....[17]

The *Ocean Lilly* was a tern schooner, a vessel with three masts and fore-and-aft sails. Her dimensions were 108 ft x 25.2 ft x 9 ft and her net tonnage was 136 tons.

*The melody of the verse often varies according to how the singer wishes to interpret the lyrics. The above notation is merely a guide to follow.

1) Nuair a chunnacas a' falbh sibh   Is sgoltadh fairge 'ga rocadh
Le cri'u a bha ainmeil   Ged bu charach no blaigh ur coltas
Chuir sibh rithe a cuid aodaich   Le bhuill chaol air a' *bhuilc-head*
'S am bratach Breatannach r'iomhach   Air bh'arr a' chuinn air an *top-mast*
Ho Hi Ho Hi Ri   Ho Ri Thall

9-3 Sheet music for *Alexander.*

An Long Alexander[17]
Chorus:
Ho-Hi-Ho-Hi-Ri-Ho-Ro-Thall
Ho-Hi-Ho-Hi-Ri-Ho-Thall
Saoil an creid me o c'ach
Nach deach air b'athadh ro'n 'am.

1) Nuair a chunnacas a' falbh sibh
Is sgoltadh fairge 'ga rocadh
Le cri'u a bha ainmeil
Ged bu charach no blaigh ur coltas
Chuir sibh rithe a cuid aodaich
Le bhuill chaol air a' *bhuilc-head*
'S am bratach Breatannach r'iomhach
Air bh'arr a' chuinn air an *top-mast*

2) An darna oidhche an de'idh fh'agail
Th'ainig stoirm a bha goirt' oirr
O'n Ear agus an Ear-dheas
Chaidh an 'ardan gu bochdan
Bha MacAoghnais ag innseadh
An naidheachd fh'irinn mu dheidhinn
Nach robh riamh a leithid
Do sh'ide ann am Bras d'Or

The Schooner Alexander
Chorus:
Ho-Hi-Ho-Hi-Ri-Ho-Thall
Ho-Hi-Ho-Hi-Ri-Ho-Thall
I think as do others
They were drowned before their time

1) With splitting waves and rocking
With a crew that was renouned
Although cunning was part of your looks
You put up the sails
With neat effect on her bulk-head
And with the elegant British flag
Over the rigging on the top-mast

2) The second night after leaving
There came a storm that was notable
The winds from the east and south east
The sea became mountainous
The son of Angus was telling
The true story about it
That there was never the like
Of such weather on the Bras d'Or

3) Tha MacLachlainn ro-bhr`onach
Ann a she`ombar 'na shuidhe
On nach cluinn e an st`oraidh
Nach eil comh-luchd a' tighinn
Chuir e air a chuid bhr`ogan
'S ruith e do'n st`oir le deal
Ghlas e fhe'in le a sh`oas
Ged nach `oladh e pr`is dheth

4) Gur e mise tha bochd dheth
Gun sporran ga'm fh`agail
On nach urrain dhol treabhadh
A dheanadh coltach ri nabaidh
Gun fiodh poidhle son fheansaidh
No gun clachair gu te`arnadh
'Se gach n`ith gu h-`iosal
Gun mac dhuinn ann an l`athair.

5) Tha do pharantan tuirseach
Tha do pheathraichean dubhach
Tha do ch`airdean fo thrioblaid
'S mor an litir a sgr`iob iad
"Se Alexander an dunaich
Ma rinn thu builleach air b`athadh
Dia df'fh`ag thu fo ch`uram
Ma tha air chunntas an l`athair.

6) Clann Alasdair mac Lachlainn
Bha iad smiorail `s tapaidh
'S gu sgairteil `s a h-uile fear
A chaidh a mach as an `aite
'Se Eachann gobha an sgiobair
Gu math r`eite nuair dh'fh`ag e
Gun do ghleus gu sti`uireach
'S lig e sm`uid dheth gun fh`aile
Chorus.

3) Mac Lachlan is sorrowful
Sitting in his room
Since he wouldn't get the story
That his crew was returning
He put on his shoes
And he ran to the store with zeal
He locked himself with his comfort
Although he wouldn't drink what he had spent

4) It is me that who is badly off
Without a purse with anything left
Since I cannot do the plowing
As well as my neighbour
Without a pole for a fence
Or a worker to nail it
Is what left me so low
Without a son of ours in our presence

5) Your parents are sad
Your sisters are tearful
Your friends are in trouble
Many a letter they wrote
It's Alexander the misfortune
That was the cause of all the drowning
God left you under care
If that is reckoned in his presence

6) Children of Alexander MacLachlann
You are energetic and clever
And as diligent as others
Who have gone away from this place?
Hector the skipper
Had the ship in good order when they left
He was attuned to the steering
Leaving an odorless spray in her wake
Chorus.

Jimmy (Dan) MacKinnon (1905-1992) claimed the *Ocean Lilly* was built during 1885 on the pioneer property of Rory J. MacDonald, along the shore of *Peigag ni'n Ruairidh* landing, which lies between the former Devoe and Jim Alec MacDougall properties. Malcolm (Murdock) MacLeod of Cain's Mountain did the caulking on the ship. Malcolm had learned this art from his father Murdock and this was the third or fourth vessel on which he had plied his craft. Some Washabuck men found suitable wood on their woodlots for the vessel's bracing knee timbers. For these they were paid one dollar per knee. The scuttlebutt around the community was that the *Ocean Lilly* was owned by someone in Halifax. Upon her launch she nearly struck the opposite shore of Washabuck River before being safely secured. According to Jimmy (Dan) MacKinnon once the vessel sailed, no one in the Washabuck community ever heard of her again.[18]

Robert Elmsley notes in his diary August 10, 1886, "*Ocean Lilly*, 135 tons, 3 masts, owner K. McDonald, came to Baddeck on Friday 13th August."[19, 20]

MacIver Vessel

Archie MacIver (1898-1984) recalls hearing that the MacIver family of Washabuck had built a schooner on the shoreline of MacIver's Cove in Washabuck and then sailed her to Newfoundland on at least one voyage. Upon her return she was frozen in the ice in MacIver's Cove during the winter months and the owners later sold her in North Sydney.[21] Murdock MacInnis also related a story about a MacIver vessel that returned with a load of coal to South Cove and remained frozen in the ice there. She supplied coal to that community for the winter. He reports further, that John E. MacIver (Archie's father), was an astute navigator. "Bye Jeez, when help was looked for, he could be awakened from a deep sleep, take a glance at a starry sky, and on the dot tell the helmsman where they were," exclaimed an animated Murdock.[22]

So was this the same vessel? Possibly.

9-4 Jimmy MacKinnon and Walter MacDougall.

9-5 MacLean fishermen and sailors L-R: Michael A., Joe (Red Rory), Martin, Murdock, and Peter F. MacLean. Front center is Peter's son-in-law, Larry Nestman, Halifax. The occasion was the annual launching of Peter F's twenty-six foot sloop. The yacht was designed by Peter and built by brother, Murdock, Washabuck Centre, August 1977.

10 – Transportation: Water, Land and Air

Wharves

A May 1985 community-based economic development study for Central Cape Breton, identified weaknesses within its communities and outlined groundwork challenges and hurdles to be over-come during the ensuing decades.

One of the key economic sectors highlighted in the document referred to Bras d'Or Lake and the role it played from a historical and developmental perspective of the region and the potential they held into the future. The early transportation corridor throughout Central Cape Breton was of course via water.

At least fifteen communities bordering the shoreline of Central Cape Breton benefited economically from bustling government wharves during the opening seven decades of the 20th century. These wharves were located in the communities of Boisdale, Shenacadie, Christmas Island, Benacadie, Grand Narrows, Estmere, Ottawa Brook, Iona, Grass Cove,[1] Pine Brook, MacKay Point, Washabuck Centre, Washabuck River, South Cove and Little Narrows, which sported two wharves. Regrettably, by 1985 all of these government wharves, with the sole exception of Iona, had disappeared.

There were also three corporate shipping piers, one situated at each of the three gypsum quarries on the peninsula, Grass Cove, Ottawa Brook and Little Narrows.[2] Only the Little Narrows pier survives.

It is within this historical background that one can better understand how these smaller settlements encircling the shorelines of Central Cape Breton sustained themselves, developed, and even flourished economically as rural entities. They achieved this success effectively and were able to efficiently move and market their commodities, pulpwood, lumber, livestock, produce, fish and shellfish, via this network of community wharves, while expediting passage for travellers along the same corridor.

Washabuck, through its main entry and exit points with government wharves located at Pine Brook, MacKay Point, Washabuck Centre and Washabuck River, provided convenient, practical, and pivotal sites for the general populace to network more easily with one another. Just as importantly, these wharves provided the outports of Central Cape Breton with the same vital transportation links that had previously only been accessible to larger communities on the northern side of the lake, such as Baddeck, Nyanza, Whycocomagh and Grand Narrows on the Barra Strait. The more exotic destinations of the Sydneys, Ingonish, St. Peter's, Mulgrave, Georgetown PEI,

and ultimately Boston, were now just as easily accessible to the Washabuck community as they had been earlier to the larger settlements. By 1890, with the advent of the railroad and its interconnecting services, delivering people and packages to the villages of Iona and Grand Narrows became ever more expeditious, as those communities were transfer depots for all of Central Cape Breton.

10-1 At one time, fifteen communities in Central Cape Breton were served by government wharves.

In these lakeside communities where traditional forestry, farming and fishing activities were the principal industries, wharves provided basic and essential pieces of infrastructure. The funding for the construction of these wharves was provided by the federal government responding to petitions from local activists. Grateful residents were to be well served by these bustling wharves for the best part of the ensuing seven decades. Washabuck was a classic example.

Pine Brook Wharf

Five kilometres south of MacKay Point, Pine Brook flows eastward from Washabuck Mountain and empties into the Bras d'Or Lake. When lake steamers plied the waters delivering mail, freight, livestock and passengers, there was a continuous need for them to replenish their water tanks, as the water supplied steam for power. The Pine Brook location provided a convenient source of fresh water for this very purpose. Apparently, there was very little mineralization in Pine Brook's water, an important factor for a steamer's boilers. For this reason, the wharf was referred to as the "Watering Wharf." A six-inch pipe ran from the brook, the length of the wharf, to the end where it was connected to the steamer's own onboard piping system and tanks, ensuring quick and convenient access to the limitless and precious commodity.

The government wharf was constructed at the south side of the mouth of the brook specifically for this purpose. The wharf also conveniently attended the needs of the residents of the community of *Rubh' a' Phonaidh*, or as it is now known Ponys Point, near the entrance to Maskells Harbour. The wharf, built in 1896, served the community of 15-20 families living there at that time. It is thought this wharf was built before the MacKay Point wharf. However, no government documentation has been obtained despite in-depth searches. Joe (Red Rory) MacLean maintained that the wharf was about 150 feet in length.[3] It was repaired on several occasions by local residents including William MacKenzie, Red Rory MacLean and Neil P. S. MacLean.[4]

Malcolm (Stephen) MacLean and Murdock (Vincent) MacLean also repaired the wharf during its last years. They would row to Pine Brook and remain there for three or four days living in a tent, before returning home to replenish their larder. There was no direct road over Washabuck Mountain to Pine Brook. Neil P. S. MacLean had obtained government funding to carry out these necessary repairs. The SS *Blue Hill* was the last lake steamer to use the watering wharf.[5]

The wharf's location, which was near Hector Campbell's residence, proved to be a great site for trout fishing and was known as a favorite casting spot. Sadie (Michael Charlie) MacLean (1884- 1956) of Baddeck commented to James (Joseph Klondike) MacDonald of Baddeck that as a youngster, she and her friends would ride the steamer *Blue Hill* to the watering wharf and remain there angling while the boat continued on to Iona. Then, they would contentedly thumb a ride back to Baddeck on the steamer's return, usually with a

10-2 The SS *Blue Hill* taking on passengers and water for the engines at Pine Brook, *Rubh' a' Phonaidh*. Note the steel pipe that carried water from the brook to the boat. Courtesy of James MacDonald, Twining Street, Baddeck.

bountiful gad of trout.⁶ Local residents would ship their cream and farm produce to Baddeck and the wharf provided a convenient transfer depot for this transportation of goods and people. The SS *Blue Hill* called at Pine Brook wharf at least twice a week.⁷

Mary (Dan D.) MacNeil (1916-2005) of Grass Cove shared an interesting bit of lore about how the point may have gotten its name. Mary recalled reading a letter to the editor in a Sydney paper (probably *The Sydney Post-Record*) from Mary Campbell a resident of Boston, but formerly of *Rubh' a' Phonaidh*. She wrote the name was the result of a Frenchman having lived on its shores for an entire winter, and the closest the Gàidhlig speaking people of the area could come to pronouncing his name was something that sounded like *Rubh' a' Phonaidh*, hence the name.⁸ It is also possible that the area was originally known as *Rubha Sheonaidh* which simply translates to Johnny's Point.

The more recent English appellation of Ponys Point (ca. 1952) is a Gàidhlig translation, perhaps initiated by the Russell family for the herd of horses that free-ranged over these vacant homesteads in the 1940s and 1950s. The Edward Russell family of Washington, DC, bought much of these vacant lands during this time and has summered there for more than five decades. For a number of years during the late 1950s the family operated a kiln that experimented with the commercial production of charcoal. Washabuck resident Francis B. MacDonald, a Russell employee, oversaw the day-to-day management of this operation.⁹

MacKay Point Wharf

In February 1882 the Honourable Members of the Nova Scotia House of Assembly received a signed petition from the residents of Washabuck and Baddeck requesting monies to build a wharf at MacKay Point, Washabuck.

> That your petitioners are separated by two miles of water from the town of Baddeck; the nearest place at which a steamer calls;
>
> That your petitioners labour under great disadvantages in having their freights landed at Baddeck and having to cross the said channel in shipping their produce;

10-3 Ponies roam free on Pony's Point (*Rubh' a' Phonaidh*) in 1955. Burnt Point can be seen to the northeast and Beinn Bhreagh in the far distance. The Pine Brook wharf was located to the left of the lone spruce. Courtesy of the Edward Russell Family, Washington, DC.

That steamers and sailing vessels in going to Baddeck pass around the eastern end of the said peninsula within one hundred yards of the land at MacKays Point;

Your petitioners therefore pray that the sum of two hundred dollars be granted to build a wharf at MacKays Point in said Washabuck and your petitioners as in duty bound will even pray.[10] (See appendix 8, wharf petition)

Eventually, two decades later, a fiat from an extract of a Report of the Committee of the Honourable the Privy Council, approved by the Governor General on December 21, 1903 that reads:

…that it is necessary to acquire the required land for an approach to the proposed wharf at McKays Point Victoria County, N.S. towards the construction of which Parliament at its last session voted the sum of $6000.[11] [T]he Minister therefore recommends that authority be given to purchase from Mr. Vincent MacLean for the sum of fifty dollars the land required for an approach to the proposed public wharf at McKays Point;[12] … containing an area of about one-half an acre."[13]

The MacKay Point wharf was built 1903-04. It consisted of a block and span configuration 120 feet in length and 20 feet wide (36.5 m x 6 m) with an ell block 40 ft x 20 ft (12 m x 6 m) at the outer end extending towards the west. The blocks were constructed of ballasted, native timber cribwork, and the block forming the ell was sheathed.[14] A freight shed was erected in 1908. Repairs to the wharf were carried out in the 1930s, in 1943 and in 1953.

Because of its location its exposure to severe nor'easters and formidable springtime ice break-up stresses, by 1959 the wharf had begun to deteriorate. In the government's view, the wharf was underutilized. So by 1964, a barricade was erected at the head of the wharf to prevent vehicles from entering, ensuring public safety.[15] A 1959 fisheries report declared:

…shows five small gasoline boats operating from this wharf with a total fish landing in recent years ranging from $3 - $4 thousand annually consisting almost entirely of lobsters. The wharf is also used as a place of call for the ferry-passenger boat *Shenacadie* which operates out of Baddeck.[16]

In January 1971, the federal government sold the remnants of the land, wharf and freight shed to Michael A. MacLean, son of the original land owner.[17] Michael A. MacLean recalled that his father had provided most of the ballast and much of the timber for the structure, which was obtained locally. Initially there was a fence and gate at the entrance to the wharf. A contractor by the name of Samson from St. Peter's may have been the original builder of the wharf.

Baled hay, general freight, livestock, lobsters, cream, produce, lumber and pulp wood were some of products shipped via the wharf. Because of its convenient location between Baddeck and Iona and with the mail boat running between these two ports twice-a-day, six days a week, MacKay Point wharf proved to be a very popular embarking and jumping off spot for travellers. Angus N. MacDonald from South Cove, quite some distance away, was one of the dedicated farmers who continued to ship cream via the mail-boat from MacKay Point to the Baddeck Creamery, once the SS *Lakeview* ceased calling at Washabuck Centre wharf.[18]

10-4 MacKay Point government wharf, looking shoreward from its outer ell; cotton salmon nets are hung on poles to dry, clean, and repair. At the shoreline, the ice-house with both the old and new barns visible on hillside, ca. 1938. Courtesy of Michael A. MacLean, Washabuck.

Saltwater Cream

Marine transportation is subjected to the variants of ice, wind and tide, resulting in unending challenges for seafarers and sometimes unexpected contests even for landlubbers. Such a situation evolved at MacKay Point wharf, with milk cow Daisy in the early 1930s. Local men were involved in a major reconstruction of the Point's wharf, installing new stringers and planking. They had started their renovations at the shoreline and were working their way out toward the outer ell, a distance of some 120 feet (36.5 metres).

One afternoon Mina, a girl from next door landed onsite with a heavy-duty milk cow with orders from her mother Sarah MacLean, to ship the cow to Iona on the afternoon mail boat. The cow had been seconded to take up winter residence in Iona. Mina, as per the accepted protocol, raised the on-wharf flag to signal the boat's Captain that he was expected to call at the wharf, and then she promptly returned home, leaving her mother's milk cow in care and control of the wharf gang. The work crew included neighbours Jimmy (1906-1972) and Tommy (Billy) MacKenzie, Joe (Red Rory), Michael A. (Vincent) and Archie (Malcolm Stephen) MacLean, as well as, Quentin (Rory Ranald) MacDonald.

As some of the wharf's decking had already been removed, the crew managed to construct a temporary catwalk to accommodate the heavy cow and so, with a lot of care and concern, abetted with hands and bodies assisting from all sides and ends, they gradually eased the animal out onto the outer ell of the wharf from where she could then be safely loaded onto the expected boat. However, the wind freshened from the east, so much so that the boat could not dock either at the MacKay Point wharf or (as was later learned) at the Iona wharf but she sailed instead to Shenacadie wharf, where it proved protection enough for her to tie up briefly, by-passing the regular ports-of-call before returning to Baddeck.

So what was the work crew to do with Daisy? They would either have to babysit her for the night at the end of the wharf or somehow take her back ashore. This they did not dare risk a second time as she had almost slipped off the catwalk on her arrival; only some strong arms and shoulders in the right places had prevented a catastrophe.

A scheme was hatched. A sturdy line was secured from a nearby boat house, a long one, long enough to reach ashore, and its working end was securely fastened around the bovine's head and horns. The men then gently positioned Daisy facing seaward and when all were ready they, with a collective grunt and heave-ho, launched Daisy off the end of the wharf into the deeps. Like a great whale she sounded, and in due course breached with a noisy expellant of air amidst a spectacular eruption of swirling water, shit and bubbles. On taking her bearing she steered toward dry land, where in no time flat, she stood safe and steady upon newly acquired sea legs, with no obvious evidence of the bends.

A dispatch was delivered to Sarah explaining the situation and the need for her cow to remain lodged in Washabuck for a few days more, until the wharf was made safer. In due course, Daisy was successfully forwarded to her destination, glistening and still splendid, where she earned her keep providing Iona tea drinkers with the best of cream during the ensuing winter season.[19]

Washabuck Centre Wharf

Deeds registered on June 30, 1902, and January 30, 1903, set the scene for the construction of the Washabuck Centre wharf. Neil Peter and wife Marjory MacLean deeded the land to the Federal Department of Public Works. One deed described the approach to the wharf and the second deed described the water lot site upon which the wharf was erected. For these transactions the couple received a total of $21 from the Crown. The approach contained 1/8 of an acre (500 sq. m) while the water lot contained 1/5 of an acre (800 sq. m).

The wharf was described as 218 ft in length and 20 ft in width (66 m x 6 m) with a 20 ft x 20 ft ell section (6 m x 6 m) extending eastward from its outer end. A 10 ft x 10 ft (3 m x 3 m) freight shed was erected upon the ell. It was built of timber cribwork and block and span construction. The wharf was erected between 1903-1905, and at its outer end, the structure was 19 feet (6 m) in height.

The Department of Public Works engineering reports for 1954-1955 describe some repair work taking place including the replacement of stringers, untreated deck plank and rock ballast. "This wharf is a port of call for the subsidized boat MV *Arev* plying between Sydney and the Bras d'Or Lake ports," runs the brief description accompanying the 1954 estimate of repair (including labour) that totaled $2,500 by the Department of Public Works Canada office in Halifax and signed by O. S. Cox, District Engineer.[20]

10-5 Washabuck Centre wharf with unidentified vessel alongside, ca. 1950. Courtesy of Marjorie Andrews, New Hampshire, USA, and Carmie MacLean, Washabuck.

In 1969 the Department of Public Works, in the interest of public safety, barricaded the approach as the wharf was in poor condition. The department cited the cessation of freight boats on the lakes as the reason, "for insufficient economic justification to maintain the facilities."[21]

The wharf and freight shed were declared surplus and disposed of through federal Crown disposals to the Nova Scotia Department of Lands and Forests for the nominal sum of $100 in October 1970. Later, ca.1985, the Nova Scotia government had the remnants of the structure and ballast removed in the interest of public safety. The contractor was D. W. Matheson and Sons of Little Narrows.

Victory Lap

Dan MacRae of Baddeck was captain of the SS *Lakeview*. In 1928, he required a good deckhand and he asked Vincent MacLean of MacKay Point if any of his boys might be interested in the job. As it turned out none of his boys were available, but MacLean recommended neighbour Michael Dan "Mickey" MacLean. Mickey, a great worker, was indeed interested; he signed on and worked many years as deckhand, cheerfully taking a regular turn at the helm of the *Lakeview* with the consummate skill of a longtime skipper.

During the fall in early 1930s, repair work was being carried out on the Washabuck Centre wharf. There had been frost most every night. Much of the repair work was completed, except for the 10 in x 10 in (3 cm x 3 cm) bumper-railings that denoted the edge of the re-decked wharf. These new railings had just been put in position by the wharf crew, and were to be spiked down the following morning.

It was early morning when the *Lakeview* tied up at the Washabuck Centre wharf, having sailed from Whycocomagh at daybreak. The wharf's deck was still white with the night's frost. The cargo to be loaded this morning included a sizeable herd of nine-month old heifers. Unruly, bawling, cantankerous heifers, that were about half grown, strong and lively, having being out on the summer's grass since early spring.

Mickey was an old pro at handling these types of animals. He was a tall, slim man, tough and wiry. He had grown up on a farm and worked around animals most of his life, so there wasn't much he wouldn't tackle or handle. This particular morning Mickey was in charge of loading the heifers. He had the process down to a system. Take a lead calf by the halter, while allowing only so many others to follow the leader out of the corral, which was adjacent to John MacNeil's general store. Mickey's plan, mimicking the Pied Piper, was to get them right into their assigned pen aboard the *Lakeview*. No problem. And so it went.

The system worked fine until the final pilgrimage, for as Mickey was leading the last group aboard, the halter line broke and the heifer immediately made a dash for freedom. Mickey instinctively grabbed the animal by its tail. Perhaps sensing that its liberty might be permanently curtailed, the critter had no intention of stopping of its own accord. It headed full bore for the end of the 220-ft (67 m) wharf with Mickey steering from behind as a counter-drag. Mickey recounted later that he figured he still had care-and-control of the situation, but as events played out, he couldn't get a firm enough grip on the decking because of the morning's frost, and he was not aware that the wharf's new bumpers had yet to be spiked down, not that that would have made any real difference, given the bizarre circumstances.

The drama unfolded like a scene right out of a cartoon and Mickey followed the animal right into the frigid October lake. Like most mariners, Mickey couldn't swim a stroke, so he had little choice but to hang on to the "life line" for dear life. The heifer, initially set a northerly course for Inlet on the opposite side of the Lake, but eventually changed direction and gradually made a half-lap, with Mickey bringing up the rear. Finally the duo reached dry land about a hundred yards east of the wharf and vessel.

Meanwhile, all work had ceased with the wharf and boat crews watching, with much speculation about how this early morning caper would ultimately play out. Captain Dan MacRae witnessing the whole event from the bridge of the *Lakeview*, laughed unceasingly at the absurd exhibition that unfolded in front of everyone. Mickey persevered and on securing landfall, determinedly steered the wayward animal via tail and ear back onto the *Lakeview*, amidst much hooting and shouting, witless cries and good natured ribbing.

"Get some dry clothes on you MacLean and then get your hide up here! I want to see you on the bridge pronto!" shouted the Captain.

Mickey did as he was commanded and not quite knowing what to expect when he encountered the laughing skipper who handed him a generous tumbler full of hot grog. "Drink this," the captain ordered, still shaking his head in disbelief. He declared the early morning's escapade had surpassed any spectacle he had ever witnessed either on land, or at sea in all his years of sailing.

"I'll tell you MacLean, that's one time a piece of tail sure came in handy for you!" said the still chuckling MacRae.

Mickey and Captain Dan shared many a laugh about the incident over the years, as Mickey continued his seafaring career aboard the SS *Lakeview*.[22]

Washabuck River Wharf

On November 9, 1910, government approval was granted to purchase a lot of land from Michael MacDougall of Upper Washabuck for the sum of $10.00. The lot was required to build a wharf at that location for which the federal parliament had recently approved the sum of $1,800.00 for its construction. The title transfer for the lot occurred on July 28, 1911. The lot, a tenth of an acre (400 sq m), was surveyed by Joseph S. MacLean, Deputy Surveyor of Victoria County.[23] No other details have been found regarding this wharf.

10-6 Washabuck River wharf looking down the river from Jim Alec MacDougall's property. Pleasant Point is clearly visible on the river's north side, ca. 1940. Courtesy of Frances MacDougall, Mabou, and Marlene MacDonald, Melford, CB.

Washabuck Freight and Passenger Ferries

From the earliest days of settlement in Washabuck, it seems there was a ferry service linking Washabuck with the Baddeck area. Neil P. S. MacLean comments:

> Concerning the ferry between Washabuck and Baddeck it was John [*Eòin*] MacNeil, grandfather of Mrs. Vincent [Theresa] MacLean that was the first ferryman.[24]

Eòin MacNeil undoubtedly provided the service from the shoreline of his own property, now called Washabuck Centre. Baddeck was some 90 kilometres away over difficult roads via an overland trip around Whycocomagh Bay, while it was but three kilometres across St. Patrick's Channel. Initially the ferry carried livestock, produce and passengers and used sail, oars (or both), whatever the occasion demanded and weather permitted. The mails were added in later years.

Neil P. S. continues his discussion about Peter S. and Neil P. S. MacLean, ferrymen:

> I am not quite sure why the ferry was transferred to Malcolm MacLean, but I have a letter in my possession, that was on my father's file when he died. It was written to him by John MacKinnon (*Eòin a' Griasaiche*), Christmas Island, stating that he built a scow for Malcolm MacLean, ferryman in 1861. Evidently the ferryman was not getting control of the subsidy to pay for the scow and he tendered his resignation to the county council in 1867. His resignation was accepted and after a due deliberation, the sessions through their customs called for tenders for the ferry office resigned by Malcolm MacLean. Peter S. MacLean tendered. His was the only tender and he was appointed and held the appointment till two years before his death in 1916.[25] His son Neil P. S. then ran the ferry until November, 1934, when Roddie D. MacLean took over.[26]

Michael Dan (Red Rory) MacLean, Ferryman

Malcolm MacLean, the first postmaster at MacKay Point (and later his son Michael) operated the ferry between Washabuck and Baddeck for which they were paid an annual subsidy. Michael Dan MacLean (Mickey) relates the following account:

> I took over the ferry system to Baddeck from my father [Red Rory] in 1947. I ran it for seven years turning it over to my brother Joe. I'd take her into the Little Harbour whenever there was a nor'wester or nor'easter blowing. Once you got into the Little Harbour, it was like being inside a milk bottle. Later, I used to use the Western Cove, and only used MacKays Point when ferrying Father Rankin.

> I had three boats. The first one was an eighteen footer. She was a double-ender with a 3-hp Acadia one-lunger. I bought one from Alex Taylor in Baddeck. She was a twenty-four footer (7 m) with a 3-hp Atlantic. I later sold it to Jimmy MacKenzie. The third one I bought from Jamie Fownes in Baddeck who had bought it from John D. MacLean of Washabuck. It also had a 3-hp Atlantic for power.

> In 1947 I was getting $200 per year from the province for running the ferry. I charged 25 cents per passenger each way. Fifty cents return trip. At the end I was getting about $800 from the province. The request had to be passed by Municipal Council first though.

Ferry Tales

I remember one day in December I was ferrying Dr. MacMillan to Andrew MacLean's at the Lighthouse, and the fuel line froze on me, right off MacKays Point. It was as cold as hell that day! Part of the line was exposed near where it was connected to the carburetor and I couldn't get her started. As a last straw, I pissed on the spot. I needed a leak anyway and my aim was still pretty good at that time, and it worked. I got her going and delivered the Doc safe and sound. MacMillan was impressed! He wanted to include the story in his book but I changed his mind. We were getting a lot of water in the gas at that time, even though we were extra careful by straining it through a felt hat. You could tell the line was frozen because that part of the line would feel different when you felt it with your hand.

I solved a similar problem the same way, only that time it was on the trunk lock of my car. I had a flat tire at one in the morning near Joe MacDougall's. I told Archie [MacLean] what I did, and the next time he was in Baddeck he bought himself a blow torch. I guess he felt it was much more decent, but it certainly was not any more effective!"

I went to Baddeck one Sunday afternoon to pick up Father Hughie D. MacDonald. [ca. 1953]. Agatha Moore came back with us. It blew up a real dirty easterly gale around 2 p.m. just before we started back for the Point. It was the fall of the year and I had the boat I'd bought from Alex Taylor.

Oh, the sea was pretty high alright and Father MacDonald got scared. And he brought out the Rosary and started praying. Agatha was sitting on the thwart nearest the bow and Father MacDonald was on a second thwart amidships, each of them facing me. She leaned over his shoulder and asked him what he was going to do with those things, meaning the beads. He got pretty angry with her. Anyway, we made it safely to the Point.[27]

In 2009, fifty-six years later, Father Hughie D., was at that time the oldest active priest in the Diocese of Antigonish serving as Pastor in Creignish. He remembered the incident. He laughed and commented that Mickey's rendition was correct, and then with another laugh, added that there was a sequel.

When we arrived at Agatha's home, she related to her adoptive parents about how rough the crossing was, and then nonchalantly added, "Oh, but we had the priest with us!" which prompted her mother, Flora MacKenzie, to admonish her, "Agatha dear, that doesn't make any difference; priests can sink too!"

Father Hughie had a great chuckle reminiscing about the incident.[28]

Lighthouses

Michael Dan (Red Rory) MacLean continues:

> Errr, there were no lighthouses [in Washabuck]. We couldn't even get a buoy with a light on it. Just one old black spar buoy that you'd have trouble seeing on a clear day, let alone on a foggy night! I remember one night it was thick o'fog and I set out for home in the double-ender with the Acadia. I didn't know for sure where I was and after quite some time the motor quit. It was foggy and dark as Hell. A bit of dirt had got on the igniter, which would occasionally happen, and she'd quit. Anyway, I got her going but just before that, I saw two large white birches looming out of the darkness. I didn't recognize them, but after I got her going, I realized I was just about four hundred feet west of my own landing. The boat could have turned around on me and I'd be on the lake all night. Lucky! Another foggy night that old black spar buoy hit me right on my arse pocket as I went by.[29]

As Mickey mentioned, there were no lighthouses along the Washabuck shoreline. Baddeck received its first lighthouse in 1875 located on the eastern end of Kidston Island. It was later replaced by a taller version around 1915. In 1921 the original was transferred over the frozen lake to Shenacadie where it performed a similar function.[30] In 2011 the lights were declared surplus property and the government of Canada divested the Kidston Island lighthouses to the village of Baddeck.[31]

Gillis Point Lighthouse

In 1935, St. Columba Pastor (1926-1953), Father Duncan Rankin, wrote in the *Victoria-Inverness Bulletin newspaper*, that:

> Philip B. MacNeil from Gillis Point taught school and was clerking in a store in Baddeck for a number of years. When he married he opened a store at the Harbour [Maskells] at Gillis Point where he did business for a few years. He represented district No.18 [Washabuck] on the Municipal Council for a term or two [1883-1895]. [I]t was solely through his efforts that the Government of the day was forced to see the necessity of building a lighthouse, at the mouth of Mask ill [sic] Harbour, at Gillis Point. He himself was the first keeper of the lighthouse, [but] as the patronage system was at its best those days at the first change of government, he was removed. He took up residence in Baddeck and got on very well indeed. He died from a fractured spine which he received when a scaffolding on which he was working gave away, felling him to the ground.[32]

The Gillis Point lighthouse, located on the southwestern side of the entrance of Maskells Harbour was constructed in 1895. The tower is 37 feet in height (11 m) and raises to a full 74 feet (22.5 m) above the harbour's surface. The light is a seasonal navigational aid that displays a flashing white light every four seconds and is visible for six nautical miles (10.6 km). An attached dwelling, which was a family home for all the light-keepers, was removed in 1978.

Gillis Point light-keepers are as follows: F. X. MacNeil (1895-1896), Philip E. [sic] MacNeil 1896-1897), Hector MacLean (1898-1916), Catherine (MacDonald) MacLean, Hector's widow (1916-1939) and finally Hector and Catherine's son Andrew M. MacLean (1939-1967). The beacon had been on automatic service from 1967 until de-commissioned in 2011.[33]

Two other local lighthouses were located on the Washabuck Peninsula, one at Uniacke Point at Iona and the other at the eastern entrance at Little Narrows.[34]

10-7 Young MacLean siblings arrive home from school in front of their long-time residence, the Gillis Point Lighthouse. (L-R) Kenzie, Gordon and Roslyn, ca. 1950.

Maskells Harbour

Washabuck River provides a glorious anchorage as does Maskells Harbour, a popular harbour that provides a sanctuary abutting the Washabuck shoreline. Located about halfway between MacKay Point and Iona, the ancient Mi'kmaq called it *Moolasaatchkt*.[35] The harbour had been adorned with two other names, Port Elliott and Boulaceet. In *Samuel Holland's Description of Cape Breton and Other Documents*, Holland's survey 1765-1767 by historian D. C. Harvey, Holland refers to this harbour as Port Elliott and describes it as follows:

10-8 A two-masted schooner alongside the government wharf at Little Narrows. This was one of two government wharves in the community, ca. 1933. In the background, the community's second Presbyterian Church (1856-1950). Courtesy of Murdell MacNeil, Iona, Cape Breton.

> Port Elliott is the only Safe Harbor along this part of the Coast, the Entrance of which is seven fathoms, and shoals regularly to two fathoms close to the Head; on the East side a sandy neck runs out for about forty yards, which forms a small Bason [sic], where vessels, May ride secure from all winds in three fathoms Waters: the Soil and Woods the same as

TRANSPORTATION

10-9 A recent picture of the entrance to Maskells Harbour.

aforementioned (with poor, stony soil in most Places, the woods small and coast partly rocky and bluff...) with high lands.[36]

The yachter's guide to the Bras d'Or Lakes entitled *Cruise Cape Breton* succeeds as well in capturing the essence of the refuge:

> Completely cradled by steep rolling hills and almost completely landlocked by a sandbar stretching across the mouth, plus the unspoiled beauty of Maskells Harbour, makes a sanctuary for yachters:[37]

The Cruising Club of America [CCA] was founded in 1922 "to promote and facilitate cruising by amateurs" and "stimulate an interesting [*sic*] in seamanship and the navigation and handling of small vessels." Perhaps not surprisingly, "the idea of such a club was begun in informal discussions onboard the famous Bell family yacht, *The Elsie* in Maskells Harbour on the Bras d'Or Lakes."[38]

As for the name (which endures various spellings), the following parody of its humble origins is offered by sailors Scot and Mary Flanders as taken from their blog Captain's Log, onboard their Nordhavn Cruiser *Egret*. It seems that:

10-10 Maskells Harbour, a popular haven for relaxing sailors, July 1993.

> Mr. Maskell, after whom Maskells Harbour was called by people in the area, owned a house and forge near the shore. Early one winter morning Mr. M. went out in his nightshirt and cap to get some firewood, slipped on the frozen snow and crashed and burned down the steep slope all the way to the shore. Fortunately, M didn't get thrashed on the descent but was chilling fast. Because of the ice he couldn't climb back up the slope so was basically [stymied] and had to find another way home before his stuff froze. So Mr. M. decided to walk the shore towards Gillis Point Lighthouse and get help from the lighthouse keeper dude. When lighthouse dude ... saw this apparition coming he locked his seven daughters in the

lighthouse before offering assistance. He did, Mr. M. got home a bit shaken and cool, but made it he did."[39]

The Canadian Hydrographic Service officially changed the name from Boulaceet to Maskells Harbour in 1960.[40]

Gordon MacLean whose grandparents and parents were the lightkeepers for a seventy year span, recalls that "Maskells" was how his people, and the seamen and sailors who frequented the MacLean's lighthouse residence, always referred to the Harbour.[41] Whatever the name of preference, the Harbour as Samuel Holland described it in 1765, remains a tranquil haven where vessels still, "may ride secure from all winds..."[42]

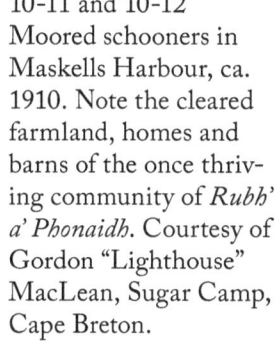

10-11 and 10-12 Moored schooners in Maskells Harbour, ca. 1910. Note the cleared farmland, homes and barns of the once thriving community of *Rubh' a' Phonaidh*. Courtesy of Gordon "Lighthouse" MacLean, Sugar Camp, Cape Breton.

Joe (Red Rory) MacLean - Ferryman

Michael Dan MacLean's younger brother Joe (1912-1998) relates his own ferry tales.

> I ran the Washabuck Ferry for fourteen seasons. I finished in the fall of 1968. I used four different boats in that time. The first ferry boat I bought from Michael A. MacLean. It was his father (Vincent's) old sailboat. It was built on Boularderie Island by K. Dugas. It was designed by Vincent. The second one was a twenty-four footer from Boularderie. The third was a cabin cruiser also twenty-four feet.... I bought her from the Kennedy brothers of Alba. The fourth one, *The Baba,* was a [gaff-rigged ketch] twenty-seven footer [with a Gray marine engine] that I bought from Edgar Forgeron of Arichat.

The passenger fee was a quarter each way. The season ran from May first until December first. The first number of years I'd ferry about 450 passengers. After the new liquor store opened in Baddeck [1967] the passenger numbers increased to 500. It was twenty-four hour service. You'd be ferrying practically all night if you had Dr. MacMillan and [nurse] Miss Lytle. Gee whiz, the hour meant nothing to them.

I ran the last five or six years from MacKays Point [Harbour] to Baddeck. Before that it was always from the Western Cove on my property. But it was such a long walk out on the beach and then you had that steep hill to climb on the way back. Besides, it must have been one-half mile longer sail to town and it was always a more difficult run against a nor'west wind than if you were heading for the Point.[43]

Charles H. Vilas, an American summer resident, lifetime sailor and owner of the esteemed cruising cutter *Direction*, describes Skipper Joe MacLean and his family's history operating the Washabuck passenger ferry in an online article entitled "Sails Backstop Mechanics on Washabuckt's Only Ferry." Vilas asked Joe why he tacked the *Baba* upwind at right angles until he was in the lee of Allen's [Bone] Island, before bearing off to MacKay Point, instead of heading directly for port. Joe replied:

...I work up to weather so I can make port under sail should I have to. I have a responsibility for the comfort and safety of my passengers, you know.[44]

Joe's recollections continue:

The County Council gave me a grant of $200 - $300 annually [Joe may have meant to say $800] at the beginning and it was $1200.00 at the last. It was little enough though when you think you had to buy your boat and fuel out of that. At first, a barrel of marked gas [45-gallon drum, 170 litres] I could get for around $10.00. You'd pay well over $100.00 for it today [1984].

My grandfather Michael (Malcolm) MacLean ferried first and then my father "Red Rory" and then my brother Mickey until I took over in 1954. [It seems to have been Malcolm, Joe and Mickey's great-grandfather that was the family's first ferryman]. The first mail that went to Baddeck from Orangedale, Murdock Gillis, the mailman of Estmere, would deliver it [here] by horse and wagon or sleigh. Three times a week to my grandfather Michael (Malcolm). My grandfather would deliver it to Baddeck. That was before the railroad came through and the mail boats started running from Baddeck to Iona.

June First

Ghee whiz, I recall one winter I was operating the snow plow then and I was ploughing through Washabuck near the graveyard and I met this man walking. I stopped and who was it but Dan Brown heading home with a couple of chunks of pork under his arm. [Salt pork that had been given to him by whatever kind soul he had been visiting.] He wasn't having any problem but he asked me if I'd be ferrying next spring and I said yes. He said, "I'll be down on June first." We parted and I never thought anymore of it.

Well, on May 31st, that evening, I had to ferry Neil James and Margaret MacNeil of Gillis Point to Baddeck for a gathering. We were late leaving Baddeck, around midnight, and on the way out of the harbour, Captain John Parker of North Sydney had his boat moored to some kind of stick or log with some large excess rope floating on the surface. Well, I hit that stick just as I gave her the throttle and we all fell over one another. There was no damage done except I fouled the rope on the prop and cut it off, and so ended up towing the rope home with me. I left it that way and went to bed.

The next morning at 6 a.m. who lands at the door but Dan Brown. "Uh, uh, it's June first, I got business in Baddeck!" Well I wasn't blessing him, but the discussion of our wintry meeting flashed through my mind. I had to get him to help me take the hawser from the around the propeller. I convinced him to turn the flywheel [on the one-lunger] counterclockwise and gradually the rope backed off and we headed to Baddeck.

10-13 The last of the Washabuck ferrymen, Skipper Joe (Red Rory) MacLean in the Baba, ca. 1968. Clipping from *National Fisherman* January, 1969. Courtesy of Charles H. Vilas, USA.

We got to Baddeck and there wasn't a damn store open. It was only 8:15 and the stores usually didn't open before 9 and the bank not before 10. Well, Dan Brown wasn't too happy about that. He couldn't understand anything not being open at that hour of the morning. Of course, Dan was probably up at 4 a.m., and then had hoofed it to my place [10 kilometres]. He had already put in half a day before the bankers would see him.

10-14 Brothers Michael (1889-1974) and Dan Brown (1891-1971) beside their neighbour, Mary MacDougall, ca. 1945. Courtesy of Donnie MacKinnon and Cheryl Myette, Washabuck.

My other grandfather Donald (Rory) MacLean helped his brother Peter (Rory) ferry a scow to and from Baddeck. It was some kind of a Barra Boat [*sgoth*] I guess. It reminded me of those first ferries they had on the Barra Strait. No sail. Just a couple of sets of oars – and heavy! They would haul freight and animals but no mail.[45] This was before the mail system started anyway. They ran out of the Western Cove and I think they got some kind of grant from the government to assist them. There were three breakwaters built in the Western Cove to protect the beach. This was federal money.[46]

The Little Harbour

Joe continues his recollections about Little Harbour:

> The Little Harbour fell out of use in the late 1940s. It had a great breakwater. A man from Upper Washabuck could leave his horse at Malcolm (Stephen) MacLean's and borrow a row boat and row himself to Baddeck when there was no ferry operating. The use of the Little Harbour became more frequent with the migration of most of Neil P. S.'s eight sons, who had always assisted their father with the ferry business. This resulted in Red Rory and his sons gradually ferrying more passengers from the Little Harbour. There was a rock wall built at the "Little Harbour" [fronting on Rory J. MacLean's property]. This was federal money too but this happened before my time.[47]

When asked, Archie MacLean (1919-2010) could not recall any repair work being done to the Little Harbour during his lifetime.[48]

Wintertime Travel

The main highway for winter travel was the frozen lake which was bushed every 50 paces for safety purposes. Bushing the ice was a county appointment, with remuneration ranging from $2.50 to $25.00 a day, recalls Joe Mac-Lean.[49] Freight and mail were moved by ice as well as just about everything else. The quality of the ice was always the subject of wintertime conversation and discussion. Although there was good ice almost everywhere, there was danger for the careless and unwary user. In daylight, drifting snow caused whiteouts that could easily and quickly disorient the user. Nighttime was worse. A fresh fall of snow would create the appearance of all ice being the same quality, with dire consequences for the unwary. At the beginning of spring thaws, warming temperatures could create pressure ridges. After the onset of a heavy freshet some locations would open much more quickly than others with the agitated underwater currents eroding ice underneath while the surface may have looked fine, especially around channels, giving the carefree traveller a false sense of security. Caution was the watchword, so bushes were essential. Michael A. MacLean recalls:

> [The] ice was bushed from Plaster Mines to Kempt Head; from Baddeck to Shunacadie and from the Maskells Harbour to Shunacadie and at times from the Grass Cove/Gillis Point area over to Christmas Island.[50] Freight and sometimes mail would cross overland from Iona to Washabuck Centre and then across the ice from Washabuck Centre to Inlet in early winter, and later on into the winter season, from Baddeck to Shunacadie; in more recent decades the ice was bushed instead from MacIver's Cove, west of Holy Rosary Church, across to Inlet; and always from MacKays Point to Graveyard Point at Baddeck and from Beinn Bhreagh to Baddeck.[51] Even Benacadie Pond was bushed.[52]

10-15 Survey sketch indicating location of the "Little Harbour" fronting on the Rory J. (Stephen) MacLean property, Lower Washabuck. Survey by Joseph S. MacLean, March 25, 1899. Courtesy of Registry of Deeds, Baddeck.

Later in the winter season, all of Big Baddeck and Middle River would order railroad car-loads of baled hay from Truro. It would arrive at Shunacadie and the convoys of teams with sleighs of every description would be seen heading from the Baddeck area to Shunacadie for the hay. They had large farms, a lot of cattle, and their own hay would be running low so numerous loads of hay would be required. It was an annual occurrence. Red Rory [MacLean] built truck-sleighs for everyone in Middle River, Big Baddeck and Washabuck. He used yellow birch

TRANSPORTATION

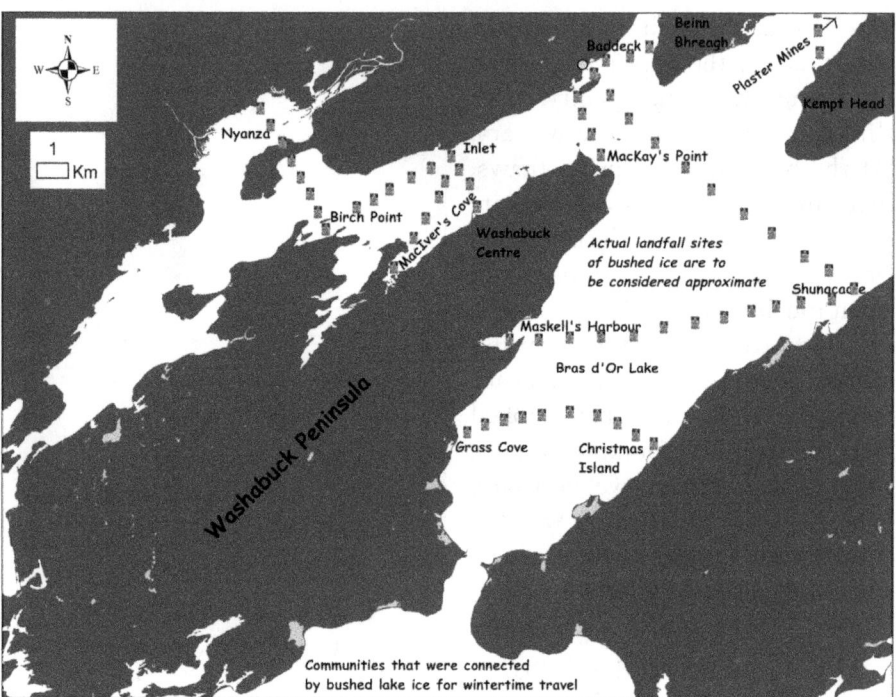

10-16 Map displaying the various locations where the lake ice was regularly bushed for safe winter passage.

for the natural shaped runners. You were taking cream to the Baddeck creamery three times a week, so everyone in Washabuck knew everyone in Baddeck because of meeting them there so frequently.[53]

Jessie (MacInnis) MacKinnon, Little Narrows, recalls:

On the western end of St. Patrick's Channel, the ice was bushed at a couple of locations. From Sheep Island in MacInnis's Cove over to Inlet, close to where Ella Mae and her brother John Hugh MacLean lived, and from Deadmans Point over to Morris Point,[Cow Point] west of Cow Bay. We'd walk across Morris Point and then don our skates again and skate across Nyanza Bay which was bushed as well, to the stores at Nyanza.[54] Bushes also ran across Whycocomagh Bay from Johnny Sandy Matheson's beach, well above the Strait of Julia channel at Little Narrows, to come ashore near the old manse property at Aberdeen.[55]

Freight Couriers

Long-time Iona resident Honey MacNeil (1921-2008) relates her memorable experiences delivering freight with her intrepid uncles.

I'd come home from school and my uncle John S. MacNeil would say, "You'll have to come to Baddeck with me this evening." This would be around 1933 or '35. His brother Angus didn't want to go. The train [from the west] would arrive in the evening at 5 p.m. If there was any freight coming on the Express we'd wait for it before leaving. There would be freight for [J. P.] MacLeod's store in Baddeck and for many others as well. This was in the winter time of course, so we'd harness up the horses. We dressed warmly. There were no slacks allowed in those days, so we'd use the big buffalo robes to keep us warm. We had some close calls on the ice. John S. once lost a horse through the ice before I started travelling with him.

John S. would lead the way with the dark coloured horse and I'd follow him with the old white one. Each sleigh had a load of freight. We did not carry the mail as the Baddeckers had their own people coming from Baddeck to Iona with the mail. We'd deliver the express freight with the truck-sleighs; [go] around snow banks, no snow plows then, and get on the ice at Washabuck Centre at the ball field. If the ice was not already bushed, it would be in a matter of days. I was twelve to fourteen years old. We'd deliver the freight to the stores or to wherever the load was to be delivered. We were paid by the Baddeck merchants. On the return trip, we'd call at Johnny Paul's [MacLean, on the Baddeck Shore Road]. He and his wife would always want us to stop and they would invite us in. We'd put the horses in the barn for a rest, and a bite to eat. They would be glad to see us, make us the tea and have a chat. They also had a big "baby grand" piano and John S. would play it, sing, and perform. We wouldn't get home until maybe 10 p.m. after leaving Iona around 4:30 or 5 if we had waited for the express. Then we would feed and brush the horses down after we got them in the barn.

John S. delivered freight to the mail-boat at Iona just like his father (F. X. S.) had done. Loading bags of animal feed and flour off the railroad cars into the hole of the mail boats. John S. and his brothers worked hard transferring those heavy bags from the cars to the boat. The boat in those times would be docked by 8 a.m. and would have to be loaded by 10 a.m. when she sailed with the mail back to Baddeck.[56]

A Mare's Tale

"Red Rory" MacLean of Lower Washabuck had a little mare which weighed maybe 950 pounds (430 kg). The mother had died and the filly was brought up on the bottle and was a real pet, as well as being considered a really intelligent animal. Red Rory was back and forth across the lake-ice to Baddeck numerous times that winter as was his custom and as a result he knew the condition of the ice well, better than anyone else from either community.

This particular day Red Rory told his young sons Joe and Johnny to take the mare and truck-sleigh to Baddeck for a load. The boys did as they were told and not far from the Washabuck shoreline, a bit eastward of the normal route, when suddenly, down through the ice went the mare.

The brothers quickly unhooked the animal from the sleigh and pulled it back out of the way. Joe then reached down, grabbed one of the mare's shod front feet, managing to bend it first backwards and then slightly sideways, and succeeded in getting the animal's leg up onto the solid ice in front of her. He told Johnny to take the ends of the reins and give the mare a sharp crack across her arse, while at the same time Joe strained on the bridle. Johnny did as he was told and sure enough, the mare pulled herself right out of the lake.

They returned home with the mare and sled none-the-worse for wear and told their father what had happened. He wouldn't believe them. Nonetheless, he grabbed an axe and they all headed back to the location. A thin layer of snow had covered the opening, which was the result of an underwater spring. A chastened but grateful Red Rory found a bush nearby and placed it in the hole to mark the site, at least for that winter.[57]

"Crack" Feed

Neil P. S. MacLean of Lower Washabuck had a sled-load of animal feed to come home from the railway station at Iona. It was getting late in the winter, the snow was melting and the lake ice was beginning to soften. He told his sons, Jimmy and Matt, to take the horse and truck-sleigh and head for Iona by road to fetch the load. He told them to make darn sure they kept away from the lake-ice.

Once the boys got to Iona, they loaded their cargo and headed for home. When they hit hard sledding with gravel poking through on the road at Grass Cove, they ignored their father's advice and decided to take the ice from there to MacKay Point for a faster, smoother and less torturous return trip, thinking that the old fellow would be none-the-wiser to their scheme.

Everything went well until they hit a crack at Burnt Point, where the horse, sled and feed, partially ended up in the drink. Matt stayed with the horse while Jimmy high-tailed it for help at Vincent MacLean's at MacKay Point. As luck would have it, Vincent and his son Leo were just coming home from the woods with their horse and truck-sleigh. They grabbed a length of rope and raced back to Burnt Point where they succeeded in rescuing the animal, sled and payload from out of the chasm. Then, just as quickly, made the return trip back to the barn at the Point. The animal was uninjured.

The horse was put in the barn, rubbed down, covered with a rug, watered and fed. Later, after the boys themselves had a bite to eat, they headed home, this time on dry land, with their freight intact. They arrived home, unloaded the bags of feed in the barn, and put everything away as normal. The feed was fine as it was only the outer bags that had gotten wet, and those had frozen instantly creating an icy-coating over the exterior, protecting the rest of the feed. In addition, the outer bags seemed to have protected the balance of the load from getting wet.

The brothers' turbulent venture ended tranquilly, as the horse and sleigh were fine; there was essentially little damage to the feed, and gratefully, no retribution for the rebellious diversion. And if their old man ever suspected anything amiss, he never said a word to them.[58]

A Changing Climate

Neil P. S. MacLean notes in his diary dated April 25, 1923:

> The ice on St. Patrick's Channel is still fit for teams and there is lots of snow on the roads and through the country. The older residents have recollections of pedestrians crossing the channel on May 8, and in the spring of '82 [1882] workmen at Plaster Mines below Beinn Bhreagh walked on the ice to Gillis Point, near Iona, on the first day of May in that spring.[59]

Murdock MacInnis of Washabuck Bridge recalls hearing about Malcolm (William) MacDonald, who had been lumbering at Lower Washabuck, take his team and bobsleighs home to Middle River across the ice of St. Patrick's Channel on May 12, in either 1926 or 1927.[60]

Washabuck resident Roddie (Malkie) MacDonald sporting a new 1955 Chevrolet half-ton, accompanied by neighbour Michael Dan MacLean, drove to Baddeck from MacKay Point via the lake ice early on the morning of April 9, 1956 for a load of hay. Since hay was unavailable in Big Baddeck, they proceeded to North Sydney where they loaded 1,300 pounds (590 kg) of baled hay and retraced their tracks to MacKay Point via the ice. Although, by noon time they noted, the ice had softened considerably from its earlier morning firmness.[61]

February 23, 1959, saw a horde of local sightseers in cars and trucks as well as a few farmers with their horses and sleighs, trek across the lake ice from MacKay Point to Baddeck Bay to witness the 50th Anniversary of the flight of the *Silver Dart*. The winter had a lot of snow and there was at least 30 inches of ice all over the lake (76 cm). The weather that day was clear and cold, with piercing winds. On that same day, Aloysius MacKinnon of Barra Glen drove his car from Jamesville, near Iona to St. Peter's and back, via the lake ice. In 2009, the 100th anniversary of the 1909 flight saw just enough of an icy platform on Baddeck Bay to enable a re-enactment of the flight. With the exception of small ponds and coves, there was practically no ice elsewhere on the lake.

Charlotte MacLean of MacKay Point was one of the last Washabuck residents that crossed the lake ice, driving her vehicle to and from work crossing St. Patrick's Channel between Washabuck and Baddeck while nursing at Victoria County Memorial Hospital during the winter of 1992. Since that year, whatever lake ice has formed on St. Patrick's Channel, it has been unsafe for motor vehicle use. Climate change has become profoundly evident over the intervening two decades. Dramatic weather changes have evolved with warmer temperatures, less snow, little ice, fiercer wind storms, sea surges, amplified tides, and increased coastal erosion. These, together with cooler springs, later summers and extended fall seasons are changes readily obvious to permanent residents who inhabit the Bras d'Or Lake watershed.

[As if to belie the climate observations noted in this chapter, as this work is being tweaked in February 2014, St. Patrick's Channel has frozen again, due as much to an escorting lack of wind as freezing temperatures. Could this be the dying gasps of what our ancestors called *Am Faoilleach*, the intensity of the Gàidhlig winter that traditionally spanned the weeks between mid-January and mid-February? Time will tell.]

Bras d'Or Lake Steamers

SS *Banshee*

For decades, the communities on Bras d'Or Lake, and certainly those along the transportation corridor encompassing St. Patrick's Channel, were well served by what are referred to as the Bras d'Or Lake steamers. Robert Elmsley, an early postmaster and chronicler in Baddeck, noted the earliest arrival of a steamer in May 1855, when he recorded the *Banshee* rounding the point of Red Head and steaming into Baddeck Harbour. The *Banshee* was said to be the first steam-powered paddleboat built on Cape Breton Island. Constructed in 1851 at Big Bras d'Or, by master shipbuilder George Auld, it had a galvanized hull and was built to ferry passengers from North Sydney across the harbour to Sydney. It was soon transferred to the lake run.[62]

Alex D. MacLean records in his manuscript, History of Victoria County:

> I was told by Michael [Charlie] MacLean that he was but a boy of thirteen or fourteen when his father took him from his home at Washabuckt to see the marvel of the age, a boat driven by steam power, and without the use of sails. Mr. MacLean told me that the town was crowded with people who had come from Big Baddeck, Middle River, the St. Anne's district, and other sections of the county to witness her arrival. The news of her coming had been noised about for days in advance. He told me the *Banshee* did not have a deck; the passengers, freight and crew, were all contained in the hull in close proximity to the boiler and engine.[63]

In her manuscript, *History of Baddeck*, Effie Bain provides a concise summary of these Lake Boats.

The *Banshee* was followed by a series of steam driven ships. The *Lady of the Lake*, *Neptune* (1878), *May Queen*, *Magnolia*, and *G.S. Burchill* were owned by Victoria Steamship Ltd. The *Lake View* [it ceased operations] in 1952. Some of these steamers would go through the lake to St. Peter's and back to Sydney tri-weekly. Other ships came from Halifax and Boston. In 1885, SS *Lady of the Lake* and SS *Banshee* both retired from the Bras d'Or Lakes and then provided Sydney-North Sydney ferry services, making several trips a day. The SS *Neptune* left in early morning for a trip to St. Peter's, picking up passengers and freight from the railway at Mulgrave, returning the following morning after a night run back through the lakes.[64]

Michael Charlie's son, Charles J. MacLean of Baddeck, adds that, the *Harlow* and the *Pro Patria* were two other ships that made Baddeck a regular port of call.[65]

SS *May Queen*

Baddeck historian Jocelyn Bethune adds the following about the *May Queen*:

> This little steamer, originally christened the *Mayflower*, was an iron-hulled boat built in 1868 by Sir Stanford Fleming, the engineer responsible for the railway route across Canada and the creator of standard time. The boat was used during the construction of the Intercolonial Railway, and later to ferry passengers, freight, and mail near Pictou, Nova Scotia.... About 1880, the *Mayflower* arrived in Bras d'Or Lake and was renamed the *May Queen*. The 38-metre-(125-foot-) long, side-paddle steamer could carry up to sixty passengers and made frequent stops in Baddeck, Whycocomagh, Grand Narrows, Little Bras d'Or and West Bay. In April 1883 Robert Elmsley noted that ice in the lake was preventing the *May Queen* from leaving Baddeck for its destination in Whycocomagh. The boat came to an unceremonious end when it burned on the shore of Kidstons Island in 1898.[66]

10-17 SS *May Queen*, Baddeck, CB. Courtesy of Beaton Institute, Cape Breton University, Sydney, Cape Breton.

SS *Marion*

Effie Bain writes that in 1885, the SS *Marion*, the side-paddle wheeler, made a tri-weekly run; connecting at Baddeck with the *May Queen* whose regular schedule was from Christie's wharf [Little Bras d'Or] to Whycocomagh. The *Marion* often brought cattle to

North Sydney where they were kept until slaughtered for food and the hides sent to tanneries.

The *Lakeview* was the last of the boats to make regular visits. Her route was from North Sydney to Whycocomagh with stops en route.[67]

Bethune writes about the *Marion*:

> The steamship *Marion* was arguably the finest vessel of the Bras d'Or steamer fleet. Outfitted with a saloon, large staterooms, and a dining room, it carried passengers and freight between Bras d'Or Lake ports and Sydney. The *Marion* was built in New York City in 1876. The ship was 43 metres (142 feet) long, with a tonnage of 478. Before arriving in Cape Breton in the early 1880s, the *Marion* was an excursion boat on the Hudson River, plying the same upstate New York waters once traversed by Jonathan Jones, Baddeck's earliest settler.[68]

> [...]On October 30, 1922 while the vessel was docked at Whycocomagh, a fire broke out on board. After several failed attempts to contain the fire, the majestic boat was cut from its mooring and set adrift. Its final lake-run ended ninety metres from the wharf, where it ran aground and burned. The hull of the ship remained visible in Whycocomagh Harbour for decades afterwards.[69]

10-18 SS *Marion*. Courtesy of Beaton Institute, Cape Breton University, Sydney, Cape Breton.

Bethune describes the steamship service on the Bras d'Or:

> Vital transportation links, these wide-bodied ships were both work horses and pleasure craft. A page in a 1902 ledger book detailed a typical trip and the cargo carried: a horse and a cow (prepaid freight, seventy-five cents each), a horse and wagon (a dollar to come from Iona), a box of helmets for the 94th militia regiment, two cases of corsets for the McKay, McAskill Company, a sofa, a piano, and one case of dry goods for Hart's Store.

> The ships were people movers too, travelers to the Iona train station, Whycocomagh, and Sydney, and bringing visitors from West Bay and North Sydney. During a typical month in 1907, almost five hundred people traveled between Baddeck and Iona aboard just one of the steamships in operation.[70]

> The Victoria Steamship Company and the Bras d'Or Steamship Company operated a number of boats including *Blue Hill*, *Marion*, *Neptune*, *May Queen*, and *Magnolia*. The steamer *Blue Hill* offered regular moonlight excursions to tourists in 1906 and was available for hire.

[I]n 1917 the two steamship companies merged to form the Baddeck Steamship Company.⁷¹ A. H. Sutherland was the owner of the Baddeck Steamship Company.⁷²

SS *Blue Hill*

The steamer SS *Blue Hill* called for water at Pine Brook wharf at least twice a week. Local residents from Ponys Point, MacNeils Vale and Gillis Point would ship their cream to Baddeck from there and of course passengers sailed from that location. According to Joe (Red Rory) MacLean there were 15 to 20 families living in the Ponys Point area prior to the turn of the last century.⁷³

Honey MacNeil describes a typical Iona scenario:

The *Blue Hill* would run twice a day to meet the train in Iona. In the morning it arrived at 8:30 a.m. to unload freight and mail for the train which arrived at 9:00 a.m. on its way to Halifax via Truro. A siding-track ran out onto the government wharf so that rail cars could be shunted closer the vessel so the freight was more easily transferred.

The *Blue Hill* was scheduled to sail at 9:30 a.m., but some days there was so much freight that she could not sail before 10:30. Then she returned at 4:00 p.m. to meet the 4:40 train arriving from Halifax on its way to Sydney. The transfer of freight occurred once again with the *Blue Hill* normally returning to Baddeck at 5:15 p.m.⁷⁴

10-19 SS *Blue Hill*.

SS *Lakeview*

The SS *Lakeview* ran from North Sydney and called at Baddeck, Nyanza, South Cove, Little Narrows and stayed overnight at Whycocomagh. On the return trip, she called at Washabuck Centre and the wharf east of Coffin Island near Kempt Head on Boularderie Island. She did not regularly call at MacKay Point, or Iona, except for an unusual delivery or on a special occasion.⁷⁵

These lake boats provided convenience for the local residents in smaller communities around the watershed. K. R. MacDonald of Middle River had two hogsheads of molasses delivered to the Whycocomagh wharf before a Christmas season by the *Lakeview*. MacDonald trucked it to Middle River where the molasses was placed on tap in his father's store. It quickly disappeared by the end of the Christmas season.⁷⁶ Once the *Lakeview* ceased its regular run and call at South Cove, and Washabuck Centre, Angus N.

MacDonald a South Cove farmer, and his neighbour, "Little" Norman MacIver of Hazeldale, would tote their cream all the way to MacKay Point, to ship it to the Baddeck Creamery via the Baddeck-Iona mail boat.[77]

Historian Rannie Gillis of North Sydney notes that it was the New Bras d'Or Steamship Company that operated the SS *Lakeview*, "a small steamship which ran between Sydney, Boularderie Island, Whycocomagh and Baddeck."[78]

Nor'easter Tryst

10-20 SS *Lakeview*. Courtesy of Eileen and Walter Matheson, Little Narrows.

Perhaps, this is as good a time as any to spin another SS *Lakeview* yarn that again involves Michael Dan "Mickey" MacLean and Captain Dan MacRae. The general standing order was that the *Lakeview* would anchor overnight at Kelly's Cove, on the Big Bras d'Or channel whenever there was a howling nor'easter blowing and proceed to Sydney only when the seas had eased.

It was dangerous to broach the vessel to the unrelenting heavy breakers when it came time to steer into Sydney Harbour. There was always the chance that the vessel would founder in the broaching seas. So the general conceded standing order was that the *Lakeview* would anchor overnight in the lee at Big Bras d'Or and proceed to Sydney only when the seas had eased.

This type of layover though always posed several problems for the crew. Despite being anchored in relatively quiet waters, the crew could get no sleep during the night with a shipload full of livestock and the unceasing bleating and bawling of the barnyard choir. There was the added work of watering the animals and with the load of sheep and cattle, the morning's deck would be covered from one end to the other with an ample accumulation of slippery shit, and shovelling it overboard was the tedious task facing the ship's crew at the crack of dawn.

On this particular occasion another nor'easter was brewing and it looked like a typical layover night, accompanied with the usual discomfort for the crew. No one was terribly enthused about overnighting at Kelly's Cove, least of all Mickey. So Mickey, who was noted for his superb helmsmanship, told Captain Dan that he thought they could make it safely into Sydney Harbour. The skipper was dubious at first but relented, telling Mickey, "You take the wheel MacLean and go for it!"

Well, the nor'easter was even fiercer than anyone had anticipated and Mickey ran the *Lakeview* out an extra distance, further out past Point Aconi than usual, awaiting his chance to safely bring the ship about for the easier run into port. They were running out of time and room however, when Mickey finally glimpsed what he thought was a slight lull in the wind and sea so he immediately put the wheel hard to starboard; but the *Lakeview* was slow to respond and the broaching seas caught her savagely amidships with crushing accuracy, smashing in the galley's portholes with great crashing sounds while swiping clean the ship's decks and the evening's table with whatever pots and dishes the frightened cook had attempted to arrange. As the violent seas broke over the ship's decks old Captain Dan became rattled and challenged Mickey: "You've lost her MacLean! You've lost her!"

Mickey displaying more coolness on the outside than he later said he was feeling inside calmly retorted, "Errr, no damn way skipper, I haven't lost her; I haven't lost her at all!" Soon the SS *Lakeview* was safely on her new heading into Sydney Harbour.

Well, if the nor'easter experienced in Sydney bight was a blistering one, so proved to be the one that the *Lakeview*'s owner delivered as a welcoming salvo to the spent crew as they tied up dockside.

> Well the old bastard was livid, chuckled Mickey. He was just beside himself, fit to be tied! He was wild about the broken glass and the deck damage, which was really only minor, the water aboard and the broken dishes, mostly trifling stuff that had occurred. He chastised Captain Dan and the crew for being so foolhardy, for not waiting out the storm as their sister ship and crew had done. He raved and raged, went on flailing his arms and was relentless in his condemnation of the entire episode.

Well when finally the owner eased off, Captain Dan saw his chance and he let fly back at the owner with some of his own choice words. He pointedly stated something to the effect:

> At least the owner has one vessel with a good and capable crew and that there are no chicken-shit sailors under his command. We are here, he continued, and the boat and livestock are here, safe and sound. There are seamen aboard this vessel - goddamn good capable seamen – and you should be grateful that you have them and they are still working for you. That's all that really matters!

So taken aback with that unexpected broadside, the still muttering owner retreated; and like the late evening winds, things gradually returned to normal.

Mickey chuckled again as he finished off with a sequel. "Errr, I never did tell Captain Dan that I was kind of anxious to get ashore myself. I had a date bargained with a young one in town that evening. I was glad we made it!"[79]

MV *Shenacadie*

The MV *Shenacadie* started its mail-boat run in the mid-1940s. Originally christened the *Tomahawk,* she was owned by Wint MacDonald of Sydney who had been involved with coal mining in the Bras d'Or area. Four Baddeck investors, Walter Pinaud, George P. Fraser, Gordon S. Harvey and Gordon MacAulay bought her from MacDonald and placed her on the mail route for twice-a-day sailings between the Baddeck and Iona, stopping when required with freight and passengers at MacKay Point, and whenever an easterly was blowing too viciously, substituting the Iona wharf with the more sheltered one at Shunacadie. The *Shenacadie* succeeded the MV *Pearl Cann,* and ran until the mid-1960s, when the mail began to be delivered exclusively via highway. The *Pearl Cann* was had been skippered by Captain Carmichael. It is thought that the Baddeck-Iona mail boat and freight service began ca.1891.

Alec MacDonald was one of the vessel's engineers. Other members that served as engineers and crewed over two decades included Wishie Rose, Todd Taylor, Donnie Ryan, and Andrew Morrison. Skippers included Danny (Murdock) MacDonald and George Dolmont.

Diluted Wine

James MacDonald of Baddeck crewed on the *Shenacadie* as a young lad. He recounts one occasion when he was with Captain Dolmont in the wheelhouse as they approached the Iona wharf. "There was no response from the engine room when the Captain rang the bell for the engineer to slow the engines," says James. On the skipper's urgent command James scampered down into the engine room to ascertain what the problem might be. There he found the engineer fast asleep on a metal folding chair between the ship's two big diesel engines. Without time to throttle back the engines' revolutions, James immediately shoved the engine controls into full reverse, knowingly afraid that his action could tear out both transmissions. A glance through the engine room's porthole displayed the Iona wharf speeding by, just as he encountered the gut-wrenching jolt and sounds of the vessel grinding to what in the end, proved to be a reasonably soft landing on the Iona beach. "A bit more time and water would have resulted in really no grounding at all," recalls James.

Young James's quick action and boat handling awareness prevented any serious damage to the vessel whose engines then easily reversed the boat off the gravel beach and delivered its crew and mail safely back to home port that evening. Captain Dolmont's rueful, and curt, aside directed toward the by-now fully rousted engineer summed up the incident succinctly:

> At last sir, you have finally succeeded in putting the *Shenacadie* almost onto the altar of the St. Columba church![80]

Perhaps a little more water in the wine could have prevented the mishap altogether.

Imagine the Adventure!

Ron Gillis whose father Martin was railroad station agent at Iona in the 1940s and early 50s, is quoted in *The Victoria Standard* in the preamble to a piece of poetry entitled, "Village Boy."

> Also mentioned in the "Village Boy" are two personalities, John S. MacNeil, an Iona teamster, and Captain Dan MacDonald, skipper of the mail and passenger boat called the *Shenacadie*, which derived her name from that small community.... The *Shenacadie* made two trips daily from Baddeck to Iona. It arrived at 9 am to meet the No. 9 train, and at 5 pm to meet the No. 5 train to transport mail and passengers via Washabuck and Baddeck.... John S. was the local freight hauler with his horse, September, and wagon, transported mail and freight to the *Shenacadie* moored at the Government Wharf.

Ron, then 8 years old, adds:

> I was a constant companion, riding on top of cargo, sometimes accompanied by Captain Dan. Captain Dan ... hailed from Baddeck. He, along with crew member Wishie Rose, also from Baddeck ... would often invite my brother and me along to accompany them across the lake. Sometimes Captain Dan would let me take the wheel. Imagine the adventure![81]

Captain George Dolmont of North Sydney took over command as the *Shenacadie*'s new skipper upon Captain Dan MacDonald's retirement and he served in that capacity until the mail boat service was finally discontinued in the mid-1960s.

10-21 The MV *Tomahawk* at the Iona wharf. The boat was later renamed the Shenacadie and delivered mail on the Lake. L-R: Wishie Rose with his faithful companion, Tippy; Dan Malcolm MacKinnon, Barra Glen, and John S. MacNeil, Iona, with his horse September, ca. 1949.

TRANSPORTATION

Washabuck River

Within recent geological times there has been but little tidal exchange to the waters of Bras d'Or Lake, fluctuating from about .1 to .3 metres on a large tide; this consequently has little impact on water levels on Washabuck River. Nonetheless, recent decades have definitely seen higher amplitude "tides" not only from normal lunar impact but also due to more volatile pressure fronts passing through the Atlantic region, and the consequence of stronger sustained winds, particularly nor'easters, creating uncommon sea-surges on the lakes.

10-22 An aerial view looking eastward from the mouth of Washabuck River. MacDonalds Cove can be seen at the near right, while MacIvers Cove is to the far right of Murphys Point. Jeannies Cove is to the near left and Baddeck visible in the distance on the far shore. Courtesy of David Gillis, Scotsville, CB, October 17, 2007.

The Washabuck River is fed partially by the Washabuck waterfalls and its waters mingle with the Baddeck, Middle and Humes Rivers as they empty into the Bras d'Or Lake's north basin. Washabuck River effectively drains the Washabuck peninsula watershed, diluting the saltiness of the Lake, if only marginally. Geologically speaking the Washabuck River watershed is fairly complicated. Draining an area of ~24 km^2, the northwest half of the watershed is underlain mainly with gypsum and shale with many sink holes, while the south and east sides are underlain by more resistant rock types such as hard sandstone, siltstones, shales and slates.[82]

In his 2004 Geological Thesis entitled, *Geology of The Washabuck Peninsula,* Acadia University graduate Darin Wasylik writes:

> The Washabuck Peninsula lies in the central part of the Bras d'Or Terrane which is comprised of four main pre-Carboniferous components.[83] [T]he Washabuck peninsula has shown economic importance with gypsum and lead-zinc showings in the Carboniferous units. The presence of an old gold mine and several smaller exploration pits on the Maskells Harbour property indicates that the pre-Carboniferous rocks may have economic potential as well.[84]

Washabuck River is perhaps best noted for its recreational activities: swimming, angling, bird-hunting and boating. The river's plump oyster quality trumps those found elsewhere within Atlantic Canada. For generations, they had been highlighted as the pre-eminent natural oyster by the mollusk's discriminating connoisseur. Then in 2002, the near-shore industry was decimated by the uncontrollable marine pathogen MSX. Although it is not hazardous for humans, the parasite caused two problems for the oyster: restrictions on its movement and its mortality. Until that time, oyster farming in the microclimates of Washabuck River and nearby MacIver's Cove had been a long-time cottage industry for residents with government leases.[85]

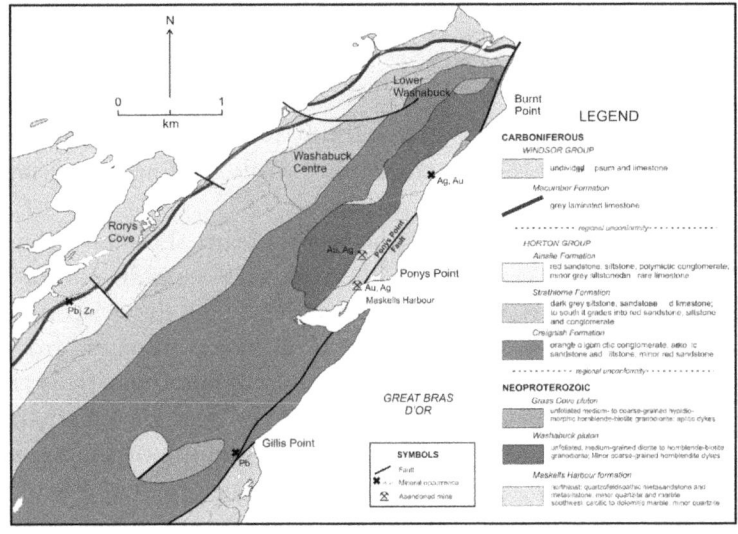

10-23 Geological map of the Washabuck Peninsula, simplified from Darin Wasylik's science degree thesis, Acadia University, 2004.

Easily accessible from along the Washabuck highway, much of the graceful river system has been a favourite trout fishing habitat and has succeeded in luring the island's sport fishermen and women. The river's peaceful shoreline is a perennial nesting domain for the bald eagle, the blue heron and more recently, the occasional family of osprey. These majestic birds share the river's viands with the migratory flocks of nesting duck and geese, while the river's coves and inlets provide select hunting camouflages for bird hunters.

In earlier times, the winter provided easier movement of man and beast throughout the sections of the community bordering the river. Unlike today, a hundred and fifty years ago both sides of the river were moderately populated. Across-the-river travel for teamsters with their teams and sleighs, utilizing the frozen river made for comparatively shorter, faster and unencumbered mobility, a vast improvement over the otherwise narrow, tormented, snow-banked "roads" during those challenging days. The movement of forest products, including firewood, commercially sawn-logs and pit-props, was made significantly easier by the use of the frozen river. Recreational ice-fishing and skating were other traditional winter activities enjoyed on the river's glib surface.

Nerve Centre

The *Ocean Lilly*, a 136-ton tern schooner, was built upon the river's bank in 1885. But it was the erection of a lumber mill and the construction of a privately built wharf at Cole Point in 1909 that the Washabuck River became a bustling nerve centre. New Brunswick lumberman William C. Dryden built the wharf for the transport of his own lumber. A few years later, in 1911, the construction of the government wharf nearby made the river a main medium of communication and transportation, with vessels disembarking passengers and crews, unloading essential products and general supplies while loading newly sawn lumber for delivery to more exotic Atlantic ports.

The shrill scream of the saw, the resounding chatter and rant of edging saws, the sounds of neighing horse teams delivering log-laden bobsleighs reverberating through the crisp morning air and the snorting horses responding to urgent commands from their harried teamsters. These were sounds of economic progress. This clatter, snarled with the clash of sharp-shod hooves upon frost-glazed wharf planking and cries from the bustling mill crew, locals and imports alike, jumbled with the whiff of freshly sawn lumber and the ever-growing pile of orange sawdust, meant cold hard cash for the community. It meant money being made. It meant progress.

Throughout those Dryden years, during the springtime logging drives, the Washabuck River was spanned with a boom, from Cole Point[86] reaching

10-24 and 10-25 Cole Point then and now. In the background (North side Washabuck River) the vacant homesteads of Joe MacKenzie (left) and Johnny Campbell's (right) can be seen. "Then" photo ca. 1930, courtesy of Frances MacDougall, Mabou, CB.

across to Tom's Point[87] on the river's north side, filled with a winter's-worth of saw logs.

St. Patrick vs. Jack Frost

The River's beguiling north side is known as Pleasant Point, with its lower-lying bank the beneficiary of eons of fertile silt deposits, passively awaiting the pioneers' calloused hand. Enjoying a southern exposure to late winter and early spring sunshine and sheltered from the chilling blasts of northerly winds, this area had proven to be as viable a farming area as any in the extended district. Perhaps, it's due too, to what Nova Scotia geological surveyor and mapper Hugh Fletcher describes when he writes: "The best farms of Baddeck, the Great and Little Narrows, Washaback [sic], East Bay and other districts have a rich marl or calcareous Lower Carboniferous bottom."[88] These marl deposits at an earlier time manifested themselves for local farmers with modest pits located in Cain's Mountain, Upper Washabuck and Washabuck Centre.

The following is undoubtedly an isolated example but, nonetheless, one that hints at that area's potential for yielding early harvests. Pat Murphy, a north-side river resident, invoked Providence and St. Patrick one season by planting potato seed on the 17th of March in some of the local luxuriant soil he had transferred into a derelict dory. With its skeletal hulk broached precariously upon the river's bank, partially filled with this loam of profusion, and coaxed by the early sunshine and unseasonably mild weather, and despite wrangling with the *Latha Giobagan* (the knifing March winds), the early weather had coerced the enterprising Irishman to lead by foremost example his neighbours' dilatory ways. Within a couple of weeks this venture of aberration had prevailed auspiciously with the appearance of early tops, when alas, an impetuous Jack Frost brought the budding to a hostile and ruinous end.[89] One can only imagine what jarring disillusionment the hijacked caper brought to the sprightly potato beetle! (Might they have been Irish cobblers?)

10-26 Johnny Campbell's Cove is a backdrop for the rafted flotilla of Cruising Club of America yachts in Washabuck River, July 18 1975. This spectacular photo was captured by Pony's Point summer resident Diana Russell, from atop *Windigo*'s 80- foot mast. The homesteads of Jim Alec MacDougall and John A. MacDougall can be seen in the background. Courtesy of Diana Russell and *National Geographic*. (See also appendix 9).

Arguably harbouring some of the finest coves and inlets on all the spectacular Bras d'Or, Washabuck's meandering river provides a plethora of safe, secluded havens, with discrete mooring sites for the discriminating mariner. For millennia the domain of the Mi'kmaq, this humble river's unsullied rendezvous for rafting and mug-ups, the river's snug coves – Jeannie and Johnny Campbell's besides the yawning and insulated, Indian and Deep coves – these havens have been long-time favourite anchorages for the Cruising Club of America, Atlantic Canada yachtsman and now the more recently established Ocean Cruising Club.

Washabuck River Nature Reserve

A 67-hectare swath of land on the most northern end of Birch Point near South Cove has been designated as an ecological site to be known as Washabuck River Nature Reserve.[90] In 2006, owners Henry W. Fuller of Baddeck and Dr. James V. O'Brien of Big Harbour placed the land under the *Special Places Protection Act* of Nova Scotia. Birch Point was a special place for Hebridean pioneers two centuries ago and it is gratifying to know that a portion of it is now officially designated to permanently remain that way.

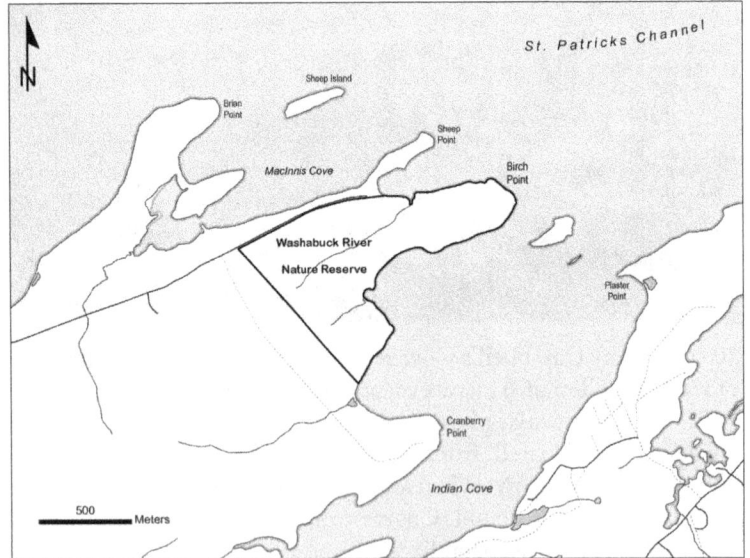

10-27 Map displaying outline of Washabuck River Nature Reserve at Birch Point. Image courtesy of Nova Scotia Environment © 2014.

10-28 Birch Point highway sign.

Twilight on the Washabuck

In the heart of our highlands cool poplars are whispering
Clear skies meet the purple of mountains below
Herons wing without signs of a great mediation
To their nest and their rest they must go
The Glen keeps its secrets as the cattle comes homeward
Bells ring a toneless tho' heartwarming lay
Soon they'll stand or lie dreaming of things cattle dream of
And sigh as their day goes away

Fragrant hay mown today that will soon be dew covered
Lies in rows as perfect as soldiers in dress
It waits for the new day and the move to new station
Its mother the good earth will rest
Stillness surrounds the old farm and its neighbours
An owl hoots as questing, it goes on the wing
On a lonely verandah a guitar is strumming
And a muted voice soothingly sings

The stars in the heavens now fight for attention
'Gainst light of dim windows now faintly a glare
The day has now dawned in faraway places
And the night comes to us from o'er there
We have found blessed peace in a world that seems crazy
Cool evening breezes lull each to his rest
We have no great care for mind bending bustle
This home by our river is best.

Charles A. "Brother" MacKenzie (1924-1989)
Washabuck Bridge

10-29 Dan Joe MacKenzie, Birch Point/Ottawa Brook; Danny Murphy, Upper Washabuck and Joe MacKenzie, Washabuck/Highland Hill, CB, ca. 1950.

10-30 Charles A. "Brother" MacKenzie (1924-1989) Washabuck Bridge.

Early Roads and Bridges

It was decades after the arrival of the pioneers before anything resembling a road existed in any local community. Throughout Lower Washabuck, footpaths wound their way along the shoreline of St. Patrick's Channel. In Upper Washabuck, toward Washabuck Bridge, pathways followed both banks of the Washabuck River.

Footpaths and shortcuts eventually connected most of the neighbouring homesteads. Brush fences delineating property lines and animal enclosures frequently impeded passageway along the trails. Easy and quick access to the main waterway was essential, although often a challenge. Gradually the pathways were widened for the benefit of oxen and later horses weighted with sleighs and carts. Swollen streams and brooks were traversed with care as freshets made them particularly hazardous to navigate. The Washabuck River itself had to be forded cautiously. Lives were lost through treacherous river and lake ice.

Early in the 20th century the Nova Scotia Government embarked on a program of bridge construction.[91] Robert Musgrave and Son of North Sydney was a particularly knowledgeable bridge-building firm and won many contracts in those early days. The iron bridge that spanned Washabuck River was erected as early as 1905. It is referred to (somewhat confusingly) in Department of Transportation records as Morrison Bridge. After collapsing in February 1966, the 50-ft (15 m) pony-truss iron bridge was replaced with a creosote timber structure at a cost of $4,481.[92]

In 1895, a large number of residents from Rear Upper Washabuck and Rear Grand Narrows [St. Columba] signed a petition to the Honourable members of the House of Assembly requesting the completion of a road upgrade.

> That about ten years ago a committee appointed by the Municipal Council of Victoria County established a line for a new road to connect the road that leads from Washabuck River to the Bras d'Or Lake with the road that leads from Grand Narrows to McKinnon's Harbour. That in the years 1891 and 1892 the government granted the sum of two hundred and fifty dollars in all for the opening of this line. That said sum was expended to the best advantage, but that a portion of the road remains yet unfinished and is serviceable only during a part of the winter. That the finishing of said road would be most beneficial to a large number of the inhabitants of these districts, affording easy access to their markets and mills besides to the general advantage to the public. That petitioners would beg leave to state that the sum of two hundred dollars would be adequate to finish the said road….[93]

Another petition accompanied with a roughly drawn sketch in 1904 by South Cove residents to the Assembly of Nova Scotia reads:

> The petition of Norman McRitchie, Kenneth A. McRitchie and others of South Side St. Patrick's Channel in the County of Victoria, respectfully showeth serious inconvenience owing to the want of road leading westward from Washabuck Bridge and the north side of Washabuck River through petitioners property which is inaccessible to without said road and to connect with the Jubilee Settlement a distance of three miles off by such road the general public would be greatly accommodated and travelling facilitated to communicate with the boat at the new wharf at Washabuck Centre the direction in which petitioners generally communicate … pray that your honourable Body … grant an equivalent sum for the opening said road. The proposed land is both level and inviting….

Signed,
Norman McRitchie,
Kenneth A. McRitchie, South Cove,
D. J. McRitchie, Little Narrows Vic. Co.; along with thirty-four additional signatures.[94]

10-31 Washabuck Bridge highway sign.

Over a long period and where it proved convenient, the Washabuck "main road" was gradually relocated away from the lake shoreline and became more aligned with newer permanent residences. By 1920, the provincial government had taken over sole responsibility for highways in the province,[95] ending participation by municipal councils in bridge and highway matters, as did the requirements of statute labour.[96] All males between the ages of twenty-one and sixty years were to perform two days' work on the local roads as a poll-tax. Fines were imposed for failure to provide the service but a person would be relieved of his duty by paying fifty cents in cash in lieu of each day's labour shirked.[97] Road changes, upgrades and improvements all marched to a sluggish drummer.

"Ka-ching"

What could be classed as major road construction was carried out through Washabuck between 1947 and 1949, under the supervision of the Department of Highways. The new construction extended from Dan MacDougall's at Washabuck Bridge eastward to Washabuck Centre. The highway superintendent was Murdock Buchanan of Baddeck, followed by Hector MacKenzie of Boularderie and finally a Mr. Stevenson who was a one-time Mayor of Glace Bay. He oversaw the project through to its completion. Francis B. MacDonald of Lower Washabuck was local foreman. Hector MacKenzie, boarded at the home of Jimmy and Annie MacKenzie while the Stevenson family rented William and *Beatag* MacKenzie's home in Lower Washabuck, the residence that shortly afterward became the permanent home of their own son Tommy his wife Cassie and their family.

Government equipment included a gasoline shovel which was operated by a Mr. Morrison from St. Peter's and later by Cecil MacInnis from Little Narrows. Cecil was known as a particularly capable operator. Tragically, he was killed in an industrial accident some years later while working in the Sydney area. Udovan Brothers from Glace Bay provided the balance of the construction equipment which included a front-end loader and a newly acquired $8,000 bulldozer that required an auxiliary engine to start its main engine. Mr. Stevenson's son operated a piece of this heavy equipment. He also drove a new dump truck, the only truck on the project with a steel box.

Pit-run aggregate was excavated from a site on the south-side of Holy Rosary Cemetery and the balance was secured from a pit on the Murdock Paul MacLean property. The quarry drilling and shooting was deftly executed by Clarence "The Bear" MacLeod from Middle River, a Second World War veteran, and legend throughout the County of Victoria and beyond.

Local truckers included the Murphy brothers Peter, Hughie, Donald and Roddie from McKinnons Harbour driving a Fargo truck. Francis (Dan A.) MacDonald of Iona piloted a Mercury truck while Duncan Campbell ran a Maple Leaf. Rod N. Matheson from Little Narrows, a beloved individual who was never too busy to stop and pick up school children along the way, operated a Ford truck while Duncan Campbell of Cain's Mountain owned two trucks. A. N. MacLean of Little Narrows drove for him. A. N. is remembered as a particularly fine man, who struggled with a severe hearing disability. The only way he could be sure that the truck's motor was still running was by observing whether or not its hood ornament was vibrating.

Johnny (Angus Ranald) MacDonald of Upper Washabuck had just returned from a two-year mining stint in Northern Ontario. He operated a new 1948 International truck purchased for $2,700 from Sampson Motors in Sydney. Two years later he bought a 1950 International from dealer John Michael MacLean in Baddeck, who then sold the trade-in to Lloyd Matheson of Little Narrows. All of the project's trucks had hoists, wooden boxes and were classed as two-ton trucks.

Mickey MacDougall of Washabuck Bridge maneuvered a second-hand 1947 Ford bought for $1,400, financed from his muskrat trap-line earnings. Pete Norton of Little Narrows owned two trucks, a Fargo and 1947 Mercury. Joe MacDougall drove a 1946 Chevrolet, which was claimed by his colleagues, to be the best truck on the project. Hugh Campbell from St. Columba and Archie MacDonald from Middle River both operated Dodge trucks as did Douglas Russell of Estmere with his 1948 Dodge. Many of these local truckers were veterans who had recently returned from overseas and the perils of the Second World War.

Labourers were paid fifty cents an hour for a nine-hour day, while the water-boys, Andy and Roddie MacDonald were reimbursed at the rate of forty cents an hour. Culverts were constructed out of local timber and then coated with hot creosote by Peter MacKenzie and Danny Murphy. Drift bolts were shaped and sized by blacksmith Ranald MacDonald, who was often assisted by his nephew Raymond. Truckers received $20.00 a day, with $5 going toward the gasoline bill.

Roddie MacDonald recalls a special "Ka-ching" moment at the local post office when he witnessed trucker Joe MacDougall, a wounded veteran, display his just-received pay cheque – $218.40 for two weeks employment. "A comfortable issue!" exclaimed the jubilant Joe, flashing his beguiling smile. He promptly celebrated the pecuniary proceeds with an exuberant three-day spree. He was not alone.[98] Accumulated expenditures of the 5.5 miles of road construction spanning the three year period amounted in excess of $91,000.[99]

Asphalt

Further major road construction and the paving of the Washabuck road occurred during 1981-1983 with LeVatte Construction and Municipal Spraying and Contracting Ltd. of Sydney winning the tender. William D. MacLean was the Department of Transportation's project engineer. The road was reconstructed from Washabuck Bridge through to MacKay Point, a distance of 13.3 kilometres. Equipment and operators were provided by LeVatte's, but a few local men were hired as skilled operators, including Larry (Murdock) MacNeil of Iona, James Andre MacKinnon of MacKinnon Harbour and Norman Matheson of Little Narrows.

Pit-run material was obtained from nearby pits located at properties owned by Rose and Ronald MacDonald, Malkie MacDonald, at *Peigag n'in Ruairidh* MacDonald's in Upper Washabuck and at Jimmy and Annie MacKenzie's in Lower Washabuck. The paving of the newly constructed road was completed on October 6, 1983. Total gross expenditure amounted to $843,263, including construction, gravelling and the acquisition of lands. The paving of 6.5 kilometres of the Gillis Point road between Washabuck and Maskells Harbour was completed by Willow Contracting Ltd. at the same time at a cost of $518,752.[100] This road was not reconstructed prior to paving.

Pride of Place

Three momentous transportation developments occurred close by and had huge long-term repercussions in Cape Breton, in Canada, indeed around the globe. These relevant events took place but a stone's throw from Washabuck shorelines, during the decades straddling the turn of the last century.

Railroad

In 1890, the commencement of railway service throughout Cape Breton Island was launched with the completion of the Inter-Colonial Railway (ICR). After vigorous debate in Parliament the national government designated that the rail line was to take the central route through Cape Breton Island. This decision had a positive impact on the communities throughout Central Cape Breton, resulting in employment for local residents. First during the construction of the rail line and the Grand Narrows Railway Bridge that spans the Barra Strait. Upon their completion, local residents continued to be employed as local Bridge and Building (B&B) operators and Extra-Gang maintenance crews.

With the advent of the railroad came the easier movement of passengers, freight and Royal Mail, having particular impact on the nearby communities of Iona and Grand Narrows, each with its own lively railroad station. The Grand Narrows Hotel was built, as were two restaurants, one on each side of the Barra Strait. These, and other service-oriented businesses, catered to the tourist, stimulating the growth of a burgeoning industry. Marine steamer connections throughout the lakes were now massaged to mesh with regular train schedules and suddenly the world became more accessible for all Island residents, including those beating the bushes throughout the outposts of Central Cape Breton.

Wooden pit-props, gypsum and, in later decades with the arrival of refrigeration cars, live lobster, were now marketable to national and international consumers via this ribbon of steel. The weekly delivery of railcars carrying coal to the Iona siding, where they were in-turn shunted via spur-line to nearby Grass Cove, enabled a cooking and drying process that made for a viable value-added plaster industry. The resulting plaster was marketed in bags and barrels and shipped via bulk carrier and railroad, to consumers. As many as a hundred workers were employed annually at the Grass Cove operation for a couple of decades, until the plant's closure in 1931.[101]

10-32 A Grass Cove Gypsum Company work crew, ca. 1921-1931. Front Row L-R: Johnny MacLean, Washabuck; Peter F. MacLean, Washabuck/Iona; Dan D. MacNeil, Grass Cove. Centre Row L-R: Alex Campbell, Gillis Point East; Peter MacLean, Washabuck Centre; Ambrose MacNeil, Gillis Point; John N. MacNeil, MacNeil's Vale; Frank MacNeil, Gillis Point; John Allan MacNeil, MacNeil's Vale; Joe MacLaughlan, St. John, NB. Back Row L-R: John MacNeil, Christmas Island; Bill McGovern, Saint John, NB; Michael Campbell, Gillis Point East; Neil A. MacNeil, Gillis Point; Joe MacNeil, Iona; Neil S. MacLean, Washabuck Centre; John MacNeil, Gillis Point; Rory MacNeil, MacNeil's Vale; Allan Austin MacNeil, Gillis Point. Names provided by F. X. MacNeil, Iona, to Grade 12 Rankin Memorial School students Janet Gillis, Jamesville, Brenda MacDonald and Beverly MacLean, Washabuck. Photo courtesy of Carmie MacLean, Washabuck.

Silver Dart

Although it took Canadians some time to realize it, Canada and the all the world were impacted by the first heavier-than-air powered flight in the British Empire. Led by inventor Alexander Graham Bell and his similar-

10-33 H. F. MacDougall, MP for Christmas Island, is joined by a legion of dignitaries aboard the flatcar making the first crossing of the Grand Narrows Railroad Bridge. The locomotive behind is piloted by Governor-General Lord Stanley, October 18, 1890. Courtesy of Beaton Institute.

minded team of enthusiastic visionaries, the first powered flight of a flying machine was piloted by J. A. Douglas McCurdy on February 23, 1909, on ice-covered Baddeck Bay. The *Silver Dart* claimed the gold medal for Canadian aviation initiative and ingenuity that eventually spawned the colossal global aviation industry.

Grasping the keen observations of his astute wife Mabel, Dr. Bell endorsed her idea of forming an Aerial Experiment Association (AEA), a "co-operative, scientific association, not for gain but for the love of art and doing what we can to help one another."[102] He assembled a team which Mabel funded with monies from a recent inheritance.

While some Washabuck residents may have failed to realize the significance of that day in history, a scan of the various names listed as witnesses of McCurdy's first flight of the Silver Dart, as compiled by a Mr. Alec MacDonald in February 1909, displays such names as, John McKay, Michael McLean, Hector P. McNeil, M. C. McLean and Dan Campbell, who were originally from Washabuck and/or Gillis Point, many of them long-time employees of Professor Bell. (See Appendix 10 – List of *Silver Dart* Witnesses, Courtesy of Parks Canada/Alexander Graham Bell National Historic Site.)

Fifteen years later, Neil P. S. MacLean of Lower Washabuck noted in his diary on October 14, 1924, "...first seaplane seen here flying in the air and alighting in Baddeck Harbour."[103] Rare are the communities, that can claim to having witnessed such a consummate moment in Canadian and Commonwealth aviation history, one that unfolded so splendidly a century ago, parallel to its own shores.

Hydrofoil

Similarly, another noteworthy world-class achievement that Dr. Bell and his team accomplished was the development of the hydrofoil and the testing of the *HD-4*, which was the fastest marine craft in the world in 1919. The term "hydrodrome" translates from the Greek as "watercraft," hence the initials *HD*. Bell had dreamed of designing and building a fast boat, one that would "go over, instead of through the water."[104] Over a period of years, assisted by his intrepid colleague Casey Baldwin, a series of hydrofoil craft were designed and tested on the waters of Baddeck Bay.

The following description was written by Edward Grosvenor and Morgan Wesson, authors of *Alexander Graham Bell*, a beautiful book about the inventor. It succinctly encapsulates a description of the *HD-4*, the last in the series, and its record breaking feat.

> By 1919 they had constructed a huge, streamlined, cigar-shaped boat with three stout hydrofoils below swept-wing splashguards that gave the HD-4 a modernistic look. With the roar of two powerful 350-horsepower Liberty engines, the sleek, sixty-foot craft made an unforgettable impression. As the boat passed fifteen miles per hour, it slowly lifted out of the water, and then "clear of the drag she drives ahead with an acceleration that makes you grip your seat to keep from being left behind," said one observer. It reached the remarkable speed of 70.86 miles per hour, a world record it held for over ten years.[105]

Again, a world-class occurrence exhibited upon St. Patrick's Channel, a couple of kilometers from Washabuck's shoreline, a determined, triumphing feat of marine vision.

11 – Communications

Newspapers

Victoria County's first newspaper began in 1884 with Arthur McCurdy editing the *Island Reporter* in Baddeck until it's folding in 1887. The *Reporter* was followed by the *Baddeck Telephone,* first published by Charles Peppy in 1898, that ran until its demise in 1900. In 1909, Charles E. Gilman, a Boston born American, began editing and publishing the *Victoria News*, which functioned until 1927. This paper later morphed into the *Victoria-Inverness Bulletin* and, later still, *The Scotia Sun*.[1]

It was with the *Victoria News* that Neil F. MacNeil (1891-1969) of Washabuck got his start in journalism with his appointment as he puts it as the paper's "Washabuckt correspondent."

> Weekly I gathered local personal items and mailed them to the editor; for which I got no pay but the honor and experience. I shall never forget the thrill of seeing my first efforts in type. I was also thrilled by the fame and dignity my writing brought me in the community. Perhaps, journalism was in my blood; anyway it became my life's work.[2]

Neil F. went on to spend more than three decades as a newspaper man, serving as the *New York Times* managing editor for twenty-one years.

Today, Victoria County is again enriched with its own county paper. The first issue of *The Victoria Standard* was printed in March 1993. James Morrow of Middle River is editor and general manager and the paper is published fortnightly by Bras d'Or Graphic Marketing.[3]

Telegraph

The 19th century witnessed the onset of a communication revolution that had a profound impact on the world. Samuel Morse (1791-1872) demonstrated a working model of the telegraph in 1837 and by 1844 there existed a 40-mile-long telegraph line connecting the American cities of Baltimore and Washington.[4] Transatlantic cable communications commenced on July 27 1866, connecting the Europe with North America at the cable station at Heart's Content, Newfoundland.[5]

Nova Scotia historian A. A. (Tony) MacKenzie (1926-2004), writes of the introduction of the early telegraph system into Nova Scotia. MacKenzie, like his father before him, had been a telegraph and telephone lineman for much of his early life, prior to his professorship at St. Francis Xavier University.

> Geography made Nova Scotia a vital link in telegraph and cable systems that connected the Old World and the New. In 1850, even before the first Atlantic cable existed, the Nova Scotia Electric Telegraph Company erected a line, nine-gauge iron wire on native poles, linking Cape Breton Island with a line already in service across New Brunswick to Calais, Maine. Very soon afterwards that company and the Dominion Telegraph Company had lines through Antigonish connecting with the Atlantic Cable in Aspy Bay, Cape Breton, and the direct cable at Tor Bay near Larry's River. The American communication colossus, Western Union Telegraph and Cable, took over the Nova Scotia Electric Telegraph Company in 1871 and opened a cable station at North Sydney soon afterward. Within ten years Western Union also had a cable station at Canso. Its monopoly of transatlantic communication was soon threatened by commercial cable which opened a cable station at Hazel Hill in 1884.... By 1910 telegraph and/or telephone poles ran along most roads and railroad lines.[6]

Charles Dudley Warner, in his 1874 travelogue *Baddeck, and that Sort of Thing*, mentions that he wired Baddeck from Plaster Cove [Port Hastings] informing them of his pending arrival.

> We telegraphed our coming to Baddeck, and departed. For twenty-five cents one can send a dispatch to any part of the Dominion except the region where Western Union has still a foothold.[7]

In December 1881, Robert Elmsley writes that "Telegraph poles put up here [Baddeck] today, 50 yards apart. One man puts in 8 a day, four feet deep."[8] By Christmas of that year there were seventy-five poles extending from the courthouse at the centre of Chebucto Street eastward towards Mrs. Tom Haliburton's gate, a distance of well over two miles.[9]

David A. and Catherine (McGrath) Dunlop arrived in Baddeck in 1858 or 1859. David was a native of Scotland who was employed in the laying of the Atlantic cable from Scotland to Newfoundland, and the Overland Telegraph from Newfoundland to Cape North, Victoria County. When the Cable was laid to Cape North, Mr. Dunlop was placed in charge of laying the wires overland from Cape North to Port Hastings.[10] His wife, Catherine, who was from Maggoty Cove, Newfoundland, immediately saw the potential in the developing town for a boarding house with a telegraph office. By 1860 they had the Telegraph House constructed on Chebucto Street.[11] Upon completion of the stringing of the overland wires David then was placed in charge of the telegraph office operation which he ran out of the Telegraph House, hence the name.

A change in government resulted in the telegraph being transferred to the Bras d'Or House in 1899. A subsequent change of government returned telegraph central office to the Telegraph House some years later. Mrs. Maud (Dunlop) MacKenzie was the operator at that time.

According to Mary (Alfred) MacDonald (1909-2011) the telegraph system was located in the very cold annex on the eastern side of the Telegraph House. Accommodations were available there as well. Marie Samson of St. Peter's arrived in Baddeck to temporarily operate the telegraph system while she trained a squad of potential local candidates in Morse code for the position. Ms. Samson apparently had no intention of becoming a permanent resident of the Baddeck community.

Janie Campbell (1897-1990), a daughter of Dan and Annie Campbell of Baddeck was among four or five trainees. Janie's mother was Annie MacLean, from MacKay Point. Janie was the only successful graduate and was subsequently offered and accepted the position as the community's full-time telegraph operator. Janie ran the wire operation out of the Telegraph House annex from 1916 until 1922, when she was given permission by Superintendent Simms to relocate the office to a building on her father's property on Cameron Street. Simms agreed, but on a rent-free basis. The office remained there until 1926.

Fire

In September 1926, as so much of Baddeck burned in a disastrous town fire, it became obvious to Dan Campbell that he and his family were about to lose their own home. It so happened that there was a navy ship in the harbour that night. Dan Campbell solicited the naval crew who had come ashore to assist in fighting the fire any way they could, to help him remove furniture and equipment out of his home and transfer it to the Telegraph House, which the fire left unscathed. There, the Campbell family lived in the annex until December when they moved into their rebuilt home.

Dan Campbell was a painter and carpenter. The day following the fire, he hired some help, and immediately started the clean-up and rebuilding process. His new house built on the same lot, included an enclosed veranda fronting on Cameron Street. Once their new home was completed, Janie Campbell received permission once again, to relocate telegraph central from the annex at the Telegraph House into the veranda area of her parent's new home.[12]

It was from this location that Janie ran the telegraph office operation until she retired in 1958, after serving as telegraph operator for forty-two years. Initially the telegraph operators received no salary, but operated on a commission basis. In 1930, they were classed as Civil Service employees and paid salaries. Officially the telegraph system in Cape Breton was phased out March 31 1959,[13] as the telephone and wireless radio had made it redundant.

11-1 Janie Campbell, Baddeck's telegraph operator of forty-two years, stands in front of her Cameron Street home (ca. 1980). It was from here that she ran Telegraph Central. Courtesy of Mary (Alfred) MacDonald, Baddeck, CB.

Via Wire and Wireless

The Canadian federal election of 1988 was fought essentially between the two main federal party leaders, Progressive Conservative Prime Minister Brian Mulroney and Liberal Party Leader John Turner. The election revolved around the contentious issue of "free trade" between Canada and the United States. Peter F. MacLean (1899-1996) a Washabuck native, then in his 89th year was living at his longtime Iona residence. Peter had been a solid supporter of the Progressive Conservative party for well over half a century. However, it hadn't always been the case.

Reminiscing over a beverage and in his characteristic drawl, Peter F. drew ironic parallels between the federal election debate of 1988 and the one he remembered as a twelve-year-old youth back in 1911, and the poignant impact the telegraph dramatically played on his memories of that election. This time around however, the parties' stances and their leaders' roles were reversed, although the divisive issue was the same. This time, the federal Liberal party was now emphatically leading the opposition against a hotly contested "free trade" agreement between Canada and the United States proposed by the Brian Mulroney-lead Progressive Conservative government.[14]

Peter F. reflected on Wilfred Laurier's 1896 federal election win that saw the Liberal party forming the government of Canada for the next fifteen years. Peter's parents were steadfast supporters of the Liberal party and his father Vincent, a fisherman and farmer, had shared in whatever patronage was disbursed to loyal rural party supporters of those times. In 1910-1911, a burning issue had arisen. Termed "reciprocity," it involved free trade between Canada and the United States. Robert Borden was the leader of the federal Progressive Conservatives and he and his party ran a vigorous campaign opposing reciprocity with a slogan of, "No truck or trade with the Yankees!" Prime Minister Laurier and his Liberal government advocated for reciprocity, even though, his own party was split on the issue.

Election Day was September 21, 1911. It was a quiet evening at MacKay Point. Vincent suggested to Peter, who was the eldest of the family that they row across St. Patrick's Channel to Baddeck and spend the evening around the telegraph office where they could glean the early election returns when they began to roll in on the wire.

Peter F. recalled the town of Baddeck was overrun with electors that night:

> People were arriving in town from the far-flung districts of the riding ... Big Baddeck, Little Narrows, Middle River, South Haven ... standing and milling around outside the Telegraph Office ... imbibing on election rum, laughing, cajoling with one another ... we witnessed a couple of brawls. It was still only early in the evening. Of course everyone was edgy and nervously hopeful for their own party's victory.

The MacLean's were eagerly anticipating another Liberal victory. The early results out of the Maritimes were not as robust for Laurier as they had been in previous elections, but nevertheless were still encouraging. Vincent, now a mite more appeased, and sensing another Liberal victory, suggested to Peter that they head back home across the lake, since it would be another hour before the returns from Quebec and Ontario would arrive.

Peter F. recalled how clear and bright that night was; how the surface of the calmed lake glistened in the glory of the unclouded moon, while the only sound that ruptured the idyllic passage was that of oars vigorously bending the waters as they propelled themselves homeward. The distance between the two communities, a tad shy of three kilometers was energetically closed by the strong-armed fishermen.

The rowboat was securely beached and the men walked casually from the shore up the hill toward their home, when suddenly, the serene night setting was shattered by a THUNDEROUS ROAR, followed by a VOLLEY OF DISTINCT HOOTS, WILD WHOOPS, and EXUBERANT YELLS from across the lake.

Both men stopped instantly in their tracks – turned their gaze toward the town so recently departed, and, mesmerized, stood there, in the exalted silence of the moment ... before Vincent turned towards his son and dishearteningly lamented:

"Peter, I think we have just lost the election."

Lost the election indeed! The election of the Progressive Conservatives was confirmed by newspaper reports in the ensuing days. Robert Borden and his party had swept victoriously through the provinces of Quebec, Ontario and British Columbia resulting in a decisive victory and a new government for Canada.

And that was how Peter F. MacLean, with the retrospection of 77 years, differentiated between the two national elections; pitted over the same volcanic issue of free trade, the acute stance adopted by each federal party in the discordant campaigns, the acerbic rhetoric of their political leaders and the similar outcomes of the elections, each won by the Progressive Conservatives, the party that successfully polarized the electorates into supporting its differing stances on the fiery proposition.

Undeniably, the keenest contrast Peter F. attested to was the state of current technology, teetering as it was on the cusp of the digital tsunami, versus the telegraph wire-system of yesteryear. And although those contrasts were obvious, Peter couldn't help but chuckle about how the polling results, such as they were of that historic 1911 Canadian election, were delivered to the Washabuck fishermen, bush-telegraphed – with such jarring, jolting, and wireless immediacy, an immediacy that unwittingly augured the coming of wireless.[15]

The Borden Song

Michael Charlie MacLean (1843-1934) was a blacksmith. He was born in Washabuck, the son of Charles (Hector *Gobha*) MacLean and Ann MacDonald. He relocated to Baddeck in 1873 where he ran a forge for several years. He later opened an establishment with rooms-for-let and dispensed strong drink – for those who appreciated beverages of that sort – until 1926, when his business was wiped out by the disastrous town fire. He married Euphemia Nicholson of Gairloch Mountain and they raised a family of eight children. Michael Charlie was clever, a Gàidhlig scholar, wit, fiddler, genealogist, church warden, businessman and generally a well-liked, well-known and highly respected citizen of the widespread community. He was noted especially for his poignant Gàidhlig compositions and had the ability as well, to compose a satirical or humourous song on a moment's notice. The following composition de-crying some early actions of the new federal administration was composed shortly after the 1911 election that saw the incumbent Liberal government under Wilfred Laurier defeated by Robert Borden and his Progressive Conservatives. [16,17]

Am Oran Bhorden
The Borden Song

11-2 Sheet music for "The Borden Song."

Am Oran Bhorden

1) Tha Borden an drasd' ann am Parlamaid Ottawa
Le moran de na cairdean a b'abhaest bhith aig Laurier
Gur e mhil a phartaidh bhith 'n fabhar reciprocity
Tha ceist lile n'drasd ann, chan fhearn l na 'n Temera
Gur e na Grits a fhuar an clisgeadh nuair a' bhrist an governme
Cha bhiodh e iongatch's am bith, sioma fear bha 'n office dhuibh
Tha Laurier's an opposition, s ni e segiam air chaereigin
'S mar dean e spairn dhuinn, bidh plaigh air na h-adhaircean.

The Borden Song

1) Borden is now in the Ottawa Parliament
By many of the friends who used to be Laurier's
What hurt the party was they favored reciprocity
There's a new question now, it's not manly what is Temera
It's the Grits who were startled when the government was defeated
It wouldn't be any wonder if it was everyone in office
Laurier is in opposition and he will come up with some scheme
And if he doesn't make an effort for us there will be a plague on their horns

2) Nis o'n fhuair thu fhein I chaidh t'eubhach 'n ad Premier
Tha long agad ri stiuradh 's cha churs' air a chairt agad
Bidh stoirm is muir dumhail 's ceo dluth a' tigh'n thairs ort
'S ma ghlaidheas tu do chursa, cha churam nach cala dhuit
Mam dean thu sin, 's ann dhutsa 's miosa leigeil air na cladaichean
Bidh do chairdean a thug dhuit I duilich mar a thachaid huit
'S fhad o'n chuala sinn am facal, "cha bheir gad air aithreachas"
'S ma leigeas thu dha'n ghrunnd I, bidh upraid am badaigin

3) Nuair chaidh thu measg nam Frangach, s tu 'n geall air na ballotan
Ag innse nach robh feum air an Navy an Canada
Chuidich iad thu an uair sin, 's ann suas air na geallaidhean
'Sa dh' aindeoin do chuid subhach, bidh Navy an Canada
Gheall thu lagh na sgoil a rinn na Grits a chur an ionad math dhuinne
'S dh' fhairtlich sin ort comh'ri tuilleadh mar a thubhairt Laurier
'S fhasa 'n gealladh a thoirt seachad mar a's tric na choirmhionadh
Lagh na sgoil a reiteach, an Navy's an Temera

4) Chaidh thu air gnothach araidh gu Parlamaid Shasuinn dhuinn
A chur air doigh 's a reiteach gach ni a dh'fheumadh Canada
Bha do chainnt cho eutrom ri guth faolaig a' glagadaich
Thill thu mar a dh'fhalbh thu 's gu dearbh, b'e mo bhrail e
Cha robh annad ach am burraidh, 's e sin a thuirt Bourassa riut
Cuir an airgead bhuineadh dhuinne chuideachadh nan Sasunnach
Na m bu Phremier math thusa, chumadh tu e 'n Canada
Is mheall thu air do chairdean, 's bidh bhladh ort an ath thurus

5) Gheall MacCoinnich dhuinn an railroad 's bhot thu fhein an uraidh leis
Am bliadhna thug thu cul ris, 's chuibhle stiuradh agadsa
Ma leanas thu do chursa, 'g ar diuladh, 's a mealladh oirnn
Theid thusa chuir air chul an am cunntais nam ballotan
Gheibh thu 'n uair sin an defeat, is thig an rithist Laurier
Suidhidh esan far bheil thusa, 's bidh thusa far an coltach dhuit
Ma thig thu mach airson ar mealladh anns gach ni a gheall thu dhuinn
Chan fhaicear thu gu brach ann am Parlamaid Ottawa

6) An grant a fhuair D. D. dhuinn le cinnt bho an Ghovernment
Gu cuideachadh an railroad tha feumail na cearnan seo
Rinn thusa do thoil fhein ris, thig eubh air, 's chan fhad uge
'S ann chuir 'n Hudson Bay e 's gu d'chairdean fhein an Halifax
Clach air thuranaini, 's chan urrainn gu ri bidh fureach fad aice
Bidh car a fuireach, 's dha le bruthach gu ruig I na claiseachan
'S ann mar sin a dh'eireas dhutsa, tha cuid a cur a mhanidh ort
Sin an uair a chi thu cho neo-chinnteach 's a tha politics

7) Gun tair a thoirt do Mhember, 's e 'm Member MacCoinnich again
Gin cha d'ruith 's a Chounty's cho pongail ceann-labhoirt ris
Mar a bodh an diutaidh a thionndach cho ealamh ris
Bhiodh carbad na smuide a' bunich troimh 'n bhaile seo
Nuair gheibh Laurier a' chuibhle theid cuisean atharrachdh
Theid an railroad dheanamh ullach's bidh 'n t-each dubh n a ghalap oirr
Bidh hip hurra am bial gach duine, 's cuid ag gathaid passage oirr
Sios gu Bagh St. Lawrence chuir failt air na ceinnaichean

2) Now that you received it and are proclaimed Premier
You have a ship to steer and there's a course on your chart
There will be storms and crowded seas and thick fog coming close to you
And if you keep your course I'm uneasy of you making port
If you don't do that, it will be worse for you letting it on the shores
Your friends who gave you this are sorry for what happened to you
It's long since we heard the words, "Nothing lasts but regrets"
And if you let it to the bottom, there will be an uproar in bunches

3) When you went among the French, you got their promise on the ballots
Telling them there was no need for a Navy in Canada
They helped you at that time, it was up with the promises
And despite your rejoicing, there will be a Navy in Canada
You promised the law of the school made by the Grits to put in place what is good for us
You failed to do that and more as Laurier said
It's easier to give out promises and as often as many others
The law of the school is settled, the Navy is in Temera

4) You went on peculiar business to the English Parliament for us
Putting in order and agreeing to everything needed in Canada
Your conversation was as giddy as the sound of a seagull scraping
You returned the way you went, and indeed my opinion was
You were only a fool and that's what Bourassa said to you
Putting the money belonging to us, helping the English
If you were a good Premier, you would keep it in Canada
You deceived your friends, and there will be a blow on you the next time

5) MacKenzie promised us the railroad, and you voted against it last year
The year you put your back to it, and you now have the steering wheel
If you follow this course of failing and deceiving us
You will be left behind at the time the ballots are counted
Then you will get the defeat, and Laurier will come again
He will sit where you are, and you will be where it's likely for you
If you come out to deceive us in everything you promised to us
We will never see you again in Ottawa's Parliament

6) The grant D. D. got for us for certain from the government
To help the railroad that's needed in these quarters
You did your own wish with it, a cry will come, but not say where
You put it to Hudson Bay and your own friends in Halifax
A stone on grief, cannot be waiting long for her
A friend will be waiting and has to make an ascent until he reaches the trenches
Something like that will happen to you, some are putting a wish on you
That's the time when you will see how uncertain politics are

7) Without taking from your Member, MacKenzie is the Member we have
Any who ran in the County were not so articulate and eloquent as he was
If his duty wasn't turned so quickly against him
The smoking train would be roaring through this community
When Laurier will get the wheel, the courses will be changed
The railroad will be completed and the black horse will gallop on it
There will be hip-hurra on the mouth of everyone and some will take passage on it
Down to Bay St. Lawrence, giving a welcome on the buyers

8) Chuir thu uidheam stìmidh a' sgrìobadh nam
cladaichean
'G obair leis a' charbad a b' àbhaist bhith aig Aileag
Beag
Thog i leaba bheag nam musgan 's dun dhi na clachan
as
Thig trìtearan a' ghuail uige nuas far 'm bu mhath leis iad
Am balaist a bh' o'n Rudha Chìdeasn, 's iongatach mar
thachair dha
'N àite chur gu fada muigh 's ann chuireadh e 's an
acarsaid
Dh' fhàg e 'n channal iann cho cumhann 's gann go
ruith am Marion
'S tha Moffat leis a' chrìn 's iad a' maoidheadh gu damain
ort

9) Chaidh i null 'n a h-aimlisg gu lambruig a'
ghovernment
'S rinn i barrachd fuaim ann 's a fhuair ich de chosnadh
aiseig
Cha tug i clach an àirde, bha 'n cairean cho lag innte
Na Tories 's iad ag ràitinn nach nar a thachair dhuinn
Na 'm biodh nigh'n na bitsich gu tighinn idèr cha bhiodh-
a-dhuinn cho dorrannach
'S ann mar sin a gheibh na Grits fios an sin air thoiseadh
oirnn
Gum bidh cuid dhuibh gu math busy chuir litrichean gu
Ottawa
Ag innse nach eil feum innt' gu reiteach na h-acarsaid

10) Glainich i ant-iasg a bha riamh mu na bangaichean
'G obair leis an driamlach a' sgrìobadh nam
cladaichean
Cha do rinn i feum ann, o 'n fheudar a chantuinn riut
'S an fheadhainn a chuir ann i, tha 'n t-am n' cuir 'n am
faireachadh
Nuair thèid an t-uisage ris a' chuibhle 's a' chlach
mhulinn car chur dhi
Thèid na Tories a chur uile 'muin air mhuin 's an
drabhailte
Thèid an-sgiolag, thèid an lomadh, thèid am pronnadh
aithghearrach
'S nuair ruigeas iad an criathar, cho bhidh sian an
sadach ann

8) You put a steam engine scraping the beaches
Working with a machine that used to be with Little Alex's
She lifted the little bed of mussels and is now shut off
from the village
The coal freighters will come down to it where they
would like to be
The ballast that was on Kidson's Point, is strange what
happened to it
Instead of putting it far enough out, it was put in the
harbor
This left the channel so narrow, the Marion will barely
pass through it
And Moffat is with the crane and they are begrudging
and damning you

9) She went over in confusion to groping of the
government
And she made more noise, in what they got of their back
earnings
She could not lift a rock high, the gear was so weak in
her
The Tories, they are saying 'Isn't it shameful what
happened to us'
If the girl of the beach had not come at all, it wouldn't be
nearly so gloomily for us
It's like that the Grits will get knowledge of that and get
ahead of us
Some of them will be quite busy sending letters to
Ottawa
Saying there is no need to clean up the harbor

10) She cleaned up the fish that were always around
these banks
Workin' with a fishing line, scraping the beaches
She didn't do any good I must say to you
And the people who put her there, it's time to wake them
When the water will go to the wheel and the mill-stones
are turning
All the Tories will be put back-to-back on the grain holder
They will be shelled, they will be sheared, they will be
mashed and cut again
And when they will reach the sieve, there won't be
anything but the mill dust

Michael Charlie MacLean
(1843-1934)
Washabuck and Baddeck

11-3 Michael Charlie MacLean, Washabuck/Baddeck. Detail from photo of Beinn Bhreagh Lab Workers, July 12, 1907. Courtesy Parks Canada, AGBNHS: Baddeck, CB.

Radio

Guglielmo Marconi, (1874-1937) the Italian scientist had been experimenting with transmitting radio waves since 1894. In 1901 Marconi sent a transatlantic radio message from Cornwall, England to St. John's Newfoundland.[18] In 1902, Marconi, with the financial help of the Canadian government, built a station at Table Head near Glace Bay. On December 21 the first message was sent from Cape Breton to England.[19]

During the springtime of 1922 while still in Washington, DC, and shortly before his death later that August at Beinn Bhreagh, Alexander Graham Bell acquired a radio – the latest scientific wonder of the world. Bell listened to the "wireless set" with the aid of headphones.[20]

In Lower Washabuck, Michael Hector MacKenzie (1909-2000), who was employed in Detroit, returned home for a visit with what is believed to be the community's first radio as a gift to his parents William and *Beatag*. Mary (Alfred) MacDonald (1909-2011), Baddeck, daughter of Vincent and Theresa MacLean of MacKay Point recalls she was about sixteen years old and in her first year of teaching school at Lower Washabuck when the MacKenzie radio arrived.[21] The year would have been about 1925. "It created quite a buzz in the community," she said. "All the neighbours were dropping in to marvel and have a listen." Her father Vincent refused to believe in the magical powers of a radio. He exclaimed, "I'll believe it only when I see it!" laughed Mary.

11-4 Michael Hector MacKenzie (1909-2000) with nephew Carlie, Washabuck, August, 1995.

Mary's eldest brother, Peter F., was living and working in Iona in the early 1920s and his initial entrepreneurial endeavours included being the area's agent for radio sales. One of the first radio sets he sold in 1928 was to Arthur Campbell, who bought it as a gift for his adoptive mother Mary (MacDonald) MacNeil in Barra Glen. Mary was a sister to Dan A. MacDonald of St. Columba, later of Iona, and she was Rod C. MacNeil's maternal grandmother, who relates this account.

Arthur was employed with the railroad Bridge and Builders earning the going rate of $1.10 per day. In appreciation for her maternal kindness toward him, he bought her a radio, which he paid the sizeable sum of $215, a price that had been discounted $10.00. The new-fangled apparatus, an Atwood Kent model, consisted of a receiver and an "A" battery which was about the size of a car battery; a series of dry-cell "B" batteries and another dry-cell "C" battery. The device required an outside antenna which Rod C. MacNeil remembers reached a height of 25 feet (7.6 m).

Battery power consumption was ever a concern, so the use of this "latest technology" was restricted. It was used judiciously, for short periods each day and for special occasions, just long enough to catch the evening news and weather forecasts from CJCB Radio Sydney, which transmitted with an output of about 50 watts. Late night USA radio broadcast stations could be picked up with surprisingly clear reception. WJZ New York and WOR New York had higher outputs, approaching 1000 watts.

The broadcasting of the heavyweight boxing championship bouts always drew in a crowd of late-night visitors. Champions and contenders alike, boxers sporting names like Baer, Schmeling, Carnera and Sharkey, were spoken about in as familiar terms as next door neighbours. At that time there was a windmill operation at Grand Narrows which ran a generator that among its many tasks was recharging the radio "A" batteries.[22] When Barra Glen resident John Anderson heard mention of the then unfamiliar frequency wave speed, boasting some 200 kilohertz, he drolly quipped, "Well by-the-gosh, some scut!"[23]

John R. Campbell owned one of the first radios in Jamesville.[24] In Upper Washabuck, Joe (Dolly) MacIver was the first to own a radio set.[25] At Washabuck Bridge, a Philco model was owned by Murdock MacInnis's parents John and Annie. The radio naturally was quite the novelty. Neighbours never needed an excuse for visiting one another as it was just the thing to do in all rural communities, but with the advent of the radio, well, this was an added incentive to drop by, to view, listen to, and marvel, at this latest of inventions.

After his first admiring encounter and in-depth examination of the newfangled "talking contraption" Jim Alec MacDougall, sagely advised his neighbour Murdock MacInnis: "Well now gee MacInnis, you keep that instrument level with lots of oil in it and it will last you a lifetime!"[26] Another American station that was frequently tuned in by Washabuck enthusiasts during late evenings was the Wheeling West Virginia radio station WWVA, well-known for its country and western music.

11-5 MacDougall brothers, Washabuck Bridge ca. 1930. L-R: Standing: Jim Alec, Hughie Archie Kneeling: Hector and Dan. Courtesy of Lawrence MacDougall, Washabuck.

Telephone

The first telephone installed in Baddeck was a line established by William F. McCurdy. McCurdy had visited the Centennial Exhibition in Philadelphia in 1876 where he viewed the earliest model of Bell's very basic telephone that was exhibited there for the first time. A year later in 1877, Bell conducted the first-ever long distance telephone call, between Brantford and Paris, Ontario, a distance of eight miles.[27]

McCurdy was obviously impressed with the new invention. In Boston during his homeward trek, he placed an order for three telephones to be delivered to him at Baddeck as soon as production began. The incredulous wholesaler could not believe that such an instrument actually existed. In due course, the telephones arrived in Baddeck, together with the material necessary to install them. By 1880, McCurdy had one phone in his store, one in his residence, and the third phone was placed in his father's home. This, according to Alex D. MacLean, was not just the first telephone system in Baddeck, but likely the first telephone system in the province of Nova Scotia.[28]

It was at the *Island Reporter* newspaper office that Mr. Bell on his first visit to Baddeck in 1885, much to his surprise, saw his invention in use. Dr. Bell not about to be out-done himself – after all it was *his* invention – shortly afterwards had the next local telephone system installed as a private line, that connected the Baddeck McKay, McAskill & Co.'s store with his own early residence at Crescent Grove.[29]

In December 1898, the newspaper *Baddeck Telephone* reported that phone service had come to town: "Baddeck, Little Narrows, Orangedale and Whycocomagh [are] now connected by telephone."[30] Alex D. MacLean writes that the Inverness and Victoria Telephone Company was first organized in 1903 or 1904 to give the citizens of Baddeck and vicinity general telephone service. Its head office was in Baddeck. Most of the first subscribers were professionals and business people.

After a period of time that company was absorbed by The Nova Scotia Telephone Company. Then the two major telephone companies in Nova Scotia, the Eastern Telephone Company and the Nova Scotia Telephone Company merged. They were taken over in 1910 by the newly formed Maritime Telegraph & Telephone Company.[31]

"Teas and Meals"

Gordon MacLennan (1932-2002) of Little Narrows, worked on the Washabuck telephone system for a number of years alongside his father Alec, during the 1950s. He recalls:

> There was a Joe Logue from North Sydney who used to come up
> this way for the phone company. He was the representative for the

"Government Tel and Tel" as it was referred to at that time. My father might have started work with them around 1927. Alec MacLennan was responsible for the telephone system on the Washabuck peninsula, Orangedale and Lake Ainslie areas. He worked right down to Wreck Cove when he was first employed with them; those were the horse and wagon days. The system was government run initially, but Maritime T & T bought them out in 1961.[32]

Gordon worked with the telephone company until about 1960. His father Alec had retired in 1958. Gordon continues:

Three or four local men worked with my father on a regular basis.

Grant MacLean, D. W. Matheson and Duncan Ross worked with us some of the time. But then we hired local men in each community to cut the poles. This was not so much a government decree, as it was expected and required by the local councillors who picked those men. This was how local politics was involved. A change in provincial governments did not interfere with our operations. Alec R. Campbell supervised the Inverness area; George Hardy was in Ingonish and of course Dad and I looked after Iona, Little Narrows and Washabuck. Someone else was in charge of Louisbourg.

Originally it was a one-wire, grounded system with spruce poles. We had the local men cut the poles, usually 25-foot poles which we would then modify according to the lay-of-the-land. During the 1950s the suppliers were probably paid $1.50 per pole. The poles did not last very long. If they did not rot off at ground level, the ants would eat them off. We would then rescue them, cut them off at ground level and reuse them at least once.

The two-wire system came in with MT&T. It provided better service. It was clearer; you could hear better on the two-wire system. The only problem [with the new system] was that of trees falling on both wires, fouling the line and causing shorts. There was not the noise on it as was on the steel wire. We did run some copper wire through Washabuck, but we reverted back to the steel wire for a while because the copper wire was not very strong. That old steel wire was durable but it was hard to work with and to splice.

We changed to cedar poles during the mid-to-late 1950s before MT&T took over the system. Any line we built or rebuilt during that period, well we put in cedar poles, and when MT&T took over operations they started using treated poles. With the coming of electricity to these communities you had a duplicate system of poles. We sometimes used to run the telephone line to the houses on the power poles, mainly to reduce the number of poles in the farmers' fields. The power poles were on one side of the road and the telephone poles were on the opposite side. We never buried the lines. The Little Narrows Strait was spanned with an underwater cable however, and the only other underwater cable we ran was out to Goldthwaite's Island off South Cove.

We never took much abuse when the lines went down. People were very understanding. They realized we had a large service area. In some communities there existed what was called the "Farmer's Line," where the local residents ran their own telephone system. It was like a co-op group, where a bunch of residents from a community banded together and ran their own telephone system. Barra Glen and Middle River are two areas that come to mind. When a storm came and created damage, we repaired both systems. We had the equipment. They usually had only a ladder. We didn't usually bill them. We just repaired it for them.[33] We repaired it in Middle River quite a bit. MT&T eventually took over all those rural telephone line systems.

The Central operator in Bucklaw was Catherine Ross, Frank Ross's wife. Mrs. John P. MacNeil was the Central operator in Iona and later her daughter Cassie took over from her. Margaret MacRitchie, Alistair's wife ran the switchboard in Little Narrows, having taken over from Catherine Ross upon her retirement. Then when MT&T took over, everything was moved to Whycocomagh and ran from that community.

It was a great county to go around in. You never had to take a lunch with you. There were always teas and meals. Everywhere was the same. You were always offered something to eat. The people would be glad to see you anyway but especially if they were getting their telephone repaired. We used to stay overnight in a trailer near the brook and ball field at Washabuck Centre, and we boarded on occasion at Neil Stephen MacLean's in the old home.

Telephone Infidelity: Practically everyone listened in on their neighbours conversations. There was one home in Washabuck, where the residents had a rag rolled up tightly in the form of a plug wrapped with a piece of string, with the other end fastened to the transmitter itself. This way they could then plug the transmitter when they were tapping into the neighbours' conversations without having to hold their hand continually over the transmitter.[34]

But telephone infidelity, such as it was, was perhaps best described by Charlotte Gray in her biography of Dr. Bell. "In rural areas, the early party-line system created a virtual community, as farmers gathered by their phones each evening to exchange news and gossip."[35]

In the rural community of Piper's Glen near Upper Margaree in Inverness County, the promise of the coming telephone system was perpetually dangled as an election carrot. The election promise never became a reality but its proposal was humourously captured in a marvelous piece of poetry entitled, "The Telephone Song," composed by Walter Scott MacFarlane (1896-1979), an entertaining Bard from that community. Mrs. MacDonnell's opinion cited in one of the thirteen verses, poses a bit of counterpoint to Ms. Gray's observation.

> Mrs. John MacDonnell, she should know what is good;
> She has traveled this world from Margaree to Port Hood.
> She considers the phone and its use a disgrace,
> Since one speaks to a man while not seeing his face.[36]

In a similar vein, piper, fiddler and Gàidhlig Bard, Hugh F. MacKenzie (1895-1971), of *Cùl Eilean na Nollaig* (Rear Christmas Island) whose wife was from Barra Glen, composed a fittingly similar song entitled, "Oran an Telephone an Barra Glen." One of its fifteen verses refers to John Rory MacNeil of Barra Glen, whose wife Betty was the daughter of Red Rory and Ellie Ann MacLean from Lower Washabuck:

Tha eagal air Iain Ruairidh	John Rory is concerned
Gun dèan am bocsa tuasaid	That the box will cause a row
'S gun toir Ruairidh Ruadh leis	And that Red Rory will take home
A' ghruagach a thug e nall	The girl he had brought across[37]

Gordon MacLennan continues his recollections:

11-6 Gordon MacLennan (1932-2002). Courtesy of Eileen and Walter Matheson, Little Narrows, CB.

> All the old telephones we had, we ended up hauling them to the dump. It was just a few years later that so many people wanted them for antiques. The actual phone changed from the long-bodied type to a shorten one with a crank and then later to a cradle one with a small black box which contained the generator. Those old phones were quite reliable, good phones, awkward maybe and they took up a lot of room, but they were reliable.[38]

Early Phones

In Iona, Honey MacNeil ran Central (ca. 1964-1976) after Cassie (John P.) MacNeil retired. Honey's husband F. X. MacNeil (1911-1994) who grew up in MacNeil's Vale relates his memories of the early telephone system.

The telephone came to MacNeils Vale in 1922. Mary Ann Morrison, John Rory Morrison and my parents [Dan S.'s] had the phone. We then moved to Grass Cove in 1923. At Grass Cove, the Gypsum Plant, Allan Austin MacNeil, John D. MacNeil, Dan S. MacNeil and John Archie MacDonald in St. Columba all had the phone. Malcolm Dan MacNeil also had the phone in his store and home. My brother John Hector worked for Alec MacLennan and looked after light repair work for him on the telephone system from Iona to MacKays Point. In Iona, Michael D. MacNeil, Mrs. John P. MacNeil and Father Rankin all had the phone installed at that time. In Barra Glen the people there had their own system; they maintained it and collected their own bills.[39]

For a period of time there were three separate telephone systems handled from the Iona switchboard: the government system, MT&T and the Mutual that was initiated in Barra Glen in 1948.[40]

In Washabuck, the provincial government installed the first telephones in the community in 1927, recalled Michael Anthony MacLean.

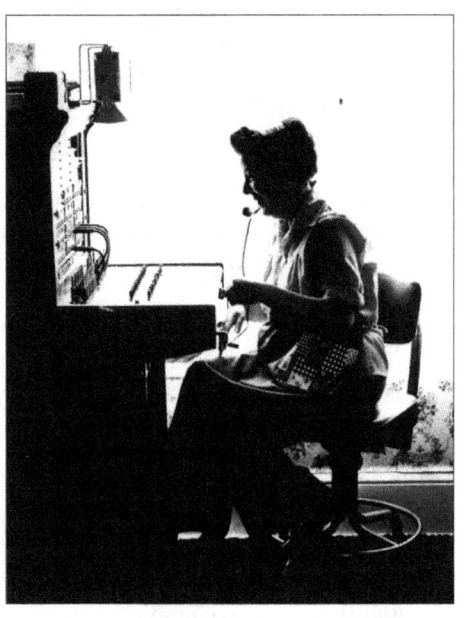

11-7 Catherine "Honey" MacNeil, Telephone Central operator (1964-1976) Iona, CB. Courtesy of Sharon MacNeil, Iona.

There were three customers on that first party line, namely John Dan and Margaret MacRitchie at Washabuck Bridge, John and Mary MacNeil at Washabuck Centre and Vincent and Theresa MacLean at MacKay's Point.[41]

Then, by the spring of 1928, Neil P. S. MacLean in Lower Washabuck had a telephone installed in his residence, as well.[42]

Juxtaposed Disparity

As late as 1986 and to the chagrin of furious telephone customers of Washabuck and surrounding Central Cape Breton communities they were still subjected to four customers to a party line. The situation had become intolerable and there were many complaints, including numerous exchanges within a short radius, which resulted in long distance charges to simply chat with one's neighbour. MT&T's maintenance repair record for the area was atrocious. The high percentage of party lines found in rural Central Cape Breton remained the outstanding issue of dissension.

The problem had been clearly defined in a 1985 LEAD[43] community-based economic development study for Central Cape Breton which identi-

Iona

MISS CATHERINE McNEIL - Agent

PUBLIC PAY STATION AT — CN Railway Stn

SUBSCRIBERS

C

Campbell Arthur J Iona 3-5
Campbell D F MacKinnon's Hbr 1-11
Campbell Eliza A Mrs r St Columbia 6-12
Campbell John R Genl Store Jamesville W. 9-13
Candn National Railways Iona 3-2

D

Dept of Highways Ottawa Brook 2-2
Dept of Highways Ottawa Brook 2-13

G

Gillis John Y McKinnon's Harbour 2-3
Gillis Neil H McKinnon's Harbour 9-24
Gillis Neil J Jamesville 9-12
Gillis Point Co-operative Stn Iona 3-21
Gillis Rod Jamesville 9-21

I

Iona Co-op Ltd Genl Store Iona 3-4
Iona Co-op Ltd Ottawa Brook 2-5
Iona Co-op Ltd Washabuck Centre 7-2

L

Leonard John Iona 5-31

Mc

MacCormick W L Iona 31
MacDonald Dan A Iona 5-4
MacDonald Dan F Upper Washabuck 7-13
MacDonald Florence Mrs Washabuck Centre 6-4
MacDonald Francis B r Lr Washabuck 7-5
MacDonald John A St Columbia 6-11
MacDonald John D Ottawa Brook 2-33
MacDonald Malcolm R Mrs Up Washabuck ... 7-21
MacDonald Stephen Iona 5-13
MacDougall Jim Alex Upper Washabuck 7-22
MacDougall Michael R Lr Washabuck 7-23
McKinnon Dan A Up Washabuck 7-14
MacKinnon Dan M Iona Rear 5-11
MacKinnon James A McKinnon Harbour 9-14
MacKinnon Jerome r Highland Hill 1-14
MacKinnon John r Red Point Rd 1-12
MacKinnon John M r MacKinnon Harbour ... 1-32
MacKinnon Veronica Mrs r Iona Rear 5-21
MacLean Alex C Iona 9-32
MacLean Hugh Ottawa Brook 2-16
MacLean James A Lr Washabuck 7-31
MacLean Michael A MacKay's Point 7-6
MacLean Michael D Ferryman
    Lr Washabuck 7-32
MacLean Neil S r Washabuck Centre 6-15

MacLEAN'S ESSO SERVICE
| Atlas Accessories — Tires and Batteries |
| GENERAL REPAIRS |
| Iona .... Iona 3-12 |

MacLellan Peter A Ottawa Brook 2-12
McLeod Joseph MacKinnon Hbr 2-23
MacNeil Allan A r Gillis Point East 6-24
MacNeil Andrew r Ottawa Brook 2-15
MacNeil Annie C Gillis Point 6-2
MacNeil Dan A Iona 3-3
MacNeil Dan Murdock Highland Hill 1-24
McNeil Dan R r Red Point Rd 1-2
McNeil Donald J r Grass Cove 6-43
MacNeil Edmund Capt Iona 3-22
MacNeil Francis J Iona 3-14
McNeil Francis X Iona 9-3
McNeil Frank Grass Cove 6-3
McNeil Hector Iona 9-4
McNeil J L Red Point Rd 1-3

MacNeil J W M......... 2-24
MacNeil James St 6-21
MacNeil James C 5-15
MacNeil James S Grass ... 6-211
MacNeil John Alexander .. 1-23
MacNeil John J 9-31
MacNeil John Joseph 5-22
McNeil John M r Red Point Rd ... 1-4
McNeil John Malcolm r Iona 3-6
McNeil John R r Barra Glen 5-3
MacNeil Malcolm Iona 9-16
McNeil Margaret Mrs 3-31
MacNeil Michael J 9-2
MacNeil Michael J Iona 9-5
MacNeil Murdock r Iona 3-13
MacNeil Murdock D r Barra Glen . 1-13
McNeil Neil James r Gillis Point 6-42
MacNeil Peter M r Up Washabuck . 7-111
MacNeil Rod Mrs r Ottawa Brook Iona 2-31
MacNeil Roddie C Barra Glen 5-2
MacNeil S R r Barra Glen 5-1
MacNeil Sadie Mrs Iona Rear 5-12
McNeil Stephen r Grass Cove 6-33
McNeil Stephen J Jamesville 1-21

M

Martell's Const Ltd Ottawa Brook 2-14
Mosher Const Co Iona 12
Murphy H J MacKinnon's Harbour 9-23

O

O'Donnell Philip Jamesville West 9-22

R

Russell Edward W Pony's Point 6-112

S

St Columba Parish Glebe Iona 8
St Mary Rev Sister Iona 13

W

Walker Dan Ottawa Brook 2-22

11-8 MT&T telephone directory for Iona, 1963.

fied the seriousness of the telephone service problem. Fifty two per cent of the local telephone customers had expressed strong dissatisfaction with their telephone service, while twenty-two percent were dissatisfied with their Nova Scotia Power electrical service,[44] a difference of 30 per cent.

Backed by supporters, residents and local politicians, the Grand Narrows and District Board of Trade brought the matter to the Nova Scotia Board of Public Utilities. President and local businessman J. Bruce MacNeil delivered a strong and emphatic public presentation for improved telephone service at the MacKinnon Harbour Hall in December 1987.

Within three years, the outstanding issues were satisfactorily resolved, including the installation of private telephone lines.

On October 10, 1990, the private-line system was inaugurated throughout Washabuck and surrounding district. That evening I peered through the darkened living room window of our MacKay Point home and observed a dim light burning in Alexander Graham Bell's residence. The "The Big House," of Beinn Bhreagh lies directly across St. Patrick's Channel, a distance of about three kilometres. I found the phone number and dialed. A gruff voice answered. I introduced myself and asked if I could speak with Dr. Mabel Grosvenor (1905-2006), Dr. Bell's grand-daughter. She was then a woman of 85 and our family had the pleasure of meeting her on a number of occasions.

Dr. Mabel readily recalled our meetings and so I related the achievement the Washabuck community had accomplished that day. I said that I considered it a privilege to chat with a grand-daughter of Dr. Bell's at any time, but especially this evening via a private-line; to be able to thank personally, if not her grandfather (who was a contemporary and friend of both our grandparents and great-grandfather), at least her, for his marvelous invention. Dr. Mabel expressed delight with the call, the achievement of the occasion, and we shared a laugh or two about the time-lapse between the dates of 1876 and 1990.[45] Progress, no matter how nearby, can sometimes take more than a century. Now, if only we could wrap our heads around these smart phones!

Broadband / Community Access Program (C@P)

Dial-up Internet services were first introduced in Victoria County in the early 1990s by Auracom.com. It was replaced by Sympatico Internet service

11-9 Cape Breton's portal banner from 2006. Photo by Joanne MacKinnon, Grass Cove/Whycocomagh, CB. Courtesy of Gerard MacNeil, Washabuck.

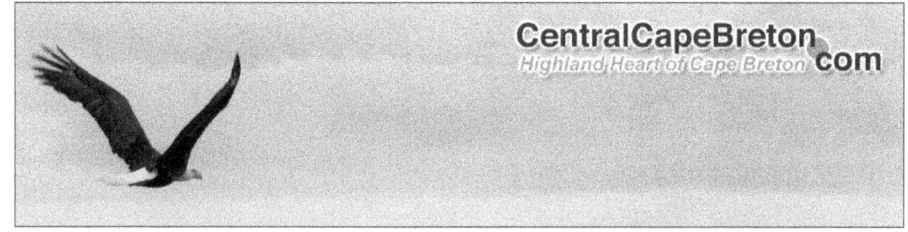

provider. The Community Access Program (CAP) sites were introduced to the county in the late 1990s and soon there was an interest in high-speed internet and broadband. Today's many computer applications and activities require high-speed Internet connections (greater bandwidth).

Washabuck resident, and Internet enthusiast Gerard MacNeil, worked in close collaboration with Victoria County Director of Recreation & Tourism, Tom Wilson, and the County Broadband committee to champion the introduction of high-speed internet and broadband in 2002. A business plan was developed utilizing a public/private partnership and funding proposals were successful.

Phase 1 of Victoria County's broadband project began in 2004 with Bell Aliant providing DSL technology to 11 sites and 30 communities. Industry Canada used the Victoria County model as the best practice example for its implementation throughout the rest of rural Canada.

Phase 2 began in 2006 and 9 more sites were added utilizing Bell Aliant DSL technology providing 25 plus more communities with high-speed Internet. This brought the high-speed coverage to about two-thirds of the communities served in Victoria County.

In 2006-2007, Gerard MacNeil was successful in enlisting sections of the Washabuck community to be a pilot project with Seaside Communications, for high-speed wireless Internet. The success of this project using wireless technology provided Victoria County the incentive and confidence to proceed with Phase 3 of its broadband project and developed another public/private partnership.

Phase 3 began in 2007 with Seaside Wireless and was completed in 2010 with 27 sites developed and networked, providing the remaining communities in Victoria County with high-speed internet. Victoria County became at the time, the most-connected rural county in North America with completion of Phase 3.

The following year, Victoria County developed a further 5-year strategy for broadband applications and infrastructure. This strategy has introduced online meetings, webinars and online conferences, for rural communities and has now begun to increase the speeds for broadband.[46]

Victoria County Community Access Program Sites Association (VC-CAPS) was formed in 1998 as an umbrella organization for all C@P sites in Victoria County. First introduced across Canada in 1995, C@P sites act as the local access point for people to get help via the internet. The original plan for implementing the C@P movement was to ensure all Canadian citizens and visitors to our communities, would have free or low-cost public access to Internet communication, especially in rural areas.[47] VCCAPS helps manage projects and support funds available to the C@P sites through an Industry Canada Initiative. Federal funding for the program however, was withdrawn in April 2012.

Nine C@P sites throughout the county assist communities and visitors with a mandate that includes, public Internet access, familiarizing with computers, and high-speed Internet, as well as offering access to information, IT training needs, the provision of cyber and special camps for children, as part of a youth initiative program.[48] The nearest C@P site serving the Washabuck Community is located at Rankin School of the Narrows in Iona.

11-10 An assembly of Upper Washabuck men, friends and relatives gather on the occasion of Dan Alec MacKinnon's marriage to Martha MacDougall, October 12, 1942. Back Row L-R: Rod MacIsaac, Dan MacKinnon, John Stephen MacKenzie, R. C. MacDonald, Roderick MacKenzie, Joe MacMullin (Sydney), Charlie Beaton (Port Hastings), Jim Alec MacDougall. Front Row: Danny Murphy, Murdock MacKinnon, Walter MacDougall, Groom Dan Alec MacKinnon, and Johnny MacKinnon. Photo taken at Jim Alec MacDougall's, Upper Washabuck (note government wharf in background). Courtesy of Hector MacKenzie, Washabuck Bridge.

12 – Alphas and Omegas

First Vehicles

Henry Ford built his first car in 1893.[1] According to Effie Bain's *History of Baddeck*, in 1915 in Victoria County you were not allowed to operate a car on its roadways, on Sunday, Monday, Friday and Saturday. Top speed was restricted to 10 mph and the car must stop on seeing an approaching team of horses. Fines were imposed and increased on each new offence. By April 1925, the number of cars had increased, so horses were no longer given top consideration.[2]

Vincent MacLean (1872-1943) owned the first car in Lower Washabuck. He purchased the car through his son, Peter F. who was a sub-agent for Norman Bethune. Bethune had the 1931 nut-brown Model-A Ford coach on display at his Baddeck Ford dealership. It was purchased at a discounted price of $600. Since there was no snow plowing of roads in those days, the car was placed on jacks in a building during winter months. Vincent's son John Alec was the first member of the MacLean dynasty venturesome enough to drive the mechanical chariot.[3]

12-1 Michael A. MacLean behind the wheel of his parent's new car, a 1931 Model-A Ford Coach.

Wilson Wright of Hazeldale, John Charlie MacIvor of Washabuck Bridge and Annie and Angus N. MacDonald, South Cove, owned some of the earliest cars. Peter MacDonald, a brother of John Archie of St. Columba and Allan Austin MacNeil in Gillis Point both owned early cars in those nearby communities, as did Councillors Roddie James MacLean and Frank B. MacDonald of Lower Washabuck, who a few years later was the proud owner of a new 1937 Chevrolet.[4] Mick-John (Lighthouse) MacLean had returned to Gillis Point ca. 1950 having being employed in New Bedford, Massachusetts, driving a black 1928 Buick sedan. He continued to use it for years until it became increasingly difficult to obtain tires for it. The same MacLean family later drove a 1937 Oldsmobile which they used well into the late 1950s.[5] Angus J. (Angus Ranald) MacDonald owned the first new half-ton pick-up in Washabuck. It was a blue 1952, six-cylinder International, which he purchased for just under $2,000 from Baddeck dealer John Michael MacLean.[6]

A Winter's Supply

Peter F. MacLean operated a service station in Iona during his long lifetime. In a chat in 1994, he recounted a story about his initial operation and one of the hurdles he encountered during those early days of motor travel. "Well now I'll just tell you, it was November 11, either 1922 or '23," Peter said, as he pensively stroked a close-shaven jaw. He'd been operating a small convenience store with a gas pump at Iona near the ferry docks at the Barra Strait. The building later became an early residence and convenience store for Victor and Catherine Jankowski.

"It started to snow that morning and it snowed steadily for the rest of the day," he recalled. Baddeck businessman Norman Bethune delivered fuel in the morning and filled the gas pump tank. Bethune later related to Peter that because of the heavy snowfall, he had just made it back to Baddeck. The snow stayed and accumulated that November, and Peter ruefully lamented, as a result, he did not sell a single gallon of that newly delivered fuel until the following spring.[7] As things turned out, there would be no snowplow around the district for another two and a half decades.

First Plow/Early Grader

The first plow began operating throughout Washabuck and district ca. 1947. The first plow operators were Danny (Michael D.) MacNeil of Iona; brothers Roddie, Donald and Hughie-Jim Murphy of MacKinnon Harbour and Francis (Michael D) MacNeil of Iona. The first plow was a D-6 caterpillar that operated on narrow crawler tracks. Pushing a V-blade it advanced at a sluggish, measured pace.[8] The rate of plowing was not really an issue, as the country roads were abominable and were less than half the width of today's roads. Realistically, there were few motor vehicles to use them.

Kenny (John A.) MacDonald from Middle River and Dougald Matheson from Little Narrows, were two of the first operators who ran the early road-grader throughout the area. It was towed with the same D-6 Caterpillar. Other grader operators included Francis (Michael D) MacNeil of Iona and Donnie (Danny, John D) MacNeil of Grass Cove.[9]

First Hearse

The first hearse to arrive in Washabuck carried the body of Johnny Brown in April 1959, under the direction of Whycocomagh funeral directors Everett Waddling and Tom MacLean.[10] Prior to that date, human remains, rested in homemade wooden coffins and were transported by horse-drawn cortèges. After 1947, they were usually carried in the box of a truck.

Canned Entertainment

Gramophones became part of the Washabuck culture and home furnishings, during the early 1930s. Three decades earlier in 1897, Emile Berliner of Montreal had taken out a patent on the Gramophone and began manufacturing the talking machines with 10-inch discs in 1901 and the double-sided records in 1908.[11] Berliner had bought the rights to the famous "His Master's Voice" logo, featuring the painting by Francis Burraud that showed Burraud's dog, Nipper, looking down the horn of a phonograph.[12]

Washabuck residences exhibiting this cutting-edge technology included those of John Stephen MacKenzie, Neil Peter MacLean, Neil P. S. MacLean, Rory (Ranald) MacDonald and Vincent MacLean. Some early 78 rpm recordings found in Washabuck homes included Irish fiddlers Michael Coleman, James Morrison and Paddy Killoran; Cape Breton-born,

12-2 Early Cape Breton 78 rpm fiddling record, released under the Decca Label, ca. 1933. Courtesy of David Gillis, Scotsville, CB. Disc 1 is titled Inverness Gathering, March: Alick Gillis and His Inverness Serenaders.

12-3 Early Cape Breton 78 rpm fiddling record - Close to the Floor: Schollar: Gillis Favorite: Reels; Alick Gillis and His Inverness Serenaders.

12-4: Early Cape Breton 78 rpm fiddling record Violin with Piano/ King George The IV/ Strathspey: King's And Lochiel's Reels/ Alick Gillis Accompanied by Elizabeth Mallet at Piano.

Boston-based fiddler, Alick Gillis and his Inverness Serenaders, from Upper Margaree. In fact, Gillis, accompanied by pianist Elizabeth Mallet are found on a 1933 fiddling record, on the Decca label. This was one of the first Cape Breton recordings which presaged the wave of Celtic music releases that were to follow from Island musicians – recordings that provided listening and dance music at literally the drop of a needle, entertaining and delighting local Gàidhlig-rooted audiences.[13]

Electrification

Electricity had been introduced to Sydney in 1888. By 1900, the Sydney Gas and Electric light Company, the first electric utility, was bought out by the Cape Breton Electric Company.[14] In 1928, Norman Bethune, provided electric power to a portion of Baddeck by means of his own generators.[15] Rural Nova Scotia had only 14 per cent of its homes wired for electricity by 1936. With the passage of the *Rural Electrification Act* of 1937, the provincial government agreed to pay a portion of the cost of supplying power to rural districts that had enough potential customers to pay the balance, resulting in Nova Scotia Light and Power taking up that challenge.[16]

In 1937, St. Patrick's Day was celebrated as usual by many Irish people. But in Barra Glen, local residents were attending a Study-Club meeting. Before the meeting got underway, John S. MacNeil of Iona and the Barra Glen student choir entertained the audience with a selection of Irish ballads and Gàidhlig songs, culminating with a few tunes by Gillis Point fiddler, John Angus MacNeil. Study-Club meetings were held in several surrounding communities in an attempt to identify key infrastructure issues around which the larger extended community could benefit. In addition to Barra Glen, the communities of Iona, Jamesville, MacKinnon Harbour, Gillis Point and Washabuck were all part of the same initiative.

Some of the topics explored included the availability of a better oat seed – one that would ripen earlier. It was a Jamesville meeting, though, that spawned the concept of bringing electrification onto the peninsula, a suggestion made by long-time Jamesville resident, Neil John Gillis. The continent however remained in the grip of The Depression and the Second World War was about to erupt. So, the suggestion ended up on the back-burner for a further decade.

The Iona Federation of Agriculture became quite active within the community during the late 1940s. Under its influence, a poll taken on its behalf by John Dan MacNeil of Barra Glen which indicated that 90 per cent of residents were interested in obtaining electricity for their respective communities. The end result was the introduction of electricity to Little Narrows in July 1948.[17] It was 1949 before the communities of Ottawa

Brook, MacKinnon Harbour, Jamesville and Iona were electrified while electricity arrived in Barra Glen in 1950 and Washabuck in October 1952. The Washabuck line was built under the foremanship of Lauchie Chisholm of Antigonish, a capable and likeable linesman, who developed an appreciation for hunting and angling and found Washabuck, its environs and residents most accommodating in that regard.[18]

Benny (Neil, P. S.) MacLean with the assistance of his son Ben and brother-in-law Hector MacKenzie wired a number of the homes throughout Washabuck. Benny received training as a radar-technician while in Montreal with the Radio Flying Corp, Canadian Military and while deployed to the U.K. where he installed and repaired this latest technology in allied aircraft. After the war, Benny attended St. FX University and worked as a summer apprentice with an Antigonish area electrician named Gogan. He put his experience and training to practical use, wiring a number of homes on the Washabuck peninsula[19] in his spare time. Murdock MacAulay of nearby Hazeldale and Gordon (Electric) MacDonald of Baddeck also wired homes in the area.

Television

The first television set in Upper Washabuck was owned by Angus MacDonald and his mother Sarah Eliza (Angus Ranald) in 1956. The first one in Lower Washabuck was enjoyed by James A. and Irene MacLean and family at about the same time. Both homes became instant hang-outs for local enthusiasts of the original-six NHL Saturday night hockey games, for midget wrestling matches and for late-night Friday boxing bouts. The tea was graciously served and no one ever went home hungry. Welterweight and middleweight division boxing champions and would-be-champions, the likes of Sugar Ray Robinson and Carmen Basilio, two boxers amongst an international fleet of contenders, were admired and vainly imitated by up-start Washabuck pugilists.

Refrigeration

The first refrigerator was a propane appliance owned by Jimmy and Annie MacKenzie of Lower Washabuck, while the first electric refrigerator arrived in 1952 and was owned by Michael and Rose MacLean of the same community. Until that time, ice-houses (and snow banks) provided the only means of refrigeration for residents. Ice houses were modest windowless buildings built with double walls, this helped in preserving blocks of ice that were cut from nearby fresh water ponds during winter months. If freshwater ice was not easily available, then saltwater ice sufficed. Saltwater ice will melt much more quickly of course, but once the lake froze, any additional build-up of ice atop the initial layer was essentially accumulated from further snow and rain and proved to be as good as the freshwater ice from ponds.

The stacked blocks of ice were separated with a layer of sawdust providing a long lasting, cool and secure environment for freshly netted fish or meat from any recently slaughtered animal, often preserving the meat into late spring and early summer. Obviously, fresh fish and meat provided a welcomed variety of sustenance and nourishment to a family's usual winter diet of predominantly salt fare. Some families simply used their nearby icehouses as rustic refrigerators, conveniently keeping their eggs, milk and produce cool.

Municipal Services

Municipal street lighting gradually became part of the Washabuck community landscape when the Community Centre grounds were first lit during the mid-1970s. With each succeeding year, local councillors were entitled to use their annual street-light allotment of four new lights placed on existing power poles, installing them first at the public road intersections and subsequently at private driveways. Municipal garbage collection began throughout the area during the mid-1970s as well.

Blacksmiths

Blacksmiths were an admired and integral part of pioneer communities, with novices serving several years apprenticeship under a veteran's tutorship. The village Blacksmith ranked in esteem alongside the minister and priest and the community's piper and fiddler. Blacksmith services were always in demand for all facets of pioneer life. Seafaring vessels of all description required expert ironwork services. The gradual advent of oxen and horses to Cape Breton's farming and forestry industries resulted in an immense demand for carts, carriages, spring wagons or "buggies" and riding sleighs, all requiring the services of accomplished blacksmiths. The shoeing of horses became a full-time career for many a skilled farrier. Door hardware, latches and hinges and wrought iron fireplace tools, were the domain of the ingenious village blacksmith.

Blacksmithing was a prevalent trade amongst the pioneers who arrived from Barra. Certainly among the MacLeans of Lower Washabuck, Alexander and his sons were noted as shipwrights, skilled with the adze and in blacksmithing. Some years later, on north side Washabuck River, Charles (Hector) *Gobha*, a nephew of Lachlan MacLean was engaged in blacksmithing as were his sons John who died in 1867 at 38 years of age, and Michael Charlie who followed the trade while living in Washabuck, and then later in Baddeck, where the family relocated in 1873. Hector MacKenzie remarks that as a youth he found the middens of a forge between the river and the public road at his own property at Washabuck Bridge. No one today recalls there ever being a forge there, but it certainly would have been a convenient and advantageous site, especially for those *Gobha* living as they were, on the river's north side 150 years ago.

In more recent times, Michael D. (Red Mike) MacNeil of Iona, John D. MacNeil of Grass Cove, Johnny (Dudley) Matheson, "Big" Kenny MacLeod (who had relocated from Sydney Mines)[20] and John P. Matheson of Little Narrows were highly respected blacksmiths, and the last of their ilk, in their respective communities. Worthy of note, John P. Matheson had four brothers who as young men had turned their hand to blacksmithing too, although mostly away from the local area.[21] Their family forge was near where the Department of Transportation garage is located today at Little Narrows. At one time, Malcolm Matheson, referred to as Griffin, plied the blacksmithing trade in Cain's Mountain.[22]

The last two blacksmiths that served the Washabuck community were Dan Henry (Dolly) MacIver and Ranald (Angus Ranald) MacDonald, both of Upper Washabuck. Dan Henry operated a forge on the MacIver property until he relocated in the 1920s to Millville, Cape Breton County. Ranald, a Second World War veteran, closed-up his forge during the mid-1960s. By then, horse-shoeing was no longer the specialty it had once been and a bustling blacksmithing career ended.

12-5 Washabuck's last forge provides a backdrop for Washabuck's last blacksmith, Ranald (Angus Ranald) MacDonald. He is seen here enjoying a cup of tea and small talk with his neighbourly sister-in-law, Rose MacDonald and her young family. L-R: Zina, Gwen, Cheryl, John S. (in front), Quentin (Ranald's son) with the family dog, Kelly, and Denise in her mother's lap, ca. 1966. Courtesy of Rose MacDonald, Washabuck.

13 – Fires, Firefighters and Fire Chiefs

Fires

The scourge of house and barn fires destroyed many buildings in the Washabuck community over the decades. The following list itemizes known fires and the approximate dates when they occurred.

1) A major grass and forest fire occurred at Sand Point, Lower Washabuck ca. 1860. No known buildings were lost but there was major damage to the surrounding forest.

2) Dan A. MacDonald's home burned at St. Columba, ca. 1895.

3) Hughie Archie MacDougall's home burned at Washabuck Bridge, date unknown.

4) Dan MacDougall's barn burned at Washabuck Bridge, during the early 1920s.

5) Effie Morrison's general store burned at Washabuck Bridge, date unknown.

6) "Little" Jimmy MacDonald's home burned at Upper Washabuck, 1925.

7) Rory J. MacNeil's home burned at Upper Washabuck, 1926.

8) John Dan MacRitchie's general store burned at Washabuck Bridge 1927.[1]

9) Michael E. MacDonald's home at St. Columba burned in May 1931.

10) A vacant MacRitchie house burned near Washabuck Bridge, date unknown.

11) Angus Ranald MacDonald's barn burned at Upper Washabuck, October 31, 1933.[2]

12) Roderick MacKenzie's home burned at Washabuck Bridge, 1934.

13) Duncan Campbell's home burned at Cain's Mountain, during the early 1940s.

14) Ellen (Devoe) MacLean's home burned at Upper Washabuck, March 1, 1948.

15) Joe MacKenzie's vacant house burned at north side Washabuck River, during the early 1950s.

16) Pat Murphy's vacant house burned at northside Washabuck River, date unknown.

17) Michael Rory and Rita MacDougall's home burned at Lower Washabuck, October, 1950.

18) Malcolm Campbell's barn burned at St. Columba, 1957.

19) Peter and Flora MacKenzie's home burned at Upper Washabuck, 1957.

20) Murdock MacInnis's home burned at Washabuck Bridge, 1970.

21) Dan and Michael Brown's vacant house burned at Upper Washabuck, 1971.

22) Dan Hughie MacDougall's barn burned at Washabuck Bridge, 1980.

23) The vacant Washabuck Co-operative store was burned at Washabuck Centre in a controlled burn, April 23, 1989.

24) Angus and Florence MacDonald's vacant house at Washabuck Centre was burned in a controlled burn October 27, 1989.

25) Red Rory MacLean's vacant house was burned at Lower Washabuck in a controlled burn, 1994.

26) Peter Malcolm MacNeil's vacant house was burned at Upper Washabuck in a controlled burn in 2000.

30) Dan Francis and Kathleen MacDonald's vacant house was burned at Upper Washabuck in a controlled burn on April 3, 2011.

31) Dan MacDougall's vacant house in Upper Washabuck was burned in a controlled burn in October, 2011.[3]

Firefighter Department Services (1959-2009)

In May 2009, the Iona Volunteer Fire Department celebrated its fiftieth anniversary of providing fire protection services to Iona and all communities on the Washabuck Peninsula. Fire Chief Colin MacNeil observed in his message fronting an Anniversary booklet that: "Fifty years ago, in 1959 … the biggest and most important requirement that was needed to start and maintain a fire protection service was volunteers." Quickly, dedicated volunteers graciously provided such services.

Rod C. MacNeil of Barra Glen, a founding member of the Iona Volunteer Fire Department, recalled that prior to 1959, rural communities depended on extemporized bucket brigades to extinguish any fire that became a threat. Most buildings were roofed with wooden shingles and sparks were a constant cause of concern for the homeowner. Careless smoking and disposal of hot ashes from woodstoves, lightning strikes and even spontaneous combustion, certainly in barns, were other common causes. With the arrival of electricity to the Washabuck peninsula in the early 1950s, it too, became an entirely different source for potential fires.

An initial community meeting was convened on April 27, 1959, at Rankin Memorial School. It was chaired by St. Columba Pastor, Father Dan E. MacDonald, and attended by local residents, Department of Lands and Forests personnel and Baddeck Fire Department volunteers. Through the assistance of local MP Robert Muir, early efforts were successful for securing a suitable used truck from Lipton's Dealership in Sydney and obtaining permission from the federal government to use the heated freight-shed on the Iona government wharf proved successful. The Royal Bank consented to a request for a development loan. In 1965 the fire department bought the wharf's freight-shed and relocated it to a parcel of land donated by Iona resident Mrs. Mary (Roddie Frank) MacNeil.

In 1977 Catherine (MacNeil) Jankowski (1917-1985) become the new fire chief. In addition to serving as Victoria County's first female municipal councillor (1973-1984) and being a strong community leader, Mrs. Jankowski also gained the distinction of being the first female Fire Chief in Nova Scotia. A new fire hall was built in 1977, with the financial assistance of a federal government LIP grant.[4] Construction was carried out under the supervision of local artisan Francis (Dan A) MacDonald and the new edifice was officially opened on June 9 1978, by local MP and Deputy Prime Minister of Canada, Allan J. MacEachen.

The Iona Volunteer Fire Department was incorporated on May 14, 1981. Training in fire and rescue techniques for active members continues, and "Ice Rescue" has been recently added to the department's list of capa-

13-1 Members of the Iona Volunteer Fire Department stand with local M. P. and Deputy Prime Minister Allan J. MacEachen at the official opening of the new hall in June 1978. Courtesy of Iona Volunteer Fire Department and Chief Colin MacNeil.

bilities. A fire department sub-station is now situated in Little Narrows and a designated helicopter emergency helipad has been developed at MacKinnon Harbour, in partnership with the Shock Trauma Air Rescue Society (STARS).[5]

Iona Volunteer Fire Department Fire Chiefs

1959-1965	Arthur J. Campbell
1965-1968	Michael B. MacDonald
1968-1973	Peter Murphy
1973-1975	Roddie (Frank) MacNeil
1975-1977	Catherine Jankowski*
1977-1980	Michael B. MacDonald
1980-1984	James H. MacNeil
1984-1986	Alex MacLeod
1986-1989	Columba MacNeil
1989-1992	Michael A. MacNeil
1992-Present	Colin MacNeil

*Catherine Jankowski was doubly distinguished by being the first female volunteer Fire Chief in Nova Scotia.[6]

14 – Forestry, Farming and Fishing

It can be said that Jonathan Jones Jr. was Washabuck's first entrepreneur when he established a sawmill operation here in 1811. It was the first sawmill to be erected anywhere in the surrounding countryside, 40 years before Victoria County was created. Jonathan Jones Jr. was the son of Captain Jonathan Jones who settled the "Big Farm" area on the Baddeck River ca. 1785. No further information regarding how long Mr. Jones operated the mill or how successful an operation it was, has been found. He petitioned the Crown for the 600 acres (242 ha) in 1811.[1] Jonathan Jones's mill was located at the base of Washabuck Falls.

Neil W.'s Shingle Mill

Decades after the Jones's mill, Hughie Campbell's grand-uncle Neil W. MacKenzie, purchased the eastern 100 acres (40 ha) of the original 600 acres of this Jones property, and operated his own sawmill on the original site.[2]

It is unknown why Neil W. erected his mill further out on the Washabuck River bank, west of the waterfall property but this area eventually flooded. So he relocated the mill to the Washabuck falls. Roderick (1878-1945) was a nephew of Neil W. and he inherited his uncle's property. Pioneer Mary *Bàn* MacNeil, had lived on property adjacent to and east of the Washabuck waterfalls. So the falls that Jones and Neil W. used for their source of power, are referred to interchangeably as, Mary *Bàn's* falls, St. Columba falls, and of course, Washabuck falls (see back cover), but the brook that feeds the falls is referred to simply as, "Roderick's."

Neil W. was a brother of "Red" Archie MacKenzie. They were sons of Donald and grandsons of pioneer Archibald (*mac Eachainn*), who settled at Birch Point in 1821. S. R. MacNeil recalls: "Neil W. would be operating this short shingle mill around 1889."[3] He built the water wheel himself all out of wood, and by all accounts made a beautiful job of it.[4] Neil W. was an architect and contractor of note. Among his outstanding buildings were St. Columba parish's second glebe house (1904-1974) and St. Barra's third church at Christmas Island which was destroyed by fire in 1972.

S. R. MacNeil recollects:

> Stephen Dunn MacNeil of Barra Glen bought saw logs from Dan A. MacDonald while Dan A. was still living in St. Columba. Stephen Dunn then brought the logs to Neil W. to saw into shingles. The logs had been cut exactly 8 ft and 16 ft in length (2.4 and 4.8 m). There had been no allowance made for a saw kerf, but Neil W. solved this problem by simply cutting each block a bit less than 16 inches, the usual length of a shingle. So, the first shingles on Alec Rory (Stephen Dunn) MacNeil's house in Barra Glen were sawn on Neil W's shingle mill.[5]

Peter Murphy's Mill

Peter Murphy (2) came to Cape Breton from Prince Edward Island. It is thought that he set up and operated his mill first in the community of St. Patrick's Channel, but later moved it by vessel to Washabuck Bridge. He erected the mill in the early 1900s at the junction of the Cain's Mountain and St. Columba roads adjacent to Washabuck River.

The steam mill was a big outfit and well laid out. It was a two-story operation with the mill on the top story and the shingle-mill below. It had a very large boiler that was brick all around its exterior. There was an equally large steam engine. Neillie Devoe (1895-1981) of Washabuck worked for Murphy and "Little" Stephen Campbell from Gillis Point was the fireman. The Murphy operation either had a "Dutch oven" or his boiler burnt the sawdust.[6] Peter Murphy's son Jack, a teacher by profession, worked around the mill with his father. Jack taught school in PEI, but because he developed "sleeping sickness" he had to give it up. Even about the mill, his father would not let Jack near the saw because of his illness.[7]

Peter Murphy was a stout man and noted as a great sawyer. He was a very fair man to do business with. As he grew older, however and because of Jack's illness, the mill became run down. S. R. MacNeil recalls, "I remember myself when Jack Murphy was sawing shingles there in 1915. Murphy promised us shingles for our barn here in 1915. He got sick, let the mill go and died shortly after that." The old boiler was in due course cut up for scrap and hauled to the Sydney steel plant during the First World War.[8]

Another boiler, this one an upright one, that also spent time at Washabuck Bridge, was bought from Dan A. MacDonald by Neil M. MacNeil who was the manager of the Iona Gypsum Company at Grass Cove. Neil M. was from Big Pond and he lived in a big house situated above the old Post Office in Iona. He was eventually replaced at the Grass Cove operation ca. 1925 by a new manager named William Buckley. The original Iona Gypsum Company was taken over by the Canadian Gypsum Company.[9]

Employees were earning about $1.75 a day. It was around this time that Neil M. started his own gypsum crushing operation behind the Barra Glen pond and he used the existing railroad spur-line to deliver the crushed rock to the main CN line in Iona. How the boiler came to be there involved an adventurous trek over the lake ice from Washabuck Bridge to Grass Cove. He lost it first through the ice at Hughie Archie MacDougall's in Lower Washabuck, and after retrieving it from there with much difficulty, it was lost a second time through the crack at MacKay Point.[10]

The Saga of Neil M's Boiler

Michael A. MacLean describes the tale of the boiler:

On the way down the lake on the ice from Washabuck River they stopped at Jimmy MacKenzie's for a fresh horse. It was late in April and late in the afternoon and by cripers because of the extreme weight of the boiler, the sled runners were cutting right into the ice. So the fresh horse came in handy. I think John Alec "The Fiddler" [MacNeil] from Gillis Point also lent them his horse to make for a fresh team.

When my father saw them heading for the point he knew the ice was bad around the crack and that they should not attempt to complete the trip that day. The treacherous crack at the Point was about three feet wide but nevertheless, they decided to cross it anyway. [The crack was continually changing in width because of the current and frequently impassable.] But first they borrowed a long hawser [a thick nautical rope] from my father. They undid the team from the shaft, gingerly took the team across the crack and some distance beyond it [with the help of a couple of make-shift wooden ramps] and then tied the hawser to the team and the other end to the shaft. As soon as the front of the sled started to cross the crack, the divide began to widen and by cripers, the nose of the runners dug right into the lip of the ice under the heavy weight and the sleigh and boiler immediately headed for the bottom.

Now, the field commanders had nonetheless anticipated and prepared for this possibility, by providing John Alec "The Fiddler" with an axe to sever the hawser should the need arise. John Alec was an affable bachelor, a well-liked, highly respected individual, fiddler, story teller, an accomplished framer, and finish carpenter. He stood at the ready with puffs of white smoke emanating from his ever-lit, and tightly-clenched, crooked-stem pipe. Well, arise the need did – and quickly. To the nervous cries from all around him, John Alec was being yelled at to:

"CUT THE HAWSER!"

But, John Alec was having trouble. As the boiler was quickly settling towards the bottom, the horses were being pulled backwards towards the crack, and the strain on the line was keeping the hawser taut about a foot or so above the surface of the ice.

"CUT THE HAWSER, JOHN ALEC! CUT THE HAWSER!"

Every clip John Alec got at the hawser resulted in the axe ineffectively bouncing off the heavy rope causing only a strand or two of the line to be severed, and by the time he got another crack at the hawser, it had slipped further backward towards the lip of the ice and so he had to start anew.

All the while, the clamor was becoming louder, shriller, more animated.

"CUT THE GODDAMN HAWSER MACNEIL!" was the one exalted cry that rang shrill, clear and crisp throughout the harshness of shouts.

The apprehensive teamsters were unsure whether or not there was enough length of hawser for the boiler to reach bottom before the team itself would be pulled into the crack.

Finally, the boiler struck bottom and the strain eased. The hawser instantly laid flat on the ice. John Alec, shrouded in pipe smoke, with the intensity of the moment and to the vigorous howls of the prodding crew, took a vengeful final smash, severing the hawser and succeeding in burying the double-bitted axe. The whole fiasco proved to be a vehement and amusing scene for all involved, with the probable exceptions of John Alec and Neil M., and perhaps the team.

The following summer a couple of divers from St. Peters, and a crew of locals and others, spent the best part of a week at the Point, some of them boarding at Vincent's. They rigged and anchored a large raft lashed to empty barrels above the boiler. An opening was made in the centre of the raft with a roller attached at the hole. A hawser was then run through the opening. The divers hooked the hawser to the boiler and a crew on the shore used neighbour Malcolm (Stephen) MacLean's stump-puller to slowly, an ... inch ... at ... a ... time, lift the heavyweight boiler just high enough off the bottom so that it could then, gradually, be pulled to shore by a team. The Grand Narrows ferry captained by John S. MacNeil was seconded for a day down to the Point and assisted in finally delivering the well-travelled and overdue boiler to its destined place of work.[11]

The William Dryden Era

William Dryden was a lumberman from New Brunswick. He came to Washabuck around 1909.[12] He lumbered here for at least four years but possibly for as long as ten years. Some of the local workers later left his operations to enlist in the army at the outbreak of the First World War hostilities in 1914. Jimmy MacKinnon relates his version of the Dryden years.

Dryden ran a big and impressive operation. He set up his mill operation at Cole Point on the south side of Washabuck River. Apparently, he did not own the point but he obviously had some lease agreement with the property owner at that time which would have been Michael MacDougall.

His mill, cookhouse, store and horse hobble, were located between the public road and the river. A bunkhouse was located across the road on the high side. All of this was located just below Michael MacDougall's homestead. Dryden also built his own wharf at Cole Point[13] from where he loaded and shipped his lumber. Dryden's wharf was not as large as the Washabuck River government wharf, but the water there is known to be very bold adjacent to the Cole Point shoreline. According to Walter MacDougall, the wharf extended eastward from Cole Point. In addition, Dryden had a tugboat built in Baddeck which he used for guiding the lumber laden schooners away from his wharf into the river's channel.

"He shipped an awful lot of lumber out of there," recalled Malkie MacDonald."[14]

Dan MacKinnon [1864-1949] and "Little" Jimmy (Stephen) MacDonald [1874-1946] built the store for Dryden. There was a big upstairs in it, and a fellow by the name of Murray Steeves who was Dryden's wood scaler had married John Dan MacRitchie's sister, Cassie. They lived on the second level and ran the store at ground level.

During the first year of operation, Dryden hired Angus (Ranald) MacDonald to haul water for the mill's boiler, from "Little" Jimmy's spring at Washabuck Bridge, with his horse with a cart-load of barrels. In the following summers, Dryden had the water piped from the spring down to the mill. John Brown worked for Dryden for a short time and so did his sons Johnny, Angus and Dan. Pay was $1.00 per ten-hour day. They had the task of taking the slabs out of the mill on a rack and pile them outside. The slabs were free for anyone who wanted them.

Among the many properties Dryden lumbered were those of John C. MacNeil's [The Bones][15] property, first owned by Jonathan Jones Jr.

Dan MacKinnon sold him a piece of land in Cain's Mountain as did Baddeck surveyor Joe S.

14-1 L-R: Neil Stephen MacLean, Stephen (Rory Ranald) MacDonald, Neil Peter MacLean, Angus Ranald MacDonald. Courtesy of Carmie MacLean.

MacLean, who owned a piece of land between Dan MacKinnon's house and the river. Dryden put another camp on this site.

Both hardwood and softwood was lumbered. The hardwood was hauled directly to the mill site by a team while the softwood logs were hauled to brows all along the river. [One of the more likely sites for a brow would have been along a precipitous bank, located along the north side of the river. This site is yet referred to as the, "Tumbling Bank."] In the spring the logs were sent down the river on "the drive." A boom was strung across the river from Cole Point to Tom Murphy's Point on the opposite north side. The river was flooded with logs from the bridge down to the mill.[16] When the boom was full of logs a person could walk from one side of the river to the other on them. John Stephen MacKenzie's job at the mill was getting five or six logs into position with a pike pole, and then maneuvering a heavy chain around them so that they could be hauled out of the water and onto the carriage. They sawed 16-18 thousand board feet a day (approx. 5,000 sq m).

Angus N. MacDonald of South Cove, Dougald Matheson of Little Narrows and George MacKenzie of Cain's Mountain, each had teams working for Dryden. There were a lot of horses used throughout the whole operation and they were well-trained. The lumber was hauled by team the short distance from the mill to the vessels at the wharf. The teamsters could guide their teams' backwards out onto the wharf and alongside the vessel, simply using voice commands like, "gee" "haw," "whoa." The horses' hooves always made a lot of noise on the wharf. The vessels were then loaded by hand.

Two Thousand

Jimmy MacKinnon tells a tale about "Dimmie Yang" a New Brunswicker who was the woods foreman.

> Jack Steele was a scaler also. He was missing a couple of fingers. Dimmie Yang had a big horse that he got from PEI. The horse came to MacKays Point by vessel and Jim Alec MacDougall [1880-1963] brought him up to the mill. John Dan MacRitchie, a shrewd Washabuck Bridge merchant, lost a five dollar bet to Dimmie Yang when he claimed that the horse couldn't haul two thousand board feet of logs on a single load. Jack Steele measured the load and sure

14-2 Tumbling bank, north side Washabuck River.

enough, the horse had pulled the two thousand board feet to the mill so, "Bye-goth, John Dan was forced to pay up!"

Dryden provided room and board, saws and axes and all supplies. Washabuckers, Joe MacIver, Angus (Rory) MacKinnon and Hector MacKinnon, and John Murdock MacNeil (Allan Alec's brother) from Gillis Point all worked for Dryden in the bush. John Murdock was noted for being a big, strong, able man. Dan A. MacDonald's twin brother, Stephen, after he moved back from the States, also worked for Dryden.[17] A chopper had to produce 1000 board feet a day to make it pay.

Dryden's operation did not have a "Dutch" oven (one used for burning sawdust). The sawdust was not used, and the government inspectors were strict about safeguarding that it did not get into the river. Apparently, the sharp edges of sawdust, when eaten, will quickly kill fish.[18]

The sawdust was hauled out of the mill by horse and cart. Malkie MacDonald mentioned that the sawdust was placed in a large hole in a nearby marsh and Malkie's son, Roddie, recalls as a lad, seeing the remnants of the sawdust pile on Cole Point ca. 1940.

Dryden moved his mill operations to Black River/West Bay area when he left Washabuck.

Robert MacLeod from Baddeck Bay later bought the large cast iron lumber planer, and received great service from it for many more years.[19] After Dryden left Washabuck, the store building was taken on the lake ice from Washabuck to Iona and situated next to the glebe house where it was used for a garage and dynamo shop. John Neillie (*Hamish* Neil) MacNeil from Gillis Point was in charge of that moving project.

Glen MacKenzie (1938-2007) of Hazeldale recalled hearing stories about Dryden having a dam located out at Murdock Neil MacLeod's property in Cain's Mountain. There is a large marsh in that area, which apparently was flooded with the dam waters. In later years, marsh-hay was harvested off the same area. Glen thought that it was Dryden that had initially corduroyed what became known as "The MacKinnon Road."[20]

Dryden and his wife and family lived in Baddeck. According to his headstone in Greenwood Cemetery, Baddeck, he died September 26, 1919, at the age of 81 years.

Malcolm (William) MacDonald

Malcolm (William) MacDonald from the Yankee Line near Middle River and A. K. MacKenzie from Nyanza were for a number of years in partnership in the lumber business. Joe (Red Rory) MacLean thought that Malcolm MacDonald first cut in Lower Washabuck in the fall of 1925. He hauled out that winter; cut again the fall of '26.

Malcolm MacDonald had bought Dan A. MacDonald's steam engine that had been the original Peter Murphy steam engine used earlier at Washabuck Bridge. "There was lots of power, with slabs for steam, and MacDonald had his own boiler, a horizontal one." According to Joe "Red Rory" a seasoned seaman, "the boiler on the SS *Lakeview* was a horizontal type, while the boiler on the SS *Aspy* was vertical one. They were not fired the same. There were two fireboxes in each boiler and two fires in each firebox, but the vertical boiler according to Joe, "was the easier one to fire."[21]

Three for the price of two

Mickey relates a story from Dan Alec MacKinnon. Dan Alec, Joe (Dolly) and Tom MacKenzie worked a contract together. Dan Alec and Joe (Dolly) broke a crosscut saw. The saw was worth $7.50, so each man would contribute $3.75 to pay for it. When they eventually all got squared up with their pay, Tom was mad as hell because Malcolm MacDonald had charged him for the broken saw as well. Malcolm took full advantage. "Malcolm was just too smart for those fellows," said Mickey.[22]

Joe MacLean outlines:

After the deal was hauled to MacKays Point, it was loaded on a three-master schooner, which was bound for England. Because the vessel was so large, it was partially loaded at the MacKays Point government wharf, and then moved further offshore into deeper water, where the balance of the load was rafted out and loaded upon her at anchor.

The Kennedy Brothers of Alba [of boat-building fame] had sawed a cut at MacKays Point area around the same time. Their lumber was cut on the lakeshore side of the Boyd property and then boomed down the Lake to the Point, where it was sawed. Michael Dan and Joe MacDonald worked for the Kennedy brothers, at that time.

A bit later, Malcolm MacDonald put in a final cut and sawed that lumber with the loan of the Kennedy brothers' gas engine powered sawmill, that was already set up on the shore at MacKays Point, while he was relocating his own saw operation to Boisdale. MacDonald, had in the meantime been awarded a railroad-ties contract and was in the process of setting up his sawmill operation in that community. Michael Dan and Michael A. worked as teamsters for Malcolm on this last occasion, hauling those logs down along the MacKay Brook wood-road, and out across the frozen pond, before sawing commenced during the spring months.[23]

Vincent MacLean also hauled out logs that Malcolm MacDonald cut on Boyd's place. He hauled them down the brook road and across the frozen pond. Malcolm then pulled [his own sawmill] out. It was not worth his while to set up again for the small amount of lumber that was down there, so Malcolm got a loan of Kennedy's mill, at MacKays Point. It was mostly black spruce, awful hard blocks of stuff. You'd take the board off and "she twist" ... Joe MacDonald was the teamster. He was hauling it out over the ice-covered pond.[24]

Atlantic Pulp Company:

The Atlantic Pulp Company spent a couple of winters lumbering properties, one that was referred to "The Company's Place," on lands along the "Camp Road" between St. Columba and Highland Hill. That was sometime between 1926 and 1930. Dan A. MacDonald sold them the lumber and the land on his 100-acre (40-ha) property located immediately to the west of John Stephen's.[25] They also lumbered the large tract of Crown land in that same area. Many of the local men worked for them along with outsiders, including some from the Inverness area. Cutters were paid $3.50 per cord by the Atlantic pulp company.

Michael Anthony MacLean recalls that brothers Malcolm and Rory (Stephen) MacLean cut 14 cords of pulp on Black [Bone] Island at that time. They swam their horse out alongside the rowboat; piled the wood on the southern point of the Island and later tossed it into a boom, where it was subsequently loaded aboard the steamer anchored off MacKay Point. A platform on the water was tied to the vessel with an opening in the platform designed to float the wood close to the men who directed the pulp onto a treadmill system onside the vessel. The same thing was done for about another 1,000 cords, some of it cut by Johnny Fownes and his crew on lands [*Rubha Dearg*] today owned by Ned Crosby, and the lands at that time owned by Rory (Stephen) MacLean.[26]

Bully-Beef Special

Roddie MacDonald recalls hearing his father Malkie with some of the neighbours, reminiscing about the Atlantic Pulp Company lumbering on Murphy Point for a summer, probably during the late '20s. There were bunk camps and a cook-shack set up on the Point. Malkie, and Dan Alec MacKinnon lived at home, but ate at the camp. Fresh meat was scarce and the company somehow got a special on a spent bull that had been slaughtered in a neighbouring community and brought it to the camp's cookhouse. Of course the crew was delighted to get a feed of fresh meat, but after hoeing into the beef that proved to be tainted, the results were dreadfully bowel-loosing, or as the debacle was described by the "wood cats," they developed a brutal case of "flying axe-handles." There was just one "john" on the premises patronized by the distressed lineup, coupled with a great demand for Eaton and Simpson catalogues. For a day or two the incensed men were squatting enough to question their own gender. "You had to be careful where you stepped amongst the bushes for a spell after that fiasco," ruefully observed Malkie MacDonald.[27]

Murdock and Sandy MacRae: (The Rabbits)

Murdock and Alexander "Sandy" MacRae of Middle River Victoria County lumbered for two winters in Washabuck 1945-1947. They were affectionately referred to as "The Rabbits." They and their crew lumbered the property referred to as "The MacAulay Place," the property originally granted to Donald "Piper" MacAulay, pioneer. Murdock was in charge of the woods operation while Sandy, a capable mechanic, was in charge of the sawing side of the operation.

During the fall and winter months the MacRae brothers employed about ten choppers and teamsters in the woods operation. Murdock MacRae recalls:

> The property was not a difficult one to lumber. We bought the property and buildings which included the house and barn and we lumbered approximately 350,000 board feet [each year] of softwood off it.
>
> We had bunk beds upstairs in the old house and so provided room and board for the crew. On the Washabuck job the men ate their three meals a day at the house. We were close enough to the camp so that they could get home for the noon meal. Pepin Arsenault was the cook for the sawing crew during the summer season.
>
> The crew usually worked a 10-hour day except in the late fall and winter when it was from daylight to dark. The wages were roughly two dollars per man per day with the teamsters receiving a bit more than the choppers because they were up an hour earlier at 5 a.m. to feed the horses. In addition to providing the room and board, we supplied the cross-cut saws and double-bitted axes and axe handles. The buck-saw didn't become popular until later years. Most of our major supplies we bought from Cape Breton Wholesalers in Sydney.
>
> Red Rory MacLean from Lower Washabuck was our saw-filer, and a good saw-filer he was too, and a very fine man as well! I had an agreement with him to come to the camp once a week to sharpen our saws. He'd probably sharpen six saws each time. We had a couple of spares in case something happened any of the saws…. During the summer, Sandy and I, we each had a three-ton Chevrolet truck and we trucked the lumber to Iona where we loaded it into the box cars. We would put about 3,000 BF (board feet) on a truck-load and 38 to 40 000 BF in each box car, depending on the length of the lumber. The lumber went to Halifax where we had sold it to a broker who was shipping it overseas, mostly to England. The Second World War was on and there was no trouble during the war years to export lumber.

"A Good Bunch"

Michael Dan (Red Rory) MacLean reminisces about his winter working for "The Rabbits" in Washabuck:

One day Long Dan and I took down 250 logs. We struck a good bunch on the side of the mountain. We just about finished it. There were forty loads left in the woods that day. The old rabbit [Murdock] wasn't too pleased with the young fellow's snigging that day, and he thought that maybe somehow we had help, you know! So the next morning we went out and George Peters was helping the other fellow snigging out, because George's own choppers did not have as good a stand as we had struck.

Anyway, we worked until about 9 o'clock when Murdock came to us and said, "I have to take you fellows to get me some stringers." Those were logs about twenty inches in diameter on the stump and they had to be 16 feet long, as he needed them for different things, like bridge stringers and dump-truck boxes. So the best we did that day was fifteen of these logs. It snowed like the devil and we had to walk half a mile here and there to pick out these logs and that was a hell of a job. George Peters snigged them away. He had a dandy fifteen-hundred-pound, brown horse, just a wonderful animal, he could leap and he was strong. We had to turn the log small end ahead so it wouldn't catch so much snow.

When we came in that evening and I turned the tally in to Murdock he smirked, "Well you fellas didn't act quite as swift today as you did yesterday!" It was quite a drop alright from 250 to 15, but we didn't count what we had cut before 9 o'clock, before he moved us. We got no credit for those. That was another thirty logs, but I never thought of it at the time.

"The Long Saw"

Murdock and Sandy were good to work for, the very best – very, very, cool. They wanted you to work and they never bothered you at all. "Long" Dan was a great chopper but a poor axe-man as far as branches went. He never cut a branch off close to the trunk. There'd be snags "that long" on them. Murdock finally got after him. "Dan, you'll have to cut those branches off," he says, "or you'll kill the poor horse snigging and dragging everything." "Ahh to hell with her," laughed "Long" Dan with his queer twang, "The long saw [big saw] won't take long taking them off!" Dan just wouldn't clip a branch close to the tree trunk.

"Poor Dan," chuckles Mickey, "you know, he would be over at Murphy's all evening looking at all those young women over there! [Danny and Mary Ann Murphy lived next door and they had a fleet of eleven children including three sets of twins, seven of them beautiful girls, an endearing trait that even today displays itself in their descendants.] He'd get up in the morning still lovesick and all he could eat was an egg, and by about nine o'clock he'd be beat out, recalls Mickey with a laugh.[28]

Roddie MacDonald a Nova Scotia Land Surveyor from Washabuck recalled the reason the MacRae Brothers were christened "The Rabbits" evolved from a habit Sandy developed while he was still a youth. He would be observed wriggling his nose like a rabbit while sitting on a stump, apparently contemplating how he was going to get his logs out of the woods. Others claim that the nick-name simply evolved because the brothers were such keen woodsmen and spent so much time engaged in the lumbering business.

4-3 (L) Jimmy MacKinnon and (R) Michael Dan "Mickey" MacLean.

According to Ranald (Angus Ranald) MacDonald (1914-1983), the last year the Rabbits used their steam mill was on the Washabuck job. Subsequently, when they switched to the gasoline engine they were able to saw 14,000 BF during a ten hour day.[29]

Mersey Paper Company

The Mersey Paper Company set up business in Liverpool, Nova Scotia in December 1929. It was not until the middle '40s that the company made much of an impact on the Washabuck area of Cape Breton Island. Around that time, they bought vacant properties that were heavily forested and began buying four-foot length pulpwood from private woodlot owners. This was a welcomed opportunity for the unemployed or the under-employed local men, many of whom had recently returned from overseas and the Second World War.

MacDonald Brothers

Between then and 1960 most of the local residents cut their woodlots for 4-ft (1.2 m) pulpwood and sold it to the *Mersey Paper Company*. While each woodlot owner cut whatever amount, time and woodlot constraints permitted them during the winter months, the Angus Ranald MacDonald brothers of Upper Washabuck made it a full-time business. Between the late 1940s and the mid-1960s the six brothers worked in various combinations among themselves, cutting pulp on their own woodlots and paying stumpage for pulp they lumbered on numerous vacant, private woodlots and Crown properties, all for the Mersey Paper Company. Brothers Ranald, Roddie, Johnny and Alec worked a few years together with Angus and Dan

Francis, but it was the latter two who tenaciously prevailed throughout that era for many more years of pulp cutting. These two brothers were noted as particularly hard men to follow when it came to woods work.

Roddie J. MacDonald, a close friend and neighbour, worked with Angus and Dan F. for a number of those years, before becoming a Nova Scotia Land Surveyor, a career he would eventually spend forty years in, conducting forestry surveys for government and corporate interests, in seventeen counties around the province.

Roddie recollects:

> The Macaulay brothers from Baddeck, Gordon and Alec, had an agreement with the Mersey and acted as their local agents. Gordon Macaulay [1912-2011] was receiving $3.00/cord for the pulp from the Mersey while paying his choppers $2.65/cord, ca. 1950. This would be from cuttings on the Mersey's own properties. In addition, Gordon was selling Ford trucks at his dealership. It was during this time period that Agnes MacDonald, Malkie's wife remarked to a visiting Gordon Macaulay, "You have certainly come a long way from the time I first remember you selling *Family Herald* subscriptions, Mr. Macaulay."[30] Indeed he had! Gordon – an astute and successful businessman – never looked back.
>
> Malkie MacDonald, with his son Buddy as well as neighbour Alec (Angus Ranald) MacDonald worked for Alec Macaulay loading his trucks with pulp from daylight to dark for $8.00 a day. Alec Macaulay was also running the parts division of the dealership and the general chit-chat expressed amongst the woods' cats at that time was that "Alec Macaulay was making more money selling truck parts (particularly brakes) than his brother Gordon was, selling trucks." A woodlot owner at that time was receiving $9.50 a cord for peeled wood and $8.00 for rough wood.[31]

The Boom

Most of the Washabuck pulp (1948-1960) was dumped directly into a boom where the secluded river fronts along that portion of the Upper Washabuck road. Today this area is still referred to as "The Boom."

> When the boom was full it was towed by tugboat into Nyanza Bay where the pulp was loaded onto boats anchored off-shore by means of a log roller. "There were literally thousands of cords in the Nyanza boom – the whole of Nyanza bay was all pulp,"[32] recalled Ewen MacLean.

Ewen MacLean of Baddeck Bridge hauled countless cords of pulp to the Washabuck boom during those years leading up to 1960. He was usually accompanied by Willie Bernard, a stocky Mi'kmaw from the First Nation reserve of Wagamatcook. Willie, much like Ewen himself, always had a twinkle in his eye and they both endeared themselves to everyone

14-4 (Right) "The Boom," Washabuck River.

14-5 (Below, right) Booms in Nyanza Bay, Victoria County, filled with Mersey Paper Company pulpwood, ca. 1957. Courtesy of Ewen MacLean, Baddeck Bridge, CB.

14-6 (Below) Willie Bernard at the helm of Gordon MacAulay's tractor, with unidentified assistant, Hunter's Mountain, ca. 1958. Courtesy of Ewen MacLean, Baddeck Bridge, CB.

14-7 L-R: John Bernard (Willie's brother), Ewen MacLean, and Trevor Salisbury are pictured with young fellow Charles MacDermid (Kenny MacDermid's son). It is Kenny's wood on the truck. The photo was taken along Baddeck Bay road in the late 1950s. This Ford truck was bought by Gordon MacAulay from Lipton, a dealer in Sydney. The horns on the cab were removed from the mail-boat, MV *Shenacadie* when the boat received new ones. The truck could handle approximately nine cords, with double rows of four-foot wood. Its box was sixteen feet long with a trailing axel. "When we shifted to the trailer, it could handle twelve-and–a-half cords," recalled Ewen. He used this trailer to haul to the boom his last year in Washabuck, 1960. Courtesy of Ewen MacLean, Baddeck Bridge, CB.

FORESTRY, FARMING AND FISHING

they encountered. "He was an excellent worker," says Ewen, speaking of Bernard.

Ewen relates this story about Willie Bernard and he loading the truck, this time in North River, in the early morning and delivering it to the boom in Nyanza before the pulp owner had risen for the day. When they returned for the second load, the owner revealed to them that none of the wood had been scaled, so the teamsters proceeded to fill the rack again, but this time with an extra-large load. Upon meeting the scalar, they heralded the fact that the first load had been just as big, so in the end, the pulp owner ended up with an extra good scale. It wasn't every day that one got the jump on the Mersey Paper Company.

Reid MacKay of Big Baddeck recalled that, after the Mersey Paper Company left Cape Breton ca. 1957, the PEI Produce Company took over buying pulpwood. Leonard Harvey of Baddeck, was one of the buyers.[33]

Red Point Contractors

In 1970 Red Point Contractors was founded by brothers Melvin and Michael Dan MacNeil who had been in the woods business themselves since they were ten years old, cutting pit props, booms, chuck blocks, saw logs and of course pulp.

Michael Dan relates that, John Henderson a Montreal businessman, and buyer of export wood among other products in Atlantic Canada, reached an agreement with Red Point Contractors. Red Point purchased a five-acre (2-ha) property in Barra Glen for yard purposes, while Henderson purchased another property in Iona and in turn leased it to Red Point Contractors. This property was originally owned by Hector (Josie) MacNeil. In 1975 Red Point Contractors bought a new pulp porter for $33,000 and in 1985 bought yet another yard, this one at Jamesville. Red Point had by then, built its own debarking machine which resulted in an increase in wood peeling capacity from 15 cords per-ten-hour-day to 100 cords a day, with just two men handling the job. Prior to that time, wood had been de-barked in the yard by a mechanism running off a tractor's PTO (power take-off). With winter tips on the de-barker, wood was now successfully peeled throughout the year.

14-8 First pulp boat to load for Red Point Contractors at the refurbished Iona Port wharf, July 1989.

In 1992, because of the pinewood beetle scare, a ban was placed on softwood exported to Europe from Canada that was not kiln-dried. So the last boatload of export wood sailed out of the Iona port in 1992. Until that time, 25,000 cords of softwood had been loaded and delivered annually to overseas markets, averaging six shipments yearly.[34]

Shingle Mills and Sawmills

A lumberman by the name of Mooreshitt harvested the area between Grass Cove and St. Columba sometime in the early 1900s. He had his steam-driven sawmill located near where the brook empties into John Alec (The Fiddler) MacNeil's pond at Grass Cove.[35] In 1933, Rod N. Matheson relocated his saw mill from Hazeldale to Washabuck Bridge, and sawed logs for Murdock MacInnis's new barn.[36] Murdock MacAulay of Hazeldale ran his sawmill at Peter MacKenzie's in Upper Washabuck during the summer of 1937.[37] John A. MacDougall operated a shingle mill on Cole Point ca. 1939. He used an old Nash engine for power and sawed 24-inch (60 cm) shingles, some of which were used to shingle John Stephen MacKenzie and Murdock MacInnis's barns.[38]

Dan Michael MacKenzie handled a marginal sawmill operation near his father's (Peter) property for a short time, while another family of MacKenzie's, the brothers, Dan Murdock, A. K. and John, managed a successful sawmill venture for years, as did Laurier MacLeod, another especially capable lumberman, all at nearby Cain's Mountain.[39]

After the Second World War, many residents were cutting logs. The main buyers were the two building-supply firms, Chappell's and Stevens in Sydney, who paid $40 to $45 per thousand (300 m) board feet for lumber of various lengths, widths and thicknesses. Hardwood chuck-blocks measuring 6 in x 6 in x 2½ ft (15 x 15 x 76 cm) were bought by the Steel Plant, while there was also an intermittent demand for pit props and 12-16-ft (3.6-4.8 m) booms for the mines.

The railroad required railway ties. The MacDonald brothers including Ranald and Angus cut pulp and hemlock logs for railway ties during the winters of 1945 and

14-9 Washabuck women visit sawyers on the Brown property on north-side Washabuck River during summer of 1945. L-R: Mary Agnes MacDonald, Alec MacDonald, Kathleen Murphy, Theresa MacDougall (hidden), Dan F. MacDonald, along with mill owner in front, John Neillie (Hamish Neil) MacNeil, Gillis Point. Courtesy of Quentin MacDonald, Washabuck.

1946. They had logged the Brown and Norman (Rory) MacLeod properties on the river's north side, those two winters. John Allan (Hamish Neil) MacNeil of Gillis Point provided the sawing on site with his portable mill, for the MacDonald's.[40]

John Archie MacDonald carried on a sawmill operation in St. Columba for years. Although he was not regarded as a great sawyer, he nonetheless received government contracts for bridge and culvert planking, which kept his operation functioning for years.

Hughie Campbell operated his sawmill in Highland Hill near Peter B. MacNeil's throughout the summer of 1951. He also sawed in St. Columba, Cains Mountain and Upper Washabuck. He later relocated his sawmill to Washabuck Bridge.[41] The men were using bucksaws and the newly minted Precision chainsaw. The Precision, a heavy, cantankerous and awkward two-man chainsaw that sold for $400, became popular – if not endeared - by many woodlot owners during that era.

Joe (Red Rory) MacLean, a talented millwright who could turn a proficient hand to practically any venture, including water divining, worked a modest sawmill operation in Lower Washabuck and operated it on a sporadic basis, spanning the decades from the mid-1940s to the mid-1980s. Today, both Ben MacLean and Quentin MacDonald serve the community, on a part-time basis, with their portable sawmills.

14-10 Sawyer Hughie Campbell at Highland Hill during the summer of 1951. Courtesy of Hector MacKenzie, Washabuck Bridge.

Firewood Co-operative

A firewood and thrashing co-operative was active throughout the Washabuck area for at least a decade during the early 1940s. The communal effort involved the bucking of firewood during spring months and the thrashing and crushing of oats and barley in the fall. Jimmy (Neil P. S.) MacLean was the first manager of the operation. He left the position when he signed up for overseas duty in the Second World War. Malcolm Campbell of St. Columba then took charge and ran the operation during subsequent years. During the off-season the equipment was stored in the church-owned barn that was located behind Holy Rosary Church. Eventually the co-operative operation shut down and disbanded. Joe (Red Rory) MacLean bought the thrasher, Kenny Matheson of Jubilee bought the crusher and Hughie Campbell bought the engine.[42]

Malcolm Campbell would begin bucking operations with a large crew of men in early spring when the snow was still on the ground. The purpose was simple, to cut logs into sizes that would fit in the homeowners stove. As much as six to eight cords of hardwood logs, often ten to twelve feet in length had already been brought home on the winter's snow, by the homeowner.

The men would assist in lifting the logs into position onto the saw bench where they would be quickly "bucked" to the owner's desired stove length. An adjustable device attached to the bench permitted the blocks of wood to be cut the required length.

The crew received no pay, but they were well fed at the homes and that was all the pay that was expected. And naturally, as the operation moved from home to home, the whole event proved to be an exciting social cauldron for all concerned. The manager, however, received $1.00 an hour for running the operation, which included the supply of gasoline. The activity usually commenced at Dan MacKinnon's in Cain's Mountain and then moved eastward through the community, as they accommodated each owner's needs.

The thrashing of oats was achieved in much the same manner. Thrashing was always a dusty task. If cash was unavailable for payment, not unlike the shingle mill method of payment, the number of barrels of oats was split 50/50 between the farmer and the co-operative.[43]

Route 223 Forest Management Co-op Ltd

Many Washabuck and area woodlot owners became members of a forestry co-operative in Central Cape Breton in 1985. Membership eventually expanded to 135 members. These woodlot owners were interested in improving their woodlots in a general and sustainable manner, while maximizing economic benefits and promoting increased awareness of the value of a productive healthy forest for future generations. Approximately 100,000 acres (40,400 ha) were placed under forest management during a fifteen period from 1985-2000.

The Co-op's first official slate of officers was: President, Vince MacLean; Vice-President, Malcolm MacNeil; Secretary, Kenny Boyd; and Directors, Foncie Farrell, Frank Beaton, Maxie MacNeil, Brian Arseneau and Michael MacKenzie. Michael Dan MacNeil became manager, while office supervising duties were handled by Louise MacKenzie with Michael A. MacNeil acting as field supervisor and Bruce Stewart hired on as the co-op's professional forester.

The woodlots were professionally managed. This work included the development of 145 forest management plans and their implementation. The planned activities included building access roads, bridges and fire ponds; establishing boundary lines with surveys and line-renewals; harvesting of both hardwood and softwood and marketing the products. Silviculture treatments included tree planting, thinning, cleanings, site clearing, weeding and raking. Funding came from joint federal and provincial forestry agreements put in place to offset severe spruce budworm damage. Private-owner harvesting revenues complemented the government assistance. Between the co-op and local contractors, 25 people were employed implementing the forest improvement work, while a further 40 seasonal workers and contractors were employed in peak season.

Specific silviculture treatments and service work on members' woodlots included: site-clearing of 968 acres (391 ha), remnant felling on 1,070 acres (433 ha), tree planting on 2,100 acres (849 ha) with 302 acres (122 ha) of shelter-wood development. Services included the building of 57 miles (92 km) of access wood roads, 34 bridges, 15 fire ponds and 63 miles (100 km) of boundary line surveys. Over a fifteen-year period the economic benefit to local communities including Washabuck amounted in excess of nine million dollars. In 2000, the federal and provincial government funding ended and the members agreed to dissolve the co-operative, with dividends being disbursed pro-rata, to the membership after all financial and legal requirements were met.[44]

Farming

Ticket of Location

As soon as the pioneers obtained their "Ticket of Location" (and often before), they began the tedious task of clearing sections of "their property." This was part of the general agreement between the Crown and the settler. In order to obtain a permanent claim to their domain they were required to clear three acres (1 ha) during the first year of occupation. Certainly, the pioneers were keen for clearing land, using the cut timber for firewood and log buildings, while burning the remnants to make way for planting. At first they planted potato and root vegetables, then later, depending on personal circumstances, crops of barley, wheat and timothy. The burnt lands among the stumps provided fertile, if brutal soil, for those early harvests. It was usually the portions of land that fronted the lakeshore that were cleared and cultivated. In countless instances, the rear portions of their 100-200 acre (40-80 ha) lots were seldom cleared because of distance and a lack of accessibility.

Their building tools were primitive. Agrarian tools were non-existent with the exception of the sickle *(corran)* and the *cas chrom,* a crooked stick generally made of hardwood. Later, a better tool fashioned in the same principle evolved and this became the forerunner of the horse-drawn plough. Axes were prized due to their scarcity while the hand-scythe did not become available until later.

In early times, every family used a hand mill to grind their oats and flour. These primitive hand-mills were brought over by the pioneers and were called *brà*. The Loyalist settlers at Baddeck River for example would call the same mill, a "quern- stone." These stones were of different sizes. The majority of them were about two feet (60 cm) in diameter. The complete implement consisted of two large round stones, very much resembling a grind stone. The lower stone had a roughened surface, which served to break the grain as it was crushed and ground under the weight of the upper stone. The upper stone was made to revolve on an axis that was solidly set in the lower stone and fitted with a handle, most often a wooden peg set in it near the outer rim and used to turn it. These stones usually rested upon a wooden frame, but sometimes a smaller edition was made that could be rested on a table. There were outlets at several different locations along the rim where the ground meal poured out as it was being ground.

The meal turned out in this way was much coarser than the genetically-modified flour we customarily use today. Before being ground, the grain was dried in a long pan which was suspended over the fire place. Called a drier, this pan consisted of a wooden frame with a perforated bottom of sheep skin, stretched and attached to the frame. Sometimes a piece of perforated sheet metal was used instead of the sheep skin. Later, when grist mills were erected throughout the countryside, these hand-mills were laid aside.[45]

14-11 (27 section) Aerial view of Washabuck and Baddeck, 1939. Courtesy of National Air Photo Library, Ottawa, ON.

14-12 (27 section) Close up of Washabuck in aerial view, 1939. Courtesy of National Air Photo Library, Ottawa, ON.

FORESTRY, FARMING AND FISHING

14-13 (68) Aerial View, 1939. Courtesy of National Air Photo Library, Ottawa, ON.

14-14 (66) Aerial View, 1939. Courtesy of National Air Photo Library, Ottawa, ON.

And so it was that from the outset in pioneer days, little-by-little the amount of cleared acreage of each land owner's property grew with succeeding generations gradually enlarging it further. It was said that during the 1940s it was possible to scan Washabuck with an unobtrusive view from the top of the farmland at MacKay Point on the most eastern end of Washabuck from the residence of Murdock MacInnis at Washabuck Bridge on the western end, a distance of about thirteen kilometers.[46] Early aerial photographs appear to affirm this claim.

Scottish pioneers were not noted for their farming proficiency. Farming techniques after the pioneers' arrival in Cape Breton were such that they

14-15 (64) Aerial View, 1939. Courtesy of National Air Photo Library, Ottawa, ON.

Image 14-16 (56) Aerial View, 1939. Courtesy of National Air Photo Library, Ottawa, ON.

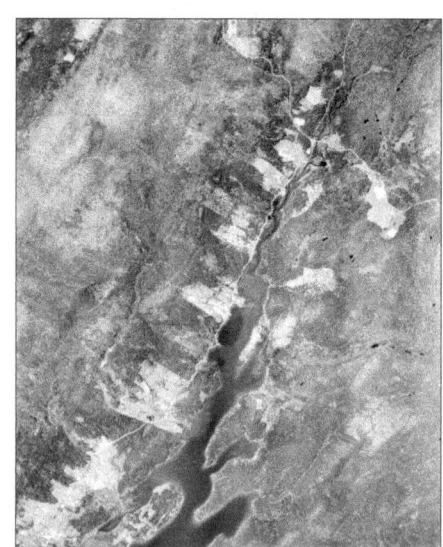

provided mainly for a family's subsistence. Over time, a cow was bought, a newborn calf would arrive, and oxen and carts preceded horses with their ploughs, mowing machines and rakers. Sheep provided wool, and the annual sale of lambs, would result in the happy arrival of the late-fall "lamb cheque." Those families who were considered as having gainful farming operations, whether because of location, soil conditions, or a farmer's own industriousness, were few and isolated. The Scottish homestead remained a subsistence one, rather than a viable commercial venture.

Horse-Tail Ingenuity

Ingenuity prevailed because cash was scarce. Homestead items such as a horse harness for example, were handmade with seal skin. Mick-John (Lighthouse) MacLean recalls his uncle John MacLean from Washabuck Centre Rear saving horse hair. When he had enough, he would weave it making a pliable, very strong, rot-proof and beautiful looking set of traces to dress-off the horse collar.[47]

"Mick" John MacLean (1897-1982) recalled that his uncle John MacLean used to make rope out of birch sticks:

> The slender sticks were cut 3 or 4 feet in length. He would leave them in the brook for several days, which caused them to swell. He would then remove them and beat them with a hammer which caused them to swell more. This process was repeated several times, whereupon the wood would then begin to peel off in strips. He would then weave and braid the thin strips into net and kelleg ropes and boat lines. It was durable and could last several seasons. It was kept inside when not in use. The rope proved to be a bit rough on the hands, it being about five-eighths of an inch – the diameter of one's finger, and it was very strong.[48]

Elizabeth MacLean (1868-1961) daughter of Peter Francis MacLean at MacKay Point recalled during her twilight years that her father's field, between the barn and the shoreline, was littered with 150-pound bales (68 kg) of hay awaiting shipment to Newfoundland. It would be shipped by sailing vessel from the MacKay Point government wharf. The hay had been wire-bound with a hand press. At that time, straddling the decades of the last century, the greatest amount of hay was harvested from farms at Murdock MacDonald's in Upper Washabuck, Vincent MacLean's at MacKay Point and on the MacKinnon Harbour interval properties of the peninsula.[49]

Michael A. MacLean recalls:

> Fifty-two barrels of oats were threshed at Vincent MacLean's one fall. Half of the crop paid for the threshing. The balance was fed mostly to the horses. The farm had three horses. Everyone travelled everywhere by horse with sleigh or wagon. You'd take oats with you to feed the horse while you visited. You stopped for water along the route. The locations of the roadside springs were well known. *Fuaran* they were called in

Gàidhlig. Horses were working all the time and were always treated with due care and respect. The balance of oats was kept for seed for next spring's planting.[50]

Milk was separated for its cream. Cream was kept in cans weighing perhaps forty pounds (18 kg) when full. These were stored in the homestead's spring or nearby brook before being shipped via lake boat to the Baddeck creamery. Prior to the 1930s, milk was placed in dedicated wooden pails called keelers, about a foot high and 18 inches in diameter (30 x 45 cm), with the cream being skimmed off after it thickened.[51] The cream was churned for butter, with any extra beyond family needs, being moulded and wrapped in one pound blocks and retailed along with farm eggs for cash. Roddie MacDonald vividly recalls severe lightning storms playing havoc with the cream, curdling the product, that was being kept cool in the brook,[52] and perhaps too as a consequent of the damp, humid, weather that preceded such thunderstorms.[53] Frequent, and severe summer thunder storms were the norm, certainly during the decades of the 1940s and '50s.

14-17 The remains of Murdock MacInnis's barn in 2012, stands defiant to the vicissitudes of time and weather at its Washabuck Bridge location. Built for MacInnis in 1934 by Jimmy MacKinnon and Neillie Devoe, the barn stood as a tortured symbol of an unfortunate decline, one that has besieged the once-bustling farming industry throughout the Washabuck community and much of rural Cape Breton Island.

Fishing

"The Wealth of My Store"[54]

Fishing was a mainstay for the pioneers. This was a livelihood with which the Barra and Lewis people were quite familiar. Boats, fishing gear, fish handling and curing their catch, were second nature to these sea-faring pioneers. For countless generations, fishing played a significant role in their daily lives; they were acutely in-tune with the vagaries of weather and the sea. Those pioneers that were fortunate enough to obtain a property abutting the Bras d'Or Lake shoreline made quick and practical use of the lake. Even the settlers on the "backlands" found themselves access to the lake's resources. It was their primary mode for transportation, and was immediately exploited as a source of protein. Very often the single staple available to a pioneer's larder, over time it proved beneficial for modest commercial return.

The pioneer boats were heavily built, their canvas sails burdened and cumbersome, and oars coarse and long. Nevertheless, these seafaring people were unrelenting and rigorous in their pursuit of Neptune's bounty. Joe (Red Rory) MacLean (1912-1998) recalls as a youth seeing the remnants of what he called a "Barra Boat" at William MacKenzie's shore in Lower Washabuck. "It was about 30 feet in length and 10-12 feet wide (10 x 3 m). It could handle a cow or a horse. It was powered by oars and probably could be rigged with a sail as well," remembered Joe.[55]

Grandsons of the pioneer *Eòin* MacNeil, who had settled at Washabuck Centre, made their way to the eastern seaboard's American fishing capital Glouster, Massachusetts. In time, both Alec (1858-1924) and Michael became captains of fishing schooners, and were known to occasionally sail their vessels into the Bras d'Or Lake while on their way to the Newfoundland banks, to spend an overnight visit with family and friends.[56]

"Mick" John (Lighthouse) MacLean (1897-1982) related that in "olden days" some local fishermen arose at 3 a.m. to go fishing. Some had to walk a mile or more to get to the shore.

Glumag

Neil Peter MacLean (1859-1940), often accompanied by his young daughters, Annie Mae and Mary Theresa, would leave in early morning from Washabuck Centre following a twenty minute walk to the shoreline. They would row with 16-foot (4.5 m) oars for about six miles to the *glumag*, a rich, fishing hole between MacKay Point and Shenacadie, where the fishers would bait and set trawl-lines, jig and hand-line for cod. They would row back, sometimes aided with a tattered sail should the wind freshen from a favourable quarter, dress (which included removing the backbone) and salt their catch. The routine was repeated for days, weeks even. The fish would be toted home from the shoreline to be dried. When weather was favourable the salted fish was placed on flakes to dry and either covered or returned inside before darkness fell. In those days, September was considered the best month for drying fish as the sun's rays were not as acute and the fish was less likely to burn.

Eels were a staple. They were speared from a boat or through a pond's winter's ice. Eels, during their winter hibernation, burrow into muddy bottoms particularly wherever eelgrass is present.

Mick-John MacLean remembered spearing eels at night:

> We would start at Washabuck Centre [by boat] on a calm evening after dark, and work our way around MacKays Point back to Maskells Harbour at Gillis Point. Layers of birch bark, each piece the circumference of the tree and about 4 inches wide were slipped in between a split

green alder and lit. One torch for each side of the boat, and this would attract the eels and make spearing them possible. These torches would burn for about ten minutes and then be replaced. A soft-bottom spear was used for spearing the muddy bottoms while the hard-bottom spear displaying a slightly different configuration was used, of course, for spearing the harder bottoms.[57]

A Teeming Lake

Mick-John recalled hearing Alex D. MacLean recounting that the old-timers would wade along the shoreline with legs bared. The fish were so plentiful in early times that the white legs would attract their attention. Like giant blue herons, the waders would stoop over, stealthily slide their arms into the water alongside their legs and suddenly flip the curious fish onto the nearby shoreline. Certainly, during the years of the disastrous potato famine in Cape Breton beginning ca. 1845, the abundance of fish helped immeasurably in sustaining the lives of the pioneers and their families.[58]

The Lakes were teeming with fish in the early days, including lobster and salmon. Commercially, even if there was a market, prices were very low. Michael A. MacLean (1911-2007) recalled that as a kid, he'd fix up one of his father's discarded traps and set it in shallow water just off their shoreline on the sandy bottom. Lobsters seldom frequent sandy bottom and are found most often on rocky shoals; nonetheless, the next morning he had trapped six lobsters. With lobsters so plentiful, they were considered to be poor people's food. It reflected poorly upon one's social and economic standing within certain circles if you were observed eating lobster.

In 2004, Michael A. MacLean was interviewed by Fisheries and Oceans Canada biologist John Tremblay about his lobster fishing experiences that covered a 56-year period (1926-1982). He recalled that between 1920-1940, lobsters fetched two cents per pound (450 g) and were purchased by fishing smacks that had made their way to-and-from the Big Bras d'Or area. If you were lucky, you'd load them onto a fishing smack, and be glad to get rid of them. Michael recalls on one occasion that his father did not have enough crates to contain all the lobsters he was catching. In those days his father fished about sixty traps out of an open boat with a "one-lunger" engine. An average catch in those days was 100 pounds (45 kg) in 60 traps.

Later, between 1940-1980 there were seven or eight lobster fishermen from Lower Washabuck fishing 70-80 traps apiece. Neighbouring lobster fishermen were often from the same family and included brothers; such as Archie and Stephen MacLean; Tommy (1905-1962) and Jimmy MacKenzie; Joe and Michael Dan MacLean, and Murdock MacLean, Michael A.'s brother. Lobsters were shipped weekly via the mail-boat from MacKay Point to Iona [until the mid '60s] where they were placed in a refrigerated rail-car and shipped to Boston wholesalers, Dent and Harvey, for the

American market. Lobstermen fished out of neighbouring communities of Gillis Point, Iona and Baddeck as well.[59]

"That Salmon"

Atlantic salmon were plentiful. Those fishermen who had fishing berths enjoyed a bountiful food fishery and to a lesser extent a commercial enterprise, in season. The spring salmon-run occurred around the Lakes at practically the same time. So, salmon fishermen very often had an abundance of salmon to sell, at matching times and to the same markets. This was well before the days of refrigeration, or at least electrification and family ice-houses maintained meat and fish in a cool, secure and sheltered atmosphere.

The village of Baddeck with its industrious waterfront and summer tourists provided the local hotels with a brisk business, resulting in a good vender's venue for fresh salmon and lobster. Sometimes, even that nearby market was over supplied, and could not handle the abundance of freshly caught salmon.

Michael A. MacLean relates a tale from the mid-1920s when his father netted a large run of salmon, as had his competition. When the salmon were running you could have a couple of dozen fish each time you checked the berth. These were on average 18-20-pound (8 kg) fish.

The usual bustling Baddeck market was saturated. Michael and his father had no choice but to dress and salt down their catch, enough salmon to fill a large barrel. To do the procedure properly, included removing the backbone, was a three-day process.

Not sure of how he might sell the catch, his father phoned Washabuck Bridge merchant John Dan MacRitchie and asked if he might be interested in buying the barrel of salted salmon. "Bring it up!" he exclaimed. So, the father-son team somehow wrestled the barrel of salmon into their open boat, motored to Washabuck River, rowed the boat the last short distance to MacRitchie's general store and delivered their cargo unto the store's rear landing which fronted on the river. A few days later MacRitchie phoned back inquiring if they had any more of "that salmon." He had sold the lot of it. The salmon which

14-18 Washabuck fisherman Vincent MacLean, MacKay Point, relaxes with his wife Theresa (Michael Eoin) on left and his sister, Elizabeth, while visiting Allen's Island, [Bone Island] ca. 1940.

turns a dark crimson when salted, had evidently proven to be an immediate hit with his patrons.

Salmon nets were treated prior to being set. These were cotton nets and they required special treatment, a task that disappeared with the advent of the nylon mesh. The nets were tanned usually in a spent molasses barrel. The puncheon was placed on its side, a sizeable hole was cut out of it midsection. The net or a portion of it was stuffed inside and then heated tanning liquid was poured in, completely covering the webbing. The hole was re-covered and left for about twenty-four hours. The tanning liquid was simply a mixture of cutch, a tannin used on sails and hot water. In even earlier times, the bark of the hemlock tree was used to achieve a similar result.[60] The process darkened the cotton mesh and resulted in the nets remaining cleaner for longer periods. The "setting-out" and "taking-in" of a salmon net was a labour intensive task and the longer a net remained clean, the better it fished and bettered the lot of the fisherman.[61]

A Rough Roll[62]

When Peter F. MacLean, Michael A.'s oldest brother, was in his ninety-sixth year, he reminisced about his fishing exploits as a boy of thirteen. He would rise about 4 a.m. to check the herring net set in front of his parent's home at MacKay Point, while his father tended some early barn chores. This was early springtime, late April and early May, just after the lake ice would leave. In the mornings, the lake was cold and the net would be filled with herring. As a rule, onshore winds would not freshen until about 10 a.m., so an early start to the day meant calmer seas. Peter and his father would row – or sail, if a breeze was fair – the couple of miles (3 km) to the fishing-hole the Gaels christened the *Glumag* and run a 700-hook trawl-line. Neighbouring fishermen, Captain Alec MacNeil and Neil Peter MacLean would journey even further from Washabuck Centre, an additional three miles (4.5 km), to tend their fishing gear at the same location.

Peter F.'s task in the stern of the boat was cutting herring for bait while the raucous sea gulls swooped

14-19 Seagulls circle above Little Narrows lobsterman Charlie Ellis and his fishing boat, as it returns to harbour at MacKay Point, 2000. Ellis and crew are the last in a long line of small-craft commercial fishermen that once patronized Washabuck's shoreline.

and screamed about. His father un-hooked the caught fish and re-baited the trawl. They would return home close to noon, after running the lobster traps, dress and salt the codfish they had not already used as lobster bait. During the warmer days, they would place the cod on flakes to dry, covering it before nightfall. A further chore for Peter F. involved cooking a portion of the lobster catch in a large boiler on the lakeshore that his father would later peddle in the afternoon to Baddeck customers.[63]

Michael A. said the largest salmon Vincent MacLean claimed to have caught weighed 44 pounds (20 kg). Obviously, a fish of this size could not mesh but had simply entangled itself in the trap's webbing.[64]

The fishermen would check their nets every few hours when salmon were running especially to rescue meshed salmon from ravaging eels. Eels devour the seafood delicacy rapidly simply by burrowing inside the fish, leaving nothing but the empty shell of skin and skeleton. Eels were abundant too.

Michael A. recalled one occasion when he and his father were running the salmon net. They had checked the lead of the net out from the shoreline toward the trap area where they were dismayed to spot the remnants of a large salmon. Suddenly, they realized eels were still burrowing inside the fish, so his father gently pulled the net around the salmon, enclosing it, and then together the men suddenly heaved that part of the net aboard, resulting in seven large eels making an unexpected and unhappy exit onto the floor boards. The afternoon trek wasn't a total loss.[65]

Make-and-Break

Neil P. S. MacLean owned the first "one-lunger" (single-piston) marine engine in Washabuck. It was thought to have been a 1915 Imperial model. At that time he ran the local passenger ferry from his own shore in Washabuck to Baddeck. Peter Campbell, a First World War veteran and a son of Dan Campbell, owned a pleasure boat and he was one of the first individuals from the Baddeck area to sport a one-lunger. Peter's sister, Janie, ran the telegraph office in Baddeck. In 1923, when Vincent MacLean saw Peter's, he had to have one as well, so brother-in-law Dan Campbell and a friend installed a new three-horsepower Fairbanks into MacLean's fishing boat.

Also known as the "make-and-break," the engine proved to be a lifesaver for rowers, as Vincent had three salmon berths, a lobster trap-line with a hundred traps and trawl lines along with mackerel and herring nets. Everybody was rowing everywhere up until that time. Jack MacFarlane who ran MacFarlane's Garage in Baddeck had a similar type engine. Naturally, the folks at Beinn Bhreagh [The Bells] had engines ahead of everyone else from the area.[66]

Gradually, from that time onward, most Washabuck fishermen invested in the Lunenburg-built Acadia one-lunger. They proved to be simple to operate, dependable and economical gas engines appreciated, respected and widely used by small craft owners for the ensuing decades.

Oyster Farming *à la Détresse*

It was early in the 1970s that the Industrial Division (ID) of the federal government agency known as DEVCO initiated a plan to develop among Cape Breton Island's rural communities, cottage industries based upon the natural fish and shellfish industry.

Marine co-operatives were established in those communities under the guidance of the St. Francis Xavier University extension department and an umbrella Company known first as Devco Marine Farming, that morphed into Cape Breton Primary Production and finally into Cape Breton Marine Farming Ltd. Co-operatives were established in Aspy Bay which held a large membership of 160 members, West Bay, Seal Island, D'Escousse, Washabuck, Mabou, Petit Etang, Baddeck and Orangedale.[67]

The science component of the company fell under the supervision of Roy Drinnan. Philip Drinnan was responsible for the fish production and Robin Stuart upheld responsibilities for the shellfish side of operations. These individuals were recruited because of their expertise and background knowledge and their previous enhancement work with oyster development in the province of PEI. The fledging Cape Breton industry involved parallel and compatible farming efforts of clam, oyster, trout, salmon, eel and Irish moss farming, in what was hoped were harmonious communities.[68]

The Washabuck Co-op had approximately thirty members and was dedicated specifically to oyster farming. Charlie Murphy (1919-1982) a local, knowledgeable, old-time oyster harvester supervised the aquatic monitoring of the Washabuck operation, monitoring that included the selection of appropriate raft sites and the regular recording of salinity levels and water temperatures.[69]

A Womanly Workforce

It was mostly females who were employed in the budding Washabuck oyster enterprise; mothers mostly, including Marie, Irene, Josie and Rose – all MacLeans, along with Margaret MacDonald and Mary Agnes MacDougall. The workforce was in due course augmented with Jean MacDonald of Estmere, Jessie MacKinnon of Hazeldale and Shirley Terrace of Little Narrows. Josie MacLean was the gifted spokesperson for the local co-op. Other outside workers included Scoggy Watson, Robert Garland and Tony MacLean from the Baddeck area.

The work involved the tedious task of stringing half-inch (13 mm) plastic spacers and spent scallop shells onto a wire string with 49 spacers and 50 shells per line. The shells were first holed with a punching machine. The string was a vinyl-coated galvanized wire. Completed lines in due course were hung on T-Bars that were affixed to modified aluminium rafts sporting pontoons 12 inches or 19 inches in diameter (30 or 48 cm). These rafts were in turn towed to advantageous sites and anchored in calm coves noted for favourable oyster-spat production.

Workers earned minimum wage with the incentive of being paid an additional 10 cents a string. Each worker strived to complete the lofty goal of 100 strings a shift. The vacant, then privately-owned Upper Washabuck schoolhouse was the original operating base for the first summer and fall season. Subsequently, all operations were relocated to another abandoned school building boasting an additional structure close by, this time at Estmere, where the work continued throughout the year.

Although the workers were warmly clad, they had no idea what winter working conditions would be encountered. As it turned out conditions were less than comfortable. With desolate buildings that were uninsulated and poorly heated, and the work itself described as, "dirty, cold and smelly." Original workers, who had little workplace skills, did not know what to expect. One worker naively showed up in the workplace with pink coloured, fleece-lined slippers. Shells were brought in covered with snow and dumped on the wet floor. "The sharp-edged, scallop shells tore rubber gloves to shreds and your hands were cut, bleeding, always sore, as they never got a chance to heal. We reeked!" recalled Marie MacLean describing the challenging work. "This shellfish related work was certainly the first gainful employment that had ever become available for women in this area."[70]

For a variety of reasons, the DEVCO initiative never reached its anticipated economic potential and failed to become a lasting venture. The last co-operative in Orangedale functioned until 1980. The Washabuck Co-op folded after a three-year stint. Oysters taken off the scallop shell after only two years were large, but thin-shelled and easily damaged. There was a problem of too much spat adhering to the shells, causing logistical cleaning problems. Although the co-operatives had plenty of members, very few of them helped out, leaving most of the tedious work and responsibility to a few, except when it came time when dividends were to be doled out. This caused friction. Perhaps the real problem from the outset was the fact that there was no equity investment required of the membership, so there was little reason for members to take a real interest in the co-op's success. The final straw came when a change in federal governments in 1984, saw the withdrawal of any further funding for the DEVCO sponsored enterprise.[71]

Harbinger

According to Robin Stuart, although the over-all enterprise proved economically unsuccessful, the operation had been initially established as a demonstration farm and, when viewed from this perspective, it proved to be profoundly successful. Successful aquaculture today has been essentially built upon the lessons learned and the experiences endured, first here, on Cape Breton Island, long before fish-farming became a fact and way-of-life in Norway or anywhere else in the Americas.

After forty years, the accumulated water temperature data, gleaned from the enterprise's scientific monitoring – especially the data from within Bras d'Or Lake, has displayed evidence of the rising temperatures now being reflected in this century's oceans. Today, the fundamental lessons learned from the Cape Breton shellfish farming initiative are accepted as standard practice worldwide and have proven to be economically invaluable for the current billion dollar international fish-farming industry.[72]

14-20 An assembly of Upper Washabuck women on the occasion of Martha MacDougall's marriage to Dan Alec MacKinnon, October 12, 1942. Back Row L-R: Sadie Jane (Mrs. Jim Alec MacDougall), Annie (Mrs. Joe MacMullin), "Red" Mary (Mrs. Jack Murphy), Mary Ann (Mrs. Danny Murphy, *Ceiteig* (Mrs. Rory MacKinnon), Sarah Liza (Mrs. Angus Ranald MacDonald) and Mary Ann (Mrs. John Stephen MacKenzie). Front Row: Agnes (Mrs. Malcolm MacDonald), Mary MacDougall, and Joan (Mrs. Ranald MacDonald). Courtesy of Hector MacKenzie, Washabuck Bridge.

15 – Murder

A Washabuck Tragedy

The following tale is revealed by Alex D. MacLean.

My grandfather's house was the scene of a murder many years ago, in 1878 if my information is correct, and I am now relating the facts as they were passed on to me by an eye witness.... Two of the principals were John MacNeil (d. 1882) and Peter MacNeil two brothers on the one side, and Hector MacNeil and his brother Alexander sons of Angus (*Eòin*) MacNeil, on the other. Bad feelings had existed between two of the MacNeil's, Alexander and John, for some time, and a few days before the tragedy in which Hector MacNeil lost his life, John MacNeil had bested Alexander in a fistic encounter. It was in the fall of the year that matters came to a head.

My grandfather Donald MacLean held a "ploughing frolic" on his small farm at Washabuck Centre. As was customary, the neighbours who assisted with the ploughing were to enjoy a dance at my grandfather's house that night. Early in the evening, those who were invited gathered at the dance and among those were Alexander MacNeil and his brother Hector. The latter was to assist in furnishing violin music for the party.

The dancing was in progress but a short time, when the other two MacNeil brothers, John and Peter arrived. They took seats near the entrance. Suddenly, the pleasant past time was interrupted by Alexander, who had been dancing up until then, turning towards John MacNeil and asking him, "Do you consider yourself to be as good a man as you were the other day?" Soon after that the two men were fighting, and seeing that Alexander was getting the worst of the argument, his father Angus – [*Eòin*], although not invited as he has a reputation of been quarrelsome – asked his son Hector to go to his brother Alexander's assistance.

My eyewitness states that Hector, who was always inclined to be peaceful and not of a contentious nature, hesitated for a considerable time, in fact shook his head negatively two or three times, before he finally acceded to is father's request.

The small house was now in an uproar. It was only a small building and the dancing [had been] in progress in the only room in the lower part of the house. The women and children present quickly got out of the way, some of them got out, and some more climbed on the loom that stood in the corner of the room. One of those who watched the fight from this vantage point ... told me that in the meantime that John MacNeil had obtained the assistance of his brother Peter, and the four MacNeils were huddled together in a corner of the room, near the fireplace, and it was impossible for her to see what they were doing.

Finally, Hector MacNeil disengaged himself from the fight, and walked towards the door, remarking in Gaelic, (the common tongue) as he went out, "My arm is broken." He was seen to be holding his arm. The next to leave the huddle was Peter MacNeil, who was a cripple, and he was covered with blood. Hector MacNeil had no broken arm [but] he evidently felt his arm to be weakening as he had lost a great quantity of blood. He had been stabbed several times under the left armpit.... He collapsed outside, and was carried back into the house, where he passed away before a priest or medical assistance could be brought to him. It was discovered that Peter MacNeil, the unfortunate cripple who had gone to the assistance of his brother, had been forced to use his knife in self-defense as he was being unmercifully beaten. Shortly before he died, Hector addressed his brother Alexander, who was beside him, and said, "I have this on your account Alex."

Needless to say this occurrence caused much sorrow and sadness in the community. What had given promise of an enjoyable dance had been turned into a tragedy. No blame was attached or could be attached to anyone but the principals. Peter MacNeil gave himself up to the Magistrates of the District early that morning. The Magistrates were Peter S. MacLean and John C. Boyd, the local school master. After these officials had concluded a preliminary hearing, the accused was taken to the county *gaol* in Baddeck.

At a subsequent hearing before the Supreme Court, Peter was sentenced to a term of five years in Kingston Penitentiary. (At that time the Maritime Penitentiary in Dorchester, NB, had not been built.) A severer sentence was not passed on him, as the charge had been reduced to manslaughter, and it was also brought out in the evidence that the killing was occasioned solely in self-defense, and moreover, it was apparent to all that the crime was not premeditated.

Indeed, it is difficult to understand how Peter MacNeil could be convicted at all, as one of the principal witnesses for the Crown, Alexander MacNeil, who, it will be remembered was the aggressor, gave his evidence in such a way as to shoulder much of the blame himself. I have often heard it remarked and I record it here as something that will stand to his everlasting credit, that he had such regard and respect for the sanctity of his oath, that when giving his evidence, he did not endeavor to mitigate his own part in the tragedy, but told the truth in every particular. His evidence elicited the comment from the presiding Justice that, "Alexander MacNeil, and not the prisoner at the bar, should have been charged."

Peter MacNeil did not serve the full term of five years. He was allowed to return to his home long before that time, as he was in poor health, and he received time off for good behaviour. He died within a few years his return. His home was near the residence of Malcolm (Paul) MacLean at Washabuck Centre.[1]

Diarist Robert Elmsley of Baddeck included the following terse entry dated June 13, 1879. "Court closed. Murderer sentenced to 5 years."[2] Alexander Munro the noted educator of Boularderie Island fame and Inspector of Schools for Victoria County served as Coroner for the county for many years. It was he who presided in that capacity at the inquest on the murdered remains of Hector MacNeil.[3]

Potato "Peals"

Alex D. MacLean relates the following sequel to the above terrible happening.

Peter MacKenzie of Upper Washabuck told me a very moving story in connection with the return of Peter MacNeil from Kingston. Mr. MacKenzie was only a young boy at the time, and a few days after Peter MacNeil had returned ... his brother John came to Donald MacKenzie's, (young Peter's father) and asked him if he would let [young] Peter go to work with him to assist in digging potatoes. Peter was allowed to go ... and the next day he toiled in the potato field, along with the two brothers John and Peter MacNeil. Being only a young boy and hearing so many different tales about the awful murder for which Peter had served a penitentiary term, he was very much afraid of him, and would keep as far away from him as he possibly could. That night, soon after supper, it was noticed that the boy was tired as a result of his steady labour in the fields, and he was directed to bed. He was soon sound asleep. He was awakened to find Peter MacNeil making preparations to occupy the same bed with him. He was so terrified that his screams roused the household. No one could understand what was the matter with him, until finally poor Peter himself thought of [his murder rap] and asked young Peter MacKenzie if he was afraid of him? The boy replied that he was. He told me that the poor man knelt by the side of the bed and began to weep, telling him that he need not be afraid of him, as he would not kill a fly.[4] Peter *Dubh* MacNeil died in 1886.

Mutiny at Burnt Point

Hector MacKenzie of Washabuck Bridge recalls having heard this grim account spun by the well-known Iona genealogist, Francis Hector MacNeil during a wake-house vigil at Gillis Point in 1950.

It seems two young men from the Arichat area of Isle Madame rowed their boat from Arichat to St. Peter's and down the length of the waters of Bras d'Or Lake to Baddeck. It was during the late summer season and they had hopes of finding work in the hay fields of that wide-spread farming community with their hand-scythes. In those times there were large farming operations at Big Farm and Big Baddeck areas. Good scythe-men were appreciated and often hard to find when needed, so the youthful pair lucked-out and spent the balance of the harvesting season slashing crops of hay and oats for local farmers who gladly provided the willing workers with room, board and wages for services rendered.

Later, with the harvesting season at an end, and the crops stowed, the men headed home for Arichat in their rowboat, but not before making purchases from the local liquor vendor in Baddeck. Soon after leaving Baddeck the two became embroiled in a vicious argument off MacKay Point and the duo went ashore at Burnt Point beach to settle the dispute. The last man out of the boat grabbed a hand-scythe and slew his partner with it before his mate had any chance to defend himself. The culprit then disposed of the body in the pond behind the beach. He removed all evidence of the crime and continued the return trek to Arichat, alone.

On arrival at home, the murderer explained the absence of his friend by stating he had jumped the train at the Iona railway station and headed west (The first time-table passenger express was run from Sydney to Point Tupper on June 22, 1891[5]). The explanation made reasonable sense to his family and nothing further was ever thought about the missing youth until

15-1 Upper Washabuck residents Murdock MacKinnon stands behind his nephew Bernie (Angus) MacKinnon (left) and neighbour Johnny (Angus Ranald) MacDonald, ca. 1940.

upon his deathbed, the killer confessed to the murder of his companion.[6] The date and names of the principals remain unknown.

Michael Anthony MacLean (1911-2007) who spent his entire lifetime at MacKay Point was quizzed whether he had ever heard of a murder being committed in the general area of the homestead. Upon brief reflection he commented that yes, as a young fellow he had heard a story related by his mother [who was from Washabuck Centre] about someone being murdered there, "and the body having been disposed of in the pond behind the beach at Burnt Point." Although Michael A. was definitive about having heard about the crime, he was as just as resolute about not having heard any further details about the sordid deed.[7]

Bludgeoned Phantom

Along the shores of Washabuck, one of the long-time preferred ice-fishing locations for smelts (and the occasional trout) is near Murphy's Point in MacIver's Cove, opposite Holy Rosary Church. The location is a favourite feeding site for harbour and grey seals that follow schools of fish around the lake. Herds of seals, often numbering in the hundreds are habitual visitors to St. Patrick's Channel. A long time ago this site was the scene of a dramatic occurrence that captured in a horrific way, the collective imagination of the commonly stoic community.

A stone's throw west of the Washabuck Church, Murdock Paul MacLean's brook empties into the estuary called MacIver's Cove. In earlier times, the public road looped and wound its way paralleling the brook prior to a new highway bridge being built; later still, the bridge was replaced by a large culvert, resulting in a realigned, shortened and straightened roadway.

15-2 Murphy Point Road sign.
15-3 MacIver's Cove, Upper Washabuck.

One winter's night, a couple of Lower Washabuck MacDonald brothers, (Quentin and another – there were six others) were visiting their uncle and aunt, Angus Ranald and Sarah Eliza MacDonald in Upper Washabuck. The clear night turned suddenly very cold, with the temperature plummeting in a matter of hours. Modern-day meteorologists may call it a flash freeze, but then, it was called *Am Faoilleach,* stormy weather that occurs in the depth of the Gàidhlig winter, spanning the weeks between mid-January to mid-February. Having spent a pleasurable evening with their kin, the brothers bundled-up, retrieved their mare from their uncle's barn, hitched her quickly in the shafts of the cutter, and pulling a buffalo robe around themselves headed at a warming pace for home, a distance of some four miles (6 km), under a starlit heaven.

15-4 (L-R) *Ceiteig* (Mrs. Rory MacKinnon), Murdock (Paul) MacLean, with his sister Ellie-Ann. Courtesy of Hector MacKenzie.

Everything was fine until they arrived at Murdock Paul's brook where the mare suddenly reared up, spooked and snorting, she veered off to the side of the road. It took a bit of constraint on the part of the brothers to get the animal calmed and back under control, but once they did, they secured her bridle to a nearby tree and went to investigate what was the cause of the mare's dread. It didn't take the brothers long to find the cause of her fright. There, on the ice along the bank of the running brook was a large seal, caught out-of-water by the sudden night-time freeze and its air hole had frozen over. It had either smelled or sensed the running water in the nearby brook and had propelled its way ashore where its presence had so startled the mare.

The MacDonald brothers immediately devised a scheme. The boys broke off a pole from a panel of Murdock Paul's line-fence and using it as a hakapic bludgeoned the hapless seal. With the ice and snow around the site now tinctured red from the massacre, the lads grabbed an axe from the back of the sleigh and proceeded to drag the dispatched seal over scrunching granules onto the lake ice, trailing blood all the way across MacIver's Cove to Murphy's Point, a distance of about seven hundred feet. Here under the starlight, they located a host of now frozen-over fishing holes, one of which they enlarged to several times its normal size and ensuring the opening was well stained. The culprits retraced their tracks, dragging their victim behind them. When they reached the sleigh, they tossed the carcass and axe into it and under the chilling night sky casually continued their homeward trek.

Well, the saga could have ended there, but it didn't. Early the same morning, bachelor Murdock Paul, discovered the broken fence panel, erupted into a stream of Gàidhlig invective, "*A Mhuire, Mhuire! Is e an Deamhan fhéin a th'ann!*" spewing the fieriest of afflictions upon the unknown perpetrators even before stumbling upon the blood-stained ice and snow along the brook. The broken fence quickly forgotten, Murdock promptly followed the bloodied trail out to the point and although stymied with what may have transpired, before long deduced the worst.

Murdock with wind in his jib, headed to the home of his neighbour and long-time bosom buddy, Danny Murphy, a distance of about half a mile (800 m). He arrived intense, agitated, out of breath and had to roust Danny out of his bed. Murphy listened groggily to Murdock's animated tale detailing the broken fence and his description of the blood-smeared scene and that he had followed the trail out to the point, where he chanced-upon the enlarged opening and the blots of bloodied ice.

It was early and still cold, as the rays of the morning sun had yet to make much impact, but soon, Murphy had the kitchen stove alight and a cup of tepid tea made for them both. Murphy then donned his winter coat and faithful fedora and followed the early-morning sleuth, retracing under Murdock's animated guidance the gory trail from one blood-soaked border to the other.

Murdock Paul's own suspicions of murder were soon confirmed by Danny who by now was himself convinced that a savage crime had indeed been perpetrated.

"Be-heavens Mister," burst out Murphy giving his barren headgear a warming tug, "Sure enough MacLean, somebody has been slaughtered here!"

"*A Mhuire, Mhuire! Nighean Sheanmhair Ifrinn,*" exploded Murdock, again breaking into harsh expletives, "*Is e an Deamhan fhein a th' ann!*" It's damn clear to me too friend, someone has been butchered here! Murdered to death right here – on my own farm! What else it could have been?" The blood-spattered evidence, they agreed, indicated that the victim's remains had been deposed off through the ice at the Point, consigned to the inscrutable depths and eels in MacIver's Cove.

So the yarn erupted. The breaking news required no Internet. For nearly a week jabber around the entire community was aflame, devoted to conjecture about the gruesome incident. Curiously though, no one seemed to be missing. Who could it have been? Who were the assailants? Why such a massacre?

Of course, the MacDonald brothers added to the consternation, adding speculative fuel anywhere an opportunity presented itself. Their ruse had worked spectacularly. Sluggishly, as bits and pieces of the shadowy drama oozed out, reality set in, and talk about the incident withered away.

Murphy calmly returned to his greatest loves, a beautiful family and harvesting oysters, while Murdock Paul, his capacity for pungent language un-restrained, beseeched corrosive blessings upon the perpetrating infidels as he maintained an ever keener surveillance on his property's defences. As for the MacDonald brothers, well they continued their vigorous lifestyle too, vigilantly awaiting an opportunity for their next impulsive caper. Normalcy returned. The community's ramparts remained inviolate. Everyone again felt safe and snug.[8]

16 – Melodic Memories

In June 1996 I was asked by Dr. Mark Wilson, Rounder Records[1] producer to draft some liner notes for a Cape Breton Fiddle Anthology, to accompany a four-series CD set. In addition to being a producer of North American folk-fiddle music, Wilson is also a Professor of Philosophy at the University of Pittsburg. He asked for my reminiscences of the musical events through the Washabuck community between the mid-1940s and the mid-1960s. Many of the following observations were included as part of that monologue.

Since their arrival on the Cape Breton shores, generations of Scots have soothed, enchanted and entertained, family, friends and neighbours – and themselves – with their talent, creative ingenuity and interpretation of Celtic music and dance. Some of them were noted composers, some displayed harmonic voices; others played a palette of instruments, such as the traditional pipes and fiddle, a guitar, a pump-organ and the upstart piano (would you believe the sax, drum and pipe-organ too). Each composition reflecting the influence of the lyrical Gàidhlig language in its own ingenious way and delighting world audiences with deft, vigorous and melodic arrangements. Over the generations, the Washabuck community has shared generously, in advancing Celtic culture to the masses. Here then are a few scattered memories from those far off decades in Washabuck, when we were younger and the fiddle was king.

Close-to-the-Floor

"I'm going for a quick visit to Hector MacKenzie's. Would you like to come with me?" asked my fiddling uncle Joe MacLean. Would I? I was about eight years old as this was I think, 1952. My paternal grandmother had passed away the previous June. (Both of my grandmothers as well as my future mother-in-law were fluent Gàidhlig speakers and respected Gàidhlig singers.) Electricians were now wiring homes for electricity throughout the community. The lights would be turned on in October of that year. Uncle Joe (or Joe W. as our family and close friends referred to him) was visiting us at the ancestral homestead at MacKay Point; he was on a few days R&R from his day job as conductor with the CN railroad out of Sydney.

"Would I? Well yes, yes!" Before that, the furthest I recall being away from home was visiting the old ram pasture on the back forty.

So away we went in Joe's car eight miles away to visit Hector at the "Bridge." The MacKenzie homestead was commonly referred to as the "Bridge" simply because it was located adjacent to the rusty iron highway bridge that spanned Washabuck River. Joe did the visiting and I remained in the car. Joe's mission was simple. Get Hector to bring his guitar and come with us, back to the Point, for an evening of music.

16-1 Mary Ann (Devoe) MacKenzie (1901-1983) Washabuck Bridge.

The evening's racket was further enhanced with the arrival of "Red" Rory MacLean, long-time neighbour, friend, contemporary of my grandparents and devotee of fiddle music. My Dad (Michael Anthony MacLean) and Joe W. played fiddles; Hector accompanied with his guitar and played fiddle too.

And "Red" Rory, he danced.

Oh, "Red" Rory played a tune or two, but he really shone when it came to step-dancing. As soon as a fiddler struck up a strathspey or reel, Red Rory was on the floor. He just couldn't abide to strathspeys and reels being played without dancing to them. He was a classy dancer with a wonderful talent for close-to-the-floor, neat, tidy, footwork, that was picked-up and carried-on in resounding style by his youngest son, Johnny "Washabuck," and daughter, Aggie MacLennan. That early evening stretched into a late night session, and in spite of my tender years, the occasion seared itself indelibly upon my soul.

Radio Airs

Growing up during the forties coincided with the beginning of CJFX Antigonish, a new radio station that went on-air in March 1943. We grew up listening to station manager Clyde Nunn, (at times accompanied by a quick-witted, home-grown, entertainer, Percy Baker) hosting his program *Fun at Five;* promoting whatever recorded and live fiddle music was available for him to unleash over Celtic airwaves to a grateful listening audience. Music from fiddlers Colin J. Boyd, Hughie A. MacDonald, Angus Allan Gillis, Wilfred Gillis, Dan J. Campbell, Angus Chisholm, Winston Fitzgerald, Bill Lamey, Carl MacKenzie, "Little" Jack MacDonald, Buddy MacMaster and Joe MacLean. Each record was eagerly awaited, appreciated and listened to keenly, in those early days of Radio Antigonish.

Over at CJCB Radio in Sydney, the Thursday evening *MacDonald Lassie* program featured Winston Fitzgerald, accompanied by guitarist Estwood Davidson and pianist Beattie Wallace. That "Picnic Reel" theme reverberates throughout my being still. That was *my* "hit parade"! Television didn't made its debut at home until 1958 (maybe) and although it proved to be a fascinating new medium, *Leave it to Beaver,* ran a distant second to fiddle music and square dancing, at least in my books.

Certainly, before there was Celtic music on the radio there was Celtic music at fundraising church picnics and parish concerts and at most community events. There were the best of Cape Breton pipers, fiddlers, dancers, and Gàidhlig singers. One of the last outdoor church concerts I recall occurred in 1961 on the St. Columba parish grounds at Iona. Performers included singer Charlie MacKenzie with his distinguished baritone voice and his fiddling brother Carl. Charlie was a fine fiddle, guitar and piano player too. Another fiddler, brother Hector, emceed the affair. From that occasion forward, he had a successful forty-year career emceeing Celtic concerts Island-wide and beyond. Sydney piper Francis MacKenzie bent the ear of the appreciative crowd, while brothers Bernie and Stanley Campbell from Iona, and sisters Joan MacDonald and Jean MacNeil of Washabuck, all proved to be nimble-footed step-dancers. Winston Fitzgerald, Joe W. and "Big" Archie MacKenzie each displayed their fiddling dexterity to the enthusiastic evening crowd.

The annual *Highland Village Day* concert at Iona was launched the next year in August 1962 and has since demonstrated an adeptness at showcasing new talent and returning Cape Breton Celtic artists to a world audience. Consequently, this annual festival holds a special place in the hearts and memories of Island residents, visiting relatives "home for the summer," and the appreciative tourist.

Fiddle music at our home was a regular occurrence. Dad played the fiddle several evenings a week including at local community dances, at any number of house rackets and during lazy Sunday afternoons. Fiddle playing for us was simply a part of our growing up. Just as for those who live near a body of water, whether it's the ocean, a lake or a river, that aquatic entity somehow, unwittingly, forever becomes an intrinsic part of one's psyche. The same can be said I believe, about music, and its influence upon a person's own self.

So as a family, we grew up listening to fiddle music broadcast over the radio waves; we heard and danced to it regularly around home and it proved to be a very enjoyable facet of our youth. Visitors dropped by frequently for a tune. Ma faithfully provided the tea. A party is simply not a party without music and in this particular case – fiddle music.

I recall late-night fiddle parties with Dolly and Murdena MacNeil – endearing school teachers from Big Beach – with their admiring chauffeurs Ray MacDonald and Simon MacKenzie and chaperon Joe "Red Rory" MacLean. Those times made for some sleepy-headed students and groggy-headed teachers on more than a few school-day mornings. Those early memories of fiddle music, dancing and laughter will live on as long as there's a pulse.

As is the case in all musical homes, other musicians dropped by. Neighbours, "Little" Stephen MacLean and Johnny "Washabuck" MacLean were fine fiddlers and frequent visitors who sometimes played together for local dances. Stephen's uncle Rory (Stephen) (1870-1935) and Johnny's father "Red" Rory (1880-1953) were mean fiddlers in their own right and generation. Later on, when Stephen and Johnny worked in Sydney, they were oft times featured playing on CJCB Radio, sometimes accompanied by John Willie Campbell. Campbell was another good fiddler, who made many a safari to Washabuck to oblige the appreciative Murphy, MacKenzie and MacLean families with his playing, particularly own favourite jig, "Maggie Brown." More MacLeans – Peter F., Murdock and John Alec – played the fiddle, although not as openly as their sister Theresa, and brothers Joe W. and Michael Anthony. Today, Stephen's nephew Daniel, plays the fiddle and Johnny "Washabuck's" own son John MacLean, is a notable world champion piper and a much sought after piping instructor.

16-2 Iona resident Peter F. MacLean jams with Jean MacNeil at a Washabuck housewarming, 1975.

Lawrence MacDougall, a favourite side-kick of mine during my teen years, spent a lot of his time with his grandfather Dan MacDougall, who lived next door to the musical MacKenzie family at Washabuck Bridge. Lawrence had a keen desire to learn to play the fiddle and he did. He developed into a delightful fiddler displaying a light touch combined with that old-time *blas math* flavor, before leaving home to become the community's first lawman serving out a long successful career with the RCMP. And now some forty years later he has returned to Washabuck in semi-retirement mode, to gratefully entertain us once more.

Gordon "Lighthouse" MacLean who grew up next door in Gillis Point learned to play on the parlor organ at his home and became one of the Island's noted pianists, with his distinctive accompanying light touch and own evocative compositions. There was always music at Gordon's lighthouse home, as his Uncles Hector and Mick-John and Aunt Veronica were fiddlers and other uncles, Joe and Stephen, were banjo and accordion instrumentalists. Gordon's sister Jacinta is an earnest fiddler and she and her sister Charlene are distinguished for their harmonic vocals, as is the melodious, great family of Benny and Annie "Sister" MacLean, via Washabuck and Sydney Mines.

16-3 RCMP Corporal J. Lawrence MacDougall, Washabuck's first lawman.

John Y. Gillis from MacKinnon Harbour made many a trip to Washabuck with his fiddle, entertaining everyone in typical John Y. fashion, a visit that could sometimes last a week. Iona's John S. MacNeil, an accomplished singer, choirmaster and organist shared his musical talents willingly with all, many, many, times in Washabuck church and home, until his passing in 1960. His niece Honey MacNeil of Iona continued in her uncle's refined organ and piano accompaniment tradition.

Magi

Dad always spoke glowingly about the local fiddlers that influenced him and his horde of siblings. Dan MacKinnon (1864-1949) of Cain's Mountain via Washabuck, John Francis Campbell of Iona and John Alec "The Fiddler" MacNeil of Gillis Point were frequently mentioned with an aura of awe. Unfortunately, I never had the privilege of meeting, or even hearing these local Magi play, as they had passed on before my teen years.

Spirit and Water

Fiddling for old-time dances required a lot of enthusiasm and stamina. Dances usually started in late evening and often went to early dawn. There was seldom a piano and definitely no amplifier to assist a valiant, lonely fiddler, sawing away to provide volume in the overcrowded, dusty, venues. A drink is appreciated by most fiddlers, bushed or not, but was not always guaranteed, even at weddings. But then, the opposite could occur and the fiddler could be, "killed with kindness." A duo of fiddlers was welcomed, not just by the merry-making dancers, but by the fiddlers themselves, who ordinarily treasured each other's accompaniment.

Annie Hamish from MacNeil's Vale, was a well-liked square-dance fiddler. She liked her drink too, if a comment she made while taking a breather from, "playing her heart out" at a Birch Point wedding reception a long time ago, is any indication. She was overheard to exclaim: "How is one supposed to play all night on just the spirit and the water?" Of course by that time, according to the keen-eared informant, she was "drunk as hell!"[1] Maybe she was referring to a spirit of a more exotic sort!

I recall Hector MacKinnon dropping by occasionally. He was the eldest son of Dan and Catherine MacKinnon's large family from Cain's Mountain. He was a dancer and fiddler. Dad claimed that Hector was a good fiddler, but not as good a dance player as Hector's own father had been. But for me, he was certainly a winning step-dancer, displaying that same neat ankle work for which that whole MacKinnon clan was noted. Like his brother Murdock, he was a veteran of both world wars and he was laid to rest in Holy Rosary Cemetery, Washabuck in 1995 on his ninety-eight birthday.

Fiddlers Johnny Brown and Wilfred Prosper would also drop by from time-to-time. Brothers Angus and Hughie Campbell from St. Columba played for dances in the local halls. Hughie was a long-time member of the Cape Breton Fiddlers Association until his passing in 2003.

Angus Gardiner, a homespun-kitchen-fiddler of fond memory, was memorialized in jig-time, by Hector MacKenzie, with his expressive and popular composition, "Corporal A. B."

Joe W. visited MacKay Point quite often. He was accompanied by his brother-in-law Ronnie (Jim Hughie) MacNeil who performed in the role of designated driver in those times. Joe usually brought along a piano accompanist for the day. Marie MacLellan and Mary Jessie MacDonald were a couple of everyone's favourites, as was Jean MacKenzie of Washabuck Bridge. Fiddler Bill Lamey dropped by on occasion, as did Johnny Archie MacDonald visiting from Detroit with his piano-playing daughter Barbara.

It was a delight to see fiddler Mary MacDonald of New Waterford (Mary Jessie's mother) arrive at the house as it was Queensville's Dan Hughie MacEachern. He would make an annual trek to Washabuck that could last several days, playing and sharing the best of traditional tunes interspersed with his latest compositions and quaint, droll, yarns. Tunes like "The Kennedy Street March," "Hector MacKenzie's Jig," "Jean MacKenzie's Jig" and "The Pork Chop Reel" are a few of Dan Hughie's many compositions that were forged by Washabuck influences.

Affable dance fiddler Angus Allan Gillis displaying his bowing prowess, along with his next door neighbours from Upper Margaree, brothers Jack, Jimmy and Ambrose Gillis, were always welcomed fiddlers to Washabuck; a tradition that continues to this day with their entertaining, melodic descendants.

16-4 Washabuck fiddler Angus Gardiner (1912-1961) takes a cigarette break at a MacKenzie family kitchen racket, ca. 1959. Courtesy of Hector MacKenzie, Washabuck Bridge.

Even one of Cape Breton's most prolific composers, Dan R. MacDonald included Washabuck on his itinerant route, making sporadic visits, particularly to the Murphy homestead. He even put in an appearance, if only a cameo, at a prominent 1946 Washabuck wedding. And speaking of Washabuck weddings, Theresa and Marie MacLellan played for a wonderful outdoor wedding replete with merriment at the Murphy residence in September 1964, when Rita, the baby of the large Murphy clan, and Morris Campbell were married. Theresa and Marie's father "Big" Ranald MacLellan was himself no stranger to Washabuck, having decades earlier been a welcome visitor at the celebrated Dan MacKinnon home.

16-5 Fiddler Joe W. MacLean entertains at the home of Tic and Emily Butler, Sydney, CB, September, 1981. Courtesy of Cyril MacInnis, videographer, Big Pond CB. / Surrey BC.

Haywire Strings

Another annual visitor was guitarist J. D. MacKenzie, a brother to fiddler "Big" Archie MacKenzie from Ottawa Brook, whose people were originally from Birch Point, a community that in pioneer days was part of Washabuck. J. D. would arrive home from Detroit where he was employed, usually in the middle of hay-making season. His arrival at our home was the only event that I can recall that would bring the god-forsaken and sacrosanct hay-making to an immediate halt. As teens we were overjoyed to see him, as his arrival meant an unrepentant break from that incessant summertime obligation. More importantly, J. D. always had the car trunk full of reel-to-reel tapes of the best fiddle music, recorded and collected by him during his colourful, tune-filled pilgrimage that spanned the previous twelve months. Dad, and all of us, truly, looked forward with anticipation to J. D.'s excursions to Washabuck.

I began attending local square dances about 1958 at the old Legion Hall at Iona. "Big" Archie MacKenzie was the fiddler and at that time he was accompanied by his sister-in-law Jemina (John H.) MacNeil of Jamesville. That was how I spent my Saturday nights for the next four summers. For the first couple of years I had no driver's license but thanks to our thoughtful and sharp-witted neighbour, Michael Dan (Red Rory) MacLean, he would ask me to come along, a gesture for which I'll always be grateful.

These were great dances. Archie was a dynamic fiddler with two tempos, fast and full throttle. His liveliness just seemed to enthuse the dancers even more, as the floor was instantly filled with five or six sets, spiritedly dancing from nine to twelve. It was a good dance hall, a retired school house really, with a great hardwood floor. Its only failing was that because of the ravages of time, the far end of the building was a bit lower than the stage. So you had to adjust your dancing accordingly or the six sets could end up on top of one another at the back end of the hall. Great music, great dances and great memories!

Fiddling Liqueurs

By 1958, Winston, Joe W. and Carl MacKenzie had each played at the same Legion hall to standing room only crowds. Jean MacKenzie accompanied Joe W. on the piano for one full summer of dances. She accompanied Archie MacKenzie the following summer season and chorded there with her brother Carl, for yet another season. Carl played for his first dance at the Iona Legion when he was fifteen. And during the winter months of 1957 and '58 Jean accompanied her fiddling brother Hector at Saturday night dances in Smithy's Hall in Whycocomagh.

16-6 Christmas house racket at Mary Ann MacKenzie's, Washabuck Bridge, ca. 1958. L-R: Michael A. MacLean, Charlotte MacKenzie, Rose MacKenzie, Marie (Neville) MacKinnon, Hector MacKenzie, Roddie MacLean (back), Duncan MacDonald, Rita Murphy, Neillie Devoe, Jean MacKenzie (back), Joan MacDonald, (back) Kathleen MacDonald, Carl MacKenzie, Dan Alec MacKinnon and hostess, Mary Ann MacKenzie. Courtesy of Hector MacKenzie, Washabuck Bridge.

Prior to his years playing at Iona, Winston Fitzgerald played at the Whycocomagh Legion Hall on Thursday nights after he, Beattie Wallace and Estwood, would finish the live *MacDonald Lassie* CJCB Radio program in Sydney. I recall Dad, my older brother Raymond, and another fiddling member of the MacKenzie family, Simon, faithfully making that weekly excursion to Whycocomagh for Winston's dances. Simon, in addition to his own fiddling talents, had perfected the making of home brew to which Winston was particularly partial, and so the dynamic fiddler always looked forward to the arrival of the Washabuck dancers with added anticipation.

I remember attending only one of Winston's dances and that was at the Ashby Legion Hall in Sydney in the early 1960s and attending a house party at fiddler Sonny and Margie Murray's home near East Bay, where Winston entertained. Sonny, a good fiddler and guitarist himself, spent a ration of time in Washabuck sharing in numerous music-filled weekends.

St. FX University beckoned me in 1962. John Allan Cameron arrived there at the same time. Carl MacKenzie had graduated from TUNS in Halifax in 1959 and was now residing in Port Hawkesbury working as an engineer with the local pulp and paper mill. John Allan teamed-up with Carl for the next couple of summer seasons, and together with John Allan's piano-playing sister Jessie Ann, they entertained at weekly square dances in Southwest Margaree, Port Hood, Creignish, Lower River Inhabitants and the West Bay communities.

John Allan Cameron made a number of forays to Washabuck during those days, entertaining in his distinctive role of minstrel boy. The future godfather of Cape Breton Celtic had stormed onto the musical landscape alongside a revitalization of fiddle players and the music, a revival that was about to unfold amazingly into innovative directions, during the following four decades.

Merry-Making *Gu leòir*

The next forty years included a legion of superb musicians, most of whom spent some time visiting and entertaining throughout the Washabuck area. The following names all come to mind: Wilfred Prosper, Charlie MacCuspic,

16-7 Christmas soiree at Charlie Murphy's residence, Upper Washabuck, ca. 1963. Front Row L-R: Gus MacLean (partially hidden), Billy MacKenzie, Morris Campbell, Ann Murphy, Betty Murphy, Roddie MacDonald, Jack MacNeil. Back Row: Charlotte MacKenzie, Vince MacLean, Joe MacDonald, Bernie MacLean, Carmie MacLean, Buddy MacDonald and Ben MacLean. Photo by Rita Murphy, Courtesy of Wendy Campbell, Port Hastings, CB.

Carl Hamm, "Bussy" MacLeod, Lee Cremo, Maynard MacKenzie and Ray Ellis (these last two being ingenious composers as well). Ray Ellis's grand-niece, Little Narrows Anita MacDonald, is a more recent fiddler and proponent of Gàidhlig traditions from the area. She released a terrific new CD entitled *Stepping Stone* in 2011. Margaree's Black Watch piper, fiddler, bard, composer, Francis (Rory Sis) MacDonald and his accompanist wife Corrine, along with their musical family, frequented many a Washabuck racket.

The "Tin Sandwich" man, the beloved harmonica player and stepdancer Tommy Basker, was always a most welcomed entertainer along with the "Rocky Shore" musicians: fiddlers Otis Tomas with guitarist wife Deanie Cox, David Papazian (Papper); Celtic music proponent extraordinaire, Paul Cranford with wife Sarah Beck; and guitarist Paul MacDonald. Piper Paul K. MacNeil and his keyboardist wife Tracey Dares continue to wow everyone at all venues.

Washabuck troubadour John MacDonald has always generously shared his talents at kitchen rackets and with church choirs; as have piano players, Hilda Chiasson, Father George MacInnis, Doug MacPhee, Susan MacLean, and Janet Cameron of Boisdale (Janet accompanying the Boisdale Trio, which consisted of her fiddling brother Father Francis, Joe Peter MacLean and Paul Wukitsch). Caribou Marsh balladeer John Ferguson attended many a soiree, entertaining throughout the wilds of Washabuck as has long-time, CJCB Celtic radio host, Sydney serenader, Donnie Campbell and Clifford Morais, founding member of the band The Sons of Skye.

Pictou County inhabitant and Highland Village Pipe Band drumming instructor, the late Sammy MacDougall even boarded in Washabuck for a time, tutoring Washabuck protégés, Quentin MacDonald and "lighthouse" sisters Grace and Charlene MacLean. Quentin's niece, Stephanie MacDonald from Whycocomagh is a keen fiddler and step-dancer. Fiddling instructor *par excellence*, Stan Chapman – the fiddlers' fiddler from Antigonish – has been a pleasurable part of Washabuck's more recent melodic decades.

Newfoundland Flavour

A band of Irish musicians known as Ryan's Fancy arrived in Washabuck via St. John's, Newfoundland, during the late 1970s. The well-liked trio of Denis Ryan, Dermot O'Reilly and Fergus O'Byrne hosted a popular national CBC weekly television show which featured guest musicians, performing at selected Atlantic Canada locales alongside their fun-loving hosts. The 1977 Washabuck show featured the fiddling tradition of the MacKenzie family of Washabuck Bridge accompanied by a number of nieces and nephews including the now internationally acclaimed Barra MacNeils. This show, as did all their shows, brought national attention to traditional musicians, their

16-8 The fiddling MacKenzie Family of Washabuck Bridge. Top photo: A beaming Winnie (Simon's wife) endorses Charlie's fiddling efforts and another milestone with a sparkling birthday cake. Right: Hector, a long-time and outstanding Cape Breton Emcee, entertains at a Christmas house racket. Bottom: Sister Jean is accompanied by brothers Simon and Carl.

music and their respective communities. Under the vision of producer and director Jack Kellum the productions also helped to display the formative influences and mentoring roles; how formal methods and casual tutoring revealed their knacks to the up-and-coming performer. Washabuck has played a role fostering that enthusiasm.

Washabuck Connection

Between 1991 and 1994, a new generation of musicians performed in Cape Breton dance halls and Celtic concert stages. The Washabuck Connection was a foursome of Washabuck teens who played the fiddle and the piano and performed dance routines. Sisters, Susan and Jill MacLean, with cousin, Martia MacLean and close family friend Bhreagh MacDonald of nearby Big Beach debuted to an approving audience at the 1992 annual Highland Village Day concert.

Under the early tutorship of intrepid dancing teachers, Betty Matheson, Jean MacNeil and Bonnie Jean MacDonald, the enthusiastic troupe played around the island. Performance requests came from the Middle River

Celtic Concert, Glace Bay Savoy Theatre, Iona Legion Hall, St. Ann's Fiddle Festival, Ben Eoin Folk Festival, Canadian Coast Guard College Campus, and the Pictou DeCoste Centre. They were even interviewed on CBC Radio. The "Connection's" unofficial demise occurred as university beckoned the girls, but not before the quartet was invited to participate in a concert series celebrating the first-place international win by the *Colaisde na Gàidhlig* Pipe Band at the 1994 World Piping Championships, held earlier that summer in Scotland.

16-9 The Washabuck Connection foursome. L-R: Fiddlers, Bhreagh MacDonald, Martia MacLean, Jill MacLean, accompanied at piano by Susan MacLean. The group are performing at the annual Highland Village Day concert at Hector's Point, Iona, August 1991.

The Tradition Continues

William and *Beatag* MacKenzie's home in Lower Washabuck was a noted site for music, dancing and Gàidhlig singing. William (1857-1933) was a good Gàidhlig singer and his lyrical wife *Beatag* (1866-1937) was adept at harmonizing. The couple enjoyed dancing and so their home was a warm and congenial gathering place where the youth of the day regularly frequented. It is not surprising, that two of their many great-grand children are prominent musicians. Rosie, a fiddler, and her guitarist brother Jimmy MacKenzie were founding members of The Cottars, a Cape Breton Celtic quartet and recipients of outstanding achievement awards and distinguished for their international performances. In 2009, Rosie released her own solo CD, *The MacKenzie Project* featuring herself on fiddle accompanied by an exuberant bevy of accomplished Cape Breton artists.

Since 1999, Washabuck native Nancy MacLean, a granddaughter of Red Rory and Ellie Ann MacLean has showcased emerging and seasoned Cape Breton musicians, to residents and tourists alike, at her annual series Baddeck Gathering Ceilidhs. The up-lifting and entertaining Celtic production runs seven nights at St. Michaels Parish Hall in Baddeck each summer. *Cum suas an ceòl!*

A melodious treasury of Celtic music has been entrusted to future generations by musicians with Washabuck roots. Alex MacLean of Iona, with his three piano releases, produced by Celtic Records in 1962, is thought to be the first recorded album of piano music devoted to the music of the Cape Breton Scot. Joe W. MacLean wrote ten compositions. Unfortunately, he christening but a few of them. There is "Peter MacKay's Hornpipe" which he named for the Scotsville mail-driver, his long-time friend, and "Grace MacKenzie," a strathspey he named for Jean MacKenzie's step-dancing. Joe W., who was admired for his dexterous playing of strathspeys, released a number of 78s, and LPs. On his passing, he bequeathed his highly prized collection of rare fiddle manuscripts and books to the Nova Scotia Highland Village Museum.

Carl MacKenzie has composed more than fifty striking tunes, released a dozen albums and CDs, and has participated in fiddle workshops worldwide. Theresa Morrison, widow of touted Sydney Pipe Major Peter Morrison[2], (and Joe W. and Michael Anthony's baby sister), decided to wait until she had it just right. She released two remarkable CDs, each displaying a symphony of fine playing and evocative compositions after reaching her eightieth birthday. A double disc of Michael Anthony's fiddle playing legacy was released posthumously in 2009.

Jean MacKenzie married Columba MacNeil from Grass Cove and settled in Sydney Mines. Their offspring, known collectively as the Barra MacNeils, have consummated a twenty-five year career with a multitude of achievement awards, the release of twenty distinguished albums and CDs, and they continue to perpetuate international awareness and admiration wherever they perform. The much-acclaimed

16-10 The Barra MacNeils. L-R: Stewart, Lucy, Ryan, Boyd, Kyle, Sheumas. Photo by Lee Brown. Courtesy of the Barra MacNeils, Sydney Mines, CB.

instrumental and vocalist band continue to bring Cape Breton music to the world's stage.

The tradition continues.

Of my experiences, I've been privileged and it's been a blast![3]

It's In Your Blood You Know

So where did you learn to play?
It's in your blood you know.
The Cape Breton fiddle tunes,
from generation to generation flow.
Just ask my grandfather, Michael Anthony,
"From my Father," he will say.
And his children – and his children's
children will answer the same way.

It started with just one fiddle;
twelve children all waiting their turn
-eagerly watching elders before them
for every motion and tune they could learn.
Why did they practice for hours
and play, "till their fingers were sore"?
Just eating the dust at dance halls
with only three dollars to score.

It wasn't for the money.
It was a passion they couldn't resist,
and thank heavens for this – just think of
what we would have missed.
So as each generation is born
into a family already with this gift,
a prayer of thanks to heaven
is what each of us will lift.

You taught us to love the music;
to honour it with care,
so that long after you are gone,
your influence will always be there.
It's in your blood they say and what a
gift to give. You put it in my blood and
through generations you will continue to live.[4]

SOCAN @Susan MacLean, December, 2005

16-11 Susan MacLean, Washabuck.

17 – Islands

St. Patrick's Channel's earliest navigators were the Mi'kmaq, but these waters became the Scottish pioneers' primary mode of transportation during early decades of settlement. The lake provided sustenance and income, if scant, from their fishing endeavours. In this century, this arm of the Bras d'Or provides a corridor of water sufficiently deep to easily accommodate the huge bulk carriers that, since 1935, have navigated its length to load with gypsum ore at the Little Narrows Gypsum Company pier at Little Narrows.

> It is not the height and grandeur of the hills, nor the wide expanse of water, that gives to these lakes and their surroundings their peculiar charm, but the countless combinations of land and water, which afford new scenes of beauty at every turn….

So wrote the geological surveyor and highly regarded mapper Hugh Fletcher about the Bras d'Or Lakes in his 1876 annual report to the Geological Survey of Canada.[1]

St. Patrick's Channel displays a picturesque collection of the summits and aquatic combinations that Fletcher references and provides exceptional sailing waters for mariners. For generations, the channel has been a sailing Mecca for yachtsmen, local and far-flung. Seasoned sailors enjoy all that the Bras d'Or has to offer unencumbered – stretches of deep water, essentially fog-free, coaxed by steady southerly winds and warm tender

17-1 Bras d'Or Lakes Scenic Drive sign.

17-2 Graham Bell's yacht, *Elsie*, yields her marine obligation to a U.S. Gypsum Company's chartered bulk carrier wending her way westward through St. Patrick's Channel and past Spectacle Island to its loading pier at Little Narrows, ca. 2000.

breezes of a Cape Breton summer – all while safely cradled within the lake's majestic watershed.

So, it was in June 2011 UNESCO (the United Nations Educational, Scientific and Cultural Organization) officially recognized and designated Bras d'Or Lake and its watershed as their newest member among its distinguished global Biosphere Reserve network.[2] The ancient Mi'kmaq called these ecologically remarkable waters with their biodiversity and unique habitats, *Pitupo'q*, which means "inland sea."[3] Not surprisingly, the first seafaring Gaels of Barra who inhabited its watershed more than two centuries ago, saw fit to admiringly christened it, *Loch Mór Nam Barrach* (The Big Loch of the Barramen).[4]

A number of islands adorn St. Patrick's Channel shoreline along the Washabuck, Baddeck and Boularderie communities. Turbulent waters and tireless coastal erosion is a fact of life in seaside regions and this channel is not exempt. Time, currents and relentless wave action, have gnawed these islands to a point where two of them have virtually disappeared; a third one is drowning fast, while two others have been resuscitated by dedicated owners. A century or so ago, each of these islands played a modest, if individualistic and colourful role, in influencing a rural lifestyle that is long since history.

17-3 Bras d'Or Lake Biosphere Logo, 2012. The blue reflects the waters of the lake while the green reflects its watershed. The entire shape suggests a human being, highlighting that people are an integral part of the biosphere. Designed by Wendy Burns-Morrison, Baddeck, CB. Courtesy of Bras d'Or Lake Biosphere Association.

Spectacle Island

Spectacle Island was granted by the Crown to spinster Alice McKay of Baddeck in October 1888, for the sum of $20.00. It is described as:

> A lot of land containing seven acres ... in the county of Victoria and bounded as follows.... Being an Island known as Bird Island lying in the Bras d'Or Lake between Baddeck Village and McKay's Point Watchabuck, [sic] about Sixty chains north of said Point.

The survey was executed by Joseph S. MacLean, Deputy Surveyor for the County of Victoria. The sketch states the land mass is called "Bird Island or McKay's Island." MacLean's field notes state further: "An Island in Bras D'or Lakes situated 60 Chs. Northeasterly from George McKay's Point, Watchabuck [sic] and known as Bird Island or McKay's Island containing seven acres more or less...."

Improvements

> "Said Island has been improved by the father [John McKay] and grandfather [George McKay] of your petitioner and all that can be cultivated has been cultivated. No objection that I know of." [5]

An interesting detail gleaned from the documentation is a sketch of the island, which displays it as one elongated body of land containing seven acres. The island has been referred to colloquially as "Toothbrush Island" as a result of its evolving appearance over the past century. The western portion of the island was forested with coniferous trees while the eastern end supported reeds and grasses, giving it the appearance of an upturned toothbrush. Cartographer A. F. Church on his Victoria County map ca. 1887 refers to it as Double Island. Similarly, the current name, Spectacle (The Specks), derives from the island appearing like an old fashioned set of spectacles.

Spectacle Island is a favoured nesting site for sea birds, which ironically has led to the demise of vegetation there and increased the rapid rate of erosion.

In 1998, Kenny MacAskill, then MLA and provincial Minister of the Department of Natural

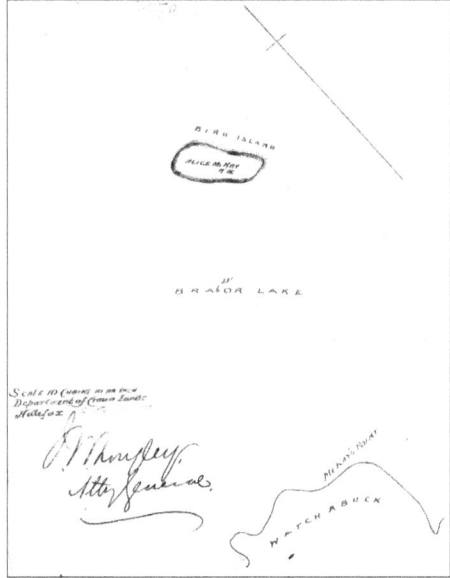

17-4 Detail of a return of survey for Spectacle Island (a.k.a. Bird Island) showing the island as having seven acres in 1888. Courtesy Registry of Deeds, Baddeck, CB.

Resources, replied to the Grand Narrows and District Board of Trade regarding concerns about erosion on Spectacle Island:

> Cormorants have nested on Spectacle Island for many years. Indeed, the island was deeded to the Province of Nova Scotia by an individual on the condition that it be designated a Wildlife Sanctuary, to protect their nesting colony. The latest census (1995) counted five hundred and twenty-four pairs of cormorants and 31 pairs of black-backed gulls nesting on the island.
>
> [...]Due to acid, leaching from the thick layer of cormorant guano, the coniferous trees on the western part of the island died; their roots no longer binding the denuded soil resulted in the acceleration of the island's erosion to the point where within another decade its western end will be awash as a shoal and just a memory. The island's large cormorant colony has been decimated and most have relocated to smaller nesting venues within the lake. It is safe to say that most local residents would have preferred smaller numbers of the fish-scouring bird as desirable.[6]

Elizabeth MacLean of MacKay Point (1868-1961) related oral traditions from the "old people" to her nephew Michael A. MacLean about remnants of fish-flakes found on Spectacle Island. It was believed that European fishermen used the island to dry fish in an earlier era, an understanding that was reinforced by the experience of the Gaels, "that there were fewer flies in that area simply because it was an island."[7]

Peter Francis MacLean (1824-1898) and later his son Vincent MacLean (1871-1943), the subsequent owners of MacKay Point, harvested marsh hay from the eastern part of the Island. Using hand-scythes, they would slash the rough hay at the end of the summer season, dry it thoroughly, stack it into a large haystack and cover it as best they could with pieces of canvas or whatever other material might be available, lashing it down securely. Then in early spring as the barn's hay was dwindling and while the lake-ice was still intact, the enterprising farmers would haul the enduring, coarse crop home with their team and sleigh, providing for their flock of sheep for the balance of the late winter season.[8]

Carol Myers, a grand-daughter of Alexander Graham Bell, bought Spectacle Island at a county tax sale in 1926. In 1968, she transferred ownership to the provincial government. Subsequently, in June 1969 the government designated it, "Spectacle Island Game Sanctuary."[9]

During the 1990s Spectacle Island separated into two, individual

17-5 Spectacle Island in healthier days, ca. 1950. Note in the foreground, MacKay Point government wharf with freight shanty.

hillocks with a connecting sand bar enclosing a pond. Generations before the island was designated as a bird sanctuary, this pond had been a favorite duck and goose hunting site, and its shoreline an erstwhile lavish location for cranberry and gooseberry pickers.

But like a battle-fatigued fighter, each passing year saw the western portion, a one-time coniferous-treed knoll now completely defoliated, eroding ever more quickly from relentless pounding of each ensuing storm. So it was during the 2010 winter solstice that coincided with a new moon, the "toothbrush component" of Spectacle Island succumbed to the tireless gnawing of a vicious two-day sou'easter and disappeared. With the breaking of dawn on December 22, there emerged a barely visible sea-level shoal marked by a contingent of double-crested cormorants. Time, weather and the resilient cormorant, the ultimate victors.

Stony Island

Stony Island has been submerged under the waters of St. Patrick's Channel for over a century. Located about 300 metres offshore from the western end of Baddeck village, the shoal is included here because of its proximity to Washabuck's own shoreline and is a well-known navigational hazard to boaters plying the channel's waters.

Early in the 19th century before its eventual immersion it played a piquant role in the area's pioneer history. Alex D. MacLean records this tale of Jonathan Jones, the Big Baddeck settler of Loyalist leanings.[10]

> We know that Captain Jonathan Jones had two sons, the elder William, and Jonathan Jr. the younger. He also had two daughters, Esther and Sarah. Now Captain Jones's neighbour John Leaver was well supplied with daughters. Between the eldest members of these two "first families" a warm attachment sprang up, which Captain Jones was more than anxious to discourage. Just why he should take this attitude is not clear. It appears that the Leaver family w[as]quite equal of the Jones family by any standard by which they could be judged. They owned property that was worth considerable, and I am informed that they were financially well off. It must also be borne in mind that the eldest Leaver was a Land surveyor, a holding appointment of the Crown, and that meant very, very much in those days. Suffice to say that any feelings of superiority that Captain Jones may have entertained existed only in his imagination and vanity. It may well be that it was he who originated the expression, "Keeping up with the Jones."

> Hoping to divert his son's affections, he gave him, in the year 1806, the command of a ship laden with produce, and ordered him to sail to Newfoundland. The son was also given, "secret orders" to the effect that on arriving at Newfoundland, he was not only to dispose of the cargo,

but was to dispose of the vessel as well, and with the proceeds thus gained, was to go to Ontario, where two of his father's brothers lived, and to settle with them. In this way did Captain Jonathan Jones plan to set aside or break up the romantic attachment between his son William, and Mary, the elder daughter of his neighbour, John Leaver.

The scheming did not have the desired effect, but it made the place and manner of the nuptials a curious one. As the little craft sailed slowly down St. Patrick's Channel, a boat shot out from the shore, containing a clergyman, the intended bride and the necessary witnesses, together with a party of the bride's relatives who were armed in keeping with the occasion. The schooner was compelled to drop anchor, and the parties most interested, with necessary attendants, landed on the little island that used to be visible at the entrance of St. Patrick's Channel. This small island ... was known as Stony. Today, the island has disappeared, and the only thing that marks it is a buoy that is placed to warn ships of the shoal water. [MacLean] well remembers when it was a fairly large island, with a couple of trees growing on it. I am informed that at one time, sheep were kept on it.

The officiating clergyman was the Rev. Mr. Cossit ... who was the chaplain of the garrison then stationed in Sydney. It appears that his services were hurriedly requisitioned by the Leaver family, when they learned of the impending departure of William Jones. The marriage ceremony was performed, and the newly made bride went back to the bosom of her family – and the vessel went on its way.

William Jones never returned to Cape Breton. Acting on his father's wishes, he disposed of the vessel and cargo in Newfoundland. From there he went to Ontario (then known as Canada) where he found his father's brothers, who had remained loyal to the British Crown, and had been obliged to change their place of residence from New York State to Ontario. [It was] with them he settled, and, in the course of time, took unto himself a second wife – the first, and legal wife being still alive. The late William Jones – the William Jones the younger – was a love child, the off-spring by his first wife. The romantic, if unconventional marriage on Stony Island in 1806, which we have just described, was nevertheless important.

In 1870 shortly after the death of William Jones in Ontario, an attorney from the latter place, Mr. Hutchins, came to Baddeck to claim the property of the deceased for his children living in Ontario. The legal gentleman received a shock when the son of the first marriage, William Jones, who [was very much alive], promptly produced the marriage certificate which was executed on Stony Island in 1806. The certificate was properly drawn up and signed, and it was plain that it settled William Jones's claim to the estate, and at the same time, [it] crushed any hopes that the Ontario heirs may have entertained with regard to the father's vast estates in Cape Breton Island.

An amusing sequel pertaining to the above Alex D. account is cited in a newspaper article in *The Victoria Standard*, by Baddeck historian Jocelyn Bethune. She relates that:

> The legend says that following the wedding, a powerful thunder and lightning storm hit. In the morning, Stoney [sic] Island was gone; an elevated shoal just below the wave tops was all that remained.[11]

(See Stony Island on the A. F. Church map pages 415, 416.)[12]

Coffin Island

Another island that foils any private ownership information is known as Coffin Island, as title searches have proved futile.[13] Located at the most easterly end of St. Patrick's Channel, near the Bras d'Or estuary as it begins to narrow into the Great Bras d'Or Channel. Coffin Island is five kilometres east of MacKay Point and about a kilometre offshore from Kempt Head, northside Boularderie Island. At one time, the Kempt Head government wharf was located east of this shoal. Former Kempt Head resident John Willie MacKenzie recalled hearing that Coffin Island had occasionally been used as a sheep pasture, or that he had simply seen sheep on the island.[14] Today, like Stony Island, it is better described as a ruthless shoal rather than an island. Generations ago it included an archipelagic of rocks encircling a bleak windswept centre, a good place to hunt seals.

17-6 Malcolm (Stephen) MacLean (1872-1971) of Lower Washabuck (centre) is flanked on the left by his neighbour Jimmy MacKenzie, his daughter Mary Margaret "Peggy" MacKenzie, (Boston) and Jeanette MacKenzie (Montreal). On the far right is son Archie and his wife Marie. Stony Island shoal is located near the opposite shore in the background, ca. 1970. Photo by Leonard MacKenzie, Montreal. Courtesy of Karen MacLean, Washabuck/Halifax, NS.

The island was said to resemble that of an old-time wooden coffin. The island's windswept core was approximately a hundred meters long, while its highest elevation reached about three metres.[15] Because of its location approaching the Great Bras d'Or Channel, Coffin Island waters teemed with an abundance of more than twenty different species of fish; this was an obvious lure for seals, enticed there by the site's convenience, accessibility, and relative security.

The Rev. Richard John Uniacke in *Sketches of Cape Breton* (1862-1865) commenting on the state of religion on Cape Breton Island, makes a brief referral about a travelling missionary he once encountered:

> I have often heard the Travelling Missionary the Rev. W. Porter, speak of these distant expeditions, and of the fatigue of officiating in these out-lying stations. Whilst steaming over the waters of the Bras d'Or Straits a few years ago, on a confirmation tour, he once pointed out to me a desolate spot called Coffin Island upon or near which he was obliged to spend the whole night, with no other shelter than a boat turned bottom-upwards.[16]

The dory would have made a very thin quilt indeed. The gaunt sheep at least had the fleeciness of their wool to warm them. For Washabuck sealers though, Coffin Island was simply an advantageous haunt that favoured the successful pursuit of a useful sea-going quarry.

Trois à la Axe

17-7 Aerial view of Kempt Head, Boularderie Island, with Coffin Island off shore, ca. 1935. To the far left MacKay Point. Courtesy of National Air Photo Library, Ottawa, ON.

In the early 1930s Vincent MacLean (1871-1943) and his son Peter F. and neighbouring brothers Malcolm and Rory (Stephen) MacLean set out for a day of seal hunting to Coffin Island. There was a lot of ice that winter. It had arrived earlier than usual and a quick freeze had trapped a large number of seals in the lake for the winter. Much of the herd wintered around Coffin Island while many lived along a large pressure crack that always ran from Burnt Point towards Kempt Head. Fluctuating current and tidal movements kept the crack partially ajar, ensuring the seals survival.

On the first day of this annual event, the sealers didn't have much success. There were too many blowholes around Coffin Island which provided the seals with a multitude of air vents. The following day the men returned, determined to have a more successful day. They brought a collection of small fir bushes, which they used to plug most of the holes. Vincent, Peter F. and Malcolm each had a steel gaff securely attached to a wooden shaft but Rory (Stephen) had brought only an axe. In the midst of the hunt Peter F. gaffed an unusually large seal that promptly pulled the gaff out of his hands. The seal and the gaff were gone in an instance. Rory (Stephen) decided to move to a larger opening in the ice that was about 12 feet (3.6 m) square, nearer the shoreline.

He waited patiently and eventually detected the sound of the wooden-handled gaff rubbing on the underside of the ice as the wounded seal made its way toward the larger opening. When the harpooned seal popped up Rory nailed it with the blunt end of his axe and immediately hauled it aboard the icy deck with the salvaged gaff, very much intact. Rory peeked into the opening and discovered that the lake bottom in the shallower water was festooned with dead codfish. He was able to salvage six of them with his axe. Upon further inspection he detected that each of the recently killed cod had simply a single bite taken out of their stomach with only its liver missing.[17] The seals were obviously noshing well. Later in the day, Rory observed a large mink inquisitively popping in and out of its den in the Island's bank. Again Rory awaited his chance and successfully slayed the mink with a deft clip of the axe to its head.

So as the day's expedition drew to a triumphant close, Rory Stephen headed homeward having dispatched a seal and a mink, retrieved six edible codfish, and rescued Peter F.'s gaff, all amassed with the aid of his trusty pole-axe, while his colleagues-in-arms, had to be placidly content with seals.

The following morning Vincent hitched his small red mare to the truck-sleigh and toted home the previous day's loot of 17 seals. Although heavy, the weight of the cargo posed little problem for the sharp shod mare, as the ice was glib. The sealers, sharing equally in the booty, proceeded to render the blubber, a tedious process, which involved skinning and gutting the carcasses, chopping the fatty torsos into chunks which were tossed into a make-shift, boiling cauldron, fired by a nearby woodpile. This rendering process demanded several days of smoky and smelly drudgery, before it was finished.

The resulting seal oil was used as a lubricant for farm equipment but more significantly, sold as a source of vitamin for horses. A bit of seal oil, when it was available, was added to the horses' ration of oats. Seal oil was in big demand by teamsters, including those from Big Baddeck and Middle River who visited Baddeck regularly and who enthusiastically sought the elixir for their teams. It sold for a dollar a gallon. And although seal meat was never looked upon as a delicacy by the Gaels, it was used around homesteads for fur-trapping bait, used to feed domestically raised mink, while scraps would be tossed to the farm hens and entrails left for scavenging birds. Seal skins were used to fashion leather products, particularly horse harness. Very little was wasted.[18] To that end, our pioneers had brought with them from the old sod a lamp called a *cruisgean* that was fitted with a spout that held a wick to burn fish and seal oil. This provided them a malodorous light.[19]

Bone Island

The grant describing Bone Island states:

> A lot of land containing one and three quarters acres situate lying and being in the County of Victoria and bounded as follows: Being an Island in Little Bras d'Or Lake lying off McKay's Point Washabuckt & known as Black Island.[20]

Victoria County surveyor Joseph S. MacLean in his petition field notes for Bone Island describes it as being:

> …six chains and fifty links north from *Rue À Storr* [Store Point] containing in all 1 ¾ acres.[21]

Generations later, *Rue À Storr* [sic] is now commonly referred to as Sand Point. *Rubh' a' Stòr* was the site of Washabuck's first store.

This description accompanied the grant from the Crown to Arthur W. McCurdy of Baddeck dated April 4, 1905. The island reverted to the Municipality from the estate of Mr. McCurdy. It was later conveyed to Joe H. Murphy of Baddeck, who in 1930 sold it to Arthur S. Allen of New York. In that deed, the island is referred to again as Black Island.

At one time, the island was completely covered with coniferous trees, giving it a very dark profile perhaps explaining that name. Once Mr. Allen became its owner, local residents began to call it Allen's Island. Prior to Mr. Allen's ownership, the Island's timber had been harvested, at least one occasion.[22] In 1947, the island was conveyed by Mr. Allen's widow Clara Allen, to Mary S. Goldthwaite. Bone Island is currently owned by the Mary's grandson Stephen Goldthwaite, of New Jersey.

Arthur Allen had a summer cottage built for him and his family on the island. Potable water was available on site from a couple of artesian wells. Mr. Allen, a successful and well respected American businessman earned the respect of the Washabuck and Baddeck communities as well, a jovial and benevolent neighbour, prior to his untimely passing in 1943.

17-8 Arthur S. Allen owner of Bone Island (1930-1943) stands between his employees, brothers Michael A. and Murdock MacLean, MacKay Point, as they build a protective breakwater for the island, ca. 1938.

Allen upgraded the island, first by protecting the shoreline with a barrier of armour stone; placed by the deft manipulation of manpower and horsepower, combined with the delicate maneuvering of motor boat and scow. He augmented the island's native growth by importing exotic poplar seedlings that prospered fabulously. They adorned the island until their recent harvesting. Approximately a third of the southern portion of the island he had groomed into an attractive green pitch that accommodated the playing of croquet. Inevitably, again due to the ravages of time and wave action, the island is now but two-thirds the size it was a century ago.

Baddeck boatyard owner and master shipwright Walter Pinaud built the cottage for Mr. Allen in 1930. Allen employed two Washabuck MacLean brothers, Murdock and Michael A. for four and seven years respectively, as hired hands and caretakers. A community minded gentleman, Mr. Allen donated funds for the concrete steps that front St. Michael's Catholic Church in Baddeck in 1934. He and his wife Clara had a son and daughter, but sadly their son died while still a young man.

Since 2000, Stephen Goldthwaite has been the current and enthusiastic owner of Bone Island. He has built an admirable new home on it for him and his family, replacing the obsolescent Allen cottage. Attractive upgrades to the island's topography along with the addition of new armour stone at the water's edge ensure that Bone Island will remain a picturesque piece of marine real estate along the Washabuck waterfront for future generations.

"Goldthwaite's" Island

Goldthwaite's Island was owned by Duval Richard (D. R.) and Mary Goldthwaite, a prominent American couple who made a demonstrable impact on the local community by employing Washabuck residents during their period of ownership.

17-9 A couple of elegantly attired ladies enjoying summer tranquility on a well-groomed Allen's Island, [Bone Island], ca. 1941.

Baddeck resident James MacDonald of Twining Street recalls that the Goldthwaite's first came to Cape Breton in the early 1930s, returning seasonally for the next two decades, until D. R.'s passing in the early 1950s. The Goldthwaite's had three children, a daughter Ward and two sons Duval and Richard.

Goldthwaite hired Baddeck boatyard owner and shipwright Walter Pinaud to construct his island residence and several outbuildings. Pinaud was assisted by Washabuck native, Joseph (Rory Ranald) MacDonald, who by this time had become a Baddeck resident. Most of the beautiful wide pine boards that adorn the interior of the Island's main building were harvested from Hunter's Mountain *Cùl* (Rear), then milled and dressed in the Pinaud boatyard shop.

Subsequently, Washabuck brothers Jimmy and Tommy MacKenzie became long-time hired hands. Later still, neighbour Joe (Red Rory) MacLean joined them. So for a period of nearly two decades these four Washabuck natives found seasonal employment working for the American businessman and his wife.[23] Goldthwaite's wife Mary was described as a very kind, down to earth person who delighted in taking photographs.

In addition to the erection of buildings, a considerable amount of landscaping was required, resulting in a well-groomed lawn which was used for a croquet pitch. The Americans had also developed an enthusiasm for vegetable gardening, which required regular attention. Foreman Joe MacDonald's son James, spent his summers as a youth, propelling a heavy push-mower around the island. In later years, extensive flowerbeds were planted annually that required an abundance of TLC. Goldthwaite had purchased land at Murphy's Point in Upper Washabuck at the same time as he had bought the island. It was from this site that topsoil was loaded by the four employees; shovelled into steel-wheeled barrows, wheeled onto a small barge, and then towed by motor boat to the island, where the loam was unloaded, spread and worked around the grounds, for lawn and garden purposes.

17-10 D. R. and Mary Goldthwaite's island cottage near Birch Point, ca. 1950. Courtesy of James MacDonald, Twining Street, Baddeck, CB.

In the early 1950s, electric power and a telephone line were brought to the island by a submarine cable. Prior to this, a gasoline generator and later a diesel generator provided power: the island's refrigerators were powered by propane. One of these appliances eventually made its way to Washabuck, to the Jimmy MacKenzie household, becoming the first refrigerator on the mainland Washabuck community.

"What Water?"

Water was piped via a three-quarter inch copper pipe across the bottom of the channel from the mainland, where Goldthwaite owned adjacent acreage. A windmill attached to a fifty-foot steel tower pumped the water across the 1400-foot (425 m) channel where it was emptied into a wooden storage tank that measured twelve feet in diameter and eight feet in height. Each fall as the property was closed for the winter, the tank was drained and the water system shut down. Each spring the tank was cleaned and prepared and the ritual was reversed. This was Tom MacKenzie's task.

One spring, by chance, Tom was absent on the day of the annual tank cleaning, so the other team members tended to the chore. The next morning Joe MacDonald mischievously suggested to Tom that maybe he should clean out the tank. Tom, unaware that the tank had been already cleaned and filled with fresh water, catapulted over the tank's side, and promptly doused himself in its frigid waters. Such pranks, jest, and constant banter, helped the foursome discharge their onerous labours with humour, good cheer and dispatch.

A well-known proclivity of Mr. Goldthwaite's was his standing order for a case of Scotch whisky to be delivered to his island on Friday evenings. The well-travelled case of Johnny Walker would arrive, probably from Halifax, certainly on the eastbound evening Express to the Iona railway station, where it was eyed enviously by the mail-boat crew before being transferred to Baddeck. Finally it was safely relayed by Joe MacDonald (1906-1992) via motor boat to the island's owner, who eagerly awaited the weekly delivery of the precious commodity.

According to James MacDonald, citing information gleaned from an old map, the island was originally referred to as Deadman's Island. On A. F. Church's 1887 topographical map the land adjacent to Island on the western side of Birch Point is Deadman Pt. but the island itself is unnamed. The surrounding area is referred to as MacInnis Cove.

The little island has had a lot of names. A legal description states

17-11 Washabuck natives Joe MacDonald with brothers Jimmy and Tommy MacKenzie are joined on the far left by Val Goldthwaite as they take a break from target shooting on Goldthwaite's Island, ca. 1950. Missing is the fourth employee Joe (Red Rory) MacLean who probably snapped the photo. Courtesy of James MacDonald, Baddeck, CB.

the name of the island is Sheep Island, also known as Black Island. Jessie (MacInnis) MacKinnon now of Little Narrows[24] maintains that her people from South Cove always referred to the island as Black Island. However, when the Goldthwaite's bought it, they called it Ark Island, but today, it is still referred to colloquially as Goldthwaite's Island or simply, The Island.[25,26,27]

The Island was purchased by Stanley Johnson, a Montreal engineer, who was involved in the design and building of the Point Tupper Pulp Mill in 1959 -1961 era. Johnson later sold the island to C. H. Hulme, another Montreal resident, whose son Grant is currently its proud owner.[28]

Bras d'Or Lakes

Lovely lakes! I sing thy praise
Through an harp unsung before
N'er had minstrel for his lays
Nobler theme than thou, Bras d'Or.

Winding through a Paradise
Of Cape Breton's heart the core
How could'st thou be otherwise
Than good and beautiful, Bras d'Or.

That sweet land for beauty famed
Those dear people on thy shore
Enhance thy glory, thou well named
'Arm of Gold' wondrous, Bras d'Or.

Though thy waves are turbulent when
Echoing Atlantic's roar
Grand, majestic thou art then
Awe inspiring, Great, Bras d'Or.

When thy waves are peaceful, mild
In thy cradle angels o'er
Thou art like a sleeping child
Smiling in a dream, Bras d'Or.

Happy he who still can hear
Thy lapping surf, the dip of oar
Ah! He know not while thou'rt near
How he loves thee sweet, Bras d'Or.

But if he should wander far
Every breeze that passes o'er
His land of pilgrimage shall bring
Memories of thee, Bras d'Or.

When the way seems hard and long
He will yearn to be once more
Lulled to sleep with mother's song
And thy lullaby, Bras d'Or.

As for her, she'll yearn for thee
If not life, Death may restore
The weary child to her to be
Laid to sleep near thee, Bras d'Or.[1]

Lucy (MacLean) Bush
(1902-1998) Washabuck

17-12 Lucy (MacLean) Bush (1902-1998) MacKay Point, Washabuck, ca. 1922.

17-13 Central Cape Breton Barra Strait.

18 – Community Organizations

Baseball

A baseball league was started on the Washabuck peninsula in 1926. Initially, it seems that an individual "from away" that was associated with the Grass Cove Gypsum operation introduced his own love of baseball to the youth of the area. His name is not known. Then Father Alexander J. MacDonald (better known as Father Alex "The Devil") arrived from Antigonish, he was assigned curate to the St. Columba pastorate in Iona. Father Alex received his sobriquet from his time working as an ink-devil's apprentice at the Antigonish newspaper, *The Casket* during his university years. He was enthusiastic about sports and during his four-year posting to Iona, he developed an exciting baseball league. He also introduced soccer. The Iona soccer field was located where the St. Columba parish church parking lot is today.

The Iona baseball field was located to the south of the former Rankin Memorial School site. Local teams included Iona, Barra Glen, MacKinnon Harbour, Washabuck and Gillis Point. Mi'kmaw teams from Eskasoni and Wagamatcook occasionally played as did the railroad workers, which all-in-all resulted in good quality baseball. The Harbour's field was located near the Jamesville's beach, while the Barra Glen field was located at Stephen Mickey MacNeil's property at the Barra Glen crossing.[1] Quentin (Rory Ranald) MacDonald played for Washabuck. He was known as an outstanding southpaw hurler, delivering a vicious curve ball. It was the generally held opinion, that if an authentic opportunity had arisen, he easily could have become a professional pitcher.

Buttermilk Sunday

Before the Second World War, a number of competitive exhibition games were played between a Mi'kmaw team from Wagamatcook and the Washabuck Wallopers. The Wagmatcook team were keen baseball players and they always came away victorious in these friendly contests. The Washabuck team was losing morale and the situation called for drastic action. Michael A. MacLean recalled what unfolded.

> The next game was scheduled for Sunday afternoon at the Washabuck field that was located at Rory (Ranald) MacDonald's, just east of where the Community Centre is today.
>
> Neil P. S. MacLean lived close to the field so, as was the usual practice, the Mi'kmaw team would paddle their canoes across St. Patrick's Channel to his property that extended further into the lake by a long narrow beach. There, the Mi'kmaq beached their craft upon its fine sand, proceeded to hike across the beach shore, up a long, steep footpath through the woods, and across a wide hayfield, before arriving at the MacLean residence. Neil was waiting for them, and invited them to rest awhile in the shade of his yard trees, as the afternoon had turned blistering hot and the Indians were all-in, from the paddle across the lake and their long up-hill trek.
>
> But Neil P. S. had a further offering for these formidable ball players. Discreetly, inquiring of his visitors if they would appreciate a drink of cold buttermilk, they uproariously agreed. Neil then drew three, one-gallon crocks of buttermilk out of his nearby spring, and the flagons were passed amongst the parched Indians who promptly proceeded to flatten the cooling elixir. In due course, the contingent proceeded to the nearby ball-field. The game proved to be anti-climactic as the Washabuck Wallopers defeated the Wagmatcook team who were no longer fleet-of-foot, burdened down as they were with buttermilk. "By cripers, it was simply a case of hit but no can run, chuckled Michael A."[2] And that's the candid tale of how the Washabuck Wallopers finally succeeded in routing their worthy opponents.

This baseball league folded shortly before the beginning of the Second World War, and a few years later Father Alex was reassigned.

15-5 The Born Loser cartoon, reprinted by permission. Courtesy of Newspaper Enterprise Association, Inc. United Media/Reprint Rights Sales, New York, NY. 1/9/2002.

Coalition League

A second baseball league was initiated some years later during the Second World War. It apparently did not develop into a rigorous league because so many of the area's youth were overseas. It was an assortment of ad-hoc teams, made up of the better available players from the various communities and they played for three or four seasons. Although he did not play himself, Jerome MacKinnon of Barra Glen was instrumental in reviving this baseball effort. The teams made use of baseball gear salvaged from the previous league. Again, teams from Iona, Eskasoni, Barra Glen, Washabuck, Gillis Point and MacKinnons Harbour participated. Both Neillie Gillis from MacKinnon Harbour, and Bob MacPherson, a CN bridge tender, who played for Iona, were particularly admired because of their superb pitching abilities.[3] The Barra Glen field was at *Ceiteig's*, located on the Fraser Road. *Ceiteig* was a sister to Peter B. (*Cursty*) MacNeil's wife of Highland Hill and R. C. MacDonald's wife Elizabeth, of Upper Washabuck , all three were daughters of *Iain Calum* MacNeil from that area.

Neil Stephen (Neil Peter) MacLean and his wife Kaye (Angus Ranald MacDonald) had returned to their ancestral community of Washabuck from Detroit in 1939 with their new son Roddie in tow. Neil had been employed for years in the American city. Ever the avid baseball enthusiast and player, Neil helped immeasurably in re-establishing the Washabuck baseball team in that league until it folded in 1946. Neil's daughter Carmie recalls hearing her Dad Neil Stephen, speak about a game played between Washabuck and Gillis Point. Her father was the first baseman.

> A youngster, substituting for an injured player from the opposing team, managed somehow to get to first base. Neil Stephen slyly suggested to the lad that it would be better for him to make a quicker trip to home plate if the batter got a hit, by taking a shortcut via the infield, directly from first to third; and this is exactly what unfolded, a hit, a mad dash straight across the pitcher's mound to third and then to home, with the resulting hilarity and uproarious recriminations.[4]

There was seldom a dull moment in any Washabuck ball game.

The Harbour baseball team and their fans, would load onto an empty hay wagon guided usually by Jimmy (*Eoise*) MacNeil from Red Point. Powered by a first-class team of horses belonging to the Walker family (they were noted for always having beautiful teams of horses) and they would travel out the Walker Road, through to Cain's Mountain, then onto Washabuck Bridge and finally to Lower Washabuck to Rory Ranald's field. After the game, a complimentary meal was provided the visiting team and their supporters, prior to their return trek.[5] Hector MacKenzie of Washabuck Bridge recalls having attended the last game of this coalition league, played on *Ceiteig's* field on the Fraser Road in 1946.[6]

Softball

In addition to baseball, a softball league developed on the peninsula after the Second World War. The Washabuck field was on the "old MacAulay Place" property in Upper Washabuck, the same property lumbered by "The Rabbits," and perhaps better known to the current generation simply as "Kettach's Place."

Many of the teams were rostered by players recently returned from overseas. The Washabuck team included Angus MacDonald pitching and Bobby Beers catching. Raymond MacDonald was known as a good all-around player. Angus's brothers, Johnny and Alec, (Angus Ranald) MacDonald played at this time as well, as did Andy, Buddy and Roddie MacDonald and Gussie Murphy. Roddie (Neil Stephen) MacLean and Carl MacKenzie were youthful players with this team where only the catcher wore a glove.

18-1 A number of "old-time" Washabuck softball players pose for this photo with several players from rival teams, at the "MacAulay Place" ball field, Upper Washabuck, ca. 1952. Back Row L-R: Carl MacKenzie, Roddie MacLean, Andy MacDonald, Gussie Murphy, Pius Campbell (Jamesville), and Alec MacDonald Front Row: Hugh Campbell (Iona), Raymond MacDonald, Francis Campbell (Jamesville), Buddy MacDonald, Roddie Francis MacNeil (Iona Rear) and Angus MacDonald. Courtesy of Hector MacKenzie, Washabuck Bridge.

For the "little kids," the big attraction was not the ball games, but rather, the huge nearby sawdust pile left behind by the recently departed MacRae Brothers lumber operation. Sunday afternoons were spent burrowing, charging up and rolling down its slopes, while chasing one another like squirrels, around this huge inverted cone of orange sawdust.[7] Every schoolyard should have one.

In 1952, ball enthusiast, Michael B. MacDonald of Iona would take Washabuck players, Raymond, Andy and Buddy MacDonald with him to complement a contingent of Iona player's when they played exhibition games against the Whycocomagh Mi'kmaw team.[8] Over the decades, Washabuck played numerous exhibition games with teams from outside communities including, River Bourgeois, St. Joseph du Moine, Baddeck, Whycocomagh, Nyanza, Eskasoni and Whitney Pier. However, it was the nearby Benacadie teams, that always seemed to be Washabuck's most zealous opponents, and whether they won or lost, they proved consistently to be great enthusiasts, great players and, together with their supporters, great sports.

Two Out

Ben MacLean recalls the slickest feat he ever witnessed, at a Washabuck softball game occurred with Bernie MacLean pitching. Washabuck was playing the MacKinnon Harbour team. They had a player on third and the batter returned Bernie's pitch with a zinger in the gap between the mound and third base. Somehow in one fluid motion, Bernie snagged the line-drive and while still in mid-flight managed to ambush the runner who, having broken early from third, was just a-toe-nailing-it for home.[9]

Bernie proved himself to be an extraordinary athlete. He was a proficient all-around softball player and a particularly superb, strong-armed pitcher, within the entire Central Cape Breton League. He also excelled in varsity football, as an offensive guard with the Don Loney-coached X-Men, while attending St. Francis Xavier University. Bernie's team went on to win several Atlantic Football Conference banners and Atlantic Bowl titles. He crowned his playing career in 1966 when the X-Men posted a 40-14 triumph over Waterloo Lutheran in the Canadian College Bowl, now called the Vanier Cup.[10]

18-2 Bernie MacLean, Washabuck Centre was the Offensive Guard with St. FX University varsity football X-Men, 1964-1966. In 1966 the team won the Vanier Cup Championship. Courtesy of Bernie MacLean, Canso, NS.

Cache Creek

In a game against Iona, played at Washabuck on a hot Sunday afternoon, pitcher Bernie MacLean inadvertently "beaned" Iona batter F. X. MacNeil. A felled F. X. took first base with the help of his teammates. While on first base he kept asking absurd questions such as, what team they were playing, what base he was on, what inning it was. The Washabuck players were as concerned over his well-being as were his teammates, so much so, that no one made an effort to tag him out at any base, resulting in him scoring the run with Iona

18-3 The Washabuck Saints, ca. 1963. Back Row L-R: Martin MacLean, Cyril MacLean, Roddie MacDonald, Joe MacLean, Joey MacLean, Francis MacNeil, Danny MacNeil, Ben MacLean. Front Row: Hector MacLean, Bernie MacLean, Leo MacDougall, Jim MacLean, Tony MacLean.

COMMUNITY ORGANIZATIONS

eventually winning the game. After the game, F. X. was taken for a medical examination to a Baddeck doctor, who found him to be alright and further indicated that his memory and lucidity would improve in due course, so he was given clearance to return home. The actual consternation amongst all the players though, it was later revealed, stemmed from the fact that prior to the game, F. X. had stealthily concealed a 2-4 of Keith's Ale somewhere in the nearby brook, but due to the injury he couldn't recall where the cache was stashed. A subsequent search proved the Doctor right.[11]

No Quarter

Charlie Murphy was unable to play ball due to a number of physical injuries sustained from a glut of errant exuberances as a youth. Nonetheless, he displayed his ingenious temperament, serving as the community's designated umpire calling balls and strikes from behind home base for most Washabuck softball games, where he effectively humoured verbal harassments with a sly smile and droll Irish wit. Saturday night trysts with barrels of home-made bull-beer, resulted in Washabuck players and their beloved on-field umpire, being in less-then-stellar condition for Sunday afternoon performances. Now and again his calls were debatable, and often vociferously contested.

Neil Stephen MacLean, a stalwart, long-time Washabuck player was attempting to score from third base during a tight contest. A teammate drilled a smash to the shortstop and the play was at home. Neil Stephen and the ball arrived at home base simultaneously resulting in an empathic "OUT!" from Charlie.

"I'm not OUT," roared an enraged Neil Stephen. "I'm SAFE! SAFE as a CHURCH!"

"You're OUT!" repeated the unflappable Murph, "You're OUT! OUT by a MILE!"

"I may be out by A FOOT," fired back Neil Stephen, "BUT I'M NOT OUT BY A MILE!"

Charlie's umpiring, displayed sufficient bleariness, for him to make errant calls with absolute conviction. Such were the travails of a Sunday afternoon umpire.[12]

Thou Shalt Not Steal

Father Dan E. MacDonald, Pastor of St. Columba Parish (1956-1960) played for the Washabuck softball team. His presence added a capable lustre to the Washabuck roster and always heightened the games' enthusiasm, among the competing teams and their raucous supporters. Here was a youthful, beloved and respected man, priest and sport enthusiast, playing catcher with the Washabuck Sinners. (And to think that he'd even question the stealing of a base because it might be deceitful.) It was shortly after the good Father's untimely death in 1960, that Washabuck management

18-4 Rev. Dan E. MacDonald (1915-1960), Requiescat in pace.

changed the team's moniker to Washabuck Saints. Unfortunately, the name upgrade did nothing to improve their record for winning championship titles.

Little League / Women's Softball

It was not long before Father MacDonald's passing that he became instrumental in championing the formation of a little league on the peninsula. A foursome of teams from Little Narrows, MacKinnon Harbour, Iona and Washabuck comprised the league. Angus (Angus Ranald) MacDonald, the senior team's very decent southpaw pitcher, had fallen heir to coaching the junior team. He enthusiastically encouraged the eager youths, as he generously chauffeured the up-and-coming prospects about the communities in his latest pick-up truck. Bernie MacLean's exceptional pitching ability shone bright and steady, as did the lumber, leather, and stealing exploits of shortstop, Gus MacLean. The league provided outstanding entertainment for the supportive and appreciative widespread community, at the same time succeeding in molding a dedicated bunch of eager players for their senior years.[13]

During the 1970s, the young women of Washabuck, played games

18-5 In August 2010, a smattering of Washabuck "Old-Timer" players are joined by Washabuck Saints players, some up-and-coming wannabes along with long-time dedicated supporters. Back Row L-R: Scott MacDonald, Sheldon MacNeil, Dan Franklin, Curtis MacNeil, Stephen MacLean, Vince MacLean, Hector MacNeil, Lawrence MacDougall, Robert MacLean, Ernest MacDougall, Lauchie MacLean. Centre Row: Paul MacNeil, Gus MacLean, Jimmy MacNeil, Roddie MacKinnon, Cyril MacLean, Ben MacLean, Dan E. MacDougall, Leo MacDougall, Quentin MacDonald. Front Row: Dave MacLean, Bernie MacLean, Josie MacLean, Irene MacLean, Jim MacLean, Joey MacLean, Martin MacLean, Danny MacNeil. Courtesy of Louise MacKenzie, Hazeldale, CB.

of softball, against Iona and Christmas Island teams. Finding a sufficient number of female players to complete a full roster was a recurring challenge so when needed, the lads were "permitted" to augment their roster. Players included, Loretta, Joanne, Teresa, Maureen, Bernadette, Karen, Beverly, all MacLeans and Marybelle, a MacKenzie. Coincidently or otherwise, the team's fostering coaches Martin, Joey, and Tony MacLean, were the other gender.[14]

4-H

4-H Clubs arrived in Upper and Lower Washabuck in 1950. Carmie MacLean became the first president of the Lower Washabuck Club. With the opening of the new school in Lower Washabuck in September 1949, teacher Teresa (Hughie) MacNeil of Gillis Point oversaw the club's fledging efforts. Subsequent teachers Dolly MacNeil, Agnes and Margaret MacDonald, continued these initial labours with equal enthusiasm.

The program was assisted throughout the region under the leadership and guidance of Agricultural College summer students from Truro. These individuals included Lorne Cox, Alvin Blades, Kaye Sutherland and Enid Fullerton. Henry Austin, the Agricultural representative, supervised the College students as they assisted in overseeing local programs. Henry Austin was a sociable and much admired representative, highly respected by the students, teachers, and parents, with everyone delighting in his knowledge, leadership, and amicable disposition. In 1957, Henry's replacement, Malcolm "Mac" Fuller (1929-2008), of Yarmouth County, proved to be an equally capable representative and likeable individual.

18-6 Norma MacNeil of Upper Washabuck, proudly displays her championship-winning calf at the North Sydney Agriculture Exhibition grounds, September 1959. As the winning entrant amongst 100 contestants, Norma won a purebred Holstein female calf. She is shown here joined by Victoria County's agricultural representative, Malcolm "Mac" Fuller on the left and J. C. F. MacDonnell, Antigonish County's agricultural representative, on the right. Courtesy of Norma MacNeil, Antigonish, NS.

Under the guidance of teachers, Friday afternoon would see a break from regular scheduling and efforts were directed into 4-H activities. These initial activities included learning proper procedures and skills for the orderly conduct of meetings. These proved to be quite successful, so much so that when Lorne Cox first arrived to provide "conduct of meeting" instruction, he was amazed and pleasantly surprised that Washabuck students already knew how to conduct basic meetings according to rules of order. The school grades ran from Primary to Grade 7 and the student body numbered close to thirty. In addition to developing proper conduct-of-meeting procedures, other skills were nurtured through sewing, woodworking, garden and livestock components.

Most families lived on farms, cultivated their own garden plot while many also had livestock, so the 4-H effort was simply an extension of what had already been happening for generations. Now, the students were assisted by more formal instruction that nurtured leadership. Girls and boys tried their hand with all the activities first, succeeding to varying degrees. Some went on to excel in a particular field of interest. Additional competitiveness came from students of Upper Washabuck School. Keen interest ensued among most of the youth, and in a few cases even keener rivalry displayed itself amongst parents as they prepared for the annual exhibition day held during early fall, when ribbons and prizes would be handed out to the top three winning entrants in each category. Vegetables were evaluated for their quality, uniformity and presentation, while calves were assessed on their bearing, stance, grooming, general overall appearance, willingness to be easily led and their potential to become good milk producers.[15]

Washabuck Community Centre Association

Lower Washabuck School closed its doors for good in June 1972. The community residents felt however, that the land and building should be maintained for community purposes. So in April 1973, the property was transferred from the Municipality of Victoria County to the newly formed Washabuck Community Centre Association, with the expressed purpose that the premises be used for the benefit of the community. The property lot which was purchased in 1946 from the MacDonald family measures an acre in size.

The Association's minutes on file date from 1970, when Frank B. MacDonald was president. The 1971 annual meeting shows Joe (Red Rory) MacLean was incoming president. Discussion revolved around the purchasing of the school building for a community centre. At a subsequent special meeting, the group agreed to lease the building for a year for the sum of $1.00 until a more permanent arrangement could be finalized. Michael R. MacDougall (1910-1982) became the incoming president in June 1972, as Annie MacDonald (1929-2014) retired from the secretary/treasurer position having served the association during the previous two years.

As owners, the group now agreed to purchase insurance for the building and its contents. Weekly card games had begun in 1970, and these continued as a means of raising funds for the maintenance of the building. A decision was made in 1975 to hold a square dance as a fundraiser on the eve of the annual Highland Village Day Concert. Forty years later this annual soirée continues and is considered, by all who have attended, to be the cultural highlight of the community's summer season. It too has proven to be a successful fundraiser. Over time, additional fundraisers have included card games, lobster suppers, pork chop BBQs, etc.

An application for a provincial government grant in 1977 totaling $9,000 under the "Little Red School House" program, proved successful and was utilized to replace old windows, repair ceiling tile, relocate an oil tank, build a wet bar, provide for additional kitchen cupboards and a cloak closet. A building-wide, 12-foot (3.5 m) addition almost doubled the floor space in 1983. Further construction occurred in 1985 that involved damp-proofing, the placing of weeping tile around the exterior basement walls, drilling a new well, expanding kitchen counter and shelf space, erecting a wheelchair ramp, exterior painting and general ground improvements. Costs totaled $35,000 with federal funding provided by the Department of Employment and Immigration assisting to the tune of $10,000.

During 1997, new upstairs washroom facilities were added, the first since the building was constructed as a school in 1949. Finally, a major addition in 2004, added a complete modern kitchen with basement, the relocation of basement stairs, re-shingling of the entire roof, installation of exterior siding and the construction of an outside deck. Pearo Brothers from River Denys, were successful bidders for the tendered contract. Costs totaled $108,000 with the federal agency ECBC providing a contribution of $101,000. Further in-house refinements were carried out to washrooms during early months of 2011, by local carpenters Leo MacDougall and Gus MacLean while Paul MacLean and Daniel Matheson, respectively, addressed the plumbing and electrical requirements. These costs were split equally between ECBC and the WCC Association.

18-7 Washabuck Community Centre, 2005.

In 1977, permission was granted to a local sports club to use the premises for the community's youth. The Association has provided modest, yet important, financial support for school trips and an annual Red Cross swimming instruction program. The Centre has served as a wake-house, a meeting place and is available for family gatherings. In 1979 the Association hosted the Clan MacLean during the provincial International Gathering of the Clans festival. During 2002, the Association played an integral role in the Central Cape Breton's Bicentennial Festival, The Barraman's Feast and, since 2009, has been the focal station for Along the Shores of Washabuck, a ten-day summer festival.

The Centre continues to serve well, the community's needs.[16]

In 2000, the Washabuck Community Centre Association (WCCA) was incorporated under the Societies Act of Nova Scotia.

Tour de Washabuck

The Tour de Washabuck mountain bike race was envisioned by Greg Bungay, Allan MacDougall and Pius MacLean. They are the friend, the son-in-law and son, respectively, of Benny and "Sister" MacLean of Washabuck and Sydney Mines. The boys felt it would be worthy to have an annual family activity take place during the Highland Village Day weekend, when so many of their large family, extended clan, and friends, were vacationing in the community.

In 1987, they decided that the bike race would be held on the morning of the annual Highland Village Day concert, the first Saturday in August, and it would be open to everybody, not just family. The race started at Joe (Dolly's) MacIver's (now 3474 Washabuck Road, the current residence of Craig and his late wife Jackie Reid), at 10 a.m. The route was: westward along Washabuck Road to the Washabuck Bridge intersection; proceed through the Cain's Mountain dirt road towards Jubilee; past the Little Narrows Gypsum quarry to the paved road; east through Hazeldale to the South Cove intersection, before finishing at the place of departure, a distance of 26 kilometres. To make it a fair competition and because of the rigours that Cain's Mountain road presented, all contestants were required to ride a mountain bike.

In the first few years, the race began at the top of the hill at Joe Dolly's with "Sister" (Annie MacLean) the clan's Matriarch, signalling the start by beating a green alder on an empty oil drum. The eager participants had a very sharp left turn to negotiate at the bottom of the driveway, where more than one racer's hopes of a winning performance were dashed as they hurtled into the alders and bull rushes on the opposite side of the road. Another factor that often had an impact on the hopes of aspiring champions was that the race occurred the morning after the annual Washabuck square dance. This created a handicap for those competitors who delighted previous evening's festivities and could then use that as an excuse for not winning.

Pius MacLean recalls that he Greg Bungay first talked about starting a bike race in Washabuck similar to what to one that Bungay had been involved with in PEI. The boys said the one thing they didn't consider was doing the race with a hangover. A second thing they hadn't considered was the route. Pius outlines the conundrum:

The morning of the first race we were still talking about it – thank God for Allan [MacDougall]! He got a map of the area from Mom and found that old road out through Cain's Mountain that gave us a loop, or else we might have ended up going over Cain's Mountain to Iona and back through the crossroads, which many of us would not have returned from. If Francis [MacLean] hadn't picked up on the challenge, it might never have taken off as well. He told everyone he was going to kick our butts so there no letting it slide. He still kicked our butts, but at least I beat Bungay, who says his downfall was not having gladiator type rotating blades on his wheels that would take out the opponents' tires [reminiscences of Ben Hur]. I told him that that sounded fine in theory but in practice he would have to be able to pass someone for it to work.

A quarter-century of statistics include:

The winner of the inaugural 1987 race was Joe MacInnis with a time of 61 minutes.

The greatest number of participants was 17 in 1992.

Allan MacDougall has ridden in the most races, missing but one since its

18-8 Kevin MacDougall of Sydney Mines, crosses the finish line, surviving another Tour de Washabuck, August 8, 2008. Courtesy of Allan MacDougall, Sydney Mines, CB.

inception.

The youngest person to ride the race was MacKenzie Fontana, Craig and Jackie Reid's grandson, who was 6 years old.

The longest time recorded to finish was 12 year old Katie (Taylor) Young, when she took a wrong turn which resulted in a time of 2 hours 14 minutes and 55 seconds in the 1998 race.

The fastest race time posted was completed by Joanne MacLean with a time of 56:45 in 2003. (It must be remembered, however, that her father was the official timer.)

Paul MacLean had learned as an aspiring plumber, a fair bit about making belt buckles from an old Italian tig welder. So when the notion of crafting a permanent Winner's Trophy presented itself, the enterprising Paul took a piece of stainless steel, nearly manhole-cover size, and fashioned it into a belt buckle design, encircling the outer edge with tigged up, braided-wire, before polishing off the bucolic masterpiece with a permanent buffing. Voila! Similarly, both second and third place trophies were fashioned into medallions from 5/8-inch (16 mm) stainless steel round-stock, 4-inch and 3-inch respectively (10 and 7.6 cm), likewise decorated and buffed to a splendid sheen.

Then, in cahoots with eldest brother Ben, the boys salvaged a hood ornament, once saved from their father's derelict Renault car that they promptly affixed as the crowning center piece to the winning trophy. Second prize was similarly adorned with a ram's-head hood-ornament from brother, Francis's, exhausted half-ton Dodge. Finally, as the treasure chest's loot waned, Ben rescued from his beloved's jewellery trove, a sparkling brooch bearing the MacLean clan crest that topped off the third place trophy, just perfectly. Job done. Now, the boys were just awaiting the admiration and congratulations all around at the presentations, when from the border of the winners' circle came a distraught EEEEEK! emanating from Ben's partner, Carmie. "IS THAT MY BROOCH?"

Before the trophies were created, prizes were medallions of a less durable material, the terminal end of spent Clark's bean cans dangling from a colourful lanyard, each inscribed by felt-marker exhibiting, name, year, finishing time and placement of race participant. These medals are still used and awarded to all those who participate. When the serrated-edged medal-

18-9 Participants of the 22nd annual Tour de Washabuck mountain-bike race, sporting official Tour T-shirts and associated bling, 2008. L-R: Foncie Farrell, Josh Farrell, Craig Reed (draped with second prize), Allan MacDougall and Kevin MacDougall, in front of Craig's home and the former Joe (Dolly) MacIver homestead. Courtesy of Allan MacDougall, Sydney Mines, CB.

18-10 "Along the Shores of Washabuck" on-line banner, August 2011. Courtesy of Gerard MacNeil, Washabuck.

lion is delicately draped around the receiving neck, the recipient makes sure to take care, ensuring no untoward mishap will mar the euphoria of such an august occasion.

All participants also receive an official Tour de Washabuck T-shirt donated by sponsoring family members. Although Debbie (MacLean) MacDougall has held the grand, if unpaid, position of official statistician since the race's inception, the fact that she has not ridden in any races herself, lends somewhat to her credibility as the source of many of these facts.[17] Only in Washabuck you say? Pity!

Festival

Under the dynamic vision of Washabuck residents, Gerard MacNeil and wife Zina, a summer festival was conceived, developed and delivered in August 2009. An enthusiastic group of residents eagerly endorsed the concept. A successful yearly summertime square dance had been happening at the community centre since 1975, on the Friday night before the annual Highland Village Day concert at Iona. Then, in 2009, the 100th anniversary of the opening of Holy Rosary Church was to be celebrated the following weekend, the community agreed to host a variety of activities on the intervening days to provide family and friends "from away" who normally vacation during that time-frame, a more varied and complete fun-filled stay.

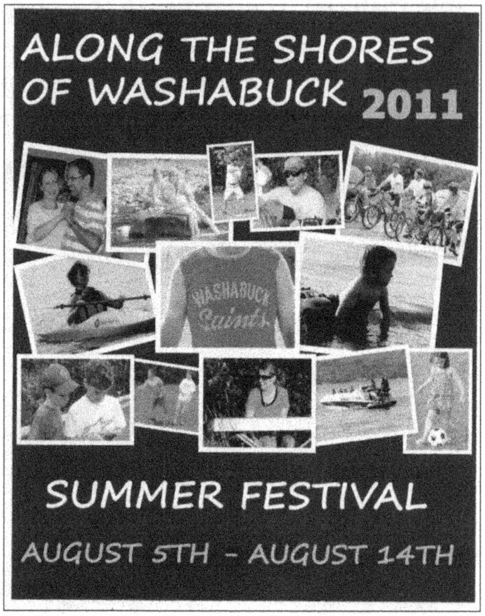

Image 18-11 "Along the Shores of Washabuck," summer festival poster, 2011

An investigation revealed that modest government funding was available for festivals of the nature proposed. Furthermore, District Councillor Paul MacNeil was partial to the concept and he assisted in a variety of ways. Quentin MacDonald's suggestion, that the festival be officially called, "Along the Shores of Washabuck" was readily acceded to, and so, the ten-day festival quickly became a reality. University student, Chrissy MacNeil, was hired in the role of Activity Director and under her dedicated direction the festival unfolded smoothly, aided further with a gaggle of enthused volunteers. Its success that first year led to the easy decision to make the festival an annual event.

In addition to the regular square dance and a pub night anchoring the weekends, other activities include beach days with Red Cross guided swimming lessons, guided nature walks, BBQs, children's activities, church and

Image 18-12 WestJet Provincial Festival Award, 2012.

Image 18-13 Music sheet, "Along the Shores of Washabuck."

cemetery services, genealogy workshops, old-timers softball games, geo-caching, card games and golf tournaments resulting in a fun-filled ten-day program. It has taken a lot of dedicated planning and effort, but the festival has given the community a new vitality and heightened profile, with its "Brown's Bear" Facebook page and each morning's "Internet Café." The fête has become an encouraging social cauldron and provincial award-winning festival, as it provides an economic boost that is most gratifying for the association. Let's see that it continues!

There are various renditions for this song, but celebrated song-writer and author, Allister MacGillivray, vaunting the folk song in *The Highlander*, a one-time Cape Breton weekly writes:

> This song is a true folk song in that it deals with people and events in a specific community over an extended period of time and was composed and performed by these people. It had its beginnings in the late '40s, blossomed in the '50s, and to this day you may hear it sung at parties with fresh verses being added.[18]

Allister quotes Hector MacKenzie, its acclaimed self-effacing author, as saying, "I'm often cited as the author but I decline the honour. I recall putting together a number of the original verses and others through the years … [but] there were many contributors to this open-ended song.[19,20]

Image 18-14 Hector MacKenzie.

1) Down in old Cape Isle
There you'll find a friendly smile;
But you'll not find in many a mile
A better place than Washabuck.

Refrain: (After each verse)
 Hill inn ha, eil ean hi,
Hill inn ha, eil inn ho
Faill il eil eadh's ho ro hi,
Gu de ni mi mur faigh mi thu?

2) Here they come from far and near
To catch the first fish of the year;
But salty pork and sour beer
Is all you'll get in Washabuck.

3) Murdock MacInnis cutting logs
Up in those plaster-holes and bogs;
From dawn to dark he's hammering dogs
Along the shores of Washabuck.

4) Hear the noise on Effie's hill
Hughie Campbell with his mill;
Hear the chanter loud and shrill
Resounding all through Washabuck.

5) Dan MacDougall on the hill
Always votes for Angus L.;
All the Tories go to hell
Along the shores of Washabuck.

6) Doctor Danial cutting ties
He is good at telling lies;
Hughie Campbell will black his eyes
Along the shores of Washabuck.

7) Joe MacDougall with his stud
He can barely chew his cud;
He'll be good for plowing mud
Along the shores of Washabuck.

8) Peter Malcolm lost his gate
Some devils dumped it in the lake;
He called the Mounties for to make
Them take it back to Washabuck.

9) Although he didn't get his gate
He got a visit from 'Big' Kate;
They say she's looking for a mate
Along the shores of Washabuck.

10) One night Dan Rory, pretty full
Brought his girl a bag of wool;
She asked him if he'd kindly pull
His carcass out of Washabuck.

11) Raymond MacDonald as you all know
The noted hunter from down below;
There won't be a beaver, buck or doe
Or boomer left in Washabuck.

12) Sarah Liza was the first
To get her licence as a nurse;
If things are going from bad to worse
Just cable Upper Washabuck.

13) All along the southern shore
There's MacDonalds by the score;
Mary Agnes and some more
Along the shores of Washabuck.

14) Johnny MacDonald with the curls
He's the devil for the girls;
He's got one in Big Baddeck
And several more in Washabuck.

15) Charlie Murphy is home at last
With his leg up in a cast;
But he can drink the beer as fast
As any man in Washabuck.

16) Charlie Murphy with his Dodge
Starter stuck and gas line plugged;
You're liable to see the bastard lodged
On every hill in Washabuck.

17) Dolly MacNeil, she stays at Joe's
That's where Raymond always goes;
What they do there, no one knows
Along the shores of Washabuck.

18) Dan Francis MacDonald got so poor
He had to go to Labrador;
So he could buy stuff in the store
When he got back to Washabuck.

19) Ranald MacDonald by the brook
Can shoe a horse or make a hook;
They say that he's the biggest crook
From River Dean to Washabuck.

20) Election coming in the fall
The Grit's are going to the wall;
It's all for one and one for all
Along the shores of Washabuck.

21) If you want some ice cold beer
I'll tell you where you aught to steer;
For Michael Anthony's Frigidaire
On the eastern end of Washabuck.

22) Down the road is our Co-Op
It is quite the little shop;
Lots of tea and lots of pop
But goddamn little dividends.

23) There's lots of salty cod to eat,
But you can't mark it with your teeth;
The yellow-eyed beans are five cents each
At our Co-Op in Washabuck.

24) I guess you all know Alex D
Although he's mighty hard to see;
He thinks he's better than you or me
Or anyone here in Washabuck.

25) It was the first trip of the year
The boys went down to get some beer;
With rabbits and an engineer
To get them back to Washabuck.

26) Here's a toast to Peter F.
He's getting old, a little deaf;
But he can have whatever's left
When we get back to Washabuck.

27) John Y. Gillis sure can play
Jigs and reels and old strathspeys;
I guess he'd never forget the day
That he came down to Washabuck.

28) John Neillie losing all his sense
As well as all his wire fence;
For Simom hooks it every dance
And takes it back to Washabuck.

29) Then there was a famous man
Who wrote a book about his clan;
He tried his best to understand
The Highland Heart in Washabuck.

30) I'm not a poet, don't you see,
I haven't even a degree;
But poems are made by fools like me
Along the shores of Washabuck.

19 – Military Salute

First World War: Killed In Action / Buried Overseas

J. Murdock MacNeil (1895-1916) Regimental Number: 67630

"Killed In Action." So reads the terse O.C. Battalion Reports for Private John Murdock MacNeil; Reg'l No. 67630, Unit: 25th. Battalion, for June 10, 1916.[1]

Three words may describe their deaths, but there was much more to their lives.

J. Murdock MacNeil descended from pioneer stock. *Eòin* and his wife Mary (MacLean) MacNeil settled in Washabuck Centre in 1817. Their son, Michael, married Lucy (MacNeil) of Washabuck Bridge and they raised a family of nine children, one of whom they christened John A. John A. married Catherine, a daughter of John (Rory, Neil) and Helen (Murphy) MacNeil, another distinct MacNeil family with Washabuck Centre roots, and they had a family of five, three who lived beyond infancy. They lived in Boston where John A. was a building contractor. When their marriage collapsed, the three children, Neil F., Murdock and Lucy, were taken to Washabuck ca. 1896 by his sister Theresa, to live with the children's grandparents. Consequently, it was in Washabuck that Murdock with his siblings spent their early youth.

Murdock was born in Dorchester, Massachusetts, on April 26, 1895. He arrived in Washabuck a few months later and lived with his grandparents on their farm until 1910 when his father sent him to live with relatives in Boston to continue his education. Murdock also worked for brief periods of time in Henry Siegel's department store in East Boston before returning to Nova Scotia in the fall of 1911. He lived in Antigonish and attended St.

FX High School for two years. He did not graduate from St. FX University, but had been enrolled as an Arts student at the outbreak of the War.[2]

Murdock enlisted November 26, 1914, with the 94th Nova Scotia Regiment, which was stationed in the old rink on Blowers Street in North Sydney, under the command of Capt. A. J. MacNeil. He transferred to the Signal Section of the 25th Battalion of the Fifth Infantry Brigade of the Canadian Expeditionary Force, when he learned that the unit was going overseas.[3]

Murdock sailed from Halifax for England on the SS *Saxonia*, just days after his 20th birthday, on April 29, 1915, and subsequently embarked for France on September 15, 1915.

A news dispatch in a Boston newspaper following his death had the following headline below his photo:

> Private Murdock MacNeil of Boston, the only American to be recommended for a Victoria Cross has been killed in battle.

The article continues:

> Private Michael MacNeil … standing in a British trench, stuck his head up over the parapet and to his dismay saw his major lying wounded near the German trenches, 50 yards away. Hesitating not a moment and yet realizing that to cross the territory known as "No Man's Land" meant certain death, MacNeil leaped over the parapet and trailing his gun ran toward the German front line. Immediately rifle shots began to land around him, but some kind Providence seemed to be watching over him and he reached the side of his beloved officer in safety.
>
> Hastily tying his handkerchief around the wounded officer's neck, where he had been shot, MacNeil picked him up on his shoulder, and taking a zig-zag course rushed back to his own lines, all-the-while dodging the enemy's fire. Officers from the British trenches saw and applauded MacNeil, and immediately he was recommended for a Victoria Cross, the most coveted decoration in the British army.[4]
>
> The 25th Battalion's War Diary "Summary of Events and Information" for 18 March, 1916, reads: "Majors Bauld and Bates seriously wounded while looking over new trenches." Could either one of these soldiers have been the rescued Major?[5]
>
> […]But the time Private MacNeil brought back his officer was not the only occasion upon which he displayed great bravery. Once, he was carrying a wounded man back to get treatment at a distributing station, and the man was killed while he was on MacNeil's back.[6]

After ten months of warfare MacNeil fell in a charge that retook the muddy trenches in the second battle of Ypres, in Belgium, June 10, 1916. Contrary to reports carried by both Boston and North Sydney newspapers

19-1 Pte. J Murdock MacNeil (1895-1916).

of the day under banner headlines, MacNeil never was awarded the Victoria Cross. According to his nephew Neil MacNeil (1923-2008), long-time chief congressional correspondent for *Time* magazine, Murdock's medals which are currently in possession of his grand-nephew and namesake, consisted of two campaign medals, and the 1914-1915 Mons Star that is awarded for heroism.[7]

Why did MacNeil not receive the Victoria Cross? It has been surmised that he had only been recommended to be awarded the medal, and perhaps upon further investigation, the British realized that Murdock, although having lived in Washabuck, Cape Breton for most of his young life and having enlisted with a Canadian Battalion, was in fact, an American citizen. Had the recommendation been realized, J. Murdock MacNeil would have been the first American citizen and first Cape Bretoner, to be awarded the prestigious Victoria Cross.[8] Murdock's name is inscribed on the Menin Gate Memorial, Belgium, and in the Book of Remembrance, page 130[9], in the Peace Tower on Parliament Hill, Ottawa.[10]

John Jay MacLean (1896-1918) Regimental Number: 469662

John Jay MacLean was the great grandson of pioneer Neil *Lachlann* Mac-Lean and his wife Annie (Neil *Geal* MacNeil) who, arrived in Washabuck in 1817. They had a family of ten children. Their son Michael married Sarah (Allan, Donald *Bàn* MacKinnon) of MacKinnon Harbour. They too had a family of ten and lived in Washabuck Centre. Their son John married Elizabeth "Bessie" (Neil, Hector, MacNeil) of Gillis Point East, the parents of Private John Jay MacLean.

19-2 Pte. John Jay MacLean (1896-1918).

John was born in Washabuck Centre on New Year's Day, 1896. He served with the 85th and 64th Battalions, Canadian Infantry. While serving with the New Brunswick Regiment, the 26th Battalion, he was wounded. He died from his wounds on August 11, 1918. He is buried in Villers-Bretonneux Military Cemetery, Fouilloy, France. John Jay's name is inscribed on page 462 of the Book of Remembrance, Parliament Hill; Ottawa, Ontario.[11]

Angus Roderick MacNeil (1888-1918) Regimental Number: 222416, DCM

Angus MacNeil was named for his grandfather. The senior Angus was born in Scotland and was one of eight children of *Eòin* and Mary (MacLean) MacNeil, original pioneers that settled in Washabuck Centre in 1817. Angus married Christina (Rory, Miller) MacDougall of Big Beach, lived at Washabuck Centre and raised a family that included five boys and three daughters. One of the boys Alexander J., "Sandy" remained on his parent's property, married Elizabeth "Lizzie" (last name unknown). Their son, Angus Roderick, was born at Washabuck Centre on May 2, 1888. Angus's parents moved their family to Whitney Pier in 1906 Angus R. was 18.

19-3 Sgt. Angus Roderick MacNeil (1888-1918), DCM.

His occupation was listed as miner and boilermaker when he enlisted in Sydney with the 85th Battalion, Canadian Overseas Expeditionary Force on October 14, 1915. His previous military experience included 13 months with the 94th Regiment. His next of kin is listed as his wife, Mary Margaret MacNeil, living at Whitney Pier.[12] Angus's military papers list his promotion to rank of Corporal in June 1916. He sailed from Halifax to England on the SS *Olympic* on October 12, 1916. By February 1917, he had joined the fighting ranks in France. Angus Roderick was awarded the DCM for bravery under fire at Eleu dit Leauvette. MacNeil's citation reads:

> Awarded the Distinguished Conduct Medal for conspicuous gallantry and devotion to duty. During an attack and the subsequent consolidation, he handled his men with the utmost skill, showing great courage and a quick initiative in placing posts where they were required. During the night he secured valuable information by patrolling the ground to his front, and on the following day he went out with a daylight patrol under heavy machine gun fire, though he already been on duty continuously for 36 hours and taken part in two attacks. He showed a very fine spirit of keenness and devotion to duty.[13]

By the October 21, 1917, Angus Roderick MacNeil had been promoted to the rank of Sergeant. A week later he grappled with a gunshot wound to his left hand, which required several weeks' hospitalization. On the September 2, 1918, Angus was killed in action at the battle of Arras. He is buried at Dury Mill British Cemetery, Arras, France. Angus Roderick's name is inscribed on page 462 in the Book of Remembrance, Parliament Hill, Ottawa.[14]

Name (Dates), Location, Parents, Regiment and Number, Buried

(*Asterisk indicates service in both wars)

1. Campbell, Malcolm R., Sergeant (1880-1969), St. Columba, 94th Reg.

2. Fraser, James, 715 478, 106th Battalion, Boston.

3. MacDonald, Alex, St. Columba, 94th, 18901972, Iona.

4. MacDonald, Alexander J. (1884-?), St. Columba, Lieutenant, 94th, North Sydney.

5. MacDonald, John Allan (1875-1955), St. Columba, 94th and 6th.

6. MacDonald, John Archie (1894-1974), St. Columba, 94th, Iona.

7. MacDonald, M. A. J., Major, (1863-1925) St. Columba, 94th and 6th, Iona.

8. MacDonald, Malcolm, Sgt. (1881-?), 185th, 877277, Washabuck.

9. MacDonald, Michael John (1896-1916), St. Columba, 106th, 715536.

 10. MacDougall, Hector (1882-1958), 185th and 85th, 878031, Glace Bay.

 11. MacInnis, Danny (1892-1924), 94th and 1st Depot, 3180011, Little Narrows.

 12. MacIver, Joe "Dolly" (1899-1972), Washabuck, 94th.

 13. MacKenzie, John Stephen (1895-1945) 94th Battalion.

 14. MacKinnon, Angus (1895-1961), 94th Battalion, New York.

 15. *MacKinnon, Hector (1891-1995), Cain's Mtn. 1st Depot, Can. Medical Corp, CEF, 17th Reserve.

 16. *MacKinnon, Murdock (1898-?), Cain's Mtn. Royal Canadian & 1st Depot Battalion.

 17. MacLean, Francis A., Gunner (1885-1938), Detroit.

 18. *MacLean, John D. (1895-1961), 1st Depot Battalion, 3180474, Washabuck.

 19. MacLean, John Jay (1896-1918), 85th, 64th and 26th Battalions, 469662.

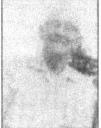 20. MacLean, John Joseph (1898-?), 40th Battalion, 482017, Detroit.

 21. MacLean, Neil S. (1896-?), 185th Battalion, 877296.

 22. MacLean, Peter A. (1895-?), 185th Battalion, 877279, Florida.

23. MacLean, Peter Neil (1898-1921) 1st Depot Battalion, 3181750.

 24. MacLean, Roddie J. (1898-1974), 185th Battalion, 878336, Sydney.

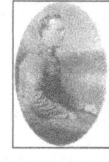 25. MacNeil, Allan Austin, Sgt. (1891-1969), St. Columba, 94th Regiment, Iona.

 26. MacNeil, Angus Roderick, Sgt. (1888-1918), 85th, Arras, France.

 27. MacNeil, J. Murdock (1895-1916), 94th and 25th, 67630, Belgium.

 28. MacNeil, Neil Archie, St. Columba, 94th, Roderick & Elizabeth MacNeil.

 29. MacNeil, Neil F., Sgt. (1891-1969), U.S. Army, New York.

Better Wrong Than Right!

The following item was carried by the *Legion Magazine* in its November/December 2003 issue. It is perhaps not so surprising that humour, became the primary recollections of returned veterans, many scarred both mentally and physically by the ravages and horrors of war. The following item is offered in that vein.

Hector MacKenzie of [Washabuck Bridge], N.S., remembered back in the '40s, when he was much younger, he hastened to add, a booklet arrived one day in a Department of Veterans Affairs mailing to his father, a WWI pensioner. The booklet included a picture of the Altar of Remembrance in the Parliament Buildings in Ottawa and a caption indicating that the Book of Remembrance resting on the altar contained the names of all 60,661 Canadians killed in the Great War.

MacKenzie's parents remarked that this sad piece of information would be a worthwhile statistic for the children to commit to memory, challenging them to file it away so that someday when somebody posed the question they could instantly respond: "60,661."

He took up the challenge, determined that he would not forget it and that one day his big chance would come. A few years later his Grade 8 history textbook gave the number of Canadian WWI casualties as "around 70 000." While basically correct, it offended our student's sense of accuracy and he smirked inwardly.

At the end of the school year the opportunity for which MacKenzie had hungered had arrived. The final examination paper in History asked: "How many Canadian servicemen were killed in the First World War?"

Our lad wrote with a firm and confident hand, "60,661".

His mark for the answer? A big round zero. He tells us that he was later informed that pertinent information is constantly adjusted in the Books of Remembrance.

While this is true, one wonders whether an innocent pupil was being fed a line by a rationalizing pedagogue who had merely expected the regurgitation of a figure from the textbook. Perhaps the teacher did not even know the exact total. The second edition of The Canadian Encyclopedia still agrees with the number a young Hector MacKenzie committed to memory– 60,661.[15]

In Flanders Fields

In Flanders fields the poppies blow
Between the crosses, row on row,
That mark our place; and in the sky
The Larks, still bravely singing, fly
Scarce heard amid the guns below.

We are the Dead. Short days ago
We lived, felt dawn, saw sunset glow,
Loved and were loved, and now we lie,
In Flanders fields.

Take up our quarrel with the foe:
To you from failing hands we throw
The torch; be yours to hold it high.
If ye break faith with us who die
We shall not sleep, though poppies grow
In Flanders fields.

~John McCrae, 1915

Second World War

Sergeant Michael Bernard MacDonald (1921- 2005) F54680, DCM

He was called Michael B. by everyone that knew him. He was decorated with the Distinguished Conduct Medal in 1945 for daring and courage at Delfzijl, Holland.

On the night of 30 April/May, 1945, Sergeant Macdonald [*sic*] was a platoon sergeant in D Company, The Cape Breton Highlanders, who were attacking the key strong point in the defenses of the port of DELFZIJL. The strong-point was sited at the top of a dyke 30 feet high and its guns commanded all approaches across the flat open ground. The strong-point consisted of four 105mm guns, two 20mm guns, and many machine guns and 300 infantry. Some of the enemy infantry were firing from concrete pill-boxes at the foot of the dyke.

Sergeant MacDonald's platoon at dawn had fought its way into the centre of the enemy position, and had cleared and occupied a trench within 50 yards of the 105mm gun positions. The enemy were then firing at the platoon from all sides, with every weapon that could be brought to bear on the trench. Sergeant MacDonald, with five of his comrades, disregarding the intense enemy fire dashed forward a further 35 yards and occupied another enemy trench. Here they were subjected to the direct fire of the bazooka and the two machine guns fifty yards away. Enemy entrenched at the top of the dyke threw grenades down into the trench. Two of Sergeant MacDonald's comrades in the trench were killed and a third was mortally wounded. In the confusion of the exploding grenades and bazooka bombs two of the enemy crept up unnoticed and, reaching the edge of the trench, demanded surrender. Sergeant MacDonald and two of his remaining comrades, with their ammunition exhausted and covered by the enemy's weapons appeared to have no alternative but to surrender. As they climbed out of the trench Sergeant MacDonald said to his comrades, "While the rest of the company is still fighting, we won't give up; make a break for it," upon which Sergeant MacDonald knocked down the nearest enemy with his fist, seized his rifle and put the second German to flight.

19-4 Sergeant Michael Bernard MacDonald 1921-2005 DCM. Courtesy of Beatrice (MacNeil) MacDonald, East Bay, NS.

As a result of this act, the enemy in the pill-boxes again opened fire and Sergeant MacDonald fell, seriously wounded in both legs. With great fortitude he crawled back to the trench in which his two comrades had already taken up positions and remained with them for more than seven hours. Sergeant MacDonald's daring attack unarmed on his armed captor allowed his comrades to reach safety. His supreme courage and cheerfulness during the long hours when he lay wounded in the trench encouraged his comrades to hold, their well-nigh untenable position until they were relieved seven hours later.[16]

Michael B. MacDonald was born in St. Columba, August 21, 1921. He was the youngest of nine children born to Dan A. and Isabella (MacNeil) MacDonald. The family moved to Iona in 1924. Michael B he worked in the woods cutting logs and milling lumber with his father, prior to his enlisting with the Cape Breton Highlanders on September 2, 1939, at the age of 18.[17] Before enlisting he had been a member of the Militia for a three-year period.[18]

Although he required periodic hospitalization for his leg wounds after returning to Iona following the war, he remained active. He worked in the woods, drove the school conveyance between Washabuck and Iona, and played softball, a passtime in which he held a particularly keen interest. Always interested and appreciative of young people, at the age of 69 he enrolled at what is now Cape Breton University under the "mature students" program.

He said:

I've long wished I could further my education. I have always had a deep interest, in history, political happenings and the lives of the Scottish people....[19]

In his later life, Michael B. served faithfully in the role of president for the Grandona Legion, Iona Branch 124, where he doubled as the Legion's affable, avid and long-time bartender. Michael B. was married to well-known Cape Breton novelist and playwright Beatrice MacNeil. He passed away in the "Year of the Veteran" on May 23, 2005. Michael B. is buried in St. Columba Parish Cemetery, Iona.

Private Margaret MacDonald

There is but one female among all 61 Washabuck enlistees that served in the two World Wars. Margaret MacDonald was the daughter of Angus Ranald and Sarah Liza (MacNeil) MacDonald of Upper Washabuck. She was one of fourteen children. Four of her brothers, Ranald, Roddie, Dan Francis, and Johnny served overseas during the Second World War. Private MacDonald was born on May 31, 1922 and served in the Canadian Women's Army Corps in Canada. During the balance of her working life she was employed with Bell Canada in Montreal. Unmarried, Margaret died on June 25, 1990 and is buried in Holy Rosary Cemetery, Washabuck.[20]

19-5 Private Margaret MacDonald (1922-1990).

Enlistees Second World War

Name (Dates), Location, Parents, Regiment, Number, Buried

1. Campbell, Angus, St. Columba.

8. MacDonald, Roderick C. (1918-1996), West Nova Reg., CBH, North Novas, Vancouver.

15. MacIsaac, Donald, Royal Canadian Engineers, Sydney.

2. Gardiner, Angus B., Corp. (1912-1961), Cape Breton Highlanders [CBH], F55276.

9. MacDonald, Stephen (?-1983), St. Columba, Calgary Highlanders, F56524.

16. MacIvor, Daniel "Buster," Married to Lillian MacLean, Washabuck.

3. MacDonald, Francis (?-1980), St. Columba, Royal Winnipeg Rifles, A117741.

10. MacDonald, Dan F. (1923-1997), Royal Canadian Artillery (ACK-ACK), Canadian Forestry Corp, F56375.

17. MacKinnon, Columbus, One of six brothers who served, CBH, Yukon.

4. MacDonald, John B. (1926-1978), North Nova Scotia Highlanders, Carlton York. Image

11. MacDougall, Dougald, CBH, Canadian Merchant Navy, Toronto.

18. MacKinnon, Dan Joe, One of six brothers who served CBH & West Nova Scotia Regiment, Yukon.

5. MacDonald, Margaret (1922-1990), Canadian women's Army Corp.

12. MacDougall, James, Lance Corporal (1918-1953), North Nova Scotia Highlanders, Canadian Provost Corp.

19. *MacKinnon, Hector (1897-1995), One of six brothers who served.

6. MacDonald, Sergeant Michael B. (1921-1995), St. Columba, CBH, F54680, DCM Iona.

13. MacDougall, Joseph H. (1918-1993), CBH, F3916.

20. MacKinnon, John Neil, Hamilton, One of Six brothers who served.

7. MacDonald, Ranald (1914-1983), CBH, F54988.

14. MacDougall, Philip (1911-1986), CBH, Royal Canadian Engineers.

21. *MacKinnon, Murdock (1898-?), One of six brothers who served.

 22. MacKinnon, Philip, One of six brothers who served. Royal Canadian Engineers, F77677, Windsor.

 23. MacKinnon, Roddie (1922-1991), Royal Canadian Artillery, St. Catherines.

 24. MacLean, Benny (1919-1980), CBH, RCAF.

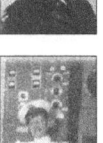 25. MacLean, Hector (1912-?), Gillis Point, Merchant Marine, 4459, Liverpool, NS.

 26. MacLean, James A., Sgt. (1902-1981), CBH, C.Q.M.

 27. MacLean, Joe I. Major, Gillis Point, CBH, Christmas Island.

 28. MacLean, John Charles (1925-1984), Canadian Army, 721188, 1945-46, First Canadian Guards, 1954-1957, Washabuck.

 29. *MacLean, John D., Sgt. Major (1895-1961), FWW, CBH, F54917.

 30. MacLean, Michael D. (1910-1992), Royal Canadian Naval Reserve Newfoundland and Canada A1368, Baddeck.

 31. MacNeil, Benny "Paul," CBH, Montreal.

 32. Murphy, Charlie (1919-1982), Pictou Highlanders.

They served in both wars

19-6 Pte. Hector MacKinnon, Cain's Mountain.

19-7 Sgt. Major John D. MacLean, Washabuck Centre.

19-8 Pte. Murdock MacKinnon, Cain's Mountain

MILITARY SALUTE

19-9 Group photo at Iona Cenotaph, November 11, 1993. Photo by Vince MacLean.

>In Grateful Tribute
>To the Men of this Area
>Who Sacrificed Their Lives
>In Our Country's Wars
>And In Everlasting
>Gratitude
>To Those Who Daring To Die
>Survived[21]

20 – Politics

The Formation of Victoria County

The separation of the new county of Victoria from the county of Cape Breton was accomplished in 1851 without much effort, fanfare or agitation. So comments Alex D. MacLean:[1]

> The demand for separation was confined principally to the settlements of Big Baddeck, Little Baddeck, and North Side Grand Narrows, which last named district included the polling districts of Iona and Washabuckt.[2]

A Bill to divide the County of Cape Breton, and to Regulate the Representation Thereof, was introduced by the representatives of the united counties in February 1851 and signed into law on April 7, 1851. The Lieutenant Governor in his speech proroguing the House mentioned that among the bills:

> ...well calculated to supply the wants and increase the prosperity of and happiness of the people, [was] for the erection of a new County in Cape Breton, conferring an increase of representation, and more efficiency in the management of local affairs.[3]

The first Court of General sessions was composed of Justices of the Peace as resided within the limits of that part of the county that had been set off as Victoria County. Donald MacLean represented the Washabuck district. Donald was the grandfather of Alex D. MacLean. The first *Custos Rotulorum*, Master of the Rolls, was Murdock MacAskill of Little Narrows. MacAskill, a native of the Isle of Lewis, immigrated to Nova Scotia, and for a period of time was employed as a school teacher in Antigonish County.[4]

Cape Breton historian, Jim St.Clair describes the political system of the times:

> Prior to 1851 and until 1879, the directors of the new county's activities were the Justices of the Peace to be found in all parts of the district. They had for some time been designated to receive oaths, witness legal documents, and represent the area in the application for funds for new roads and new ferries..... In 1879, an act was passed by the Nova Scotia Legislative Assembly to establish incorporated counties throughout Nova Scotia with municipal councils presided over by wardens and with established districts, each with its own councilor.
>
> But from 1851 until the new structure came into being, an official known as the "Custos Rotulorum" (guardian of the records) chaired the meetings of the Justices of the Peace in the so-called Court of Sessions. MacAskill was well received as the first Custos Rolulorum and respected for his orderliness and involvement in projects which promoted the development of the County of Victoria.[5]

Victoria County Municipal Councillors
District of Washabuck (1889-2012)
Councillors for District 18 – includes

Hector P. MacNeil	1889-1892
Philip B. MacNeil	1893-1895
Peter S. MacLean	1896-1901
John D. MacNeil	1902-1913
Neil A. MacNeil	1914-1919
Alexander MacDonald	1920-1925
Allan A. MacNeil	1926-1934
Roderick J. MacLean	1935-1937
Francis B. MacDonald	1938-1955
Neil S. MacLean	1956-1967
Arthur J. Campbell (districts reduced from 18 to 12)	1968-1972
Catherine Jankowski*	1973-1984
Michael Dan MacNeil	1985-1994
Foncie Farrell (districts reduced from 12 to 8)	1994-1997
Gerald Yetman	1997-2000
Dan E. MacNeil	2000-2007
Paul (F. X.) MacNeil	2007-2012

Image 20-1 Catherine "Kata" (MacNeil) Jankowski, Iona. In addition to being the first female municipal councillor in Victoria County (1973-1984), she was also the first female Fire Chief in Nova Scotia (1975-1977). Courtesy of Vince Jankowski, Boisdale, NS

A Call to Remembrance

Elections, whether federal, provincial or local were taken seriously by the Washabuck electorate. A handful of key individuals would be directly involved with the rallying of troops from within their traditional political fold, while being ever alert to the possible allurement of the disillusioned from a rival party. Others in the community felt less compelled to become overtly involved, but all made a Herculean effort to vote. Missed church services could perhaps be overlooked on occasion, but on Election Day, everyone of age was expected to make it to the polls. Cash was a scarce commodity, so the temptation and reward of political patronage played a keen if not crucial role with every election.

To the winner and his supporters went the spoils of road maintenance work, the repairing of wharves or the bushing of lake-ice. Sheep-valuers, weed-inspectors and fence-viewers, were other positions of pride and patronage whose exalted titles belied their actual importance. Nonetheless, these snippets of entitlement meant cash in one's pocket, money for basic family needs, cold hard currency, in an economic system that relied so much on barter.

The following is a humourous narrative from the hand of Alex D. MacLean. Alex D. was a staunch supporter of the Progressive Conservative party, a fact that will become obvious to the reader as MacLean renders his accounting of this anguished old-time election. The factions were unusual as it pitted Liberal party supporters against Liberal party supporters, each vying for power and the spoils,

This spectacle filled Alex D.with political glee while he sat back, absorbing the unfolding Liberal cataclysm, prior to setting pen to paper. Thankfully, he captured not only the broad stokes of the election itself, but also as relevantly, the humourous depictions and personal nuances as they played themselves out. He mocked the principals, their seconds and the party in turn, with his mischievous political banter and sarcasm.

This election was one to be remembered. MacLean's account is replicated exactly as he wrote it, including, names, blanks, initials, purposeful misspellings and grammatical imprecisions.

The "Three Rory's" Election[6]

This epochal event took place in the year of grace, 1937. This year will always be a memorable one for the people of Washabuckt, – aye, and for many residing in other parts of the county of Victoria. There were two elections in that year. The first was a contest between John M. Campbell, Liberal, and F. W. "Casey" Baldwin, Conservative, both of Baddeck, for the county seat in the House of Assembly. This election did not disturb the political surface of Washabuckt to any extent. It seemed as though the electors were reserving their vim and vitality for the council election scheduled to come later in the year. This second election, and let it be again understood, the most important from a Washabuckt view-point, was the contest between Roderick J. MacLean (hereinafter to be known as Rory J. for the sake of smoother explaining in this bit of prose) of Washabuckt Centre, and Francis B. MacDonald of Lower Washabuckt, (hereinafter referred to as Frank).

This council election created lots of excitement, oodles of it, and plenty spleen and bitterness, with no little amusement for the Tories who contented themselves by standing on the side-lines, or who from time to time, motivated by some devilish impulse, stirred up the embers of strife and hatred when they seemed to be dying down. Both candidates, Rory J. and Frank, were natives of the district, born within a few years of each other. Their educational ability, or mental ability for that matter, was of the type that could be called mediocre. To add zest and ginger to the campaign, they were both Liberal in politics. (They pronounced it Liperal.)

Now to get at the background of all this, and in order to understand how it was that such a deplorable schism came about in the ranks of the Liberal party in Washabuckt district, we must go back a bit. The reader will, we know, be patient with us. In 1934 Rory J. was elected by popular acclaim to represent his native district in the Municipal Council at Baddeck. He felt, and there were many who felt with him, that this was a deserving honour. Had he not served his King and Country during the Great War of 1914-1918 and bore scars to show that he had been wounded in action? At the end of the war, bearing these honourable scars, he had returned home, but only remained for a brief period. He left for the United States, finally locating in Detroit, then the Mecca of most Cape Bretoners. After a time, the busy city of Detroit experienced the depression that became general throughout the United States about that time. Our hero returned to his native heath, now accompanied by the wife of whom he had wed in the Michigan City. He proceeded to settle down on a farm.

It was in 1932 that the leaders of the great Liberal party in Washabuckt decided that he was the man they wanted to represent them in the Council. Accordingly a meeting of the Executives was called, (they pronounced it "Ex-e-cutives", with the accent on the "U") and "the Patronage," that precious possession of any party in power, was placed in the keeping of Rory J.

Now let it be understood. The Patronage is in theory supposed to be used for the sole benefit of the "The Party" as a whole. But only in theory. In fact, that is to use a legal phrase de facto, it is to be used solely for the benefit of the few who are included in the ring. By ring we mean those most instrumental in placing the patronage in the hands of its custodian. Of course it is always understood that a candidate, if he is compelled to face an election, shall use the patronage to the best advantage to secure his election, but after the election, "the public be hanged" and the "Ring" takes over.

From participation in "the patronage" all Conservatives were rigidly excluded.

In 1934 came the election, and as I have already pointed out, our battle-scarred veteran was elected by acclamation. If this election by acclamation was very much unexpected by all, it was a very pleasant and unexpected surprise to Rory J. He at once concluded that his unopposed election was due to only one reason – or two reasons rather. The first, his reputation as a politician, proven in the provincial elections of only a few months before and the second, his enviable war record. Of course everybody was by this time aware of the fact that himself and the Premier of the Province, Angus L. Macdonald had fought side by side in the trenches of France and Flanders. Was it not common knowledge that himself and the Premier and Rory J. were closer to each other than the Siamese twins?

To him, his election by acclamation meant only one thing. He had secured a mandate to carry on. Consequently he was a busy man. He could be seen running about in his gasoline buggy from one section of his district to another, supervising the activities of road construction and bridge-building gangs. On approaching one of these construction gangs his procedure was to run his gasoline chariot about one hundred feet ahead, apply the brakes, and then wait there in his car, until the sub-foreman came up to him hat at side, in hand. This was in keeping with the methods he had observed when the august and honourable Minister of Highways, A. A. MacMillian, would be on a tour of inspection. At the same time Rory J. felt that he was doing a wise thing in keeping at a distance from personnel of the road crews – familiarity breeds contempt you know.

On Sunday he would be seen near the church, standing apart from the ordinary everyday people, and in close consultation with Vincent MacLean, who was regarded by many as his right power, but who, in reality, was his "boss." Sometimes this group would be augmented by the addition of Rory D. and Rory C. This would usually be around election times, when there would be need of calling a meeting. Then everyone was democratic and above board, in the best "Liberal" tradition. However, if it was a case of matters of patronage being discussed, there was no publicity until the requirements and demands of the "Ring" were first satisfied.

It was at a "big gathering," like a Grit convention at Baddeck or one at North Sydney that he really felt in his element. The other delegates used to have a peep at him once in a while through the half open door of a committee room, where he always appeared to be in deep consultation with some of the big-wigs. Generally at these conventions his right hand men or "yes-men" were Rory C. and Malcolm Paul. Never did "Cheap Jack" come down from the metropolitan city of Halifax, but what Rory J. would be one of the first [to] contact him to report "on the condition (politically) of the district since I took over".

The Liberal, (or Liperal) organization in his district was a more or less efficient place of political machinery. It consisted of a President, Vice President, Secretary, and several Ex-e-cutives. There was also a Chairman, but how his duties compared with those of the President was, I believe, never fully divulged. Meetings were usually held in camera, and took after the Ku Klux Klan in this respect. Now let us observe that no chain is stronger than its weakest link. Not a few of the faithful Liperals felt that they were not getting their share of the pickings to be had from the patronage through. Many were asking: why is Vincent getting everything? Why was Rory C having the job of guardian angel of the highway tractors all the time?

Now, all this was perfectly true. Vincent Mac, always wanted, and got, more than his share. It was also true that Rory C. or some member of his family were, year in and year out, guardians of the caravan of highway tractor, grader, and supply truck. A stranger passing by his property of a summer's evening would think that Barnum & Bailey's had arrived when he caught sight of the red painted caravan that was always parked opposite Rory C's premises after the crew would be through with their eight hours stint on the highways. This family held the pleasant sinecure of being permanent guardians of the highway equipment at so much per hour, per night. It was a sinecure without doubt; they drew pay while they slept. There would be nothing to disturb the highway outfit in that remote and secluded spot.

These examples of favouritism tend to awaken long dormant jealousies. Some of the neighbours, (themselves good Liperals when the Liperals were "IN") murmured among themselves. Of all this poor Rory C. was unconscious, and as for Rory J. who had the patronage in his keeping he proceeded on the theory that the King can do no wrong.

All of a sudden he realized that another election was creeping up behind him. He awakened from his lethargy and saw that he must distribute "the patronage" a little more evenly. He must give "hand-outs" to the politically hungry and neglected. Now this is where the rub was. In order to do this, his needs must "take away" from some and "give to" others. When this he attempted to do, the storm broke and anything [taken] away from his was very much like trying to take a hunk of meat from a hungry lion. Also, it was out of the question to transfer the Barmun & Bailey's tractor outfit from the keeping of Rory C's family, at least, not until after the election. What to do? What to do?

Suddenly the storm grew worse. It now was reaching the proportions of a small cyclone or tornado. Loud rumbling of discontent were heard, and it was numbered that the "Have-gots" were determined to hang on to what they had previously enjoyed. Shrewdly the "Have-got," with Vincent Mac among them, had reasoned that if they transferred their allegiance and support to a new man, that they would be entitled to enjoy the spoils for another while, if their new political "light of love" would be successful at the polls. This they thought could be "arranged." Now let it be understood that these "Have-gots" cared little for party politics. They were good Liperals when the Liperals were in power, and they could just as easily adjust themselves as to be good Tories when it came to the turn of the Tories to be "In." The Vicar of Gray was a back number when compared to them. In other words they were good Grits only when compared to them. In other words they were good Grits only when the wind blew from that quarter.

Rory J. was not without a certain amount of political acclaim. He had observed when he was in the United States, and he had often read of incidents, whereby political conventions were sometimes "packed," and manipulated to suit the needs of the posers that be. If there was such a thing as a "packed" convention to engineer the nomination of a member for Ottawa or Halifax, why [could there not be] a "packed meeting" to nominate a district councilor? Accordingly he made his plans.

Generating the by-laws of the district Liperals Clup (club to most of us) which must have been in the keeping of some mysterious oracle, as very, very few [of] you have ever laid eyes on them, he found that it provided that a meeting could be called at any time by giving a few days" notice. It was allegedly provided that this could be done by posting notice in five or more places throughout the district, these notices to state the objects, time and place of meeting. These posters were prepared and posted.

When we say posted, that is true enough, but they were seen by very few outside of the few who prepared and posted them unless it was by the cattle and sheep who had occasion to wander through the thick woods that fringed some of the deserted farms, or the deer as they skipped nimbly through the woods. We can imagine the mild radiant look on a bovine as [she] gravely considered this poster – possibly wondering what it was all about. Thus the requirements of the Law were observed in letters if not in spirit.

The next move was to secure the presence of a majority favourable to the nomination of Rory J. This was all attended to in best machine-approved, or Tamratry Hall style. For this purpose all sorts of motor-vehicles were pressed into service to convey the voters to the designated place on the evening selected for the meeting. This date was fixed for Sept. 10th 1937. The time was seven thirty, and the place was Upper Washabuckt school house.

Rory J. and his friends had planned everything in secrecy, and they fairly imagined that it was a secret still. They thought that it would not be until the meeting was over and done with that the opposition would wake up to the fact that he had stolen a march on them, and had been re-nominated. He and his friends plastered the crestfallen looks of this opposition on the morning of Sept. 11th – AFTER the meeting. Alas! They had not taken into consideration the propensity of some of the weaker sex to blab and gossip. Evidently some member of the cabal had spoken in his home of the doings. To this day some of them have a suspicion that it was full force the truth of the words credited to the impartial, immortal Guns to the effects that "the best laid plans of men sat mice gang aft aglee." Their plans were betrayed to the enemy.

By this time the opposition had become a formidable number. It included Vincent Mac- - -, Neil B. S. _ _, the MacDonald's of St. Columba, John D. MacNeil of Grass Cove, together with his two stalwart sons, Daniel J. B., and James J. D. The wonder of it all was that this opposition could agree on anything, [as] they had been for many years at each other throats, (politically speaking) and it was thought impossible that they could ever be brought together. To find the MacDonald's of St. Columba and the John D. MacNeil faction (this faction was composed of father and son) fighting shoulder to shoulder was reminiscent of the Scriptural story of the lion and the lamb. Add to this the opposition the Gillis Point Tories who were thirsting for revenge. They had been treated like pariahs and something worse. They welcomed the opportunity of "ganging up" on their oppressor.

As I have said, the cat was cut out of the bag. The other faction was aware of the plan of Rory J. and his henchmen. Frank got busy and made a visit to every home in the district. He made no exceptions. He visited the Tories as well as the Grits. His method was to be a general man with a cruel plan. He told the people that he called on that there was to be a general meeting, "open to all," irrespective of political opinions, in the Upper Washabuckt school house on the evening of Sept. 10th. He said further that the object of this meeting was to nominate a "non-partisan" man for the council. He said also that transportation would be provided to bring them to this meeting.

Came the evening of Sept. 10th. Along the roads, from Washabuckt Bridge to the Upper Washabuckt School – from the Gillis Point and of the district to the Upper Washabuckt School – there came all kinds of motor vehicles. Good cars – second-hand jalopies, even trucks that had been provided with planks to make seats – all carrying their load of humanity. Included in this human mass were old ladies who had not been away from their firesides in years. Old ladies who had thought that they would be allowed to pass their declining years in peace, saying their beads as was their wont. But this was denied them. The urgency of the political situation and the keen rivalry for the nomination of a councilor for Washabuckt district on the Liperal ticket was too important for that.

When the hour set for the meeting approached, the school was packed to the doors. It was only a small building – about the size of the average country school – but the "Standing room only" sign could be hung out. Every seat was occupied, and every aisle was jammed. Never had the oldest inhabitant remembered of seeing such a multitude of gathering under this roof. I cannot say definitely who the chairman was. I think that before the meeting was over that half a dozen chairmen had taken turns at attempting to preside.

Now when the Rory J. supporters looked about them they saw many hostile faces. Also there were many Tories gathered there. This was the last straw, and they emitted howls of rage, and proceeded to purge the meeting of these pariahs, but not without a protest. Frank and his henchman wanted the Tories to remain, as they were certain that they could count on their support if they were permitted to vote in this meeting. The opposite faction then proceeded to categorize each suspected person present. Sometimes it was only necessary for them to point at one and say "You're a Tory!," and the person addressed not making any denial, would withdraw. Some of them would put up a fight, and say that this was a matter that would have to be proved. The late lamented Neil Peter was present, and when he was charged with being a Tory, he contented himself with saying: "You prove it!" Now it was out of the question for any person to prove how another had voted, although it was a well-known fact that Neil Peter voted for Baldwin in the provincial election of June 1937. Then some bright individual had a brilliant idea. There was one or two Justice of the Peace present, and it would be a simple matter for any one accused of being a Tory to make a short declaration to the affect that this accusation was false. However, none availed themselves of this opportunity. Most of the Tories withdrew, and contented themselves by standing outside and peering in through the windows.

Finally some semblance of order was reached, although at its quietest period the meeting resembled a meeting of the Constituent Assembly of Paris during the stormiest period of the French Revolution.

Of course there was a blackboard in the school. The first suggestion as to how the vote was to be taken was put forward by the supporters of Rory J. This was that the names of both candidates would be written on the blackboard, and then the voters would advance, one at a time, and place an "X" below the name of the candidates they were voting for. This suggestion was howled down by the supporters of Frank. They were willing to have a secret ballot taken, but the other side was not – they were certain that the Tories who had refused to leave the meeting would vote for Frank, and they did not want this at all. All efforts to find a way of taking a vote were seemingly, and actually were, beyond solution. The meeting up this time was stormy enough. Now it began to get rougher. At one time, with half a dozen or more trying to air their views at one and the same time, with half a dozen others, the veteran John D. MacNeil of Grass Cove tried to calm the multitude. He pointed to the blackboard, at the same time crying: "Luke

luke (look look) at the blackboard!" But just then a stalwart from Rory J's side approached and shook his fist at his nose. Just at this junction, one of the doors opened, and John appeared, with his sleeves rolled up, and saying: Let us clean her out!"

It looked like war and the old women began to look for a way of escape. But they were packed like sardines; there was no way of reaching the door. Even if there had been, you may be sure that fifty percent of them would have made their exit long before. One old lady, Big Alex's wife from Gillis Point was caught in this human wedge. She thought that murder was about to be committed, and she looked wildly about her, making the sign of the cross, and at the same time, exclaiming in Gaelic: *"Caite Dhia, Caite Dhia! Am bheil an dorus?"* (My God, My God! Where is the door?).

No business could be transacted at a meeting of this kind. It could not be called a meeting. It was more like a gathering of howling dervishes. It resulted in a confusion. Some say that a motion to adjourn was carried. Others say not. This will always be a matter of dispute. Rory J. and his supporters left in a body, but Frank's henchmen remained and took possession of the meeting. Then they passed a motion placing Frank in the field as candidate for the council as the Liberal nominee. This did not stop Rory J. He declared himself the only candidate of the Liperal party, and took out nomination papers. The fight was on, and boys, what an election campaign. There was never anything like it in the most turbulent part of the Dominion of Canada or the U.S.

Both sides had their lines drawn. Supporting Frank we found Vincent MacLean, Neil B. S.; Tommy and Jimmy "Billy"; Daniel Murphy; the MacDonald's of St. Columba; John D. MacNeil and his crew from Grass Cove, and a lot of lesser light, and the majority of the Tories of the entire district.

Supporting Rory J. were John Stephen from the Bridge; Rory C. from Upper Washabuckt; Rory D. from Lower Washabuckt; Malcolm Paul; John Alex the Fiddler of Gillis Point, the latter's brothers, and a few scattered Tories, who evidently preferred him, as they regarded Frank as the real Grit of the two.

Rory D. was a strong support[er] of Rory J. We may say that he acted the part towards Rory J. that Marshal Ney played in relation to Napoleon. This comparison is most appropriate. Did not Marshal Ney desert Napoleon when the fortunes withdrew their sails? But more about this later.

It was at this point that the schism in the Liperal ranks became more pronounced. Both factions formed "clups" (clubs to us) and each side claimed that they and they alone possessed the real Simon-pure Grit organization. Rory J. pointed with pride to the fact that he had never polled a Tory vote, and Frank could say that in his kitchen was hanging an almost life-size portrait of Sir Wilfred Laurier. The reader can arrive at his own conclusions. Personally, I am of the opinion that there is not, and never was a real Grit in Washabuckt.

The campaign was now on in full swing. Cars were on the road at all hours of the day and night – but mostly at night. Nothing was left undone, to secure the lone vote. There was, for instance, much rivalry to secure the favour of Michael Brown's vote. It was known that Michael was very susceptible to the influence and blandishments of the fair sex. Supporters of Frank assured him that they were able to bring about the marriage of him and the "fair Theresa." This caused the said Michael to look with favour on Frank's side of the argument. The other side got wind of this scheme, with the result that Rory J's friends interviewed him and assured him that they could bring about the betroth-of himself and a sister of John Alex, the fiddler. Now it was pointed out to Michael that this lady was a particularly good catch. She had been to the "Boston States" – in fact, she had only recently returned from there, and in addition to a certain amount of multitude, he was told that she had plenty of folding money – and last, but by no means least, that she had a decided crush on, and a leaning for Michael, whose renown seems to have penetrated even to the States of the American Union. This decided the outcomes as far as Michael was concerned. I am told that his ballot was cast for Rory J. (He is still enjoying single blessedness.)

About this time the most venerable body, the Liberal Association of the County of Victoria met in annual session. Among those present from Washabuckt were Rory J. and Frank both flanked by their henchmen from whom they sprung. The thrice puissant Liberal Association was faced with a situation that would tax the judicial powers of a Solomon. It was manifestly out of the question to recognize BOTH belligerents as official candidates of the Liberal party. Here it was that Mr. John R. Campbell of Jamesville, in the county of Victoria, demonstrated to the admiring assembly that he had plenty of grey matter, and that he knew how to use it. His solution was that as far as Washabuckt is concerned that no decision be made until AFTER the election. This of course is the adopted policy of the Liberal party in most matters of a controversial matter or nature. They are able to straddle the fence. It is much better than passing the buck. This decision of the Liberal Association was in effect something like this: "Rory J. and Frank are both good Grits – may they both win. If they don't both win, the WINNER will be the official party nominee." It seems that both candidates were satisfied with this arrangement. They were both confident of winning.

The two rival "clups" in Washabuckt were busy. The scribe of that following Frank was Mr. Daniel J. B. MacNeil of Grass Cove. The "clup" that adhered to Rory J. was happy in having the services of Mr. Rory C. as secretary. It must be confessed that as secretaries they were not of the type that could be considered as suitable for modern business where speed is a requisite. They were both of that leisurely style that was more appropriate to the time of the late King Tutankhamen of Egypt, when secretaries, (then better known as amanuensis) kept their records on stone tablets, and took their time, while recording with the aid of a hammer and cold chisel.

In practically every election in Victoria County – aye, in their every election everywhere – potent liquid refreshments have always had their place. This was well known to the two contending parties, who by this time bore the same relation to each other as the Germans do to the Poles and Russians. It was decided to fight the devil with firewater; both parties obtained their supplies from private vendors in or near the vicinity of Sydney Mines. They did not patronize the usual channels, i.e., the Government Control stores for their supplies, as they were well aware that they could obtain rum of more potent kick and much better quality from the private vendor, or bootlegger, than they could from the Government controlled source.

To obtain their ammunition, Rory J. and Rory D. proceed by motor to the town of Sydney Mines where they interviewed a gentleman, Bruno McCormick by name; they ascertained from him that he was able to fill their requirements for stimulating beverages, and for the price of fifty dollars they were accommodated with a five gallon keg. When all arrangements were completed as to quality, price etc. Mr., McCormick produced a dollar bill which he tore in two. He gave one part to Rory J. retaining the other half himself. He then told them to proceed out on the Bras d'Or road, and to stop when they reached the end of the concrete pavement. They were told that presently another car would exhibit the other half of the dollar bill, (the half retained by McCormick) and, on their handing him the half that they had in their possession, he would deliver to them the keg with contents intact. This was the procedure followed. They motored out to the end of the concrete pavement, and after a short time the other car arrived they took possession of the keg and started for home.

It was evening when they were passing through that section between Iona and Grass Cove. They knew that on that evening the nuptials of a damsel by the name of Flora Paul had been celebrated that morning, and that the invited guests were making merry at Malcolm Dan's. They decided to look in on the wedding celebration for a few minutes. They were not there very long when one thing was noticed by them. They remembered the passage of the Scriptures, and the poignant remark recorded therein: "They have no wine." Our heroes knew what they could do. The secured four empty quart flagons, and went to the car, tapped the keg, and left four full quarts with the wedding party. This was not only a beautiful gesture of friendship and good-will it was good, sound, political strategy. Was not most of the group their friends, and would it not be possible to whip over to their side some of the doubtful ones?

Eventually the booze was carried home. And securely hidden in a place close at hand, and where it could be watched at all times, and easily drawn on for inspiration. It was rather late when our fiends arrived at Rory J.'s domicile and out of the question to assemble the Ex-e-cutives that night. The next morning messages were sent out to the four corners of the district, and the members of the "ex-e-cutive" were assembled. The contents of the keg was sampled, and pronounced excellent. After each "round" it was noticed that the political fever and enthusiasm of the members of the group increased. It was thereupon decided that the "Ex-e-cutive" was thus to meet in daily session thereafter until the election campaign was over. At this time, the election was just about ten days away.

Every day, at an early hour of the morning, the members of the Ex-e-cutive committee arrived for the daily session. Most mornings their spirits would be low until revived by a copious draught of the ardent spirit contained in the keg. This was usually the case after an arduous session the day before – a session that was posted and prolonged until late at night. Visitors to the home of Rory J. while the Ex-e-cutive was thus deliberating saw them but very, very seldom. These dignitaries would be absconded in the sitting room, which for the time had been converted into an Executive Chamber.

From this Executive Chamber would drift snatches of conversation or debate; "I move that" or "I would move in amendment that" – Frequently plans of campaign and estimates of the overall vote would be discussed, [and] then we would hear words that sounded like, "forty majority," "twenty five majority," etc., etc. As I have observed, these committee members assembled in session very early each morning. Therefore it is not to be wondered at that around ten a.m. they would be feeling in need of a little entertainment and relaxation. It was then that Rory C. would be called upon to drop his secretarial duties and to regale them with words of a Gaelic song. Rory C. has a repertoire of choice Gaelic songs, and he delights in entertaining. At all these meetings Rory C., Rory D., and John Stephen were most assiduous in their attendance. When evening would come they would all get in Rory J.'s gasoline chariot and take off for some part of the district, where they would visit their supporters. On these jaunts they would take along a little from the keg. It was late in the season, but still some of them had vowed that they had seen snakes lurking about in various places. Due to the uncertainty of these reptiles being poisonous or not, they always had a little "snake-bite remedy" with them.

In Frank's camp, things were progressing about the same way. It was noticeable however that all talk of a big majority over Rory J. was now restrained. At first they were talking in astronomical figures; first fifty majority then forty majority. Now they said very little. The reason for this was that Rory J. still had the "patronage" under his control, and he was working the poor patronage overtime. Tractors and graders with their supply trucks were cavorting all over the district. Old roads were being repaired

– new ones were being made, and others were promised. In addition to this there was a "wharf-job." Since the latter part of August, gangs had been employed on the Washabuckt Centre wharf, under the foremanship of Peter D. MacKenzie of Upper Washabuckt. Peter D. was nominally a Tory, but it was noted that his enthusiasm for the principles of Toryism always evaporated when the Tory party was not in power. In fact he had not voted at a local or Federal election since 1930. It was a strange co-incident that he would be sounded as their preference for Rory J. or Frank. It was noticed that those expressing their preference for Frank did not work very long. It always happened that soon after letting it become known that Frank was their choice, that the regretful foremen would approach the men and tell them that due to lack of material, etc., he would have to lay a few off for a while. They would find themselves included in "the few to be laid off." The benevolent god "patronage" was working overtime for Rory J.

Time marched on! Election Day arrived! The poll had been set up in Rory J.'s house. This was considered a good arrangement as it was the man's own home and [surely be considered traitorous to] cast an unfriendly ballot against him.

John Neil [*Hamish* Neil MacNeil] was the presiding officer. The hour for voting had arrived. The election officials were assembled. The ballot box, sealed, was in position. That ballot box that is often the receptacle for ballots cast in revenge, ballots cast only given vent to fancied slights, and ballots cast in return "for a price" or the promise of a job. It is safe to say that most of the ballots cast this day were in that category. Of course a few friendly ballots were cast, but they were few.

Very soon after the poll opened motor cars were thundering along the road. Every car in the district was requisitioned, and they were augmented by cars hired in the town of Baddeck by the contending parties. Each car as it drove up to the poll was packed to the roof. Voters young and old came to mark their ballots. Old men and old women some of them approaching the century mark, or at least only a few years from it; voters who spoke only Gaelic, and who would require the services of an interpreter. Standing in the vicinity – a vicinity – charged with the ectoplasm of hatred, spleen and rancour were the workers for the two parties. Some of them worked up with a little shot of the potent brew. Very few smiles; everything frowns and grim.

Here approached Neil B. S. to cast his vote. He was still smarting over the loss of the ferry. He was for Frank of course. Here comes another voter with a big grievance. He wanted ALL the buoys, and was only given two. He was for Frank. If Frank got in, he might still have a chance to hog the words and works. Gillis Point Tories bent on working all the mischief they could in the Liperal ranks. In they straggled; all sorts of voters who had made a good thing out of the road work or on the wharf job, these latter were for Rory J. – strong supporters of his.

The day wore on. It was nip and tuck. The ballot box held the secret but was saying nothing. Inside the booth, the quietness was punctuated by squabbles from time to time. Oaths would be administered to some voters. Some were challenged on account of being resident in other districts. One or two were challenged on account of being suspected of being American citizens. Everybody challenged voted however.

The last hours during which the poll was opened and dragged back wearily: the last vote had been polled around four O'clock. A record breaking number of voters had come to the polls, or had been driven there rather. Six O'clock. The zero hour. You can imagine the tenseness of everybody at his tabulating card and pencil, and the alert scrutinizers. The count proceeded with that monotonous regularity characteristic of election counts. MacLean, – MacDonald. MacDonald, – MacLean. Sometimes Rory J. would have a lead, but only for a short time. Then Frank would have the lead. Again Rory J. would creep ahead. They were all on tender-hooks. Finally it was received in silence by the men assembled. [The margin of victory was less than five votes.][7] Suddenly as [found in a] best-seller, [from] an adjoining room, Rory J.'s wife was indulging in a fit of hysterics. She raved and ranted. She raved about them taking the bread out of her mouth. Finally she cooled off.

Through it all, Rory J. maintained a stoical calm. He still had more aces up his sleeve. He could call his defeat on nothing but a Tory victory. He was aware of the fact that the majority of Frank's supporters were Tory persuasion. He would make representations to the great Liberal Association of Victoria Country to this effect. They could not put anything over on him. This was the beginning of a political tug-of-war that lasted until two years later. It is true that Rory J. succeeded in holding on the patronage until the next spring, but when Frank finally got control of the patronage, he still had to face a lot of wrangling and ill feeling.

Image 20-2 (Left) Rory J. MacLean (1898-1974).

Image 20-3 (Right) Francis B. "Frank" MacDonald (1907-1971).

One case to illustrate: When the election was over Frank tried to put some of his own men on the wharf job. He failed. The foreman would take none there, or anywhere else, nor would he discharge any but on the word of Rory J. Finally Frank in desperation went to Sydney Mines where he interviewed the great Matthew MacLean, Liberal member of the House of Commons, for the dual constituency of North Cape Breton and

Victoria. Mr. Matthew MacLean listened to his story, was sympathetic, and gave him written authority to order all work on the Washabuckt wharf discontinued until he could have the construction gang replaced by men of his own thinking. He returned in triumph, went to the wharf, and with much flourishing of arms, told them that they were discharged. It was near evening anyway, and they did not mind. They were expecting something of the kind anyway, and they departed for their homes.

But Rory J. was speedily apprised of what happened. That night, while the discharged men slumbered, Rory J. got out his trusty gasoline chariot, and saying: "Steed, do your stuff!" Over the roads he chugged, his headlights lighting up the trees and the desert-highways. Presently, he arrived at the town of Sydney Mines, where he routed the great Matthew MacLean, the Grit oracle, from his bed. Swiftly and graphically he outlined to him the great injustice that he had been perpetrated on him and the men who had been employed on the wharf. He convinced Matthew that he and he alone had the backing of the Liperal ex-e-cutives. The great man there upon wrote out another order, countermanding the one that he and Frank had furnished. Triumphantly, Rory J. went back to his motor steed, and soon had navigated the distance between Sydney Mines and Upper Washabuckt. Arriving there in the early hours of the morning, he awakened his sleeping henchmen, and the result was that the next morning all the men who had been discharged the previous day were back on the job. Incidents like these were common. All that fall Rory J. supervised the road work. Nothing delighted him more than to send a fleet of trucks to load gravel at Grass Cove right under the nose of John D. MacNeil and his opponents residing there.

Of course there were repercussions. All these things were duly reported to the august Executive of the Liberal Association with headquarters at Baddeck. The sitting member for the House of Assembly, Mr. John A. Campbell, was on the verge of a nervous breakdown. He was continuously besieged by rival delegations from Washabuckt district. Everyday motor boats could be seen chugging their way across from the ferry at Lower Washabuckt, or from McKay's Point. Some of these boats went "put-put-put," as if in a hurry – and a damned big hurry. Some of them were slow and deliberate as they came "chug-chug-chug" across the lake. At last it got so that the members of the great Liberal Ex-e-cutive in Baddeck, and the sitting member hated to hear the sound of a motor on the water. It was said that Johnny Sam, as the local member was familiarly known, experience species of "shell-shock," and used to dive under the bed every time he heard the sputter of a motor boat.

The Liberal Executive then did a cruel thing. They took the patronage away from the custody of Rory J., and they gave it over to the tender care of Frank; this was a terrible shock to the supporters of the former. Be it remembered that they were devoted followers who worshipped at the shrine wherein "patronage" that it was kept. This devotion was so strong, they were so faithful to "the patronage" that it was seen that it was but a matter of time when they would be worshipping at the new shrine it was rendered that Frank was to set up.

So it happened. The first to fall by the wayside was Rory D. like Marshal Ney he was faithful to his leader until his leader was shorn of power – in this case "the Patronage." He chose to follow his idol. Rory D. began a coy flirtation with Frank. Next to go was Rory C. and his family. Always strong worshippers of "the Patronage" they followed it no matter where it was in keeping. If it was in the Tory keeping – they were Tories – if it was held by the Grits – they were Grits. Truly such devotion to "the Patronage" is unexcelled. John Stephen hesitated for a long time. He gazed on "the Patronage" from afar off, and finally came nearer. It called to him one day, and he could not resist. He pitched his tent along-side that of Frank.

(14) M. W. McLeod, Upper Baddeck; (15) J. M. McLean, Upper Baddeck; (16) Murdoch Nicholson, South Side.

District No. 17—Big Bras d'Or

Presiding Officer—J. H. McKenzie, Big Bras d'Or.

Assessor—John A. McDonald, Black Rock.

Collector—Wm. D.McDonald, Boularderie East.

Board of Health—John Squires, Big Bras d'Or; J. F. McDonald, Big Bras d'Or; Norman Morrison, Big Bras d'Or.

Overseers of Poor—Dan Grant, Boularderie East; Laughlin Patterson, Boularderie East; J. H. McKenzie, Big Bras d'Or.

Officer to serve District Appointments—J. A. McLean, Big Bras d'Or.

Magistrate to execute Collectors Bond—J. F. McKenzie, Big Bras d'Or.

Sheep Valuer—Abel Stephenson, Black Rock.

Constable in and for the County of Victoria—John A. McLean, Big Bras d'Or.

Pound Keeper—John A. McLean, Big Bras d'Or.

Overseers of Highway—(1) Kenneth McAulay, Table; (2) Archie Carmichael, Black Rock; (3) Donald McDonald, Big Bras d'Or; (4) John A. McLean, Big Bras d'Or; (5) James McPhee, Boularderie East; (6) John D. McDonald, Boularderie East; (7) Gaven Stephenson, Big Bras d'Or Rear.

District No. 18—Washabuckt

Presiding Officer—John A. McDonald, St. Columba.

Assessor—Hector McDonald, Grass Cove.

Collector — Dan Murphy, Upper Washabuckt.

Officer to serve District appointments—James McKenzie, Lower Washabuckt.

Sheep Valuer—Alex McDonald, St. Columba.

Bushing Ice—Neil P. McLean, Washabuckt Centre.

Ferryman—R. D. McLean, Lower Washabuckt.

Magistrate to execute Collectors Bond—Neil P. S. McLean, Lower Washabuckt.

Constable in and for the County of Victoria—Dan Alex McKinnon, Upper Washabuckt; Dan J. D. McNeil, Grass Cove.

Board of Health—Vincent McLean, Lower Washabuckt; Murdoch A. McNeil, Gillis Point; Murdoch McKinnon, Upper Washabuckt.

Board of Fire Escapes—Donald McNeil, Grass Cove; P. M. McNeil, Upper Washabuckt; Tom McKenzie, Lower Washabuckt.

Overseers of Poor—Dan J. D. McNeil, Grass Cove; John A. McDonald, St. Columba; Neil A. McNeil, Gillis Point.

Fence Viewers—Michael A. McLean, Lower Washabuckt; M. T. McNeil, Gillis Point; James A. McDougall, Upper Washabuckt.

Overseers of Highway—(1) Frank McNeil, Grass Cove; (2) Johnnie McNeil, Gillis Point; (3) Hector Campbell, Gillis Point East; (4) Rod J. McLean, Washabuckt Centre; (5) Dan Murphy, Upper Washabuckt; (6) Rod D. McLean, Lower Washabuckt; (7) Malcolm McDonald, Upper Washabuckt;(8) John S. McKenzie, Washabuckt Bridge; (9) John Allen McNeil, McNeils Vale.

Upon motion the Council adjourned to 10 o'clock tomorrow morning.

SANFORD G. BURKE, Warden,
CHAS. W. K. McCURDY, Clerk.

25

John Grant, Boularderie East; (6) James Campbell, Boularderie East; (7) Gaven Stephenson, Backlands.

District No. 18—Washabuckt

Presiding Officer—John N. McNeil, McNeil's Vale.

Assessor—Malcolm B. McLean, Lr. Washabuckt.

Collector—Hector Campbell—Gillis Point East.

Officers to serve District appointments—John R. Nash, St. Columba.

Sheep Valuer—R. C. McDonald, Upper Washabuckt.

To Bush Ice—M. J. McLean, Washabuckt Centre.

Ferryman—R. D. McLean, Lower Washabuckt.

Magistrate to execute collectors, Bonds—John D. McNeil, Grass Cove.

Constables in and for the County of Victoria—John S. McKenzie, Upper, Washabuckt; James J. D. McNeil. Grass Cove.

Board of Health—Vincent McLean, Lr. Washabuckt; Andrew McLean, Gillis Point; Dan Murphy, Upper Washabuckt.

Board of Fire Escapes—Frank McNeil, Grass Cove; Allan Alex McNeil, Gillis Point; Neil F. Devoe, Upper Washabuckt.

Overseers of Poor—John Alex McNeil, Grass Cove; John A. McDonald, St. Columba; Neil A. McNeil, Gillis Point West.

Fence Viewers—Thomas McKenzie, Lr. Washabuckt; Dan Alex McKinnon, Upper Washabuckt; Malcolm P. McLean, Washabuckt Centre.

Overseers of Highways Sub. Sec.—(1) Donald McNeil, Grass Cove; (2) John H. McNeil, Gillis Point; (3) Hector Campbell, Gillis Point East; (4) John D. McLean, Washabuckt Centre; (5) Dan A. McKinnon, Upper Washabuckt; (6) John J. McKenzie, Lower Washabuckt; (7) P. M. McNeil, Upper Washabuckt; (8) Dan J. McDougall, Washabuckt Bridge; (9) Michael S. McNeil, McNeil's Vale.

.Upon motion council adjourned to 10 o'clock tomorrow forenoon.

D. B. McLEOD, Warden,
CHAS. W. K. McCURDY, Clerk.

Image 20-4 (Above, left) List of Officers appointed at the January Session for District No. 18 Washabuckt, Victoria County, 1937 and 1938. Courtesy of Joan MacInnes, Victoria County Archivist, Baddeck, CB.

Image 20- 5 (Above, right) List of Officers.

The Liperal Clup that was once the pride of Rory J. meets no more. The secretary and the chairman have gone over to reside near the patronage. It is rumoured that the secretary took the minutes with him when he took his departure and that they are now in some museum. As for Rory J., he refused to be beguiled by the call of that siren, "the Patronage." He found her an unfaithful, fickle jade, and cut clear from all entanglements. It is not expected that he will get into a political campaign again until such time as the stability of men [demonstrate] such, as to make their world reliable. He often says that he now knows exactly how many liars there are in his district.

Appendix 1

Explanation of conjectural painting.

"The Barraman's Feast"- Confrontation and Appeasement

"The Barraman's Feast" mural was commissioned to celebrate the 200th anniversary of the settlement of central Cape Breton Island by Gaelic speaking Scots from the Isle of Barra in the Outer Hebrides. It depicts the legend of settlement

The imposing military figure clad in the tunic of the Fraser Highlanders at the centre is Donald "Og" MacNeil from the Isle of Barra. Donald "Og" sailed through the Bras d'Or Lakes while serving on a British-man-of-war vessel after the Siege of Louisbourg, 1758. He became so enamoured with the area now known as Iona that upon arrival home to Barra he told stories of its beauty. Donald "Og" was killed after hoisting the British flag upon victory on the Plains of Abraham, Quebec in 1759.

Forty-four years after Donald "Og's" death in 1802, recalling the tales of their ancestor, four MacNeil men from Barra came to the Bras d'Or Lakes. They cleared the land, which is now Iona, after receiving a land grant from King George III. During the clearance of the land the Mi'kmaq peoples who inhabited the shores of the Bras d'Or Lakes confronted the MacNeils.

Altered by smoke from burning trees, the Mi'kmaq people came to investigate the MacNeil's activities. Using body language and broken French, the Mi'kmaq Chief questioned the Gaelic speaking MacNeils about clearing the land.

Fearing for their lives, Eoin MacNeil fell to his knees and blessed himself. Almost immediately the Mi'kmaq appeared more friendly and asked if the MacNeils were Catholic. The MacNeils showed their crucifixes around their necks the Mi'kmaq Chief. The Chief smiled, blessed himself and exclaimed, "We are brothers!" French Jesuit Missionaries and Christianized the Mi'kmaq people decades earlier.

The Mi'kmaq Chief cooked eels to share with the MacNeils. The MacNeils shared the eels but sprinkled them with salt. The Mi'kmaq were not acquainted with common salt and had relied on salt water for cooking. The Chief was pleased with the taste of this new salt and asked for some to take with him. The MacNeils obliged this request.

It is important to note, in the intervening 200 years, peace and harmony have existed between the Mi'kmaq and the Gaels. In some instances, cross culture sharing has taken place. Furthermore, these events occurred on the site where stands today the parish church Iona dedicated to the patronage of St. Columba of Iona, Scotland.

The scene located in the upper left corner depicts a traditional Mi'kmaq encampment on the Bras d'Or Lakes circa 1500 A.D. The emblem means, "Remember the old Mi'kmaq."

The log church being erected occurred in Christmas Island just prior to Bishop Plessis' visit to the Brad d'Or Lake Mission in June of 1815. This was the Highlander's first Catholic Church on the Bras d'Or Lakes.

The two clergymen depict St. Columba pastors, Father Roderick MacKenzie (1901-1926) and Father Duncan Rankin (1926-1953), beloved, respected and long serving priest both of whom are interred in the St. Columba parish cemetery.

The bottom scene depicts some everyday activities in the life of the Cape Breton Gael with a traditional céilidh occurring in the bottom right corner after a successful day of new construction, circa 1860.

Appendix 2

Copy of letter to Wanda MacDougall, regarding recovered artifacts. From Jim Campbell, Archaeology Collection Supervisor, Fortress Louisbourg, 1994. Courtesy of Wanda MacDougall, Washabuck.

P.O. Box 160
Louisbourg, N.S. B0A 1M0
Sept. 22, 1994.

Your file   Votre référence
8440-100
Our file   Notre référence

Dear Mrs. MacDougall,

Thank you for your inquiry concerning artifacts from Washabuck that were on display in the 1970's at the Fortress of Louisbourg. It is rewarding to know that people remember some specific artifacts several years after visiting the Fortress.

A search of our records showed there were two artifacts received from Washabuck. A bayonet probably 19th century, donated in 1958. A sword which appears to 18th century, donated in 1964. Unfortunately, there is no mention by whom they were donated. Both of these were part of the Katherine McLennnan Exhibits located mainly in the Old Museum building. However, there was a period when they were relocated to the King's Bastion.

I am enclosing Polaroid photographs of the two artifacts.

I hope I was able to answer your questions.

Sincerely,

Jim Campbell

Jim Campbell
Archaeology Collection Supervisor
Washabuckt River

Canada

Appendix 3

Merchants Who Were In Business At Grand Narrows, Excerpt from The History of Christmas Island Parish, Cape Breton, 1926, pp. 144-45, by Archibald J. MacKenzie.

MERCHANTS WHO WERE IN BUSINESS AT GRAND NARROWS.

The first merchant at Grand Narrows was Robert K. Masters, a native of Truro. He granted the beach opposite the land of Donald McNeil, Red, for the purpose of using it in his fishing business.

The second was Peter McIntyre who bought the acre lot on which the stores and residence of McNeil Bros. now stand. When he failed in business, his principal creditor, James Campbell, of Arichat, offered Allan McNeil, Blacksmith, the whole of the real estate of McIntyre,—land, store and residence, for three pounds sterling. This was in 1838.

The third was James Campbell. He built one or two vessels on the beach.

The fourth was Francis Kelley. He built some vessels,—there were seven in all built at Grand Narrows.

The fifth was Darby McDonald.

The sixth were the McGillivarys, Joseph, Hugh and Augustine, brothers of Rev. Alexander McGillivray, who was parish priest here.

The seventh was Hector McKinnon, "Spike," a brother-in-law of "John the Hill."

The eighth were Dougald and Stephen McPherson. The latter was known as "Stephen Mor."

The nineth was William Murray, a Lowland Scotchman, and a Presbyterian in religion. He came here from Halifax. His wife was a native of Pictou, and her Christian name was Jane. They had a family: William Hardy, Robert, George H., Frederick and two daughters who died in childhood. When each of the girls died, many of the people of Grand Narrows went in the funeral procession to the Presbyterian cemetry at Sydney Mines and Mr. Murray and his wife appreciated highly the kindness of their Catholic neighbours. Their son Robert is the chief Physician of Mt. Hope Asylum, Halifax.

George H. was born at Grand Narrows in 1861. He studied Law; and soon after his admission to the Bar, he went into politics. He fought many hard campaigns, federal and provincial, in this County. The great fight he put up against Sir Charles Tupper, "the War Horse of Cumberland," in the by-election campaign of 1896, earned for Mr. Murray a Dominion-wide reputation. When Hon. Mr. Fielding resigned the Premiership to become Minister of Finance in the Cabinet of Sir Wilfred Laurier in 1896, Hon. George H. Murray became Premier and Provincial Secretary of this Province, and he held the position for twenty-six years, a record unequalled by that of any other statesman under the British Crown. So Grand Narrows may well be proud of the honour of being the birth-place of Hon. G. H. Murray.

The Murrays moved to Sydney Mines in 1869.

The next merchant at Grand Narrows was Rory McNeil, son of Michael McNeil, Blacksmith. He was married to Josephine, daughter of Norman McNeil (Malcolm), Arichat. After the death of her husband, Mrs. McNeil and her brother, Edward A. McNeil, continued the business until it was taken over by the firm of McDougall and MacNeil. The members of this firm were the late H. F. McDougall, M. P., and Edward A. McNeil.

In 1888 the firm of McNeil Bros. commenced business at Grand Narrows. Messrs. John C. and Rory McNeil are the members of this firm; and it appears that Fortune has favoured them better than it did the majority of their predecessors because they have been able, so far, to steer clear of the shoals and reefs of bankruptcy.

Appendix 4

Photocopy of 1830 Washabuck School register. Courtesy of Nova Scotia Archives, Halifax.

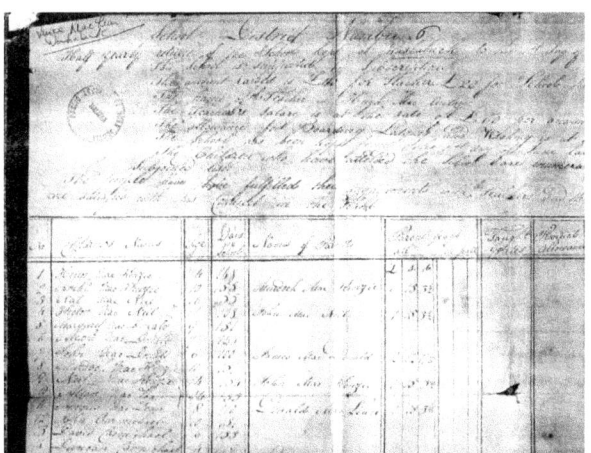

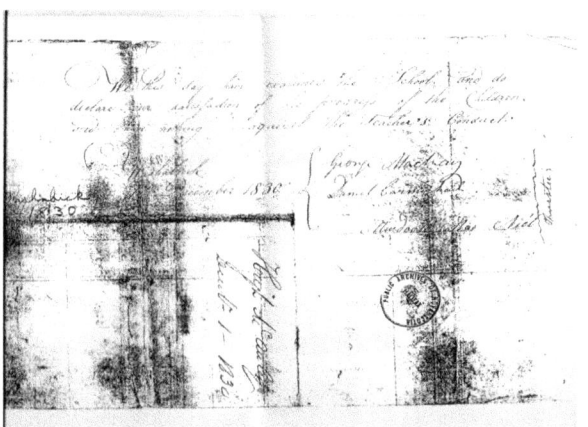
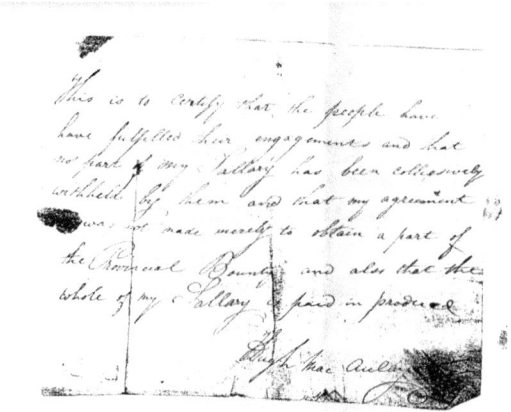

Appendix 5

Remnants of MacKenzie's School Register, Section 94, 1898, north side Washabuck River. Courtesy of Roslyn MacRae, Baddeck.

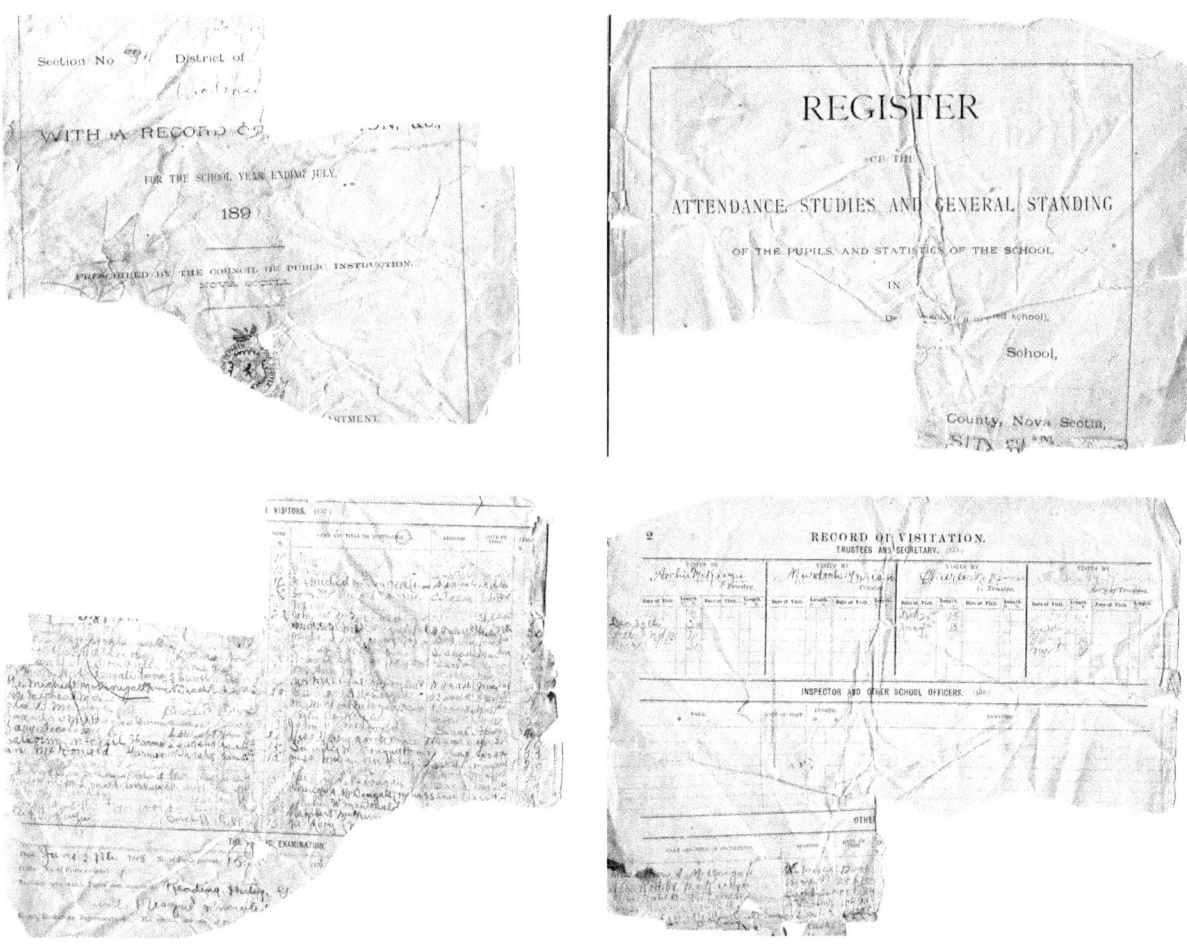

Appendix 6

Collector's Roll for St. Columba School Section # 19, 1924-25, 1928-29 and 1929-30. Courtesy of Jean MacNeil, Sydney Mines, CB.

Appendix 7

Transcription of Cape Breton Baptismal Records (Washabuck)
From records of Belfast Church, PEI:

Baptisms by Rev. John McLennan, Belfast PEI. Baptism Records; Wagamadkook, 25, Sept. 1827:

McFarlane, Alex, son of Donald McFarlane and Christy McLeod, Washbug, 27, April, 1827

McRitchie, Anne, dau. of Murdo McRitchie and Ann Morison, Washpug [sic] 28, Feb. 1827

Washabuck children baptised at Little Brodick (Baddeck) on 28 August, 1829:

28 August, 1829: Matheson, Elizabeth, dau. of William Matheson and Ann McLeod, Washbug [sic] b. 25 December, 1824

McDonald, Christy, dau. of Malcolm McDonald and Christy McDonald, Washbug, b. 15 June, 1828

McInnes, Elizabeth, dau. of Donald McInnes and Mary –Iver, Washbug, b.12 February, 1827

McRitchie, Catherine, dau. of Murdock McRitchie and Henrietta Morison, dau. b. 10 Feb. 1829 Washbug

McInnes, Angus, son of Malcolm McInnes and Janet McAulay, Washbug, b. 20 May, 1827

McInnes, Duncan, son of Malcolm McInnes and Janet McAulay, Washbug, b. 8 May, 1829

Then on the following day, 29, August, 1829, same location:

McKay, Dougald, M. son of George McKay and Mary Gray, Brodick Point, (maybe MacKay's Point) b.18, Feb. 1828

Then on the next day 30 August,1829 at Wagamadcook (Middle River):

Carmichael, Flora, dau. of Daniel Carmichael and Sarah Ross, Washbug, b.21 March, 1828

McDonald, James, son of Norman McDonald and Barbara Robertson, Washbug, b. 15 Sept. 1828

McDonald, John, son of John McDonald and Marion McRitchie, Washbug, b. 15 Sept. 1828

McIver, Angus, son of John McIver and Annie McInnis, Washbug, b. 3 August, 1828

McDonald, Donald, son of Angus McDonald and Ann Smith, Washbug, b.22 April, 1829

Baptisms by Rev. John McLennan, Belfast P.E.I. Baptism Records; Little Bradeck on the 17, Sept. 1831:

Carmichael, Catherine, dau. of David [*sic*] Carmichael and Sarah Ross, Washbug, 26, March 1831

McIver, Hester, dau. of Colin McIver and Margaret [Hayden], 24 Dec. 1826

McIver, Christin, dau. of Colin McIver and Margaret [Hayden], Washbug, 1, Mar. 1829

McIver, George, son of Colin McIver and Margaret [Hayden], Washbug, 31, Aug. 1831

Munro, Mary Gray, dau. of William Munro and Marg McIver, Washbug, 2, Feb. 1828

Special thanks to Jim St. Clair of Mull River, Inverness for a copy of this transcription.

Appendix 8

Resident's petition for a wharf at MacKay Wharf, February 13, 1882. Courtesy of Public Archives of Nova Scotia.

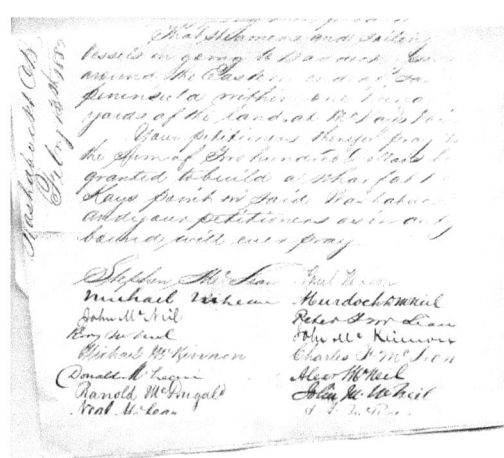
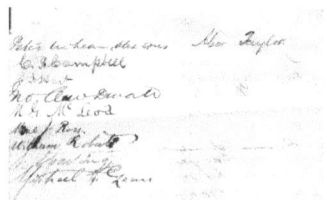

Appendix 9

Listing of Yachts names as outlined in National Geographic article.

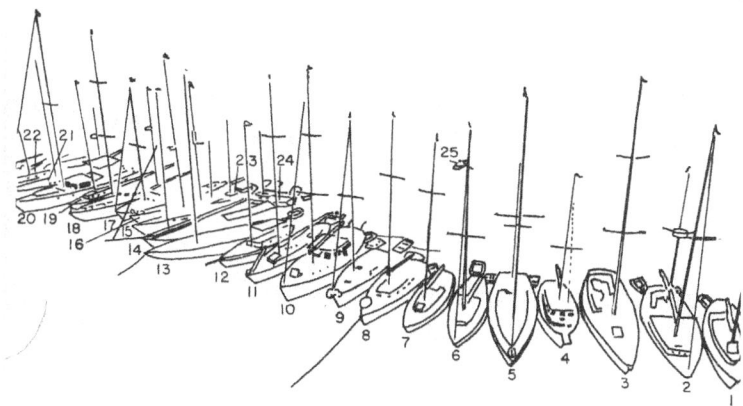

ARE WE A CRUISING CLUB?
(Photo by Diana Russell from *Windigo*'s 80 foot mast)

24 of the forty boats attending the July 18th 1975 Rendezvous of the CCA in the Washabuckt River, Bras D'Or Lakes, Cape Breton Island, Nova Scotia from the main raft around Bras D'Or Post Captain's host boat *Direction* flanked by honored vessel *Elsie*, *Silver Heels*, belonging to Cruise Chairman Jonsey, Vice Commodore's *Hokulele* and Mel Grosvener's *White Mist*. It was a memorable event with most boats cruising at least a thousand miles of foggy coastline to get there. Boats identified by number as follows:

1. *Eggemoggin* Ben Emery, Judy and Kristen Emery
2. *Baroda* Stu and Betty-Anne Caldera, Tom Hume, Betty Snaith
3. *Gesture II* Jim and Pauline Madden, Anne and Michael Madden, Andy and Peggy Marshal, Al and Susie Size
4. *Nimrod* Bob and Rhoda Hall, Lee and Audrey Geyer, and Tom Smith, Jr.
5. *Loch Naw* Bennett and Elsie Fisher, Chick and Harriett Whittelsey, Aubrey and Jo Whittemore, Sandy Kellog
6. *Malay* Dan and Marion Strohmeier
7. *Yuan Lin* (Guest Boat) Harry and Mary Harper
8. *Decibel* (Guest Boat) Bob and Ann Watson, Teeny Lemmerman
9. *Laughing Gull* (Guest Boat) Harry and Joan Sullivan
10. *Avelinda* Tom and Virginia Cabot, Bob and Barbara Livermore, Sander Black
11. *White Mist* Mel and Anne Grosvenor
12. *Direction* Carl and Margaret Vilas, Perry and Trudy Curtiss, Hank and Betty Meneely
13. *Elsie* Carol Grosvener Myers, Paul and Carol Sheldon, Lilo and Barbara Muller, Sandy and Elva Fairchild
14. *Silver Heels* Jonsey and Betsy Jones, Foxy and Liz Fox, Nancy and Doug MacLeod
15. *Hokulele* Stan and Martie Livingston, Laurie & Anne Wallace
16. *The Hawk* Peter and Charlotte Comstock, Dan and Julia Bickford
17. *Sirius* Hank and Nancy Boschen, George and Kay Hinman
18. *Auk V* Charlie and Bee Adams, Nat and Janice Goodhue and Alison Robinson
19. *Conquest* Avery and Jean Seaman
20. *Tioga* Brad and Gail Noyes
21. *Night Heron* Press and Sarah Huntington, Douglas and Sally Fletcher, Sigourney and Jean Romaine
22. *H.M.S. Day* Bob and Teta Gunther
23. *Nima* Jack Parker (Official organizer of the raft)
24. Under charter, Alan and Chapie Bemis
25. Dinghy (From *Direction*) Perry Curtiss

Appendix 10

List of Silver Dart Witnesses, Courtesy of Parks Canada/Alexander Graham Bell National Historic Site, Baddeck, NS.

Bulletin No. XXXV   18

WITNESSES OF McCURDY'S FIRST FLIGHT IN THE SILVER-DART ON BADDECK BAY, FEB. 23, 1909.

(Compiled by Mr. Alec. MacDonald).

Surname	Title	Given Name	Surname	Title	Given Name
Anderson	Miss	Annie	Hart	Mr	Joseph
Anderson	Miss	Emeline	Hutchinson	Mr	Dan
Archibald	Mr	John			
Arsenault	Miss	Esther	Ingraham	Mr	K
Arsenault	Mr	John	Ingraham	Mrs	K
			Insddor	Mr	George
Bedwin	Mr	Wm F	Irving	Mr	J A
Bell	Dr	A Graham			
Bell	Mrs	A Graham	Kidston	Miss	Jennie
Bell	Mr	Gardiner H	Keily	Mr	John
Benner	Mr	H M	Keily	Miss	Sarah
Bethune	Mrs	John L			
Bethune	Mr	Gordon	McAskill	Mr	E G
Bethune	Mr	Norman	McAskill	Mrs	E G
Bingay	Mr	A	McAskill	Miss	Marguerite
Blanchard	Mr	H P	McAulay	Mr	D W
Bowers	Mr	Willie	McAulay	Mr	Farquhar
Burke	Mr	Sanford	McAulay	Mr	Ian
Byrnes	Mr	Charles	McAulay	Mr	Murdock
Byrnes	Mrs	Charles	McAulay	Mr	Peter
Byrnes	Mr	Tom	McCurdy	Mr	J A D
			McCurdy	Miss	Mabel B
Cadell	Miss	Inez	McDermid	Mr	John
Campbell	Mr	Bert	McDermid	Mr	Neil
Campbell	Mr	Dan	McDonald	Mr	Angus J
Campbell	Mr	John	McDonald	Mrs	Angus J
Campbell	Mr	John E	McDonald	Miss	Annie
Campbell	Miss	Lena	McDonald	Mr	A S
Campbell	Miss	Maggie	McDonald	Mr	Dan
Campbell	Mr	S C	McDonald	Mr	D M
Campbell	Miss	Susie	McDonald	Mr	Donald
Cox	Mr	Chas R	McDonald	Mr	Dougald
Crocker	Miss	Elizabeth	McDonald	Mr	Ian
Crocker	Miss	Nellie	McDonald	Mr	John
Crowdis	Miss	Frances	McDonald	Mr	Murdock
Crowdis	Miss	Louise	McDonald	Mr	R S
Crowdis	Mrs	M	McDonald	Miss	Ruth
Curtiss	Mr	G H	McDonald	Mr	S
Curtiss	Mrs	G H	McDonald	Miss	Sarah
			McDonald	Mr	Stanley
Davidson	Mr	John G	McFarlan	Mr	John
Dunlop	Mr	Graham	McFarlan	Mr	M
Dunlop	Mr	J G	McFarlan	Mr	P L
Dunlop	Mrs	J G	McIntosh	Rev	C C
			McIntosh	Mrs	C C
Ferguson	Mr	Angus	McIver	Dr	
Ferguson	Mr	Angus Jr	McIver	Mr	John
Ferguson	Mr	Murdock	McIver	Mrs	N A
Franks	Mr	Richard	McIver	Mr	Philip
Fraser	Mr	James	McKay	Mr	Edward
Fraser	Mrs	James	McKay	Mrs	Edward
Fraser	Mr	Douglas	McKay	Miss	Fanny
Fraser	Mr	Harry	McKay	Mr	Floyd

Bulletin No. XXXV   -2-

McKay	Mr	John		Oram	Mr	Charles
McKay	Mrs	K J				
McKay	Mr	Wilson		Ross	Mr	A
McKenzie	Mr	Charles		Rudderham	Mr	W E
McKenzie	Mr	John				
McKillop	Mr	A M		Smith	Mr	Duncan
McLean	Mr	J		Stewart	Mr	W
McLean	Mr	John		Sutherland	Mr	A H
McLean	Mrs	John				
McLean	Mr	M C		Taylor	Mr	Alex
McLean	Mr	Michael		Thompson	Mr	E A
McLean	Mr	R J				
McLean	Mr	Stephen		Watson	Mr	Bobby
McLean	Miss	Tena		Watson	Miss	Mary
McLennan	Mr	Fred		Watson	Mr	R
McLeod	Miss	Agnes				
McLeod	Mr	Daniel				
McLeod	Mr	James				
McLeod	Mr	John				
McLeod	Mrs	M				
McLeod	Mr	M G				
McLeod	Mr	Philip				
McLeod	Mr	William				
McNeil	Mr	Alex				
McNeil	Mr	Daniel				
McNeil	Mr	Hector P				
McNeil	Mr	John D				
McNeil	Mr	P B				
McPherson	Mr	Robert				
McRae	Mr	Alex				
McRae	Rev	D				
McRae	Mrs	D				
McRae	Mr	Kenzie				
Manuel	Mr	James				
Manuel	Mr	Rod				
Morrison	Mr	Dan				
Morrison	Mr	Dan J				

----------oOo----------

Notes

Notes to Introduction

1. Neil MacNeil, *The Highland Heart in Nova Scotia*, 50.
2. Ibid.
3. Copies of Francis Hector's two monographs were initially given to me (ca. 1969) by my cousin, Vincent J. MacLean, East Bay, who obtained them from amongst the estate papers of his grandfather, Jim Hughie MacNeil, who was originally from Grass Cove, CB.
4. Conversation with Hector MacKenzie, Washabuck Bridge, November 27, 2004.

Notes to Chapter 1

1. Ferguson, *Places of Nova Scotia*, 709; Brown, *Place-Names of the Province of Nova Scotia*, 150.

Notes to Chapter 2 – Early Residents, Visitors, Neighbours

1. Davis, *Mi'kmaq: Peoples of the Maritimes,* 6.
2. MacDonald, *Patterson's History of Victoria County,* 11.
3. MacLean, *A History of Victoria County,* 14-17. A two hundred page typewritten unpublished manuscript, ca.1973 from the author's private collection. These translations come from the hand of Catholic Missionary Father Pacifique of the Capuchin Order who had spent a lifetime among the Mi'kmaq on Cape Breton Island, studied their language and compiled a dictionary of their terms.
4. MacDonald, *Patterson's History*, 11; Davis, *Mi'kmaq*, 42.

5. Fergusson, *Uniacke's Sketches of Cape Breton and Other Papers Relating to Cape Breton Island,* 114.

6. Paul, *We Were Not the Savages,* 10. Paul quotes historical author Marion Robertson who in her book *Red Earth: Tales of the Micmac, with an introduction to their customs and beliefs,* cites in turn the author Roth in *Acadia and the Acadians.*

7. Morgan, Early *Cape Breton: From Founding to Famine,* 83.

8. MacNeil, *Iona's first Settlers. A* four page handwritten paper outlining the story of Iona's first settlers and their encounter with the Mi'kmaq ca.1950. From the author's collection. MacNeil was a noted genealogist and a great-grandson of Donald MacNeil one of those first four MacNeils who settled Iona. As to the number of canoes in the flotilla, the numbers vary from twenty-two to eighty.

9. Morgan, *Early Cape Breton,* 29.

10. Paul, W*e Were Not the Savages.* This book is refreshing, in-depth account of Mi'kmaq history in Atlantic Canada, vividly described from the perspective of the Mi'kmaq.

11. Davis, *Mi'kmaq: Peoples Of The Maritimes,* 32.

12. Elmsley, Unpublished Diary and Historical Papers, 2.

13. Lamb, *The Hidden Heritage,* 80.

14. Ibid., 11.

15. MacDonald, *Patterson's History of Victoria County,* 12.

16. Fergusson, *Uniacke's Sketches of Cape Breton,107.*

17. Erskine, "The Archaeology of Some Nova Scotia Indian Campsites, 6-9.

18. MacLean, *A History of Victoria County,* 18.

19. MacLean, *Pioneers of Washabuckt*, 66.

20. Fergusson, *Uniacke's Sketches of Cape Breton,* 110

21. Davis, *Mi'kmaq: Peoples Of The Maritimes,* 32

22. Lamb, *The Hidden Heritage,* 80

23. Mackenzie, *The Charm of Cape Breton Island,* National Geographic, 34.

24. Lamb, *The Hidden Heritage,* 10.

25. Ibid., 15.

26. Johnston, *Storied Shores,* 33.

27. Ibid., 40.

28. Newman, *Hudson Bay USA*, F4.

29. Ryan et al, *Along The Shores of Boularderie,* 5-6.

30. Conversations between Elizabeth MacLean (1868-1961) and her nephew Michael A. MacLean, (1911-2007) Washabuck, N.S. ca. 1960.

31. Morgan, *Speech delivered to the Iona-Grand Narrows Board of Trade,* 1-2.

32. Ibid., 1-2

33. Jim Campbell, Archaeology Collection Supervisor, Fortress Louisbourg, Louisbourg, N.S. *Correspondence with Wanda MacDougall,* Washabuck resident, September 22, 1994.

34. Morgan, *Early Cape Breton, 31-37.*

35. MacDonald, *Patterson's History of Victoria County*, 48.
36. PANS, RG 20 Series B, C. B. #1006 Sydney, 11 October 1811.
37. PANS, RG 20, Series A, 1811.

Notes to Chapter 3 – The Gaels

1. MacLean, *Early Days in Lower Washabuck*, 4.
2. Conversations with *Mairi Ceit* MacKinnon, Barra, and Barra genealogist Calum MacNeil.
3. Campey, *After The Hector* 247- 248
4. MacLean, *The Pioneers of Washabuckt*, 1.
5. Murphy, *The Story of Pioneers and Progress in Our Community*, 2.
6. MacLean, *The Pioneers of Washabuckt*, 1, 61. Simon Fraser was known as an immigration agent but maybe he doubled as a ship's Captain.
7. MacLean, *The Pioneers of Washabuckt*, 1, 61.
8. Hunter, *Scottish Record Office*, Edinburgh, Scotland, November 25, 1982, correspondence with author.
9. Harvey, 33-34.
10. MacLean, *Comments on Early Days*.
11. Hart, *History of Northeast Margaree*, 136.
12. Angus Eoin MacNeil's land grant and survey sketch is found in CB Bk.1, No. 23A, 1834.
13. MacLean, *Comments on Early Days*, Letter to the editor, The Casket, October 31, 1939.
14. Szick, *Ross Families of Margaree Cape Breton*, 19, 35.
15. MacLean, *Early Days in Lower Washabuck*, 4.
16. MacLean, Pioneers of Washabuckt, 44.
17. MacLean,. *Comments on Early Days*, The Casket, October 31, 1939.
18. MacLean, *The Pioneers of Washabuckt*, 44.
19. Ibid., 45.
20. Ibid., 45.
21. Ibid., 45.
22. MacLean, *Pioneers of Washabuckt*, 61.
23. MacDonald, *Patterson's History of Victoria County*, 60.
24. Conversation with Archie MacIver, Baddeck, March 15, 1983.
25. Ibid.,1983.
26. Frances MacDougall, in *Settlement and Development of Our District*, has Carmichael arriving in 1821, p 8.
27. Murphy, *The Story of Pioneers and Progress In Our Community*, 2.
28. MacKenzie, *History of Christmas Island Parish*, 51.
29. Ibid., 54.
30. Patterson, *History of the County of Pictou*, 80-81.

31. MacKenzie, *History of Christmas Island Parish*, 55.

32. MacNeil, Francis Hector. A type-written foolscap memo outlining this information.

33. MacLean, *Pioneers of Washabuckt*, 62.

34. Interview with S. R. MacNeil, Barra Glen.

35. Ibid., 63. There exists a possibility that William had a family "away" from a previous marriage.

36. Conversations with Carmie MacLean, Washabuck Centre, January 31, 2013; Angus (Angus Ranald) MacDonald Upper Washabuck, during the 1990s.

37. William Matheson is described as a resident of Washabuck in the 1818 census.

38. MacNeil, *All Call Iona Home*, 271.

39. Ibid., 63.

40. Telephone conversation with genealogist Bernie Jessome, New Waterford October 31, 2005. Anna Murphy mentions Daniel MacLean in *The Story of Pioneers and Progress in Our Community*.

41. Lawson, *The MacRitchies, Am Bràighe*, Autumn Edition, 1995.

42. Conversation with Mary and Clarence Roberts, Baddeck, May 23, 2012.

43. Ibid.

44. Conversation with Archie MacIver, Baddeck, March 15, 1983.

45. MacNeil, *The MacDonald's of Saint Columba and Washabuck*, 1. A similar story was related to the author by Jimmy Caluman MacNeil from St. Columba on November 18, 2001. In 1935, Frances MacDougall tells a similar version in her *Settlement and Development of Our District* project.

46. Conversation with Rod C. MacNeil, Barra Glen, December 19, 2012. Allan Austin MacNeil then of Gillis Point, in conversation with Rod C., did not know the names of these families.

47. MacDougall, *Settlement and Development of Our District*, 2.

48. Conversation with Rod C. MacNeil, Barra Glen, December 19, 2012.

49. Conversation with Donnie MacKinnon, Upper Washabuck, April 4, 2013.

50. Conversation with Mickey John H. MacNeil, Maxie MacNeil and Rod C. MacNeil, January 19, 2013.

51. Conversation with MacLean, Ibid, 63.

52. PANS *Cape Breton Land Grant Records*, 1816.

Notes to Chapter 4 – Surveyors, Land Grants and Early Land Owners

1. Morgan, *Early Cape Breton*, 50.

2. Ibid., 51.

3. Ibid.

4. Harvey, *Scottish Immigration to Cape Breton Island*, 34.

5. Ibid., 38-39.

6. Ibid., 39.

7. Ibid., 39.

8. McPherson, *Watchman Against the World*, 24.

9. Nova Scotia Archives & Management, *Land Petitions*.

10. Bain, History of Baddeck, 9.

11. Ibid., 9.

12. This original "Ticket of Location" is in possession of the author. It was given to him in 2002 by Lily MacIvor of Sydney, N.S. a great-great-granddaughter of the pioneer and progenitor, Lachlan MacLean.

13. Book P, Page 102, Sydney, 1832.

14. PANS, Jonathan Jones, 1811.

15. PANS, Holland's Description of Cape Breton Appendix B, *1818 Census Rolls Cape Breton Island*, .

16. PANS, Bruce Fergusson, *Place Names*, 709.

17. Morgan, *List of Cape Breton Loyalists*, 26.

18. PANS, Cape Breton Land Papers.

19. PANS, Return of Survey, 1825.

20. MacLean, *Comments on Early Days*, The Casket, October, 1939.

21. Family lore as recollected by some of Alastair *Glas's* great grandchildren.

22. Conversation with Roddie J. MacDonald, November, 2011.

23. MacLean, *Pioneers of Washabuckt*, 70.

24. Return of Surveys as indicated.

25. Copy of Deed transfer, *Victoria County Land Deed Archives*, Baddeck, Courtesy of Ann Marie MacNeil, Grass Cove.

26. Ibid.

27. PANS and *Return of Survey File # 3627 and # 12582*.

28. MacLean, *The Pioneers of Washabuckt*, 61.

29. The information about A. F. Church is gleaned from an article included in the 50th edition of *Cape Breton's Magazine,* entitled, *A. F. Church and His County Maps.* The author of that article had received permission from the widow of the late Provincial Archivist, C. Bruce Fergusson, a native of Port Morien, who had researched and presented the information about Mr. Church in several other venues.

30. Caplan, *Cape Breton's Magazine*, 78-82.

31. Fletcher, *Geological Survey of Canada,* 405.

32. Ibid., 406-407.

33. O'Reilly, *From the Mineral Inventory Files, Three Graves in Margaree*, 4. Thanks to DNR surveyor Simon Aucoin, Belle Cote, for advising the author about the Margaree gravesite.

34. Ibid., 4.

35. Ibid., 4.

Notes to Chapter 5 – Stores, Merchants, Shopping

1. Elmsley, *Cape Breton's Magazine*, 27.

2. MacLean, *Cape Breton's Magazine*, 30.

3. MacLean, *The Pioneers of Washabuckt*, 35-37.

4. MacKenzie, History of Christmas Island Parish, 144-145.

5. *A Search For Yesterday*, 1.

6. MacDonald, *Patterson's History of Victoria County*, 68-71.

7. *A Search For Yesterday*, 1.

8. MacDonald, *Patterson's History of Victoria County*, 71.

9. *Elmsley's Diary*, 1-3.

10. Ibid., 1-3.

11. MacLean, *History of Victoria County*, 55.

12. MacLean, *Early Days in Lower Washabuckt*, 15.

13. PANS, *Return of Survey Petition # 23278*, in favour of Arthur McCurdy for an Island in the District of McKay's Point, County of Victoria, October 10, 1904.

14. MacLean, *The Pioneers of Washabuckt*, 41. A similar recounting of the tale is included by Captain John P. Parker author of *Cape Breton Ships and Men, (*Hazel Watson & Viney Ltd, Aylesbury, Buckinghamshire, 1967, p. 92) and a Gaelic version of the same story is by Calum Iain M. MacLeoid, in Saialachdan a Albainn Nuaidh, GAIRM, Glaschu, 1969, 77.

15. Conversation with Hector MacKenzie, Washabuck Bridge, ca. 2010.

16. Conversation with Michael A. MacLean, MacKay Point, December, 22, 2001.

17. Conversation with Lucille MacKenzie, Gillis Point, 2011.

18. Information shared with the author by Frances MacDougall, Mabou, from notes from her father's diary.

19. Conversation with Hector MacKenzie, Washabuck Bridge, November 6, 2000.

20. Conversation with Michael A. MacLean, MacKay Point, December 22, 2001

21. Story related by John Dan MacRitchie while visiting with Michael A. MacLean, MacKay Point who in turn related it to this writer January 28, 2002.

22. Information shared with writer by Frances MacDougall, Mabou, from notes from her father's Diary.

23. Conversation with Michael A. MacLean, MacKay Point, December 22, 2001.

24. *Victoria-Inverness Bulletin*, 1963.

25. Washabuck Co-Op Ledger, 1942.

26. *Victoria-Inverness Bulletin*, no d-ate.

27. Joseph MacLean, Calgary, Marjorie's nephew in an *email* to his sister Carmie, Washabuck Centre, April 1, 2008.

28. Ibid

29. Conversation with Marjorie MacLean, c. 1978

30. These stories related by Michael A. MacLean, MacKay Point over a period of years.

Notes to Chapter 6 – Education

1. MacLean, Early Days in Lower Washabuckt, 15,16.

2. Hart, The History of Northeast Margaree, 19.

3. Murphy, The Story of Pioneers and Progress in Our Community, 9-10.

4. MacLean, Comments on Early Days, The Casket.

5. PANS School District # 6, Washabuck, R 614, Vol. 59, # 117

6. MacLean, Comments, *The Casket*.

7. MacLean, Early Days in Lower Washabuck, 8.

8. Ibid., 8-9.

9. The listing of these nine teachers was provided by Marjorie MacLean, Washabuck Centre, October 24,1983.

10. Cassie MacInnis was paid $90 for the year (10 Months). From Jessie MacKinnon, Cassie's niece, Little Narrows, January 13, 2013.

11. Conversation with Madeline Norton, Little Narrows, November 15, 1997.

12. Conversation with Bea (Peter F.) MacLean, Iona, March 18, 2002

13. Conversation with Annabelle MacAskill, Baddeck, December 19,1983

14. Conversation with Joe (Red Rory) MacLean, Lower Washabuck.

15. Ibid.

16. Conversation with Michael A. MacLean, MacKay Point, January 20, 1992.

17. MacNeil, S. R., Taped conversation with author, May 11, 1979.

18. MacDougall, Settlement and Development of Our District, 8.

19. Conversation with Mary Ann MacKenzie, Washabuck Bridge, April 11, 1982. This may have been the same second schoolhouse, as was built on the neighbouring Rory MacDonald property.

20. Ibid., April 11, 1982.

21. MacNeil, The Highland Heart in Nova Scotia, 97.

22. Kaye MacDonald was 17 years old. She had gone to Truro for summer teacher's training. She left for Boston after teaching that year.

23. Conversation with Mary Ann MacKenzie, April 11, 1982.

24. This information is taken from the front page and page two of the MacKenzie's School registrar, Section 94, Victoria County, N.S. for the school year ending June 27th 1898. The document was given to the writer by Roslyn (Lighthouse) MacRae, Baddeck,1999.

25. MacDougall, Settlement and Development of Our District, 5-6.

26. Conversation with Jimmy Caluman MacNeil, St. Columba, January 11, 1999

27. Conversation with S.R. MacNeil, May 11, 1979.

28. Ibid.,

29. Conversation with Jimmy Caluman MacNeil, January 11, 1999.

30. Conversation with Rod C. MacNeil, Barra Glen, March 28, 2010.

31. Conversation with Hugh Campbell, St. Columba, April 1, 1984

32. Conversation with Jimmy Caluman MacNeil, January 11, 1999.

33. Conversation with Joan (MacKenzie) Gillis, Jamesville, January, 2007.

34. Information gleaned from notes by Charlene Cossick, Nova Scotia Highland Village Museum, Artifacts Curator, in collaboration with Sarah Margaret (Campbell) Bonvie, Tracadie, Antigonish County, NS.

35. Hector MacKenzie, Washabuck Bridge, February 19, 1984.

36. A list of St. Columba students found in teacher Sarah Margaret Campbell's note book: Mary Helen MacKenzie, Hughie J. Campbell, Angus J. Campbell, Annie C. MacKenzie, Theresa MacDougall, Charlie A. MacKenzie, Johnena MacKenzie, Malcolm G. MacIver, Cathleen A. MacIver, Dan H. MacDougall:

37. Conversation with Charlotte (MacKenzie) MacLean, December 2006.

38. Documents given to author by Jean MacNeil, Sydney Mines.

39. Conversation with Lawrence MacDougall, Oromocto, N. B. and Washabuck, October 29, 2006.

40. McCarthy, Iona Federated High School 1920-1945, Commemorative Booklet, 2.

41. Ibid., 2.

42. MacKenzie, Iona Federated High School 1920 -1945, Commemorative Booklet, 12.

43. Conversation with Clare MacDonald, Lower Washabuck, December 2006.

44. Conversation with Mary E. (Alfred) MacDonald, Baddeck, December, 2006.

45. Conversation with Peter and Pat (Malcolm Dan) MacNeil, Halifax, March 1, 2005.

46. Conversation with Roderick MacNeil, Gillis Point, December 6, 2003.

47. Conversation with Peter and Mary (Malcolm Dan) MacNeil, Halifax, March 1, 2005.

48. This same story was related by Andy, Iona, and Buddy, Toronto, on separated occasions, during the year 2004.

49. Conversation with Nancy MacLean, Baddeck, 2007.

50. Conversation with Buddy MacDonald, Toronto, April, 2007.

51. Conversation with Charlotte MacLean, MacKay Point , April, 2007.

52. Conversation with Buddy MacDonald, Toronto, April, 2007.

53. Conversation with Roderick MacNeil, Gillis Point, December 6, 2003.

54. Ibid.,

55. Conversation with Quentin MacDonald, Washabuck, December 13, 2009.

56. MacLean, Early Days in Lower Washabuck, 9.

57. MacNeil, he Highland Heart in Nova Scotia, 100-101.

58. S. R. MacNeil, taped conversation with author, Barra Glen, May, 11, 1979.

59. MacLean, The Passing of The Schoolmaster - An Appreciation, Personal Diary.

60. MacNeil, S. R. Taped conversation with author, Barra Glen, July 11, 1989.

61. MacLean, History of Victoria County, 55. Historian, John Campbell writing in the Cape Breton Post, April 26.1997, p-6A, claims the crossing date was October18, 1890. This was a maiden run from Pt. Tupper to Sydney.

62. McCarthy, Times of My Life, 87. McCarthy retired as principal in 1966 after spending 38 years at the institution. He had begun his first year of teaching in Iona at the province's first federated rural high school.

63. Ibid., 115.

64. Ibid., 88.

65. Ibid., 88.

Notes to Chapter 7 – Religion

1. Stanley, *The Well-Watered Garden*, 188.

2. Ibid., 195.

3. Ibid., 177.

4. MacMillan, *Memoirs of a Cape Breton Doctor*, Preface vii.

5. Stanley, IX.

6. Ibid., X.

7. Ibid., X.

8. MacKinnon, *The History of the Presbyterian Church in Cape* Breton, 148.

9. Hart, 48.

10. Stanley, 59.

11. MacKinnon, 148.

12. Ibid., 149.

13. Ibid., 150.

14. Ibid., 150.

15. MacKinnon, 127.

16. Ibid., 127.

17. Ibid., 21.

18. *Belfast Church Baptismal Records, PEI,* Transcribed records by Jim St. Clair, Mull River, Nova Scotia, Copy shared with the author.

19. MacKinnon, 102.

20. Stanley, 134.

21. Ibid., 133.

22. Ibid., 134.

23. Ibid., 126.

24. Ibid.

25. Ibid., 145.

26. MacKinnon, 149.

27. Stanley, 134, as quoted in *Genesis of Churches* by J. Croil, Foster and Brown & Co. Montreal, 1907

28. Ibid., 129.

29. Warner, *Baddeck, and that Sort of Thing*, 126.

30. MacMillan, *Memoirs of a Cape Breton Doctor*, Preface vii.

31. Stanley, 200. As quoted from *The Home and Foreign Missionary Record of the Free Church of Scotland*, (May, 1852), pp. 347-349

32. MacKinnon, 106.

33. Conversation with Walter and Eileen Matheson, Little Narrows, March 13, 2012.

34. Stanley, 181.

35. Stanley, 78, 181, 122.

36. MacKinnon, 151.

37. PANS, *Place-Names Nova Scotia*, with Introduction by C. Bruce Fergusson, 361. Mention is made in this volume that in the settlement of Little Narrows with a population of 146 "A Presbyterian Church was built here in 1856."

38. MacKinnon, 106.

39. Conversation with Walter Matheson, March 13, 2012.

40. Conversation with Clarence and Mary Roberts, Baddeck, May 23, 2012.

41. MacKinnon, 174.

42. Correspondence with Rev. Colin MacIver, St. Andrews, Manitoba; email with biographical data, August 5, 2012.

43. Mary Catherine MacDonald (1919-2009), Upper Washabuck, November 7, 2002.

44. MacNeil, *Highland Heart in Nova Scotia*, 75.

45. Conversation with Marie MacDonald, Upper Washabuck, April 29, 2010.

46. The Casket, *Pioneer Narrative,* Vol. 3 80, Issue # 46, May 5, 1938, 3; Passing mention is also mentioned by Gordon Brinkley in *Away to Cape Breton*, Dodd, Mead & Company, New York, 1940, 161

47. Nicholson et al, *Middle River: Past and Present,* 34,

48. Conversation with Joe (Red Rory) MacLean, Lower Washabuck, ca. 1990s.

49. Conversation with A. MacLean, MacKay Point, December, 13, 2006.

50. These comments by John A. Macdougall appeared in the book *Souvenir of a Centenary* in 1915 by Father Roderick MacKenzie. A portion of these comments are quoted in the historical sketch, *The History of Christmas Island Parish* by Archibald J. MacKenzie, 1926, 7.

51. MacLean, *The Pioneers of Washabuckt*, 39.

52. Johnston, *A History of the Catholic Church in Eastern Nova Scotia*, 304.

53. Ibid., 392.

54. MacLean, The Casket, Antigonish, December 22, 1938.

55. Johnston, 402.

56. Roddie C. MacNeil et al, *The Story of St. Columba Parish*, 8.

57. Stanley, *The Well-Watered Garden*, 31.

58. MacLean, *The Pioneers of Washabuckt*, 21.

59. Murphy, *The Story of Pioneers and Progress in Our Community*, 9.

60. MacLean, The *Casket,* December 22, 1938.

61. Johnston, Volume 2, 456.

62. MacLean, *Comments on Early Days*, The Casket, October 31, 1939.

63. Johnston, A. A., Volume 2, 523.

64. MacLean, *Early Days in Lower Washabuck*, 7.

65. MacLean, *Comments on Early Days*, The Casket, October 31, 1939.

66. MacLean. *Early Days in Lower Washabuck*, 7.

67. MacLean, . *Comments*.

68. *The Victoria News*, Baddeck, June 9, 1909.

69. The cost of the refurbishing was borne by Baddeck descendants of the Rory Ranald family, ca. 2008.

70. MacLean, The *Casket*, Antigonish, December 22, 1938, 8.

71. MacNeil, *The Story of St. Columba Parish*, Iona, 40.

72. MacLean, *Newspaper item from the Casket*, Antigonish, N. S., September, 1954.

73. The right-of-way was constructed by the provincial Department of Lands and Forests, with the Hon. Vincent J. MacLean, serving as Department Minister.

74. MacLean *The Pioneers of Washabuckt*, 8.

75. Ibid., 10-12.

76. Ibid., 14-15.

77. Lot A: The Catholic Episcopal Corporation of the Diocese of Antigonish, Book KK P- 498, 34, 239 Sq. Ft. Lot B: An addition to Lot A. Book 66, P-166, 24,057 Sq. Ft., Surveyed by Roddie J. MacDonald, Upper Washabuck, N.S. L. S., 1986.

78. Conversation with Mary C. MacDonald and Donnie MacKinnon, Upper Washabuck, ca. 2005.

79. Conversation with Roddie J. MacDonald, Upper Washabuck, January 31, 2008.

80. Conversation with Roddie J. MacDonald, Upper Washabuck, January 31, 2008.

81. MacLean, *Early Days in Lower Washabuckt*, 8.

82. Holy Rosary Ladies Society, *Society's Minutes*, Washabuck, (1956-1991).

83. Ibid.

84. Biographical information from *All Call Iona Home, History of Christmas Island Parish and Happenings*.

85. Biographical data from Sister of Charity Records, Rockingham, Halifax, N.S. and obituary in the Halifax Herald, January 8, 1943.

86. Correspondence from Lucy (MacNeil) Hayes, Montreal, November 1, 1982. Photo credit for these two Sisters is courtesy of Lucy Hayes, Montreal, and her nephew Neil MacNeil, Bethesda, Maryland. A newspaper obituary reports that Sister St. John passed away at the age of 74 and that she had served as Superioress in Whitney Pier, New Victoria, and New Glasgow. Her sister was referred to by the name, Sister St. Peter.

87. Biographical information from Cape Breton Post obituary and Rose MacDonald, Upper Washabuck.

88. Biographical information from Patricia Timmerman, Washabuck, March and May 16, 2012.

89. The Post Record, *Obituary*, Sydney, 1942.

90. MacNeil, *Barra MacNeil's of Nova Scotia*,19.

91. MacKenzie, Archibald J., *History of Christmas Island Parish*, 55-56.

92. MacLean, *Holy Rosary Church, Washabuck*, Casket, Antigonish, December 22, 1938, 8.

93. Ibid., 8.

94. Ibid., 9.

95. Conversation with John Rory and Betty MacNeil, Barra Glen, N. S. ca. 1979.

96. MacLean, *Happenings*, Washabuck, October, 1921.

97. Conversation with Hector MacKenzie, Washabuck Bridge and Michael A. MacLean, MacKay Point, various occasions.

98. Correspondence in possession of the author.

99. Conversation with Michael A. MacLean, MacKay Point and his sister Mary (Alfred) MacDonald, Baddeck, on several occasions.

100. Item carried in Casket, November 17, 1910.

101. *Obituary*, Rev. R. MacEachen, The New York Times, July 2, 1965; For in-depth details on this family the reader is referred to, *"Eoghan Dubh" A Pioneer's Family* by Stanley Beaton.

102. Stanley, *The Well-Watered Garden*, 30.

103. MacLean, *The Pioneers of Washabuckt*, 37. This story was related to Alex D. by Alexander "Sandy" MacLean, Georges River, a son of Paul and Ann MacLean, ca. 1937.

104. Ibid. 39.

105. MacLean, *The Pioneers of Washabuckt*, 43-44.

106. Rev. J. H. Gillis, PhD, of MacKinnon Harbour and St. F. X. University, March 13, 1993, personal correspondence with author.

Notes to Chapter 8 – Post Offices and Couriers

1. Sandra Devlin, *It's in the mail: looking at the history of postal service*, Cape Breton Post, January 21, 2005.

2. MacDonald, *The Nova Scotia Post: Its Offices, Masters and Marks*, 9.

3. Campbell, *Canada Postal History*, 1958, 141, PANS (He, 6185, C24D1, C35, 1958, c.3)

4. Ibid., 145. A Post Office Directory included within *Hutchinson's Nova Scotia Directory* by Thomas Hutchinson for 1864-65, Halifax N.S. (R.T. Muir, 125 Grandville Street) includes the listing for Washabuck, Inverness [sic] County with the forward Postal town of Plaster Cove (on page 493) and Washabetchett, Cape Breton County, with the forward Postal town of Sidney [sic].

5. Campbell, *Canada Postal History*, 142.

6. Jim St. Clair, *The Victoria Standard*, Baddeck, January 5th -18th, 2008, 8.

7. Elmsley, Robert, *Copy of Extract From Robert Elmsley's Diary*, P # 4.

8. Munden, *Post Offices of Cape Breton, Volume 3, Victoria County*, 2-4.

9. Clipping from the *Victoria-Inverness Bulletin, Iona Post Office Officially Opened by Allan MacEachen*, June 1, 1969.

10. Ibid.

11. Munden, Carl, 30.

12. Ibid., 39.

13. These dates do not correspond with the official ones from the archival files.

14. MacLean, *Early Days in Lower Washabuckt*, 10.

15. MacLean, Neil P. S., *Comment on Early Days*, Casket, October 31, 1939

16. Munden, *Post Offices of Cape Breton, Volume 3*, 50.

17. Munden, Carl, Foreword, V.

18. Munden, Carl, 48.

19. Conversation with Irene MacLean, Lower Washabuck Post Mistress, September 15, 1999.

20. Ibid.

21. MacLean, *Early Days in Lower Washabuckt*, 10

22. Conversation with Irene MacLean , Lower Washabuck, September 15, 1999.

23. Munden, Post Offices, 87- 88.

24. PANS, "An Act to change the name of a settlement in the County of Victoria; passed the 11th day of April AD, 1903; Section 1 Grand Narrows Rear to be known as St. Columba. Be it enacted by the Governor, Council and Assembly as follows: The settlement in the county of Victoria heretofore known as Grand Narrows Rear shall hereafter be known and designated as St. Columba." Ch. 102, 217

25. Munden, Post Offices, 31.

26. Ibid., 88.

27. Ibid., 88-89.

28. MacLean, Neil P.S., *Comments on Early Days*, Casket, October 31, 1939

29. MacLean, *Early Days in Lower Washabuckt*, 10-11.

30. MacLean, Neil P.S., *Comments on Early Days*, Casket, October 31, 1939.

31. St.Clair, Jim, *The Victoria Standard*, January 5th-18th, 2004, 8.

32. Part of a signed contract between Michael D. MacNeil, Iona, and the Postal Inspector's Halifax Office, 1926.

33. Ibid., 1950.

34. Conversation with Bea (Peter F.) MacLean, Iona, December 16, 1994.

35. Copies of contracts and photos provided by Anita MacNeil, Iona, granddaughter and daughter of the mail couriers, February 18, 2009.

36. Related by Roddie J. MacDonald, Upper Washabuck, June 9, 2012.

37. Conversation with Larry (Murdock) MacNeil, Little Narrows, December 4, 2011.

38. Hector MacKenzie, Washabuck Bridge, *Tribute*, May 14, 1971.

Notes to Chapter 9 – Shipbuilding

1. Elmsley, *Diary,* 188.

2. Parker, 179.

3. Ibid., 91. Anderson's nephew also drowned.

4. Elmsley, Diary, 155.

5. MacLean, *Early days in Lower Washabuckt*, 11-12.

6. Parker, 182.

7. Elmsley, 31.

8. Ibid., 32.

9. MacLean, *The Pioneers of Washabuckt*, 45.

10. Elmsley, 37.

11. MacLean, 46.

12. Archibald J. MacKenzie of Christmas Island writes in his *History of Christmas Island Parish*, that two additional men, lost their lives as well on this voyage. Their names were Alexander MacLean, a blacksmith, a son of Allan (*Leathaineach*) and Flora (MacDonald) MacLean [who may have lived in the area bordering St. Columba and Washabuck] and Neil MacKenzie a big able young man, a son of Archibald (*Gilleasbuig MacEachuinn*) and Catherine (MacKinnon) MacKenzie of Birch Point. However this information has never been confirmed. See Archibald J. MacKenzie, *History of Christmas Island Parish*, 1926, 51-52 and 68.

13. Sydney Post Record, *Lament for the Three Brothers*, May 24, 1939; also included in *The Pioneers of Washabuckt* by Alex D. MacLean, 46.

14. A conversation with Rod C. MacNeil, Barra Glen, October 26, 2003. Grateful acknowledgment is due to Jim Watson, Nova Scotia Highland Village, who assisted with some difficult parts of this translation plus his addition of the sixth verse, from his own recording of Mickey (*Ben Nellick*) MacNeil. Jim spent a lot of time locating the right recording and missing verse, but his persistence proved successful.

15. A secondary source was later located, *Sgealachdan a Albainn Nuaid,* by Calum Iain MacLeoid , GAIRM Glaschu 1969, 58-61, An Long "Alexander".

16. Parker, 189.

17. Correspondence with Captain John Parker, January 30, 1972.

18. Conversation with Jimmy MacKinnon, MacKinnon Harbour, January 27, 1985.

19. Elmsley, 166.

20A notation carried in an eight-sided Victoria County Centennial Brochure, Baddeck , N.S. 1851-1951 includes among the County's historical facts "...Ocean Lily (sic) launched on Washabuck River in 1885".

21. Conversation with Archie MacIver, Baddeck, March 15, 1983. No other details known. In Robert Elmsley's diary (page 39) for April 9, 1860, he notes '*Jessy*" returned from Nashabuck (sic). Fine Day." Could this have been the MacIver vessel? However, on page 188 he lists vessels "Built in and About Baddeck, Cape Breton" and includes "Jessie' [Owner] A. McAully, 1866". Elmsley also includes a vessel

called "Wasubuck' [sic] built between 1880 and 1883 and possibly owned by C. J. Campbell. No other information is given.

22. Murdock MacInnis, Washabuck Bridge, as related by Clarence Roberts; Baddeck, May 23, 2012.

Notes to Chapter 10 – Transportation

1. The underwater pilings of the Grass Cove wharf were removed under government tender in December 2012.

2. *Central Cape Breton Economic Development Study*, 1985.

3. Conversation with Joe (Red Rory) MacLean, Lower Washabuck, February 3, 1992.

4. Conversation with Michael A. MacLean, December 22, 2001.

5. Ibid.

6. Conversation with James MacDonald, Twining Street, Baddeck, December, 2001.

7. Conversation with Michael A. MacLean, December 22, 2001.

8. Conversation with Mary (Dan D.) MacNeil, Grass Cove, November 30, 1994.

9. Cape Breton Post, July 18th, 1957, 7. Provided by Sadie Marie MacNeil, Ottawa Brook.

10. Stephen McLean et al, *Public Archives of Nova Scotia*, Vol. 118, No. 20.

11. Report of the Committee of the Honourable the Privy Council, approved by the Governor General on the 21st December 1903.

12. Ibid,.

13. *Registry of Deeds*, County of Victoria, Baddeck. The deed was registered on February 15, 1904.

14. Brown, *Engineering Report* August 26, 1959.

15. Brown, correspondence January 3, 1964.

16. Brown, August 26, 1959.

17. Federal Crown Assets Disposal, January, 1971.

18. Conversation with MacLean, Michael A., January 29, 1992.

19. Conversation with MacLean, Michael A., March 26, 2002.

20. DPW Records August 1954.

21. Bright, *Memorandum*, November 13, 1969.

22. Michael Dan "Mickey" MacLean in conversation with Michael A. MacLean. Story related in turn by Michael A. MacLean, c.1986.

23. Victoria County Registry of Deeds, Baddeck.

24. MacLean, Neil P. S., *Comments on Early Days*, Casket, October 31, 1939.

25. Ibid.

26. MacLean, Neil P. S., *Happenings*, November 8, 1934.

27. Conversation with Michael D. MacLean, Baddeck, March 3, 1984.

28. Conversation with Rev. Hughie D. MacDonald, Creignish, Inverness County, January 20, 2009.

29. Conversation with MacLean, Michael Dan, March 3, 1984.

30. Bethune, *Historic Baddeck*, 44. Also see *Victoria Standard*, Baddeck, August 24-September 6, 2009.

31. Ibid., January 9-22, 9.

32. Rankin, *The Genealogical History of Victoria County*, The *Victoria -Inverness Bulletin*, 1.

33. There appears to be some discrepancy between the information in Father Rankin's writings above and those on the website. However, Philip MacNeil's middle initial was B. and not E. as listed on website lighthouse database. See www.lighthousedepot.com

34. MacLean, *History of Victoria County*. Data on lighthouses taken from Belcher's Almanac for 1919, 3-4.

35. *Mackinlay's Map of Nova Scotia*, 1862.

36. D. C. Harvey, *Description of Cape Breton and Other Documents*, Halifax, 70. This data researched by Henry H. Anderson, Newport Rhode Island, 1995. A.F. Church's *Topographical Map of Victoria* c.1877 shows Maskells Harbour as "Boulaceet'.

37. *Cruise Cape Breton*, 115.

38. Ibid., 218.

39. Scot & Mary Flanders, *Captain's Log, Voyage of the Egret*, Fort Lauderdale, Fla; August 17, 2011; www.nordhavn.com/egrat/captains_log_aug17.php Modified story from its original source, *Maskells Harbour, Cruising Guide To The Nova Scotia Coast*, Charles A. Westropp, Editor, 2012, 173.

40. Westropp, *Cruising Guide To The Nova Scotia Coast,* 173. Story related to "Cruising Guide" by Diana Russell, Ponys Point, Cape Breton Island.

41. Conversation with Gordon MacLean, Sugar Camp, Inverness County, N. S. April 16, 2010.

42. Holland's, 70.

43. Conversation with Joe (Red Rory) MacLean, Lower Washabuck, January 25, 1984.

44. Vilas, "Sails Backstop Mechanics on Washabuckt's Only Ferry." *National Fisherman* January, 1969.

45. Conversation with Joe (Red Rory) MacLean. Joe had seen the remnants of the beached scow as a kid.

46. Conversation with MacLean, Joe (Red Rory), January 25, 1984.

47. Ibid.

48. Conversation with Archie A. MacLean, Lower Washabuck, December 4, 2003.

49. Conversation with MacLean, Joe (Red Rory), Lower Washabuck, January 25, 1984.

50. Conversations with Joseph Neil and Jean MacNeil, Grass Cove, February 5, 2012 and Michael A. MacLean. Information affirmed by John Hughie (The Bar-

ber) MacNeil, Shunacadie, June 22, 2012, and Dena MacDonald, Iona, February, 2013.

51. Conversation with Michael A. MacLean, MacKay Point, March 8, 2004.

52. Conversation with Hughie and Mary Lou MacNeil, Benacadie, N. S. February 5, 2012.

53. Conversation with Michael A. MacLean, MacKay Point, March 8, 2004.

54. Conversation with Jessie MacKinnon, Little Narrows, October 9, 2011 and January 13, 2013.

55. Conversation with Walter Matheson, Little Narrows, March 13, 2012.

56. Conversation with Honey MacNeil, Iona, February 8, 1999.

57. Conversation with Joe (Red Rory) MacLean, Lower Washabuck, in conversation with Michael A. and Vince MacLean December 3, 1997.

58. Conversation with Michael A. MacLean, December 3, 1997.

59. MacLean, *Lower Washabuck Happenings, April 25, 1923.*

60. Conversation with Roddie J. MacDonald, Upper Washabuck, November 24, 2011.

61. Ibid.

62. Bethune, *Historic Baddeck*, 40.

63. MacLean, *History of Victoria County*, 91- 92.

64. Bain, *History of Baddeck,* 33.

65. MacLean, *Remembering Baddeck Away Back.* A 6-page hand-written remembrance about Baddeck (1890-1920).

66. Bethune, Historic Baddeck, 42.

67. Bain, History of Baddeck, 33.

68. Bethune, Historic Baddeck, 189.

69. Ibid., 40.

70. Ibid., 49.

71. Ibid., 49.

72. Ibid., 78.

73. Conversation with Joe (Red Rory) MacLean, February 3, 1992.

74. Honey MacNeil to Elizabeth MacPherson, Beaton Institute, Sydney. Tape Conversation # 667, n.d.,

75. Conversation with MacLean, Michael A. MacKay Point, December 22, 2001

76. Michael A. MacLean in conversation with Alfred (K.R.) MacDonald, Middle River, in turn related to the author December 22, 2001.

77. Ibid.

78. Rannie Gillis, *Cape Breton Post*, March 8, 2008.

79. MacLean, Michael A. relating Michael Dan MacLean's telling of his tale, to the author, December 22, 2001.

80. Conversation with James MacDonald, Baddeck, May 4, 2010.

81. Gillis, The Victoria Standard December 2004 - January 2, 2005, 14.

82. Baechler, Lynn. Hydrologist, Johnstown, N. S. Emails with author, March 24 and 25, 2010.

83. Wasylik, *Geology of the Washabuck Peninsula*, 4.

84. Ibid., 1.

85. Beresford, *Distinction*, 11.

86. The source of this name is unknown.

87. Named after resident Tom Murphy.

88. Fletcher, *Reports of Exploration and Surveys,* 449.

89. Conversations with Mary Ann MacKenzie and daughter Charlotte, Washabuck Bridge, various occasions.

90. Government of Nova Scotia Special Places Protection Act, July 24, 2006.

91. Hart, *The History of Northeast Margaree*, 27.

92. DOT records for bridges, Victoria County, 1967-1969.

93. Nova Scotia Archives and Records Management.

94. Nova Scotia Archives and Records Management.

95. Bain, Effie, *History of Baddeck*, 24.

96. Hart, 26.

97. Ibid. 26.

98. Conversations with Roddie J. MacDonald, Upper Washabuck, February, 21, March 13, 2007 and January 16, 2010.

99. Nova Scotia Archives and Records Management; Dept. of Highways and Public Works.

100. DOT annual road construction reports.

101. Interview with Rod C. MacNeil, Barra Glen, March 28, 2010.

102. John Boileau, *The Silver Dart's dream team*; Bell's own words as quoted in *The Nova Scotian*, The Chronicle Herald, February, 22, 2009, P-5.

103. MacLean, Neil P. S., *Happenings*, October 14, 1924.

104. Edwin S. Grosvenor and Morgan Wesson, *Alexander Graham Bell*, 258.

105. Ibid., 259.

Notes to Chapter 11 – Communications

1. Bain, *History of Baddeck*, 42, 43.

2. MacNeil, *The Highland Heart in Nova Scotia*, 124, 125. MacNeil ended his distinguished newspaper career as managing editor of the *New York Times*.

3. Bain, *History of Baddeck*, 42, 43.

4. *Kingfisher Science Encyclopedia*, 471.

5. Rowe, *Connecting the Continents: Heart's Content and the Atlantic Cable* as reviewed in The Nova Scotian, Chronicle Herald, December 27, 2009, 13.

6. MacKenzie, *The Linemen of Antigonish and Guysbourgh,* Scottish Lights, 113-114. In an entry dated October 1, 1856, Robert Elmsley notes in his diary, "Telegraph open to C.N." On the 7th he notes further, "First Telegraph Dispatch from

St. John's to Mr. A. F. McGovern". The following day he records that a dispatch sent to the Newfoundland city was answered just fifteen minutes later.

7. Warner, *Baddeck, and that Sort of Thing*, 105.

8. Elmsley, 139.

9. Ibid.

10. MacLean, *History of Victoria County*, 101.

11. Bethune, *Historic Baddeck*, 4.

12. Conversation with Mary (Alfred) MacDonald (1909 -2011), Baddeck. May 3, 2001, August 30, 2007. Mary was a cousin, contemporary, and a lifetime friend of Janie Campbell.

13. Bain, *History of Baddeck*, 34, 35.

14. For the benefit of political history it should be made clear that John Turner was not opposed to free trade per se, but only Mulroney's interpretation of it.

15. Conversation with Peter F. MacLean, Iona, 1988.

16. The entire song was lost to the *Gàidhlig* fraternity for several decades. A couple of retrieved, fatigued, audio recordings resulted in a determined attempt to revive it, but the effort was a challenge due to quality problems of recordings, when suddenly and thankfully - a long-lost, faded, type-written copy was resurrected by Rod C. MacNeil of Barra Glen and son Paul K , from amongst a mislaid file in July 2011.

17. Special thanks are extended to these local *Gàidhlig* enthusiasts: Maxie (Dan Angus) MacNeil, Rod C. (John Dan) MacNeil, Mickey (John H) MacNeil, Seumas Watson and Peter (Jack) MacLean (1913-2013), who worked so diligently to resuscitate this marvelous piece of Canadiana. *Slàinte!* The lyrics are sung to the melody of *Cabar Feigh* portrayed by a stag's head on the Clan MacKenzie Chief's Coat of Arms, a compelling up-tempo piece of music, by an unknown composer ca. 1750.

18. Kingfisher Science Encyclopedia, 425.

19. Morgan,, *Rise Again! The Story of Cape Breton Island*, Book 2, 25.

20. Gray, *Reluctant Genius*, 418.

21. Conversation with MacDonald, Mary (Alfred), Baddeck, November 5, 2009.

22. Conversation with Rod C. MacNeil, Barra Glen, November 3, 2009.

23. Conversation with Maxie MacNeil, Highland Hill, N. S. January, 2010.

24. Conversation with Rod C. MacNeil, November 3, 2009.

25. Conversation with Hector MacKenzie, Washabuck Bridge, December 3, 2009.

26. Ibid., November 6, 2009.

27. Gray, . *Reluctant Genius*, 399.

28. MacLean, *History of Victoria County*, 116.

29. Ibid., 116.

30. Bethune, *Historic Baddeck*, 54.

31. MacLean, 117.

32. Conversation with Gordon MacLennan, Little Narrows, March 4, 1991.

33. In Barra Glen, the telephone residents repaired their own Mutual system, Rod C. MacNeil, January 2, 2013

34. Conversation with Gordon MacLennan.

35. Gray, *Reluctant Genius*, 428.

36. Walter Scott MacFarlane, *"Songs of the Valley"*, Edited by Kay MacDonald and Pat MacFarlane, 20-21.

37. Hugh F. MacKenzie & Rod C. MacNeil, (Compiled by Kim Ells) *Mar a b" àbhaist "S a" Ghleann* (As it was in the Glen) Casket Printing and Publishing, Antigonish, NS, 2012, 93-97.

38. Conversation with Gordon MacLennan, Little Narrows, March 4, 1991.

39. Conversation with F. X. and Honey MacNeil, Iona, March 4, 1991.

40. Conversation with Rod C. MacNeil, Barra Glen, January 2, 2013.

41. MacLean, *Rural residents highly dissatisfied with telephone service*, Cape Breton Post, Sydney, April 26, 1986.

42. MacLean, Neil P. S., Lower Washabuck, *Happenings*, May 5, 1928. Neil notes: "Installed the telephone, our house at the rate of $9.00 per year & the Government to supply one set of batteries every year."

43. LEAD is an acronym for a federal government funded economic initiative.

44. *Community Economic Development Study*, Central Cape Breton, 1.60.

45. Dr. Mabel Grosvenor, *Beinn Bhreagh*, Telephone conversation, October 10, 1990.

46. Conversation with Tom Wilson, Recreation Director, Municipality of Victoria, Baddeck, May 30, 2012 and Gerard MacNeil, Washabuck, May 2012.

47. Donna MacDonald, Regional Coordinator, VCCAPS, *The Victoria Standard*, Baddeck, April 16 to April 30, 2012, Page 1.

48. MacLeod, Ken, *More to CAP program than browsing the Internet*, Cape Breton Post, April 28, 2012, C1.

Notes to Chapter 12 – Alphas and Omegas

1. Gray, *Reluctant Genius*, 310.

2. Bain, *History of Baddeck*, 24.

3. John Alec MacLean of Detroit, in conversation with his sister Mary (Alfred) MacDonald, Baddeck who in turn related it to this writer, May 6, 2008.

4. Conversations with Hector MacKenzie, Washabuck Bridge; Michael A. MacLean, MacKay Point; Roddie J. MacDonald Upper Washabuck, and Walter Matheson, Little Narrows all provided pieces of information.

5. Conversation with Gordon (Lighthouse) MacLean, December 28, 2009.

6. Conversation with Roddie J. MacDonald, Upper Washabuck, January 27, 2010.

7. Conversation with Peter F. MacLean, Iona, November 11, 1994.

8. Conversation with Hector (Frankie) MacNeil, Iona, May 28, 2011.

9. Ibid.

10. Conversation with Allister and D.W. Matheson, Little Narrows, January 20, 2013. Everette Waddling was from originally from New Brunswick.

11. *Chronicle Herald*, January 2, 2010, A2.

12. *Chronicle Herald*, May 28, 2010, A2.

13. Conversation with David Gillis, Scotsville, Inverness County, December 22, 2012.

14. Morgan, *Rise Again! The Story of Cape Breton Island*, Book Two, 88.

15. Ibid. 89.

16. Ibid., 89, 90; AND Jenkins, Nova Scotia at Work, British Canadian Co-operative Society, *History of the British Canadian Co-operative and its Branches*, 150.

17. Conversation with Rod C. MacNeil Barra Glen, January 13, 2010.

18. Conversation with Raymond MacDonald, Vancouver, B. C., December, 2011.

19. Conversation with Ben MacLean, Washabuck Centre, January 13, 2010.

20. Hector MacKenzie says MacLeod was from Grand River, December 9, 2012.

21. Conversation with Allister Matheson, Blues Mills, January 21, 2013.

22. Conversations with Hector MacKenzie, Washabuck Bridge, and Walter and Eileen Matheson, Little Narrows, May 3, 2012.

Notes to Chapter 13 - Fires, Firefighters and Fire Chiefs

1. John Dan built a new store in Little Narrows ca. 1929.

2. Rod C. Mac Neil, Barra Glen. The fire could be seen from John Dan MacNeil's residence in Barra Glen that Halloween night.

3. Hector MacKenzie, Washabuck Bridge. This listing of community fires was provided by Hector in March, 2001. A few additions have been made since that date.

4. LIP is the acronym for the Federal government grant *Local Initiative Project*.

5. *Iona Volunteer Fire Department, Fifty Years of Service, 1959 – 2009*, Thirty page booklet, Edited by Randy Pointkoski, Iona, May 2, 2009.

6. Ibid., 25.

Notes to Chapter 14 – Forestry, Farming and Fishing

1. PANS, RG 20 Series B, CB # 1006, Jonathan Jones.

2. Conversation with Hector MacKenzie, Washabuck Bridge, September 24, 2000.

3. Taped conversation with S. R. MacNeil, Barra Glen, January 12, 1979.

4. Conversation with Hector MacKenzie, Washabuck Bridge.

5. Conversation with S.R. MacNeil, January, 12, 1979.

6. Conversation with Jimmy MacKinnon, MacKinnon Harbour, January 27, 1985.

7. Conversation with S.R. MacNeil.

8. Ibid.

9. Ibid.

10. Ibid.

11. Conversation with Michael A. MacLean, January 31, 1985. Conversation with S. R. MacNeil, Barra Glen, January 12, 1979. S.R. affirmed that indeed, the boiler was ultimately delivered to the beach at the Barra Glen crossing.

12. Conversation with S.R. MacNeil, January 12, 1979.

13. The source of the name of Cole Point is unknown.

14. Conversation with Malkie MacDonald, February 11, 1983.

15. This property was originally owned by Jonathan Jones but subsequently referred to locally as "The Bones', perhaps, because at one time it was also owned by man named Bona.

16. S. R. MacNeil also made reference in a conversation to the boom spanning the river, February 10, 1979.

17. Ibid.

18. Conversation with Jimmy MacKinnon, January 27, 1985.

19. Conversation with Hector MacKenzie, Washabuck Bridge.

20. Conversation with Glen MacKenzie, Hazeldale, February 10, 2007.

21. Conversation with Joe (Red Rory) MacLean, May, 1985.

22. Ibid.

23. Conversation with Joe (Red Rory) MacLean May 1985.

24. Conversation with Michael Dan MacLean, June 25, 1985.

25. Conversation with Hector MacKenzie, Washabuck Bridge, February 8, 2008.

26. Conversation with Michael A. MacLean, October 1, 2003.

27. Conversation with Roddie MacDonald, Upper Washabuck, January 24, 2008.

28. Conversation with Michael Dan MacLean, Baddeck, June 25, 1985.

29. Conversation with Ranald (Angus Ranald) MacDonald, Upper Washabuck, A passing comment mentioned and overheard.

30. Quoted by Roddie MacDonald, November 22, 2008.

31. Ibid.

32. Conversation with Ewen MacLean, Baddeck, November 22, 2007.

33. Conversation with Reid MacKay, Big Baddeck, June 25, 2008.

34. Conversation with Michael Dan MacNeil, Jamesville, N. S. December 5, 2011.

35. Conversation with Columba MacNeil, Sydney Mines, February 9, 2008.

36. Conversation with Hector MacKenzie, August, 21, 2012.

37. Conversation with MacDonald, Roddie, January, 24, 2008.

38. Conversation with Hector MacKenzie, February 17, 2007.

39. Conversation with Maxie MacNeil, Highland Hill, February 25, 2013.

40. Conversation with Roddie MacDonald, January 31, 2008.

41. Conversation with Hector MacKenzie, February 17, 2007.

42. Ibid, April 7, 2007.

43. Conversation with Roddie MacDonald, April 5, 2006.

44. Information provided in an 11-page typewritten summary of Cooperative's activities upon the windup of all forestry activities in 2000. Data compiled by long-time Co-op manager Michael Dan MacNeil, Jamesville, N. S.

45. MacLean, Alex D., *The Pioneers of Washabuckt*, 51.

46. Conversation with Murdock MacInnis, Washabuck Bridge.

47. Conversation with Mick-John (Lighthouse) MacLean, Gillis Point, October, 1981.

48. Conversation with Mick-John MacLean, Gillis Point, October, 1981.

49. Conversation with Michael A. MacLean, January 29, 1992, February 21, 2002.

50. Ibid. July 4, 2006.

51. Conversation with Rod C. MacNeil, Barra Glen, January 2, 2013.

52. Conversation with Roddie J. MacDonald, February, 19, 2012.

53. Conversation with Rod C. MacNeil, Barra Glen, January 2, 2013.

54. This heading is a line from one of songwriter Allister MacGillivray's compositions, Marion Bridge, CB.

55. Conversation with Joe (Red Rory) MacLean, January 25, 1984.

56. Family lore, recounted by their nephew Neil MacNeil, Bethesda, Maryland, while visiting Washabuck cousins, during 1980s and "90s.

57. Ibid.

58. Ibid.

59. M.J. Tremblay, K. Paul and P. Lawton, *Lobsters and other invertebrates in Relation To Bottom Habitat in The Bras d'Or Lakes: Application of video and SCUBA Transects,* 12,13.

60. Conversation with Roddie J. MacDonald, Upper Washabuck, March 23, 2013.

61. Conversation with MacLean, Michael A., April 30, 2006.

62. A line from one of songwriter and entertainer Buddy MacDonald's compositions.

63. Conversation with Peter F. MacLean, Iona, October 14, 1995.

64. Conversation with MacLean, Michael A., April 30, 2006.

65. Conversation with MacLean, Michael A., April 30, 2006.

66. Ibid., February 12, 2004.

67. Telephone conversation with Robin Stuart, Englishtown, November 5, 2011.

68. Ibid.

69. Ibid.

70. Conversation with Marie MacLean, Lower Washabuck, October 10, 2011.

71. Conversation with Robin Stuart, November 5, 2011.

72. Ibid.

Notes to Chapter 15 – Murder

1. MacLean, *The Pioneers of Washabuckt*, 33-35.

2. Elmsley, June 13, 1879, 125.

3. MacLean, *History of Victoria County*, 165.

4. MacLean, *The Pioneers of Washabuck*, 35.

5. Peter MacDonald, *Many Changes in History of C. B. Railway*, Cape Breton Post, 1965.

6. The story was related to the author by Hector MacKenzie, Washabuck Bridge; he heard it told by Francis Hector MacNeil, November, 1950.

7. Conversation with Michael A. MacLean, December 13, 2004.

8. Conversation with Raymond MacDonald, Vancouver, December 16, 2004.

Notes to Chapter 16 – Melodic Reminiscences

1. Rounder Records #7039.

2. Conversation with Malkie MacDonald, Upper Washabuck, May 6, 1986.

3. Piper Major Peter Morrison was from nearby Glen Morrison, Cape Breton. He was a highly regarded piping instructor with the Glace Bay MacDougall Girls Pipe Band during the 1950-60s and later with the Pipes and Drums of the Cape Breton Gaelic Society (1983-1986).

4. Vince MacLean, MacKay's Point, *Modified Liner Notes*, Bras d'Or House, Traditional Fiddle Music of Cape Breton, Rounder Records, #7039, August 14, 2006.

5. Susan J. MacLean, MacKay's Point, December, 2005. Poetry composed for her grandfather Michael A. MacLean and gifted to him Christmas, 2005.

Notes to Chapter 17 – Islands

1. Fletcher, *Report on the Geology of Part of the counties of Victoria, Cape Breton and Richmond, Nova Scotia*, 403.

2. www.blbra.ca

3. Johnston, *Storied Shores*, 2004, 17. A similar translation means "To where all waters flow'.

4. Shears, *Dance to the Piper*, 137.

5. Government of Nova Scotia, Baddeck Registry of Deeds, Bk. N. p- 276.

6. Ibid.

7. Conversation with Michael A. Mac Lean, January 29, 1992, February 21, 2002.

8. Ibid.

9. Telephone conversation with Grosvenor Blair, *Beinn Bhreagh*, N. S. April 22, 2011. Mr. Blair is a nephew of the late Mrs. Myers.

10. MacLean, *History of Victoria County*, 77.

11. Bethune, Jocelyn, *Solstice storm brings big changes to small island*, The Victoria Standard, 5.

12. Extensive research at the Baddeck Land Registry Office or the Department of Natural Resources has unearthed no information as to possible ownership of Stony Island during those earlier times. The island however, does show up on the A.F. Church map of Victoria County.

13. Title searches with DNR and Land Registry Office inquiries have proven futile.

14. Conversation with Parker Donham, Kempt Head, N.S., January 12, 2010.

15. Conversation with Michael A. MacLean, November 27, 2003.

16. *Uniacke's Sketches of Cape Breton and Other Papers Relating to Cape Breton Island,* Edited by C. Bruce Fergusson, 131-132.

17. Graeme Hamilton, *The National Post,* March 9, 1999, A1. It's more than a bit intriguing that a news item carried in the National Post referred to underwater video footage that had been recently filmed by the Newfoundland government showing the ocean floor after a group of seals crowded a school of codfish into a local bay and started feasting. The released footage, "…shows tens of thousands of cod lying on the bottom, gutted." The article quotes Jeff Hutchings a fish biologist at Dalhousie University, "…that documentation of seals having eaten only the fish stomachs suggests scientists may have underestimated how many cod seals kill. Researchers detect traces of fish in the seals" stomachs only if the entire fish has been eaten."

18. Conversation with Michael A. MacLean, July 13, 1994 and March 11, 1999.

19. MacLean, *History of Victoria County,* 53.

20. Municipality of Victoria, Grant Bk. E. 61.

21. MacLean, *Petition field notes,* # 23278.

22. The A. F. Church map refers to it as Bone Island, as does the DNR Grant Index Sheet # 123 and the Nova Scotia Atlas.

23. Goldthwaite was employed with the Inter-Chemical Paint Company in New York.

24. Conversation with Jessie (MacInnis) MacKinnon, Little Narrows, October 2, 2011.

25. Conversation with James MacDonald, Twining Street, Baddeck, May 4, 2010.

26. Registry of Deeds, Baddeck, Bk. 42, 148. "All that certain island known as "BLACK ISLAND" situate, lying and being at the south side of St. Patrick'd [sic] Channel and in front of "BIRCH POINT", so called and which said Island was granted to Nicholas Murphy, on the 19th day of June A. D. 1920, and which was conveyed by the heirs of said Nicholas Murphy to Catherine A. Murphy by deed dated December 2, A.D. 1925…..and being the same lands conveyed to Joseph H. Murphy by Catherine A. Murphy by deed dated September 12, A. D. 1933…." "Being the same premises conveyed to Mary S. Goldthwaite [Bronxville, New York] by Joseph H. Murphy by deed dated October 15, 1934…."

27. Also: A piece of the legal description reads as follows: LOT No. 1; "All that certain lot, piece or parcel of land, being "SHEEP ISLAND", otherwise known as "BLACK ISLAND', in the County of Cape Breton, in the province of Nova Scotia, and containing five and three-quarters acres and bounded as follows:

28. Conversation with James MacDonald, Baddeck, May 4, 2011.

Notes to Chapter 18 – Community Organizations

1. Conversation with Rod C. MacNeil, Barra Glen, March 28, 2010.
2. Conversation with Michael A. MacLean.
3. Conversation with Rod C. MacNeil, Barra Glen, March 28, 2010.
4. Conversation with Carmie MacLean, Washabuck Centre, Email, January 30, 2010.
5. Conversation with Rod C. MacNeil, Barra Glen, March 28, 2010.
6. Conversation with Hector MacKenzie, Washabuck Bridge, January, 2010.
7. Conversation with Carmie MacLean, January 30, 2010.
8. Conversation with Buddy MacDonald, Toronto, April, 2007.
9. Conversation with Ben MacLean, Washabuck Centre, January 13, 2010.
10. The Chronicle Herald, *Loney to be inducted in football hall*, February, 22, 2013, D3.
11. Ibid.
12. Conversation with Roddie MacDonald, Upper Washabuck, March, 2010.
13. Conversation with Martin MacLean, Millville, NS, March 11, 2012.
14. Conversation with Teresa (MacLean) MacIsaac, Halifax, Email, February 21, 2010.
15. Conversation with Carmie MacLean, January 30, 2010.
16. Minutes of *Washabuck Community Centre Association* (1972-2012).
17. Thanks to Allan and Debbie (MacLean) MacDougall, Sydney Mines, N. S. (Email, June 17, 2011), Pius MacLean, Edmonton, Alberta and Paul MacLean, Sackville, N S. Email, January 10, 2012 for contributing the information re: *Tour de Washabuck*.
18. Allister MacGillivray, Mira, N. S., *The Music*, The Highlander, Sydney, August, 1993.
19. Verses by Hector MacKenzie et al, Washabuck Bridge, N. S.; *Gàidhlig* chorus vetted in *Highlander* column August, 1993, as sung by Roddie C. MacNeil, Barra Glen, to the air: "*S E Mo Cheist An Gille Donn.* Thirty verses are included here.

Notes to Chapter 19 – Military Salute

1. Library and Archives Canada, RG 150, # 67630, seq.53, (Date: 25-1-06).
2. North Sydney Herald, Volume 44, March 22, 1916. An erroneous account.
3. MacDonald & Gardiner, *The Twenty–Fifth Battalion, Canadian Expeditionary Force*, 49. Other Military Attestation and casualty documents, Library and Archives Canada forms, RG 150.
4. Item carried in a Boston newspaper clipping. No other data available. In authors possession.
5. MacDonald and Gardiner, *The Twenty-Fifth Battalion*, 88.
6. Boston newspaper clipping.
7. Conversation with Neil MacNeil, Bethesda, Maryland, nephew of Pte J. Mur-

dock MacNeil, July 24, 1996. (Neil, a distinguished congressional historian, served as the chief congressional correspondent for *Time* magazine for thirty years.)

8. A portion of personal correspondence from the Federal Minister of Veterans Affairs, (Hon. Julian Fantino; PC, MP) in response to an inquiry by the author, April 8, 2014.

> "... With respect to private MacNeil's eligibility for the Victoria Cross, allow me to explain that this honour was issued by the British Ministry of Defence to service personnel of Commonwealth countries for individual acts of valour. At the time, the selection process was initiated by a soldier's commanding officer and went up the British military chain of command all the way to His majesty King George V. Unfortunately, not every person recommended for the Cross received it.
>
> Let me assure you that the Victoria Cross and other decorations for bravery were granted based on merit and not on an individual's birthplace or nationality. In fact, it was common for people to enlist with the forces of another country, and you may be interested to know that four Americans were awarded the Cross while serving with the Canadian Expeditionary Forces. In total, approximately 70 Canadians were granted the Cross in recognition of their heroism on the battlefields of the Great War.
>
> I should mention that in 1950, the Commonwealth governments decided that no further claims for bravery awards would be considered for actions during the First and Second World Wars. This decision was made because the passage of time had made it too difficult to obtain reliable witnesses and the necessary documentation to justify a nomination for an award."

9. Thornhill and MacDonald, *In The Morning, Veterans of Victoria County, Cape Breton*, 167.

10. *Macneil [sic] Recipients of the Victoria Cross*, The Galley, 57. According to this item in the Clan MacNeil bi-annual publication, "The only American to hold the V. C. is the Unknown Soldier of WW I buried at Arlington National cemetery."

11. Thornhill and MacDonald, *In The Morning, Veterans of Victoria County Cape Breton*, 120.

12. Attestation Papers, PAC, Ottawa, Canada.

13. Remarks taken from Military Form B. 123, Form A. 36 and other official documents.

14. Ibid and MacDonald, *Honour Roll of the Nova Scotia Overseas Highland Brigade*, 57.

15. MacKenzie, *Legion Magazine*, November/December 2003, 93.

16. Morrison and Slaney, *The Breed of Manly Men, The History of The Cape Breton Highlanders*, 394.

17. Harold Shea, *The Chronicle Herald*, November 23, 1990.

18. Telephone conversation with Beatrice MacNeil, wife of Michael B. MacDonald, East Bay, N. S., February 8, 2010.

19. Shea, *The Chronicle Herald*, November 23, 1990.

20. Thornhill, and MacDonald, *In The Morning*, 379.

21. *Cenotaph inscription*. Erected by Royal Canadian Legion, Branch 124, Iona, NS.

Notes to Chapter 20 – Politics

1. MacLean, Alex D., *History of Victoria County*, 89.

2. Ibid.

3. Ibid.

4. Ibid.

5. Jim St.Clair, *The Victoria Standard*, June 21 to July 4, 2004, 8.

6. Alex D. MacLean; *The "Three Rory's" Election*. Although Alex D. did not grace this story with his byline, there was no question throughout the extended community that he was indeed its author.

Select Bibliography

Newspapers

Cape Breton Post
The Casket
The Chronicle Herald
The Highlander
The North Sydney Herald
The Sydney Post-Record
The Victoria News
The Victoria Standard
Victoria-Inverness Bulletin

Primary Sources:

Bain, Effie, *History of Baddeck,* an 85- page typewritten unpublished manuscript, Baddeck, c.1952.

Caplan, Ron, *Cape Breton's Magazine,* # 42, 50. Devoted to the History, Natural History and Future of Cape Breton Island.

Catholic Church Parish Records of Barra. Scotland, September 23, 1805-August 3, 1821.

Eaton, Paul C. and Rankin, Angus. *Resource Study of Little Narrows, Iona, Washabuck, Boisdale, Christmas Island*: A Community Development Study.

Elmsley (sic), Willard Lyman, Author's copy of *Extracts from copy of Robert Elmsley's Diary & Historical Papers.* Baddeck, (1855-1889) (This Diary was copied from the original handwritten by Willard Lyman Elmsley, a grandson of Robert Elmsley of Peterborough, Ontario, Canada, during 1966 and 1967.

Johnston, A.J.B., *Storied Shores: Isle Madame, St. Peter's, Chapel Island in the 17th and 18th centuries.* University College of Cape Breton Press, Sydney, 2004.

Karnis, Linda and MacLean, Loretta, *Tourism Inventory on Route 223, (From Little Narrows to Boisdale)* Sponsored by the Grand Narrows and District Board of Trade, A 22 page typewritten Tourist Inventory compilation, N.d.

MacDonald, W. James, *Patterson's History of Victoria County*, College of Cape Breton Press, Sydney, 1978.

MacDougall, Frances, *Settlement and Development of Our District*, A handwritten history St. Columba School project, Grade V11 & V111, 9 pages, 1935.

MacDougall, Ricky, *Holy Rosary Cemetery*, Washabuck and *St. Columba Pioneer Cemetery*, Iona, A listing and siting of all headstones, 2010.

MacGregor Francis, *The Days That I Remember*, A 68 page typewritten manuscript, Nyanza, Cape Breton, January 1962, given to writer by author's widow Bessie.

MacKenzie, Archibald J., *History of Christmas Island Parish*, 1926.

MacKinnon, Martin et al, *Iona Federated High School 1920-1945*, Reunion Recollection, Reflections. Booklet (18 page) outlining history of first Federated Rural High School in Nova Scotia, ca. 1970.

MacKinnon, Archibald D., *The History of the Presbyterian Church in Cape Breton*, Formac Ltd. Antigonish, N.S. 1975.

MacLean, Alex D. *A History of Victoria County*, Author's copy of 174 page typewritten manuscript. (c.1936-1973).

MacLean, Alex D. *Early Days in Lower Washabuckt*. A 16 page typeset monograph, c.1939.

MacLean, Alex D. *The Pioneers of Washabuckt:* A typewritten 70 page foolscap manuscript, September 15, Baddeck, 1939 Author's copy; (A limited additional copies of the original manuscript were privately printed by Vincent J. MacLean of East Bay in 1976 and Daniel J. MacNeil Grass Cove in 1988).

MacLean, Alex D., *The "Three Rory's" Election*, A 11 page foolscap typewritten monologue, No author's name but without question an authentic Alex D. production, ca. 1937.

MacLean, Charles J., (1886-1947), *Remembering Baddeck Away Back*, A six page hand written remembrance about Baddeck (1890-1920).

MacLean, Neil P. S. and MacLean, Alex D., *The Genealogy of the MacLean's of Washabuckt:* A 7 page foolscap compilation by authors of Lower Washabuckt, and Baddeck, respectively, March 1935. Revised and corrected by Alex D. MacLean, Baddeck, March, 1937; revised and corrected further by Alex D. MacLean, Baddeck, 10 regular typewritten pages, September 15, 1940.

MacLean, Neil P. S. *Comments on "Early Days"* A letter to the editor of *The Casket*, October 31, 1939.

MacLean, Neil P. S., *Happenings (1915-1943)*, A personal Diary, Compiled and transcribed by granddaughter Sharon MacLean, Sydney Mines, and formatted by great- granddaughter Colleen MacLean, Washabuck and Ontario.

MacLean, Vince et al, *Central Cape Breton, Community Economic Development Study*, Iona, May 1885, 82 pages.

MacNeil, Francis Hector, [*A genealogical sketch of The MacNeil's of Iona*] No title, no date and no author's name but generally agreed that the 15 page typewritten document was originally written by local genealogist Francis Hector MacNeil c. 1938, Outlines genealogy and historical notes about the first Barra Strait pioneers.

MacNeil, Francis Hector, *The MacDonald's of Saint Columba and Washabuck*, A 9 page typewritten Manuscript c. 1939, No author's name and no date but generally agreed that original work was compiled by local noted genealogist Francis Hector of Iona and New Waterford.

MacNeil, Roddie C. et al, *The Story of St. Columba Parish*, Iona, City Printers, Sydney, 1994.

MacNeil, S. R., *All Call Iona Home 1800-1950*, Formac Publishing Company Ltd. Antigonish, Nova Scotia, 1979.

MacPherson, Elizabeth; *Transportation in the Grand Narrows-Iona Area;* Museum Studies 211, Submission for Mr. Terry MacLean, UCCB, December, 32 pages, 1987

McCarthy, Joseph P., *Times Of My Life*, Privately Printed, C. 1971

Morgan, Robert J., *Early Cape Breton: From Founding to Famine*, Breton Books, 2000.

Munden, Carl, *Post Offices of Cape Breton, Victoria County, Volume 3,* Published and Printed Privately, Dartmouth, NS. 1989.

Murphy, Anna, *The Story of Pioneers and Progress in Our Schools*, 11 pages Grade V111 handwritten history school project, 11 pages, ca. 1930

Nova Scotia Department of Agriculture and Marketing, 1967, 49 pages

Parker, John P., MBE/Master Mariner, *Cape Breton Ships and Men*, McGraw-Hill Ryerson Ltd. Toronto, 1967/1980.

Pinaud, Mary, *History of Baddeck,* An 8 page typewritten Manuscript, Baddeck, 1963, Revised 1997.

Pointkoski, Randy J., Editor, *Iona Volunteer Fire Department, 50 Years of Service 1959-2009*, 50th Anniversary Celebration Booklet, 32 pages, 2009.

Stanley, Laurie, *The Well-Watered Garden: The Presbyterian Church in Cape Breton, 1798-1860*, University College of Cape Breton press, Sydney, 1983.

Tremblay, M. J., K. Paul and P. Lawton, *Lobsters and other invertebrates in relation to bottom habitat in the Bras d'Or Lakes, Application of video and SCUBA transects, Canadian Technical Report of Fisheries and Aquatic Science 2645,* Her majesty the Queen, Right of Canada, 2005.

Washabuck Cooperative Store Ledger, Two Volumes, 1942-1947 and 1952-1957, Writer's Collection.

Wasylik, Darin R. G., *Geology of The Washabuck Peninsula, Central Cape Breton Island, Nova Scotia,* Bachelor of Science in Geology, Honours Thesis, Acadia University, Wolfville, N. S., 2004.

Secondary Sources

Baddeck, A Search For Yesterday, No Author, A pictorial booklet of Baddeck, July, 1981

Beaton, Stanley, "*Eoghan Dubh*" *A Pioneer's Family*, The Casket Printing and Publishing Co. Ltd., Antigonish, Nova Scotia, 2002.

Bethune, Jocelyn. *Historic Baddeck*, Nimbus Publishing Ltd., Halifax, 2009.

Campbell, Frank W., *Canada Postal History*, 1958, (PANS, HE, 6185, C24D1, C35, c.3)

Crocker, Rev. Dr. Robert D., *They Were Here, The British Army On Our Land 1785 – 1853*, Glace Bay, NS.

Cruise Cape Breton, The Yachter's Guide to the Bras d'Or Lakes, Cape Breton, Nova Scotia, 1974, 8th Printing; Diversity Special Interest Publishing Co. Ltd. Halifax, NS.

Davis, Stephen A. *Mi'Kmaq, Peoples Of The Maritimes,* Nimbus Publishing Limited, Halifax, 1997.

Erskine, J. S; *The Archaeology Of Some Nova Scotia Indian Campsites* published in Proceedings of the Nova Scotia Institute of Science, Vol. 27, Earl Whynot & Associates Limited, Halifax, NS. June 1971.

Gray, Charlotte, *Reluctant Genius, Alexander Graham Bell*, HarperCollins Publishers Ltd., Toronto, Ontario, 2006.

Grosvenor, Edwin S. and Morgan Wesson, *Alexander Graham Bell*, Harry N. Abrams, In. Publishers, New York, NY. 1997.

Hart, John F., *History of Northeast Margaree;* Printed by Lynk Printing Service, Sydney, NS. 1963.

Hutchinson, Thomas, *Hutchinson's Nova Scotia Directory for 1864-65, containing Alphabetical Directories of each place in the Province with a Post Office Directory,* Complied and Published by Thomas Hutchinson, Halifax, NS. 1865.

Johnston, A. A., *A History of the Catholic Church in Eastern Nova Scotia*, Volumes 1 & 11, Hunter Rose Co. Ltd. 1960.

Lamb, James B., *The Hidden Heritage*, Lancelot Press, Windsor, Nova Scotia, 1975

MacDonald, F. B., C. D., M D. & John J. Gardiner, *The Twenty-Fifth Battalion, Canadian Expeditionary Force, Nova Scotia's Famous Regiment In World War One*, City Printers, Sydney, 1983.

MacDonald, J. J., *The Nova Scotia Post: Its Offices, Masters and Marks: 1700-1867*, The Unitrade Press, Toronto, Ontario.

MacDonald, W. James, *Honour Roll of The Nova Scotia Overseas Highland Brigade*, Cape Breton University press, Sydney, 2007.

MacDougall, J. L., *The History of Inverness County Nova Scotia*, Mika Publishing Company, Belleville, Ontario, 1976. Original published in 1922.

MacFarlane, Walter Scott, *"Songs of The Valley",* Edited by Kay MacDonald and Pat MacFarlane, Upper Margaree, NS.

MacGillivray, Don and Tennyson, Brian, *Cape Breton Historical Essays*, College of Cape Breton Press, Sydney, 1980.

MacKenzie, A. A., *Scottish Lights, Popular Essays on Cape Breton and Eastern Nova Scotia*, Breton Books, 2003.

MacKenzie, Hugh F. and MacNeil, Rod C., (Compiled by Kim Ells) *Mar a b' àbhaist 'S a' Ghleann* (As it was in the Glen) Casket Printing & Publishing, Antigonish, NS, 2012.

MacMillan, A. J., To *The Hill of Boisdale; Pioneer Families of Boisdale, Cape Breton and Surrounding Areas*, City Printers, Sydney, 1986.

MacMillan, Dr. C. Lamont, *Memoirs of a Cape Breton Doctor*, McGraw-Hill Ryerson Limited, 1975.

MacNeil, Neil, *The Highland Heart in Nova Scotia*, Charles Scribner's Sons, New York, 1948.

MacPherson, L. B., *Nova Scotian Postal History Volume 1, Post Offices (1754-1981)* Petheric Press, Halifax, 1982.

McPherson, F., *Watchmen Against the World*, Ryerson Press, Toronto, 1962.

Morgan, Robert J., *Rise Again! The Story of Cape Breton Island, Book One,* Breton Books, 2008.

Morgan, Robert J., *Rise Again! The Story of Cape Breton Island, Book Two,* Breton Books, 2009.

Morrison, Alex, and Ted Slaney, *The Breed Of Manly Men, The History Of The Cape Breton Highlanders*, Cape Breton Printers, Sydney, NS, 1994.

National Geographic, National Geographic Society, Washington, USA, July Issue, 1920.

Nicholson, John A. et al, *Middle River Past and Present, History of a Cape Breton Community 1806-1985*, The Middle River Area Historical Society, City Printers, Sydney, 1985.

Nova Scotia Mineral Update, Winter Edition, 2009.

Paul, Daniel N., *We Were Not the Savages*, Fernwood Publishers, Halifax, 2000.

Public Archives of Nova Scotia, *Uniacke's Sketches Of Cape Breton and Other Papers Relating to Cape Breton Island*, Edited With an Introduction and Notes by C. Bruce Fergusson, Halifax, N. S. 1958

Public Archives of Nova Scotia With an Introduction by Charles Bruce Fergusson, *Place-Names and Places of Nova Scotia*, Mika Publishing Company, Belleville, Ontario, 1974.

Ryan, Laurie A. et al, Along *The Shores of Boularderie*, City Printers, Sydney, 2001

Selwyn, Alfred R. C., Director, *Geological Survey of Canada*, Reports of Exploration and Surveys, 1876-77, Dawson Bro's Montreal, Published by Authority of Parliament, 1878.

Shears, Barry W., *Dance to the Piper*, Cape Breton University Press, Sydney, 2008

Szick, Lark B., Ross Families of Margaree Cape Breton, Pioneers and Descendants, 2000.

Index

Pages numbers refer to print edition

Alexander, ship 141-42
Almon, Baptists 14
Anderson, James 43-44, 140
Andrews, Marjorie and Harold 103
Ann, ship 14-15
MV *Arev*, ship 155
Arsenault, Catherine (MacLean) (Boyd) 20, 45-46, 96
Arsenault, Joseph A. 20, 45-46
SS *Aspy*, ship 231
Astchbuckt (variant of Washabuck)
Atlantic Pulp Company 232

SS *Banshee*, ship 172
The Barra MacNeils xv, 272-73
The Barraman's Feast, painting 5
Beaver Cove 22, 73, 117, 142
Beer 47
Beinn Bhreagh vi, 2, 24, 151, 167, 171, 201, 202, 210, 251, 369, 373
Beinn Mhìcheil, near Mabou 26
Bell, Alexander Graham 3, 190-91, 202, 204, 278
Big Farm 12, 20, 224, 258
Birch Point ix, 2, 8, 20, 23, 66, 68, 101, 102, 118, 184-85, 224, 268-69, 288-89, 363
SS *Blue Hill* 102, 150, 175
Bone Island (a.k.a. Allen's Island) 286-90
"The Boom" 236-37
Boulaceet Harbour 39
Boularderie 7, 10-11, 22, 24, 41, 163, 175-76, 187, 257, 278, 283-84, 351, 382
de la Boularderie, Louis-Simon de St. Aubin, Chevaiier (ca. 1674-1738) 10-11
Boyd, John C. 20, 45-46
Brown, John 25

Brown, Johnny (1884 -1959) xxi
bush road, bushing the ice 166-67

Cain (Cain's) Mountain 2, 13, 16, 18, 51, 70, 128, 146, 183, 188, 219-20, 225, 228-30, 241, 267-68, 293, 301-302, 317
Cameron, Alexander 39
Cameron, Lt. John 34
Campbell, Angus 70
Campbell, Arthur 202
Campbell, Charles J. 19, 44, 130
Campbell, Colin 69
Campbell, Dan Joe 78
Campbell, Hector (*Eachmann Ban*) (d. 1922) 19
Campbell, Hugh 26
Campbell, Hughie 69, 134, 240
Campbell, James 42
Campbell, Jane (MacPhee) 19
Campbell, Janie 196, 251
Campbell, John R. 203
Campbell, Johnny 65
Campbell, Joseph 130
Campbell, Malcolm 26, 78, 240
Campbell, Malcolm 82
Campbell, Rory 26
Campbell, Sarah Margaret 70
Carmichael, Daniel 21, 24, 33-35, 56
Cashman, William 74
Chabert de Cogolin, Joseph-Bernard 28-29
Church, Ambrose Finson (A. F.) 37-38, 65, 279
Cladh Lachlann (cemetery) 18, 104, 106, 111
Cladh nan Leòdhasach (The Lewis Cemetery) 90
Cladh Nill Ghil See also Holy Rosary Cemetery) 18
clergy *See* chapter 7
Coffin Island 175, 283, 284

Colaisde na Gàidhlig (The Gaelic College, St. Ann's) xv
Cole Point 11, 46-47, 182, 228-30, 239, 371
Company of Cape Breton (Compagnie du Cap-Breton) 10
Cox, Captain William 29
Crawley, Captain Thomas, Surveyor General 13, 29-31, 34
Cuyler, Abraham 12

DesBarres, Joseph Frederick Wallet 29, 31
Devoe, Ellen (1868-1953) 65
Devoe, Neillie xvii, 79, 225, 246
Dollard, Rev. William 97-98
Donovan, Father Charles OMI 99
Doyle, Mr. (schoolmaster, given name unknown) 56, 66
Dryden, William 35, 46-47, 227, 230
Duffus Island See Kidston Island
Duffus, James 40, 43
Dunlop, David A. 194
Dunlop, Catherine (McGrath) 194

Elmsley, Robert 6, 40, 44, 130-31, 172, 257
Eskasoni 30, 291, 293, 294
Estmere 2, 148, 164, 252, 253

Farquharson, Reverend Alexander 88
Fast, Michael See Michael B. MacDonald, teacher
firewood co-operative 240-41
First World War See Chapter 19
Fletcher, Hugh 38-39, 277
Forrester, Rev. Alexander, DD 88
Fraser, Donald Allan 85
Fuaran Mharsailidh (natural spring) 18, 19, 108

Gammell and Christie, store 40-41

383

Gillis, Father Dougald 102
Gillis, Hugh 23
Gillis, John 23
Gillis, Rev. John Hugh, PhD, (1910-2006) 128
Gillis, Father Michael 71-73
Gillis Point vii, viii, xviii, 2, 18, 23, 51, 60-61, 67, 71, 75-76, 78-79, 102, 111, 115, 135, 137-38, 160-62, 165, 167, 171, 175, 189-91, 214, 216, 225-26, 230, 239-40, 247, 249, 258, 267, 291, 293, 298, 310, 317, 326, 328, 332, 353, 355, 357, 372
Gillis Point East 2, 115, 190, 310
Gillis Point Harbour *See* Maskells
Goldthwaite's Island 206, 286-89
Goold, William 34
Grand Narrows vi, 2, 11, 22, 23, 42, 43, 60, 66, 73, 74, 82, 95, 96, 98, 118, 131, 134, 148, 149, 173, 186, 189, 190, 191, 203, 210, 227, 280, 319, 340, 351, 362, 378, 380
Grand Narrows Rear Grand Narrows Rear *See* St. Columba 2, 134, 362
Grant, Father Roderick 100
Grass Cove vii, 2, 25, 69, 74, 76, 78, 135, 136, 138, 148, 151, 167, 170, 190, 208, 210, 215, 219, 225, 226, 239, 275, 291, 326, 327, 328, 329, 330, 334, 350, 354, 364, 365, 379
Gruaigean (a man about whom nothing else is known) 26
Haire, Alexander 29

Harbour Hill 75
Harmony, ship 15, 21-22
Hazeldale 2, 25, 49, 60, 66, 176, 214, 217, 230, 239, 252, 297, 301, 371
Hector, ship 22
Highland Hill 3, 26
Holland, Samuel 29, 161, 163
Holy Rosary Mission Church and Cemetery 18, 20, 23, 59, 90, 93, 95, 97, 101-104, 111-12, 117, 119-21, 188, 259, 304
Hope, ship 14-15
Hurd, Thomas 29

Indian Bay 7
Iona Co-op Store 51
Iona Rear (*Cùl Beag*) 3, 26

Jamesville vii, viii, 2, 23, 69, 70, 74, 171, 190, 203, 216, 217, 238, 269, 291, 294, 329, 357, 371, 372
Jankowski, Catherine (MacNeil) (1917-1985) 222, 320
John, Michael 80
John, Peter 80
Jones, Esther 12
Jones, Captain Jonathan 12-13, 281
Jones, Jonathan Jr. 12, 34, 224, 281
Jones, Sarah 12
Jones, Thomas 12
Jones, William 12
Jubilee 2, 186, 241, 301

Kempt Head 11, 41, 167, 175, 283, 284, 374
Kempt Head 11
Kempt, Sir James 32, 34
Kidston Island 6, 40-41, 43, 140, 160
Kidston, Capt. William 43-44, 130

SS *Lakeview* 153, 155-57, 174-77, 231
"Lament for the Three Brothers" 142
Lewis, Charlie 51
Little Narrows Gypsum Company 277

Long Point 7
Louisbourg 11, 12, 29, 205, 337, 339, 351

MacAskill, Annabelle 63
MacAulay, Alexander (Allie Donn) 23-24
McAulay, Allan 37
McAulay, Donald ("piper") 20, 111
MacAulay, Hugh 56, 58

MacAulay, Murdock 24, 239
McCarthy, Joseph A. 73
McCoy, Wallace 17
McCurdy, Arthur W. 45, 286
McCurdy, William F. 203
MacDonald, Alasidair (*Glas*) 21
MacDonald, Alec 80
MacDonald, Alec (Michael B.), merchant 51
MacDonald, Alexander 23
MacDonald, Rev. Alexander J. (a.k.a. Father Alex "The Devil") 291
MacDonald, Pipe Major Alexander A. 105, 111
MacDonald, Allan 115, 134
MacDonald, Andy (1937-2005) 75-76
MacDonald, Angus (*Aonghas an Tuathach*) 24
MacDonald, Father Angus R. 71
MacDonald, Angus (*Aonghas mac Ruaridh*) 99, 131
MacDonald, Angus Ranald (d. 1934) Grandfather xv, 65, 228
MacDonald, Angus J. (Angus Ranald) 78, 214, 297
MacDonald, Annie (Dan) 25
MacDonald, Annie (Ranald) (1852-1925) xiii
MacDonald, Archie 80
MacDonald, Bernard (Pastor) 113
MacDonald, Buddy 75-76
MacDonald, Catherine (MacIntyre) 26
MacDonald, Catherine (Donald) (MacKinnon) 24
MacDonald, Daniel 7
MacDonald, Dan A. 69, 232
MacDonald, Dan Angus and Margaret 61
MacDonald, Capt. Dan 179
MacDonald, Father Dan E. 112-13, 222, 296
MacDonald, Dan Francis 77, 78, 79, 236
MacDonald, Donald (son of Alexander and Margaret) 21, 23, 26
MacDonald, Donald (Calum Bàn) 118

MacDonald, Flora (daughter of Alexander and Margaret) 21, 23, 26
MacDonald, Francis B. (1907-1971) 52, 54, 132, 151, 187
MacDonald, Helen 111
MacDonald, Father Hugh D. 122, 159
MacDonald, James 21, 26
MacDonald, James (Joseph Klondike) 150-51
McDonald, James 33
MacDonald, John 68, 134
MacDonald, John A. (of Iona) 51
MacDonald, John Archie xix, 51, 81, 240
MacDonald, Johnny (Angus Ranald) 188
MacDonald, Joseph (Hector) 76
MacDonald, Malcolm (William) 171, 230-31
MacDonald, Malkie xvii, 47, 66, 79, 109
MacDonald, Margaret (Gillis) 23
MacDonald, Marie 90
MacDonald, Mary Ann 81
MacDonald, Mary C. 65
MacDonald, Mary (MacNeil) 68
MacDonald, Michael 21
MacDonald, Michael B., teacher 66, 80-82
MacDonald, Michael Bernard (1921-2005) 76, 314
MacDonald, Michael E. 26, 134
MacDonald, Michael (Mìcheal Mór mac Alasdair) 23, 26
MacDonald, Murdock (married to Effie Morrison) 48
MacDonald, Murdock (*Murchadh Alasdair Glais*) 35, 99, 109
MacDonald, Norman Peter 48, 89
MacDonald, Quentin (Rory Ranald) 79, 153
MacDonald, Ranald (*Mór*) 16, 21, 24, 37
MacDonald, Ranald (Angus Ranald) (1914-1983) 188, 235
MacDonald, Roddie 35, 79, 235
MacDonald, Roddie and Clare 58

MacDonald, Roddie and Laura 21
MacDonald, Roddie J. 109, 171, 236
MacDonald, Roderick 36
MacDonald, Roderick (*mac Alasdair*) 133
MacDonald, Ronald Stephen 14, 106-107
MacDonald, Rory (son of Alexander and Margaret) 21, 23, 26
MacDonald, Rory Ranald 58, 63, 65, 102, 114, 132
MacDonald, Rory Ranald "Klondike" 19, 132
MacDonald, Sarah (MacNeil) 115
MacDonald, Sarah E. 37
MacDonald, Sarah Liza (1886-1961) xiii
MacDonald, Stephen 20
Macdonald, Sylvester 73
MacDonald, Wanda 111
MacDonnell, John V. (*Maighstir Ian Dòmhnullach*) 36
MacDougall, Alexander 23
MacDougall, Calum William 23
MacDougall, Dan (1876-1963) 69, 72, 78
MacDougall, Frances xix, 64, 68, 71
MacDougall, Hughie Archie 226
MacDougall, James (*Seumas Muillear*) 23
MacDougall, Jane (Sìne) 26
MacDougall, Jim Alec 146, 203
MacDonald, "Little" Jimmy (Stephen) 46
MacDougall, Dan 78
MacDougall, Joe 188
MacDougall, John A. 72, 239
MacDougall, John Peter 69
MacDougall, "Big" Kate 47
MacDougall, Corporal J. Lawrence 72, 267
MacDougall, Leo and Edie 16
MacDougall, "Little" Mary 48
MacDougall and McNeil, merchants 43
MacDougall, Mickey xviii, 188
MacDougall, "Piper" Rory (1848-1936) 111
MacEachen, Rev. Roderick A. 120

MacEachern, Father Angus Bernard 100
McEachern, Donald (East Bay) 22
MacFarlane, Murdock 24
MacGillivray, Father Alexander 95, 98-100, 108
MacGregor, Dr. James 84
MacInnis, Anna Belle 24
MacInnis, Christina 24
MacInnis, Donald 17, 18
Donald MacInnis (1)(married to Peggy MacIver) 25
MacInnis, Donald (2) (married to Annie MacIver) 25
MacInnis, Donald (Henry) 24
MacInnis, Henry 24
MacInnis, Jane 18
MacInnis, Jane (Donald "Piper" MacAulay) 25
MacInnis, John 25, 134
MacInnis, Marcella 18
MacInnis, Mary 18
MacInnis, Mary Margaret 80
MacInnis, Malcolm 24-25
MacInnis, Murdock 65
MacInnis, Murdock D. A. (1899-1994) vii, 25, 89, 246
MacInnis, Peggy (MacIver) 25
MacIntosh, Msgr. Donald, VG 102
MacIntosh, pioneer family 20
MacIntyre, Ann (widow of Hugh Gills) 23
McIntyre, Peter, merchant 42
MacIntyre, Roderick (*Ruaridh Ùr*) 24, 26
MacIsaac, Father Donald 98-99, 124
MacIsaac, Roderick 37, 66-67
MacIver, Annie 25
MacIver, Archie (1898-1984) xvii, 20, 147
MacIver, Catherine (Matheson) 25
MacIver, Colin 20
MacIver, Henry 24
MacIver, Reverend James C. 89
MacIver, Joe (Dolly) (1899-1972) 89-90, 203, 301
MacIvor, Rev. John W., DD 88
MacIver, Margaret (Hayden) 20
MacIver, Mary (MacInnis) 90

McIver, George 20
MacIver, Joseph 20
MacIver, Neil 25
McKay, Angus 36, 91-93
MacKay, George (d. 1858) 17, 56
MacKay, Mary 17
MacKay (MacKay's) Point viii, xiii, 4, 11, 17, 20, 39, 44, 45, 74, 91, 93, 109, 131-32, 140-41, 148-55, 158, 161, 164, 170-71, 175-76, 178, 189, 195, 202, 210, 226, 232, 244-45, 247-50, 258-59, 264, 268, 280, 283-84, 286, 290, 355-57, 359, 361, 366, 369

MacKenzie, Alexander "Framer" 25, 118
MacKenzie, Archibald J. xx, 21, 118
MacKenzie, Archibald (*Gilleasbuig mac Eachainn*) 8, 23, 118
MacKenzie, Archibald (Ruadh) 101
MacKenzie, "Red" Archie 8-9
MacKenzie, Archie Alec xx
MacKenzie, Beatag (MacNeil) 18, 141, 187
MacKenzie, Carl 72
MacKenzie, Cassie 78, 116
MacKenzie, Catherine (MacKinnon) 118
MacKenzie, Catherine "Kate" 18
MacKenzie, Charles "Framer" xvi
MacKenzie, Rev. Charles A. 118
MacKenzie, Charlotte 48, 71, 76
MacKenzie Country Store 49
MacKenzie, Dan Michael, merchant 51, 239
MacKenzie, Donald (*Dòmhnull Eòin*) 127
McKenzie, Donald (Hector) 21
MacKenzie, Ellen, wife of Simon Devoe xvi
MacKenzie, Flora (MacLean) 20
MacKenzie, Hector 22
MacKenzie, Hector xviii, 24, 70, 116, 263
McKenzie, Hector (Archibald) 22
MacKenzie, Hugh F. (1895-1971) 105, 207

MacKenzie, J. H. 73
MacKenzie, James Murdock 18
MacKenzie, Jean 71-72
MacKenzie, Jimmy (1906-1972) 153
MacKenzie, John 22, 24
MacKenzie, John Stephen 1895-1945) xv, xvi
MacKenzie, Liza 70 (later Liza Campbell) 68
MacKenzie, Mary Ann (Devoe) (1901-1983) xv, 65, 68, 264
MacKenzie, Michael Hector (1909-2000) 202
McKenzie, Murdock 33
MacKenzie, Murdock (*Murchadh mac Eachainn*) 21
MacKenzie, Murchadh Bàn 117
MacKenzie, Neil W. 224
MacKenzie, Peter D. (1869-1956) 20, 22, 94, 100-101, 110
MacKenzie, Father Roderick 95, 100, 108
MacKenzie, Father Rory 71, 73, 95, 102, 117-19
MacKenzie, Rose 71-72
MacKenzie, Sarah 8
MacKenzie, Tommy 116, 153
MacKenzie, Wayne and Louise 49
MacKenzie, William 18, 141, 187

MacKinnon, Rev. Archibald D. (1898-1985) xv, 84, 88-89
MacKinnon, Catherine also Catherine Ranald (*Mór*) MacDonald 16
MacKinnon, Dan (son of Murdock Donald) 16, 46, 267
MacKinnon, Donald 16, 19, 105
MacKinnon, Father Donald 98
MacKinnon Harbour 3, 26, 61
MacKinnon, Jimmy (Dan) (1905-1992) xvii, 52, 146-47
MacKinnon, John 16
MacKinnon, John (*Eòin a' Griasaiche*) 158
MacKinnon, Martha (MacDougall) (Mrs. Dan Alec) 69-70
MacKinnon, Mary (daughter of Neil *Geal* MacNeil) 16, 18

MacKinnon, Murdock (Donald) 16
MacKinnon, Neil 16, 37
MacKinnon, Neil (son of Murdock Donald) 16
MacKinnon, Philip 16, 19
MacKinnon, Philip (son of Murdock Donald)
MacKinnon, Rod 101
MacKinnon, Roderick 37
MacKinnon, Rory 16
MacKinnon, Rory (John Mór) 120

MacLean, A. D. (a.k.a. Alex D., "Little Alec") (1889-1974) xvii, xviii, 7-8, 14-15, 105
MacLean, Alex 21
MacLean, Alex (Iona) 275
MacLean, Alexander 16, 32, 73
MacLean, Alexander (Lachlan) 18, 105, 116, 141
Sandy MacLean, Alexander "Sandy" (1861-1940) 125
MacLean, Allan (*Ailean Leathaineach*) 21, 24
MacLean, "California" Angus (*Aonghas Nìll Eachainn*) 25
MacLean, A. N. 188
MacLean, Ann 16
MacLean, Ann (Jessome) 24
MacLean, Annie (MacNeil) 16, 18
MacLean, Archie (Malcolm Stephen) (1919-2010) xvii, 153, 166
MacLean, Benny (Neil, P. S.) 217
MacLean, Calum 16, 32
MacLean, Calum *Calum mac Lachlainn* 45
MacLean, Carmie 23
MacLean, Catherine 21
MacLean, Catherine 69
MacLean, Catherine (MacNeil) 142
MacLean, Catriona (Christina) (*Calum 'ic Lachlain*) (1839-1933) 20, 44
MacLean, Charles (*Teàrlach Gobha*) 15-16, 23, 198
MacLean, Charlotte (MacKenzie) wife xv
MacLean, Cyril 18, 53, 109

MacLean, Daniel (b. 1834) 24
MacLean, Donald (*Aonghais "Og"* MacLean) 24
MacLean, Donald (*Dòmhnull mac Ruairidh*) 111
MacLean, Donald (*Dòmhnull Nill 'ic Lachlainn*) 60
MacLean, Elizabeth (1868 -1961) 11, 245, 280
MacLean, Ellie-Ann xx
MacLean, Flora (MacDonald) 21
MacLean, Father Alexander 101
MacLean, Francis Alexander 111
MacLean, Hector (*Eachann mac Nill Ghobha*) 142
MacLean, Charles (Hector) Gobha 218
MacLean, Gordon "Lighthouse" 267
MacLean, Irene 133
MacLean, James A. 132
MacLean, Jan 16
MacLean, Jessie (MacDonald) 114
MacLean, Jimmy (Neil P. S.) 240
MacLean, Joe (Red Rory) xvii, 15, 150, 153, 163-65, 230-31, 240, 247, 264, 266, 288-89
MacLean, Joe W. 63, 263-65, 275
MacLean, Joseph 53
McLean, Joseph S. 36, 157, 229, 279, 286
MacLean, Josie 15
MacLean, Kaye xvii, xx
MacLean, Kaye Godmother xvii
MacLean, Lachlan 15, 32, 104-105, 111
MacLean, Malcolm xx
MacLean, Malcolm (*Calum mac Lachlainn*) 131
MacLean, Malcolm (Stephen) 78, 232, 284
MacLean, Marjorie xvii, 23, 154
MacLean, "Little" Marjorie 61
MacLean, Mary (daughter of Daniel MacLean) 24
MacLean, Mary (wife of "California" Angus MacLean) 25
MacLean, Mary E. 74
MacLean, Mary (Gillis) 114
MacLean, Mary "Lighthouse" 111

MacLean, Mary (MacDougall) 116
MacLean, Mary Mhór 16, 32
MacLean, Michael 16
MacLean, Michael A. 64, 152-53, 213, 264, 280, 292
MacLean, Michael A. (1911-2007) xiii, xv, 248-49, 259
MacLean, Michael (son of Allan and Flora) 21
MacLean, Michael Charlie (1843-1934) 198-201
MacLean, Michael Dan "Mickey" 155, 176-77, 235
MacLean, Michael Dan (Red Rory) 158, 163, 234, 269
MacLean, Michael (Malcolm) 164
MacLean, Mick-John "Lighthouse" (1897-1982) xvii, 214, 245, 247
Maclean, Murdock Paul (1861-1947) xx, xxi, 23, 90, 93-94, 119, 260-61
MacLean, Neil 16, 32
MacLean, Neil (*Niall Dubh*) 24
MacLean, Neil Peter 102, 134-35, 154, 247
MacLean, Neil P. S. 17, 54, 63, 101, 150, 170, 208, 251, 292
MacLean, Neil Stephen 52, 78, 296
MacLean, Paul 59
MacLean, Paul (*Alasdair mac Lachlainn*) 123
MacLean, Peter 16, 32
MacLean, Rev. Peter 86
MacLean, Peter (Peadar mac Lachlainn) 41
MacLean, Peter F. (1899-1996) 196-98, 214, 250, 266
MacLean, Peter Francis (*Chaluim*) 17, 245
MacLean, Peter Francis (1824-1898) 280
MacLean, Peter S. (*Peadar mac Ruairidh*) 16, 17, 19, 58, 98, 101, 114, 135 141
MacLean, Roddie 18, 61, 109
MacLean, Roddie James 134
MacLean, Roderick 16, 32, 41
MacLean, Roderick D. 131

MacLean, Roderick (piper) 111
MacLean, Roderick (*Ruaridh mac Lachlainn*) 98-100
MacLean, Father Ronald 93
MacLean, "Red Rory" 169
MacLean, Rory J. (Rory "Stephen") (1870-1934) 20, 110, 167, 232, 284
MacLean, Rose (1912-1999) mother xiii
MacLean, Sadie (Michael Charlie) (1884- 1956) 150
MacLean, Sarah 20
MacLean, Stephen 114
MacLean, Susan (daughter of Daniel MacLean) 24
MacLean, Teresa 111
MacLean, Theresa (1875-1951) xiii
MacLean, Vincent (1871-1943) xv, 19, 213, 280, 284
MacLean, William D. 189

MacLennan, Gordon (1932-2002) 204
MacLennan, John 85
McLennan, Katherine 11-12
MacLeod, Ann 24
MacLeod, Major Calum I. N. (d. 1977) xv
MacLeod, Christie 39
MacLeod, Malcolm (Murdock) 146
MacLeod, Murdock Neil 230
MacLeod, Rev. Norman 85
MacMillan, Dr. C. L. 83, 87
McNab, D. B. 36-37
McNab, Deputy Surveyor Robert 30
MacNaughton, John 135

MacNeil, Alexander (Sandy) 132
MacNeil, Allan 24
McNeil, Allan, blacksmith 42
MacNeil, Allan J. 109, 116
MacNeil, Angus 26
MacNeil, Angus (*Eòin*) 17, 35, 131-32, 255
MacNeil, Ann (Stephen "Rogers") xvi

MacNeil, Ann (John [Murdock Beag] MacNeil) 19
MacNeil, Annie Catherine (Mrs. John Dan) 69
McNeil Brothers, merchants 42, 43
MacNeil, Cassie (John P.) 207
MacNeil, Catherine (Murdock Donald MacKinnon) 16
MacNeil, Catherine (daughter of Roderick) 98
MacNeil, Catherine Ann (Mrs. George MacNeil) 105
MacNeil, Chrissy (Allan Alec) 76
MacNeil, Dan Joseph and Charlene 16
MacNeil, Danny (John D.) 69
MacNeil, Donald (pioneer)
MacNeil, Donald (Eòin a' Phlant) 101
MacNeil, Donald, merchant 42
McNeil, Donald (Piper) 22
MacNeil, Eòin 16, 32, 157
MacNeil, Evelyn 78
MacNeil, Francis Hector (1867-1954) xviii, xix, 258
MacNeil, F. X. (1911-1994) 207
MacNeil, Gerard 211
MacNeil, Hector R. (d. 1925) xviii
MacNeil, Hector (*Eachann Dubh*) 97
MacNeil, Hector (Rory, Donald) xviii
MacNeil, Honey 207, 267
MacNeil, James 105
MacNeil, Janey (*Sìne an Uillt*) 18
MacNeil, J. Bruce 210
MacNeil, Jessie Ann 69
MacNeil, Jimmy Caluman 26, 68-69, 111
MacNeil, Jimmy John D xix
MacNeil, Jimmy and Gerry 58
MacNeil, Joe (1877-1948) xii
MacNeil, Joe (Allan) 51
MacNeil, John 18, 33, 37
MacNeil, John Alec xix, 239
MacNeil, John Allen xix, 240
MacNeil, John, merchant 47-48, 156
McNeil, John C. 43, 228
MacNeil, John D. 78
MacNeil, John (*Eoin*) 105

MacNeil, John (*Ian Ruadh*) 21, 24, 116
MacNeil, John (*Iain mac Ruairidh*) 46
MacNeil, Rev. John J. 24, 100, 108, 116-17
MacNeil, John Malcolm 69
MacNeil, John (*Murdock Beag*) 19
MacNeil, John Neillie xix, 230
MacNeil, John P. xix
MacNeil, John S. 168, 179, 267
MacNeil, Joseph Neil 76
MacNeil, Kate 133
MacNeil, Malcolm (*Calum Ruadh*) 23
MacNeil, Malcolm (*Calum mac Iain Ruaidh*) 23, 109
MacNeil, Malcolm Dan 74-75
MacNeil, Margaret from (Mrs. Francis B. MacDonald)
MacNeil, Margaret (Frank M.) 72
MacNeil, Mary (1865-1935), wife of Francis Hector xviii
MacNeil, Mary Bàn 109, 224
MacNeil, Mary (Dan D.) (1916-2005) 151
MacNeil, Mary (MacNeil) 115
MacNeil, "Little" Mary (MacDougall), wife of John (*Iain mac Ruairidh*) MacNeil 46, 48
MacNeil, Michael D. 110, 136
MacNeil, Michael (*Eòin*) 59, 120
MacNeil, Michael (Murdock *Beag*) 115
MacNeil, Michael (Stephen) 82
MacNeil, Mickey (*mac Bean Nìlleig*) (1917-1995) 144
MacNeil, Murdock 69
MacNeil, Murdock 33
MacNeil, Murdock 56
MacNeil, Murdock (*Dhòmhnaill Eòin*) xviii
MacNeil, Murdock A. xviii
MacNeil, Murdoch (*Murachidh Beag*) 21, 98-100
MacNeil, Murdock (Michael D.) 68, 75, 133, 136-38
MacNeil, Neil 51
MacNeil, Neil F. xi, 16, 69, 80, 193

MacNeil, Neil *Geal* 16, 18, 97, 107-108
MacNeil, "Red" Neil, *Niall Ruadh* 18, 52, 108, 144
MacNeil, Neil James 76
MacNeil, Neil M. 225
MacNeil, Norman 75
MacNeil, Peter 74, 115
MacNeil, Peter (*Niall mac Eachainn*) 115
MacNeil, Philip B. 160
MacNeil, Robert (Danny John D) 76
MacNeil Rod C. 144, 202, 221
MacNeil, Roderick (1927-2009) 75-76, 78-79
MacNeil, Roderick A. 131
MacNeil, Roderick (*Ruairidh Geal*) 108
MacNeil, Roderick and Mary 98
MacNeil, Father Roderick 100
McNeil, Rory (Governor) 22
McNeil, Rory, merchant 43
McNeil, Rory J. (*Iain `ic Ruairidh Mhóir `ic Dhòmhnaill `ic Ruairidh*) 24-25, 116, 133
MacNeil, Rory (Neil *Geal*) 19, 108, 115
MacNeil, Sarah (MacLean) 109, 116
MacNeil, Stephen B. 102, 111
MacNeil, Stephen J. (Red Stephen) 131
MacNeil, Steven Rory (S. R.) xvi, 64, 81-82, 144
MacNeil, Vince xviii
MacNeils Vale 2, 60, 71, 175, 207

MacPhee, Catherine 18
MacPhee, Dòmhnull 18
MacPhee, Donald 18, 19, 108
McPherson, Stephen 131
MacPhì, Marcella (married to Dòmhnull) 18, 108
McQuillen, David 34
MacRae, Charlotte D. 91
MacRae, Capt. Dan 156, 176-77
MacRae, Murdock (The Rabbits MacRae) 233-34

MacRae, Sandy ("The Rabbits" MacRae) 233-34
MacRitchie, Cassie 46, 228
MacRitchie, John Dan 46, 48-50, 228, 249
MacRitchie, Kenny 25
MacRitchie, Margaret 50
"Marjorie's" (Marjorie MacLean) Co-op 51-54, 79
SS *Marion*, ship 173-74
Maskells 23, 150, 160-63, 167, 181, 189, 247, 365
Masters, Robert K. 42
Matheson, Angus 24
Matheson, David (1951- 2011) 77
Matheson, Dougald 89
Matheson, Elizabeth (Betsy) 24
Matheson, Ernest 109
Matheson, Hugh G. (Hoodie) 24
Matheson, Jimmy and Judi 109
Matheson, Murdock 37
Matheson, Rebecca (Doherty) 24
Matheson, Rod N. 188, 239
Matheson, Walter (1931-2013) 88
Matheson, William 23-25
Mathewson, William 34
Mayflower, ship See SS May Queen
SS *May Queen*, ship 173
Mersey Paper Company 235-38
Mi'kmaq, Mi'kmaw 3-10, 29-30, 43, 97, 104, 161, 236, 277
Military See Chapter 19
Morris, Charles Surveyor General 31
Morrison, Donald 25
Morrison, Angus 47
Morrison, Effie, merchant 48
Morrison, Johnny 47
Morrison, Murdock 48
Morrison, Norman 47
Mowatt, Esther (sometimes cited as Moore) 17
Munro, Allan 20
Munro, Ann "Nancy" (MacNeil) 23
Munro, William (Uilleam Ailein) 23
Murphy, Anna xix, 15
Murphy, Charlie (1919-1982) 54, 78-79, 252
Murphy, Daniel 20

Murphy, Danny (1874-1955) 54, 261
Murphy, Hugh J. 51
Murphy, Peter (1) 25
Murphy, Peter (2) 25, 225
Murphy Point 2, 20, 232, 259
Murphy, Rita 75
Murray, Premier George H. 42
Murray, William, merchant 42

Napean, Major General 13, 34
Nash, Agnes 72, 76
Nash, Jonathan 26
Nash, Mick-John 116
Nash, Rachel 116
Nixy Beer 47, 48
Nova Scotia (activities) iv–xxii
Nova Scotia Highland Village Museum vii, xvi, 70, 275, 357
Nyanza *See* also Wagmatcook 9, 25, 149, 168, 175, 230, 236, 237, 238, 294, 379

Ocean Lilly, ship 144-47, 182-83
Oram, William 26-27, 109
O'Rielly, Father Eugene 98
Ottawa Brook viii, 2, 25, 51, 73, 74, 75, 106, 148, 185, 216, 269, 364

Parker, Capt. John 144
Paul, Joseph (a.k.a. Little Joe) 8
MV *Pearl Cann*, ship 178
Pleasant Point 47, 157, 183
Pony's (Pony) Point 2, 150, 151, 175, 365
Port Elliott 161

Railroad 189-90
Rankin, Father Duncan 61, 74, 106
Rankin, Mary 74
Red Head *See* Beinn Bhreagh 24, 172
Red Point (*an rubha dearg*) 2, 17, 61, 68, 238, 293
Red Point Contractors 238
Religious orders See Chapter 7
Ross, David 21
Ross, John 16, 19, 32
Ross, John (son of William Ross) 17
Ross, Mary *Òg* (MacLean) 17, 32

Ross, Peter H. 36-37
Ross, Sarah 21
Ross Settlement 17
Ross, William (b. 1768) 17, 34
Rothe, Marion (MacKenzie) xx
Route 223 Forest Management Co-op Ltd. 241
Rubh' a' Stòr 45, 286
Russell, Edward 151

Sainte-Anne, Fort 10
Sand Point 36, 45, 141, 220, 286
"The Schooner Alexander" ("*An Long Alexander*") 144-46
Second World War See Chapter 19
Shenacadie 22
SS *Shenacadie*, ship 178-79, 237
Silver Dart, the 190-91
Slàinte Mhath xv
Smith, Dougie 76
South Cove (The Grant) 3, 24, 48
Spectacle Island vi, 2, 11, 278, 279, 280, 281
St. Ann's 10-11, 35, 85, 274
St. Columba ix, xix, 2, 20-21, 23, 25-26, 36, 46-47, 51, 60-61, 65, 68-73, 76, 78, 80-81, 93-95, 98-99, 100, 103-104, 108-109, 111-13, 116-18, 122, 128, 134-38, 160, 179, 186, 188, 202, 208, 214, 220-22, 224-25, 232, 239-40, 265, 268, 291, 296, 311-12, 315-16, 326, 328, 338, 343, 353, 356-57, 359-60, 362-63, 378-79
Steeves, Murray 46
Stewart, Rev. John 85
St. Francis Xavier University (St. FX) xv, 116, 117, 128, 194, 252, 295
Stony Island 281-83, 373
Stòr a' Gràthaich 44-45
St. Peter's 10, 12, 17, 34, 44-45, 52, 106, 109, 116, 149, 152, 171, 173, 187, 195, 258, 378
Sutherland, Charles 37
Sutherland, Mary 37
Sutherland, Robert 21, 36-37

Sutherland, Robert Junior 37
Thompson, Father A. McD., VG 101
Ticket of Location 32, 34
MV *Tomahawk* See SS *Shenacadie*
Triumph, ship 140
Veterans See Chapter 19

Wagmatcook 9, 30, 85, 236, 292
Walker, Mary 51
Wall, William 17, 34-35
Wallace's Bank 17
Wallace's Clearing 17
Waserbaurkchuch (variant of Washabuck) 26
Washabuck Co-operative (a.k.a. "Marjorie's") 51-54, 79, 253
Washabuckt (variant of Washabuck) xi, xvii, 3, 59, 80, 95, 106, 107, 141, 164, 172, 193, 286, 319, 321, 322, 325, 326, 328, 329, 332, 334, 335, 351, 352, 353, 354, 355, 356, 359, 360, 361, 362, 363, 365, 372, 379
Watchabaktchkt (variant of Washabuck) 3, 33, 37
Waycobah 30
Whycocomagh i, 1, 24, 40, 48, 85, 86, 87, 88, 89, 123, 124, 125, 149, 156, 158, 168, 173, 174, 175, 176, 204, 206, 210, 215, 270, 271, 272, 294
William Tell, ship 14-15
Wosobachuk (variant of Washabuck) 3

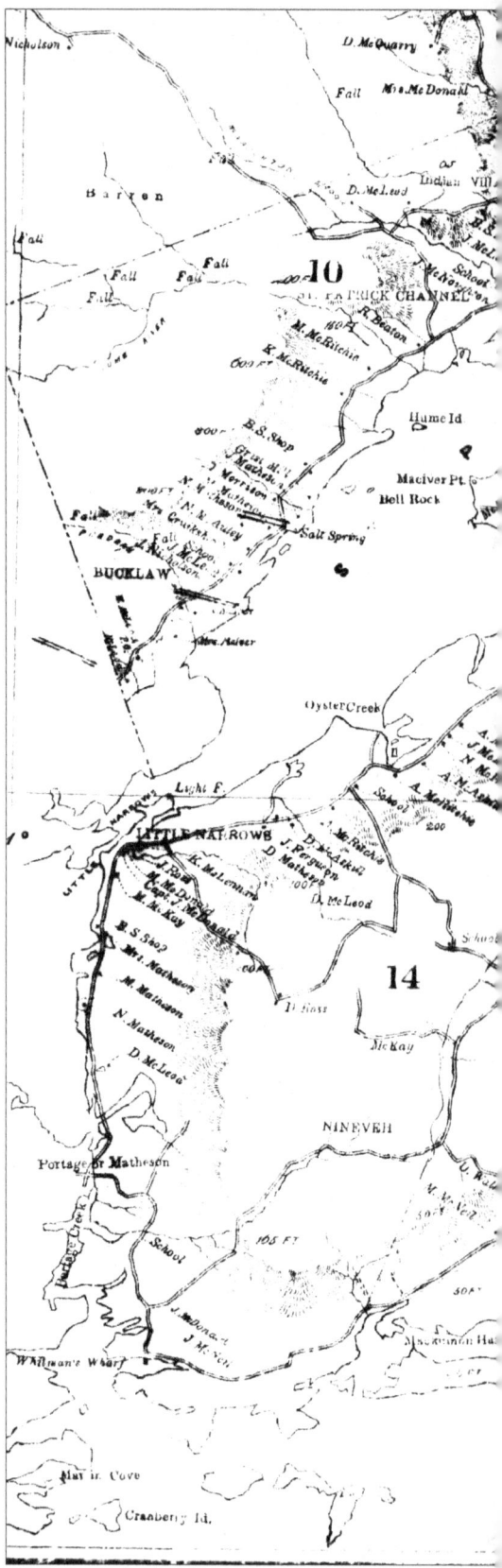

390

www.ingramcontent.com/pod-product-compliance
Lightning Source LLC
Chambersburg PA
CBHW081916180426
43199CB00036B/2681